Guide to
MODERN WORLD
LITERATURE

When Scaliger, whole years of Labour past,
Beheld his Lexicon complete at last,
And weary of his task, with wond'ring eyes,
Saw from words pil'd on words a fabric rise,
He curs'd the industry, inertly strong,
In creeping toil that could persist so long,
And if, enrag'd he cried, heav'n meant to shed
Its keenest vengeance on the guilty head,
The drudgery of words the damn'd would know,
Doom'd to write lexicons in endless woe.

From Dr. Johnson's Latin poem 'Know Yourself',
written after revising and enlarging his lexicon, or
dictionary; translated into English by Arthur Murphy,
in his *Life*, 1772.

Guide to
MODERN WORLD
LITERATURE

Martin Seymour-Smith

PAPERMAC

First edition 1973
Second edition (paperback) 1976

Third edition (completely revised) first published 1985 by
The Macmillan Press Limited

This edition published 1986 by
PAPERMAC
a division of Macmillan Publishers Limited
4 Little Essex Street London WC2R 3LF
and Basingstoke

Associated companies in Auckland, Delhi, Dublin, Gaborone,
Hamburg, Harare, Hong Kong, Johannesburg, Kuala
Lumpur, Lagos, Manzini, Melbourne, Mexico City, Nairobi,
New York, Singapore, Tokyo.

British Library Cataloguing in Publication Data

Seymour-Smith, Martin
    Macmillan guide to modern world literature.
    3rd ed.
    1. Literature, Modern–19th century–Dictionaries
    2. Literature, Modern–20th century–Dictionaries
    I. Title
    809'.034   PN41

ISBN 0-333-42794-7

Typeset by Leaper & Gard Ltd, Bristol
Printed in Hong Kong

Contents

To the memory of my Father
and
to my Mother

Acknowledgements

This third edition of Guide to Modern World Literature, first published in 1973, is some 550,000 words longer than the first and second editions – it is now way over the 1,000,000 mark; most of it has been rewritten. But I owe a great debt to those who helped me write the original work; that I mention their names here does not mean that they are tainted with my not always orthodox views. The people who helped me most particularly were: my wife, my son-in-law Colin Britt, who made things cheerful at a time when they could hardly be expected to be; my late father, my mother. Colin Britt has continued to support me in a quite unprecedented way; but he would only want me to thank him for his friendship and the benefit of his views, and so that is what I do here. I owe a great debt to my friends Robert Nye and C.H. Sisson: they are the ones with whom I have talked and corresponded about literature over a long period of time most fruitfully (for me). Istvan Siklos helped me with the revised version of the section on Hungarian Literature with great generosity – and I should think a good deal of disagreement with my views of some English writers he admires and I do not; Prince Yakamoto performed a similar service with the Japanese section at a rather earlier stage. Others who helped with enquiries, translations and even difficult books were: Cliff Ashby, B.H. Bal, George Barker, Robert Bly, Ronald Bottrall, Keith Brace, the late Edward Charlesworth, Sally Chilver, James and Angelica Dean, the late Sir William Empson, Giles Gordon, Tony Gottlieb, the late Robert Graves, the late Geoffrey Grigson, Fujio Hashima, Ivar Ivask, Solly Jacobson, Patrick Kavanagh, Andrew Maclean, James Mehoke, Wing Commander Vernon 'Coils' Pocock, Anthony Powell, the late James Reeves, Lees Roos, Michael Schmidt (tireless in his generous championship of my work), John and Hilary Spurling, the late Patrick Swift, the late Allen Tate, Anthony Thwaite, the late Anne Tibble, David Wright, Toby Zucker, and Miguel Martinéz García, to whom I owe a great deal.

I owe a special debt to the librarian, writer and bibliographer Peter Marcan; if I could not take advantage of quite all the riches he offered, then that was my fault, not his.

Another special debt I have is to the legendary and indestructible Miron Grindea, editor of *Adam;* genial, full of out-of-the-way information, generous, he helped me in every way he could.

The third edition took much longer than I had intended, quite often because I was obstinately determined to acquaint myself more thoroughly with a literature, or even the works of a particular author, than I had heretofore been; this meant that many suffered whilst I was entranced (if getting broker). I realise that this is my life, rather than that of the sufferers, and I apologise to all of them, not least to my wife, who has always, and understandably, regarded me with (almost) silent despair. Another who has regarded me with a despair, necessarily not so silent, has been my unselfish editor, Penelope Allport. All I can say about my gratitude to her for her tact and wiles is that I should never have completed this task without them. What she has done for me goes far beyond the call of duty.

Others to whom I am grateful are the sharp-eyed heroine of countless romances, Alison Mansbridge; the menacing but ultimately sweet-hearted Shaie Selzer, for believing this worthwhile in the first place; the librarians who will buy two copies of this book for each x   Acknowledgements

library, because they recognise that the book is for reading as well as reference (this in anticipation); my friend Jonathan Barker, because he knows what literature is really about; Peter Davies, likewise; Simon Jenner, for reading so much poetry over the telephone; the Arts Council of Great Britain who gave me a Bursary for a book which circumstances prevented me from writing–it helped me with this; South East Arts for awarding me a prize every penny of which went to my publishers (not Macmillan in that case); the London Library; the East Sussex County Library–especially my old friend Richard Akam of the Bexhill branch, who must have bent every rule in his efforts to make sure that I have the 360 books a week I need; the Library of the University of Sussex; and last but not least to the hundreds of people who have written to me, since 1973, from all parts of the world, and who have encouraged me to believe that this book performs a useful service in a horrible and declining age. As before, I invite further corrections, comments–and the like: I cannot always reply immediately, but I do so eventually.

Brownbread Street,
13 February 1985.   Martin Seymour-Smith

Introduction

I

The scope of this book extends to writers, of all nationalities, who survived 31 December 1899. In certain instances (e.g. Hopkins, Mallarmé) I have had, for obvious reasons, to discuss writers who died before that; but I have strictly limited these. The cut-off date is as artificial as it is necessary; but I have tried to make it as little so as possible. I have given an account of the major and most of the minor literary movements of the past century and a half; the names of these will be found in the index. The system of putting 'q.v.' after names of literary movements, philosophers, authors and titles of books is intended to be a practical aid to the reader: if he/she turns to the index the main entry should not be hard to find.

Complete accuracy in such a comprehensive work as this is impossible. Errors are repeated from reference book to reference book, and the dates of first publication of books – especially if they or versions of them first appeared in periodicals – cannot always be checked without seeing them. I have made every effort to give correct information (e.g. my dates for the birth of Tenessee Williams and E. Lasker-Schüler differ from most authorities', but are right). I have sometimes slipped up in the matter of where writers are now residing; a few move about rapidly and it is hard to catch up with them. I shall be glad to correct any errors, with acknowledgements, in future editions – as I have in this fourth paperback edition, which, although substantially a reprint of the third edition, incorporates some corrections, a few additions, and a completely revised and partly rewritten introduction. The third edition, upon which it is based, was rewritten; it was almost twice as long as the first two editions. There is a great deal of new matter.

Dates after individual books try to be of first publication in whatever form. The list of abbreviations consists mainly of books in which translations – into the question of whose merits I seldom enter – into English of works by writers discussed in the text are conveniently available. The most useful translations of poetry are almost invariably literal cribs; translations of poetry into English verse are bad as approximations to the originals, but not without exception; you should look for parallel texts where these are available. Not all the books I have listed are currently in print, but are available in libraries.

Unsigned translations are my own.

The emphasis, since in the interests of space there has to be an emphasis, is on the more universal areas of interest and language-knowledge (English, French, Spanish, German, Russian, Italian) and on the earlier rather than the latter part of the period, which may be less surely assessed. I have discussed at length some authors whom I believe to be neglected or underrated or misunderstood; and two literatures that are not well known, The Japanese and the Catalan, have received a fuller treatment. Most of the Japanese is available in translation, and Catalan is accessible to anyone who understands enough of any romance language to read it.

The book as a whole lacks a 'systematic thesis'. This has upset some critics. But its thesis is literature itself, without which criticism could not exist, and which is in itself mysterious (although not mystical) and anti-systematic and elusive of ownership. If literature could be made into a thesis then it would not be worth what it is worth. It is that way whether we like it or not. Our moods about this vary; but it is understandable if, when confronted with false theory, many cling to the mystery. Only the undefinable 'common reader' 'owns' literature, and he/she owns it only inasmuch as it is (again mysteriously) in his/her hands. What is in the common reader's hands is the true (as distinct from false, or artificially hyped) reputation. But the common reader, untrained in technical niceties, may not always be able to articulate his/her responses. So this book has been written for the common reader. But of course there is or ought to be a common reader within every professional critic or teacher of literature. Only those academics who have diminished this common reader within themselves, and made of him a mean machine which puts information and opinion above all else, need complain that I am 'anti-academic'. I am in great debt to many academics who are fine readers.

Some will note certain abrupt changes of the view taken of certain authors or even whole literatures between this and earlier editions. My only comment is that if I clung on to my own often ignorant interpretations for the sake of 'consistency' then I should be unfit to write any book. True consistency cannot be self-conscious or for its own sake. My view of literature is always changing as I seek to diminish my ignorance of it – and so is the reader's! I offer this book not in a teaching spirit but in one of candid sharing. My reader's various views are in reality as 'strong' as mine, but he may not be as used to airing them. Doubtless all views are shortcomings, but, unaired, they can become something worse than that: something authoritarian. If you suppress how you feel – and you must feel something – in the interests of a pseudo-objectivity, then you may sullenly retreat into an assumption that you have achieved real objectivity. You may then believe that you have discovered the whole truth. I therefore give you my views – because, after investigating the credentials for them as fully and as dispassionately as I could, I should be cheating if I suppressed them – and that is an end to it. They are certainly no more likely to be 'right' than anyone else's. What is important about a view is not that it should be right – we have had enough of this – but that it should be compatible with all the realities of which you can make yourself aware, and that it should be honestly held. The truth must be left to look after itself, difficult though this is. If it is not it becomes strained and distorted by zeal and self-love; a strained-after truth is no longer a truth but an ideal urged, unpleasantly or otherwise, upon others. For those who dislike my views, or are discomforted (as I am) by my scepticism, I offer information, and information about information. There is much more that you should know about this enormous subject – that is why you are reading my book. There is also, alas, very much more that I should know.

But let us not pretend. I believe in my views. One of my critics has suggested that I am an insensitive reader because I take a positive, although by no means uncritical, view of Walter de la Mare (q.v.). He also pronounces that I ignore the common reader. These are serious charges. I do not think that you can have the rejection of de la Mare *and* the common reader. . . . The sort of person who rejects de la Mare cannot be said to be what Jonson, or Virginia Woolf, meant by the common reader. The common reader is not, after all, either a mindless absorber of junk or one who is going to be put off by critical theory. The common reader is to be distinguished from the 'ordinary reader', and is as intelligent as the professional writer or the professional critic, although probably not as well informed about technicalities (which are not unimportant). But he lives his life as well or badly, as happily or unhappily, as anyone else. He knows about that – and *that* is what literature is really about: whether it is 'for its own sake' or not, life and the living of it is the material literature has to work on. Even if you are a Platonist the living of your life is possibly more about dealing with the Forms than about the Forms themselves. . . . Literature is about living. . . . It cannot be about real dying or real death because no one who is in a position to write knows what those processes are. But of course it is filled with metaphors for what we variously imagine real dying and real death may be.

What my critic is saying is that, in preserving the work of de la Mare long past its author's death, the common reader has been wrong: he needs 'guidance' of a kind I do not, and could not with a good conscience, give. But I can sympathise. For I must suppose that I myself have, in effect, even if less dogmatically, said almost the same about Rupert Brooke (q.v.) However, a *sensitive* reader of both poets, if he had the time and the space at his disposal, and was not fashion-crazed, would admit to the difficulties he was in and then perhaps attempt to discriminate further: between two sorts of qualities, both of which endure. He might point to the fact that sincere patriotism and the hot-bloodedness of youth (well expressed in metrical prose) whether ultimately specious or not, tend to appeal over long periods; but that so does real poetry over even longer ones. The critic would have been better advised to answer my claim that de la Mare, for all his archaism and tendency to lapse into outworn and poetical modes, was as 'modernist' (in the sense in which I have explained it here) as many self-consciously polemical modernists: I give my reasons, and I support my view with quotations. What I say is refutable – I hope all I say is refutable – but it has not yet been refuted. I should think that anyone prepared to sacrifice what is to be found in de la Mare in the interests of devotion to a now itself dated notion of modernism is an insensitive reader of poetry.

II

All Western literature has developed, with some national exceptions and variations, to a consistent pattern. In the succeeding brief sketch I have kept definitions as broad as possible: understanding of literature does not benefit from attempts to narrow down the meaning of terms too precisely: the terms themselves, which are usually retrospective, lose their value. They are indispensable, but become abstract when allowed to dominate individual achievement. The history of literature seen as a phenomenon in itself is valid; and there is certainly a problem, perhaps insoluble, about the extent to which men and women – writers and their readers – are the creatures of their times, and the extent to which they create those times. But the history of literature cannot be told through the use of abstract terms. Pragmatically, literature is generated by individuals, not by movements. Individual writers do shape their works to the requirements (or precisely not to the requirements) of movements as they interpret them; but movements are continually redefined by individual works. We need to look at the works first, because they supply the gist of the matter. Movements could not exist without works; works could exist without movements.

By the mid-century realism was well established in the novel. Realism in its broadest sense is an essential aim of any work of literature: it simply means verisimilitude to actuality – and points to the aspects of life the author selects as the most meaningful. But this leaves entirely open the question of how actuality is regarded: as an inward or an outward phenomenon, or both, or an illusion, or whatever. The tendency throughout the history of literature, and particularly the more recent history, has been for increasing emphasis to be put on inward phenomena, on the nature of consciousness, subconsciousness and unconsciousness. This is well exemplified by the philosophical project of Husserl (q.v.), called phenomenology: Husserl, seizing on the revival, in the philosophy of Brentano, of the medieval notion that the mind is necessarily *intentionalist* in nature – meaning not that it intends something, but that it must always be *directed towards* something – set out to explore and to define the 'lived-in space', the 'immediate data of consciousness'. The immediate data of consciousness is all we have, if we do have it, to defend ourselves against pure solipsism; so phenomenology, which eventually became somewhat philosophically idealistic in the hands of Husserl, went – like so many other twentieth-century enterprises – back to the beginning. In phenomenology it did not matter whether the objects of mental perception were 'real' or not. My idea of the Battle of Waterloo has the same status as my idea of a squared circle. That the first 'existed' in a sense that the other never yet did is irrelevant. This suited the mood of the times, and gave an inevitably psychological slant to what was at the same time, in Husserl's hands if not in those of some of his disciples such as Heidegger (q.v.), pure philosophy.

There have of course, persistently, been revolts (the French *Populism*, q.v., is but a minor example) against this tendency to look inwards, and I have recorded these. Nineteenth-century realism, the mode out of which modernism developed, does, even though it remains one of the broader literary concepts, have a less vague connotation than the word 'realism' on its own implies.

First, this nineteenth-century realism is essentially a part of romanticism, however much it may look like a reaction against it – and however certainly the romantic movement may have seemed, in the positivist Fifties, to have collapsed. We are still living in a romantic period – nor, indeed, could there ever be a full return to the limitations and artificialities of classicism, which does no more than re-assert its spirit from time to time as a necessary curb to romantic excess or, of course, to laziness and silliness which are ubiquitous but no part of the subject of this book. The only interest the common (as distinct from the ordinary) reader could have in junk literature would be as some kind of index to 'culture lag', the term used by the sociologist W.F.Ogburn to describe the differing rate at which the various elements in a culture change. Thus surrealism (q.v.), a movement in the arts, is eventually vulgarised in 'pop art' and so forth. The view that writers, in order to be effective, require technical skills as well as gifts, talents or 'inspiration' is by no means merely classicist ('inspiration' is not a classical concept at all). Classicism now implies almost eccentrically stern views about forms and properties and, above all, subject-matter. The nearest the twentieth century has had to a classical critic is Yvor Winters (q.v.); but his motivations were anything but classical. In fact the term 'classical' *(scriptor classicus)* was first used by Aulus Gellius, in *Noctes Atticae*, in the second century of our era, as an alternative to *scriptor proletarius*: it meant no more than 'aristocratic', i.e. for the, to anticipate Stendhal, 'happy few'. (The common reader could be seen as one of these.) Notions of 'learned in the classics of Greece and Rome', and then 'worthy to be preserved in the academies' were understandable but erroneous later misinterpretations. Eventually the word came to be applied to works of literature which preserved allegedly eternal standards of beauty by means of precedents; therefore the uglinesses, and the search for originality of expression, of the romantics were banished. Classicism is now employed most usefully in a noncommittal historical sense.

True literature is 'given', in the first place – this is essentially a romantic notion – but the vast extent of the hard work and 'art' to which the 'given' work has to be subjected is well known to writers, if not to their inferior imitators. The position taken in this book is that the admittedly too vague term 'inspiration' is to be preferred to the lie perpetrated by the notion that literature can be manufactured by anyone who can acquire literary skills, and nowadays of course, even by those who cannot. In the rare cases when a text is simply 'given' – is written out immediately and in a white heat – then it is still a reward for hard work, even if that has been earlier expended on what would not come out right. Lack of care has never produced a body of good work, although apparent lack of heed has.

Realism, the nineteenth-century literary movement said to begin in England with George Eliot, in America with Howells (q.v.) and in Europe with Balzac, has no significant relationship to the literary classicism of antiquity or even to the neo-classicism (which had some romantic tendencies) of the eighteenth century. It originates in the age-old tendency towards accuracy of representation (usually manifesting itself as an anti- or non-classical depiction of plebeian life – Cervantes, Jonson, Shakespeare, Smollett – or as regionalism, in Spanish terminology *costumbristo*), and in philosophical pragmatism and all proto-pragmatic and proto-utilitarian inclinations. Nineteenth-century realism, at various times and in various writers, exhibited the following characteristics: objectivity (in the sense of concentration on facts rather than interpretation of them); lucidity (rather than style or rhetoric); a search for an immediate, verifiable truth, even if this be no more than relativistic; secularism; emphasis on the psychological motivations of the characters, often but certainly not always at the expense of 'plot'; matter-of-fact style, in order to give the illusion that the story is true. It was mostly in the picaresque novel that plot was neglected or eschewed in the interests of individual psychology. This genre was initiated much earlier than realism: in the seventeenth century by the anonymous author of *Lazarillo de Tormes*. The hero of a picaresque novel is a *picaro* (a Spanish word meaning, roughly, rogue). This kind of novel was very successful in France, Germany and England, and has been revived in the twentieth century. But what it now means, out of its original context, is 'rambling, would-be-lively narrative about an amoral likeable person'.

In general the good realist authors (e.g. George Eliot, Henry James, q.v.), had good and even idealistic intentions towards their readers; but they refused to uplift their hearts, thus raising false hopes. A few realists (paradigmatically Flaubert) had more aggressive intentions towards the bourgeois. Bad intentions towards the bourgeois (which term I use in this book not in the Marxian but in the Flaubertian sense) are a characteristic of most literature that likes to feel itself modern; but few are as aggressive as Flaubert. In so far as the bourgeois read such literature it has bad intentions towards itself; but then most writers, too, are bourgeois in this sense of the word, and so know about being bourgeois even if they are (hopefully) ignorant of *sottise*. The milieu chosen by realist writers was emphatically middle-class, in any case. If a guide to the mood of this guide were required, then it would certainly be Flaubert's *Dictionary of Accepted Ideas*, which forms an appendix to his warm-hearted but crushing unfinished novel *Bouvard et Pécuchet*.

In many countries, but most notably in France, realism shaded into naturalism. This term is frequently used, not only by literary journalists and theatre columnists but also by those who should know better, as a synonym for realism. This is misleading. Naturalism is a more precise term than realism, and there was less confusion about its programme. It should not be confused with its philosophical meaning. In literature it represents a narrowing-down of realism. Zola's (q.v.) programme (described in the account of him) was entirely naturalist; but he did not believe in his own programme, and his practice was not. Naturalist fiction is guided, or thinks it is guided, by the principles of scientific determinism. This arose largely from 'Darwinism', a movement or climate of thought that has less to do with Charles Darwin, from whom it derives its name, than might seem immediately apparent. Darwin gave a new and viable interpretation of the theory of 'transformism'; according to Darwinism he invented it and proved it. Actually it went back as a theory to at least 550 BC. The naturalists extracted from Darwinism the notion of man-as-animal, of his life as essentially a bloody struggle (this had already been stated with more confidence, and without falsification of biological evidence, in Hobbes' proto–behaviourist but perhaps partially ironic *Leviathan*): 'the strongest, the swiftest and the cunningest live to fight another day,' pronounced T.H. Huxley, as though it were a law of nature. This persistent fallacy has been given the name of 'Social Darwinism'. It was dominant in American thought in the first years of this century, and is by no means dead today. In point of fact the fittest may be neither 'strong' nor 'swift' nor 'cunning'. . . . They may be weak and slow, but none the less able to adapt to certain environments more successfully than the strong and fast. But our anthropomorphism is irresistible, so that there is a Social Darwinist within each of us. The lives of the poor, to the depiction of which the naturalists turned, seemed to give ample justification for this crude misinterpretation of the facts. However, the best naturalists, while intellectually convinced of the rightness of their point of view, have in practice transcended it. Zola is as romantic and indeed at times proto-surrealist (q.v.) as he is naturalistic; and Dreiser (q.v.) is massively and poignantly puzzled as well as philosophically awkward and occasionally sentimental. Both writers are undoubtedly to be classed as naturalists, it is true; but both gain their ultimate effects from features unconnected with their stated 'philosophies of life'. Hardy (q.v.) seems very near to naturalism, especially in *Jude the Obscure*; but he had other virtues, and the cosmic determinism which he substitutes for biological determinism is subtler, richer and more relevant to his achievement than it looks. Nevertheless his brutal frankness (the pig incident; the death of the children) are genuinely and aggressively naturalist. The difference is that Hardy was far more bitter about his naturalist feelings than Zola or even Dreiser; this feeling of bitterness did not arise from a perusal of theory, but from the quality of Hardy's experience.

The other distinguishing feature of naturalism is that it deals more self-consciously with the working classes than realism ever did. In this sense the Goncourts – themselves neither democratic nor socialist nor even liberal – are the pioneers, in *Germanie Lacerteux* (1864). In the preface to that depressing and excellent novel they made many remarks pertinent to naturalism: 'The public loves fictitious novels! This one is true. It loves books which pretend to introduce their readers to fashionable society. This book deals with the life of the streets.' And so it did. The Goncourts had asked themselves whether the 'lower classes' had any rights in the novel, and had answered in the affirmative. *Soeur Philomène* (1861) had come first, but, a study of hospital life the research for which made both brothers ill, it was less thoroughgoing and less effective. '*Humanity*' they proclaimed in 1864: 'it needs no other warrant than the consciousness that that is its right.' And the novel was indeed 'true' in the sense that they based its central figure on the life – of which they had known nothing – of their own (deceased) servant. Their decision to write in this way was made in the interests of aestheticism, not political passion.

The so-called neo-romanticism, and then decadence, that manifested itself in almost all the Western literatures between about 1885 and 1905 was not as remote from either realism or naturalism as its practitioners felt. All great literary movements initially outrage or at least offend, are later accepted and dominate, and then decline. They all eventually deteriorate: into preciosity, self-consciousness, trivial scholarship, cultivation of debility and, of course, whatever society may at the time determine as perverse behaviour. The perversity of a dying movement is different from that of a new one: the former is passive and weak, the latter aggressive and energetic. There is also always a 'culture lag' between what general readers think about the literary situation and what critics think about it. The literary critics regard themselves as being 'ahead'. In a certain sense they are. But they do not determine taste, and criticism – if not all critics – tends to become prescriptive and dogmatic.

The so-called decadence of the late nineteenth and early twentieth centuries, more of a tendency than a movement, is also called *fin de siècle*. It is characteristic of all literary movements, though, in the sense that it resembles earlier ones in their decline; indeed, it exaggerates this feature. Decadence is as much a development, or an etiolation, of Parnassianism and Symbolism (qq.v.) – or their less dogmatic equivalents in countries other than France – as it is a reaction against positivism and the ostensibly 'scientific' elements in naturalism. But naturalism itself, in imaginatively capable hands, shaded easily into decadence, because if you are a gifted writer and you are writing about squalor and decay you tend to relish it: the imagination cannot function at all unless it affirms something, even if the polemical or the political aspects of the subject-matter make you wholly indignant. There is nothing polemical or political about the Bosch-like vitality and vivacity of Zola's Rabelaisian crowd scenes; but there is just a touch of *fin de siècle* about them. . . . There is no touch of decadence about the realist Flaubert (who, however, opposed the representatives of the official realist movement, and who was opposed even more vigorously by them); yet he wrote in a letter of 1857 to Mlle de Chantepie, 'In order to survive, one must give up having clear-cut opinions about anything at all. *Humanity is like that*; it is not a question of changing it, but of knowing it. . . Give up all hope of a solution. . . Life is such a hideous business that the only method of bearing it is to avoid it.' This is very different from rejecting life altogether – and no decadent could ever have said, as Flaubert so often did, *'Compel yourself to regular, exhausting work'.*

Decadence developed not only out of the more robust Flaubertian disgust but also out of what is called the 'aesthetic movement', which was mainly French but which had its roots in part of the philosophy of Kant. While the respectable Kant, who tried to cover all eventualities, was propounding an aesthetic theory according to which the artistic 'object' should be perceived without reference to reality or morality, the enraptured American drunkard Edgar Allan Poe, so terribly important to the French, was heralding the 'poem for the poem's sake'. Art, in other words, existed for itself alone, and had no usefulness in society. (Flaubert did not say much about the usefulness or otherwise of art: he was concerned with the plight of the individual in this 'hideous' life.) Baudelaire (q.v.) and lesser writers consciously embraced decay and decline, which they celebrated as sweet. They were devoted to such eras as those of the decline of the Roman Empire and Byzantine Greece, to which they compared their own. They revelled in unnatural states, and some took drugs to induce them. The gifted boy Rimbaud, much influenced by Baudelaire, developed the notion of a 'systematic derangement of the senses' (this became sacred text for the surrealists, q.v.). But it should be noted that it is generally conceded that Baudelaire as a thinker and systemetiser, in comparison to his mature achievement as an imaginative writer, was but a child; and that Rimbaud, almost before he reached adulthood, dropped his deliberately corrupt practices, and all interest in literature – as though they were childish things. It is often forgotten that Rimbaud, although an extraordinary writer of great achievement, was never a mature poet: he is the poet of precocious adolescence. He is not less good because of that, since doubtless no one ever grows up completely; nonetheless, he is more derivative (especially from Baudelaire) than has been acknowledged, and there is little more to be got from him than adolescence offers. A lesser figure such as Lautréamont was and still is overrated simply because he was precocious, sick and died young. He was talented and representative but not gifted: the surface of his prose-poetry sparkles with the iridescence of decay, but it has no depths. Yet Remy de Gourmant, a programmatic *symboliste*, praised Lautréamont's *Maldoror* as a 'universal blasphemy'. Lautréamont, too, later became a surrealist hero. The essence of so paradigmatically decadent a novel as Wilde's (q.v.) *The Picture of Dorian Gray* is not, well done though it is, in its depths, for it has none; but it does set up resonances in those readers who are capable of experiencing them. There are other more robust works of that kind (perhaps *Death in Venice*, q.v., is one of them, although it was written with more aplomb than *The Picture of Dorian Gray*: Mann was throughout his life torn between the decadence without which he was convinced art could not exist, and responsible humanism – which he cultivated slowly and with difficulty). A hero of the French Symbolists, the more polemical of whom were assuredly decadent, was Villiers de L'Isle Adam. Villiers (one of his characters famously remarked, 'Living: we will leave the servants to do that for us') was exemplary in that he led an absurd and pathetic life, of grinding poverty. He dreamed of living off a rich and aristocratic wife, but actually lived with a charwoman, and so forth. He developed his slight talent to the full in his least self-conscious tales, yet was totally artificial. Mallarmé dedicated an entire symbolist conference to his memory. But Mallarmé, although 'ridiculous' in his capacity as a schoolmaster (he could not keep order), was not typical: the more gifted are always exceptional and do not need to fit into a mould. Villiers, the 'supernaturalist', is nowadays (as the obscure author of translated collections rather than as himself) a hero of pseudo-literary 'fantasy' junk writers (a perfect example of culture lag: decadence run wild), and translations from him provide them with a useful source from which to draw their 'plots'. Villiers' cult of the horrific was infantile even in its own time, although deliberately so; his best stories are well recognised by informed readers as being precisely those which are not 'horrific'.

Symbolism (the French literary movement, q.v.) contained or fulfilled the function of religious or 'Platonic' impulses in human beings during the realist-naturalist period. (Whether religion is 'true' or not, the manifestation of it represents something that cannot be replaced except by the genuinely religious: thus, in Godless Russia, people either go on worshipping God or they regard Marx with a truly religious awe – and the régime is beginning to recognise this, because it is clearly thinking of rehabilitating the Russian Orthodox Church in some modified form.) The decadent writers – they range from the partly decadent such as Verlaine to the completely decadent such as Dowson (q.v.) – were nearly all 'religious', if only in the sense that they embraced 'Satanism' and died incense-sniffing semi-repentent Catholics. They saw the life of their times as in headlong decay rather than in growth: they worshipped entropy, degeneration, disorder. They transformed the romantic cult of the individual into the romantic-decadent cult of the self (narcissism); hence their interest in or cultivation of homosexuality, which, whether it originates in narcissism as woman-avoidance or not, often involves more narcissistic contemplation than heterosexuality does. (We now discover from his diaries that the quasi-decadent Mann actively indulged his homosexual impulses, and remained obsessed by them; on the subject of homosexuality he was clearly ambivalent.) The decadents worshipped the urban because of the ugliness it offered; but they worshipped it in a deliberately perverse spirit. They turned the notion of mimesis on its head: for them life imitated art. They neurasthenically worshipped the erotic, and hurled themselves into hopeless loves. Imitating what they believed was Greek practice, they made a cult of the beautiful boy (this is seen developed to its fullest extent in the

George, q.v., circle, a case of late decadence not seeing itself as such). They romanticised the then dominant principle of the Second Law of Thermodynamics ('The Heat Death of the Universe'), seeing it as operative in the evolutionary sphere. ('The Heat Death of the Universe' has now lost its credibility, because although entropy 'works' in a closed system, it is not clear that the universe is a closed system.) They were deliberately hysterical, and even liked to be syphilitic, blind, crippled, consumptive or maimed (though not too much so if possible). They cultivated artificiality. The mood and the depressive stance persisted in such writers as Mann (q.v.); occasionally it degenerated into an aggressive, cheap and ignorant pseudo-nihilism.

The foregoing are the characteristics of decadence in general. No single writer manifests all of them, not even the exquisitely trivial Firbank (q.v.), who was so feeble as a person as hardly to be able to realise his own homosexual impulses. (There is an instructive and attractive treatment of him, from a very different point of view, by Brigid Brophy, q.v., in *Prancing Novelist.*) In its less extreme form the neo-romantic spirit – a reaction to the positivism of the Fifties – began to pervade the works of the realists and then the naturalists; but this, while it is connected with thoroughgoing decadence, should not be confused with it.

In the course of time literary movements provoke reactions to themselves. But these reactions absorb the essences, the genuine discoveries (apprehensions of change) of what preceded them. To give a simplified illustration: romanticism at its best contains the truth of classicism as it eventually came to be understood. Doubtless there are eternal qualities; but we do not know what they are. . . . The best neo-romantic writers had learned the lessons of realism. And it was, perhaps, most essentially from neo-romanticism, a sort of romantic revival and confirmation of the completeness of the recovery from the eighteenth-century rationalism, that what is now called 'modernism' arose. Literature is now, broadly, romantic. But the critics tend to lean enviously towards all kinds of positivism. Nor has the situation in that respect ever been worse. It is a pity to have to recognise that so much criticism arises from an envy of creativity; but is absolutely necessary to understand that it is so, if only because it is hardly ever acknowledged. The envy of creativity exists not only within those who feel that they have never created anything, but also within the temporarily disabled imaginative writer. . . . Too often the elaborations and over-systematisations of contemporary criticism are a defensive strategy: to take literature, with its natural vitality, away from the common reader – by a process of intimidation. This book is certainly written in an attempt to return literature to its owner: to the responsible and creative reader, to whom one may confess one's preferences, but for whom it is sinful to prescribe. Without such readers there would be nothing. Everything would lack energy. Not a few modern writers exist by virtue of being unreadable (e.g. Barth, Pynchon, qq.v.) by such readers; their great strength lies in their massive unreadability. They exist as threats waved at readers by certain critics: 'if you do not enjoy these texts then you do not understand literature'. They do not exist because they have been read with true attention and true curiosity, or because they are truly loved; they exist because they could not be. And it is not really such authors who are at fault: it is the critics who have created their reputations.

Such apparent denunciations as this are frequently, and quite rightly, suspected of being motivated by simplicity and ignorance of the 'modern'. They often are so motivated. But the modernism discussed in this book – it is in very large part what the literature of our century is about – has now itself become a sort of decadence. This demonstrates itself. There is no longer anything 'new' in the sense Ezra Pound (q.v.) or any other highly self-conscious modernist of the early years of the century meant this word. The chief feature of our own age is the intimidated common reader. Someone who is brave enough to assume that he is not wholly unsophisticated should put out a helping – but perhaps it is really a welcoming – hand to such good-willed but bewildered readers. This is all the more relevant now that the age of deconstructionism (q.v.) is upon us. It is difficult to see what professional critics could venture upon next. Someone therefore has to declare that the author is not wholly dead – even as he has to admit the truth of the sense in which he always has been. . . . It is not as if deconstructionism were simply nonsense – or as if such notions should never have been put forward. But those who take literature seriously should be anxious about the manner in which it has been received: timidly and without thought.

Modernism as a term can be descriptive, prescriptive or pejorative. It depends on who you are and what you think you think (how you 're-arrange your prejudices', as William James, q.v., put it). Modernism is 'good' for 'progressive' critics, and 'bad' for 'old-fashioned' ones. It is not altogether different from anything else that was once new, although it is often taken to be. But the notion of 'newness' – and the more dubious one, of 'up-to-dateness' – is comparatively recent.

The chief technique of literary modernism can most usefully be described, in general terms, as expressionism. But Expressionism was also the name of a specifically German movement, one which I have fully described in the section devoted to German literature. Modernism is the name given to distinguish the literature which developed out of the First World War, or, really, the conditions out of which that war inevitably arose. (Sometimes the term 'post-modernism' is over-hopefully employed to describe the literary reaction to the shock caused by the Second World War.) Modernism deliberately broke with Western traditions of certainty, when these collapsed. It came into being as they were collapsing. It challenged all the old modes. Important precursors of modernism are Nietzsche, Unamuno (qq.v.), Freud and Marx – all of whom, in varying degrees, rejected certainties in religion, philosophy, psychology and politics. Armchair anthropologists such as Sir James Frazer (an anthropologist, in this book, is someone who has worked in the field) questioned the certainties of the Christian religion by pointing out that it had arisen directly from 'barbarism', 'superstition' and 'primitivism': from the rituals and disparate beliefs of ancient peoples. Writers came to distrust the stability, coherence and order traditionally assumed in earlier literary works: they could not account for lack of social stability, coherence and order. Therefore works such as Eliot's *The Waste Land* (qq.v.), which has an enormous importance in the history of literature, were organised so as to be 'disorganised', and thus to reflect social, political and religious chaos. It was significant, too, that *The Waste Land* should draw upon pre-Christian myth. Later writers, mainly surrealist, took an even more radical approach. But none of this became standard practice until after the Second World War. When it did become standard practice modernism was dead. The term 'post-modernism' is not very useful, since there is too great a continuity between modernism and it. But it can be said that after the Second World War, which represented a temporary – not, hopefully, a permanent – triumph of barbarism, 'existentialism' became a standard attitude. By then 'modernism' was no longer modern – or adequate to its age. And such old modernists as Joyce, Pound and Eliot (qq.v.) were either dead, had gone mad, or had turned into conservative traditionalists.

Henry James (q.v.) called the modern tradition (which was – for we may now speak of it as in the past – anti-traditional, for reasons obvious enough) an 'imagination of disaster'. This was not an attack upon it, but an alarmed description. James himself was the last of the realists, more or less committed to a nineteenth-century 'mimetic' approach, but aware of how inadequate it would be when the war he did not survive had ended. Looking back, it is easy for us to see modernism as it was: variously ambiguous, nihilistic, defiantly and over-nervously self-sufficient, and perverse. But it did not fail: this book is very largely a record of the individual triumphs of modernism. The achievement of our own age, hopefully designated by the term – for those who employ it – 'post-modernism', is a more dubious one. Proust (q.v.) is a more important and gifted novelist than Robbe-Grillet (q.v.), but then so are Montherlant or Romains (qq.v.), both of whom are modernistic but not in an obvious manner. Ford (q.v.) is greatly superior to Fowles (q.v.) in all the ways that matter; but then so is Maugham (q.v.). This pattern is generally true for all countries (in America: Faulkner, Gass – say – and Farrell, qq.v., fit it), although it is hardly true of Döblin, Grass and (say) Arnold Zweig (qq.v.). But then Grass has a much warmer feeling – something of a different quality altogether, which is actually evident in his texts – for Döblin than Fowles has for Ford, or Robbe-Grillet for anyone but himself. . . . Grass *is* 'post-modernism'.

It should be remembered that in so far as Expressionism implies 'inside-out' – i.e. the expression of internal emotions or other processes in external and often 'realistically impossible' terms – so a vast quantity of the literature of the past, as of the present, may be described as 'expressionist'. The only difference between the old and the newer is that the former almost always represents the external action, whatever that is, as coherent. This does not mean that it does not also represent internal processes. . . . Many passages in Shakespeare could thus be called expressionist. But no text by Shakespeare depends for its viability on an expressionist interpretation. Many of the plays thrown up by German Expressionism – mostly the ones that are now forgotten – were not credible unless they were thus understood. Otherwise they had to be taken as farces. A good many serious Expressionist plays now do read like farces. . . . The first readers of Homer did not look for external representations of internal processes. But it can now be argued that they are nonetheless present. . . . Whether the imaginations of its contemporary readers (or audience) grasped this without being conscious of it, and whether that is a good way to read (or listen), is another matter altogether.

Modernism, which as a phenomenon still arouses (because of 'culture lag') destructive impulses, does share certain features with other 'movements' which were 'new' in their time. But it has unique features. Like any new movement or approach, it rebels against the old. But it also, in its first phase, seeks to destroy the old because it takes it to be not only inadequate but also repulsive and misguided. There was never such a total rebellion in literary history. Modernism is nihilistic, and tends to believe in its own self-sufficiency. It also seeks to go behind what precedes it, and to re-discover primitivism. It is for the most part specifically anti-Christian (Eliot was not a Christian when he wrote *The Waste Land*), if only because Christianity was the prevailing religion of the Western world. New developments in literature had always, before modernism, accepted traditional ethics, and been for the status quo. Realism, just after it began to shade off into naturalism, opposed the status quo. This, the writers started to say, is *not* how things ought to be. Readers were now asked to look into themselves, to establish their real connections with the world and to ignore the rules of religion and society. Modernism wants therefore to break the old connections, because it believes that these are artificial or exploitative. (It seeks to renew the *real* connections, and so is attracted to Pre-Socratic philosophers such as Heraclitus, who said that apparent connections were less powerful than hidden ones. . . .) Modernism is therefore in itself aesthetic, and has no use for rules or forms. It seeks to persuade people to construct their own moralities, and is thus anarchistic (even when its proponents are not). It sees itself as humane, but sees both the structure of society and those who uphold it as inhuman, greedy and unnatural. Of course any writer who held all those attitudes simultaneously was an entirely trivial one, or was simply a critic or a charlatan. The more absolutely a writer is under the sway of a movement to which he belongs, the feebler he is likely to be. The major writers move with their times, but they move in unforeseen ways.

Realism – like its last great wholehearted proponent, James – although it contained the seeds of modernism, remained committed, increasingly subtly, to a mimetic theory: literature is an imitation or a photograph of life. A mimetic theory is the opposite of a symbolic one and, in the sense that it encourages the emulation of earlier models (one of the chief features of 'classicism'), discourages originality. Modernism is more thoroughgoingly anti- or at least non-mimetic. In its extremist form it may resolutely omit all that is regarded as 'essential' in societal, communal or simply representational terms. On the other hand, it will stress precisely what is regarded as unessential in those terms (eventually to the point of perversity). (Of all the modernist movements, probably the most thoroughly programmed, surrealism, q.v., is paradigmatic.) This, again, amounts to an emphasis on the inner life, and therefore on the life of individuals (cf. Expressionism). Causality, carefully observed by nineteenth-century realists, is eschewed or quite deliberately deleted. This does not mean that it is rejected. It means that it is not an essential part of what the modernist writer is trying to draw attention to. Emphasis on it is no longer required. It is not an accident that the surrealists drew so much attention to premonitions and chance.

I should explain that the term mimetic, from mimesis (Greek for *imitation*), is of necessity used unsubtly when it is linked to crude realist aspirations. In Auerbach's book *Mimesis* the fragmentation of exterior action that has taken place in fiction is seen, fruitfully although too often obscurely, as an essentially mimetic process. That it is such can be very persuasively argued. But we must retain the less subtle distinction between 'photographic' intentions (or expectations), which are simplistic, and 'expressionist' ones, which are not. Much popular literature of the ephemeral sort pretends to act as a camera. It manipulates reality in the interests of quick, easy gratification, and assumes a mesmerised reader who wants to believe in its 'world' as he/she believes in a tinted photograph.

It thus aids and abets fantasy. Yet it relies on the assumption that a narrative can represent reality like a photograph, which itself only appears to represent what was in the viewfinder when the picture was taken. The assumptions behind 'photographic realism' call for a descriptive unsubtlety to match them. . . . Whenever merely photographic assumptions are implicit then so is bad faith and ill will. What we are really being offered is a fantasy – even one that we are reading a 'literary' work. . . . However, no serious writer ever had merely photographic assumptions, even if he thought he did.

Mimesis as a term is first seen in Plato, who used it pejoratively to describe the pale imitations of poets, whose works but feebly reflect a feeble reflection. Aristotle, perhaps correcting him, used it to mean a concrete manifestation of that natural order of things which exists but is concealed in 'ordinary' life. He saw this (still very influentially) as peaking in the the Sophoclean tragedy, and thereafter declining.

The nineteenth-century realists, then, were by no means photographic in their imaginative assumptions. Photographic assumptions characterise the vulgar popular novel, which has never been acceptable to the 'common reader'. There is no such assumption built into the Aristotelian definition of art (Aristotle thought that music was the 'most mimetic' of the arts). Plato would have required a symbolic theory, which might have satisifed even him. Aristotle required nothing. The imaginations of the realists knew very well that they could not take either true or even trick photographs of society. But they chose the photographic (really simply the representational) method as the most effective metaphor at their disposal. In every case there is an extra-photographic element in their achievement: in Dickens a proto-Kafkaesque (q.v.) vitality, in George Eliot a brooding moral fervour, in Gissing a drabness of atmosphere which is so severe that it is richly suggestive. . . . But in the now forgotten popular junk of that day there were no extra-photographic assumptions.

Modernism goes beyond realism in being rebellious, anti-traditional, futurist, 'dehumanising' (cf. Ortega, q.v.) and crisis-conscious. But there are not only modernist writers; there are also contemporary writers (those who adequately represent their times, but do not seem to employ modernist techniques). Some critics look at modernism as an essentially timeless concept, perhaps in order to describe such writers as Sterne as modernist in spirit; but modernism is essentially timebound, even if it is by no means clear when exactly it began. Suffice it to say that certain writers are less modernist than they appear (e.g. Cummings, q.v.), while the opposite applies to others (e.g. Powell, q.v.); and that modernism is now a thing of the past. The crises of the 'death of God' and of progressive dehumanisation persist; but modernism is dead, and little has taken its place. There was nothing 'new' about the 'new novel' except its self-consciousness; and 'happenings' were no more than a pop takeover of old surrealist normalities. The revolution in the arts did not, after all, affect the world outside the arts. It only affected the arts themselves, and then inferior imitations.

Because modernism – for all the legacy it has left us – is dead, formlessness, absolute carelessness, has also had its day. Nothing has been done in the 'post-modernist' period that was not done by the surrealists or by such heroes of theirs as Roussel (q.v.). Writers like Burroughs (q.v.) are most distinguished by their unoriginality and conventionality. They rely for their inflated reputations upon perversity, thoughtlessness, ignorance and superficiality. For no poem or book – or painting or piece of music – was ever entirely chaotic. It would be remarkable if such a work could be achieved. It is difficult even to understand the concept of absolute chaos, total entropy. No anarchist ever thought along such lines. An anarchist may well be seen as a nobly pathetic believer in natural form. The imagination generates its own forms, even though these may seem from time to time strange and unfamiliar. The modernists did of course turn to myth; and, even if modernism is dead, myth is not. It could be that in this new positivistic and trivial age, myth is no longer coming into being. But this is unlikely, because there is much resistance to positivism – although unfortunately it seldom, yet, comes from those who are as well informed as the positivists themselves are, at least in their own fields. But the kind of forms the imagination generates are still intimately connected with myth. This is the case whether we believe, with Malinowski, that myths are functions which defend rights, systems and laws, or whether we believe, with the anthropological structuralists, that myths are necessary to man. For Malinowski himself said that myths are 'statements of reality, products of a living faith, intimately connecting word and deed'. The myth-making capacity would only die if the capacity to imagine died. Life itself, in its 'hideous' sense as defined by Flaubert, is and perhaps always has been an enemy of the imagination. But, as he made clear in what have often been taken – and by people who greatly admire Flaubert's novels – as a series of immature and over-romantic posturings, there is always also a sense of life *as it ought to be*. In his letter to Mlle Leroyer Chantepie, from which I quoted above, Flaubert also wrote: 'You are in revolt against the injustice of the world, against its baseness, its tyranny and all the vileness and corruption of life'. Now if another kind of life were not possible, then Flaubert could not talk in this way. But he makes this clearer: 'I believe in the perpetual evolution of humanity and in its ever-changing forms, and consequently I abominate all those frames which men try to cram it into by main force, all the formulas by which they define it, and all the plans they devise for it'. It was dogma that Flaubert did not like; clearly he did not think it was good for humanity or art. 'Life is a rose which withers in the iron fist of dogma,' George Moore (q.v.) wrote. There are many conflicting dogmas about transcendental powers and the origins of the universe and of society. Flaubert did not like these. But he accepted myth inasmuch as this generalised in a metaphorical, not a literal, way about such matters. Myth is sure in its outlines, but somehow not dogmatic. The manifold various accounts of creation – from the famous ones to those hardly known – do not conflict. Perhaps Lévi-Strauss is right and it is not their detail but their structure which should be studied. But perhaps they are, as Cassirer and Frankfort believed, an 'emotional recognition of values' (but it is likely that Frankfort was wrong in his view of myth-making as 'primitive', and in his belief that 'thought' is something superior, which came later). More likely, these views can to a certain extent be reconciled. Whatever myth is, it has about it an unmistakable air of the sacred. Scientism, itself an abuse of knowledge, cannot desacralise the world, however successful it may seem to be in trivialising it in the interests of metaphors (formulations) about the nature of nature, which it naïvely understands to be literal statements. It is well established that literature arose from whatever religion is; it will continue to partake of the religious. Pseudo-literature, the modern 'romance', the 'horror story', and so forth, seeks to destroy the spirit by feeding the impossible: as Anthony Burgess (q.v.) has written, the end of writing a best-selling novel 'is the writing of a best-selling novel. Responses of the reader of a best-selling novel have, strictly speaking, nothing to do with literature. . . . The words of *Lace* . . . are minimal triggers for the explosion of sex and violence. The reader does most of the work, building his voluptuous dreams of rape or mayhem with the least possible artistic assistance from the author. He would resent complexity, poetry, any verbal construct above the level of the near-cliché'. And, he goes on, it takes a 'talent of deprivation' to provide this kind of fare: an inability to look beyond the 'glands, muscles, and the vocabulary of technical processes'. The reader who does not resent inventiveness, the common reader, also works hard, but he does not *use* - - as people use pornography – the serious text, written by the writer who has wrestled with his creation: he is himself with it and lives in it. He works in a certain sort of harmony even when he feels himself to be intellectually 'against' the writer. Writing which has been done only for money and vanity, and which is in no way compelled from its author, is a pornography of the mind, which deprives everyone of their imaginative capabilities, and thus violates life itself in the interests of fantasy. And all but the very greatest of literature occasionally strays into that territory. It was territory Flaubert was trying to avoid in his project of *Madame Bovary*. There is much that he affirms about human life in this terrible and painful record of its unwitting negation. (It is, of course, romances that lead not only Don Quixote but also Madame Bovary into error.)

So the real rather than the merely wishful post-modernism looks for the new in the old, sometimes unsuccessfully but at others successfully. In our ending, in these final years of gloom, doom and decline, is, it seems, our possible beginning, too. It makes for a not unexciting inner life.

III

As we have seen, the fully fledged modernisms that followed realism all broke, in varying degrees, with literary conventions.

History itself has not allowed the writers to, so to say, recover from this blow to the artistic in themselves. The always startling, unfamiliar and yet structured forms of myth saved more or less conservative-minded modernists such as Eliot, Yeats, Pound and of course Graves (qq.v.) from chaos. Myth, being timeless, defeated time. . . . It seemed to be the only effective enemy of the historical process. Less conservative and more sceptical men, such as Robert Musil (q.v.), could not complete their work; but they, too, had resort to myth – in Musil's case, as in others', to the myth of incest. The 'progressive' minded, such as Nexø or Leonov (qq.v.) – though the latter might not have chosen that path had he been other than a Soviet citizen – returned to convention and relied or pretended to rely on the form provided by Marxist-Leninist dogma. But one important break with convention which I have not so far mentioned deserves a section to itself; it seems natural enough in view of the other breaches of convention, but it has vexed and puzzled many readers. I am speaking of the manner in which modern writers have dealt with the notion of time.

Time appears to be a straightforward and common-sense concept. But it is not. All children – natural if unsophisticated metaphysicians – puzzle over it. (Childhood is the only period in life in which metaphysics is natural.) They ask themselves why there is any time: is it not enough that things simply happen (cf. Heraclitus' view of time: there is no permanence; only change is real – but Heraclitus, in spite of his famous remark comparing time to a river, which flows, still seems to have regarded time as a succession of discrete moments, although its substance and symbol for him was fire)? They ask themselves why it moves at different rates despite the evidence of the clock. They ask themselves why it cannot go backwards (although in Newton's universe there was nothing to prevent this). They ask themselves if we just 'come upon' events 'already written'. From not being aware of time at all, they come effortlessly to speculate on the lines of the Pre-Socratic philosophers, agreeing now with Heraclitus and then with Parmenides, who believed only permanence was real. . . .

Wells (q.v.) managed to deal, with great imaginativeness and purity, and just before the public became aware of Einstein, with all these child-like questions, although he gave himself an apparently adult frame in which to do it (his explanation of why there cannot be an 'instantaneous cube' is satisfying to every child, and his time fiction dispenses with almost all of the fiction of that nature which followed it, simply because he anticipated most eventualities). But Wells in his non-speculative fiction did not try to go beyond chronology.

In my comments on the French *nouveau roman* I have explained at some length how and why modernist novelists jettisoned conventional chronology, especially in its aspect as simply a means of manipulating reality into emotionally acceptable forms. By 'acceptable forms' I mean the way time is treated (notoriously) in the 'modern' ('up-to-date') world: only the present is important. This makes time into a commodity, in Marxist terms 'fetishes' it – or, to use Lukács' term, 'reifies' it. Max Lerner wrote: 'American culture cuts away the sensitivity to death and grief, to suicide and immortality, emphasising the here-and-now as it emphasises youth and action'. Time is measured by fascination with mere process, and illusory progress. Thus our attitude to it becomes fraught with anxiety. It was this bland aspect of conventional chronology that the modernists rejected.

It is here that the work of the French philosopher Henri Bergson is relevant. Bergson did not 'discover' either unconventional time or stream-of-consciousness; but his philosophy reflected much contemporary thinking. Bergson is a part of the neo-romantic revolt against positivism; he is anti-intellectual; he also complements the phenomenology of Husserl (q.v.) inasmuch as he concentrates upon the concrete rather than the abstract (Husserl himself was not interested in this problem; but the effect of his work was to draw attention to perceptual actualities). It is appropriate that Bergson, although not a creative writer, should have been awarded the Nobel Prize for literature (1928): his influence on literature – as well as, alas, on Hitler and others of his ilk – has been wide and deep. He demanded a return to the 'immediate data of consciousness'. He has been dismissed by regular philosophers as a mere vitalist, and his notion of 'creative evolution' was somewhat vulgarised by Shaw (q.v.), who was lacking in the intuitive and imaginative faculties. But certain forms of vitalism (usually new versions of holism) are now being canvassed again. Bergson is most profitably regarded as a sort of romantic phenomenologist (although his work only complements the much more meticulous and philosophically respectable investigations of Husserl) who emphasises the difference between our conception of the world and our actual consciousness of it. (Bergson's 'consciousness', originally put forward before Freud had published any books, embraces what we understand by the unconscious.) Modernism follows Bergson in concentrating on the latter – if only, in some cases, through sheer desperation. Indeed, if we survey his philosophy – it is really a form of psychological speculation rather than philosophy in the Anglo-Saxon sense – in more detail, it becomes immediately apparent why he was so influential. When we look at the world intellectually – conceptually, analytically – we see it not as a whole but as a series of discrete units. The intellect gives us a mechanical view of time: as a succession of happenings spread out in *space*. The solution of the paradox on motion mischievously set forth by Zeno of Elea (q.v.) lies in the application of the infinitesimal calculus. But this is not an imaginative answer: the calculus itself only *assumes* that a series of small intervals are continuous. . . . In a psychological sense the infinitesimal calculus is a trick. . . . Bergson was therefore justified in holding that the intellect 'spatialises', and conceives 'geometrically'. Its measuring-rod is a conventional clock. By contrast, the 'intuitive consciousness' experiences the flow of real time *(la durée)* as continuous. This is why it really does – according to the immediate data of consciousness – go at different rates. Beforeness interpenetrates afterness, and vice versa.

Bergson insisted that this 'Intuition' could dispense with symbols. Inasmuch as it is pure *feeling* that he is considering, perhaps it can. But he used symbols and metaphors to discuss Intuition – and wasted some time in vainly trying to prove that this was not really the case. He compared what he called 'metaphysical intuition' to literary creation: something more is needed, after all the study has been done, the notes completed and gathered together, to get started. So Bergson saw human character not as a bundle of attributes or even as personality, but as a process of 'ceaseless becoming'. However, he believed that such a process could only be experienced if 'our ego lets itself *live*, when it refrains from separating its present states from its former states' – i.e. when it frees itself from geometry. It is by no means a long step from this state to the existentialist one of *authenticity* (now, alas, almost a household word), which, among other things, insists that we do allow our egos to thus 'live'. And it was Sartre (q.v.) who well summarised Bergson's position: 'on going into the past an event does not cease to be; it merely ceases to act and remains 'in its place' at its date for eternity. In this way being has been restored to the past, and it is very well done; we even affirm that duration is a multiplicity of interpenetration and that the past is continually organised with the present'. (Sartre was thinking of the 'sticky viscosity' of the past, like a flypaper – a concept which I have discussed in connection with him.) If we look for any sort of rigour in Bergson, as distinct from romantic speculativeness, we shall be disappointed. But ultimately he was prepared to describe his negentropic 'life force', 'élan vital', as 'love'.

The term 'stream of consciousness' originated with Henry James's brother, William, in his *Principles of Psychology* (1890). This provided modernists with a new means of reportage. Henry James reported the conscious and ordered thinking of his characters (or some of them) as though it were the natural process of consciousness. This kind of reportage, since it does not resemble the way in which human beings actually think and feel, is a metaphor or representation – one which puts a metaphorical order and coherence into the ceaseless and by no means altogether rational or explicable flow of feeling-mixed-with-thought which is human experience. But modernists wished to avoid (and sometimes to evade) authorial intrusiveness, with its tendency to make moral judgements.

Sometimes stream-of-consciousness is first-person (as in Joyce's *Ulysses*), at others it is embodied in a third-person narrative. Interior monologue is, in practice, synonymous with it. The two terms can be used interchangeably, and usually are; but strictly speaking stream-of-consciousness refers to the subject-matter and interior monologue to the technique. The technique may be unrelieved or spasmodic. The first thoroughgoing stream-of-consciousness novel was Sterne's *Tristram Shandy*, and so was by no means modern. But it has been charged that he 'did not get below the speech level' in this epoch-making work. From this assumption certain problems arise, not the least of which is, can that be done?

It is generally understood that serious writers who employ the interior monologue technique do so because they find more meaning in the internal lives of people than in their external lives flatly or otherwise described; they also never try to represent this internal life as rational. This is perhaps true. But it is more problematical whether, as is so often assumed, they can put emphasis on the 'pre-verbal' part of human experience. They are said to achieve this by making the necessarily inarticulate (*pre*-verbal) articulate by means of the judicious use of 'images'. Wagner, with his continually repeated musical motifs, deeply influenced the first thoroughgoingly stream-of-consciousness novel, Dujardin's *Les Lauriers sont coupée* (qq.v.). But it is possible that we cannot have, in our human capacity, 'pre-verbal' experiences. It is language that makes us human. At the animal level we appear to have non-verbal experiences such as anger, fear, hunger or pain. But as soon as we consider them we articulate them into speech. This investigation at the animal level (scarcely separable from the speech – or human – level in experience) does not seem to have been what the practitioners of interior monologue wanted to describe. They seemed, rather, to want to describe feelings, which they assumed were inarticulate. But can feelings even come into being – as humanly such – without verbal articulation? The question as to whether thought was possible without language was often asked in the nineteenth century. William James was certain that it was. He thought that the case of Ballard, a deaf-mute instructor at the National College at Washington, showed it 'to be perfectly possible'. The case may well be, though, that if there is any thinking that is not 'inner speech', then even this acts as a function of language, and is thus structured by it. The question will never be fully answered. But the novelists we are considering do not seem to have been investigating this psychological territory. They were more interested in articulating the unconscious in the manner in which Freud had 'articulated' dreams, all of which are a series of 'images'. The main purport of the interior monologue technique is certainly to investigate and reveal motivations and drives. The practitioners of it probably also intuited the fact that by allowing ourselves to become slaves of clocks and conventional chronology our sense of real time has become atrophied. We don't have a better but a 'worse' sense of time than animals. It has been pointed out that *talitrus*, a minute beach crab with only a millimetre of nerve substance, can 'calculate' the 'time of day, the course of an hour, as well as the angle formed by its bodily axis and the position of the sun'. Our own inner clocks would like to be, could be, different and more meticulous than our outer clocks. . . .

There are, however, two very distinct kinds of interior monologue, although they do from time to time get mixed up with each other. The distinction is seldom acknowledged. One is realistic in technique; the other is not. The first is simply an attempt to record – laboriously, you may think – the 'passing of seconds' (cf. *sekundenstil*, q.v.). There is no serious attempt here to penetrate the unconscious, or to portray the mind in its entirety (as we memorably find in, say, Faulkner's portrait of the idiot Benjy in *The Sound and the Fury*). This was the aim of Holz (q.v.). It usually produces the kind of dull text most forgettably presented by Dorothy M. Richardson in her interminable *Pilgrimage*, one of the critically most overrated – if least read – novels of this century in any language. Little imagination is exercised in this type of what might be called pseudo-interior monologue. The other has been described above; it is genuinely experimental, although by no means simply for the sake of experimentation. James and Proust hover at the very edge of this sort of experimentation, James because in extreme moments (such as when Strether, in *The Ambassadors*, actually walks into a picture – the only way in which James can describe an exceedingly complex mental and emotional process) he is driven to employ techniques akin to that of interior monologue, and Proust because he investigates the role of free association in the process of memory. But neither is a true stream-of-consciousness novelist. Some novelists such as Virginia Woolf (q.v.) may have wanted to rely wholly on stream-of-consciousness; but this would have been impossible, not only because the flow of consciousness is *endless*, but also because it is impossible to avoid some principle of selectiveness. Needless to say, stream-of-consciousness records time in a phenomenological and not a chronological manner.

Bergson is important above all for his anti-intellectualism and his continual suggestion that there are ways of seeing ourselves in the world other than the conventional. 'There is one reality, at least', he wrote, 'which we all seize from within, by intuition and not by simple analysis. It is our own personality in its flowing through time – our self which endures'.

IV

I have referred throughout to a number of concepts, or used certain terms, or persisted in pursuing certain themes, which require initial definition or explanation.

I have characterised some writers as *naïve* and others as *sentimentive*. In 1795 Goethe's friend the German poet, dramatist and critic Friedrich Schiller published his essay *On Naïve and Sentimentive Poetry* (*Über naive und sentimentalische Dichtung*). I have followed the sensible practice of translating 'sentimentalische' as 'sentimentive'; 'naïve' is misleading, too, but 'simple' is even more so – at least 'sentimentive' avoids 'sentimental'. This essay has not had, in the English-speaking world, the recognition it deserves. Of all the familiar antitheses – the antique and modern of Schlegel, Dionysian and Apollonian of Nietzsche (q.v.), classical and baroque of Wölfflin – it is the most fruitful. However, the questions of Schiller's exact intentions and motivations are not, strictly speaking, relevant here. What I have done, with the minimum of explanation, is to borrow Schiller's terms and to simplify them for the purposes of this book. For, even in my modified and restricted usage, they convey indispensable information that is not contained in the more familiar classical-romantic opposition.

For Schiller the naïve poet is one who is in perfect harmony with nature; he is, in the familiar cliché, 'attuned to the universe'. Thus his somewhat brutal personality is scarcely to be found in his poetry: he often seems to be 'repulsive', 'callous', 'invisible'. (To take our own example: Goethe's *Roman Elegies* express none of the guilts or doubts of the lover: they enter unanxiously and with salacious ease into the lover's world.)

The sentimentive poet, on the other hand, has lost his contact with and even faith in nature, for whose simplicities he therefore yearns.

Naïve poetry, Schiller writes, is characteristic of the ancients such as Homer: an immediate, inspired, detailed representation of the sensuous surface of life. The sentimentive poet is everywhere present: he is self-conscious, the object 'does not possess him utterly'.

On Naïve and Sentimentive Poetry was originally prompted by the example of Goethe, whom Schiller saw as a serene and naïve poet born out of his time. It was Goethe, too, who made the most profound comment on the essay: '. . . He plagued himself with the design of perfectly separating sentimentive from naïve poetry.. . . as if . . . sentimentive poetry could exist at all without the naïve ground in which. . . it has its root'. One notes Goethe's effortless wisdom as one notes Schiller's tormented and intellectual struggle with himself. Both styles of being are equally exemplary.

Schiller was contrasting the objective (naïve) poetry written in the early, progressive stages of a culture, and the subjective (self-conscious: sentimentive) poetry written in its decline. (If cultures do flourish and decline – and our view of their doing so does not appear to be a subjective error – then our own is certainly in a state of decline.) Goethe, again, summed up the matter: 'All eras in a state of decline and dissolution are subjective . . . all progressive eras have an objective tendency'. Thus, in the poetry of Homer or Shakespeare there is a centrifugal tendency (called by Goethe 'healthy'), an inwards-outwards movement; in most of the poetry of Schiller's contemporaries (and successors) there is a centripetal tendency, an outwards-inwards movement.

Now Schiller wished, very understandably and properly, to defend his own sentimentive poetry in the light of what he took to be Goethe's naïve poetry. His precise concerns in his own context need not be ours. It is enough to say that he felt, about Goethe's poetry, somewhat as we feel about Homer's. Babel felt like this about Tolstoy (qq.v.). 'Reading Tolstoy', he said, 'I always have the feeling the world is writing through him. . . . His books convey the feeling that the existence of a great number of the most varied people – and not only people, but animals, plants, clouds, mountains, and constellations – has been poured out on paper through him. . . . As in electricity, there are writers who are almost ideal "conductors". Tolstoy was an ideal conductor because he consisted entirely of pure literature.'

Here I mean by the naïve writer the writer whose vision has something of the uncomplicated and direct about it. Suffering is certainly torn out of him. His writings are not. His view of life is uncluttered by intellectual considerations. Of course there can be no truly naïve writer now; and in any case all writers, as Goethe pointed out, are ultimately naïve. The more naïve, and therefore more powerful, writers of the nineteenth and twentieth centuries have been poor as thinkers: Dreiser, Sherwood Anderson, Hardy (qq.v.). . . . I have made a good deal of this fact. The naïve writer cannot proceed by thought, even if he thinks he does. The phenomenon can still only be explained by recourse to Schiller's distinction.

I mean by the sentimentive writer – always mindful of Goethe's remark about his rootedness in the naïve – the writer who is sophisticated, trained in thinking, self-conscious. Thomas Mann (q.v.) is paradigmatic in this respect; yet his naïve roots are equally obvious. This sort of writer is suspect to himself and to others.

Schiller's distinction enriches our understanding of modern literature because it points the way towards an invaluable definition of modernism (the sentimentive), without denigrating it. The more naïve writer is happier or 'better' than his counterpart – or so his counterpart feels. Hauptmann and Giono (qq.v.) are two good examples of how naïve writers can be misled in our age: wrecked and corrupted.

In this age the sentimentive writer desperately searches for his naïve roots. The wheel has come full circle. Dream, myth, certainty, affirmation, belief, 'beauty', 'truth' – all those things so reprehensible to the sullen, resentful, reticently superstitious, hell-fearing positivist mind, saturated as it is with journalistic triviality – are now as 'offensive' as modernism was fifty years ago. Then Joyce's *Ulysses* shocked and horrified 'traditionalists'. The book had to be fought for every inch of the way. Today the very people who take it for granted, as orthodox, are themselves shocked by the genuinely naïve, the lyrical, the affirmative! Emotion has become embarrassing, the truly feminine absurd. Some substantial part of what passes for 'feminism' consists of woman's rejection of her own femininity and search for a new, inevitably artificial phallocentrism of her own. This, promoted by Man, suits him so well that he has made it into a new orthodoxy, which insists that male and female are similarly desexed, neutral, colourless 'persons'; the strident woman wearing a flamboyant penis is a tolerated, patronised and attractive novelty.

*

The contrast I have occasionally made between poetry 'direct' and 'oblique' is slightly different – and at a much more elementary, almost pre-critical, level – although the antithesis is of a similar nature.

Direct poetry, clearly, tends towards the naïve, whereas oblique poetry tends towards the sentimentive. You take such poems as Blake's lyrics on trust ('dance with them'), at least when you begin to read or re-read them, rather than get bogged down in analysis of their 'symbolism'. Of course, just as there are no purely 'romantic' or 'naïve' poets, so there are no purely 'direct' poets. The contrast raises stimulating questions: does the apparently direct manner of Williams (q.v.) conceal sentimentive longing? Is there anything false about Perse (q.v.)? Is he oblique trying to seem direct? How much cunning is there in his work – and, if there is a great deal more than meets the eye, then does it detract from its quality? How much wisdom is there really in him? In order to know our own true answers to these questions, it is necessary to be able to approach all poets (and writers) as, in the first instance, direct and naïve. There is much dishonesty and timidity in declared literary response. No one is really an 'expert' in this field.

*

I have often spoken of works having a middlebrow appeal. This term is embarrassing and irritating, as well as difficult to explain without appearing to be over-solemn, humourless or portentous. No definition of 'middlebrow' is to be found in dictionaries of literary terms: it is too elusive. The one essay on it, by Dwight Macdonald – he called it 'midcult' – was inadequate, although on target in characterising the glossy, clever, readable *New Yorker* as middlebrow.

Middlebrow is a broad term which is not, essentially, pejorative. It ought always to be prefaced by a modifier. Those who use it often seem, understandably, to be arrogant and discomfortingly superior. Yet it is quite often used by weekend reviewers, and – an apt example – by the middlebrow movie expert Leslie Halliwell when he wants to characterise certain movies. Thought is very seldom taken as to what it really means, so that some defend themselves (as middlebrow) without knowing what they are defending beside a sense of inferiority; others employ it as a casual term of dismissal. Few pause to think it through; but the common reader's own taste in this respect is (or used to be) unerring. There is general agreement that Margaret Mitchell's hugely successful romance *Gone With the Wind* is middlebrow. *Gone With the Wind* is not a serious book: it falsifies history, is psychologically shallow, and appeals to appetites which can never be satisfied. But it has fluency and a sort of readability. It is contemptible but not quite beneath contempt. It possesses the sort of attraction that is exercised by the image of going with a prostitute (or with a gigolo); and of course the experience never matches up to the image. *Gone With the Wind* offers a convenient example of pure middlebrowism. Certain of its readers are unaware that it is a bad book; others, who are aware of its badness, may acknowledge that they have enjoyed it at a certain level; still others (such as myself) are unable to read it. Another paradigmatic purveyor of not wholly disagreeable rubbish – not quite junk – is Irving Stone, who writes quasi-informed fantasy about such real-life figures as Freud, Van Gogh, and so forth. His function is to turn anguish into boulevard kitsch.

Middlebrow is distinct from junk. Junk is inoffensive (insofar as psychologically inept manipulation of reality can be inoffensive – but it does not do to be too fussy) when it is not ill-willed. It is not usually ill-willed, although it may be foolish, loudly pretentious and sickly. Its socio-anthropological interest lies in the definitions it provides of the nature of fantasy: the day-dreams of the man who sees himself as a war-hero, or of the woman who guiltily yearns to be taken violently, and so forth. Such material may be exploited by serious writers. A decent example is offered by Geoffrey Cotterell's novel *Go Said the Bird*, about a fantasist. Wyndham Lewis (q.v.) used junk-like structures for some of his more realistic novels. Unfortunately it is now a fashionable pastime of criticasters to investigate this sort of material, and pretend that its interestingness is literary (the tedious cult of James Bond is an example). But the connection between junk and literature is as tenuous as the connection between anything else and literature. Anita Brookner's *Hotel du Lac*, a prizewinning novel which exactly caught the spirit of its time, is a clever and able example of an autobiography disguised as *bon ton* fiction: the protagonist is a sexually helpless and hapless writer of junk romances. This rather nasty but goodish book could be the prelude to a series of exquisitely observed light novels, or to one of increasingly pretentious arch ones. Its first successor points to the latter. But Ms Brookner for the time being, through little fault of her own, rules supreme in the middlebrow world, so that her qualities – or lack of them – are usefully indicative.

Middlebrows always call other middlebrows middlebrow. The truth is that everyone has at least a touch of the middlebrow. There are two main reasons for this. First, we all have at times a need for entertainment that does not tax the mind or emotions; secondly, none of us is able, in any case, to face much reality. But our partial weakness does not (or should not) involve subscription to gutter culture, which is now on the ascendant. Somerset Maugham (q.v.) is a good writer, within his limitations, who has a wide appeal to middlebrows. Charles Morgan or Iris Murdoch (qq.v.) are bad (pretentious) writers who also have a fairly wide appeal to middlebrows. You cannot infer much from the fact that a writer has this kind of appeal, which is *in itself* positive, not negative. The difficulty is that it cannot be taken *in itself*. It could (tactlessly) put like this: it is best to read Maugham, but, if you must read bad books – perhaps because you want to feel literary – then *Gone With the Wind*, which is plain awful but not very pretentious, is preferable to Morgan or Murdoch, who are (somewhat modestly beautiful) lilies that have festered. . . . But the literary world saw through Morgan many years ago, and is in the process of seeing through Murdoch. The question is, will it ever see through their younger and increasingly repulsive counterparts?

Wide appeal *in itself* is a useful indication of quality only when it is considered along with other evidence. The paradigmatic middlebrow enjoys narrative (one of the hallmarks of the common reader), but simultaneously desires to suppress those features of writing which leave him unconsoled. The middlebrow (who, needless to say, seldom if ever exists in pure form) is a sort of Pangloss, inasmuch as the best of all possible worlds is the present one. His vociferous complaints about the lack of quality of modern life are fashionable and mechanical, and reflect the 'concern' of the 'quality press', which has all but vanished. His feminism is false and equally fashionable, and seeks to represent both sexes as identically 'wired' (the demonstrable falsity of this is ignored in much of the literature that passes for feminist, and, alas, you cannot found a viable programme on an untruth). The pure middlebrow is a glib pseudo-liberal, superior but cowed, and determined to avoid both sides of any question. He is, politically, of the 'extreme centre' (e.g. Bradbury, q.v., the SDP's Shadow Minister of Culture), is enthusiastic about prizes, and about the subsidisation of literature in general: if governments can control the unpredictable imagination then they can absorb and render harmless (to them) the inevitably subversive effects of literature (literature says, however unobtrusively: this is *not* the best of all possible worlds: it is funny where you think it is serious, and it is serious or pathetic where you think it is funny). The winning of a prize of any kind is indicative neither of merit or of its opposite (so long as one does not go in for it). It is not always even an indication that an author is widely read: the abject Gjellerup (q.v.) offers an excellent example. The Nobel Committee once gave its Prize for Literature to the good-hearted Pearl Buck, for her philanthropic intentions – and ignored Cather, Riding, Akhmatova and countless other women! The history of the Booker Prize in Great Britain, partly chosen by show-business 'personalities', politicians and over-ambitious entrepreneurs, demonstrates that it has no relevance (either way) to literature. But the awarding of prizes causes middlebrows to talk about what they believe to be literature. The precisely middlebrow element in middlebrow material, if it could exist in absolute isolation, manipulates reality in the interests of ignoble comfort and inertia. But in order to masquerade as literature, the 'real thing' – so that the reader, now transformed into a *consumer*, may feel that he has had an authentic cultural experience – it is required to be 'tragic', 'cruel' and so forth. Hence the current popularity of certain subjects: the holocaust, concentration camps – and espionage, in real life the most tedious of activities, carried out, for the most part, by childish and greedy psychopaths or bores. The arch-middlebrow John Le Carré has it both ways: he spins skilful fantasies in which grown-up men behave like murderous schoolboys, and yet preserves an attitude of disgust towards espionage. His success is based on his absolute lack of seriousness, but also, simultaneously, on the crass insensitivity and self-confidence of his assumption that he is serious; his increasing pomposity and vanity, and his tendency towards kitsch, are not irrelevant in this connection. But middlebrow books as bad, even, as Le Carré's, do contain admirable features, spoiled though they may be. Two common ones are the presence of the ability to tell a story in a significant way, and stylistic skill; but authors often distort these gifts – perhaps with unintentionally comic portentousness, like Charles Morgan, or, perhaps more culpably, like Fowles's (q.v.) attempts to dress up his appealing romances as profound modernist works – in order to ingratiate themselves with 'cultured' audiences. No reader is wholly impervious to the middlebrow, although some are certainly impervious to it in its more pretentious forms. Usually the middlebrow novel could be improved (and more modest) if it were in some way changed: Durrell's (q.v.) tetralogy would be interesting as a straightforwardly realistic novel, Fowles's later books would be excellent as lively pastiche of Victorian masters, Le Carré would be all right if he did not take himself seriously. . . . Yet middlebrowism, for all its attractive features and its ubiquitousness, is ultimately, in the terminology of Sartrian (q.v.) existentialism, 'viscous'; it helps human beings to remain *salauds*. That terminology is now outdated; but it is perhaps the most appropriate one to use, for all its sensationalism. However, there is much else besides middlebrowism which acts in this way upon human beings.

Middlebrow material is never wholly junk – junk is Cartland, Danielle Steele, Mills and Boon – but neither can it be wholly literature. Furthermore, as we have seen, some true literature has middlebrow appeal. Middlebrowism is ubiquitous because a part of ourselves is intent upon suppressing energy, which is disturbing and threatens inertia. As Arthur Hugh Clough wrote in *Amours du Voyage*:

I do not wish to be moved, but growing where I was growing,
There more truly to grow, to live where as yet I had languished.
I do not like being moved, for the will is excited; and action
Is a most dangerous thing; I tremble for something factitious,
Some malpractice of heart and illegitimate process;
We are so prone to these things with our terrible notions of duty.

Thus readers (and books) are either more or less middlebrow – never simply middlebrow or not-middlebrow. The solution provided by concientious highbrowism is not often wholly convincing. But that is not because we 'need' the false elements of middlebrowism 'in order to know what kind of world we live in' (a defence frequently encountered). Insofar as reading offers such knowledge, it offers it only in the form of literature, because the possession of that quality is one of the many definitions of literature. The self-conscious highbrow frequently denies himself legitimate pleasure, or is narrow. We need intelligent light entertainment (in order to rest) and we have to get some of it from middlebrow books as well as from those popular writers who somehow elude the category: examples are John Buchan (for very subtle reasons beyond the scope of this book), Wodehouse, Conan Doyle. Such writers are becoming rarer.

Boulevard culture, a swaggering form of middlebrowism, is a term taken of course from the theatre; it is self-explanatory. It is more comic than offensive. It takes different forms in different countries. In Great Britain it is typified by the plays of Tom Stoppard (q.v.), a talented writer for the stage who satisfies audiences because he pleases them for a few hours with fashionable platitudes but has nothing to say. People attend his plays and come away feeling that they have had a profound experience, which they have not. The theatre is the most ephemeral form of literature, and attracts the shallowest audiences. The audiences at popular (and sometimes enjoyable and entertaining) plays are liable to believe that they *discuss* such authors as Umberto Eco, George Steiner (popular because he is taken as profoundly concerned with Heidegger and concentration camps, and because he has a suitably heavy tone), Iris Murdoch or John Fowles during the intermissions. But all that is 'wrong' with the theatre is that it is almost always overvalued.

Middlebrowism becomes truly offensive only when it veers into glaring pretentiousness, or takes on certain characteristics of gutter culture, a sinister phenomenon which is of extreme interest, but which has no connection with literature. It must be mentioned here only because it is beginning to take over middlebrow territory, which (as we have seen) does have literary features.

To describe gutter culture and its intrusion into literature I must have recourse to a somewhat bizarre comparison. Let us suppose that there existed, in reality, a large group of people who could not play soccer, who were too stupid to understand the rules, and who lacked the slightest degree of coordination or skill. They could do no more than merely kick the ball ineffectively. During the game they played – a parody, a static interlude of shockingly uncomic ineptitude – nothing would happen except a series of tricklings of the ball and tacklings of appalling clumsiness.

Let us further suppose that these people formed themselves into teams consisting of eleven people of both (identically wired) sexes, each calling itself by the name of a famous first-division club (Arsenal, Spurs, Everton, and so forth), that they attracted huge numbers of spectators (and drunken hooligans, murderers and policemen), and that they played actual ninety-minute games which they and the spectators believed (not made-believe) were of the quality of first-division matches. Everything except the football would be the same as it is in real football – except the game.

The teams are the gutter writers, and the spectators are 'readers' whose cheer-leaders write articles in publications such as *Time Out*, a collection of fatuous trivia, combined with information about entertainment, published weekly in London. These spectators are content to be told, in the most unauthoritative and cliché-ridden terms, what to think they think about verse, fiction and, of course, the theatre.

Unfortunately this comparison is nearer to the truth than it is to caricature; nor is it hyberbolic. As yet the purveyors of gutter fiction are very seldom acknowledged by those who would like to feel themselves decent and literate. But here is where the ghostly soccer teams come in: there is an unfortunate if somewhat furtive, hapless and haphazard layer of society, 'spectators', who treat it, not as the hateful or pathetic garbage that it is, but as serious writing. . . . There are meetings, readings and mindlessly enthusiastic notices in publications not (now) unknown to the literate public.

All this would be irrelevant, cruel comedy, part of the history of sub-culture, if writing of this low calibre were not now creeping into middlebrowism, and confusing the familiar picture. Of course truly awful writing covers a wide spectrum. At the one end of it are innocently bad 'local' writers; at the other pseudo-sophisticated psychopaths. The worst are characterised by lack of sensibility, facetiousness, meretriciousness, tendency to pastiche, ignorance of what literature is – and, above all, infantilism. Thus 'blood' and 'death' are 'horrifying', and the exposure of them in their raw, unexperienced form is designed to raise applause and approval. Reviewers of the *Time Out* sort, and others, are beginning to fail to be able to distinguish between this kind of material and the seriously intended. There is a touch of this sort of infantile nastiness even in Martin Amis (q.v.), and in a growing number of others. It is as if the human race had given up in the face of the existence of evil, and so decided to try to reduce literature to an inert thing, an object, with neither energy or moral sensibility. It is too silly to be called evil; but it is nonetheless hateful, and it draws on the hateful. The appallingly innocent or supremely egocentric authors of it are less to blame than is the lack of judgement exhibited by those who work for the media. D.M. Thomas' *The White Hotel*, one of the few successes of this sort to be treated as having literary quality, reads as though it were the desperate plagiarism of a professional masturbator. Yet it was hysterically applauded, mostly by emotionally disappointed women, as though reading it were an important experience. In fact merely elementary literary criticism demonstrates it to be devoid of merit. It was popular, however, because it showed how to succeed in sex-business-'literature' without really trying. Its status is that of a masturbation fantasy, and the world it inhabits is a pornotopia suitably furnished with the appurtenances of oppression. To appear to take this seriously involves a considerable degree of self-deception and shrill falsity: a straining of the human faculties. It is not as if we did not all share some of the horrible features of even the worst books. It is unfortunate that the world of *The White Hotel* is not very far from the shabby, dead world of those books, although it does lack that world's impudent facetiousness and total imperviousness to taste and experience.

But there can never be any point in any writing in which, in Keats' famous term, the 'disagreeables' do not evaporate. It may be as well to recollect what Keats actually wrote: 'The excellency of every art is its intensity, capable of making all disagreeables evaporate, from their being in close relationship with Beauty and Truth'. Keats, writing to his brothers, had been looking at a picture, 'Death on a Pale Horse', by Benjamin West. He compared it with *Lear*, in which 'you will find this exemplified throughout' – 'but in this picture we have unpleasantness without any momentous depth of speculation, in which to bury its repulsiveness'. Literature can be nothing if it does not belong to the common reader. And the common reader, and no one else, maintains the precious life and energy in such books as possess them. Either what Keats said is true for all time or it is not true at all. It is therefore incumbent on the common reader to resist the fashionably disgusting: that which adds torture and falsity to a world already almost destroyed by them. We may say we have enjoyed the ephemeral; we may ignore the innocently fatuous; but lazy tolerance of what denies humanity is equivalent to welcoming death. The delights of middlebrow 'profundity' are bad enough, because they are insidious and corrupting. The passive acceptance of the hateful is worse. It numbs us to the life within us. Readers need to be on the lookout – and, most especially, for what is both fatuous and ugly. This is an age of triviality and pretence; thus, works which possess the right admixture of the truly obnoxious, the unskilled, the trivial, the sexually infantile (such as many Germans indulged themselves in, when Hitler gave them an opportunity to involve themselves in a seemingly endless trip into pornotopia) exercise a peculiar appeal. They offer avenues of escape from reality that seem not merely innocuous, but intellectually respectable. Resistance to this kind of material does not involve external or internal censorship; it involves instant recognition. Harsh and persistent ridicule of it, and of its purveyors and supporters, is perhaps the most effective remedy.

*

The term objective correlative was coined by the American painter Washington Allston in a lecture which was published posthumously in 1850; T.S. Eliot (q.v.) revived it – without acknowledgement – in 1919. It has been much criticised as either putting too much or too little emphasis on the alleged objectivity of works of literature. . . .

I am not concerned with this here. I have adapted and simplified the term; in my usage its meaning is unambiguous. I mean by it: equation for personal emotion. Thus, if a writer has an emotion about having killed his wife, and composes a work about a toad eating dry, red eggs, then that fictitious situation is the objective correlative for his emotion about killing his wife. I do thus assume that, in at least the cases in which I employ the term, an equivalent for personal emotion can exist in literary texts. Apart from that assumption, my use of the term is wholly descriptive.

*

Gnosticism was a 'heresy' that arose at about the same time as Jesus Christ. Each record of gnosticism is subtly different, but has something in common with the others. All gnosticisms involve the acceptance of the co-existence of good and evil as elemental forces in the universe. Death may be overcome only by superior *knowledge*. Thus the questions of emotional tone and behaviour ('good works') are or can be ignored. Whether gnosticism arose as a result of Christianity, or whether it preceded it as a form of Greek astralism, is simply not known. But certainly all gnosticisms partake of elements of Greek magic.

The gnosticisms (as they should be called) are mysterious. This is largely because they consist of irrational, pessimistic intuitions re-cast into more or less rational forms. It makes their scriptures read very peculiarly. Gnosticism was the last desperate fling of sceptical magicians against the certainties being put about (God is good and is watching you personally), to cure the age of its terrible uncertainties, by priests. Augustine, first a gnostic (a Manichean), struggled with noble hysterical zeal to conquer these tendencies in himself. He ended by being sure about a good God, but unsure about how to explain him. But gnosticism persisted. It always went against the stream. It managed to combine terrible courage with rigorous intellectualism and magic. People, not themselves intellectuals, died agonising deaths in order to demonstrate that salvation depended on a total rejection of the material world, of creation itself. Creation is, in gnosticism, an accident by which good became (literally) imprisoned in evil. The element of hatred of the material, of substance, that characterises gnosticism is in Plato, Platonism and Neo-platonism; but the Neoplatonists were seldom gnostics. Gnosticism is unflinchingly complex, intellectually meticulous, unappealing and (frequently) highly scatological. 'Perfect salvation is the cognition itself of the ineffable greatness: for since through "Ignorance" came about defect and "Passion" the whole system springing from the Ignorance is dissolved by knowledge.' Salvation is not physical, since the body is corrupt; but neither is it 'psychical', since 'even the soul is a product of the defect'. Thus the 'Valentinian Speculation'.

Gnosticism, persisting in the Cabala, Catharism and other 'heresies', came to be mixed up with vulgar occultism and confidence trickery. Gnosticism is at the heart of alchemy, both of its serious and its disreputable features. It has itself two sides, the one singularly pure and impressive, the other garish and shallow (the 'magick' of the pathetic crook Crowley and his successors). These two aspects of it have become almost, although perhaps not quite, inseparable.

Anyone who calls himself a gnostic is a fraud. We do not understand enough about it even to begin to debate its 'truth'. But what can be said is that it persists as an attitude, and that it does question the potent myth of the good and beneficent God. It seems realistic (in the modern world) in its insistent pessimism and lack of consolation. Yet it seems impossible to practise because it demands a total denial of the material which can only be attained (if it can be attained) by magic. Somehow it is both religious and profoundly irreligious.

More recently gnosticism has emerged into the secular world. The popular philosophy of existentialism (q.v.) is a form of gnosticism. 'Authenticity' is a secularisation of the gnostic concept of salvation. Gnosticism also lies at the heart of modern nihilism. The nihilism of modernism was the 'heresy' of the old, traditional realism. The parallels between our own eschatological age and the one which saw the invention of Christianity are too important to be missed, although I have not been able to give more than a hint of them in this book. They offer food for thought, not least on the subject of how mankind can do, if it can, without religion. Heidegger, a Nazi who became disappointed with Nazism but never apologised for his considerable involvement in it, offered a brand of gnosticism, perhaps of the spurious kind. Hardy, and perhaps Nietzsche (qq.v.) in part, offered another and less opportunistic kind. But these and other writers cannot be represented as 'gnostics', only as modern men tormented by what may be described as religious nihilism.

*

Madness has always been closely related to literature, if only because not a few writers (such as myself) have been quite widely regarded as mad. But writers are not more subject to madness than the rest of the community. They are usually sensitive; but then so are other people (for example, readers). But writers are more prone to histrionic behaviour. (The phenomenon of 'split personality' has nothing to do with schizophrenia, as is popularly supposed: it is a rare manifestation of hysteria, and inevitably involves acting out a role. There is no such condition as 'two personalities occupying one body', although there is profit in the notion.)

Hysteria (now usually called histrionic behaviour) is more wilful than we are usually led to believe. Writers are wilful people. Hysteria is inevitably 'cured' when no attention whatsoever is paid to it. It is therefore seldom cured. If attention is paid to it, and it often has to be, then it can mimic all sorts of illnesses. This is not an old-fashioned condemnation of hysteria as characterising the behaviour of people whom the physicians of a few years ago used to describe as 'poor stuff'. It is merely a realistic corrective to the glib, contemporary pseudo-liberal tendency to indulge bad behaviour on factless grounds. Most people, given the chance, will behave in a manipulative or histrionic manner. Those who do not seem to do so are often authoritarian, and so indulge themselves in a far more sinister manner: they have already gained the attention that the hysteric desperately needs.

One of the illnesses that histrionic behaviour can closely resemble is what ought to be called the schizophrenias. The success of R.D. Laing – unfortunately much heeded by writers – is entirely owed to this. Laing started as an 'anti-psychiatrist' usefully critical of official psychiatry, and of the authoritarian style in which it treated its victims. This was admirable. But Laing became over-ambitious, and, employing an obscure and gnomic style (what he says seldom means anything, wherein lies its attraction) he began to pretend that because the world is mad – which it undoubtedly is – those people characterised by it as 'mad' are really 'sane'. This is not true. It is, indeed, ruthless and cruel nonsense. It is fallacious because 'mad', in the two statements, is used in two distinct senses.

Laing maintains that mad people, whom he calls schizophrenics (he has never seemed to show much interest in affective disorders) are creative. But most of Laing's schizophrenics, whom he wrongly represents as victims of their families, are clearly people of histrionic personality subject (occasionally) to schizophreniform episodes. His view of insanity and its function has been very widely influential, especially on writers of a mindlessly existentialist or (indeed) histrionic bent. What I say about madness in this book runs directly counter to what Laing says – so I should explain myself, and one or two other assumptions I have made. After all, there is a significant relationship between the lunatic, the lover and the poet. But it is not what Laing, drawing for the most part on the writings of others such as Binswanger, thinks it is. And his approach is anything but humane.

The world is indeed mad. But its madness does not resemble the madness which afflicts individuals. The world, as the misunderstood ironic Italian sociologist Pareto pointed out most clearly – at least in sociological terms – is a partly irrational place pretending to be completely rational. One of the chief functions of literature is to try to describe, explain or reconcile the difference between reality and this illusion of rationality. However, the world cannot be described as suffering from schizophrenia or affective illness. Individuals *are* afflicted by various forms of affective illness (depression, mania – no doubt a special case of the former – hypomania, panic and disappointment reactions, acute anxiety, intolerable fear; and by various combinations of these), which was once called 'manic-depressive psychosis' – or by one or other of the many forms of schizophrenia. The Americans tended, at least until the advent of lithium therapy (which alleviates affective illness but is almost certainly not helpful in schizophrenia: it is thus, incidentially, a valuable diagnostic tool), to classify people who were suffering from affective disorders, or who were just exhausted, as schizophrenic. This practice led critics who knew less about psychiatry than even American psychiatrists to 'diagnose' most of the writers known to have suffered from madness as schizophrenic. This has proved to be mistaken. The difference between the schizophrenias and the affective disorders is that the former tend to destroy the personality, which disintegrates. In the affective disorders there is no systematic deterioration of the personality, although, under the shattering effects of deep depressions and manic attacks it may become somewhat worn out. It is true that many experience schizophrenic attacks and recover completely, but the general tendency of the group of diseases called schizophrenia is towards total disintegration of the personality ('chronic schizophrenia', alleviated but not 'cured' by anti-psychotic drugs). It was through observing this difference in the prognosis that Kraepelin first made the distinction between the two types of illness. He called it *dementia praecox*; subsequently Eugene Bleuler (1857-1939) re-named the group (already divided by Kraepelin) schizophrenia. He did not mean to imply by this resort to the Greek word for *split*, that the split was into 'two personalities'. He meant that the personality fragments under pressure of bizarre emotion and persecuting ideation. People suffering from states of depression, mania, or a mixture of the two can experience hallucinations and paranoid emotions – but their behaviour seldom exhibits the emotionally incongruous 'flatness' or 'bluntedness' peculiar to schizophrenics, who cannot handle reality appropriately, and might laugh at the tragic and cry at the comic.

It is impossible to generalise about mental illness. But, although some writers (and creative people) might experience schizophrenic attacks and recover, schizophrenia is *not* a 'creative' illness, nor is it (as Laing, who does of course recognise the suffering involved in it, would have it) a bizarre and painful representation of that reality which the world wrongly avoids. Known in all societies, including those fortunate enough not to have experienced the process called civilisation, it is a destructive and anti-creative illness.

What schizophrenics create is bizarre, child-like and actually avoidant of any kind of reality. The personality withdraws into panic and atrocious fear; finally, unless the process is arrested by drugs, it fragments. Sometimes the schizophrenic becomes 'burnt out': he still believes that the radiators are controlling him (or whatever he believes), but can tolerate it. At others he becomes catatonic, a vegetable. The 'word-salads' produced by schizophrenics are pathetic documents which evade reality by every manner of trick: echolalia, repetition, flat and emotionally blunted avoidance of logicality or any sort of coherence: the product of incapacitated imaginations.

Thus the idea that schizophrenia, of all the states that might be chosen, represents a positive or creative process is utterly wrong. Laing began by sympathising with schizophrenics. But he then over-ambitiously developed a derivative psycho-social theory in which psychiatrists were identified with the existing political order (or disorder), and schizophrenics were identified with its 'victims'. But schizophrenia is an enemy of life, and of the energy that makes life worth living. That literature which has been modelled on his ideas is occasionally good-hearted but mostly deadly and self-indulgent junk.

Most writers who have been 'mad' have suffered from affective disorders; but most have been misdiagnosed by biographers. Thus the poet John Clare, clearly a hypersensitive 'manic-depressive' whose episodes of illness were triggered by disappointment reactions, was until recently described as a schizophrenic. Campana (q.v.), diagnosed as schizophrenic by the Florence hospital in which he spent his last years, was almost as obviously a manic-depressive who suffered from severe and debilitating 'mixed states'. Hardly anything about schizophrenia is understood; and there are some invaluable insights into the condition in literature: for example, in modern Hebrew fiction. And those who have suffered from schizophreniform episodes have been able to describe something of their anguish. But no literature could come from sufferers from chronic schizophrenia, and the state does not (as it happens) stem from social evils or wicked families (there is no evidence for the Langian myth of the evil family; there is much more for a genetic predisposition triggered by concatenations of circumstances, which of course may include difficult mothers and fathers).

Further on this subject: it is often asserted that Lowell, Berryman (qq.v.) and some other American poets, suffered from affective disorders as well as alcoholism. But what these two and many like them suffered from were, mainly, gross hysteria and hyperbolic self-love. There is no reason to withhold sympathy from them on that account: many of us are or have been in the same case. But it is as well to have the facts straight in an age in which writers aspire – to the cost of their achievement – to the status of film stars, and drive themselves reprehensibly crazy in the process.

*

For a truly viable theatre to exist there must be a truly viable audience. Such a theatre existed in Belgium, at least until recently. A theatre dominated by a star system cannot really be viable, and – to their credit – some companies in Great Britain have made half-hearted efforts to avoid this. But the theatre of today is largely in the hands of directors (hence the term 'directors' theatre'), who do not work in true conjunction with the authors of plays, but rather as 'commercial realists' who manipulate such texts as fall into their hands to meet the needs of middlebrow audiences. The genuine dramatist has to survive this and assert himself. There are two tests of a genuine dramatist: his work must be playable on the stage, in some form, at any time during or after his lifetime; and it must stand the test of reading as well as viewing. Perhaps a score of twentieth-century dramatists fulfil these requirements. I have discussed these and a number of other interesting ones. But it must be remembered that this is a guide to literature and not to the entertainment industry, however intelligently motivated or amusing this may occasionally be. My remarks on certain dramatists have been taken by some as over-severe; but they are directed not towards the authors but towards the bad habit of taking them over-seriously.

*

Another concept that I have used freely is what I have christened *Künstlerschuld*: artist-guilt. Increasingly in this century writers have been beset by the fear that literature fulfils no useful or humane, but only a selfish, function. Rilke, Mann, Broch (qq.v.) are examples. The writers who have felt like this have usually been dedicated to literature to the exclusion of anything else. The question is as old as Plato, but in the past hundred years it has become crucial. If literature is not obviously a political weapon – and it is obviously not, as 'socialist realism' (q.v.) makes clear – then has it a social function? Is the writer an outcast or an unacknowledged legislator or neither? Is the imagination the enemy of all political order, and not just Marxist order? This phenomenon has not been picked up by critics, perhaps because they would like to be creative writers and think that the life is all delight and ease. But if a hatred or at least a distrust of your enterprises is actually built into them, then this is clearly paradoxical and interesting.

    The approach of this book affirms literature as humane, but sees it as continually menaced by insights into evil which are, however, necessary for the maintenance of its very humaneness. It also, while attempting to retain a sense of balance, sees it as threatened (by trivialisation) from another quarter: the fatuous, mendacious and deliberately unintelligent media. Writers have always needed money as much as anyone else; now some of them (not me, alas) are in danger of getting too much. It is in the interests of inertia to create, or allow to come into being, a mockery of literature. But that is only going to look like the real thing to fools.

*

It is towards the truly mysterious and yet authentic that the creative writer must aim. That is why so much of the best literature came, until recently, from Latin America: an exotic and largely unexplored region of the world which well matches our own equally exotic and largely unexplored interiors. But Latin-American literature is now getting dangerously near to parodying itself. Recourse to the purely surreal can now lead to nothing better than the raw material of the dream, which, as it comes into consciousness, is censored, screened. What is needed – we see it in the best of Vallejo (q.v.) – is the real dream: the meaning of the dream in its own original, unknown, day-haunting images. This truth contains, absorbs and accepts death.

The problem is one of control as well as 'inspiration'. What kind of control must the writer exercise over his immediate impulses to return to this naïve realm? Animal cunning can be useful: the cunning art of the 'primitive' man who hunts, for food, the animals he loves and understands. This is nearer to the required sentimentive than is the cleverness of the academic critic, for all the ancient wisdom that is locked up, fossilised, inside the notions with which he plays. The way will not be fashionable, and those who take it will not be universally popular, since they must find new means of expressing lyrical simplicities not now palatable to *soi-disant* sophisticated audiences – or to the ignorant criticasters who train and drill them in conformist subversiveness. It is not enough to oppose all governments. It is necessary, if we are to think for ourselves, to oppose all official oppositions. 'Whatever it is,' sang Groucho Marx, 'I'm against it.' People can only read well if they are independent, and they can only agree when they have agreed to disagree – and be themselves. At the same time writers (and their readers) must avoid a return to the immediate pre-modernist past. Modernism, which really forms the subject of this book, is over; but it had lessons to offer. Its successor is likely to look very strange indeed; but it will be recognisable, and it will possess satirical laughter.

Blandford Forum–Salonika   Martin Seymour-Smith
23 June 1984–17 March 1986

Abbreviations

AD: *Absurd Drama*, P. Meyer, 1965

abd.: abridged

ad: adapted

add.: with additional matter

AGD: *Avant-Garde Drama*, 13.F. Dukore and D.C. Gerould, 1969

AL: *Albanian Literature*, S.E. Mann, 1955

AMEP: *Anthology of Modern Estonian Poetry*, W.K. Matthews, 1955

AMHP: *Anthology of Modern Hebrew Poetry*, A. Birman, 1968

AMYP: *Anthology of Modern Yugoslav Poetry*, J. Lavrin, 1963

ANZP: *Anthology of New Zealand Poetry*, V. O'Sullivan, 1970

AP: *Africa in Prose*, O.R. Dathorne and W. Feuser, 1969

ARL: *Anthology of Russian Literature in the Soviet Period*, B.G. Guerney, 1960

ASP: Apollinaire: *Selected Poems*, O. Bernard, 1965

AU: *Agenda*, vol. 8, no. 2, Ungaretti Special Issue, Spring 1970

AW: *Australian Writing Today*, C. Higham, 1968

AWT: *African Writing Today*, E. Mphahlele, 1967

BAP: Bella Akmadulina: *Fever and Other Poems*, G. Dutton and I. Mezhakov-Koriakin, 1970

BAV: *Book of Australian Verse*, J. Wright, 1956

BEJD: Josef Brodsky: *Elegy for John Donne and Other Poems*, N. Bethell, 1967

BISS: *Penguin Book of Italian Short Stories*, G. Waldman, 1969

BP: Bertolt Brecht: *Plays*, 2 vols, J. Willett and E. Bentley, 1960-62

BRV: *Book of Russian Verse*, C.M. Bowra, 1943

BRV2: *Second Book of Russian Verse*, C.M. Bowra, 1948

BSP: André Breton: *Selected Poems*, K. White, 1969

CCD: *Chief Contemporary Dramatists*, 3 vols, T.H. Dickinson, 1915-30

CDP: *Contemporary Danish Plays*, E. Bredsdorff, 1955

CFP: *Contemporary French Poetry*, A. Aspel and D. Justice, 1965

CGP: *Contemporary German Poetry*, J. Bithell, 1909

CGPD: *Contemporary German Poetry*, B. Deutsch and A. Yarinolinsky, 1923

CIP: *Contemporary Italian Poetry*, C.L. Golino, 1962

CIV: *Contemporary Italian Verse*, G. Singh, 1968

CLP: *Century of Latvian Poetry*, W.K. Matthews, 1957

CP: Anton Chekhov, *Plays*, 1959

CRP: *Anthology of Contemporary Rumanian Poetry*, R. MacGregor-Hastie, 1969

CTP: Albert Camus: *Caligula and Three Other Plays*, S. Gilbert, 1958

CV: *Caribbean Verse*, O.R. Dathorne, 1967

CWT: *Canadian Writing Today*, M. Richler, 1970

DFP: Friedrich Dürrenmatt: *Four Plays*, G. Nellhaus et al, 1964

ed.: edited by

EOWYO: *Envy and Other Works of Yuri Olesha*, A. MacAndrew, 1963

ESW: Paul Eluard: *Selected Writings*, L. Alexander, 1951

FBS: Marcel Raymond: *From Baudelaire to Surrealism*, 1950

FCP: *Five Centuries of Polish Poetry*, J. Peterkiewicz, Burns Singer and J. Stallworthy, 1970

FGP: *Four Greek Poets*, E. Keeley and P. Sherrard, 1966

FMR: *From the Modern Repertoire*, 3 vols, E. Bentley, 1949-56

Fr.: French

FSP: *Four Soviet Plays*, B. Blake, 1937

FTP: Max Frisch: *Three Plays*, M. Bullock, 1962

FTS: Frank Wedekind: *Five Tragedies of Sex*, B. Fawcett and S. Spender, 1952

FWT: *French Writing Today*, S.W. Taylor, 1968

GED: *Anthology of German Expressionist Drama*, W.H. Sokel, 1963

Ger.: German

GMS: *Plays of Gregorio Martinez Sierra*, H. Granville-Barker and J.G. Underhill, 1923

GSP: Michel de Ghelderode: *Seven Plays*, G. Hauger and G. Hopkins, 1960

GSS: *German Short Stories*, R. Newnham, 1964

GWT: *German Writing Today*, C. Middleton, 1967

HE: *Heart of Europe*, T. Mann and H. Kesten, 1943

HSS: *Hungarian Short Stories*, 1967

HW: René Char: *Hypnos Waking*, J. Matthews, 1956

HWL: Joseph Reményi, *Hungarian Writers as Literature*, 1964

IMPL: *Introduction to Modern Polish Literature*, A. Gillon and L. Krzyzanowski, 1964

IMSL: *Introduction to Modern Spanish Literature*, K. Schwartz, 1968

IN: P.J. Jouve: *An Idiom of Night*, K. Bosley, 1968

IP4: Eugene Ionesco: *4 Plays*, D. Watson, 1958

IQ: *Italian Quartet*, R. Fulton, 1966

ISS: *Italian Short Stories*, R. Trevelyan, 1965

IWT: *Italian Writing Today*, R. Trevelyan, 1967

JDP: Max Jacob: *Drawings and Poems*, S.J. Collier, 1951

JLME: Y. Okazakix: *Japanese Literature in the Meiji Era*, V.H. Vigliemo, 1955

LAP: *Anthology of Latin-American Poetry*, D. Fitts, 1942

LTT: Federico García Lorca: *Three Tragedies*, J. Graham-Luján and R.L. O'Connell, 1961

LWLF: *An Anthology of Byelorussian Poetry from 1928 until the Present Day*, 1971

LWT: *Latin-American Writing Today*, J.M. Cohen, 1967

MAP: *Modern African Prose*, R. Rive, 1964

MBL: *Introduction to Modern Bulgarian Literature*, N. Kirilov and F. Kirk, 1969

MBSP: V. Mayakovsky: *The Bedbug and Selected Poetry*, P. Blake, 1961

MEP: *Modern European Poetry*, W. Barnstone, 1966

MFC: *Four Modern French Comedies*, A. Bermel, 1960

MGL: *Introduction to Modern Greek Literature*, M.P. Gianos, 1969

MGP: *Modern German Poetry*, M. Hamburger and C. Middleton, 1962

MHP: *Mayakovsky and his Poetry*, H. Marshall, 1965

MJL: *Modern Japanese Literature*, D. Keene, 1956

MJS: *Modern Japanese Stories*, I. Morris, 1961

MPA: *Modern Poetry from Africa*, G. Moore and U. Beier, 1963

MRD: *Masterpieces of Russian Drama*, 1933

MRP: *Modern Russian Poetry*, V. Markov and M. Sparks, 1966

MRPC: *Modern Rumanian Poetry*, N. Catanoy, 1967

MSP: Oscar Venceslas de Lubicz Milosz: *14 Poems*, K. Rexroth, 1952

MST: *Modern Spanish Theatre*, M. Benedikt and G.E. Wellwarth, 1968

MSW: Henri Michaux: *Selected Writings*, R. Ellmann, 1968
MT: *Modern Theatre*, 6 vols, E. Bentley, 1955-60
NIP: *The New Italian Poetry*, L. Smith, 1981
NTE: *The New Theatre in Europe*, R.W. Lorrigan, 1962
NVSP: *Selected Poems of Neruda and Vallejo*, R. Bly, 1970
NWC: *New Writing in Czechoslovakia*, G. Theiner, 1969
NWP: *New Writing from the Philippines*, L. Caspar, 1966
NWSD: *The New Wave Spanish Drama*, G.E. Wellwarth, 1970
NWY: *New Writing in Yugoslavia*, B. Johnson, 1970
OBCV: *The Oxford Book of Canadian Verse*, A.J.M. Smith, 1960
orig: originally
OW: *Ocean at the Window*, A. Tezla, 1980
PAWT: *African Writing Today*, E. Mphahlele, 1967
PBFV3, PBFV4: *Penguin Book of French Verse 3, 4*, A. Hartley, 1957, 1959
PBGV: *Penguin Book of Greek Verse*, C. Trypanis, 1971
PC: Anton Chekhov: *Plays*, E. Fen, 1959
PGV: *Penguin Book of German Verse*, L. Forster, 1957
PI: *Poem Itself*, S. Burnshaw, 1960
PIV: *Penguin Book of Italian Verse*, G. Kay, 1965
PJV: *Penguin Book of Japanese Verse*, G. Bownas and A. Thwaite, 1964
PKM: Kai Munk: *Five Plays*, R.P. Keigwin, 1953
PLAV: *Penguin Book of Latin-American Verse*, E. Caracciolo-Trejo, 1971
PLJ: *Poetry of Living Japan*, D.J. Enright and T. Ninomiya, 1957
POM: *The Prose of Osip Mandelstham*, C. Brown, 1965
PNT: *Plays for a New Theatre*, A.S. Weineger and C.J. Atkinson, 1966
PP: Alfred French: *The Poets of Prague*, 1969
PPPP: *Post-War Polish Poetry*, C. Milosz, 1965
PRP: Robert Pinget: *Plays*, 2 vols, S. Beckett, B. Bray, 1965-7
PRV: *Penguin Book of Russian Verse*, D. Obolensky, 1965
ps.: pseudonym of
PSAV: *Penguin Book of South-African Verse*, J. Cope and U. Krige, 1968
PSV: *Penguin Book of Spanish Verse*, J.M. Cohen, 1956
pt.: part
PTP: Luigi Pirandello: *Three Plays*, A. Livingstone, 1923
PWT: *Polish Writing Today*, C. Wieniewska, 1967
rev.: revised
RP: *Russian Poetry 1917-55*, J. Lindsay, 1956
RSP: Pierre Reverdy: *Poems*, A. Greet, 1968
SAWT: *South-African Writing Today*, N. Gordimer and L. Abraham, 1967
SCO: *Swan, Cygnets and owl*, M.E. Johnson, 1956
sel.: selected by
SL: *Soviet Literature, an Anthology*, G. Reavey and M. Slonim, 1933
SP: Bert Brecht: *Seven Plays*, E. Bentley, 1961
SSP: *Six Soviet Plays*, E. Lyons, 1934
SSW: Jules Supervielle: *Selected Writings*, 1967
TC: Anton Chekhov: *The Tales*, 13 vols, C. Garnett, 1916-22
TCG: *Penguin Book of Twentieth Century German Verse*, P. Bridgwater, 1963
TCGV: *Twentieth Century German Verse*, H. Salinger, 1952
TCSP: *20th Century Scandinavian Poetry*, M.S. Allwood, 1950
TGBP: *Two Great Belgian Plays about Love*, 1966

TMCP: *Three Modern Czech Poets*, E. Osers and G. Theiner, 1971
TMP: *Twenty-five Modern Plays*, S.F. Tucker, 1931
TNM: *Two Novels of Mexico*, L.B. Simpson, 1964
TPAVL: *Three Plays of A. V. Lunacherski*, 1923
tr.: translated by
TSP: *Three Soviet Plays*, M. Glenny, 1966
TT: *Tellers of Tales*, W.S. Maugham, 1939
UP: *Ukranian Poets*, W. Kirkconnell and C.H. Andrusyshen, 1963
VA: Andrey Voznesensky: *Antiworlds*, P. Blake and M. Hayward, 1967
VCW: Paul Valéry: *Collected Works*, J. Matthews, 1962
VSW: Paul Valéry: *Selected Writings*, 1950
VTT: Paul Éluard: *Thorns of Thunder*, G. Reavey, S. Beckett, 1936
WNC: *Writers in the New Cuba*, J.M. Cohen, 1967
ZS: Nikolay Zabolotsky: *Scrolls*, D. Weissbert, 1970

African and Caribbean Literature

I

The emergence of a people, oppressed for centuries, into articulate awareness of their insulted and traumatic history is a matter of concern to everyone. But the matter is a highly complex one, as one learns most easily of all, perhaps, from V.S. Naipaul's (q.v.) essays *The Overcrowded Barracoon* (1972), in which he shows how not only the foundation of the British Empire but also its dissolution caused untold suffering. One can extend his humane concern and explanations to other empires and other places than those he deals with. The literature of Black Africa is, of course, only one aspect of this confused but increasingly evident emergence. But its intrinsic literary importance has sometimes – with every justification – been somewhat exaggerated. Such works (I take a random example) as the Ethiopian **Sahle Sellasie**'s (1936) *Shinega's Village: Scenes of Ethiopian Life* (1964; tr. 1970), the first work written in Chaha – a hitherto unwritten Ethiopian dialect which Sellasie used an Arabic script to transcribe – are important in sociological and historical terms. So is his *The Afersata* (1969), written in English, describing how a remote Ethiopian community with no police force investigates an outbreak of arson by its age-old 'Afersata' method. But neither is a work of great literary importance. Even the more famous African writers, such as Senghor (q.v.), have had exaggerated claims made for them. These writers will be important figures in the history of the literature now emerging; but the intrinsic importance of their work – as literature – will surely be seen to be smaller than is now apparent. I mean that no indisputably major poets or novelists, with the possible or probable exceptions of those I have chosen – out of a hundred or so – to discuss here, have yet emerged. I have quoted the South African writer Ezekiel Mphahlele's (q.v.) reasons for his holding of a similar view in the section dealing with black South African writing, which should be read in conjunction with this.

The tensions in black literature are acute. What black man, who is also a writer, is to assert that it is more important for him to function independently – as a writer must (but witness the fierce bitterness attracted by V.S. Naipaul for choosing to be non-political) – when he and his fellows' freedom seems to be threatened and insulted? Good writing has arisen from such tensions; interesting writing has arisen from them; as yet not a large number of unquestioned masterpieces have. But what is happening and is likely to happen in this area is important, for literature is here being put to the test. It is being put to the test as much in 'liberated' Cuba as it is in the more unequivocally oppressed Haiti.

Yet two strands are already clearly discernible in the black literature of the world: one is 'committed' to negritude (q.v.), or something akin to it or developed from it (at the most extreme, 'black power'); the other is for obvious reasons less easily definable, but it leaves writers freer and more open to attack from their colleagues. Its spokesmen (the

1

South African Ezekiel Mphahlele is one of them) are often accused, by adherents of negritude, of such crimes as 'colonialism, neo-colonialism and imperialism'. But this is an attack by political upon literary animals; it also represents a misunderstanding of the nature of literature. It may be that, in the wider context, the activists are correct; it may be that they are wrong. In the context of literature they are missing the point. Literature is made not with ideas but with imagination; and despite the arguments of committed writers, the imagination is autonomous (I do not apologize for repeating this so often), and owes no allegiance to any form of dogma, even if certain assumptions are built into it. Writers in favour of Marxist commitment call this view 'mystical'. But it is not mystical; it merely acknowledges a mystery. It is a mystery exceedingly hard even to begin to solve; only some knowledge of anthropology – and not a fashionable one at that – can help.

However, this is the situation at present. But such writers as Mphahlele and Soyinka (q.v.) – who has pointed out that tigers do not need to advertise their tigritude – readily acknowledge that negritude was a 'necessary phase'; if one did not like the word 'necessary' one could substitute 'inevitable'.

Although the concept of negritude was fully developed in Paris during the Thirties by such poets as Senghor (q.v.), it originated in the Caribbean and elsewhere: it is not in fact a French phenomenon, even if the single issue of the magazine *Légitime Défense* (June 1932) launched the actual movement (the editors, young French West Indians such as Étienne Léro, did not become well known). In the French islands the Africans were as violently alienated from their original nature as any black men anywhere: displaced, separated from their immediate families, forced into the Roman Catholicism of their masters, they either developed secret systems such as Voodoo (in Haiti) – a distorted means of asserting their essential Africanity – or they tried to become, by imitation, the very thing that oppressed them. The French were always glad to bestow upon a 'good', Catholic, educated, 'civilized' black the ultimate honour: to be a 'black Frenchman' (*'évolué'*). But this system of 'assimilation', until recently practised by the Portuguese (*'assimilado'*), does not allow for French (or Portuguese) black men. ... Nor was it ever sincere: it was just a patronizing reward-system: a false payment to a man for selling his soul and his self. Thus, the 'good' black slaves of the French were told of their 'Gallic' ancestry. Assimilation is based on the anthropologically erroneous assumption (convenient to master-races engaged in economic exploitation, and therefore primarily a Victorian notion) that the concept of evolution can be applied to the 'progress' of human species. The insult contained in such an attitude – 'you are a primitive non-European, a version of my unperfected self' – is both loveless and humanly wounding. Only now are we beginning to realize that so-called 'primitive' societies are too complex for 'civilized' people to understand with either ease or confidence. Some (myself included) prefer some of them, though this attitude is not at all easy to maintain – societies differ in so many ways – and it is best described as emotional and subjective.

Negritude expressed itself mainly, but not entirely, in poetry. Ironically it got its first chance in Cuba – as *negrismo* – when there was a European craze for all things African. (This craze did not represent a sudden awareness of the riches of African culture, but a reaction to the First World War.) In Haiti there was a similar revival. Caribbean Africans, thus encouraged, began to look at their true heritage. There were magazines – in Cuba *Revista de Avance* (1927–30) and in Haiti *La Revue Indigène*. Then, in Paris, a group of students, including Césaire (q.v.) and Senghor, published one issue of a magazine called *The Black Student*; later Volontés printed Césaire's *Return to My Native Land* (1939; tr. 1947 as *Memorandum on My Martinique* – the best translation; tr. not recommended for its English, 1979). This was ignored at the time; but André Breton (q.v.) found a roneoed copy of it in 1940, visited Césaire in Martinique in 1942, and publicized the poem when he returned to France. When it was republished in 1956 it was already famous both as a surrealist poem and as the quintessential expression of negritude.

However, it must be added that a great deal of nonsense has been written about negritude – and that, although the term has had a concrete meaning to some writers, it is in fact an abstraction. Even Senghor has written very foolishly on the subject, as when he stated that the African was 'non-intellectual' – for which remark a Ghanaian critic called him an 'apologist of France speaking to Africa'! Yet on another occasion he said, 'Claude McKay [q.v.] can rightfully be considered the spiritual father of negritude.' Apart from tracing the history of the movement – which was of course to alienate many writers later on – the only useful definition of negritude is that it represented a conscious effort to reach back to traditional roots, whether it was thus defined or not. Obviously the integration of the 'traditional' (an anthropological concept of the utmost difficulty) into Westernized countries was going to present enormous problems and produce violent arguments. L. Hughes (q.v.) and McKay are as important in the development of negritude as Senghor or Césaire. ...

Aimé Césaire (1913) was born in the kind of circumstances suffered by most poor African peasants in Martinique. His house was 'a shack splitting open with blisters like a peach-tree tormented by blight, and the roof worn thin, mended with bits of petrol cans, this roof pisses swamps of rust on to the grey sordid stinking mass of straw. ...' His own status turns out, in fact, not to have been as bad as this (the Césaires were almost an elite within their own society); but the exaggeration is excusable. Césaire was a communist, but left the party in 1956. Now he is a deputy to the French Assembly, representing the independent revolutionary party of Martinique (which has an association with France – it was he who gained its transfer from colony to overseas department in 1946). *Return to My Native Land* is his main work, though he has written much else. Its style has been profoundly influenced by surrealism (q.v.) – the logical weapon with which to assail the polite and dreamless language of the oppressor – but it is misleading to call it a surrealist poem: its structure, and much of its content, is too immediately comprehensible to the rational, conscious mind. But it is disorganized enough – in terms of what 'poetry-loving', paternalistic colonials would expect – for its purpose. Césaire's negritude is here a state of the soul: 'I want to rediscover the secret of great speech and of great burning ... The man who couldn't understand me couldn't understand the roaring of a tiger'; 'my negritude riddles with holes/the dense affliction of its worthy patience'.

Césaire's later work, much of which is in dramatic form, is less successful than *Return to My Native Land*. He ceased to write poetry after the late Fifties. The most interesting of his plays are *A Season in the Congo* (*Un Saison au Congo*, 1966; tr. 1969), on Lumumba, and his version of *The Tempest* (*Une Tempête*, 1969), in which Caliban is the black hero and Prospero an inept colonizer. His infuriated *Letter to Maurice Thorez* (1956; tr. 1957) is important on his break with communism. His *Complete Works*, *Oeuvres complètes*, appeared in 1976 in translation. Césaire's is not a great mind, and he has borrowed much from others. But he is a generous man, and possesses true originality – even if this be less than the majority of his critics like to suppose.

Léopold Sédar Senghor (1906), until recently First President of Senegal, is often thought of as the leading apostle of negritude; but in fact his version of it now differs from his friend Césaire's (q.v.). His father was wealthy (Senghor remembers his being visited by a king); he has retained his Catholicism; and where Césaire is in many ways well to the left of organized communism, Senghor is a passionate pan-Africanist (his own experiments in federation failed) whose sympathy with Marxism is tempered by his conviction that it is an unsuitable system for under-developed peoples, and by his Roman Catholicism. In Césaire's negritude there is at least an element of what is now known as 'black power': the militant movement that advocates seizure of power, by black people, from a white society which they see as rapidly falling into a decay induced by capitalism. This comes out strongly and convincingly in *Une Saison au Congo* (q.v.), in which Lumumba is seen as a redemptive figure: 'I speak and I give Africa back to herself'. Senghor, on the contrary, is an integrationist, who has in more recent years been influenced, and not at all fruitfully, by the Jesuit Teilhard de Chardin's ideas of 'cosmic complexification': a number of organisms fitting symbiotically together to form a united whole. He would thus see the Black African states united in a federation, and, in a wider context, this federation as a part in a still larger federation. His own political record is more humanly honourable than most; for example, his erstwhile associate Mamadou Dia, tried in 1962 – after a crisis the details of which are not fully known – was imprisoned and eventually released, instead of being executed. ... 'Negritude', Senghor has written, 'is the *sum total of the values of the African world* ... intuitive reason, reason which is embrace and not reason which is eye ... the *communal warmth, the image-symbol and the cosmic rhythm which instead of dividing and sterilizing, unified and made fertile*'. Other aspects of his negritude include: rhythm (incantation); style – of sympathy; humour ('laughter to keep from crying' – as the American Negro Langston Hughes put it); the haunting presence of the dead. ... It was poetry reflecting this complex attitude – embracing non-whiteness as well as blackness – that Senghor included in his important *Anthology of New Negro and Malagasy Poetry*, introduced by Sartre (q.v.), in 1948. On the whole Sartre managed, in his introduction, to discuss the 'racist' and other difficult implications of negritude with good sense.

Senghor's poetry has appeared in several volumes, of which the first was *Songs in Shadow* (*Chants d'ombre*, 1945). There is a good English selection: *Prose and Poetry* (1964). Senghor's presentation is in the tradition of Claudel (q.v.): free verse in 'versets'. He also resembles Claudel in his use of elemental imagery and copious rhetoric. In the poem 'Chaka', however, he significantly fails to reconcile his poethood with his role as politician. It is unlikely that much of his poetry, however, will survive: it is very self-conscious, and in fact more 'intellectual' than it looks (whatever he says about 'the African' being 'non-intellectual'); it is also not without a certain rhetorical pomposity. W.E. Abraham's verdict that his verse is 'French ... interlarded with African allusions' is a fair one. That his poetry transformed negritude into a 'lonely confrontation with the self' is an assertion to be doubted. (AWT; AP)

Léon Damas (1912–78), Senghor's and Césaire's (qq.v.) associate in Paris in the Thirties, came from French Guiana. His mother was a mulatto and confused him greatly by talking about 'niggers' (there is much 'racism' between Blacks of light and dark hue). He made some successful innovations in French versification before Césaire or Senghor. *Pigments* (1937), introduced by Desnos (q.v.), the first volume of 'negritude poetry' to be published, was destroyed by the French police. Damas, once described as 'not a whole person' – because of his early 'Frenchness' – was a minor poet who was at his best when most lighthearted or sarcastic and satirical. He spent the last part of his life in America, and died in Washington. *Black-Label* (1956) was a confused collection, in which he denounces what he believes in: 'Africanism'. **Birago Diop** (1906), a Senegalese veterinary surgeon who became an ambassador, but then returned to care for animals, is usually classed as a poet of negritude; he is most distinguished, however, as a short-story writer. He was influenced by Maran (q.v.). Both his poetry and his prose incorporate Senegalese folklore in a subtle and sophisticated, and yet apparently artless, manner. He is one of Africa's most accomplished and elegant prose stylists. Birago Diop is a superior writer to Senghor (q.v.): his Africanism is much more thorough and natural, and he is never grandiose. He demonstrates the fate of those at odds with society in its 'natural' state.

The stories may be read in *Tales of Amadou Koumba* (tr. 1966), selected from three volumes written in French published in 1947, 1958 and 1963 respectively. Amadou is the *griot* (the oral storyteller), and 'his' tales are rooted in Wolof tradition; Diop renders these folktales of animals with impeccable art – and has acknowledged the genius of Amadou himself, a real person, a *griot* well known to him. His poetry is genuinely charming, but not profound as are the tales. (MPA) **David Diop** (1927–60), of mixed Senegalese-Cameroonian blood, born in France – he only visited Africa – published one book, *Coups de Pilon* (1956); all his manuscripts were lost when he died in an air crash. In Diop's poetry we see an aggressive affirmation of negritude, immature but of great power. He was aware that he did not understand his 'own Africa', and consequently drew more from Césaire (q.v.) than from other poets. Yet for a young poet he made much of his peculiar predicament. (AWT; MPA)

The Malagasy, **Jean-Joseph Rabéarivelo** (1901–37), included by Senghor (q.v.) in his 1948 anthology, was a victim of 'assimilation': the persistent refusal of French clerks to allow him to go to France, whose culture he loved, caused him first to take to drugs and then to kill himself. He may reasonably be regarded both as murdered by the stupidity of bureaucrats, and as an example of what 'assimilation' meant in practice. He is rightly regarded as the founder of modern Malagasy literature in French. He just had time to perfect his style. From self-consciously symbolist poetry in faulty French he graduated to masterly adaptations of Malagasy vernacular poetry:

> What invisible rat
> come from the walls of night
> gnaws at the milky cake of the moon?
> Tomorrow morning,
> when it has gone,
> there will be bleeding marks of teeth. ...
>
> And all will snigger
> and, staggering, will fall.
> The moon will no longer be there:
> the rat will have carried her into his hole.

(MPA)

He also wrote poetry in Spanish. In truth Rabéarivelo was not a poet of negritude at all. He was good enough to transcend categories. He was a melancholic, and his poetry is a description of the condition of melancholy, a rare sense of the beautiful and strange. He speaks of himself as having sheltered under 'apathy', of dreading eternity. *24 Poems* (tr. 1962) is a helpful guide to his unusual power. He drew much inspiration from *hain-teny*, the traditional love poetry in the Malagasy language, a member of the Malayo-Polynesian group.

Jean-Jacques Rabemananjara (1913) was luckier than his countryman Rabéarivelo (q.v.), whose disciple he early proclaimed himself: as a civil servant in Madagascar he managed to get to France on a tour of duty, and the Second World War prevented his return. He began by imitating French models; then he followed Rabéarivelo in his adaptations of popular indigenous ballads. His later style, however, imitates that of Senghor and, beyond him, Claudel (qq.v.); but rhetoric usually swamps invention. Rabemananjara was imprisoned in 1947 for his part in the uprising against the French; but he became a minister in the first independent government (1960). His most original work is contained in his plays, which include *The Malagasy Gods* (1947). His more recent work, such as *Lamba* (1956), poems, is wholly synthetic.

Flavien Ranaivo (1914), more poetically gifted, has carried on where his compatriot Rabéarivelo (q.v.) left off in the exploration of Malagasy popular poetry, particularly in *hain-teny*. His collection *My Songs of Always* (*Mes chansons de toujours*, 1955) was introduced by Senghor (q.v.). In some poems Ranaivo fails, but he has been most successful in recreating, in French, the love-poetry of his native land, since it is evident that he writes from personal experience. The whcle question of the necessity – simply because Malagasy is not and will never be accessible to most of us – of recreation into accessible languages of the secrets of less accessible ones raises innumerable problems, perhaps tragic in their implications. (MPA)

II

The novel in English in Africa came entirely from the West. There was no such thing as an indigenous novel – only folktales, although the quality of these was certainly never less than that of any novels, just as the quality of 'Homer' (whoever 'he' may have been) could not be said to be less than that of any narrative which followed it. The Africans already had, of course, both poetry and drama. But the sophistication of the novel they did not have. Realization of this can sometimes induce a feeling that, in one sense, the novel is a bad thing. But it is no more than necessary to acknowledge this feeling, which is anthropological in its nature – and too simplistically cuts out what we now are: have been made to be. Nevertheless, such a teller of tales as Birago Diop (q.v.), who transmits and transforms the spirit of his *griot* so beautifully, and with such respect, must cause us to experience such a sadness: a sadness at the loss of innocence. But then we remember that, if literature is worth anything, then we have had to have the novel, if only to record this loss in its own terms; and that the Africans (and other colonized and exploited peoples) have eventually had to have it too. Its coming into being in Africa and the Caribbean was hard.

It started late in the English language. E. Casely-Hayford's *Ethiopia Bound* (1911) was a fascinating start, but was not true fiction. More important is **R.E. Obeng**'s *Eighteenpence* (1943), a real novel – and, curiously enough, published at the author's own expense at Ilfracombe in England by the first of the English 'vanity publishers'. *Eighteenpence* is still just readable; but its extrinsic importance is not in question. It is the simple story of a too obviously virtuous man, told in language that derives quite frequently, not from the Bible, but rather from the Bible as it was taught by the missionaries to the 'ignorant' Africans. But in parts, and in some (limited) ways as a whole, it transcends its origins. The author himself emerges from his book, and was a true pioneer.

Its successors were some time in coming, although in almost all the African countries locally printed novels – looking very like the pulp fiction produced by supposedly respectable publishers in Great Britain and America today – were highly successful in market terms, and were not always at a pulp level. The first book to be published commercially in a large edition was the Nigerian Yoruba **Amos Tutuola**'s (1920) *The Palm-Wine Drinkard* [*sic*] (1952). This achieved an enormous success in English-speaking countries, but was not very popular in Nigeria. One can see both why it was so successful – and why it was so strongly disliked by Nigerians. Tutuola is an uneducated storekeeper, and his command of English is poor. Part of his appeal does indeed lie in the quaintness of his

English – and anyone who has taught Africans, whether by mail or in person, is familiar with this charming and funny quaintness. But a number of Tutuola's British readers were amused in a patronizing manner. Furthermore, he owed a very great deal to another Yoruba writer, one practically unknown outside Nigeria: **Daniel O. Fagunwa** (c 1910–63), who wrote in Yoruba and who died prematurely in a boating accident (he worked for the British publisher Heinemann in the latter part of his life). It is said that in Yoruba Fagunwa is a better writer than Tutuola (q.v.), and I have no doubt that this is true – but how many of us know or ever will know Yoruba? However, Soyinka's (q.v.) *A Hunter's Saga* (1968), from Fagunwa's 1939 novel, which is of course in Yoruba, suggests that Fagunwa is indeed at least as good as Tutuola. Tutuola, who owes much to *The Pilgrim's Progress* in English, is an intellectually simple-minded man (his Christianity is a refuge for his simple-mindedness); but he has a powerful imagination which really is his own, and *The Palm-Wine Drinkard* (if not its successors) is a remarkable book: part, as I have said, merely quaint, but part an extraordinary account of a spiritual adventure. That it is not as good as Birago Diop (q.v.) – or others whom we cannot even read – is, in pragmatic terms, beside the point.

In terms of the non-African, non-Negro, *The Palm-Wine Drinkard* is an epic masterpiece, a mixture of native lore, poetry, children's tall tale, innocently observed modernity and grotesquerie. The palm-wine drinkard loses his tapster, and goes to seek him in Dead's Town. Although the English is ungrammatical, it is real – and Tutuola's own. The work has great oral directness. When Tutuola tried again (*My Life in the Bush of Ghosts*, 1954; *The Brave African Huntress*, 1958, etc.) he found his old inspiration only in isolated passages. He is a natural, a naïve (q.v.), to whom thought – even in the sense of a professional writer's thought – is fatal. One cannot blame Tutuola's fellow Nigerians for feeling that he gave many (too many) white readers the opportunity to patronize Africanness (if not negritude, a concept wholly alien to Tutuola, who is still a good colonial servant): even at its best there is a tiny element of the 'I-am-a-funny-nigger-out-to-amuse-you-master' in his work.

The proper African novel in English developed very much later than the French, though it came earlier in the Caribbean (with McKay, q.v.). It has also been very different from the French: more integrationist in its beginnings.

Chinua Achebe (1930), born in Iboland, presents a complete contrast to any of his French counterparts, earlier or later. He is an intellectual, whose chief debt is not to any African writer but to such English novelists as George Eliot and Joseph Conrad (q.v.) – who, although a Pole, chose English as his means of literary expression. Achebe is penetratingly intelligent, and his realistic treatment of Nigerian life is as valuable anthropologically and sociologically as it is creatively. He was actively involved on Biafra's side in the Nigerian civil war. His first novel, *Things Fall Apart* (1958), is the tragic and moving story of Okonkwo and his village of Umuofia. Achebe is detached and cool – but more penetrative of the nature of both his Nigerians and his Christian missionaries than any previous African writer. *No Longer at Ease* (1960) is about Okonkwo's grandson Obi, turned into a corrupt civil servant by pressure of superstition and prejudice. *Arrow of God* (1964), set in the Twenties, in Eastern Nigeria, is about a chief priest who comes to trust an ignorant and essentially cruel British District Officer (portrayed by Achebe with great restraint). *A Man of the People* (1966) is more satirical and comic, and is not so effective as its predecessors. Its central episode is frighteningly reminiscent of the military coup in 1966, when many people were murdered. But its ending is contrived and weak. *Girls at War* (1971) collects short stories. Achebe believes that the writer should be 'in the thick of ... at the head of' 'the big social and political issues of contemporary Africa': 'I *am* a protest writer', he has said, but 'Restraint – well, that's my style, you see'.

Achebe seems, possibly temporarily, to have lost his creative powers since the Sixties. But he has published books for the young, and has concentrated exclusively on educating them. He seems to have moved from literature to enlightened and constructive politics. (AWT; MAP)

T.M. Aluko (1918) is less substantial, but in his way as interesting and important as Achebe (q.v.). He is undoubtedly a comic novelist, and there is even a sense in which he has allowed his imagination more play than Achebe has. His *One Man, One Wife* (1959) was the first genuine Anglophone novel to be published in Nigeria. He has been accused of being frivolous and uncommitted; but this is to misread his work, and to see what is really comedy for a self-indulgent lack of control. Aluko is in fact doing what is absolutely necessary, even if a certain degree of detachment from politics on his part is inevitable: he is satirical of the more absurd aspects of the African tradition, but only as this exists in the context of imperialism. The satire is affectionate; but it is also deadly. Aluko is a vastly underrated and misunderstood novelist, possessed of great but unobtrusive skill. However, his earlier novels are on the whole his best (*One Man, One Wife; One Man, One Matchet*, 1964; *Kinsman and Foreman*, 1966), because in *Chief the Honourable Minister* (1970) and *His Worshipful Majesty* (1973) he has somewhat compromised: he tries to retain his sense of humour and yet injects some of the 'philosophical' depth of Achebe into his work. But the last-named novel showed greater self-confidence, and therefore some signs of a return to the earlier manner.

Cyprian Ekwensi (1921) is not on the level of Achebe or Aluko (qq.v.); but, despite his amateurishness, is of some importance. He began by writing for the local pulp market (*When Love Whispers*, 1948): cheap pamphlets, badly printed on bad paper. *When Love Whispers* is by no means a 'juvenile' book, as it has been described in a supposedly authoritative bibliography: it is a torrid and sensationalist romance. But it has qualities which raise it above its genre, which has not yet received very full study. Ekwensi went on to develop his talents – even while remaining an entertainer by intention – and, after writing many short stories, published *People of the City* (1954; rev. 1963), his first novel, a scrambled book with a poor plot – but with some acute criticism of city life, which transcends the literature of pure entertainment. *Jagua Nana* (1961) is a great improvement, and one critic even went so far as to suggest that it was better than anything Achebe had written. This is not the case; but, because the author's vitality is never damped down by extra-literary considerations – despite its frequently poor English – one at least sees what was meant. *Iska* (1966) is another unusual novel in that it presents its female characters with possibly more subtlety and understanding than that achieved by any other Anglophone African writer. It is also prophetic in its treatment of tribal factionalism. *Survive the Peace* (1976), set at the end of Nigeria's civil war (Ekwensi, like Achebe, supported Biafra), is his most serious and 'committed' novel. *Reckless City and Christmas Gold* (1975) contains some of his best stories. Ekwensi remains a too glib novelist, still not understanding why he should not follow the example of Edgar Wallace (Simenon, q.v., his other acknowledged master, is a different matter): his ideas are not interesting. But, curiously, his depiction of people, his instincts about the clash between tribalism and integrationism, his tender understanding of women, his idea of purity in conduct (no longer mawkish or sentimental): all these are very interesting and relevant. He is an odd example of a novelist who, almost by accident, does allow his imagination full rein – but at the cost of poor English and lapses into sensationalism which are wholly inappropriate. His work offers us a strange mixture – and is important on the African scene. (MAP)

The prose of Onuora Nzekwu (1928), another Nigerian, suffers from the same kinds of defect as that of Ekwensi (q.v.), but not to such a great degree. However, though neglected (he is much less often mentioned than his contemporaries), he is not as gifted as Ekwensi. But he is a thoughtful and worthy writer. *Wand of Noble Wood* (1961), set in Lagos, resembles Achebe's *No Longer at Ease* (qq.v.), but is less profound, except that it has great documentary value in its detailed descriptions of Ibo marriage customs. Nzekwu cannot present the man torn between integrationism and the African past as Achebe does, because he is not really torn – he is a teacher, and his commitment to Westernization, or an 'Africanized' version of it, is unsophisticated and superficial; he remains exactly what he is, at heart, an Ibo who cannot come to terms with the modern. But he lacks the doubts of Achebe (and of Aluko, q.v., too, for that matter), and so his accounts of tribal customs have a dogged good heartedness, and benefit the reader by their simplicity and their understanding. It is a pity that his prose style is so dull and mechanical.

Blade among the Boys (1962) is a great improvement, though badly flawed. This deals with tribal rites (apparently 'disgusting') versus Roman Catholic 'morality'. Patrick Ikenga is the head of his family – both the living and the dead – but, educated by Catholics, he is also a novitiate. It is clear that Nzekwu intends this book to be a severe criticism of Roman Catholicism, and one can only sympathize in this context. But his treatment, though valuable as documentary, is not subtle or balanced enough. It is true that Roman Catholicism, the thing, has corrupted the truer and purer religious ceremonies of the Ibo (and of any other non-Christian tribe upon which it has forced itself). (Anthropologists who have tried to demonstrate otherwise have found themselves in deep waters indeed.) But this is not to imply, at all, that those who practise Catholicism are what Catholicism itself is, in terms of imperialism. . . . It would be ridiculous to pretend that there is no religious feeling in Catholicism – even if little of it is found in the Vatican, a merely bureaucratic headquarters. (This view is, after all, endorsed by many Catholics.) Nzekwu makes us feel that he is being unfair, in imaginative terms, even though he manages to convey the predicament of his protagonist with some sympathy. In *Highlife for Lizards* (1966), his best novel, Nzekwu has concentrated on Ibo life and its actual effect on individual persons; the language is still strained, but because the book is not polemical the sense of life is greater.

Gabriel Okara (1921), from Amatu in Nigeria, has evolved the most profound style of all the Anglophone novelists from his continent – especially in *The Voice* (1964). The protagonist, who has had a Western education, goes back to Amatu (Okara's own village, it will be recalled), in order to question everything. This is artificial in the ordinarily realistic sense; but Okara makes it convincing, not the least by his use of language. There are ways in which *The Voice* resembles a kind of *Invisible Man* (q.v. – I refer of course to Ellison's novel) – in reverse. Okolo, the protagonist, soon finds himself at odds with the conservative tradition in his native village (cf. Aluko, q.v.), and, after exiling himself to a nearby town, even finds himself in a lunatic asylum. He ends, not dead, but drifting in a canoe with, significantly, a witch (such people are the only ones who can remind him of his own values). It has been suggested that the novel fails because Okara gives no clue at all to the nature of Okolo's 'values' – but this reading also depends on the erroneous assumption that because he is set adrift he is wholly 'dead': he is just probably dead, possibly dead, feeling dead; the ambiguity is very important. This view is simplistic and lacks sensitivity: the 'it' of Okolo, his 'values', is itself just as elusive as Okara has made it. He might have written a more immediately successful novel by inventing some dogma and sticking it in place of the 'it' which so annoys simplistic critics who use authorial pessimism as a weapon to attack literary works. Okara's English, a superbly sensitive transposition of Ijaw syntax, shows this attitude to be wrong. Okolo is said by critics to be unsympathetic because he is isolated from the others; but then he is. . . . So ambitious a novel could hardly have succeeded wholly; but in saying this one remembers that nothing ambitious, in this proper sense, has ever succeeded as a whole.

It is hardly surprising that Okara is also a poet, or that a sensitive reading of his poetry illuminates *The Voice*. His first collection (though he appeared in an undistinguished anthology called *Poetry from Africa*, 1968) is *The Fisherman's Invocation* (1978). (It is not helpful that Howard Sergeant, a good-hearted man who knows nothing about the difference between poetry and verse, should be one of his exegetes.) His poetry is highly original, with a sense of personal rhythm which is rarely found in Anglophone African poetry (or anywhere else, for that matter). Okara is modest and unassuming, and he has been badly misinterpreted when he has been interpreted at all. But he is possibly the most powerful of all African poets writing today – in any language. The manner in which his poems gather up strength and then end in a mixture of puzzled serenity and submerged fury is quite inimitable ('To Paveba' affords a fine example). He is an honest writer who has paid for his honesty. But his lyricism will eventually be recognized as the most intense of any African poet of the century. He is a far superior poet, for example, to Senghor (q.v.), for all the latter's philosophical posturings.

*

French-Caribbean literature developed much earlier than African. Despite the presence of Césaire (q.v.: he made a visit to Haiti in 1944, during the course of which some say – though the fact is by no means certain – he was able to overcome a serious impediment of speech which had afflicted him until that time, under the psychological impact of 'encountering an un-self-conscious awareness of being Creole'), Haiti is the only part of the French-Caribbean (Martinique, Guadeloupe, French Guinea) to have evolved a national literature. The population of Haiti consists of a small dominant mulatto élite and some 90% Negroes, originally slaves from Africa. The official language is French, but French Creole is the language spoken by the vast majority. Since 1957 the Duvalier regime has ruled – the death of the mad 'Papa Doc', universally condemned as a criminal, has made little real difference, since his equally criminal son succeeded him (yet the Americans can invade Grenada in the interests of 'democracy', while leaving Haiti studiously alone; these Americans, exhibiting the anti-colonialist fervour for which they are famous, occupied the island from 1915 until 1934; curiously, the excuse for the invasion was not entirely different from the one used by Reagan in 1983 for the invasion of Grenada).

The dominant, and most influential figure, in Haitian literature has been **Jacques Roumain** (1907–44), who was himself of an élite mulatto family, and was educated in Europe and America. He was essayist, poet, diplomat, politician (he founded the Haitian Communist Party in 1934) but, above all, novelist. Roumain founded the *Revue Indigène* in 1927; it has been asserted that this magazine did no more than introduce French modernism into Haiti – the modernism of such as Cendrars, Marinetti or Apollinaire (qq.v.) – and that it gave its 'blessing to modern conformism in Haiti'. This may be disputed, and is certainly unfair on Roumain; suffice it to say here that Césaire (q.v.), a more derivative poet than he is usually taken to be, borrowed very heavily from a poem by Roumain in his own most famous poem. ... Elaborate reasons put forward as to why this blatant lifting of passages from Roumain's poem were not simply thefts are unconvincing – especially the one that asserts that whereas Roumain was being communist Césaire was not. Césaire was in fact then communist – and far more prone to ideological influence than Roumain, who was an ethnologist with an education and intellect far superior to those of Césaire. Roumain was an intelligent Marxian thinker; Césaire was a pragmatic Marxist activist.

Roumain wrote several novels, but by far the best is the last: *Masters of the Dew* (*Gouverneurs de la rosée*, 1944; tr. 1947), which abounds in creolisms, shows a true appreciation of the African aspect of Haiti's patrimony, and influenced *Disaffection* (1975), the first novel written in Creole – a dead end, perhaps, in itself, but a very important one – by **Frank Éttiene** (1936).

Two other important Haitians are **Jacques-Stéphen Alexis** (1922–61), whose *The Musical Trees* (*Les Arbres musiciens*, 1957) could not have been written but for the existence of Roumain – who figures in it under another name – and **René Dépestre** (1926), a poet who lives in Cuba and regularly denounces the false Haiti of the Duvalier regime, as well as the emerging Black middle classes' support of it. Alexis' *The Musical Trees* is a self-confessed exercise in 'magic realism' (q.v.), and – for all its derivations from Roumain's (q.v.) intelligently Marxian critiques of Haitian society – is really the first Haitian novel (with the exception of Roumain's last) to analyse in depth the nature of Haiti's own culture, which he perceptively sees as not merely African. Alexis was murdered – probably stoned to death – by agents of Duvalier. Dépestre's most influential poem has been *A Rainbow for the Christian West* (*Un Arc-en-ciel pour l'occident chrétien*, 1967; tr. 1972); this shows the influence of Alexis, but is far more dogmatically Marxist, and is less interesting as poetry than as polemic.

René Maran (1887–1960) has great importance in the history of the African novel. A Negro, he was born in Martinique, though of parents from French Guinea; but he lived and worked in Africa from early on – and later in his life, after writing many worthy but not outstanding books, he lost faith in everything – and he felt himself to be concerned mainly with African, and not with French-Caribbean, culture. *Batouala* (1921, with added chapter, 1948; tr. 1922), his finest book, was published at the behest of Henri de Régnier (q.v.), and won the Prix Goncourt. It is the simple story of an African chief, and its virtue lies in the fact that it is the first African novel to portray Negroes as Negroes, and not as white men in blackface. Furthermore, it demonstrates how such a society as the Ik of Uganda, well known from Colin Turnbull's account in *The Mountain People* (1972), can come into being: through utter deprivation.

*

Nothing like Maran's *Batouala* appeared before the Second World War in Francophone African fiction. However, strictly speaking, it is not an African novel, since Maran did have Caribbean parents and had lived, if only until an early age (his parents settled in Bordeaux) in Martinique: this fact does show in his text, for all its authentic Africanness. The first actually African novel in French, Bakary Diallo's *Righteous Strength* (*Force-Bonté*, 1926), was the work of an *évolué* (q.v.): it praises French colonialism in ecstatic terms, and is a fairly contemptible book.

Paul Hazoumé (1890), from Dahomey – since 1975 the People's Republic of Benin – produced a better novel, *Doguicimi* (1938), which he completed in 1935. Dahomey (known in the Thirties as the 'Latin Quarter' of French Africa because of its many intellectuals) lies between Togo and Nigeria. *Doguicimi*, which has not yet been translated into any other language, is the work of a distinguished ethnologist, but also of a product of the French colonial system; it is his only novel. To the careless reader it might seem to follow in the tradition of *Force-Bonté*; but it stems from a vastly superior mind, and those critics who have dismissed it as an apology for colonialism, and no more, are obtuse: it contains another element, even if this be submerged. It is a historical novel set in the times of King Geso (the first half of the last century), ruler of Abomey (Dahomey), and, for all that its main character, the wife of the nobleman Toffa, expresses pro-French sentiments, the novel as a whole not only contains anti-colonial sentiments (powerfully expressed by Toffa himself), but also has an authentically African rhythm to it – as John D. Erickson, most perceptive of critics of African Francophone fiction, has demonstrated (*Nommo*, 1979). In itself, the book is an African novel written in French, not a French novel written by an African. It is a subtle novel which awaits translation – and not further exegesis by anti-colonialist critics: in itself, being a creative work, it is anti-colonialist.

II

The Francophone African novel came into its own, however, with **Camara Laye** (1928–80), born in French Upper Guinea of a Malinke family. He began his literary career while he was a student in Paris. Although attacked for his alleged lack of commitment (his first book was enviously described as a 'colonialist pot-boiler' by African nationalists), he was in his lifetime the most serious French-language writer in Africa; no other novelist approached him in artistry, or in psychological insight. Laye grew up in Kouroussa, in an environment largely untouched by French colonialism. His father was a smith; since he was respected as a master not only of metalwork but also of magic, Camara Laye came to acquire a full understanding of an ancient, and now vanishing, way of life. *The Dark Child* (*L'Enfant noir*, 1953; tr. 1954) is an autobiography in fictional form: written lucidly and straightforwardly, it is a candid lament for the past; there is no resentment against colonialism. But, for all that, Laye's imagination is 'committed' to the all-important matter of the preservation of his own (black) identity. The book's chief importance is its unique evocation of Malinke traditions and customs. *The Radiance of the King* (*Le Regard du roi*, 1954; tr. 1956) is an ambitious allegory, written in colloquial style, on the theme of a white man's search for a King he wishes to serve (not, as some have suggested, God – except in an ironic, 'white' sense). Undoubtedly influenced by Kafka (q.v.), this subtle novel operates on both a serious and a comically ironic level. The white man Clarence goes to Africa, loses his money, and is enslaved. Only at the end is he redeemed. This moves out of the negritude phase and into the integrationist. It has all the mysterious life and infinite suggestiveness of a great work of art. Two of its main themes are the search, by the 'civilized' European, for the irrational that eludes him (but not the African), and the necessity for the European and the African to meet.

In 1965 Camara Laye, who had served Guinea as a cultural ambassador, became wholly disenchanted with his country, seeing President Touré and his government as technological monsters who were ruthlessly suppressing all traditional values. He expressed his horror by going into exile to Senegal and too hurriedly writing *A Dream of Africa* (*Dramouss*, 1966; tr. 1968). This is a wooden book, in effect denouncing the events in Guinea which had disillusioned him. As fiction it simply does not live up to his disillusion, however much one sympathizes. Camara was already ill with a lingering disease, and it was not until 1978 that he was able to finish *The Wordmaster* (*Le Maître de la parole*). This is a weak retelling of the Malinke story of an ancient exiled King; but its weakness is wholly understandable. Camara Laye, whose illness and despair rendered him incapable of supporting nine children (two by his second wife; seven by his first) by work at a research centre, was a victim of the cruel savagery of a section of his own people. But nothing can take from him the achievement of his first two novels. History has shown Camara Laye to be right in his assessment of his country: no one has freedom to express their own thoughts. It is appropriate that Touré should have condemned Camara to death *in absentia* – as well as spitefully and characteristically holding on to his wife in Guinea for many years.

Five more African Francophone novelists will be considered here: Ferdinand Oyono, Mongo Beti, Cheikh Hamidou Kane, Sembène Ousmane and Yambo Ouologuem. None of these is as good as Camara Laye in his first two novels, which are undoubtedly of the first order; but all possess manifold virtues and a considerable degree of versatility and originality.

Ferdinand Oyono (1929) comes from Cameroon (which became independent in 1961). He studied in Paris, worked as an actor, and then began to write. In 1961 he returned to Cameroon, where he has held a variety of diplomatic posts. He has published four novels, of which the first two are the best. *Houseboy* (*Une Vie de Boy*, 1956; tr. 1966) is a novel in the form of a diary. This diary was originally written by Oyono in Ewondo, then translated by him into French. It describes Toundi Joseph's experiences at a Catholic Mission – but there is a short prologue, narrated by another, describing his death in Spanish Guinea. The diary consists of a deadpan record of how Toundi believed in the colonialists and in their values: he wants to become a true *évolué* (q.v.). But the colonists eventually destroy him. The value of the book lies in what Oyono is able to do with the persona of Toundi, 'Boy': for in all his reverence and his belief he demonstrates to the reader just how absurd and hypocritical the colonialists really are in their attitudes. It is full of ironies ('Since the white man came we have learnt other men must not be looked on as animals'), but the authorial attitude is not unfair to the colonialists, some of whom do – in their way – actually believe in the Africans as human beings. Further, *Houseboy* may be read, not simply as a satire on colonialism, but as the parable of what happens to the innocent everywhere in the world. Toundi is almost a 'holy fool'. Short, lucid, always economical, almost perfectly judged in its humour, this novel has not really been bettered by Oyono (he wrote it in Paris). *The Old Man and the Medal* (*Le Vieux Nègre et la medaille*, 1956; tr. 1967) is a more obvious but nonetheless subtle attack (in effect – though Oyono never dehumanizes his characters to intensify his satire) on the 'good Negro' under colonialism – in other words, on the would-be *évolué*, the person who can never realize that the whole concept of 'assimilation' is a fraud, even if most often a well-intentioned one on the part of the European. It concerns a Christian cocoa farmer called Meka who is rewarded for his services to France by a medal – only when he actually receives it does he recognize its insignificance, and change his mind about his good and kindly masters. Although a comic novel, this has a serious core to it – but this, para-doxically, weakens it, not because Oyono is trying to go deeper, but because he uses somewhat over-obtrusive symbolism, and because the end is forced. *The Path to Europe* (*Chemin d'Europe*, 1961) shows a marked falling off. Oyono fell under the spell of the *nouveau roman* (q.v.), and, although this novel cannot be placed in that category, its long and tedious passages reflect its inappropriate influence. It is about a youth who wants to go to France, and eventually gets there by a process of selling himself, lock, stock and barrel, to every form of hypocrisy. *Pandemonium* (*Le Pandémonium*, 1971) shows Oyono still further lost in European techniques which are alien to his genius.

Mongo Beti (ps. **Alexandre Biyidi**, 1931) is the now established pseudonym of a French Cameroonian writer who wrote his first book (and one short story) under the name of **Eza Boto**. Unlike Oyono (q.v.), Beti has not returned to his own country since

1959, and has since vigorously attacked its politics in a full-length 1972 publication called *The Plundering of Cameroon* (*Main basse sur le Cameroun*). He lacks the artistry of Oyono, but almost though not quite compensates for it in energy and verve. He has disclaimed his first novel, *Cruel Town* (*Ville cruelle*, 1954), a sensationalist account of colonial exploitation which was promising only in its abundance of energy – the whole is very badly organized. With *The Poor Christ of Bomba* (*Le Pauvre Christ de Bomba*, 1956; tr. 1971) he matured greatly – though this is not his 'masterpiece', as it has been called. It deals with the efforts, against fierce resistance, of a French priest to convert all the people of Bomba; at the end he has to confess his failure, and is indeed condemned for his efforts. Just as in Oyono's first book, the action is viewed through the diary of a native houseboy who believes implicitly in the 'good father', who in his own way is good. *Mission to Kala* (*Mission terminée*, 1957; tr. 1958) tells of the fate of an *évolué* (q.v.) who, because he is what he is, fails when he tries to go back to his village to reclaim his heritage. But Beti's finest novel came in 1958: *King Lazarus* (*Le Roi miraculé*, tr. 1960). In this book he once again treats of missionaries; but this time he is less crude and more comic, at the same time making a serious point. This is certainly Beti's most enjoyable novel, and his least coarse. His humour is not as subtle as Oyono's, but here at least it is more robust. The Chief of the Essazem Tribe falls mysteriously ill; his surrogate mother (actually his aunt), Yosifa, a Christian convert, baptizes him (she drenches him with water). The Superior of the Catholic Mission returns, to find the Chief lingering between life and death. When he recovers, the Superior exerts pressure on him to change his ways: give up his twenty-two wives and marry the twenty-third. But he will not name the wife he will keep. ... The Chief remains transfixed between 'conversion' and 'reversion', but the tribe itself makes so much trouble that the Administrator has to tell the Superior that he must desist – and he is eventually sent away, at the Administrator's request. This is a magnificent comic novel, weak only inasmuch as it tells us little about the deeper meaning of the tribal ways, preferring to treat these, too, as merely comic.

Beti had attacked Camara Laye (q.v.) for refusing to write to a 'socialist realist' formula. But when he ran into trouble over a lawsuit in his own country, and was jailed for a short time, he fell silent as a writer of fiction. He later explained (in the Sixties) that he did not wish (surprisingly) to be confined to politics: he wanted as a fiction writer to 'feel free' (just as Camara Laye had always done ...). But by 1974 when he started to write fiction again Beti seemed to have gone back yet again on his intentions: the three novels he has produced since then are still political, if not quite so overtly as before. His theme is now the need for Africans to achieve their true independence, to discover themselves, to cast off for ever the notion of the *évolué*. But *Remember Ruben* (1974) – this title is in English – is a very uneven work, which, in its recreation of the days of the early Fifties when the Africans were fighting for their independence, contains superb passages, but also tedious and even irrelevant ones. It lacks cohesion, being a cross between a political novel and the story of one who returns and does rediscover himself – but that rediscovery, being too evidently political in its nature, does not entirely convince. Its sequel, *The Almost Laughable Ruin of a Buffoon* (*La Ruine presque cocasse d'un polichinelle*, 1979), is more of a piece, and more intellectually interesting, but is still not psychologically convincing. *Perpétué* (1974) is simply long-winded and dogmatic. Beti cannot yet resolve the conflict between his ideological convictions and his imagination, though he wants to.

Cheikh Hamidou Kane (1928), a Muslim born in Senegal, presents a complete contrast. *Ambiguous Adventure* (*L'Aventure ambiguë*, 1961; tr. 1963), which was well received and won a prize, deals at a more self-consciously philosophical – but no less imaginative – level with the ambiguous position of the African torn between his own African situation and that imposed on it, and him, by colonial (and Western) values. Kane has no clear answer, except (almost) one: only by exploring the impossibilities of negritude (q.v.) by means of the imagination can any reconciliation ever be brought about. The novel's message is the novel itself, as it should be – with the important proviso that to Kane a certain kind of specific Muslim mysticism represents the only harmony accessible to man. In this not all readers can follow him. His vision is not merely pantheistic. The protagonist, Samba (the author's own 'house name', as he was the second son), spends his early years at a Koranic school, and learns to accept the mystery of God's Way. But then a relative insists that he be sent to Paris to learn European ways, and to integrate them with those of Islam. Thus is Samba spoiled. A Parisian education destroys his faith. He returns to Senegal, but it is too late: the companion of the Master of the Koranic school where he grew up slays him when he conscientiously refuses to take part in a Muslim family ritual. The novel is perfectly balanced, wholly unpolitical, and very strong in characterization. It is exquisitely done, as every critic agrees. But acceptance of its final message depends upon belief in a specifically Muslim sort of revelation. ... So that in order for every reader, and not just Muslim mystics, to accept his religious message, Kane will somehow have to go further: to suggest a psychological state (not necessarily non-religious, but certainly more than only Islamic) in which peace on earth may be found. *Ambiguous Adventure* needs to be complemented, if Kane is to achieve what we call greatness (to which he has come almost as near as Camara Laye, q.v.). But he has still written one of the most outstanding of all African novels.

Sembène Ousmane (1923), son of a fisherman of the port of Ziguinchor, is a very different kind of Senegalese novelist. He was not educated in France; but he fought with the French army in Italy and Germany (an education in itself). He is a militant trade-unionist, and is now the best known novelist (and film-maker) in Senegal. He is a prolific and uneven novelist, much cruder than Kane (q.v.), but very effective in his way, and undoubtedly wider in his range. One thinks of James and Dreiser (qq.v.) in America: however exquisite the former, the latter supplied material that James did not. His first book, *The Black Docker* (*Le Docker noir*, 1956), based on his own experiences as a trade-union leader in Marseilles after the war, is coarse stuff, redeemed only by the vividness and sincere fury of its presentation of the plight of black dockers in France (which even under Mitterand has not much improved). *God's Bits of Wood* (*Les Bouts de bois de Dieu*, 1960; tr. 1970) is his best novel; here he learned, profitably, from Romain's *Les Hommes de bonne volonté* (qq.v.): he gives a panoramic view of various groups of people to great effect. The novel is based on the great strike of African railwaymen on the Dakar-Niger line (1947–8). The characters are full of life, and the sense of outrage (and official complacency) is rendered with a heartfelt immediacy. This is the novel of protest at its best; and in some of its moments it recalls Zola (q.v.), even though Zola was not (in fact) a novelist of protest. The Marxian approach is intelligent and well thought out (it is emphatically not 'Marxist-Leninist'), no character is manipulated in the interests of polemic, and the approach is balanced and fair. Outstanding among Sembène Ousmane's other works is the collection of stories *Man from the Volta* (*Voltaïque*, 1962). He is not a great writer, but he steadily produces good and illuminating books, and is unusual in that he can be leftist and yet not distort his material in the interests of leftist polemic. He is above all a humane and fair man, with a great gift for showing us the realities of the lives of the poor and the oppressed. This can be offensive only to *hommes de mauvaise volonté*. ... He is a very much better writer than – to choose a famous example – Nexø (q.v.), for all the latter's dreary worthiness. He can tell historians and sociologists much more than they will ever learn in the finest textbooks.

Yambo Ouologuem (c1930), from Mali, began as a poet, and his best known poem, 'When Negro Teeth Speak', gives some idea of his wildness, his anger, his range, his oddness – here are a few lines from the beginning:

> Everybody believes I'm a maneater
> But you know the way people talk
>
> Everybody sees my red gums but whose
> Are white
> Up with tomatoes
>
> Everybody says the tourist trade will decline
> Now
> But just realise
> We aren't in America and anyhow everybody
> Is skint
>
> Everybody says I'm to blame and is frightened
> But listen
> My teeth are white not red
> And I never ate a soul. . . .

Ouologuem (who is of Dogon ancestry) is prolific: he has written polemic, much lively pornography, a reader for elementary schoolchildren, and many stories, as well as poetry. But his one major work, flawed though it almost defiantly is, is *Bound to Violence* (*Le Devoir de violence*, 1968; tr. 1971). In this book Ouologuem freely borrowed from a number of writers, including Graham Greene (q.v., who made his publishers withdraw it until he deleted or rewrote the offending passages, which he has so far apparently refused to do). As I have indicated in my introduction, I think the literature of sly plagiarism is highly suspect – and no more so than in cases of creative inadequacy. But Ouologuem is different: he slings his books together (he does not 'compose' them) by drawing on whatever material happens to lie to hand. You will find Baudelaire (q.v.) by the side of an American writer of pulp thrillers, plus much that is by the author himself – and which is original (cf. Burroughs, q.v., whose own material is banal). There is no necessity to defend or attack in solemn terms Ouologuem's procedures, as was unconvincingly done in the case of the shabby, humourless British poeticule D.M. Thomas who, unable to write a properly imagined novel of his own, produced a bestseller by combining what appeared to be a set of tedious masturbation-fantasies – 'sopping cunts' and so forth – with slices out of the work of others (this was an example of gutter culture successfully posing as boulevard culture, qq.v., and had simple-minded people saying that their 'lives had been changed' – a sort of Billy-Graham effect in reverse, and as short-lasting). Ouologuem is a genuine writer, and a genuine eccentric. His *Thousand-and-one Bibles of Sex* (*Les Milles et une bibles du sexe*, 1969) is pornography proper, just as that of Apollinaire (q.v.) is: it does not pose as high art. Ouologuem's act is to respect no one and he does it with verve, violence and some humour; and, despite learned objections, is African in an authentic – although disconcertingly unique – manner.

Ouologuem's *Bound to Power* covers the period 1202–1947. It sees the history of Africa as one of almost unrelieved violence and corruption. In the first part the history of the Nakem Empire is traced; by the end of the nineteenth century Saïf ben Isaac El Heit has come to power, and is in conflict with white colonialists (he loses). In the course of all this the author draws perhaps only apparently recklessly on any source to hand, including Arabic, Christian and Jewish lore. The modern part of the novel deals mainly with the adventures of Raymond-Spartacus Kassoumi, who does about everything a man should not, and much that he could not. Ouologuem's main source for some parts of the book is a novel called *The Last of the Just* (*Le Dernier des justes*, 1959; tr. 1961), by André Schwarz-Bart, a Polish Jew who became French. He got into trouble for this, as he probably anticipated, since his publishers had issued the earlier work. But the joke (apparently never appreciated by any critic) is that Schwarz-Bart, by no means as good a novelist as Ouologuem (he is a sincere popular novelist, who is sentimental rather than 'moving', as he has been wrongly called: it is his material that is moving, not his treatment of it), had won the Prix Goncourt for this rather kitsch tale, and had himself been accused of plagiarism – and of 'exploiting' sex. It is therefore unsafe to be too serious about Ouologuem's plagiarism: he used this book as a cornerstone in a very proper if somewhat cruel contempt for it – and he chose appropriately, because its author had himself been accused of plagiarism and pornographizing. . . . The fact is that if Ouologuem plagiarized from Schwarz-Bart then Golding (q.v.) certainly plagiarized Ballantyne – but of course no one has accused him of this. Moreover, the charge of plagiarizing from Schwarz-Bart is somewhat akin to one of plagiarizing Mary Renault or Mary Stewart: this sort of thing is surely for any serious writer to make amused use of, unkind though it undoubtedly is.

Although sprawling, *Bound to Power* is not without subtlety and high satirical intelligence. It is the most savage attack on negritude (q.v.) yet made; but it does not extol Western values. It is by no means entirely nihilistic: it attempts to right the balance. Whereas most (but not the best) African writers have praised Africanism for its primitiveness and 'sublimity', Ouologuem demonstrates that the Africans are as human (i.e. both good and bad) as anyone else. It is a work not so much of excess as of exorcism (as Erickson insists): exorcism of 'idyllic Africa', a necessary process for any honest African, and a corrective to the sentimental and partly colonialistic views put forth by the essentially *évolué* Senghor (q.v.), who after all ended up as a not unpompous First President, a Catholic, and dedicated to an idealized and impracticable pan-Africanism. It hardly matters that negritude was an inevitable phase. Of course we have seen Ouologuem's message conveyed more subtly, for example in Kane's *Ambiguous Adventure* (qq.v.). But the very violence with which he has transmitted it has special value – and to take this humorous man too seriously is in any case to play into the hands of an earnestness which his work – for all its flaunted flaws and bold parodies of polite 'literature of allusion' (q.v.) – is most excellently against. It should also be noted that in his pornographic work *The Thousand-and-one Bibles of Sex* this author at least appears to portray French sexuality as pornographic and African as natural – which could be said to render this work not pornographic, but merely realistic and instructive. The contrast is between sex-with-fantasy and sex-as-sex: clearly Ouologuem is aware of it. That takes no fool.

Contemporary poetry in English and French is serious, but on the whole disappointing. This may well be because the indigenous traditions, of which Rabéarivelo (q.v.) and a few men of earlier generations were to make legitimate and less self-conscious use – they lived through a time of greater despair – are still so powerful. It must now be a little like trying to write poetry under the immediate shadow of Homer – or at least of a Homer who is still being performed.

The outstanding Nigerian poet is Gabriel Okara (q.v.), whose work has already been discussed. Others from this country are not as successful. **John Pepper Clark** (1935), perhaps at his best as a dramatist, is fluent and sweet, but his poetry lacks originality, and he has not found his own voice. **Christopher Okigbo** (1932–67), killed fighting with the Biafran army, tried too self-consciously to combine indigenous poetry with the sophisticated modernist poetry of the West: this shows up in his poem to Yeats (q.v.), 'Lament to the Masks'. A literary critic could make this seem subtle and complex, and intelligent indeed it is; but the reader of poetry knows that Okigbo's true voice is lost in it, that it is synthetic. It is all very well to assert that Okigbo dwells on 'the disparity between man's ambition and his futile attempts to become God'; but that does not make a vital poetry. One can admire and be touched, but one cannot respond as one would heartily wish. There is much to be said about the intelligence of many of these African poets in English, but, as the perusal of a good anthology such as *Modern Poetry in Africa* (1963) – which also contains French and a few Portuguese poems – demonstrates, the vast majority of these writers have not succeeded in reconciling their indigenous heritage with their Western understandings (which are often false, though for unavoidable reasons). There can be excellent technique (Clark, Okigbo, qq.v.), and a fine sophistication; but these don't make poetry.

In French much the same applies. The only contemporary Francophone poet to break partly through the barrier – and he is by no means wholly satisfying – is **Tchicaya U Tam'si** (ps. Felix Tchicaya, 1931), from Congo (Brazzaville). U Tam'si has lived mostly in France, and although he has considerable lyrical gifts and a deep understanding of Bantu poetry, the fact of his residence has given his work a heavy intellectual overlay which is hardly suitable to it. He has tried to adapt Bantu poetry, which is essentially oral, to a special kind of French oral poetry which will, however, be effective on the page as well. His earlier angry topical satire on the death of Lumumba – he was in the Congo at the time – was more effective than his 'personal' poetry. But at times his attempts to express his erotic nature do acquire vitality – a vitality apart from critical exegeses that merely tell us about the intellectual structure of his poems – and then his poetry comes to life. The influence of Césaire (q.v.) is very marked, but has not been fatal *Selected Poems* (tr. 1970).

III

The most effective Negro playwright from Africa and the Caribbean has been Césaire (q.v.), whose work has already been discussed. But the Africans have a dramatic heritage upon which to draw, and they have made better use of it than they have in poetry. Many of the earlier African plays (in both languages) tended to use African myth as an anti-colonial message; they were effective in the theatre at the time they were produced, but were more ephemeral than drama usually is. They are interesting in terms of politics, but not of literature. The least ineffective of them were adopted from Yoruba legend.

The leading African playwright is undoubtedly **Wole Soyinka** (1934); his plays have been widely performed. He is also a poet and novelist; competent and sensitive but not outstanding. His plays use much African material – as is natural – but they aim, Soyinka insists, beyond matters African. His first major play, *The Dance of the Forests* (1963), was commissioned for the Nigerian Independence Celebrations. In this work Soyinka does in dramatic form what Ouologuem (q.v.) did in *Bound to Violence*: insists that the African past is not idyllic. *The Road* (1965), which was produced in London in 1965, and is one of his best plays, is set in an impoverished republic which has long gained its independence: it is going to pieces, and so are its inhabitants. The protagonist is a half-mad professor who is trying to discover the meaning of death. *The Road* relies on an elaborate use of ritual, and is very evidently African – but Soyinka has drawn as much from Greek tragedy as he has on African material. Indeed, in 1973 he adapted Euripides' *The Bacchae*, showing that he had a thorough understanding of what he was doing in his theatre (he has been an actor, and has produced many plays). *Madmen and Specialists* (1971) is about a doctor who turns inquisitor: his father tries to show him what he has become by inventing a cannibalistic cult. Doubtless the fury expressed in this play arose from the fact that Soyinka was for two years a political prisoner (during the Biafran war), and was lucky to remain alive (*The Man Dies: Prison Notes*, 1972). When the son kills his father, the latter tries to purge him of his lack of humanity in a scene, which, once again, owes quite as much to Greek theatre as it does to African legend. Essentially Soyinka has taken the Western play as his model, and used African ritual only to a very carefully limited extent. The language of his plays is not inspired; but he remains an effective and intelligent dramatist.

John Pepper Clark (1935), whose mellifluous poetry has already been mentioned, is not a 'Renaissance Man', as someone has called him; but his plays are his best work, even though he is as concerned with criticism and poetry and teaching (at the University of Lagos). He also founded and edits *The Horn*, a magazine based at Ibadan. His best play is his first: *Song of a Goat* (1964), which was seen in London in 1965. This resembles Soyinka in that Clark takes Greek drama as his model. The story is simple: a man becomes impotent, his main wife sleeps with his younger brother, who hangs himself; but the sterile protagonist also kills himself, in shame. The play is good, but is much weakened by the attempt to make it 'Greek': Clark is not as good at this as Soyinka (q.v.), who really needs to do it, and who could not manage without it. Still, the characterization is powerful and the play genuinely tragic. The successors to this play unfortunately work much less well, and at times Clark is (as has been said) reminiscent of Fry (q.v.), a most pernicious influence and an indication that there may be something fundamentally wrong with Clark's taste.

Obi Egbuna (1938), a Nigerian who has written novels and stories as well as plays based on them, has written one interesting and original comedy: *The Anthill* (1965). This is really a farce, and it shows that Africans can write these as well as anyone else: this is bound to be played for many years to come. Egbuna is a militant advocate of 'Black Power', and was locked up in England for it (*Destroy This Temple: The Voice of Black Power in Britain*, 1971); but in *The Anthill*, which centres on a man who paints only anthills, he has produced a frothy and funny comedy almost worthy of Wilde (q.v.).

The Ghanaian **Efua Sutherland** (1924) is a woman of the theatre: the person behind most theatrical activity in her country, in which she still lives. She is particularly concerned with children's drama. She has designed two theatres. She has adapted Euripedes' *Alcestis*, as *Edufa* (1967), and has in *Foriwa* (1967) written a 'street play', a rather sentimental but effective work about the need for co-operation and the rejection of tribalism.

Ama Ata Aidoo (1942), another Ghanaian, is a more serious playwright; she has written a novel, *Our Sister Killjoy* (1977), and a collection of stories, *No Sweetness Here* (1970). She does not write in the mainstream, inasmuch as she looks for solutions in tradition, though not in any conservative manner. (The usual approach is to look for the best of both worlds in an unthoughtful way.) *The Dilemma of a Ghost* (1965) is about an African who goes to England and brings back a black American wife. It deals sensitively with the weakness of the husband, who cannot assert himself. *Anowa* (1970) is historical: set in Africa under the reign of Queen Victoria. Anowa rebels against her parents and marries a man they consider a no-good. The couple prosper in trade; but they are unable to live happily together, and each commits suicide. This play is feminist, but in a subtle and convincing – never over-strident or unrealistic – way.

But it is Soyinka (q.v.) alone who is a major dramatist in Africa. The ancient dramatic tradition of Africa, with its drums, its all-important dance, and its attendant ritual, offers a great temptation to any dramatist – but then so, of course, do the techniques of the modern theatre, and some of its stars (such as Tennessee Williams, q.v.). Only Soyinka has succeeded in making full use of the ancient tradition without falling back falsely into it.

In French only **Bernard Dadié** (1916) need be mentioned. Dadié, from the Ivory Coast, is important as a novelist and poet; but his plays are outstanding. He served in the government administration in Senegal, and set up a theatre; later he became Minister of Culture of his own country. Dadié is frankly what he is: an *évolué* and a political optimist (he produced embarrassing odes to Houphouet-Boigny, who so to say deserved them – 'You are the people/You are the Master'); but he has been sincere, and a subtle and illuminating writer. The novel *Climbié* (1956; tr. 1971) is autobiographical, and traces with dignity and skill the progress of an African whose acceptance of white rule is transformed into hatred for it. His other novels, and, in particular, his retelling of African Legends, *Légendes africaines* (1953), are excellent; but it is in the theatre that he excels: in the farce *Monsieur Thôgô-gnini* (1970), which is in form a kind of cross between Molière and Jarry (q.v.), and, above all, *Stormy Islands* (*Îles de tempête*, 1973), which deals with Toussaint L'Ouverture (the slave who became ruler of Haiti, but who hesitated over the declaration of independence too long: the Napoleon whom he admired imprisoned him). The technique of this play is modernistic, and effectively so; but what is outstanding is Dadié's ability to treat the protagonist as a human being as well as a legendary hero.

IV

African literature in Portuguese is lively and interesting, but is not well known outside the ex-Portuguese countries and Portugal itself. In poetry no one has really distinguished themselves, although as a body of work Afro-Portuguese poetry is interesting, a 'cry of agony and loss', as has been rightly said. Most of the activity has come from Angola, and the most important of Angolan writers is certainly the blind mulatto **Óscar Ribas** (1909), who has written poetry, stories and novels. Nothing better than his short-story collection *Echoes of My Land* (1951) has come out of Portuguese Africa. This, and his other work, is particularly important because there is little vernacular literature in Angola, and it is Ribas above all others who has been able to combine immense anthropological knowledge with creative ability. The rest of Afro-Portuguese literature is still in a formative phase, largely no doubt because the Portuguese were so late in hanging on in Africa – but also because of other factors. Unfortunately Ribas awaits a translator.

V

George Lamming (q.v.) pointed out in 1960 that 'the West Indian novel, by which I mean the novel written by the West Indian about the West Indian reality, is hardly twenty years old'. The main reason for this has been the high rate of illiteracy in the West Indies (I refer here to the formerly British islands, and to Guyana), the direct responsibility of British administrators, whose nineteenth-century policy towards education of the Negroes has rightly been described as 'criminal'. And it is as well to remember that the language of the West Indian novelist is an English which veers, not always easily, between what authorities call West Indian Standard (the correct language, surely, for West Indians), English Standard – and, of course, the dialects.

The first professional West Indian novelist was the Jamaican **Claude McKay** (1890–1948), who was also a poet. McKay went to America to study just before the First World War; there he discovered the American Negro W.E.B. DuBois' *The Souls of Black Folk*. (DuBois and Marcus Garvey, a Jamaican described by McKay as a charlatan, were the two great founding – and feuding – fathers of Pan-Africanism; DuBois, mocked by Garvey for his light skin, believed in the maintenance of the black diaspora; Garvey did not.) Financed by a man named Gray ('there was a greyness in his personality like the sensation of dry sponge'), McKay in 1920 visited England, but was disappointed. His poetry is in a Victorian idiom and is of little value; but his fiction, which he began writing in the late Twenties, is of more interest: his novels are: *Home to Harlem* (1928), *Banjo* (1929) and *Banana Bottom* (1933), described by Kenneth Ramchand as the 'first classic of West Indian prose'. This is a vivid and affirmative evocation of Jamaican village and town life, and a skilful portrait of a woman's achievement of freedom from social and racial fear. It contains also a memorable portrait of an itinerant musician, Crazy Bow:

> You may wrap her up in silk,
> You may trim her up with gold,
> And the prince may come after
> To ask for your daughter,
> But Crazy Bow was first.

Many West Indian novelists are now better known than McKay, but few have bettered his work.

There was a general exodus of West Indian novelists to London in the early Fifties: to a place where they could feel the presence of readers. After the Second World War the British Broadcasting Association ran a programme called 'Caribbean Voices', and magazines started up (*Bim* in Barbados, *Focus* in Jamaica, *Kyk-over-Al* in what was to become Guyana); but the obstacles to local recognition remained formidable. Two novelists were in the forefront: **Edgar Mittelholzer** (1909–65), who set fire to himself in a field after writing a novel with just such a suicide as its main incident, and **Roger Mais** (1905–55), who had already distinguished himself as a short-story writer and poet in Jamaica in the Thirties and Forties, but who did not become a novelist until the last three years of his life – two of which were spent in London, although he died in Jamaica.

Mittelholzer was an uneven, over-prolific novelist, whose work consists of ghost stories, Gothic horror tales, historical fiction and studies of decayed gentry. His novels of the past, despite fine passages, are spoilt by an indulgence in the erotic for its own sake; better is a more straightforward novel such as *A Morning at the Office* (1950), an acutely observed and painful account of racial division. In Mittelholzer the humanist observer and the neo-romantic experimentalist jostle against one another uncomfortably, and seldom work together. Possibly his best book is the autobiographical *A Swarthy Boy* (1963). It is a tragedy that his last terrible gesture should have been real as well as fictional.

Mais wrote three novels, *The Hills Were Joyful Together* (1953), *Brother Man* (1954) and

Black Lightning (1955). These have been collected as *The Three Novels of Roger Mais* (1966). The first two are grim sociological studies of poverty and prison life; they are of very high quality. The third is one of the few successful accounts in modern fiction of a Christ-like figure. Bra'Man's followers reject him; but he is saved by sexual love. This portrait of a holy man is neither Christian nor Reichian – and is convincing and original.

West Indians of a younger generation who have written good novels include: **George Lamming** (1932), from Barbados, whose finely written *In the Castle of My Skin* (1953) and *The Emigrants* (1954) are autobiographical; **Andrew Salkey** (1928), born in Panama of Jamaican parents, who gives accurate and sometimes depressing pictures of Jamaican life in *A Quality of Violence* (1959) and *Escape to an Autumn Pavement* (1960); **John Hearne** (1926), another Jamaican (born in Canada), whose *The Faces of Love* (1957) brilliantly examines the insecurity of a mulatto woman; and **H. Orlando Patterson** (1926), a sociologist, whose *The Children of Sisyphus* (1965) gives a vivid and sympathetic account of the Rastafarian cult.

Most of these novelists added fruitfully to their *œuvres*. Lamming's *Natives of My Person* (1972), his sixth novel, is probably his finest book – at least it is his most mature and original. It takes the crude and false legends of the West Indies as they exist in Western consciousness (Lamming, like so many West Indian writers, lives in London), and weaves them together into a fantastic and imaginative extravaganza, half satirical but half poetic. It is a difficult work, written in what at first sight seems to be pastiche of seventeenth-century voyagers' prose. But the style is really very much Lamming's own – which, in an age in which pastiche as a technique is far too often taken for granted, is an achievement.

Andrew Salkey wrote his best novel in *The Late Emancipation of Jerry Stover* (1968), a scarifying and heartfelt attack on the state of Jamaica in the period just before it achieved its unhappy independence. *The Adventures of Catullus Kelly* (1969) has been called 'weak'; but its experimental form, including the use of both English and dialect, was absolutely necessary – and the picture given of a young Jamaican going mad in London is quite unforgettable, and, although sometimes comic, deeply moving. This book is far more imaginative than the majority of critics granted: they saw it as polemic, quite forgetting that the most important figure in it, and the most important theme, is the personality of the used-up protagonist. Salkey has edited much West Indian material, and written a number of good books for young people. He is an author whose subtleties have not received their full due.

John Hearne has stayed in Jamaica, and his work has on the whole declined (though not for that reason). He has taken to writing crude thrillers in collaboration, and these have no point except to entertain (some): the effort has weakened his sense of reality. *The Faces of Love* remains his best book.

H. Orlando Patterson, whose fiction is certainly underrated – mainly perhaps, and very unjustly, because he has now become a sociologist of universally recognized importance: *The Sociology of Slavery* (1967) and *Ethnic Chauvinism* (1977) are both essential books. But he does something in fiction that he cannot do in his other works. There have been two new novels: *An Absence of Ruins* (1967) and *Die the Long Day* (1972). Both are bleak and pessimistic studies in absolute alienation, and are so well achieved that they reach that high level at which it can only be said that the one affirmative answer provided by them lies in the fact that they were written at all. Developments in Jamaica under Michael Manley and then under Seaga cannot have encouraged any of its enlightened natives, and perhaps these books reflect the earlier stages of the deterioration (which led to the massive election victory of the American-trained Seaga, a sinister figure whose harmfulness has not yet been fully seen, since Jamaica can never for long remain an American client-state – and for whose emergence the younger Manley must take much responsibility). But at least Patterson's protagonists do understand, if dimly, that mental freedom from slavery is possible.

But the most gifted of Caribbean novelists – he is probably as gifted in his very different way, though not as fulfilled, as V.S. Naipaul (q.v.), who has been dealt with as an English novelist – is **Wilson Harris** (1921), from Guyana. In certain respects his approach is' nearer to that of such writers as Patrick White (q.v.) – on whom he has written and by whom he has been influenced – and even Alexis (q.v.) than to his Caribbean contemporaries. He is not without a certain pretentiousness, but this, as we have seen in the case of White, is almost unavoidable. His comments on his work are not as good as the work itself. But he is superior to Carpentier (q.v.), and his novels, taken together, do something similar to what Carpentier was trying to do: to explore the interior through giving a view of the exterior. He has a few devotees (as he should), but has not yet reached the wider public which he deserves. Some criticism of him is unhelpful and obscurantist, but this may well be because his work is not as accessible as he could, without loss to its integrity, make it. *The Guiana Quartet* (*Palace of the Peacock*, 1960; *The Far Journey of Oudin*, 1961; *The Whole Armour*, 1962; *The Secret Ladder*, 1963) forms the most thorough picture of Guyana ever given or likely to be given; its re-interpretation of a complex past in contemporary terms is convincing and very rich in detail. *Ascent to Omai* (1970) and the four novels which preceded it were less successful: too mystical, too fragmented on the surface – the experimentalism of these narratives was not sufficiently compelled. Newer novels display more humour, and get away from the Caribbean – which Harris needed to do. The best are *Da Silva da Silva's Cultivated Wilderness* (1977) and its sequel *The Tree of the Sun* (1978), in which the protagonist is a painter, a kind of surrogate for Harris himself. But this important and in a sense still neglected writer needs to develop a wholly suitable language: he has never yet been quite unselfconscious enough, and his intellect has obtruded so much into his fiction that it now quite certainly needs a rest. His is an imagination that requires strict control; but not so intentionalist a one. He has written poems (*Eternity to Season*, 1954; rev. 1979) which are very ill accomplished, but which (for example 'Troy') give invaluable clues to his novels. It may be that Harris' work is somewhat vitiated by the fact of a basic pessimism which he cannot cast off: myth is greater than history, but no man can understand myth – so he tries to destroy it. It is a grand and universal enough theme.

Tom Redcam (ps. **Thomas Macdermot**, 1870–1933), novelist as well as versifier, was the unpromising colonial father of West Indian poetry. A slightly better poet was **W. Adolphe Roberts** (1886–1962), born in Kingston (CV); but it was McKay (q.v.) who – even if not a good poet – brought the necessary theme of Africa into Caribbean poetry. The best Thirties poet was Roger Mais (q.v.). The form in which he was finally to find himself, shortly before his early death, was the novel; but his free verse and his manner show that he fully realized that Caribbean verse, to achieve anything beyond 'local colour', must break free of sunlight, sea – and the Victorian poetical poesy. Love, he knew, spoke 'With accents terrible, and slow'. Clearly he had read the imagists (q.v.), and his poetry has a sharpness otherwise entirely lacking in the West Indian poetry of the period. His now celebrated 'All Men Come to the Hills' was in part an exhortation to his countrymen to give up the touristic sun and sea and look at the nature of Jamaican society. (CV)

But **Derek Walcott** (1930), born in St. Lucia, is the only truly outstanding contemporary Anglophone Caribbean poet and playwright. Walcott has a superb ear, knows his limitations (important in a poet) and is intelligent without allowing this to undermine his initial poetic impulse. As well as effective plays, he has published a dozen books of poems (*Selected Poems*, 1964, and *Selected Poems*, 1977, are the best guides to his achievement). His poetry gives a record, often in exuberant language, of growth to maturity against a West Indian background more fully and truthfully and painfully realized than in any previous West Indian poetry. His play *Dream on Monkey Mountain* was published in London (1972). But his more recent work, especially since the long poem *Another Love* (1973), an attempt to write his own *Prelude* in shorter compass, and a failure, has lessened in tension. On the other hand his plays (e.g. *O Babylon!*, 1976) are improving in theatrical effectiveness. He lives in Trinidad.

American Literature

I

Henry James' (q.v.) statement, made in a letter of 1872, that 'it's a complex fate, being an American, and one of the responsibilities it entails is fighting against a superstitious valuation of Europe' is hackneyed; but it sums up, with splendid aptness, the heart of the American dilemma at the time he wrote it. (In 'Europe', of course, he included England: the parent country whose political, but not literary, shackles had been wholly thrown off.) The Americans as a whole were slow to recognize their native geniuses: no country likes to discover its true nature too quickly. Emerson was widely acknowledged and highly influential, but, although a major writer, he was not a major creative writer. The American public took Longfellow, an inferior poet, to its heart, but was not happy with Melville; and Whitman – the first wholly American poet – was to the end of his life read only by a minority which misunderstood the nature of his achievement, leading to the establishment of a legend that took more than fifty years to dispel. Many Americans of the nineteenth century tended to regard their own literature patronizingly, as an inferior cousin of English literature: they reckoned that English earth, and not that of America itself, the new country, was the proper place for its roots.

This situation has now changed drastically. If there is a cultural capital of the English-speaking world, then it is New York – that it might be London is now no more than a joke. Since America is by far the bigger and more varied country, and since English literature has temporarily exhausted itself, it is not surprising that this state of affairs should have come about. What is more interesting is how American self-discovery developed into a major world literature. This may be seen most clearly in the way American writers discovered and achieved realism.

*

America had her indisputably great nineteenth-century writers: Melville, who failed to achieve real success and was forced to spend all but six of his last twenty-five years as a customs inspector; Whitman, who had even less popular success; Hawthorne, who did achieve fame with *The Scarlet Letter*, but who was not fully understood. But these had done their best work by the end of the Civil War: Hawthorne died (1864), Melville 'retired' to his custom-house, Whitman began his long decline into mage-hood, and added little of consequence to *Leaves of Grass*. Few in the quarter-century after the Civil War would have thought of these writers as particularly important. The fashion was first for the so-called 'Brahmin' (the name was good-naturedly applied by analogy with the highest caste of Hindus) poets and thinkers (Longfellow, J.R. Lowell, Holmes, Prescott and others), centred in Boston – once revered, then too severely misprized, now more temperately revalued as creatively limited but tolerably liberal gentlemen – and later for such popular pseudo-realist fiction as that written by 'the Beau Brummell of the Press', **Richard Harding Davis** (1864–1916), a clever newspaper reporter, the more skilful romantic novelist **F. Marion Crawford** (1854–1909), every one of whose forty-five novels has dated, the solid 'conscientious middle-class romantic' historical novelist **Winston Churchill** (1871–1947), and the more gifted **O. Henry** (ps. **William Sidney Porter**, 1862–1910), a writer of short stories of humour and technical adroitness (his speciality was the surprise ending) but no psychological depth. The more important writers were not at first much heeded. But there is a major exception: **Mark Twain** (ps. **Samuel Langhorne Clemens**, 1835–1910), a nineteenth-century figure the importance of whose legacy to the twentieth is beyond question. The 'Brahmin' James Russell Lowell as well as the so-called 'literary comedians' ('Artemus Ward', 'Josh Billings', 'Bill Arp' and so on) of the Fifties and Sixties had tried to create a truly indigenous prose style, and had failed. In *Huckleberry Finn* (1884), sequel to *Tom Sawyer* (1876), Twain portrayed a complex but free American boy, in genuinely American prose; he also wrote a great novel of innocence and experience. But, like Whitman, Twain was a naïve American novelist of the latter half of the nineteenth century. He had also lived close to nature and to the experience of action. He could always write directly and uninhibitedly of experience; but only once, in *Huckleberry Finn*, did he produce a masterpiece. The realists were, however, for the most part sentimentive (q.v.) writers. They admired Twain – Howells (q.v.) was his friend and collaborator – but could not emulate him; nor, to do them justice, could he help them much in their aims: to portray truthfully, and to anatomize psychologically, American urban society.

Howells, James (q.v.) and the other realists had honourable precursors: writers whose realism was more than nominal, superficially regional – in the sense of patronizingly recording quirks and customs – and fashionable. Such was **John William De Forest** (1826–1906), who influenced Howells. De Forest, born in Connecticut, fought as a captain on the Union side; he wrote a number of readable novels, the most important of which is *Miss Ravenel's Conversion from Secession to Loyalty* (1867). This is didactic and its plot is sentimental, but its realism consists not of photographic set pieces but of a serious examination of the origins of the 'Southern' prejudices of Lillie, daughter of an abolitionist New Orleans doctor who has voluntarily come north at the outbreak of the war. Particularly well done is the portrait of one of her suitors, John Carter, a Virginian officer in the Union army, dashing, dissipated, heroic, morally ambiguous. It was in his battle scenes, however, that De Forest was most in advance of his time. His more happily titled *Honest John Vane* (1875), about a corrupt congressman, is also realistic in its study of political background.

The clergyman **Edward Eggleston** (1837–1902), founder of a 'Church of Christian Endeavour' in New York, was one of the best of the many regionalists then writing. Encouraged by J.R. Lowell, and an important influence on Hamlin Garland (q.v.), Eggleston described Indiana backwoods life in *The Hoosier School-Master* (1871), based perhaps on the experiences of his brother. Overall this is a sentimental and didactic novel, but it is important for the author's use of Indiana dialect and the realism of some isolated passages. Eggleston wrote a number of other novels, none as good as this, but nearly all distinguished by some realist facet. **Edgar Watson Howe** (1853–1937), who was born in Indiana, was another forerunner – one who lived to see the aftermath. Howe was essentially a small-town sage, in the American tradition; a sort of provincial H.L. Mencken (q.v.). He edited newspapers and magazines, produced cynical and homely aphorisms, and wrote memoirs. But when a young man he wrote one powerful though crude novel of the midwest: *The Story of a Country Town* (1883). Howe was not a good novelist, and the plot of this book is so melodramatically pessimistic as to be absurd. It is also at times monotonous, though on the whole thoroughly readable – hence its availability in paperback. But Howe's savage misanthropy caused him to look for unpalatable facts, and since he was intelligent as well as completely sincere (as Mark Twain told him) Howe selected some facts that had not previously been presented in fiction. Howe's picture of midwestern life and human scullduddery and scullduggery (for example, the stern patrician farmer-preacher turns out to be a randy hypocrite) is not vivid – but is more truthful than anything that had preceded it in its category, and with its intended scope. It helped to set a tone for such later writers as Sherwood Anderson (q.v.). For all its faults, *The Story of a Country Town* concentrates into itself a quintessentially American attitude: politically neither 'left' nor 'right', its main thrust is at the reality of small-town life as distinct from the legend of respectability. The battle is still being fought.

William Dean Howells (1837–1920), son of a newspaperman and printer, was born in Ohio. During the middle years of his long life Howells was considered by most critics to be the doyen of American writers. He was important not only as a pioneer realist, but also as a judicious and generous – but not indulgent – critic of the American writers of half a century, and as the introducer of much vital foreign literature. As a young man Howells, who knew how to get on, was taken up and blessed by Brahmin culture. He wrote a campaign life of Lincoln (1860) and was rewarded with the consulate at Venice, where he spent the years of the Civil War. Highly thought of by his elders, Howells joined the *Atlantic* in 1866 and soon became its editor (1871), and printed both their work and that of promising newcomers such as Henry James (q.v.). During the Seventies he began to form his ideas about fiction and to write novels. The best of these came between 1881 and 1892. Howells' reputation declined during his final year, and he was in due course equated with Victorianism, prudery (it was unfairly asserted that he had 'censored' Mark Twain) and facile optimism. Now Howells was a 'gentleman', and he did not think it right to be profane, obscene or gloomy; nor did he have the genius of Mark Twain. But he was not a pre-Freudian relic: his criticism is still valuable, and the best of his fiction has subtlety and depth. It comes from a mind that, even while it believed in a 'respectable' facade, was well aware of the violent impulses that rage beneath the surface of consciousness: he knew and admitted (to Twain) that the whole 'black heart's-truth' about himself could not be told. This would be something that came later. But if Howells was 'polite', then so, it must be admitted, was James. That the whole truth could not be told was something that not more than one nineteenth-century liberal gentleman in ten thousand would admit; not many gentlemen will admit it now.

Howells' achievement is a monument to what can be done in literature without genius. To understand him it is necessary to have a taste for 'both James and Twain'. . . . Certainly, if we are levelling charges of gentility, it is grossly unjust to dismiss Howells and yet absolve James. For it was Howells above all who helped to make the decently written novel an acceptable form in America: who helped American readers to understand that fiction, too, could have a 'moral' message – that the absolutely serious writer need not confine himself, as had Howells' mentors, to the oracular essay or to verse. And his own best novels courageously, if never dynamically, examined American mores. *Dr Breen's Practice* (1881) traces the private and public fortunes of a woman doctor; it sympathizes with her ambitions, though in making her a puritan fit for satire Howells reveals, perhaps with deliberate slyness, lurking anti-feminist prejudice. Howells had a sense of the outrage men inflict on women, but could not overcome his fear. James entered into his fear, and therefore could depict women. His two best novels are *A Modern Instance* (1882) and *The Rise of Silas Lapham* (1885), both of which were more unusually subtle and penetrating for their time than is realized today. *A Modern Instance*, which handles divorce and got Howells blamed for both over-boldness and 'moral timidity', is a study in the spiritual squalidity of a relationship in which hatred has replaced attraction (not, I think, love). This, written under the direct influence of Zola (q.v.), is Howells' boldest book. In *The Rise of Silas Lapham* Howells satirized the hollow snobbishness of Brahmin families (reflecting his committedness to his own kind) and at the same time showed how a vulgar, self-made man could attain moral authority. Lapham is a brash paint-manufacturer with high social ambitions for his family. He is humbled and forced out of Boston society because, although his way to wealth has been ruthless, he refuses to commit a dishonest act; thus he grows in stature, but, as Howells remarks, 'It is certain that our manners and customs go for more in life than our qualities'. Some critics have hailed the panoramic *A Hazard of New Fortunes* (1890) as Howells' best work – and so it might be if it had the power of the psychological novels. After *An Imperative Duty* (1891) Howells' fiction became more self-consciously didactic and illustrative of the Tolstoian socialism he had now adopted. But until the very last novel, *The Leatherwood God* (1916), published when he was seventy-nine, he maintained his high standards of craftsmanship and style. It is, strangely enough, this last book – a moving study of a historical character, an Ohio smallholder of the mid-nineteenth century, who persuaded a number of women to regard him as God – that is the least didactic of them all.

It is probably right to regard Howells as one of the native sources of what we may call the naturalist (q.v.) strain in American fiction – if only because others followed where he led. But his own realism was never really naturalistic, even in *A Modern Instance*. Howe's rudimentary *The Story of a Country Town* was nearer. The fact is that there is always something 'ungentlemanly' about true naturalist fiction – even when, as it seldom is, it is written by gentlemen such as Frank Norris (q.v.). Howells was also, and more obviously, an exemplar for – and frequently an encourager of – the other American realists who eschewed naturalism. Many of these, both major and minor, were temporary or permanent expatriates. If you stayed in the new America, it seems, you thought you understood it in assured, scientific, Darwinian – evolutionary – terms: you were a sort of determinist. Otherwise your impulse was to escape from a reality that you could neither deny nor affirm.

Escapism at its most obvious is seen in the case of the eccentric **Lafcadio Hearn** (1850–1904). Hearn was born on the Aegean island of Santa Maura (once called Leucadia, hence his name) of Irish-Greek parentage, with a goodly admixture of gipsy, English and Arabic – but no American – blood. However, he spent twenty-one years (1869–90) in America as a journalist before sailing for Japan, where he married into a Japanese Samurai family, raised children, turned Buddhist, and became a lecturer in English literature at the Imperial University at Tokyo. (His successor was Natsume Soseki, q.v.). As a journalist Hearn presented himself as a believer in the evolution of human society into complex higher forms; but really he wanted to get away from the ruthless drive that this 'evolution' implied. When competitiveness became increasingly evident in the life of Meiji Japan Hearn made plans to return to the States, but died before he could put them into effect. His real inclinations are revealed in the exotic character of his novels, *Chita* (1889), about a girl who survives a tidal wave on an island in the Gulf of Mexico, and even more in *Youma* (1890), on the theme of a slave-girl's devotion – till death – to the girl whose 'mammy' she is, and whom she has promised never to desert. Hearn never showed any inclination, despite the optimism of his journalism, to harness his creative imagination to the purpose of analysing modern society. He knew that had he done so he would have taken a view too gloomy for the comfort of his social conscience.

His case is one of simple escapism. That of **Henry Adams** (1838–1918), great-grandson of the second President of the USA and grandson of the sixth, is more complicated. The two novels he wrote, *Democracy* (1880) and *Esther* (1884) – the first anonymous, the second pseudonymous – are not important as literature; but Adams as a thinker is. He was the first great American pessimist. Where his illustrious family had been public servants, he took refuge in letters. Had he, however, sought to express himself creatively rather than philosophically he would perhaps have discovered an objective correlative for the personal problems of his marriage (1872), which ended in 1885 with the suicide of his wife. But this period of his life (with the seven years following it) is missed out of his remarkable autobiography, *The Education of Henry Adams* (privately issued 1907; published 1918). Adams was a distinguished historian, and in writing his huge *History of the United States during the Administrations of Jefferson and Madison* (1889–91) he had seen something that might have looked like evolution at work; his argument here was that men cannot change the course of history. He wrote, it must be remembered, as a member of a family who had actually 'made' history. ... So he had a superior, or a stronger – less journalistic – sense of evolution than Hearn (q.v.). But, like Hearn, he sought to escape: in restless travel to Mexico, Japan, Europe. In *Mont-Saint-Michel and Chartres* (privately issued 1904; published 1913) the religiously sceptic Adams postulated a unified medieval universe, the centre of which was the Virgin. This was perhaps more fictional, if unwittingly, than either of his novels: thirteenth-century stability is to a large extent a myth in the minds of nineteenth- and early twentieth-century Catholic apologists. We find the same error in a cruder form in Belloc (q.v.). He showed the world of 1150–1250 as in equilibrium, 'pre-evolutionary', centripetal. In the *Education* he shows the modern 'multiverse' as accelerating towards disaster, centrifugal, spinning towards what in a letter he called 'an ultimate, colossal, cosmic collapse ... science is to wreck us ... our power over energy has now reached a point where it must sensibly affect the old adjustment. ...' He used the Second Law of Thermodynamics to show the individual, the victim, as so to say being whirled (by the symbol of the Dynamo, opposed to the Virgin of the earlier book), run down and dissipated into a nothingness: into entropy, disorder. Here and in the posthumous *The Degradation of the Democratic Dogma* (1919) – which was edited by his brother, the historian Brooks Adams (1848–1927), who shared his gloomy view of history – Adams rationalized his theory into an exact prophecy, with dates. This prophecy was wrong – the date of final dissolution was doubtless made early in order to fall into Adams' own lifespan – but few intelligent men reading Adams fifty years after his death are likely to find his apprehensions entirely unjustified. He published his two most important books after the first heyday of American naturalism was over; he had no influence on it. But his thinking in these books – and even more so in his *Letters* (1930; 1947), where he is at his most fascinating and vigorous – is more representative than merely influential. Of course he has nothing in him of the material or cultural optimism that was then one of the characteristics of America, nothing of the pure joy in becoming and feeling pure American, un-English, that distinguishes, say, William Carlos Williams (q.v.). But his work is a response to the same sort of mental crisis that Hofmannsthal describes in his *Chandos* letter (q.v.). Not being a poet, Adams does not see the problem in terms of language. Basically he fears for the integrity of his human, and therefore the human, personality in the face of scientific advance. The proto-fascist and futurist Marinetti (q.v.) hailed the new technology. Adams shuddered before it, his sardonic mind casting fearfully back for a static and stable paradise, for 'some great generalization which would finish one's clamour to be educated'. 'Modern politics is, at bottom, a struggle not of men, but of forces', he wrote. In the new 'multiverse' 'order [is] an accidental relation obnoxious to nature'. Adams, however, was a historian, not a creative writer: all he wanted was to get out, have nothing to do with it: 'All the historian won was a vehement wish to escape'.

Each man sees his own death differently: he colours his apprehensions of it according to his personal and historical circumstances. Adams, a historian, a scion of mighty history-makers who had more excuse than most for treating the world as his particular oyster, faced by a crazily accelerating, and already over-confident science (the 'score or two of individuals' who controlled 'mechanical power' he described as 'as dumb as their dynamos, absorbed in the economy of power'), coloured his idea of death with zestful meaninglessness. It is instructive to compare his non-creative reaction to the creative one of the first German expressionists (q.v.), with its distorting rapid wobble between ecstatic hope and horror. Adams' importance is that he shared such men's awareness of the time.

Ambrose Bierce (1842–*c*1914), born in Ohio, was as sardonic as Adams – and more creative. But although his best short stories are distinguished, he never wholly fulfilled his genius, preferring for the most part to substitute for the wisdom he could have attained a mordant but too folksy and self-indulgent cynicism. Bierce was a man of principle (he refused the back pay he had earned as a soldier in the Civil War), and a soul genuinely tortured by what Henry Adams (q.v.) called 'the persistently fiendish treatment of man by man'; but in his case journalism, and the pleasure of being literary dictator of the Pacific States (for a quarter of a century until he resigned in 1909), distracted him from literature; it was easier to indulge himself in his vitriolic epigrams – often cheap and gratuitous, and in any case never on the level of his best stories – than to write creatively. The epigrams are in *The Devil's Dictionary* (1911), originally called *The Cynic's Word Book* (1906); the stories are in *Can Such Things Be?* (1893) and, notably, in *In the Midst of Life* (1898), which was originally called *Tales of Soldiers and Civilians* (1891). The famous Civil War tales, including 'An Occurrence at Owl Creek Bridge' and 'The Horseman in the Sky', in which a young Union soldier has to shoot his father, make a valid use of Poe – and remain original, economic, appropriately macabre: they are secure minor classics. But Bierce did not want to use his imagination to grapple with the problem of contemporary America – his cynical journalism was in a sense as much of an 'escape' as Japan was for Hearn (q.v.). He made his final escape when he disappeared into Mexico, in 1911, to join Pancho Villa. He was never heard of again.

*

The achievement of **Henry James** (1843–1916), born in New York and educated mostly abroad, is so great as hardly to abide all questions of American realism. Son of a formidable, eccentric Swedenborgian father, and younger brother of William James – an important and seminal thinker – Henry offers in one sense a contrast to Howells (q.v.): his achievement is a monument to how literary genius can surmount crippling personal difficulties. For James was fated to be only an observer. His friend Henry Adams (q.v.) complained that he knew of women only from the outside – 'he never had a wife'. But, as Alfred Kazin rejoins, 'because he knew so little, he could speculate endlessly'. His mind was a brilliant and sensitive instrument of speculation. He is certainly one of those whose work transcends its psychological and historical occasions; the only question is to what extent.

James expressed one important theme of his fiction when he passionately expostulated at the unfairness of fate's treatment of Howells' daughter, Winifred, who died young after a long, disabling, mysterious and unrelieved illness: 'To be young and gentle, and do no harm, and pay for it as if it were a crime'. James as an adolescent had felt himself crushed by his father and his clever older brother; he had not gone to the war as his younger brothers had, and never felt himself able to fulfil a masculine role. His biographer Leon Edel has now revealed, for those who had not detected it from the work, that James' sexual impulses (at least as a middle-aged man) were homosexual, and that he had a bad conscience about it. Whether or not he was ever an active homosexual is an as yet unanswered question. Probably not. Hugh Walpole (q.v.), whom he fell for ('Beloved Little Hugh') and overrated as a writer, is supposed to have offered himself to the master and to have been repudiated with 'Si la vieillesse pouvait!'. These facts throw new light on such works as 'The Turn of the Screw' (printed in *The Two Magics*, 1898), *The Other House* (1896) and *What Maisie Knew* (1897), all written at the height of James' crisis of homosexuality – which coincided with his humiliation in the theatre and with the trials of Oscar Wilde. (About Wilde James was unforgivably and viciously hypocritical.) It was in 'The Turn of the Screw' above all that James (unconsciously) analysed his condition, defensively referring to it as a 'jeu d'esprit', hoping to throw himself and his readers off the scent. James' personal sexual predicament actually affects our interpretation of all his work, from his first novel *Roderick Hudson* right up until his last unfinished one, the posthumous *The Ivory Tower*. For the young novelist not only wanted to get away from America – although not from his Americanness, a different thing – but also from the 'masculine' obligations of love for a woman and the heavy commitments of marriage. The 'horrid even if ... obscure hurt', probably a strained back, he claimed to have suffered while helping to put out a fire at about the time of the outbreak of the Civil War, served him in a number of ways: it linked him with his father, who when a child had lost a leg while fighting a fire; it excused him from joining the army; it enabled him to be passive, feminine; the nature of the 'injury' was supposed to be sexual, but no one could of course ask about it directly – thus giving 'sex' the *frisson* it nearly always has in James' fiction. The hurt was 'obscure' – but mere mention of it none the less drew a kind of attention to it. It reminds us of those 'things' little Miles, in 'The Turn of the Screw', said to those he 'liked', and which were 'Too bad' 'to write home about'. ...

Europe attracted James from the beginning. He felt that America was too crude for his own artistic purposes. His first novel, *Roderick Hudson* (1876), explores his dilemma: Europe is beautiful, sinister, wicked – like Christina Light, who tortures the genius hero into 'horrible' dissipations which all, of course, as always in James, take place off-stage, and which eventually lead to his death. In *The American* (1877), not one of his most convincing novels, he rationalizes his doubts about his inadequacies. Wealthy American Christopher Newman (the name is significant) goes to Paris (where, said James elsewhere at this time, modern French books resembled 'little vases ... into which unclean things had been dropped') and falls in love with an aristocratic girl whose family are most reluctant to approve the match. Christopher finds an ally, however, in her younger brother Count Valentin. He discovers that the mother of the girl he loves is a murderess, but eventually decides not to use the information to gain his objective: he will not use such knowledge for material ends. Thus James launched himself into fully fledged writerhood.

By 1881, at the age of thirty-eight, with *The Portrait of a Lady*, he had become an undisputed master, for all his shortcomings one of the most important of all English-language novelists. It was in the Eighties that James wrote the novels of his so-called 'middle period': the most notable are *The Bostonians* (1886), *The Princess Casamassima* (1886) and *The Tragic Muse* (1890). The novels of the last period – *The Ambassadors* (1903), *The Golden Bowl* (1904) – are more difficult: the sentences are long, the motivations that are examined are ambiguous; the whole approach seems anfractuous not to say tortuous. And yet many regard *The Wings of the Dove* (1902), with good reason, as James' masterpiece. This is the story of an innocence betrayed and of the terrifying and irrevocable corruption of spirit that this betrayal brings in its wake. Kate Croy persuades her lover, a poor journalist, Morton Densher, said partly to be based on Ford (q.v.), to attach himself falsely to a rich, dying girl, Milly. He does so, and gets her money. But he cannot take it, and asks Kate to have him without it. Now herself 'infected' by the innocence of Milly, she will not do so because she rightly suspects him of loving the dead girl's memory. In this hideously accurate portrayal of how a man acts in bad faith, of unmelodramatic evil, James the detached observer triumphed – as he did in so many of his short stories (ed. L. Edel, 12 vols., 1962–5).

Right through his fiction, from *Roderick Hudson* onwards, James had maintained a technique for suggesting, without ever detailing, evil. He had not, of course, experienced evil – only his 'evil' homosexual impulses. He was highly professional, as well as emotionally rather innocent, in the way he dealt with this problem. It is one of his strengths that the horrors he hints at are not really, by normal sophisticated standards, particularly horrible at all. The point is that this highly sentimentive (q.v.) writer was not, in calling 'debauchery' 'unclean', simply being reactionary or hypocritical. It was his lack of knowledge that lamed him; but he turned it into a crutch. We do not look, in James, for any kind of enlightenment about or illumination of actual sexual matters: his fiction deals with the innocent or inexperienced preliminaries to them. They lie horribly in wait at the ends of twisting and turning corridors.

In *The Portrait of a Lady* the good and generous Isabel Archer is not experienced enough to realize that the widower Gilbert Osmond – a shallow pseudo-aesthete whose worst failing, however, is his capacity to manipulate others' emotions for his material advantage – wants her fortune. She marries him, and discovers too late that she can do nothing for him – as she had hoped to do for whatever man she might love. Eventually she admits to her former American suitor that she loves him, but nevertheless chooses to return to her husband: to give up her freedom in return for that of his bastard daughter, Pansy, whose interests she will continue to protect. The reader can and does easily fill in the missing sexuality here: Osmond is as self-indulgently and sadistically lustful for Isabel's virginity as for her money; her own disillusion is as much sexual as psychological. If any reader wonders how she could be taken in by so evidently insincere a man, then he need not wonder for long: the reason is sexual. James had the feminine sensitivity and intuition to understand these things: he earned it by the integrity of his self-analysis – for, in one aspect, all novels are either rationalizations or self-analyses. In *The Portrait of a Lady* James is Ralph Touchett, the tubercular (crippled) observer who loves Isabel, and renounces her from the start (because of his condition) but who stolidly looks after her interests. The real tragedy of the book lies in his death: James' touching account of his own death to sexual life. But he also presents himself as Isabel, who initially turns down both a straightforward New Englander and a decent English aristocrat, then falls into the snare of a cosmopolitan – finally choosing, now a natural and detached moralist, to endure him (as James chose to remain in Europe – but he was happier in England than Isabel was with Osmond, for he found there 'an arrangement of things hanging together with a romantic rightness that had the force of a revelation'). James wrote criticism of great subtlety, travel books and a number of interesting but bad plays and adaptations from his novels (*Complete Plays*, ed. L. Edel, 1949). When the First World War broke out James was agonized: 'that to have to take it all now for what the treacherous years were all the while really making for and *meaning* is too tragic for any words'. He became a British citizen, did what war-work his failing health would allow, received the Order of Merit, and died in 1916. James understood that 1914 meant the disintegration of the old order of things, but was too old to contemplate it. He was one of the greatest of the writers of that vanished world. But he has relevance to the literature of today because his fiction is ultimately a commentary, often exquisite, on what it is to be a creator. Most of the important considerations – the relationship between virtue and creativity among them –

are there. James saw with some ruefulness what he could never be; but he never hid from his creative responsibilities. There will always be controversy about the stature of his last three major books – *The Wings of the Dove, The Ambassadors, The Golden Bowl.* Are they a 'trilogy' that embraces a new form, akin to the drama of Racine? Or was the profound self-adjustment (after his failure to capture a big audience or even to avoid ignominy as a dramatist), of which these books are undoubtedly the fruit, achieved at a high cost to the universality of his art? *The Wings of the Dove* is surely exempt; of the other two novels one is less sure. But all the work of James has much more to yield. Supposing he did, in his last period, create a new kind of fiction; he was still not an innovator in the sense of clearing ground for anyone else; but he cannot be ignored because his whole life was in one way an anticipation of the practice of the writers who came after him: he created his own world, understood that he was God in it – and took his responsibilities with the utmost seriousness. He has been denigrated both by Marxist critics and by members of the indigenous 'Black Mountain' school (q.v.); there also existed in the Forties and Fifties an over-fanciful image of James that had little relationship to the man or the writer. Close study, new understanding, increase our respect for him.

James' friend **Edith Wharton** (1862–1937), although pessimistic in her view of life, was another who rejected the determinism of naturalism (q.v.). She came of a distinguished family and, like James, was introduced to Europe in childhood. Her marriage was unhappy, since Edward Wharton became mentally ill; this helped to drive her into literature. She settled in France in 1907 and five years later divorced her husband. Mrs. Wharton insisted that the duty of a novelist was to discover what the characters, 'being what they are, would make of the situation' – but in reality her people are less free than James'. In her world, usually of high society, vulgarity overwhelms fineness; the choice to go against the conventional leads to disaster; opulence corrupts; where James' women are convincing angels, Mrs. Wharton's are defeated harpies. Edith Wharton wrote well of a society she knew, but as a whole her fiction lacks tension. The author knew too well from the beginning, one feels, that vulgarity would triumph: her characters do not assert themselves strongly enough to be tragic in their defeats. The short stories (*Best Short Stories of Edith Wharton*, 1958), ironic and satiric, are slight but in this respect more satisfactory. However, there are amongst the novels some notable exceptions; and Mrs. Wharton invariably maintains a high standard. Her observation is impeccable. One compares her to James and inevitably finds her wanting; and yet she is incomparably better than the Nobel-winning Galsworthy (q.v.) was, even at his best. In her best works she partially overcomes her shortcomings, and has something entirely of her own to offer. An account of *Ethan Frome* (1911), which is one of the only two novels (*Summer*, 1917, is the other) Edith Wharton set outside polite society, makes it sound naturalist; but it is no more than bleak. The story is told wonderingly, by a stranger. Ethan Frome barely wrings a living from the barren earth of his Massachusetts farm; his hated wife Zeena (Zenobia) is a whining hypochondriac. Her cousin Mattie comes to live with them, and Ethan and she fall in love. Zeena forces her out; when Ethan is taking her to the station he yields to the impulse to end it all by crashing the sledge in which they are travelling. But the couple are crippled. Zeena is transformed into their devoted nurse, leaving Mattie to become the whining invalid and Ethan to his despair and certain economic failure. This is not absolutely convincing, but the portrait of Zeena – the nagging, loathed wife – the growth of affection between Ethan and Mattie, and the ironic ending are all beautifully done. Her two other major books are both society novels: *The Custom of the Country* (1913) and *The Age of Innocence* (1920). The character of Undine Spragg, the ruthless social climber of the first, has been objected to on the grounds that Mrs. Wharton's disgust with her type is too great to permit of psychological accuracy. This is not altogether fair. Undine Spragg is a shallow monster driven by ignoble motives; but when critics object that the drama of her marriage to a Frenchman more decent than herself is 'weakened' by this, they are in effect trying to tell novelists what kind of characters to use in order to get their plots right. But life is not as such critics want it to be, and novelists must ignore them. People like Undine Spragg do exist, and *The Custom of the Country* is better than is generally allowed. *The Age of Innocence* is an acid, ironic but touching study of a love whose happiness is destroyed by adherence to a code, and by the kind of people 'who dreaded scandal more than disease, who placed decency above courage'. *Hudson River Bracketed* (1929) is not wholly successful, but is peculiarly subtle and poignant in its portrait of the creative side of its hero, a novelist who discovers that the 'people' he understands best are the ones he has invented. ... There is something very attractive about Edith Wharton even at her worst – when she is too gloomy or when she is copying Henry James in some of her supernatural tales – for she is always intelligent and humane. Probably her best work has been underestimated and her originality not fully recognized.

*

'New England transcendentalism' is even less susceptible of exact definition than most such phenomena. But, although it was never a school, it is important, for all subsequent American movements may be seen to stem from it. Essentially it is a first religious step after the repudiation of the Christian doctrine; it can fairly be called a form of rationalistic religion. Its chief figure was Emerson, whose lecture 'The Transcendentalist' came in 1841, when transcendentalism was at its peak. One can most profitably study transcendentalism as it manifested itself in individuals – in Henry David Thoreau, in Emerson himself, in the poet Jones Very – but, while there was never a doctrine, some ideas were held in common. Every transcendentalist is a Platonist, and the inclination towards Oriental religions (exemplified in the later Emerson), 'creedless creeds', is typical. The spirit of transcendentalism was eclectic, individualist, reformist. On the specifically American subject of slavery the transcendentalists were abolitionist, although initially they were more sympathetic than active – but for the honourable reason that they were sceptical of all group action.

In the fiction of Henry James (q.v.) the implications of transcendentalism were realized. Its consistent background was a non-dogmatic – indeed, a being-sought-for – moral system, something as ghostly but as effectual as that of any Platonic realm of perfections. Thus Mrs. Wharton (q.v.), despite her gloom and her apparent belief that men's circumstances are stronger than themselves, is no naturalist: she follows James when she says: 'Every great novel must first of all be based on a profound sense of moral values. ...' And one does feel her sense of values more strongly than her gloom, which in any case does not arise from an intellectual determinism. That same moral sense lurks behind Howells' fiction, too; but in him there are more gentlemanly prejudices.

The source of naturalism (q.v.) – which only in America produced a crop of major or potentially major novelists – is, as Charles Child Walcutt has pointed out in an essay on Dreiser (q.v.), the 'Divided Stream of ... transcendentalism'. The transcendentalists, not always unconfusedly, regarded spirit and matter as two aspects of the same thing. But, as Walcutt observes:

> The monist stream did not stay One ... time and experience divided it into poles of optimism and pessimism, freedom and determinism, will and fate, social reformism and mechanistic despair ... the Nature which was assumed to be a version of a

man's spirit and therefore of his will appeared under scientific analysis as a force which first controlled man's will and presently made it seem that his freedom was an illusion, that there was no such thing as will but only chemicals performing reactions which could (theoretically at least) be predicted.

First, Walcutt continues, Americans believed that the human spirit could be liberated by mastering nature; but their 'devotion to science and fact' led them to the point where the natural law seemed to deny both freedom and spirit. ...

The atmosphere that produced the powerful movement of American naturalism was well summed up by Henry Adams in 1894 when he wrote '... if anything is radically wrong it must grow worse. ... If we are diseased, so is all the world. ... Europe is rather more in the dark than we are. ...'

But there is more in a major novelist than a philosophy or, more usually, a pseudo-philosophy. As Nietzsche (q.v.) once said, talking about realists: 'What does one see, and paint, or write? In the last analysis, what one *wishes* to see, and what one *can* see'. And so, grateful as we are to determinism and gloom for sometimes inspiring such as Dreiser, we do not go to him for his thinking (God forbid). As always, the truly gifted went altogether beyond dogmatism, to produce something certain and knowable. But let us first look at the minor novelists who anticipated or participated in naturalism.

Hamlin Garland (1860–1940) is more interesting as a pioneer than as a novelist. Harold Frederic (1856–98), a similar pioneer, produced in *Seth's Brother's Wife* (1887) and *The Damnation of Theron Ware* (1896) novels psychologically far in advance of anything of Garland's; but the latter does have his importance. An autodidact, Garland was born in Wisconsin. As a young man he sweated on the land: he knew the farmers he wrote about, and the conditions under which they worked. He was influenced by Howells (q.v.), and even more by the economist Henry George (1839–97). George, a lucid and fervent writer, was highly influential. Imbued with the Pelagianism that still characterizes most Americans, he devised an economic scheme by which he believed social justice might be ensured: a 'single tax' on land. By means of this, he believed, the community would recover what it had lost in rents. George's effect on economic thought probably amounted to little more than the stimulation of more lucid theories of rent (as an econo-mist, it is said, he was 'a little more than a child'), but his passion for justice and the style of his thinking were and to some extent still are influential (to the dismay of some econo-mists). George's theories lie behind Garland's early short stories, collected in *Prairie Folks* (1893) and *Wayside Courtships* (1897): these villainize landlords and mortgage-holders rather programmatically, in a manner of which Marx would have disapproved. In the mid-Nineties Garland put forward a theory of literature that he called 'veritism'. This was a meliorist extension of realism. It was naturalist only in that in proposing a literature that would change social conditions it assumed that those conditions determined men's lives. Garland's best work is a short novel called *A Little Norsk* (1892), about a Dakota farm-girl's hard lot; next best is the longer *Rose of Dutcher's Coolly* (1895), the story of another farm-girl – but this one studies at the University of Wisconsin and succeeds in becoming a writer in Chicago. Garland projected himself into his heroine, but then got interested in her for her own sake. The result is a convincing realist novel. Garland's most serious work was not popular, and before the turn of the century he began to write romances of the far West; after this he turned into a dull memoirist and, ultimately, weak-minded devotee of psychical phenomena.

Robert Herrick (1868–1938) was not a naturalist, but like Garland he anticipated and influenced the mood by his critical and reformist attitude. A graduate of Harvard, he was a professor of English at the University of Chicago. An older professor, writing of him in

1909, could allude to him as 'something of a pessimist, but not unwholesome'. Herrick partly made up for his lack of power and psychological penetration by his honesty. He was perhaps temperamentally a determinist, but frustrated by guilt about the consequences of such an attitude. The scientist of his first novella, 'The Man Who Wins' (1897), believes in the freedom of the will – but his very circumstances seem to deny it. Herrick did not resolve his problem, but turned to the (sometimes acute) analysis of the corruptions and strains in industrial society. In his best novels he succeeded in his aim of dealing with social problems 'less in an argumentative ... manner than as crises in human lives'. *The Web of Life* (1900), his most psychologically ambitious book, indicates the direction he might have liked to follow. Herrick was obsessed with the figure of the doctor, the healer (an inferior 1911 novel is called *The Healer*), and this early book is about one who saves the life of an alcoholic by an operation in which, however, he injures the brain. He falls in love with the man's wife; she collapses under the strain and kills herself. This was melodramatic and, except in parts, unconvincing: Herrick was wise to turn to the more social theme of *The Common Lot* (1904), his best novel, which traces the moral degradation of a young Chicago architect in his dealings with crooked builders, which finally lead to a fire and a number of deaths. His moral 'regeneration' by his wife is tacked on as a gesture. Herrick later became more ponderous, his characters less interesting. His greatest success, the sentimental novella *The Master of the Inn* (1908), is now dated and unreadable.

The prolific **Upton Sinclair** (1878–1969) was from any kind of 'Jamesian' point of view never more than a simplistic romancer, but he cannot quite be ignored – he is, as one critic has said, 'an event in nature'. *The Jungle* (1906) displays real power and concern, and is possibly the most sheerly vivid exposé in American literature of humanly intolerable economic conditions. It tells of the exploitation of an immigrant Lithuanian family in the meat-packing industry. The message is socialist, but what was heeded was the revelation of the filthy conditions in which meat was packed in Chicago – Sinclair had himself investigated the situation. The Federal Pure Food and Drug Act was hastened through, with the assistance of Theodore Roosevelt; but the lot of the workers was not improved for many years. Sinclair was humourless, a crank and an idealist – but of a personal nobility enough to make most humorous and sensible realists feel at least a pang of shame. He wrote well over one hundred books. He remained a socialist all his life, but was one of the first to rumble the nature of the Soviet regime. After *The Jungle* his best known novels are the 'Lanny Budd' series, beginning with *World's End* (1940): these feature Lanny Budd, the bastard son of a munitions king who is, in his grandiosely well-intentioned way, a kind of Yankee Jules Romains (q.v.) in that writer's unfortunate self-appointed capacity of world's chief troubleshooter. Lanny knows everyone, including the top men, and they take note of him. Sinclair, who sunk his money into or took part in several Utopian projects, including Helicon Hall (burnt down), and a single-tax colony, was at heart a big, dear romantic booby. But he was not middlebrow: he did not tell his audience anything at all they wanted to hear. And although, like Henry George (q.v.), he believed in the innate goodness of man, he was a true naturalist at least in the sense that he was able to bring to the notice of a reluctant public the evils they lived amongst.

Stephen Crane (1871–1900) was almost forgotten until some quarter of a century after his death from tuberculosis. Then the novelist, pleasantly ironic short-story writer and critic **Thomas Beer** (1889–1940) – famous for his later study of the Nineties, which he christened *The Mauve Decade* (1926) – wrote his *Stephen Crane* (1923), which was one of the initial steps in the rehabilitation of a major writer. (Beer himself combined the economy of Lytton Strachey (q.v.) with the sardonic style of Henry Adams (q.v.) and was a notable biographer; unfortunately he later came to over-sound the sardonic note, and some of

The Mauve Decade reads like self-parody.) Since Beer's book and the issue of his *Collected Works* in twelve volumes in 1926 Crane has, and without doubt properly, attained the status of a classic. The fourteenth son of a Methodist preacher and a religiously zealous, well-educated mother, Crane was a thorough rebel by the time he came of age. Part of the secret of his achievement lies in the absoluteness of his rejection of the values of his age – which went with an intelligent curiosity, a sense of humour, and a natural compassion in acute competition with a bitter and sardonic nihilism. Even when Crane seems to throw the whole of himself into what he is describing, a part of him is usually detached and amused. His style was devastatingly new and original.

Crane starved, worked as a freelance journalist, and then, in 1893, published his first book, under the name of 'Johnston Smith', at his own expense. *Maggie: A Girl of the Streets* was reprinted, in a slightly abridged form, in 1896. At the time of its first publication only Garland and Howells (qq.v.) noticed it. *Maggie*, whatever its faults, is a pretty remarkable effort for a twenty-two-year-old: what it lacks in maturity it more than makes up for in attack, candour and confidence. Critics have suggested several sources of this stark tale of a pretty girl forced by the brutal squalor of her home, and then by seduction and desertion, into prostitution and suicide: '*Madame Bovary* recast in Bowery style', the novels of Zola (q.v.), or a sermon of De Witt Talmage which visualizes the suicide of a prostitute called Maggie. ... It is not certain how much Crane had then read. But the book's tone is Crane's and no one else's. It is, as a critic said, 'violent and absurd like a primitive film' – but not, as the same critic incautiously adds, 'dated'. The 'primitive film' effect is an impressionism that anticipates the innovatory pointillism of *The Red Badge of Courage*. The scenes in which Maggie's parents quarrel are perhaps absurd; but they are also vivid and powerful – one feels how the hopelessly pretty, weak girl was deafened by them. (An old woman asks Maggie, amid shrieks, 'Is yer fader beatin' yer mudder, or yer mudder beatin' yer fader?') Regardless of whether naturalism is a 'true' philosophy or not, Crane gave an unforgettable account of one poor creature whose life was quickly snuffed out by her environment. And he strengthened his novel by bringing to it the moral indignation of his preacher father, but not the moral judgement. Its abundant irony is apparent only to the sensitive, humane reader. It remains as truthful a picture of Bowery life as could at that time have been achieved. It has the authority of imagination and a painterly exactitude that reminds one of the fine New York slum paintings of George Bellows and the 'Ashcan' group of painters whom he joined.

Encouraged by Howells and Garland, although ignored by almost everyone else, Crane continued to write. In his laconic, debunking poetry, published in *The Black Riders* (1895), *War is Kind* (1899) and collected in 1930 and again, in a variorum edition, by J. Katz (1966), Crane created a tough, rhythmical free verse: it was well fitted to accommodate what John Berryman (q.v.) has called his 'sincerity ... bluntness ... enigmatic character ... barbarity'. It is subtler than the directness of its manner makes it seem, and in it Crane has absolutely no truck with respectability – or anything that seems to him to be respectable. This poetry, influenced as much by the verbal compression of Emily Dickinson as by the cynicism of Bierce (q.v.), has not perhaps had its full due in spite of the recognition now accorded to Crane. However, he did not wholly succeed in finding his own poetic voice, which might well have combined his parabolic with his symbolist, 'Baudelairian' manner, when this had been purged of its immature neo-romantic tendencies. Crane's poetry is important, though, because in it he is investigating the meaning of his deepest and most mysterious impulses.

Crane subscribed to Garland's 'veritism', but had had no personal experience of war, the subject of *The Red Badge of Courage* (1895). This is an extraordinary demonstration of the complex nature of fiction: it may be 'realism', it may even be 'naturalism' in so far as it presents men helpless in the grip of events – but the 'reality' it embraces is evidently wider than that of mere reportage. As one of Crane's leading critics, R.W. Stallman, has pointed out, it 'is a symbolic construct'. And because it succeeds so triumphantly on the realistic level, it is also about many other things: the fearful plunge of men into maturity and responsibility, into sexuality, into the raw, chaotic unknown. Henry Fleming is not named until half-way through the book. A farm-boy, he swaggers to himself, is frightened, is reassured, is caught up in battle and runs, gains his 'red badge' by an accident, returns and becomes a demon of aggressive energy. But it is all for nothing: his regiment takes up its former position. If he has become a 'man' (as he tries to believe) then what, asks the ironic structure of the book, is a man? In a short sequel, 'The Veteran', Henry really does become a 'man' when he goes into a burning barn to rescue two horses; but after that conversion he is a dead man. Another interesting thing about Henry Fleming and some of Crane's other characters is that they have nothing dis-honestly to offer outside his own pages. As Berryman points out, they are not 'types', but they are not 'round' characters either: they move significantly only in their context, of Crane's impressionistic imagination. This not only anticipates but also disposes of all the philosophical claptrap surrounding the *nouveau roman* (q.v.). He does not tell us meaning-lessly that the sun shone red. He puts it honestly into the text that is his own picture, his invention of a battle: 'The red sun was pasted in the sky like a wafer'.

Crane's novel 'The Third Violet' (1897), on bohemian life, is more conventional than *George's Mother* (1896), a competent tale of a working-class mother whose son is the opposite of what she fondly and pathetically imagines he is. Besides novels, poetry, un-finished plays and fiction, and a mass of journalism, Crane left behind him a number of short stories as classic as *The Red Badge of Courage.* The most famous of these are 'The Open Boat', based on Crane's experiences when, sent as correspondent to cover an expedition, he was shipwrecked off Cuba, and 'The Blue Hotel', a wickedly knowing tale about a Swede who creates the death-trap, the hostility of tough Nebraskans, that he most fears.

Crane drove himself ever more frenetically towards an early death. He took jobs cover-ing the Spanish-American and the Graeco-Turkish wars, got into debt, desperately and vainly tried to write himself out of it. His last years were shared in England in a dilapi-dated manor house at Brede, Kent, with Cora Taylor, divorcee, prostitute and madame. There he made close friends of H.G. Wells, Ford Madox Ford and Joseph Conrad (qq.v.), and enjoyed as much friendship and understanding as any young writer has had. But he wore himself out entertaining on a regal scale, projecting – and writing. It was characteristic that he should have taken no heed of a serious warning (a lung haemor-rhage) six months before he died. His self-destructiveness remains enigmatic, but one senses an enormous secret despair behind the sardonic and even gay phthisic energy. We can suspect that as his Henry Fleming turned after the battle to 'tranquil skies' with 'a lover's thirst', so he turned to death. Certainly Hemingway (q.v.) was right in saying that modern American literature begins with *Huckleberry Finn*; but rivers do not come from one spring, and it is as true to say that it flows from Crane's fiction. This may become increasingly apparent. It is sometimes objected that Crane's fiction and 'perverse' poetry ultimately function only 'as a fresh symbol of the universe's indifference to human needs' (Alfred Kazin). Crane did feel that. But there is something else locked away in that blandly autonomous prose, a creative intelligence like a great bird of prey, anticipating American writing not yet seen.

Chicago, to become the centre of the new literature, was an appropriate birthplace for **Frank Norris** (1870–1902), who shared the given names of 'Benjamin Franklin', but little else, with Wedekind (q.v.). Norris did not have Crane's genius or sense of style, but he left

some powerful fiction, and usefully demonstrates the limitations of such terms as naturalism when they are allowed to apply to anything beyond conscious method: we cannot
heed Nietzsche's warning too much; 'What does one see, and paint, or write? ... what
one *wishes* to see, and what one *can* see'. Norris was a romantic who studied art in Paris at
seventeen, and while there became hooked on medieval chivalry (or what passed for it)
rather than realist or naturalist literature. Later, however, at Harvard, he chose the
naturalist method as he had observed it in the novels of Zola (q.v.) in order to have a
literary principle, and thus to get his fiction written. He carried out journalistic assign-
ments, including one in Cuba, married, and became well known as a novelist before his
death. Norris wrote his best novel, *Vandover and the Brute* (1914), while at Harvard during
1894 and 1895; the manuscript was believed lost for a time, in the San Francisco earth-
quake; it was not published until twelve years after his early death of peritonitis.
McTeague, written at about the same time, was published in 1899, after the issue of the
later and inferior *Moran of the Lady Letty* (1898). Norris' reputation rests on *Vandover*,
McTeague, and the first novel of a planned but uncompleted trilogy on the production
and distribution of wheat: *The Octopus* (1901); *The Pit* (1903), the second, is inferior. His
first published work, a long phoney-medieval poem in three cantos called *Yvernelle: A Tale
of Feudal France* (1892), is of no literary value but is useful as an indication of the romanticism that he never wholly shed.

Norris' importance has been acknowledged, but his achievement has been underrated
because he has been judged (by critics more interested in movements than individual
writers) as a naturalist and therefore by the standards of realism. Norris was, however,
like Crane, a symbolist, and his three best books are all symbolic novels; but unlike
Crane, he had no inkling of the fact, and when he announced, 'By God! I told them the
truth', he equated the telling of truth with the simple act of holding a mirror up to the
unpleasanter facts of nature. He had been very worried by the consequences of his
(apparently ordinary) sexual excesses, and suffered from some measure of the gentility
then endemic in America. The simple fact of sex existing at all haunts his fiction as a
terrifying background grossness. *McTeague* is about a huge and physically gross dentist
who is driven to bestiality, and the murder of his whining, miserly wife Trina, because of
the circumstances created when his jealous friend betrays him to the authorities for
practising illegally. *McTeague* is indebted to Zola, and even to actual incidents in his
novels, and it is plainly intended as a naturalist novel, with simple symbols (such as the
huge, gilded tooth that Trina gives McTeague for his sign: 'tremendous, overpowering
... shining dimly out ... with some mysterious light ...', or his canary). McTeague is
usually described by critics as 'stupid and brutal', and as thoroughly deserving of his fate;
and possibly Norris himself consciously thought this. Actually, however, he is initially a
very sympathetic character, not in the least brutal except when aroused – as when a
friend bites his ear. His lapse in 'grossly' kissing Trina while she is anaesthetized is not
too serious, since he goes no further – and in any case the episode too obviously arises
from Norris' own anxiety about sexual desire originating in a menacing beasthood
(which he was simultaneously trying to resolve in *Vandover*). In *McTeague* each incident
and object, and not just that gilded tooth, has symbolic force. The whole does not quite
hang together, but the clumsy and deliberate style (like that 'of a great wet dog', John
Berryman suggests) is more appropriate than is at first apparent. McTeague's degeneration – after his friend has denounced him – is convincing; but is it 'realistic'? Not more
than the detail of his carrying his little singing canary about with him under impossible
circumstances, or more than the habit he gets into of biting his wife's fingers (which have
to be amputated) to punish her.

The Octopus is a more truly realistic novel. The 'octopus' of the title is the railroad, which threatens California wheat-ranchers. The description of the battle between the farmers and the railway men is justly famous, and the whole novel – although like all of Norris' fiction it has grave faults, one of the chief of which is unconvincing and stilted dialogue – deserves its reputation. *Vandover*, however, remains his masterpiece. It deals with the descent into madness, despair and penury of a decent and well-bred man. It quite transcends its origins: Norris' fear of syphilis, which masked his even profounder terror that sexual indulgence might drive him into a mysterious insanity; and a programmatically naturalist desire to show a man at the mercy of his 'bad' heredity. This is not a moral tale, as is sometimes alleged, because Vandover's fate is ironically contrasted with the good fortune of his vulgar friend Geary, a dishonest man who sows as many wild oats as Vandover, but merely prospers. Vandover's illness is not venereal, as has been suggested, but mental: once a promising painter, he sinks into a fatal decline, ending up by prowling naked and barking like a dog, earning his living by cleaning up filth. His decent friend Haight, however, does get syphilis – apparently from a mere kiss and the accidental slippage of a court plaster. Out of a neurotic anxiety and a fairly crude programme Norris produced a satisfying comment on the nature of both sexuality and creativity. It has been objected that he was inconsistent, putting the blame for Vandover's madness variously on himself, an indifferent universe, and society. ... But Norris' creative bewilderment is honest; the pert critical objection is sterile. The book has a power and cohesiveness that cause us to take it on trust. Norris did more than enough to ensure survival.

If **Theodore Dreiser** (1871–1945), the Indiana-born son of a crippled and intermittently employed mill superintendent, had sought fame as a thinker he would have been lucky to get as far as the middle pages of a local newspaper. His fiction, the best of which is not far below the best of the century, is related to his ideas (if we care so to dignify them); but it is fatal to an understanding of the fiction to try to interpret it in terms of the ideas. Most people with such sets of notions as Dreiser possessed remain comparatively inarticulate cranks, or, at best, write books whose appeal is strictly limited to the semi-educated. But Dreiser's fiction is what his ideas were really about. And although his determinism is philosophically shabby and his 'science' a vulgarized jargon and travesty, H.L. Mencken (q.v.) was entirely justified in his remark that 'Dreiser can feel, and, feeling, he can move. The others are very skilful with words'. And when a critic as intelligent as Lionel Trilling, a cruel and treacherous academic rationalist and heartless intellectual incensed by such reactions as Mencken's, tried to demonstrate that Dreiser was not good and wrote poorly (clumsily and not like a professor) because he thought poorly (not like an ambitious rationalist professor), instead of damaging Dreiser's status (who, admiring him, does not know that his style and thinking are not models for emulation?) he most painfully and needlessly exposed his own shortcomings. Dreiser is an exception that tests almost every known rule.

Dreiser was an emotional, not an intellectual man. We have to treat his ideas as simplistic rationalization of his feelings; in his fiction they become transformed. Since his parents were poor, Dreiser was all his life profoundly moved by poverty. Few if any serious modern writers actually believe in capitalism as a system, although many do believe that liberalized forms of it may be the least of a number of evils; Dreiser, however, loathed it, and at the end of his life he joined the communist party, convinced that a Marxist revolution would provide the only just solution. On the other hand Dreiser, himself a compulsive womanizer, was obsessed by capitalist tycoons and crooks, and by the compulsive sexuality they frequently display. The character of Frank Cowperwood, the central character in the trilogy comprising *The Financier* (1912), *The Titan* (1914) and the posthumous *The Stoic* (1947), is partially based on the swindler and transport magnate Charles Yerkes. (Dreiser himself, after a year at Indiana University and some years working on newspapers, attained huge success before he became a famous writer: although his first novel failed in 1900, he went on to become editor of the women's magazine *The Delineator* at the then unprecedented salary of $25,000.) Brought up as a strict Catholic, he came to hate religion and to profess to see the workings of the mind as 'chemisms', mere predetermined chemical reactions. But he remained as interested in religion as in socialism and communism; his last novel – most of *The Stoic* was written many years before his death – *The Bulwark* (1946), some of which was written at the end of his life, has for its hero Solon Barnes, who is sympathetically portrayed as a Quaker and a seeker after religious truth. As for 'chemisms': he could never fully make up his mind about free will (what novelist really can if he tries?), and one of the strengths of his fiction is its ambiguity on this point (for all the unnecessary pseudo-philosophical asides). As Dreiser drifted into communism, he also drifted into a sympathy with the transcend-entalism of Thoreau, and with Hinduism. But it is the novels that are important – and Trilling's virulent hatred of them is instructive.

In terms of thought all this is of small interest. But when Dreiser came to write his fiction he stopped what he believed was thinking, his imagination started to work, and he dramatized the conflict within himself. Those asides that disfigure even the finest of his novels are irrelevant to them. Critics say that Dreiser in *An American Tragedy* 'makes society responsible' for the tragedy of Clyde Griffiths' execution. That is not so. Dreiser does not know. But certainly this is not the 'message' of his massive and poignant novel. He shows us Clyde's own pitiful moral weakness, the terrible unwitting callousness with which he plans Roberta's death. Beside this he shows us the hypocritical and equally callous indifference of society, concerned with procedures and not at all with understand-ing or even guilt. Dreiser's book is important in that it gives us the actual grain of, the sense of being of, a specific human being going towards extinction; it warns that 'life' is frightening because it is 'like that'; but it offers – whatever Dreiser himself may say when he abandons his proper business of rendering Clyde and his story – no easy junketing of responsibility onto society. Clyde is forced to leave Kansas and the Green-Davidson by chance (the running down of a child, for which he is not responsible); thus he meets his uncle, his good fortune – and his end. Here Dreiser offers no facile comment as to whether there is free will. There is nothing essential to the novel that demonstrates choice as an illusion – except in that universal and bitter sense which the retrospective view confers. And the book has much more subtlety than is usually allowed – for example, in its descriptions of Clyde's eyes.

Sister Carrie (1900) was accepted for Doubleday by Frank Norris (q.v.), but Doubleday himself – influenced by his wife, who was horrified because in it 'sin' is not 'punished' (it is the duty of society to keep this dark, lest the underprivileged should try it) – 'prvished' it: he kept to his contract, printed and bound one thousand copies – but did not push it at all hard. That it was not put on sale at all is a myth, doubtless propagated by Dreiser himself. So Dreiser had to wait until 1911 and the publication of *Jennie Gerhardt* for recog-nition. After the first two of the 'Trilogy of Desire' (on Cowperwood) came *The Genius* (1915). *An American Tragedy*, which was occasioned by the Chester Gillette-Grace Brown case (though it is not based on it), was published in 1925. Apart from these novels and the final posthumous two, Dreiser wrote many short stories, travel and political books, essays and (atrocious) verse.

The view (later modified) of the influential biographical critic Van Wyck Brooks (1886–1963) that American literature was impoverished by puritan dualism (isolated idealism starved by practical materialism) was over-simplified, especially since it wrote off Mark Twain and Henry James (qq.v) as failures; nor was it a new idea; but it had truth in it. Dreiser helped American literature out of the 'genteel tradition'; again, although critics do not enjoy admitting it, he offered something that Henry James could not offer. Where Dreiser is massive is in the illusions he gives of lives as they are lived, of people as they seem: Clyde weakly appealing in his good looks and ambitiousness (right from when the 'captain' at the Green-Davidson engages him as bellboy), Carrie Meeber and Jennie Gerhardt innocent – although in different ways – of the nature of the lusts they arouse in men. ... Dreiser – notwithstanding the philosophies in which he was interested, ranging from Herbert Spencer to Elmer Gates' Laboratory of Psychology and Psychurgy – can convey the texture of life itself as few other novelists can. It is the kind of 'realism' for which there will always be a place. To reject what Dreiser has to offer may well be an insult to the imagination.

Dreiser's best novels are *Sister Carrie* and *An American Tragedy*, followed by *Jennie Gerhardt* – here the heroine, whom some critics still describe as 'sinful', is morally superior to the other characters, whereas Carrie was morally neutral – and *The Financier*. Then, a long way back, come the last two of the Cowperwood trilogy. Here there are too many authorial asides – we hear too often the voice of Elmer Gates of the Laboratory of Psychurgy – and Dreiser's confusion over Cowperwood loses dramatic power. *The Genius* (1915), whose chief character Eugene Witla is a self-portrait – with some added details drawn from a painter and an art-editor Dreiser knew – was banned and then drastically rewritten. It is the odd one out of Dreiser's books. Here Dreiser tried to resolve his sexual difficulties, but pseudo-intellectual scruples interfered; there are far too many irrelevant intrusions. However, some sections of the novel – such as that describing Witla's decision, after a breakdown, to give up painting and become a manual worker – are extremely good. *The Bulwark* is interesting, but lacks creative steam.

A word about the so famously bad style and the gauche dialogue. Too much is made of this. Dreiser was not a sophisticated writer; a sophisticated or elegant style would not have suited him. His style is admirable – for its purposes. That it is rebarbative, 'as lacerating to the sensibility as the continuous grinding of pneumatic drills' (Walter Allen), is neither here nor there: so is the life and death of Clyde Griffiths, so is the fact that only a little 'ordinary' ruthlessness on his part would have brought him success, so is the transformation of the matter of his guilt or innocence into a political issue, so is the massive and never withdrawn pity. To lament that Dreiser's style was not 'better' is to miss the whole point of what Dreiser was. It is not of course sensible to praise Dreiser at the expense of a very different writer, Henry James. It is less sensible to condemn him, as Lionel Trilling tried to do, because he was not James (or, more precisely, James-as-seen-by-Trilling). Trilling sneers at the concept of Dreiser's 'great brooding pity' and attacks him for the 'failure of his mind and heart'. It is an interesting and curiously contorted bitterness in a critic that can miss Dreiser's achievement in *An American Tragedy*. What has gone wrong here? It is something more fundamental than Dreiser's doubtless hideously non-professorial notions of culture. ... In a comment on *An American Tragedy* Irving Howe shrewdly quotes George Santayana (q.v.) on one kind of religious perception, that 'power of which we profess to know nothing further', and through which we feel 'the force, the friendliness, the hostility, the unfathomableness of the world'. As Howe says, this power 'flows, in ... feverish vibration, through *An American Tragedy*'. Whoever says Dreiser's heart fails has little heart himself.

Jack London (1876–1916), bastard son of a wandering Irish astrologer whom he never saw, is wrongly regarded in Russia as a great writer. He is, however, a remarkable one, with a gift for storytelling unsurpassed in his time. Before he found fame and a huge public in the early years of the century, Jack London (he adopted his mother's husband's surname) had roughed it: had drunk heavily, whored, been to jail, poached oysters, slaved in a canning factory, prospected for gold, been a tramp, gone sealing. ... He is another writer whose achievement need not be discussed in terms of his crude attempts to systematize his reading; but he has neither the compassion nor the weight of Dreiser. London achieved enormous success, wrote fifty books in sixteen years, married twice – and finally killed himself (half-unpremeditatedly) with an overdose of morphine when ill health (uraemia), financial worry and legal troubles exerted too great a pressure upon him.

The main influences on London, apart from the fact of his bastardy, which he suppressed and which drove him to seek fame, fortune and respectability, were the writings of Kipling (q.v.) and Stevenson, then in the ascendant in America, and the ideas of Marx, Darwin (through his popularizer Haeckel) and Nietzsche (q.v.). There is usually something worthwhile in all London's fiction, if only narrative and descriptive vigour. But as he grew older he tended to dissipate his gifts in his increasingly frenetic quest for security. His best books are: *The Call of the Wild* (1903), which dealt with his own problem (compare Norris) of wildness by giving an account of a dog that returns to its ancestors, the wolves; *The Game* (1905), a boxing tale (perhaps only for those who like and have a knowledge of its subject); *The Iron Heel* (1907), which prophesied a 300-year period of fascism, followed by socialism; *Martin Eden* (1909), an autobiographical novel in which London made the more personal prophecy of his suicide seven years later; and *The Star Rover* (1915), interconnected short stories about a convict who learns to transfer himself to another body. London was acutely aware of the conflict between instinct and reason, retrogression to primitivism, progress to utopia; in his inferior fiction he too crudely advances either socialism or his misunderstanding of Nietzsche. It was in *The Call of the Wild* that he discovered his most satisfactory objective correlative. He wrote beautifully about animals, with whom he had a sympathy that extended beyond his obsessions with brutality and strength. London is not only still readable, but still worth reading (a different matter).

Sherwood Anderson (1876–1941), born in Camden, Ohio, still does not always get his due, even in America. To some extent this is understandable. At his death Lionel Trilling (once again) struck; he reprinted his vicious and patronizing obituary piece, with added material, in his widely-circulated collection of essays *The Liberal Imagination* (1950). This helped to put Anderson out of fashion. Furthermore, the best writing of his last twenty years (written off too confidently by the ignorant Trilling as a time of absolute and 'poignant' failure), the autobiographical material, was unavailable. Paul Rosenfeld's *Sherwood Anderson's Memoirs* (1942), however good its editor's intentions, was bibliographically a disgrace, consisting largely of rewritten material. Not until 1970 did *Sherwood Anderson's Memoirs: A Critical Edition*, impeccably edited by Ray Lewis White, appear. The best writing in this has the kind of impact of the stories of Anderson's undoubted and acknowledged masterpiece, *Winesburg, Ohio* (1919).

Anderson's moment of truth at the age of thirty-six is a legend. He was sitting in his paint factory in Elyria, Ohio, dictating to his secretary in the winter of 1912, when he suddenly walked out. He turned up in a Cleveland hospital four days later, with 'nervous collapse'. This myth that Anderson himself established about his escape from soulless commercialism to creative freedom contained an element of truth. For he did eventually reject the non-values of his existence as an advertising copywriter and salesman of paint and, previously, other merchandise. But he had been struggling for some years with writing before he made the famous break; and he did not give up writing advertising copy until 1923 – as he tells us in the memoirs he wrote in the Thirties, when his fame had passed. Superficially the businessman Anderson was not very different from his neighbours: public churchgoer and private out-of-town brothel-patronizer, country club member, and so on. There are similar men in almost every small town in America, and some of them even 'walk out'. But Anderson differed from them because, in the privacy of an attic, out of the way of his university-educated wife who was always informing him of his inability to become the kind of man she envisaged as a writer, he indulged himself in what at first seemed like fantasies but later turned out to be the imaginative realities of a born writer. Although the actual moment of walking out came to symbolize for him his dramatic escape from the crass materialism of America, the process really took a number of years. The walking out was the result of a real hysterical breakdown, occasioned by domestic tension and financial anxiety; these elements were played down, and led first to Anderson's being lionized as a great antiphilistine and enemy of Babbittry (q.v.), but later to his being attacked and subsequently neglected as a crude apostle of instinct. And yet in 1956 William Faulkner (q.v.) affirmed that Anderson was 'the father of my generation of American writers and the tradition of American writing which our successors will carry on', and he asked for 'a proper evaluation'.

Six of Anderson's seven novels amount to little more than a distraction from his real achievement, which lies in his short stories and in the section of autobiography collected together by Ray Lewis White. Parts of the first, *Windy McPherson's Son* (1916), are good, and in all of them, even the disastrous *Dark Laughter* (1925), there are fine passages. The best, and worth revival, is *Poor White* (1920), a successful projection of the author into Hugh McVey, a 'poor white' telegraph operator who becomes successful when he invents a corncutter. He awakens from his mathematical dreams only when Bidwell, Ohio, has been turned into a strife-torn industrial hell. *Poor White* has the faults of too glaring symbolism, but the grotesque and then distorted character of Hugh, and much of the detail of Bidwell's transformation into a factory town, are described with the power and subtlety of *Winesburg, Ohio*.

But Anderson was superior in shorter forms: the pressure put upon him to write long fiction was not good for his work. He was a lyrical and truly naïve (q.v.) writer; his outbursts against criticism, some of it sensible criticism, did not help readers to understand him or critics to follow him. Hemingway (q.v.), an inferior writer, pillaged him and then tried to parody him in his *Torrents of Spring*. After a difficult period in the Twenties, Anderson met his fourth wife, with whom he was happy, and retired from the literary scene to edit two Virginia newspapers, one democratic and the other republican. It was in this period that he did much of the autobiographical writing that provides a full answer to Trilling's charge that 'what exasperates us is his stubborn, satisfied continuance in his earliest attitudes'. After his first great success Anderson was too eager to publish whatever he wrote, and in his efforts to fulfil his genius in a novel he momentarily lapsed into the middlebrow image of himself that had been created by the widest section of his public: prophet and mystic. But he was too fond of life itself to stand the strain of this falsity for long. He refused to become or to pose as a mage – the fate of so many naïve writers, from Hauptmann through Jammes to Giono (qq.v.) – and instead, never stubbornly or satisfiedly, strove for self-knowledge. In the best of his autobiographical writings his effortful honesty comes naked off the page: it is embarrassing in so sophisticated, so intellectual and so reticent an age. But literature would entirely dry up without its stream fed so copiously by Anderson. It was this that aroused the infuriated envy of the desiccated instructor at Columbia. The *Memoirs* contain writing that is genuinely inspiring (again, an embarrassing concept today): it fills the reader with the desire to search for and try to attain a similar simplicity and similar honesty. There is very little like it in twentieth-century literature. It is beautiful in the important sense that it illuminates and adds meaning to that increasingly difficult word.

For so seminal and original a book *Winesburg, Ohio* has some strangely obvious sources. The structure is that of the poems of Edgar Lee Masters' *Spoon River Anthology* (q.v.); the self-revelatory characterization is reminiscent of Turgenev's *A Sportsman's Sketches*; the deliberately oral, indigenous style owes much to Mark Twain, though it updates him; the tone sometimes approaches Howe's in *The Story of a Country Town* (q.v.). Finally, Gertrude Stein (q.v.), whom Anderson early recognized as being essentially 'a writer's writer', liberated him from conventional usage, teaching him what she could not herself achieve: the lyrical expression of intuitions. The episodes in *Winesburg, Ohio*, all centring on the writer-figure of George Willard – a man who brings out something in each of the characters, if only the desire to confess – reveal men as both cursed and blessed by their gift of language: even as they are trapped, they live, they exist, they believe. This arises from a profound scepticism, set out in the prologue to the book and too often ignored. Anderson saw the citizens of Winesburg, and the whole of the modern world, as trapped in what Keats so famously called 'an irritable reaching out after facts and certainties'. Rejecting that multiplicity of apparently contradictory truths that is the actual sum of human knowledge – refusing to be in those 'uncertainties, mysteries, doubts' (Keats) that are proper to the human condition – we (Anderson said) grasp at and appropriate single truths; this distorts us and turns us into grotesques. Anderson's notion throws more light on the nature of society than many searchers after or possessors of systems may care to admit. There are some other short stories by Anderson that reach the level of *Winesburg, Ohio*, from *The Triumph of the Egg* (1921), *Horses and Men* (1923) and *Death in the Woods* (1933). These may be found in *Short Stories* (ed. M. Geismar, 1962). Hart Crane (q.v.) said of this unique writer that his strong sense of nature 'colours his work with the most surprising grasp of what "innocence" and "holiness" ought to mean'. Despite what we know about the financial and domestic pressures, the quiet and beautiful work of Anderson's last decade does, after all, take us back to that winter afternoon in Elyria. . . . He at least did not spoil his myth.

The connection between Anderson and **George Santayana** (ps. **Jorge Ruiz De Santayana Borrás**, 1863–1952), who was born in Spain and retained his Spanish nationality, may seem tenuous. Santayana was an intellectual, and was more important as a philosopher than as a creative writer. Yet he and Anderson are curiously bound together by the sceptical and eclectic philosophy that Santayana ambitiously formulated in *Scepticism and Animal Faith* (1923) and its successors. If Anderson typifies the naïve (q.v.) approach to a certain apprehension of reality, then Santayana typifies the sentimentive (q.v.). Santayana left Spain at the age of nine and was educated in Massachusetts. From 1889 until 1912 he was a professor at Harvard. Then, on receipt of a legacy, he resigned. After many productive years he settled (1939) in a Roman nursing home – the fascists left him alone in the war because of his Spanish nationality. Santayana has written the best prose of any philosopher of the century. His poetry, although technically graceful by the standards of its time, entirely fails to reconcile the disparate sides of his nature; had it succeeded he would have been a great poet. As it was he called himself, rightly, 'almost a poet'. His philosophy is essentially an attempted reconciliation of idealism and realism. It is rightly described by orthodox philosophers as not being thorough-going or 'of [philosophical] consequence': it is more important, though, than any sets of rigorous games, in that it may be immediately related to how men actually feel and live. It is significant that Santayana's initial approach resembles that of a philosopher who stands behind much modern literature, Husserl (q.v.): the application of strict logic results in everything being doubtable. But 'animal faith' compels us to believe in a matter from which what Santayana called 'intuitive essences' have arisen. It is a subtle philosophy, and a profoundly intelligent and ironic modification of scepticism (it is by suffering, Santayana says, that we gain the clue to matter, which we must affirm in a suitably sardonic manner); it contains anticipations and understandings of modernism in literature. Santayana wrote one distinguished and interesting novel, *The Last Puritan* (1935), in which he contrasts Oliver Alden, the last puritan of the title, with other, hedonistic characters. For a reason that no one could explain, this became a best seller.

In 1931 Santayana had written a book called *The Genteel Tradition at Bay*. This attacked, although with much more cogency, the same tradition that had been Van Wyck Brooks' (q.v.) target. But Santayana was specifically criticizing the movement of the 'new humanism', which was led by **Irving Babbitt** (1865–1933), who taught French at Harvard for most of his life, and **Paul Elmer More** (1864–1937), a more interesting figure who interrupted his teaching career to become a distinguished journalist (he edited *The Nation* 1904–14). T.S. Eliot (q.v.) was loosely associated with this movement, although critical of it. The new humanism was thin-blooded, anti-romantic, classical conservative, anti-modernist, intellectual, with some elements of authoritarianism. Essentially it was a foredoomed attempt, by men in general non-creative, to revive what they thought of as transcendentalism. It drew on Christianity, but substituted for its central tenets a universal ethical code. Babbitt advocated an 'inner principle of restraint'. This movement flourished in the Twenties but petered out, after being much attacked and defended, in the Thirties. It is one of the least distinguished of the theories that have come from the better minds of our century. Santayana revealed the new humanism, which claimed to be opposed to decadence, as itself decadent and attenuated. He was particularly withering on the question of the new humanists' supernaturalism, upon which they were vulnerable. *The Last Puritan* was conceived both as a criticism of and a satire on this continuation of the genteel tradition; it was also for Santayana a happy return to the Nineties, when he was still young enough (he said) to sympathize with youth but old enough to understand it. However, in the character of Oliver Alden, and the tragedies of his love and end, Santayana got beyond satire.

*

Four important women fiction writers emerged in this period. **Kate Chopin** (1851–1904), born in St. Louis, did not begin to write seriously until after the death of her Creole husband in 1882. She won a notoriety (unwelcome to her) with her novel *The Awakening* (1899). Interest in her has grown so much that her *Collected Works* have recently been issued in a scholarly edition, in two volumes (1970), edited by Per Seyersted. Among the many 'local-colourists' then working she is immediately distinguished by her superior objectivity and psychological conscientiousness. Her best stories are in *Bayou Folk* (1894), often poignant and sometimes ironic studies of the Creoles of Louisiana. In 'Désirée's Baby', her most famous tale, a wealthy aristocrat turns his wife and son out of the house because he suspects them of having Negro blood; then he discovers that he has; meanwhile Désirée kills herself and her child. Kate Chopin's stories are among the earliest of their kind to show real sensibility and freedom from prejudice.

Her major work, however, is her novel *The Awakening*. This tells the torrid story of Edna Pontellier, who fails in love but succeeds in lust – and kills herself. This could fairly be described as a kind of Creole *Madame Bovary* (Kate Chopin had read Flaubert), although its purpose is different. It is a tragedy that the hostile reviews of this fine book should have broken her spirit.

Another gift that deliberately confined itself to a single locality (Maine), but that displayed itself in tales rather than novels, is that of **Sarah Orne Jewett** (1849–1909). It would be impertinent to describe her as a local-colourist: her wide culture and worldly humour are always in evidence. Her novels are negligible, and the series of sketches with which she made her reputation, *Deephaven* (1877), are slight in comparison with those of her acknowledged masterpiece, *The Country of the Pointed Firs* (1896). By then she had assimilated the influence of James (q.v.) as well as of Flaubert, Tolstoy and other Europeans; but she wisely confined herself to the limits of her experience. *The Country of the Pointed Firs* consists of loosely connected tales about the people in the beautifully evoked seaport town of Dunnet. This deserves its status as a classic because in its unobtrusive way it says so much about old age (most of the characters are elderly) and the manner in which a place may embody both decay and hope, as well as about Maine. Willa Cather (q.v.) was deeply influenced by it.

Ellen Glasgow (1874–1945), born of an aristocratic family in Richmond, Virginia, came to revolt against the tradition into which she was born and in which she began – although not with absolute obedience – writing: the sentimental tradition of the old domain of the South as a lost cause, and of the Civil War as an affair between honour and commerce. Ellen Glasgow's fiction set out to investigate this legend. She had a highly developed sense of humour, and, like Sarah Orne Jewett (q.v.), she chose to write about the locality, Virginia, that she knew best. The teacher and critic H.S. Canby claimed, with justice, that Ellen Glasgow in her nineteen novels 'was a major historian of our times, who, almost singlehandedly, rescued Southern fiction from the glamorous sentimentality of the Lost Cause'. The work in which she accomplished this was mostly done in the Twenties; in old age she became over-conservative, though not unintelligently so, in the sense that she found she could not accept such manifestations of the modern age as bad manners or William Faulkner (q.v.). Her main theme was the consequences of the Southern myth on Southerners themselves. She is also notable for her resistance to the notion that all Southerners are alike. She always, in her own words, 'preferred the spirit of fortitude to the sense of futility'. To some extent Ellen Glasgow anticipated the concerns of the 'Fugitives' group (q.v.), but her approach was more mordant and even, judged just as an approach and not as a breeding ground for poems, preferable. There was not as much to recommend about life in the South before 1860 as Margaret Mitchell's best-selling romance, *Gone With the Wind*, suggests. But later Southerners, and much more intelligent and sensitive ones than Margaret Mitchell, have cherished such an image.

Like most of the novelists of her generation, Ellen Glasgow was of a pessimistic turn of mind, although it was doubtless personal experience that led her to the limiting view that life consists of specifically sexual disappointment followed by stoical acceptance. In her treatment of her thus sexually defeated people there is sometimes an element that goes beyond irony and becomes gloating and almost cheap. From the quality of this irony and of her not always successful epigrammatic writing, one may discern, in fact, that she is not of the first rank. But she is consistently adult, and her best books rise above her intentions. In *Barren Ground* (1925) the 'poor white' Dorinda Oakley, crossed in love, turns her father's barren ground into a farm with as much determination as Ellen Glasgow had put into her fiction writing just before the turn of the century; ultimately, having contracted one marriage of convenience, she marries the man, now a drunk, who turned her down, caring for him until he dies. Dorinda is a memorable creation. *The Romantic Comedians* (1926) is a surprisingly sympathetic treatment of a hypocritical and lustful old judge, Gamaliel Bland Honeywell. The book begins as he buries his wife. A respectable man who disapproves of 'sexual looseness', he marries a young cousin of his dead wife; she immediately makes him a cuckold, and runs off with her lover. The old man becomes ill and depressed, but we leave him cheered up by spring and the charms of his young nurse. Neither we nor the author dislike him half as much as we should. The Judge, shallow and self-deceiving, is rightly described by Walter Allen as a 'considerable comic creation'; but, as Allen goes on to point out, his fantasies of romantic love are – surprisingly and unusually – given a genuinely lyrical quality, so that he becomes a character actually touching in his defeat. *Vein of Iron* (1935) is not as a whole quite as psychologically acute, but contains fine passages, and effectively sums up Ellen Glasgow's attitudes to the South and to life. Her title expresses her recommended philosophy. Ada Fincastle displays this 'vein of iron' throughout all her and her loved ones' vicissitudes; it enables her to endure her father's lack of reality, the pregnancy she cannot (out of love) disclose, ostracism by the community, her husband's bitterness, poverty during the Depression. Ellen Glasgow makes an excellent 'introduction to the South' and to the more complex novels of Faulkner: she makes explicit much of the knowledge of the South that, as Walter Allen has said, Faulkner assumes in us. Certainly some dozen of her novels ought to be back in print. Those who think *Gone With the Wind* a good book need only read Glasgow.

But the most considerable woman novelist of the period was undoubtedly **Willa Cather** (1873–1947). She was born in Virginia but moved to Nebraska, whose people are the subject of most of her novels and stories, at the age of nine. She never forgot the pioneering spirit of the immigrants, who in her childhood often lived in sod houses or caves. Nor, it must be added, could her later fiction adjust itself to what America became. She was a late developer. She was educated at the University of Nebraska and had a tough journalistic apprenticeship on *McClure's Magazine* (1906–12). She had been writing verse and short stories since before the turn of the century, but did not publish her first novel, *Alexander's Bridge* (1912), until she was nearly forty. This was a failure because of a too intrusive symbolism; but the subtly flawed, nostalgic character of its engineer hero already indicated that Willa Cather's scope was larger than that of any previous American woman novelist. In the most successful *O Pioneers!* (1913) she went back to her greatest love and inspiration: the late nineteenth-century settlers in the Nebraska prairie. Like Ellen Glasgow (q.v.), Willa Cather excelled in the portraiture of strong-minded women; here Alexandra has to assume responsibility for the farm after her Swedish father dies. Her moral superiority to those around her is convincingly conveyed. The episode of 'The White Mulberry Tree' – the story of the doomed romance of Alexandra's younger brother Emil with Marie, whose husband murders them both – fits in and perfectly complements the main narrative.

In *The Song of the Lark* (1915) Willa Cather tried unsuccessfully to deal more or less directly with the subject of herself: her opera-singer Thea Kronberg is clearly based on herself, although supposed to be modelled on an actual singer's career. The author told herself that she was most interested in the way in which her heroine 'escaped' through a fortuitous falling together of commonplace events; actually she was interested in, but ultimately afraid to deal with, the nature of her sexuality. On the one hand she shows Thea as regretful of the asceticism that she feels is a penalty of art; on the other, it is clear that her irritation with men does not originate in her creativity but in lesbianism.

My Ántonia (1918) is probably Willa Cather's finest novel. It is an unhappy New York lawyer's middle-aged recollections of his Nebraska childhood, and of his dear companion, the Czech Antonia. This is one of the most moving and powerful of pastoral evocations; the lawyer Jim Burden's present unhappiness is the result of his urban existence with its betrayal of the values of his childhood. *A Lost Lady* (1923) is as moving but not as convincing: here Willa Cather is beginning to manipulate her characters in order to prove her point about urban corruption. Ántonia remains a saved character; in *A Lost Lady* Mrs. Forrester yields to the corrupting embraces of Ivy Peters, a vulgar, slick lawyer: her worth is destroyed. This is a good novel, but one may see in it the germs of

Willa Cather's sentimentalization of the pioneer age: the idealized portraits of the pioneers themselves, the too easy dismissal of those born to a commercial and urban way of life. In her great success *Death Comes for the Archbishop* (1927) she goes back to the middle of the nineteenth century and the organization of the diocese of New Mexico by two close friends, Bishop Jean Latour and his vicar Father Joseph Vaillant. This is more satisfactory because Willa Cather is writing about the era she loves: there is no temptation to load the dice against the present. In this book Willa Cather's style reached its apogee, achieving epic qualities. There is deep understanding of both the missionary Roman Catholics' and the Indians' point of view. Willa Cather was a major writer, but not one big enough to take creative account of the changes in her century. This is not to say that her hatred of urbanization was wrong; only that it was too intense. She failed to understand that some men are victims of their circumstances. She did in the end turn spinsterish and difficult. But she gallantly resisted the intrusion of journalistic vulgarity (it must be remembered that she had been a journalist) into the novel, and her best books offer a unique evocation of the midwest of her youth.

*

Finally, an unclassifiable odd man out: will anyone ever revive even the best-known novels of **James Branch Cabell** (1879–1958)? Cabell, born in Virginia, was an expert in genealogy – and was what might be described as a latter-day escapist. Hatred of modern life caused him to invent his own country, Poictesme, his epic of which is much and tiresomely concerned with the imaginary genealogy of its leading family. His books are 'naughty', and now seem desperately dated; indeed, his reputation collapsed in the Twenties because it had been founded, unfortunately, upon an unsuccessful prosecution of his novel *Jurgen* (1919). This, irritating though it is in its highly self-conscious artiness and sly phallicism, may be a book that will deserve to be looked at again. In this sceptical tale of a middle-aged Poictesme pawnbroker who has a series of fantastic adventures Cabell examined his romanticism and found it wanting. An age only a little later than our own may more easily be able to penetrate the tortuous style and discover some wisdom that it obscures. But I doubt it: Cabell was the victim of a cult and shaped his style according to it; unfortunately his bitterness when he went out of fashion did not result in any recapture of the genius underlying *Jurgen*. The only novelist remotely resembling him now, with due allowance for changing fashion, is Robert Nye (q.v.), and then only occasionally.

II

Although American poetry did not show its true strength until after the First World War, the poets from whose example its most modern manifestations spring were active before that war – and nearly all of them had to wait a long time for public recognition. The first fully and authentically American poet was Walt Whitman. But Whitman was not fully understood until as late as 1955, when Richard Chase's book *Walt Whitman Reconsidered* was published. Interest in him continued to grow after his death in 1892 and he was the rallying cry of many splinter movements; but he was treated as a mystic, a mage, a socialist, a homosexual, a 'transexualist', anything rather than as a discoverer of an American voice who was also a complicated hider behind various masks. Whitman had his faults, and his intellectual equipment was hardly superior to Dreiser's; but he and Emily Dickinson, unknown in her lifetime, were the only major American poets of the nineteenth century.

The poets most highly considered in the first decade of this century have vanished from sight; nor is there much of value or even of interest to salvage from their work. **Richard Henry Stoddard** (1825–1903), called in the year of his death 'the most distinguished of living American poets', was no more than an imitator of English Victorian poets who celebrated Abraham Lincoln in the English Victorian manner. **Thomas Bailey Aldrich** (1836–1907) was not quite undistinguished as a novelist, but as a poet was a scented and weak imitator of Tennyson. Of somewhat more account was the Ohio poet **Paul Laurence Dunbar** (1872–1906), who was at least the first Negro to use Negro dialect (he was preceded by a number of white men); but he did not know the South, and the most that can be said of his best work is that it has some grace and style.

The 'Harvard generation' of the Nineties promised much, but performed little. **William Vaughn Moody** (1869–1910) was intelligent and even tried to achieve a modicum of sexual realism; but in spite of his skill no poem he wrote deserves to survive, and his verse drama – *The Fire-Bringer* (1904) was the best known – is stilted. It is sometimes claimed that Moody influenced Wallace Stevens (q.v.), and this may be true; but only of the Wallace Stevens of juvenilia, which he destroyed. That Moody was a formative influence is unlikely. Moody's best work was done in the prose drama, and is mentioned in the section devoted to theatre.

More poetically gifted was Moody's Harvard friend [Joseph] **Trumbull Stickney** (1874–1904), whom Santayana (q.v.) recollected as one of the two most brilliant men he had ever known. Stickney's life was cosmopolitan. He was born in Switzerland, and spent his childhood in Europe. After he graduated from Harvard in 1895 he again left immediately for Europe. He was the first American to receive the *Doctorat des Lettres* from the Sorbonne. Stickney finally returned to Harvard, to the post of Instructor in Greek. After only one unhappy year of teaching he died of a brain tumour. Stickney, like his friend Moody, wrote plays: his *Dramatic Verses* (1902) made no impact whatever, but when Moody and two others collected his *Poems* (1905), interest was briefly aroused. The English poets James Reeves and Seán Haldane (qq.v.) made a selection, *Homage to Trumbull Stickney* (1968), which contains a valuable biographical and critical introduction. Messrs. Reeves and Haldane quote lines such as 'Your face possesses my despair', 'He stubborned like the massive slaughter-beast', 'That power was once our torture and our Lord' and 'I have it all through my heart, I tell you, crying' to illustrate their contention that he is 'more a rejected than a neglected American poet of genius'. Another view puts him on a level with Moody and suggests that both 'occasionally capture the modern manner, only to lose it again in a plethora of words' (Marcus Cunliffe). It seems to me that, moving though some of Stickney's poems are, his language would need to be considerably less archaic for him to be as exceptional as Reeves and Haldane claim. Cunliffe's 'the modern manner' is perhaps misleading; what Stickney needed was a language capable of expressing – primarily, indeed, of discovering – a set of highly complex prepossessions. Now Stickney certainly had a 'modern' sensibility, but in almost all his poems he tends to lapse into a diction and tone which are alien to this sensibility. Feeling in his poetry tends to be robbed of sharpness and impact by muddy, self-indulgent diction, and sometimes by an ear that is more metrical than rhythmical. He lacks a formed style. But certainly he is, as Donald Hall has said, one of America's 'great unfulfilled talents'.

While most of these poets and others – such as the Canadian-born **Bliss Carman** (1861–1929), whose 'carefree' verse now seems so laboured, the verse playwright **Percy Mackaye** (1875–1956), or **Josephine Preston Peabody** (1874–1922), who was influenced by Moody – were enjoying some esteem, **Edwin Arlington Robinson** (1869–1935) was ignored. He did not achieve real recognition until he was fifty. For the duration of the Twenties he was America's most popular poet (Frost's, q.v., ascendancy came later), but before he died of cancer in 1935 his stock had begun to go down, and between the Second World War and the beginning of the Sixties he was almost forgotten by critics (although his massive *Collected Poems* has sold consistently at about twelve copies a week since it appeared in 1937). In the last decade there has been a revival of interest: his excellent letters are now being collected, and many books have been devoted to him. Even at the height of his fame, which did not go to his head, Robinson was never at the centre of any coterie or cult, and no one knew much of his private life – except that he was unmarried, rumoured (incorrectly) to be homosexual and had an alcohol problem. Neither Eliot nor the usually percipient, just and generous Ezra Pound (qq.v.) indicated that they had troubled to read him: this was a mistake, for all of Prufrock – and more – is in him. The fact is that he was the only fully-fledged American poet to come out of the 'gilded age' (the title of Mark Twain's and Charles Dudley Warren's melodramatic novel denouncing its instability and acquisitiveness) that followed the Civil War; in this age Robinson was formed. Nor is Robinson as far behind the vastly more ambitious Frost as the difference between their reputations suggests. Robinson did not write the handful of nearly perfect poems that Frost did as a young man; but he had a wider range and wrote more penetratingly about people. He was psychologically far ahead of Frost – and ahead of him in sensibility. In many respects he remained a child of the nineteenth century, his roots in Crabbe, Hardy, Browning; but if one compares the diction of his early poems to that of Stickney's (q.v.), the best of the poets who failed to attain a twentieth-century manner, it will be obvious that Robinson did at least find a language appropriate to what he had to say. That does not of itself guarantee the value of the poems themselves; but in this case they are good poems precisely because their author has discovered a new language to say new things. In Stickney the sentimentality and easy assumptions of the age linger on – alas – in the diction and style; Robinson's manner cuts through all this like a knife. What he can do in his best poetry (the shorter ones), besides expressing some personal emotions, is to give an authentic account of what it is like trying to be a nineteenth-century man in a twentieth-century society. That is something.

He was born at Head Tide, Maine, but moved to Gardiner, in the same state, six months after his birth; this environment marked him for the rest of his life, and the Tilbury Town of his poems is Gardiner. Robinson became aware of his lonely poetic vocation there (he was an exceptionally lonely man), and there too he learned to identify himself with failure. His mother and father kept him at such a distance as to imply to him their rejection of him; his two brothers were always expected to outshine him. Ultimately, however, he was the success of the family: his father failed financially and went to pieces under the strain, and the eldest brother turned from a promising doctor into a drug addict. Robinson himself attended Harvard until the money ran out, then turned – still in his twenties – into a lonely and alcoholic drop-out. He published two books privately, and for the third, *Captain Craig* (1902), the publishers Houghton Miflin had to be guaranteed against loss. President Theodore Roosevelt was given this book to read in 1905, enthused, and obtained a sinecure for Robinson in the New York Customs House, which he retained until the change in the presidency in 1909. During that time of comparative independence Robinson drank heavily and wrote little. It was the poems of *The Man Against the Sky* (1916) which finally gained him public acceptance; but it was not until the eve of his fiftieth birthday that critics and poets alike joined together in tribute to him. From 1911 until the end of his life Robinson spent his summers at the MacDowell Colony, founded by the widow of the gifted (and, outside America, still neglected) American composer Edward A. MacDowell, as a refuge for creative artists of all kinds. He published two plays, which are interesting but not viable theatrically, and wrote fiction, all of which he destroyed. Eventually he confined himself entirely to the long verse narrative: *Tristram* (1927), a national success, completed an Arthurian trilogy; he was at work on *King Jasper* to within a few weeks of his death. It is always said that Robinson fails in these very long poems. And so he does. What is not said often enough is that he comes nearer to success in this form than any other poet writing at the time.

One of Robinson's subtlest and most characteristic poems is 'Flammonde', in which he exploits commonplace and cliché in a strategy that is quite certainly 'modern' in its implications. The wooden didact Yvor Winters dismissed it as 'repulsively sentimental'; but William J. Free, in an important essay, has shown how Robinson in this instance did succeed in finding a suitable, if ambiguous, language to express his uneasy situation. As Free says, 'he was trying to restore life to a worn-out language without abandoning that language'. Flammonde is just such an enigmatic and alienated character as Robinson felt himself to be, but Robinson ironically presents him as seen through the eyes of the townspeople: he has wisdom, but this is remarkable because he is not respectable; he has 'something royal in his walk' and has been 'accredited' 'by kings', but has been banished from that kind of life. Robinson turns Flammonde's *noblesse oblige* into a caricature by making him befriend an ex-'scarlet woman' – one of the worst clichés of the period. In his brain the kink is 'satanic'. Flammonde is the poet seen from the angle of the crowd, vulgarly mysterious, cheaply sinister, and yet necessary:

> We cannot know how much we learn
> From those who never will return,
> Until a flash of unforeseen
> Remembrance falls on what has been.
> We've each a darkening hill to climb;
> And this is why, from time to time
> In Tilbury Town, we look beyond
> Horizons for the man Flammonde.

'Flammonde' demonstrates Robinson's inability to define his poetic function directly, and incidentally explains why he invariably expressed himself through a strategy of characterizations. Thus he found his Flammonde in an Englishman called Alfred H. Louis, a well-connected failure; when in the more famous and longer *Captain Craig* he tried to be more explicit, to dissolve some of the mystery, about the objective correlative he had discovered in this person he was not quite as successful – although this, too, is an interesting poem.

Robinson wrote a number of other excellent short poems. The celebrated 'Miniver Cheevy' sums up his own situation even more tersely. It has been pointed out that the fourth 'thought' of

> Miniver scorned the gold he sought
> But sore annoyed was he without it;

> Miniver thought and thought and thought
> And thought about it

'comes as an authentic kick in the womb of a stanza that proves the existence of a live poet'; it has the touch of a master. Equally good are 'Eros Turannos', 'Isaac and Archibald', 'Saint-Nitouche' and some others. The narrative poems, naturalistic in the sense that they show people at the mercy of their passions, are unrivalled in their field – Masefield's (q.v.) aim at so much less – in that they are all, even the lushest (*Tristram*), readable and interesting; one may come across a good passage at any time. A properly selected Robinson – still lacking – would have to include some of these, as well as the best of the shorter poems and such medium length narratives as 'Isaac and Archibald'. Robinson may have been a late romantic and even a transcendentalist, who allowed a false optimism to mar much of his poetry; but his was the only nineteenth-century sensibility to express itself effectively in twentieth-century terms. His influence has been considerable although, except in the case of Robert Lowell's *The Mills of the Kavanaughs* (q.v.), unobtrusive. His stock is certainly rising.

Now for three lesser, but undoubtedly important poets, all from the state of Illinois: Edgar Lee Masters, Carl Sandburg and Vachel Lindsay (qq.v.). All of these were quintessentially American as distinct from English-style poets. In this sense, but only in this, each was superior to Robinson (q.v.). **Edgar Lee Masters** (1868–1950) was the son of a lawyer who himself became a lawyer; born in Kansas, moved to Illinois at one, he wrote much both before and after *The Spoon River Anthology* (1915), but never produced anything remotely near to it in quality. A newspaper editor gave him Mackail's *Select Epigrams from the Greek Anthology* in 1911, and this acted as the catalyst required to manufacture the acid of his own genius, compounded of an innate bitterness, a passion for truth, and a rare sympathy for human beings. Spoon River was an amalgamation of Petersburg and Lewistown. In a flat, laconic free verse Masters makes the inhabitants of the Spoon River hill cemetery state their own epitaphs. He resembles Robinson, but is more direct and less officially optimistic:

> Did you ever hear of the Circuit Judge
> Helping anyone except the 'Q' railroad,
> Or the bankers ...?

This was a poetry in the prose tradition initiated by Howe, Garland (qq.v.) and others; but the compression he learned from the Greek Anthology enabled Masters to improve on it. However, *The Spoon River Anthology* is better considered as prose than as poetry; as poetry it lacks linguistic energy.

Vachel Lindsay (1879–1931), born in Springfield, Illinois, obtained a good education, and then studied art for five years; but he failed at it, and decided to become a tramp. His drawings look like meagre and talentless imitations of Blake. Lindsay had always wanted to be a missionary, and in 1905 he alternated winter lecturing with summer tramping and declaiming; he would exchange leaflets of his poems for a bed and food. By 1913 he had become well known. Harriet Monroe began to publish his poetry, and *General William Booth Enters into Heaven and Other Poems* (1913) and *The Congo and Other Poems* (1914) were successful. For some fifteen years he enjoyed fame as declaimer of his own work all over America and in Great Britain as well. Public interest in him lessened soon after his marriage in 1925; in 1931, in despair and ill-health, he took poison.

Lindsay was a midwestern populist and revivalist whose views never altered or expanded with his experience of the greater world. His father was a Campbellite minister (member of the Church of the Disciples of Christ, which had broken away from Presbyterianism to a simplicity based solely on the Bible). Lindsay combined this evangelical creed with worship of Lincoln and other local heroes, religious ideas of Swedenborg, and the economics of Henry George (q.v.). He was vulgar and parochial, but at his best he knew it, and exploited these very failings. His sources are revivalist hymns and sermons, Whitman's manner and tone, temperance tracts, Negro jazz, all the sayings and doings of Lincoln and other lesser known, local heroes, and Salvation Army brass band music. He learnt much about the performance of poetry from the readings of S.H. Clark, a professor at the University of Chicago. His best poems succeed because they are impassioned and wholly unsophisticated. To put it at its most simple: he meant every word of them, and for a few years he found exactly the right combination of sources. He introduced a genuinely new rhythm into American poetry; he was also America's first genuine folk poet – at his best he is superior to Sandburg. Later he went to pieces and produced too much weak and self-parodic verse. The novelist Richard Hughes (q.v.) heard him at Oxford, and recorded for the British Broadcasting Corporation some remarkable and highly illuminating renderings of his poetry.

It was Harriet Monroe's *Poetry* that gave **Carl Sandburg** (1878–1967) fame. Born at Galesburg of Swedish immigrant parents, from thirteen he was an itinerant labourer all over the West; he served in the Spanish-American war, worked his way through college in his home town, and became a journalist and socialist. His master was Whitman, but although more genuinely 'of the people' than Whitman he is a minor poet by comparison, because he is never more than a reporter. He used very free forms, and his poetry resembles Masters' in that it is by no means certainly properly judged as poetry, but rather as a rhythmical prose. At his worst he is whimsical, sentimental and falsely tough; at his rare best colloquial, tender and precise. He could be defined as an ideal 'unanimist' (q.v.): he responded to and thoroughly understood the corporate longings of the new industrial folk, and he fervently believed in their happy future. His weakness is that he has no creative means of confronting evil. The famous stanza about John Brown

> They laid hands on him
> And the fool killers had a laugh
> And the necktie party was a go, by God.
> They laid hands on him and he was a goner.
>   They hammered him to pieces and he stood up.
> They buried him and he walked out of the grave, by God,
>   Asking again: Where did that blood come from?

owes all its strength to the presentation of John Brown's vitality as a folk hero; Sandburg could not cope with, and was a child in trying to deal with, the forces of evil. But his best poems reflect midwestern speech, and in rigorous selection they will continue to survive. He wrote a monumental biography of Lincoln (1926–39) and made two important collections of local American folk ballads, *The American Songbag* (1927) and *The New American Songbag* (1950).

At his death **Robert Frost** (1874–1963) was America's most famous poet and unofficial laureate. No other American has reached his eminence in letters. And yet he waited as long as – and even more bitterly than – Robinson (q.v.) for recognition. He was born in San Francisco of a New England father and a Scots mother; when he was eleven his father died, and the family moved to Salem, New Hampshire, where his mother taught in a school. Frost worked in mills and as a newspaper reporter, taught, married, spent two years at Harvard and tried to be a poultry farmer – all unsuccessfully. At the age of thirty-six he sold his farm in Derry and went to England, where he settled down to write. In England he met Wilfred Gibson, Ezra Pound, Lascelles Abercrombie and, most importantly, Edward Thomas (qq.v.), whom he encouraged to write poetry. While he was in England his first two books of poetry were accepted: *A Boy's Will* (1913) and *North of Boston* (1914). The second was published in America by Holt in the same year, and when he returned to the States early in 1915 he found he was the author of a best seller. For many years after this he spent periods as poet-in-residence in various academic institutions. The rest of the time he spent on farms he bought in Vermont and, finally, in Florida. He had much sorrow with his children: one died of puerperal fever, and his son Carol shot himself. At the end of his life, although an outspoken and fierce conservative, and a lifelong enemy of all things academic, he had twice been greeted by the Senate (on his seventy- and eighty-fifth birthdays), taken part as unofficial laureate in the inauguration of John F. Kennedy, and received nearly fifty honorary degrees (including ones from Oxford and Cambridge).

To say that Frost has been overrated is not to say that he is unimportant. He was a naïve (q.v.) poet, and when he took thought never more than a skilled folksy epigrammatist, who in order to cling on to his so hardly won fame had to write too much, and not always in his natural vein. His pose as sage seldom led to wisdom, and hardly does the true poet in him credit. The poems of *A Boy's Will* are less certain than those of *North of Boston*, his best book, and the confidence of this extends into some of the poetry of its two successors, *Mountain Interval* (1916) and *New Hampshire* (1923). After this Frost was increasingly intent on subscribing to an image of himself largely formed by people who had little knowledge of or love for the arts in general. His poems can be optimistic and cheerful when he does not really feel like that – he conceals his blackness – and he can be arch and self-consciously Yankee.

But when this has been said Frost is still a unique and original poet both in short lyrics and in certain comparatively short narrative poems. The famous 'Mending Wall' is a good enough example of his strength; it alone is enough to give pause when we are told that the claim that Frost is a major poet is 'ridiculous'. This is a genuinely tragic poem: it spells out how things are between people. Lawrence Thompson, Frost's biographer, suggests that 'the conclusion resolves the conflict in favour of the poet's view. ...' It seems to me that this judgement does not do it justice: it is more than an expression of a mere point of view, for while the wall is a real wall, it also stands for that barrier of reserve which neighbours erect between each other – to avoid being friends, or to protect themselves. We are told that 'Something there is that doesn't love a wall': frosts break it up. Hunters have the same effect. At 'spring mending-time' he gets in touch with his neighbours, and together they make the repairs, piling the boulders up. It's only a game, the narrator tells us: a wall isn't necessary at this point, since his neighbour is 'all pine' and he is apple orchard. He tackles his neighbour with this – 'Spring is the mischief in me', he explains, thus surely negating Thompson's assertion that the notion of having no wall is his seriously held point of view – but the neighbour only says 'Good fences make good neighbours'. However, mischievously he continues to taunt his neighbour, who goes on rebuilding the wall 'like an old-stone savage armed'; and the narrator concludes

> He moves in darkness as it seems to me,
> Not of woods only and the shades of trees.
> He will not go behind his father's saying,
> And he likes having thought of it so well
> He says again, 'Good fences make good neighbours'.

This is 'about' the barriers between people and the worth of love; maybe the conservative neighbour is right. Frost could and did moralize in his lesser poems; in this good one he is content to leave things as they are, tragically in balance. Yes, spring has made him challenge (with 'mischief') the notion of a wall; but there is no pat conclusion, no suggestion that it is his neighbour's state of mind that is responsible for the state of affairs. ... The poem works so well because its full meaning arises so naturally out of the situation it describes; there is no straining for a meaning in the account.

Again, it would surely be risky to dismiss the narrative 'The Death of the Hired Man', also from *North of Boston*, as only a minor poem. It is true that Frost's people are cardboard, and that they do not act upon each other or change each other; it is also true that his technical arrangements are static – the oft-made claim that he used American speech-rhythms cannot be carried far. But this account of the return of a hired man, and the differing views of a husband and wife about charity and their duty, attains such simplicity –

> 'Home is the place where, when you have to go there,
> They have to take you in.'
> 'I should have called it
> Something you somehow haven't to deserve.'

– that it cannot be ignored. It offers, for the time being, something other than the urban sophistication of Eliot (q.v.). So do a half dozen other similar narratives, most of them included in *North of Boston*. Frost is not usually a 'nature poet', for he does not observe natural objects minutely; he rather observes man in natural surroundings, and tries to find consolations for nature's indifference. He can be falsely sweet, as when he asks us to come with him while he cleans out the pasture spring (he does not mean it); but he achieves true sweetness when he reveals his desire for a valid and unsentimental universal love, as at the end of 'The Tuft of Flowers', from his first book:

> 'Men work together,' I told him from the heart,
> 'Whether they work together or apart'.

All Frost's concern with communality and love stemmed from his violent ambitiousness and black solitariness: he woke an enormous guilt in himself. Most of the poems of his last thirty years are good exercises; but while he struggled with himself, he wrote a poetry that is as secure as any.

Frost's influence on American poets of account may, surprisingly, be somewhat less than even that of Robinson (q.v.). Robinson remains enigmatic, unexplored; there does not at present seem to be very much to go to Frost for. The same can under no circumstances be said of the prince of American regionalist poets, **William Carlos Williams** (1883–1963), who was born in Rutherford, New Jersey, practised there as a doctor all his life, and died there. He studied dentistry at the University of Pennsylvania, where he met Pound (q.v.), and later went to Europe to study medicine. By 1912 he was married and settled into his lifelong practice at Rutherford, partly the Paterson of his long poem of that name.

'Williams ... is ... the most innocently tedious, insufferably monotonous, and purely mental of modern poets ... polythene verse. ... [His] form conceals that he is saying very little, and has very little to say. ...' (An English critic.)

'Williams' poems contain a generosity of spirit, a humane warmth, ability to translate daily life and ordinary objects into an unsentimental order of personal and universal significance, which are unique in modern poetry and rare at any time. ... His ear for rhythm is practically perfect. ...' (An American critic.)

The first judgement may be turned somewhat to Williams' advantage if we grant that, for all his multifarious pronouncements, Williams was a naïve (q.v.) poet – a good deal more naïve than Frost (q.v.), himself disingenuous in his intellectual pose. His overriding passion (it was never a thought) from early on was that poetry should reflect experience exactly, and that therefore rhyme and metre were falsifications: non-American, Anglophile devices. What he has to say about rhythm is neither well thought out nor interesting; mainly it is silly. He attacked Eliot (q.v.) and Pound for not staying in America, and imagism (q.v.) for being mere free verse. His 'objectivism' (q.v.) postulated the poem itself as object, presenting its meaning by its form. 'No ideas but in things', he insisted, seeking until the end to describe the universal only in the stubborn particular. He went his own singular way, inconsistent, obstinate, publishing his poetry with obscure small presses – and ended up as a grand old man of American letters, inspirer not only of Olsen, Ginsberg, Creeley (qq.v.), but, less logically, also of the formalists Roethke and Lowell (qq.v.). He wrote autobiography, impressionistic criticism (*In the American Grain*, 1925), plays, short stories and fiction.

All Williams' work flows out of his insistence upon the local and the particular. He saw the world 'contracted to a recognizable image'. His poems are his namings of the objects in his world as it unfolds itself to him. His own words, written when he was at his most energetic, and when he was hardly heeded, are incomparably the best expression of his intentions:

> There is a constant barrier between the reader and his consciousness of immediate contact with the world. ... I love my fellow creature. Jesus, how I love him ... but he doesn't exist! Neither does she. I do, in a bastardly sort of way. ... In the composition, the artist does exactly what every eye must do with life, fix the particular with the universality of his own personality. ... The only realism in art is of the imagination. It is only thus that the work escapes plagiarism after nature and becomes a creation. ... [Shakespeare] holds no mirror up to nature but with his imagination rivals nature's composition with his own. ...

That last remark gives us the clue both to Williams and the appeal he had for so many Americans. Here is a man who insists on the evidence of his own perceptions. As Marianne Moore (q.v.) shrewdly said of him: he has ' a kind of intellectual hauteur which one usually associates with the French'. Indeed, we have only to remember the philosophy behind the French *nouveau roman* (q.v.) to recognize this: but this is a doggone, non-intellectual, Yankee approach. Williams exists on the strength of his perceptions or he does not exist. After some early imitations of Keats, he began writing in the vein that he maintained until his death. It is seen at its best in 'This Is Just To Say' – surely an irresistible if relentlessly minor little lyric?

This Is Just To Say

I have eaten
the plums
that were in
the icebox

and which
you were probably
saving
for breakfast

Forgive me
they were delicious
so sweet
and so cold

Williams' long poem *Paterson* (1946–58), his attempt at an epic, in five books, is distinctly American in its attempt to recover innocence and a sense of community. It is characteristically impressionistic: in large part it consists of seemingly casual collage of undoctored raw material – heard conversation, private letters, news clippings, official reports, bald anecdotes, and so on. It contains some vigorous and compelling passages, but suffers from two contradictory defects. Williams wants to appear non-literary, ordinary, and so to this end he includes far too much unedited material in the poem; this makes it tedious. However, at the same time the essentially naïve poet artfully and disingenuously tries to superimpose a symbolic pattern on the poem: for example, an analogy is worked out between the poet's and the physicist's function, even to the extent of comparing the splitting of the atom to the splitting of the (metrical) foot. ... (this last is peculiarly tiresome and idiosyncratic). The first two books hold together better than the rest, but even these contain dull passages; the rest fails to convince or to cohere, although some enthusiastic critics have stated otherwise. Williams' technique here more closely parallels that of painters than poets: 'he strives', writes a critic, 'for a poem that will, in its own process, answer the question it continually poses.' This is no more than the old, anti-mimetic insistence on creation, the necessity he felt to 'rival nature's composition with his own. ...' It does not work, but comes near enough to doing so for us to wish that Williams had not tried to be so artful: he was not good at it.

However, Williams' anti-mimetic preoccupation is enough to demonstrate that he is no spurious modern, as the English critic quoted above has suggested. It is true that in an intellectual or metaphysical sense Williams has nothing whatever to say. But is he that kind of writer? Is he not, rather, simply a recorder of his perceptions? That these are often simplistic is beside the point. They are almost inevitably unspoiled. However, can Williams, on the strength of his best things – such fragments as 'El Hombre',

It's a strange courage
you give me ancient star:

Shine alone in the sunrise
toward which you lend no part!

– be called a major poet? As a pioneer he is obviously of importance. But is his poetry intrinsically major? The poem of his old age, of some 350 lines, called 'Asphodel, That Greeny Flower', is probably his crowning achievement. It is hard not to respond to it. But are we not perhaps responding to the integrity and sweet cussedness of personality, to a devoted life, rather than to a substantial poetic achievement? The answer to the question is not to be easily found. In my own judgement there is as much of the simple-minded as of the simple about Williams, so that he is finally a physician and minor poet rather than a major poet and a physician. He always wanted desperately to be 'average', and I think that his simplicities, too, were near the average. ... (Evidently Wordsworth's, say, weren't.) One appreciates the way he lived and felt and talked; but even 'Asphodel, That Greeny Flower' offers no insight, only a chance to applaud that performance. In order to attain to it he eschewed all alien devices, so that his poems lack tension. And a whole poetry that lacks tension is inexorably minor. Further, his rhythms lack tension: the 'practically perfect' ear is just loose, rhetorical praise.

And now, since it is relevant to most of the American poetry that follows, a word about Williams and poetic technique. Williams many times announced that he had discovered a new, American poetic technique, which he referred to as the 'variable foot'. Williams was no prosodist, and his attempted definitions of his variable foot are worthless. But it does mean something in terms of his own practice:

> Of asphodel, that greeny flower,
>   like a buttercup
>   upon its branching stem –
> save that it's green and wooden –
> I come, my sweet,
>   to sing to you.
> We lived long together
>   a life filled
>   if you will. ...

Each of those 'lines' is a 'variable foot'; at one time Williams would have called it a 'triadic foot', comprising a single 'line'. And the reader will quickly appreciate that, while Williams himself achieved a personal rhythm by writing in this way, his imitators have not. This way of writing verse should be discussed, and there are new elements in it (even though one can treat Williams' verse in terms of the various traditional approaches to prosody); but it has not been usefully discussed yet – least of all by Williams, who waded thigh deep into the old bog of confusion between accent and quantity that has bedevilled English prosodic studies since Elizabethan times. This has not often been intelligently discussed, although it has excited poets. Accent in English poetry will always be the main factor; but syllabic length adds another. Syllable-counting without reference to duration of syllable results in a purely mechanical, arhythmical verse. Williams' confused theory comes nearer to the 'temporal' prosody advanced by the American poet Sidney Lanier, who died in 1881. What is original in his practice – 'not that,' he wrote, 'I know anything about what I have myself written' – is the accommodation he gives to quantity without straining its function in the vernacular: without, as the Elizabethan Stanyhurst, and Bridges (q.v.), and even Tennyson did, trying to destroy accent. This you simply cannot do without turning your verse into a sort of quaint prose. If Williams' pronouncements on Thomas Campion are embarrassing, his poems do achieve a kind of musicality, and a new musicality at that, which many others of this century lack.

It is appropriate at this point to deal with a movement in which Williams played a major part. Objectivism never hit any headlines, even though Pound (q.v.) was officially associated with it, and besides Williams only one other 'objectivist' has since become at all well known: Louis Zukofsky (q.v.). But this small group is important both as a refinement of imagism (q.v.), and as a forerunner of a branch of American poetry exemplified in the work of Robert Duncan, Robert Creeley, Gary Snyder (qq.v.) and many others, which flourished in the Sixties and Seventies, and is only just beginning to peter out. It began when a wealthy young man (the description is Williams'), George Oppen (q.v.), decided to lose his money on publishing poetry. At first his press was called TO ('The

Objectivists'), and in 1932 it published *An "Objectivists" Anthology*, edited by Zukofsky. Then it became the Objectivist Press, with an advisory board consisting of Williams, Zukofsky and Pound; other poets involved included Carl Rakosi (ps. Callman Rawley), born in Berlin, and Charles Reznikoff, a lawyer born in New York (qq.v.). Acknowledging Williams as their master, these poets (this does not include Pound, whose relationship was avuncular and postal) published his *Collected Poems 1921–1931* (1934), with an introduction by Wallace Stevens (q.v.). But their own work has its importance in twentieth-century American poets' search for simplicity. All, though minor poets and content to be so, possess an integrity and a lack of interest in personal fame – as distinct from poetic achievement – that could be a lesson to their modern successors. There is much in the claim that while the American poetic tradition appeared to be, during the Thirties, in the hands of such as Tate and Ransom (qq.v.), it was really in the hands of these relatively obscure poets. Where it is most feeble is in its lack of emotional robustness and its relentless concentration on the trivialities of everyday existence – a kind of egotism. Only Whitman avoided this. That this tradition, stemming directly from Whitman and running through Sandburg and Williams to Creeley and others, has not yet produced a truly major poet since its originator does not constitute a negation of the claim, though American poetry is unlikely to produce this kind of poet from philistine roots.

The objectivists were agreed that imagism, having helped to get rid of mere verbiage, had 'dribbled off into so much free verse. . . . There is no such thing as free verse! Verse is measure of some sort . . . we argued, the poem . . . is an object . . . that in itself formally presents its case and its meaning by the very form it assumes . . . it must be the purpose of the poet to make of his words a new form: to invent, that is, an object consonant with his day . . .' (Williams). These words bear heeding, because they sum the credo of every kind of disciple of Williams.

Louis Zukofsky (1904–78) was a quiet, unassertive man who has been possibly the most persistent and courageous experimentalist in the English-speaking world in this century. Once again, it is his procedures that are important – as indeed one might expect in a work that 'in itself formally presents its case and its meaning by the very form it assumes. . . .' To the reader nourished on conventional pap Zukofsky's poetry and criticism seem thin and insubstantial; nor indeed does he display anything of the emotional robustness of a Williams (q.v.). But this should not distract attention from the significance of what he did. It is characteristic of Zukofsky that his chief work, the long poem – unfinished – *A*, should be continuous, a day book. For Zukofsky it is absurd to be a good poet at one point of one's life, then a bad one, and so on. So *A* is his continuous poetic reaction, as often concerned with sounds as with music. He reminds us of Gertrude Stein (q.v.) at least inasmuch as meaning in his verse is very often no more than an overtone to sound. (All the objectivists shared Gertrude Stein's notion of words as words, things-in-themselves.) Zukofsky is continually playful, and yet he is always thinking – if in a somewhat primitivistic (and why not?) sense of the word – very closely indeed about words as meaning and words as sound. The context of his work is almost always his domestic life; his wife and son Paul (now a well-known violinist) are both musicians. The theme of *A*, in fact, is marriage: marriage as a bastion against the ruins of 'civilization'. For poets at least it is always readable, always an evocation of a sweetly lived life. Some clues to the passages that look like nonsense, but which are in fact various sorts of experiments with sound, may be gathered from Zukofsky and his wife Celia's *Catullus* (1969), in which they have transliterated the entire works of Catullus from Latin into an American that 'tries . . . to breathe the "literal" meaning with him'. Thus the famous:

Odi et amo. quare id faciam, fortasse requiris.
nescio, sed fieri sentio et excrucior

becomes:

O th' hate I move love. Quarry it fact I am, for that's so re queries.
Nescience, say th' fiery scent I owe whets crookeder.

Now: can the texture of the sound of Latin be woven into that of American? Apart from one or two remarkable *tours de force*, it seems not. The vast majority, however well disposed, would consider the above transliteration, for example, a grotesque failure: not only in terms of the literal Latin meaning but also in those of the American language. But it is the failure of an intelligent man; and the experiment is not a useless or a foolish one. However, the question that wholehearted partisans of this version of Catullus (few of whom, curiously, seem to possess the Zukofskys' knowledge of Latin) need to answer is: what can be the function of such a language as is here invented? What is interesting is that an answer can be made. Just as some sense can be made of Williams' 'theory' of prosody so even 'O th' hate I move love' for 'Odi et amo' can be defended. We must consider it – and Zukofsky, even if we find against him. The poems have been collected in *All: The Collected Shorter Poems 1923–1958* (1966), *All: The Collected Shorter Poems 1956–1964* (1967), *"A" 1–12* (1967), *"A" 13–21* (1969). Criticism is in *Prepositions* (1967), and fiction (a useful method of approach to this important poet) in *Ferdinand* (1968). *Bottom: on Shakespeare* (1963) is criticism combining poetic and musical interests.

Carl Rakosi (1903), a social worker and psychotherapist, and always involved in social protest from a position well left of the usual American liberalism, is the least well known or committed of the objectivists, but his poetry is as clean as it is slight; *Selected Poems* appeared in 1941, *Amulet* in 1967, and *My Experiences in Parnassus* in 1977.

George Oppen (1908) is more substantial. *Materials* (1962) collects thirty years of his work, and he has published three collections since then. He has been described, in terms characteristic of recent criticism, as being 'one of the best and one of the worst of poets'. He has been important to some of the Black Mountain poets (q.v.) because his project has been to express his existence and the use he has made of it:

Yet I am one of those who from nothing but man's way of
thought and one of his dialects and what has happened to me
have made poetry

Oppen, unlike Zukofsky and Olson (qq.v.), has not received even belated critical recognition, despite his Pulitzer Prize of 1969. And yet his understanding of the problems of diction has been as acute as Williams' (q.v.), and since his first book appeared in 1934 he has provided an object-lesson: a poetry that 'presents its case ... by the very form it assumes'. Like Zukofsky, he aims for a full articulation of his engagement with life; he is fascinated, too, with objects-as-themselves (cf., again, the *nouveau roman*), objects not anthropomorphized. But his method is complex; cutting across his purely objectivist preoccupations are intellectual and abstract concerns that might contort the face (often the Black Mountain equivalent of raising the eyebrow) of a true disciple of Williams. Sometimes he has been guilty of smuggling thought into his poetry, in such lines as those describing women in the streets 'weakened by too much need/Of too little'; and yet careful study of his poetry shows that he, more than any other poet in his tradition, has seen the possibilities of using content to create its own form. He is not trivial, and his methods are more original than some of his admirers think. *Collected Poems 1929–1975* (1975); *Primitive* (1978).

Charles Reznikoff (1894–1980), a considerably older man, wrote distinguished prose in his novel *By the Waters of Manhattan* (1930), and in *Family Chronicle* (1963); as a poet he was more of an imagist:

> This smoky morning –
> do not despise the green jewel shining among the twigs
> because it is a traffic light.

His poetry, much of which is collected in *By the Waters of Manhattan: Selected Verse* (1962), is as enjoyable (in the full sense of the word) as any imagist's could possibly be. Though evidently sometimes impelled to widen his scope, he chose to limit himself to the minimal, with, in this case, excellent results. Reznikoff was not, like Oppen (q.v.), a pioneer; but because he decided to narrow his scope, his picture-making impulses were not frustrated, and many of his poems have the freshness of such paintings as 'Early Sunday Morning' by Edward Hopper, with whom he has indeed been compared.

Ezra Pound's (1885–1972) part in the new American poetry has been more cosmopolitan. No writer of the twentieth century has had more personal influence on modern literature, or has known and encouraged more individual poets. His importance in connection with imagism (q.v.), vorticism, W.B. Yeats, T.S. Eliot, William Carlos Williams (qq.v.) and other men and movements has been or will be noted. His immense historical importance has never been in question; the matter of his individual achievement is very much more controversial.

Pound was born in Idaho. He began to attend the University of Pennsylvania, Philadelphia, at the age of fifteen, owing to his good Latin. Here he met William Carlos Williams, then a student in dentistry. After two years he transferred to Hamilton College in New York State. By 1906, when he received his M.A., he had for some time been experimenting with various forms of verse. He had also already begun to develop the eccentric behaviour – a mixture, it seems, of exhibitionism, excitability, devotedness to his in many ways rather vague ideals and something that looks like hypomania – that was to characterize his life, and eventually lead him to incarceration in a mental hospital for thirteen years. By that time he had become ill: manic-depressive. After a short time spent in an academic job, for which he was totally unsuitable, Pound left for Europe. He published his first book of poems, *A Lume Spento* (1908; reprinted as *A Lume Spento and Other Early Poems*, 1965 – with a note by Pound addressed to William Carlos Williams referring to it as 'A collection of stale cream puffs ... why a reprint? No lessons to be learned save the depth of ignorance ...'). Soon afterwards he arrived in England and, with typical effrontery, 'took over' T.E. Hulme's (q.v.) and Henry Simpson's 'Poets' Club' of 1909 and turned it into the imagist group. In 1914 T.S. Eliot (q.v.) called on him in London; his poetry immediately aroused Pound's enthusiasm. Before this he had met Yeats (q.v.), and the Irish poet was to acknowledge his influence.

Pound was active on the English literary scene until after the end of the First World War. He helped, encouraged and publicized the work of James Joyce (q.v.), Wyndham Lewis (q.v.) and many others, a few of whom are still almost unknown today. Pound has never bothered much about reputation, and has frequently treated his own simply as a means of helping other writers' work to become recognized. In this sense he has been the most generous poet of the century. He began writing his (unfinished) Cantos in 1915, but had been planning them for some time before that. The first collection, *A Draft of XXX Cantos*, was published in Paris in 1930 (Pound's *Cantos* are now available as follows: *The*

Cantos of Ezra Pound, 1957; *Thrones: 96–109 de los Cantares*, 1959; *Drafts and Fragments of Cantos CX–CXVII*, 1970). He lived in France and then in Italy until his arrest at the end of the Second World War.

In 1918 Pound met Major C.H. Douglas, who had devised an economic scheme called Social Credit, which, he claimed, could avert economic depressions. Pound very soon became taken up with these ideas; he was convinced that in monetary reform lay the key to the creation of a society in which perfect beauty and perfect justice would co-exist. Previously his views on art and society had been less unusual: the writer was to be valued by the degree of his clarity and precision (compare the programme of imagism); of society and social systems Pound was contemptuous – only the individual deserved respect.

Douglas' ideas have never been taken seriously by economists – not necessarily an indictment of them, but perhaps of their originator's sense of tact – but they have had some influence on minority politics in Canada and elsewhere. Douglas himself was not a fascist, and he did not see his theories as being implemented either in Mussolini's Italy or in Hitler's Germany. Pound, unhappily, despite his later confused denial that he had ever been 'for Fascism', was deluded into thinking that Italy's fascist government was leading the country in the cultural direction he found desirable. Yet he knew little about contemporary Italian literature. His anti-semitism, never personal, now began to flare up dangerously; it became increasingly distasteful as the Nazi attitude towards the Jews became clearer. Pound gradually came to see all wars and social misery as a conspiracy of 'top' Jews, based in usury. Markedly greater than his anguish at the unhappiness caused to ordinary people by wars and poverty, however, was his own frustrated rage at not getting his ideas accepted. An element of grandiosity entered his calculations – or projects, as they had better be called – even as his anti-semitic language became more abrasively insulting (and puerile); he thought seriously of gaining the ear of American government officials, and at the same time developed a violent dislike of President Roosevelt. He did have some doubts about fascism, and on occasions he even tried to be fair, in his own terms, about the Jews; but more attracted him in fascism than did not, and he was clearly ideologically committed to it by the late Thirties. There was certainly a paranoid element in this commitment, though this seems only to have co-existed with, not to have been fuelled by, his mental instability and varying affect. His thoughts and utterances were a fantastic ragbag of theories both wild and sane, and indignations just and unjust. He seems to have had not the faintest idea what the war of 1939 was really about: he told the popular novelist and Nobel prizewinner Pearl Buck that it was 'mainly for moneylending and three or four metal monopolies'. When America entered the war Pound made an effort to leave Italy, but was prevented from doing so. It is likely that he found it hard to make decisions.

It is clear that Pound's mind began to cloud, seriously, from the beginning of the Thirties – although a tendency to retreat into a position from which reality was inaccessible had been apparent since early youth. In 1933 he gained an audience with Mussolini, the only one he was ever to have, and came away with the delusion – amazing in anyone of his intelligence – that the dictator really cared for poetry and beauty, and was working passionately for a just society. Pound even thought, from a polite remark, that Mussolini had read and understood the *Cantos*.

It is evident that throughout the war years Pound was in a state of considerable distress. He had been taking small sums of money – which he needed – for broadcasts from Rome radio since before the American declaration of war. He continued to do so after it. The broadcasts were rambling, ill-delivered, dense and perhaps technically treasonable. They had no adverse effect on anyone on the Allied side: since they were almost always on the subject of economics or literature, very few could have understood them. His wife could not follow them for the same reason that some of his readers cannot follow his poems: because of the abrupt jumps from one subject to another. These radio talks were clearly the work of a man at the verge of, or perhaps at times immersed in, insanity.

At the end of the war Pound was eventually arrested and sent to the Disciplinary Training Camp at Pisa. Here he suffered exceedingly, at one point collapsing into a state of 'violent and hysterical terror'. But he recovered sufficiently to write the continuation of his *Cantos*, called *The Pisan Cantos*, and published as such (1948). Brought back to America to face treason charges in 1945, he was correctly judged to be unfit to plead, and was confined to St. Elizabeth's Hospital in Washington. His state at this time was worse than it had ever been: symptoms included scattered wits, inability to concentrate, and an insistence that his new versions of Confucius were the only rational foundation upon which to build a new world. He maintained throughout that he had not committed treason; it was plain that the matter had worried his conscience at all times.

Released (after too long) in 1958, Pound went back to Italy, where he died. He suffered from periodic depressions, and was never wholly coherent. He said on several occasions that he had 'botched' his life work, and made 'errors'; but he continued to publish fragments of poetry. The *Cantos* remained unfinished.

Pound had of course aroused great controversy. This reached its height when he had not long been in St. Elizabeth's, and was awarded the Bollingen Prize for *The Pisan Cantos*. Since many of his disciples then appeared to share his political views, it was natural that his detractors, however unfairly, should identify his poetry with those views – with, in fact, a virulent brand of anti-semitic fascism. One of these erstwhile disciples, Pound's best biographer (*The Life of Ezra Pound*, 1970), Noel Stock, has put all this into a proper perspective. 'I will not dwell on the rubbish which we, his correspondents, fed to him [in St. Elizabeth's], or the rubbish which he in turn fed to us ... a good number of us ... helped to confirm him in the belief that he alone possessed a coherent view of the truth. ...'

The fact is that Pound's political views, such as he has expressed them, would not do credit to a sixth-former. They were partly inherited from the American populism of the Nineties of Pound's childhood, a movement that originated in poverty and was quickly dissipated by a return to prosperity. Like all populism, Pound's is characterized by a practicality (he had been a good handyman all his life), a love of folk poetry, a genuine love of and feeling for the very poor and a cluster of negative attitudes: ill-informedly anti-capitalistic, anti-legal, anti-semitic and (tragically and confusedly in this case) anti-intellectual. Certainly the brilliance of some of Pound's insights has been vitiated by his evident insensitivity to human suffering (e.g. the suffering going on around him in Italy during the war) and his increasing tendency towards incoherence. Fortunately this is only half the story.

Pound's first book to attract wide attention, *Personae* (1909), was attacked both for being incomprehensibly 'modern' and for being absurdly archaic. Much of the modernism was actually Browning put into a distinctly new rhythm. Here Pound writes of a down-at-heel old scholar (these lines, from 'Famam Librosque Cano', come originally from *A Lume Spento*):

> Such an one picking a ragged
> Backless copy from the stall,
> Too cheap for cataloguing,
> Loquitur,

'Ah – eh! the strange rare name ...
Ah – eh. He must be rare if even *I* have not ...'
And lost mid-page
Such age
As his pardons the habit,
He analyzes form and thought to see
How I 'scaped immortality.

But where Pound was already most original was in his method. He adapted from the Provençal, mixed archaism with modern slang, resurrected (to adapt his own words from his *Credo*) forgotten modes because he found 'some leaven' in them, and because he saw in them an element that was lacking in the poetry of his own time 'which might unite' it 'again to its sustenance, life'. The programme was impeccable – but always missing was any robustness of his own: there is never a core that is individual.

In the succeeding years Pound produced more books of short poems, and a brilliant adaptation (complete with presumably deliberate howlers, such as a rendering of the Latin 'vates' as 'votes') of the poems of Sextus Propertius called *Homage to Sextus Propertius* (1934; written 1917–18). *Hugh Selwyn Mauberley* (1920), a group of poems originally prompted by the correct conviction that the free verse movement had 'gone too far', was written just afterwards. For those critics who see the *Cantos* as a failure not substantially relieved by excellent or beautiful passages, these two works represent the height of Pound's achievement. Free verse has probably never been handled more firmly or effectively in English than in *Homage to Sextus Propertius*, which, like *Hugh Selwyn Mauberley*, has a coherence that Pound never found again. 'Mr Nixon' is as acid and yet serenely good-mannered a satire against literary opportunism, commercialism and lack of integrity as the twentieth century has seen; and the famous 'Envoi' (1919) that Pound offers as his own poetic credo is as beautiful as anything he has ever written:

Go, dumb-born book,
Tell her that sang me once that song of Lawes:
Hadst thou but song
As thou hast subjects known,
Then were there cause in thee that should condone
Even my faults that heavy upon me lie,
And build her glories their longevity.

Tell her that sheds
Such treasure in the air,
Recking naught else but that her graces give
Life to the moment,
I would bid them live
As roses might, in magic amber laid,
Red overwrought with orange and all made
One substance and one colour
Braving time.

Tell her that goes
With song upon her lips
But sings not out the song, nor knows
The maker of it, some other mouth,

> May be as fair as hers,
> Might, in new ages, gain her worshippers,
> When our two dusts with Waller's shall be laid,
> Siftings on siftings in oblivion
> Till change hath broken down
> All things save beauty alone.

And yet even in this poem, as good as anything ever written by Pound, we may see his limitations. 'Beauty' is still sensed as itself something of a generalization. There is nothing in Pound's poetry about human behaviour as such: no psychological hint as to what beauty itself might consist of, either behaviouristically or in understandable, human terms. The beauty in Pound's verse is nearly always elusive in its nature. Furthermore, utterly convincing as this is, it is pastiche: it is not Pound's own voice, and the rhythms are not his own.

Pound had previously defined the image as 'an intellectual and emotional complex in an instant of time. ... It is the presentation of such an image which gives that sudden sense of liberation; that sense of freedom from time and space limits; that sense of sudden growth, which we experience in ... the greatest works of art'. His own participation in the imagist movement had really been only a dramatization of his own developing programme; and yet, like Reznikoff (q.v.), but on an infinitely grander scale, he was to remain an 'imagist' all his life. That is what he is best at.

Pound first learned about Japanese poetry from F. S. Flint (q.v.), but he soon took over as the pioneer in the study of it. In fact, although he did not understand the Japanese language, he understood some of the more important qualities of Japanese poetry long before they were fully explained to Western readers. It is in this understanding, and the use he made of it, that his greatest achievement lies. His famous poem 'In a Station of the Metro',

> The apparition of these faces in a crowd;
> Petals on a wet, black bough

perfectly illustrates his discovery: a straightforward non-metaphorical statement is followed by a striking image, in the manner of the Japanese *haiku* (q.v.). In this 'superpository' method one idea 'is set on top of another'. The beauty and the meaning of the poem are to be discovered in the imaginative leap necessary from the statement to the metaphor for it. But perhaps almost tragically, it is not a substantial poem: it is rather a building block from which a substantial one might be made. When Pound came to construct the *Cantos*, the whole edifice failed (as he said) to cohere: it was a series of images strung onto a prose string. In a slightly longer poem, 'Coitus', Pound employs essentially the same method to describe a well-known experience:

> The gilded phaloi of the crocuses
>   are thrusting at the spring air.
> Here is there naught of dead gods
> But a procession of festival,
> A procession, O Giulio Romano,
> Fit for your spirit to dwell in.
> Dione, your nights are upon us.
>
> The dew is upon the leaf.
> The night about us is restless.

Pound's inspiration here was Japanese – specifically the Japanese *haiku*. Now this is essentially a miniature art – one that the modern Japanese poets have themselves found largely inadequate. Pound's genius perceived its possibilities for English verse, but nevertheless could not turn miniaturism into epic – which is, however, exactly what he tried to do in the *Cantos*. In the epic he hoped that his own unifying sensibility would successfully gather together all the fragmentarily presented poetries and cultures. Instead, the poem became a game for adepts, as Noel Stock has demonstrated (*Reading the Cantos*, 1967). As Stock says, they 'do not constitute a poem, but a disjointed series of short poems, passages, lines and fragments, often of exceptional beauty or interest, but uninformed, poetically or otherwise, by larger purpose'. They are, he insists, poetry – not poems. Although there are books, notably one by Donald Davie (*Ezra Pound: Poet as Sculptor*, 1964), which claim that the *Cantos* do possess a unifying purpose, these are not convincing, they have not on the whole convinced unintimidated readers (Davie is essentially a didactic bully, for all his insights), and it seems unlikely that the view they put forward will prevail. It is very difficult indeed to credit the epic poet Pound with a 'unifying sensibility' – as difficult as it is to credit the man with one; and there is, after all, his own recent view of the poem, which cannot altogether be attributed to senile depression: 'I picked out this and that thing that interested me, and then jumbled them into a bag. But that's not the way to make a *work of art*.' As Santayana (q.v.) put it to Pound in a letter in 1940: '... Your tendency to jump is so irresistible that the bond between the particulars jumped to is not always apparent'; and he himself, in Canto CXVI, has confessed: 'I cannot make it cohere'. It is both ironic and significant that Pound's greatest triumphs and failures should consist of 'leaps'. In the *Cantos* the leaps too often become impenetrable ellipses. Pound's admiration for earlier and successful epics such as the *Divine Comedy* misled him into believing that they could be written today. They cannot.

In Pound mental instability has certainly vitiated poetic achievement. His imagery of beauty and its permanence, and of light, is often strangely beautiful; but even his achievement here may ultimately be seen to have been vitiated by a lack of emotional solidity, an absence of wisdom, reflecting an inability to learn through experience. Probably his reputation has been unduly inflated, and he has certainly attracted a large number of inferior cranks.

But Pound stood notably, if never very diplomatically or tactfully, for poetic values against commercial ones; he was generous and perceptive; and he searched, as well as his wrecked mind would allow him, for the truth. Posterity may dub him a minor poet: minor because even in his best poetry he lacks solid conviction; but he will be called a vital critic (sometimes in his poetry), and the failure of his mind will always be regarded as tragic.

The novelist and poet **H.D.** (ps. **Hilda Doolittle**, 1886–1961), born in Bethlehem, Pennsylvania, went to Europe in 1911, was for a time married to the English writer Richard Aldington (q.v.) and was associated with the imagists in England; but she remained essentially an American poet in her attitudes and her use of the short line. Like Williams (q.v.), she was much influenced by the hard precision of Greek poetry. But her Greek was better than Williams', and she was a poet of more substance. Read by almost every poet of the century and recognized by them as an exquisite minor, H.D. has been extraordinarily neglected by critics. Her translation of Euripides' *Ion* (1937) is probably the best translation from Greek drama of the century – only MacNeice's (q.v.) *Agamemnon* can rival it – if faithfulness to the text be taken into consideration. H.D.'s gift, slight but tempered, survived: alone of those imagists who did not merely travel through the movement, she continued to write well. Her earlier poems subscribed exactly to the imagist programme; but she differed from the other imagists, such as her husband Richard

Aldington, in that the manner was natural to her. She did not come to imagism; imagism came to her. Her style rigidly excludes sentimentalities, and concentrates on producing objects (poems) that do not pretend to evoke, but instead present themselves as themselves. Her poems have a dateless quality, which calls attention not only to their strength but also to her general weakness: commonplace emotion may be subsumed in 'classical' style, as such lines as:

> your insight
> has driven deeper
> than the lordliest tome
> of Attic thought
> or Cyrenian logic

hint. Except at their very best, there is in her poems always an element of pastiche of late Greek classical poetry that raises suspicion. This suspicion is partly confirmed by the trilogy she wrote during the Second World War: *The Walls Do Not Fall* (1944), *Tribute to the Angels* (1945) and *Flowering of the Rod* (1946), which dealt with themes of war. In style and taste this is an impressive work; but the symbolism and thought behind it are tawdry by comparison. When H.D.'s poetry is not at its best the manner conceals this; when she is at her best the manner itself is, becomes, the poem. She wrote a number of novels, including an extremely interesting and valuable *roman a clef, Bid Me To Live* (1960), about London in 1917. This contains a portrait of D. H. Lawrence (q.v.). Her best book, though, is *Tribute to Freud* (1956 rev. 1974), about herself and her experiences with Freud.

Marianne Moore (1887–1972), who was born at St. Louis, Missouri, has been praised and loved by poets of every persuasion. It was H. D. (q.v.) and the English novelist Bryher who, unknown to the author, published her first book, *Poems* (1921), which collected twenty-four poems that had appeared in periodicals. She was editor of the magazine *The Dial* from 1925 until its demise in 1929. Hers is a reputation that has never suffered vicissitudes.

Marianne Moore's *Complete Poems* were issued in 1968, but one also needs her *Collected Poems* (1961), and her earlier volumes: her alterations are revealing. She is unique in that she alone has made a 'modern' (by means of procedures) poetry out of an experience that deliberately excludes that rawness which we associate with the modern. There is absolutely nothing of the 'redskin' (q.v.) about her. She cut, in her eighty-first year, the twenty-odd lines of her famous poem 'Poetry' to just this:

> I, too, dislike it.
>   Reading it, however, with a perfect contempt for it, one discovers in
>   it, after all, a place for the genuine.

The end of the original version, which includes the celebrated lines about 'imaginary gardens with real toads in them' (it is the real toads she eschews), runs:

> ... if you demand on the one hand
>   the raw material of poetry in
>   all its rawness and
>   that which is on the other hand
>   genuine, you are interested in poetry.

Miss Moore really does dislike it; but she is interested in it, and in a thoroughgoing, respectable manner that is not shared by many other poets. But that, of course, is not poetry at all – but criticism.

All this is not a mask. Miss Moore's external personality is what she presents it as: she is a Presbyterian (like her father) who approves of Bible classes. Hart Crane (q.v.) called her 'the Rt. Rev. Miss Mountjoy', and protested 'What strange people these – [the omission is by the editor of Crane's letters] are. Always in a flutter for fear bowels will be mentioned. ...' This aspect of Marianne Moore must, I think, be faced up to. And Crane's verdict is the right one: 'She is so prosaic that the extremity of her detachment touches, or seems to touch, a kind of inspiration'. This is the shrewdest remark ever made about her poetry, which is indeed about rejecting almost everything in modern experience – but rejecting it without loss of grace or authenticity. Out of a sensibility applied to a world she rejects she has created a genuinely poetic style, a body of work that confers vitality and meaning upon a propriety that we might otherwise reject as either incredible (in a poet) or absurdly provincial.

Her most sustained and exact and, in its way, confessional poem is 'The Pangolin'. This has been taken as a description of an animal so precise and loving that its object becomes a paradigm of a certain kind of human virtue. But it is both more and less than this. For here she describes her own life-style. And in the gentleness of the poem there is an implied rejection of an ungentle world:

> to explain grace requires
> a curious hand. If that which is at all
> were not forever,
> why would those who graced the spires
> with animals ...
> have slaved to confuse
> grace with a kindly manner, time in
> which to pay a debt
> the cure for sins ...?

In Marianne Moore's poetry the disliked 'poetry', the peerless, imaginative thing that she sees she must reject, is relentlessly eschewed by a technique that makes enjambement a rule and not an exception, and takes as often as not an almost cynical, mechanically syllabic pattern as its norm – and yet the poetry returns, as a gift, in the form of subtle rhythms and light rhymes, as delicately as a butterfly alighting.

Wallace Stevens (1879–1955), born in Pennsylvania, was admired by Williams (q.v.), but is on the whole eschewed by the 'native American' school; academic critics and poets, however, have taken him up. Stevens is not only modern in appearance – recondite, wanton in his imagery, holding back explicitness – but in substance as well. Thus two of his best-known lines are (and they are atrocious): 'The poem is the cry of its occasion/Part of the res itself and not about it'. He wasted much of his gift in meandering, ineffectual poetry ('The Man with the Blue Guitar') that is little more than an appropriate screen for the projections of ingenious critics; he needs rigorous selection; but at his second-best he is delightful, and at his rare best, superb. His first book, *Harmonium*, appeared in 1923 when he was nearly forty-four, and, unusually, he wrote the bulk of his poetry after he was fifty. He was at Harvard, then read law, and then joined the Hartford Accident and Indemnity Company in 1916; in 1934 he became its vice-president, a position which he held until his death. He was, then, a full-time business man for the whole of his life. This is often remarked upon. Perhaps the only relevant comment is that he is the only poet of the century, of comparable stature, thus to combine business with poetry; and that this is a formidable undertaking simply because the values of insurance and those of poetry do not appear to mix too easily.

Stevens' manner is polished, aesthetic, literary, exotic – at its worst whimsical and contrived – alogical and rhetorical. In terms of feeling his poetry is thin and deliberately reticent: that kind of experience is not its subject. Stevens is above all a civilized poet; his project is usually taken to be philosophical, but it can also be described as a search for a style, an answer to the question, 'How can an insurance man also be a poet?' 'What! Wally a poet', one of his illiterate colleagues exclaimed when told of it. The usual critical approach is to grant that there is what Professor Frank Kermode calls a 'poetry of abstraction', and to judge Stevens as a master of it. However, Stevens is at his best when he is being non-abstract – even if about the pains and difficulties of trying to maintain abstractness. The whimsical, recondite surface of the inferior poems is not always as masterly as it appears. As Stevens told his future wife when he was a very young man: 'Perhaps I do like to be sentimental now and then in a roundabout way. ... I certainly do dislike expressing it right and left'. Thus 'The Man with the Blue Guitar' conceals not feeling but sentimentality beneath its artful veneer of vaguely symbolist preciosity; the complex aesthetic philosophy it contains may provide grist for such interesting neo-scholiasts as Professor Frank Kermode (a fine if contentious expositor of Stevens), but poetically this is neither here nor there. Too often Stevens was practising: a business man who, instead of questioning the moral sources of his affluence, played scales on an old chocolate bassoon (as he might have put it). Kermode says: 'There is a poetry of the abstract; if you do not like it, even when it is firmly rooted in the particulars of the world, you will not like Stevens'. It is not quite as simple as that. One may dislike or not accept as valid the existence of 'a poetry of the abstract', but one may still like a little of Stevens. The trouble with 'The Man with the Blue Guitar' is that it is wholly cerebral: there is nothing to anchor it to any sort of emotional particular. 'Owl Clover', a longish poem rightly omitted from the *Collected Poems* (1954) but restored in its original version in *Opus Posthumous* (1957), shows him to least advantage: not because it maintains a poet's right to pursue his function despite politics, but because its view of Marxism, for all the sonorities, is as vulgar and insensitive and ignorant as one might expect from an insurance man (no more than an 'it', in E. E. Cummings', q.v., words, 'that stinks excuse me'). But William York Tindall has reminded us that Stevens was a 'Taft Republican who thought Eisenhower a dangerous radical', and in a poet of his sensibilities what is 'fine and private ... heroic ... the romance of lost causes finds its happiest concentration here'. However, Stevens skated on thin ice; we have good reason to suspect his aestheticism – if we are among those who do not believe the possession of genius is an excuse for lack of sensibility. 'Owl Clover' is crass reactionary propaganda from a man who never visited Europe in his life, and knew nothing of it at first hand – as bad as crass communist propaganda or tractor doggerel, and perhaps worse because wrapped up in an aestheticism that looks so advanced. (Stevens once wrote in a letter: 'The Italians have as much right to take Ethiopia from the coons as the coons had to take it from the boa-constrictors'; he then nervously qualified this by saying his own sympathy was with the coons and the boa-constrictors – but finally stated that Mussolini was 'right, practically'. This is worse than Pirandello, q.v.: it has not even cynicism or guilt in it, it is selfish and obtuse.)

Still, that is enough said. If he kept off politics, especially the kind that threatened his good living and his picture collecting (he believed, and wrongly, that people who could afford to buy pictures were better judges of them than those who could only talk about them), he was, after all, subversive: his early poetry, with its new words and gaiety, deliberately sought to annoy. 'The Emperor of Ice Cream' (equally, 'The Emperor of "I

Scream" ') analyses its material into its Freudian components in spite of himself.

Stevens' first inspiration may well have been Moody (q.v.); at all events, those poems (his juvenilia), he said, 'gave him the creeps'. The sources for his mature manner were mostly French, and perhaps his greatest debt was to Léon-Paul Fargue (q.v.), whom he sometimes resembles quite closely. His American forebears were inferior poets: **Donald Evans** (1884–1921), a now forgotten Greenwich Village decadent who killed himself, and **Alfred Kreymborg** (1883–1969), a lesser imagist and a friend of Stevens', from whom he may have gathered some more general hints. Lacking (or eschewing) a central core of experience that compelled poems from him, Stevens' chief theme is the supremacy of the creative imagination. Like Robbe-Grillet (q.v.), Stevens sees order, form, as coming only from the creators of imaginary worlds. For all his sophistication he is, as Maurius Bewley has observed, a romantic, who believes in the transmuting powers of the imagination. This faith is most succinctly defined in the sequence called 'Notes Towards a Supreme Fiction', which some would put amongst his best poems. However, 'Sunday Morning' and the subtly autobiographical 'Le Monocle de Mon Oncle', both early poems, have the feeling this often verbally beautiful, but over-cerebral sequence lacks. In both, Stevens' manner functions as vitality, but is subdued by personal concerns rather than philosophizings. Nothing touches the note of such lines as the beautiful 'but until now I never knew/That fluttering things have so distinct a shade' or 'We live in an old chaos of the sun' until the serene final poems, when the threat of death edged safe business and prime capitalist living out of the foreground:

> Ariel was glad he had written his poems.
> They were of a remembered time
> Or of something seen that he liked.

It has been claimed that Stevens is the most important poet of the first half of the century with the 'possible' exceptions of Eliot, Pound and Frost (qq.v.): 'There are no other serious competitors'. This, it seems, is to put philosophy above poetry. Williams' poetry is surely much more 'important', though it is to be granted that it is nothing like as rewarding; and Ransom's (q.v.) achievement in individual poems is as great or greater. But to exegetic critics, it is true, Stevens offers most of all; ironically, it is his best work, mostly in *Harmonium*, that most strongly resists such attentions. Stevens did have an emotional life, but could not face up to its implications; but by not thinking about it he produced some sort of record of it. His inferior, pseudo-philosophical poetry, the 'abstract' stuff which excited some critics, did provide him with a means of keeping in practice.

E. E. Cummings (1894–1962), born in Cambridge, Massachusetts, is still regarded by some as a 'modern' poet. But he was a quirky traditionalist in all respects save two: he showed that typography – visual variations – could be useful; and his ear for the vernacular was sometimes, though not always, good. There are two Cummings: a versifier who disguises his sentimentalities and sometimes irregular but always conventional metrics by typographical tricks; and a magnificently aggressive comic and satirical poet who – alas – never quite grew up. Cummings had wanted to be a painter, and he did in fact execute strangely atrocious paintings all his life (his sense of colour can only be described as horrible). Instead of maturing he surrendered to – as his photographs and self-portrait show – self-love and arrogance: his language lost its edge, and he descended increasingly into the cliché from which his love poetry had never been wholly free. No amount of critical interpretation can disguise the tawdry third-rateness of the language in the following poem (drawn from Cummings' later work):

now all the fingers of this tree (darling) have
hands, and all the hands have people; and
more each particular person is (my love)
alive than every world can understand

and now you are and i am now and we're
a mystery which will never happen again,
a miracle which has never happened before –
and shining this our now must come to then

our then shall be some darkness during which
fingers are without hands; and i have no
you: and all trees are (any more than each
leafless) its silent in forevering snow

– but never fear (my own, my beautiful
my blossoming) for also then's until

This is the work of a man who has gone soft at the centre and likes himself too much to be able to see it. (Of course, at a private level it is perfectly acceptable – no one's business; but that is the trouble.) And yet he had once been very good indeed; more, I think, than the 'slight and charming' which has been allowed by him by his detractors. He had been able to criticize false patriotism and outworn literary language to admirable effect in such poems as 'come, gaze with me upon this dome'. Cummings has always been enormous fun, and, if one sounds a dissenting note, it is only because during his lifetime he had too much attention as a serious lyrical poet. He certainly deserves respect for his part in dismantling the genteel tradition. But diligent search fails to produce a single completely effective love poem: every one is marred by tentativeness or portentousness if not by that unquestioning sentimentality that is so odd in so fierce a satirist. The early poems are full of promise, but it was a promise that did not fully materialize. Cummings' originally childlike whimsicality and tweeness ('the little/lame balloon man'; 'hist whist/little ghost-things' – and so on) need not have been offensive; but he came to indulge it and, eventually, to confuse it with lyricism. The early love poems contain hints of a manner that Cummings might have developed, but most of them only conceal, by their eccentricity – which is of course often typographical – Cummings' failure to find a language. An exception is the fifth of the 'Songs' in *Tulips & Chimneys*: 'Doll's boy's asleep', in which a nursery rhyme insouciance is transformed into a note of genuine menace. But Cummings chose not to investigate the menace in his sexual emotions – he chose to avoid the crux of sexuality – and his best energies went into a satire that can be piercingly accurate, or merely hilarious – or funny but curiously diminishing, uncompassionate and perhaps insensitive. There are many poems like the one ending 'i try if you are a gentleman not to sense something un poco putrido/when we contemplate her uneyes safely ensconced in thick glass', and they are certainly funny; but there is an absence, elsewhere in Cummings' work, of a compensating pity: perhaps he imagined that the lyrics fill this role.

The fact is that for most of the time Cummings' fun is not quite good enough: not enough – the poet has been too keen to impress. If he does not diminish he patronizes. It has, however, been salutary to have someone like Cummings to ridicule and generally slam our philistine society of politicians and business men – and the pseudo-culture that nurses and sustains it. And then there are the splendid tough-guy poems, and the descriptions of low life. Cummings is seldom as empathetic as Williams (q.v.) in his descriptions ('It really must/be Nice, never to', XIII from *Is 5*, is one of the fine exceptions), since he is concentrating on a kind of audience that Williams has rejected, but his immense gaiety and humour ('what's become of maeterlinck/now that april's here?') give him a unique importance. The oft-repeated judgement that he is 'the Catullus of the modern movement' is quite wrong; he is cheerfully and most enjoyably obscene (as in his car poem: 'she being Brand/-new; and you/know consequently a/little stiff I was/careful of her ... just as we turned the corner of Divinity/avenue i touched the accelerator and give/her the juice, good ...'), as Catullus is, but the Latin poet could never have indulged in Cummings' sentimentalities. We are grateful to Cummings; but the reservations have to be made. It is astonishing how many readers and critics take Cummings' late nineteenth-century, neo-romantic love poetry to be modern because of its careful but logical surface pyrotechnics. What has not yet been fully grasped is that Cummings' experiments are extensions of traditionalism, not reachings-forward.

Cummings went to France in the First World War as a volunteer ambulance driver; as a result of his violation of the French censorship laws in a letter home, he was arrested and spent some time in a French prison camp. *The Enormous Room* (1922) was the result, a classic of its kind – in which, incidentally, Cummings shows his capacity to master the vernacular. *Eimi* (1933), an account of a visit to Russia, is less good, but contains some memorable passages; in it, too, we see Cummings' romanticism at its strongest and least self-indulgent. *Complete Poems* (1968; expanded 1982) supersedes previous collections.

A rather more important, but less striking and less heeded writer, is **Conrad Aiken** (1889–1973), born in Savannah, Georgia. He has not yet had the thoroughgoing critical treatment he needs. Aiken is a distinguished novelist, critic and short-story writer as well as a poet. It is often said of him that he did not realize his enormous gifts. But this is to ignore too much: *Senlin* (1918), the *Preludes for Memnon* (1931) – his best poems, still undervalued – the novel *Great Circle* (1933), a number of short stories, the autobiographical *Ushant* (1953). The four main influences on Aiken have been: his physician father's killing of his mother and subsequent suicide (in 1900), music, Freud, and nineteenth-century romantic poetry (from Poe to Swinburne). This last debt makes him – in many ways a modernist – a very odd man out indeed. He combines a luxuriant style with a psychological subtlety that has not been fully appreciated. Famous for such finely simple poetry as 'Discordants' (from *Turns and Movies*, 1916):

> Music I heard with you was more than music,
> And bread I broke with you was more than bread;
> Now that I am without you, all is desolate;
> All that was once so beautiful is dead.

Aiken can sustain such feeling in more complex poetry, as in the tragic Rilkean twenty-ninth prelude, which begins:

> What shall we do – what shall we think – what shall we say –?
> Why, as the crocus does, on a March morning,
> With just such shape and brightness; such fragility;
> Such white and gold, and out of just such earth.
> Or as the cloud does on the northeast wind –
> Fluent and formless; or as the tree that withers.

It takes much to maintain such pantheistic lyricism against the harsh sense of being human.

Aiken's weakness, despite his huge and unexcelled intellectual sophistication, is his romantic imitativeness; but at his best he has – as in the lines above – been able to find his own voice. He has been neglected because he has chosen to express himself, for the most part, in long poems or sequences, and these have simply not been explored. They should be. More than any other poet, he has wanted to allow the subconscious mind to speak for itself; but – paradoxically – he has organized the surface of his poetry most elaborately to that effect. This is to say that he has modified his bland lyrical flow only by such devices as have suggested themselves at the moment of composition; but the devices themselves are often complicated.

His short stories often deal poignantly with psychotic situations; more than any others, they are the stories of a poet. *Ushant* treats of the men he has known: it was he who showed Eliot's poems to Pound (qq.v.); he who helped to orient Malcolm Lowry (q.v.) imaginatively, truthfully and yet with a tact that he may have learned during his long stay, between wars, in England. Of his novels, *Great Circle* (1933), a treatment of the catastrophe of his childhood, seems certain to be revived and admired. An 'essential Aiken', which would be a very fat volume, would contain some of the most unusual and rewarding writing of our time.

By contrast, **Robinson Jeffers** (1887–1962), though he has a few staunch admirers, seems unlikely to survive, perhaps because his extreme pessimism is uncompensated for by any linguistic energy. He was born in Pittsburgh, Pennsylvania; from 1924 he lived in a stone house and tower – in Carmel, California – which he built himself. His philosophy is not new, but is not in itself uninteresting: man's intellectual capacities are a terrible delusion and they disgrace him and lead him into trouble. Stone, the sea: these endure. Animals: these have dignity and no aspiration. But nothing whatever happens in Jeffers' language, which is cliché-ridden and more often than not suggests that he was by no means convinced of his own beliefs, which were perhaps formulated as a response to his father's theological certainties. He had some narrative gift, of an old-fashioned kind; but his poems and plays hardly bear re-reading. His *Collected Poems* was published in 1948.

Louise Bogan (1897–1970), whose *Collected Poems* (1954) shared the Bollingen Prize with Léonie Adams (q.v.), was best known for her poetry reviews in *The New Yorker*. She was skilful and precise, and did enough to win gallant accolades such as 'the most distinguished woman poet of our time' (Allen Tate); but she lacked attack, and nothing she wrote is memorable.

Léonie Adams (1899), born in Brooklyn, is a different matter. Not too well known in her own country, she remains unpublished and unknown in Great Britain. Yet she is a most distinguished and original poet. She has been called romantic, but wrongly: rather, she has preserved the metaphysical tradition in a romantic diction. Of a gull alighting without a feather being stirred she says,

> So in an air less rare than longing might
> The dreams of flying lift a marble bird.

Her best poems are in *Poems: A Selection* (1954).

Both these poets are vastly superior to **Edna St. Vincent Millay** (1892–1950), who survives in Edmund Wilson's poignant memoir of her as a person, but hardly at all as a poet. Once very widely read, her proper place is beside Rupert Brooke (q.v.). A few of her lines have descriptive precision, but she left no single satisfactory poem. Her capacities are well illustrated by her lines: 'God! we could keep this planet warm/By friction, if the sun should fail'.

III

The late nineteenth century in America was a time of highly effective, bewitching actors (Robert Mantell, William Gillette, Richard Mansfield, John Drew, Jr.), but of mediocre drama. Ibsen made a late impact, and the plays through which the Americans were introduced to realism now seem melodramatic as well as sentimental. The energetic actor-manager and dramatist **Steele MacKaye** (1842–94) developed stage machinery and lighting, and trained actors. He was, if mostly in what he aspired to, an important influence on the future American stage. But not as a playwright: his own plays were pioneer in subject (*Hazel Kirke*, 1880, is the most famous) but weak in structure and dialogue. Much of the work of the real pioneer in playwriting, **Bronson Howard** (1842–1908), does not now seem an improvement; but, although his primary purpose was always to entertain, he was one of the first to treat his material thoughtfully – and he did develop. He was also the first American to make his living by writing for the stage. The loose ends of *Young Mrs. Winthrop* (1899), first produced in 1882, are sentimentally tied up in the last act; but its situation is realistic. One who did not hinder – though he hardly helped – the emergence of a realistic theatre was **David Belasco** (1859–1931), who also wrote plays – Puccini's opera is based on his *Girl of the Golden West* (1905). **Augustus Thomas** (1857–1934) was in the main simply a successful playwright, but he did have the serious purpose of showing the United States as it was, and he did help – with, for example, *As a Man Thinks* (1911), on faith healing – to clear the way for the 'problem play'. Neither **Clyde Fitch** (1865–1909) nor **James A. Herne** (1839–1901) wrote what we should call a good play. But both contributed in a small way to a specifically American theatre. The former's best plays were his study of a pathologically jealous woman, *The Girl with the Green Eyes* (1902), and *The City* (1909), which is one of the early stage attacks on political corruption. James A. Herne's *Margaret Fleming* (1890), about adultery, is superior. It seems maudlin and artificial to us now, but its theme deeply shocked the audiences – for the adultery is forgiven. It was praised by Howells and Garland (qq.v.). It is unfortunate that all these men worked to create the star system as well as an American theatre, since the star system is in many ways one of the banes of the modern American (and British) theatre; but they had little alternative if they wanted to eat. However, by 1896, with the formation of the first Theatrical Syndicate, the days of the actor-managers were effectually at an end. Philistinism and commerce moved into the theatre: it was hardly to be wondered at that business men, seeing a potential source of profit, should move in. In the first two decades of the century philistinism was countered by the formation of groups who, in one way or another, managed to make themselves independent. Winthrop Ames (1871–1937) inherited a fortune from his father, who was a railway magnate, and made three gallant efforts to found true repertory in New York; later he built two theatres. More important was the equally non-commercial Theatre Guild (1919), which began as the Washington Square Players in 1914. And most important of all was the Provincetown Players. This was founded in 1915 by the novelist and playwright **Susan Glaspell** (1882–1948), whose plays were competent although not inspired, and her husband George Cram Cook. Their experimentalism was important for giving Eugene O'Neill (q.v.), America's only great dramatist, the chances he needed to develop without commercial restrictions. As vital an influence on American theatre was George Pierce Baker (1866–1935), a Harvard professor who in 1905 set up the '47 Workshop', a course in playwrighting that was taken by, among others, Winthrop Ames, O'Neill, Philip

Barry, John Dos Passos, S.N. Behrman, Sidney Howard, Thomas Wolfe (qq.v.). Baker went to Yale in 1925, where he continued until his death. Wolfe's Professor Hatcher, in *Of Time and the River*, is a portrait of him.

The verse plays of William Vaughn Moody (q.v.) have already been mentioned; he was an intelligent man and an able craftsman, but he did not possess enough originality to achieve a real break-through. The best of all his works are *The Great Divide* (1909), a revision of an earlier play, about a girl who marries a man who has bought her against her will, and *The Faith Healer* (1909), about a genuine faith healer whose gift is destroyed by the scepticism of those around him. It was in this latter play that Moody came nearest to a truly modern style; but he was too inhibited to try for the rhythms of ordinary speech, and this failure seriously vitiates his achievement. **Edward Sheldon** (1886–1946) had similar difficulties with language, but had had the benefit of attending George Pierce Baker's classes. He was in fact its first distinguished graduate playwright, and his *Salvation Nell* (1908) was actually produced by the group. *The Nigger* (1909) and *The Boss* (1911) were both profoundly shocking in their day, the first because a white girl finally decided to marry the governor of a Southern state who discovers that he has Negro blood. Sheldon was blind and paralysed for the last fifteen years of his life, but continued until the end to act as consultant to actors, actresses and all connected with the theatre. His worst play, *Romance* (1913), a piece of skilfully executed middlebrow trash, was easily his most popular.

Steele MacKaye's (q.v.) son Percy MacKaye (q.v.) wrote an effective verse drama called *The Scarecrow* (1908), from Hawthorne's tale 'Feathertop'; but although this was the best thing he ever did, it solved no problems for the theatre.

Towering above these, and over all his successors, is the figure of **Eugene O'Neill** (1888–1953), the New York born son of the well known romantic actor James O'Neill, who was most celebrated in the part of the Count of Monte Cristo. O'Neill's mother was a drug addict and his brother an alcoholic. O'Neill himself suffered from ill-health for most of his life, and was, besides, a tortured soul – so much so that one of his biographers called his book *The Curse of the Misbegotten* (after O'Neill's title *A Moon for the Misbegotten*), and hardly descended into melodrama. O'Neill wrote successful plays in two styles, the realistic and the expressionist (qq.v.); he also might be said to have pursued two careers in the theatre, since he was silent for the twelve years between 1934 and 1946. In 1936 he was awarded the Nobel Prize.

The theatre was in O'Neill's blood; but before he came to it he tried Princeton (a year), poetry, mining, marriage (secret and dissolved), the sea (he voyaged to South America, South Africa, several times to England), newspaper reporting, sickness, tuberculosis; and then, after writing some short plays, he joined Baker's course. In 1915 he went to Provincetown, and the Provincetown Players' performance of his one-act *Bound East for Cardiff* – on a makeshift stage in a fishermen's shack at the end of a pier, while fog seeped through the wooden walls – initiated the true birth of the American theatre. It was also the début of a playwright whom no other of his century would outdo. Baker, and the men and women of the Provincetown Players – Robert Edmond Jones, the stage designer, is important among them – had heard of what was going on in Europe: of Antoine (q.v.) in France, Reinhardt (q.v.) in Germany, Strindberg (q.v.) in Sweden, Stanislavski (q.v.) in Russia. ... The American theatre had come of age, and its chief playwright had the required genius and nerve.

O'Neill had passion, gloom and an absolutely uncompromising realism; at the end, anguished, ill and personally unhappy though he was, he achieved a mood of something like reconciliation. The key to his achievement was stated by himself in a letter he wrote about his play *Mourning Becomes Electra*:

It needed great language ... I haven't got that. And, by way of self-consolation, I don't think, from the evidence of all that is being written today, that great language is possible for anyone living in the discordant, broken, faithless rhythm of our time. The best one can do is to be pathetically eloquent by one's moving, dramatic inarticulations.

O'Neill was right. No nineteenth- or twentieth-century dramatist has come near to what he called 'great language' (perhaps he was thinking of Shakespeare, as we all do), but he alone authentically yearned after it. Brecht (q.v.) achieved great language – but in his lyrical poetry. Only O'Neill achieved a dramatic framework whose interstices surround poetic silences, and whose 'inarticulations' are truly 'pathetic'. He has been attacked for not producing 'heroes of stature'; but that is one of the reasons why he is truly modern.

Beyond the Horizon (1920), his first full-length play, is a naturalistic study of two brothers, each of whom makes the wrong choice in life, and is defeated through mistakes induced by sexual drive. *The Emperor Jones* (1921) is a piece of expressionism conceived before O'Neill knew anything of the European expressionists: a Caribbean Negro dictator flees from his victims to the sound of a relentlessly beating drum. *The Hairy Ape* (1922), another expressionistic play, deals with a brutish stoker, a sort of McTeague (q.v.) Yank, who yearns for a more human fulfilment; he ends by trying to retreat into what he thinks he is, by embracing a gorilla – which kills him.

Desire Under the Elms (1925), largely prompted by O'Neill's interest in Freudian psychology, is a return to realism, and is one of his most powerful plays.

The Great God Brown (1926) is probably too experimental for the stage, although it reads well. In it O'Neill used masks to try to define the difference between the bourgeois and the creative temperaments – but his chief character Dion Anthony (Dionysus-St. Anthony) is too symbolic, even though his anguished vacillation between pagan creativeness and Christian morality is at times most intensely and movingly conveyed. In *Marco Millions* (1928) O'Neill turned unsuccessfully to satire: this lampoon of materialism is both too obvious and tedious. There is no tension. *Dynamo* (1929) is O'Neill's worst and most theory-ridden play. Aware that he was troubled by the loss of the Catholic faith of his childhood, he tried an experiment in which he did not really believe, melodramatically showing a young man's failure to substitute faith in a dynamo for the Calvinistic faith of his childhood. *Days without End* (1934) has two actors playing the same (divided) man: a sceptic and a believer. Nothing demonstrates more clearly O'Neill's failure to rediscover Catholicism, although at the time it was widely believed that he had returned to it.

Between these two disastrous attempts, O'Neill had written the finest of all the plays of his earlier period: the trilogy, *Mourning Becomes Electra*, based on Aeschylus' Orestean trilogy. O'Neill took a New England family in the aftermath of the Civil War and fairly carefully paralleled the Greek story: the returning General Ezra Mannon is killed by his wife Christine, whose lover Adam Brant is then killed by their son Orin, egged on by their daughter, Lavinia. Christine kills herself, Orin goes mad and commits suicide, whereupon Lavinia shuts herself up for ever with an unrelievable guilty conscience in the family mansion. This was presented in relentlessly Freudian terms, which led many critics to describe it as a case-study rather than a tragedy. O'Neill has also been attacked for his prosaic language at moments of enormous stress. But may we not, in retrospect – having had the opportunity to study the 'great language' of the wretched Christopher Fry, or even that of Tennessee Williams (qq.v.) – be grateful for this alleged 'flatness'? O'Neill knew he could not attain the great language he yearned for. And so, unlike so many lesser playwrights, he did not attempt it. One suspects that his critics would too easily forgive a heady, contrived rhetoric of the kind so often produced by Tennessee Williams – a pseudo-poetry; dramatic occasions demand 'high' language. I think O'Neill was right, and that the plays are better without such language.

By 1934 O'Neill had made two more marriages, the latter of which was not unsuccessful. He went into a state of semi-permanent depression from about the mid-Thirties until the end of the war. He destroyed much that he wrote in this period, but by 1946 he felt able to release *The Iceman Cometh* (1946), which he had written in 1939. O'Neill's experiments were necessary to him, but he always returned to the realistic mode. *The Iceman Cometh*, set in a disreputable dive for down-and-outs and outcasts, is entirely realistic; no gimmicks are required. The Iceman of the title is death, which is the only release from the illusions that torment mankind. The salesman Hickey tells all the drinkers in Harry Hope's bar that their only chance of happiness is to renounce hope. Previously happy in their absurd and drunken way, they now disbelieve Hickey and go out to prove him wrong. But each returns: broken. Then Hickey turns out to have killed his wife. When he gives himself up to the police, all but one of them return to their old contentment. Like Dreiser (q.v.), though in an utterly different and more poetic manner, O'Neill here richly conveys the actual grain of life. It does not much matter if you agree with his philosophy or not. Its torpor is counteracted by the lyricism of the outcasts' hope – and of their despair.

O'Neill wrote a number of other plays, none of which was performed in his lifetime. *A Moon for the Misbegotten* (1952) was withdrawn while on trial. *More Stately Mansions* (1964), a study of the breakdown of a poetic soul into madness, has only been tried out in a cut, Swedish version. *A Touch of the Poet* (1957), the sole survivor from a projected eleven-play cycle called *A Tale of Possessors Self-Dispossessed*, contains an unforgettable portrait of a man who seems to attain stature through self-deceit and selfishness. In the one-act *Hughie* (1959) and *Long Day's Journey into Night* (1956) O'Neill rose to the heights of his achievement. In *Hughie* he perfectly captures a vernacular more difficult than that of his early sea dramas: the speech of seedy, boastful New York drifters of the Twenties. *Long Day's Journey into Night*, a semi-autobiographical family-drama, is his simplest play. Here O'Neill demonstrates his genius beyond doubt: there is no plot and no drama, the play is very long – and yet it holds the attention. Alan S. Downer has written wisely of it: 'It cannot be overemphasized that this is a play of reconciliation; the audience that has experienced *Long Day's Journey* cannot go out of the theatre without a greater capacity for tolerance and understanding. . . .'

Not one of O'Neill's American and British contemporaries and successors can be compared to him: his plays are torn from him; theirs are, at best, made. American theatre, like the British, lacked vitality in the Thirties, and this lack was made even more manifest by the example of O'Neill, who could be criticized for all sorts of faults, but never for lack of vitality or attack. Only Pirandello, Brecht, Lorca and perhaps Synge (qq.v.) are the equal of O'Neill in our century.

The verse drama does not seem to be a viable form in our century (the German habit of writing in verse is hardly relevant here), despite valiant attempts; it has been as successful in America as almost anywhere.

Archibald MacLeish (1892–1982) wrote *Nobo-daddy* (1926), the labour play *Panic* (1935), and *J.B.* (1958), his most successful play, in which a contemporary Job acts out his story in a circus tent. He also wrote several effective verse plays for radio, including *Air Raid* (1938). MacLeish began as a poet, and his *The Hamlet of A. MacLeish* (1928), one of those long poems inspired by the success of *The Waste Land* (q.v.), was taken with seriousness. He shifted from the extreme subjectivity of this poem to a somewhat simple-minded advocacy of full political 'engagement'. He was Librarian of Congress 1939–44, and was influential in the Roosevelt administration. He ranks, David Ray has written (damning with faint praise?), 'with Robinson Jeffers and Carl Sandburg in the penetration of public taste'. But not, one has to add, with Brecht (q.v.). MacLeish has written sincere and unpretentious verse, and has been an admirable public man – one of the most admirable of the time, a genuinely well-intentioned link between poets and an establishment that cannot take them into account. The poetry of his plays, however, contributes nothing whatever to them. *J.B.* was apparently personally inspiring to a number of those who watched it; this is admirable. But the nature of the inspiration is nearer to that of a good sermon or exhortation than to, say, Sherwood Anderson's (q.v.) various autobiographical writings. These are true literature because they never exhort: the author lives entirely in his imagination. MacLeish appears to have no such imaginative, internal centre.

The same applies to **Maxwell Anderson** (1888–1959), who wrote plays in verse (and, in 1925, one book of poetry) and yet who was not a poet. He tried for the 'great language' that O'Neill (q.v.) knew could not be achieved: he felt that there could be no 'great drama' without 'great poetry', and he did not claim that his own verse was well written. He may have been right about 'great drama'; the trouble was that he thought anyone could write poetry – if 'badly' – not realizing that it takes a poet. The career of Anderson, a worthy, gifted and sincere writer, and a fine craftsman of the theatre, affords an illustration of the harsh fact that art and commerce do not and cannot really mix. Art may or may not be successful in terms of the market; once a writer orients himself towards the market, however, he destroys his imaginative credibility. Anderson was a serious man who nevertheless conceived it as his duty to entertain middlebrow audiences. His and **Laurence Stallings'** (1894–1968) *What Price Glory* (1924), on the American soldiery of the First World War, was a hit. It was outspoken for its time, but its realism is in fact tawdry and its comedy as second-hand as it is second-rate. Anderson improved on this, but always conceived of a play not only as a dramatically viable entity but also as suitable fare for commercial audiences, whom he believed he could convert to his own humane point of view. And so he did; but this, like a response to Billy Graham, was temporary, because Anderson did not write from his imagination. Verse operates in his drama as an effective rhetoric. True, it is a rather less meretricious rhetoric than that of Christopher Fry (q.v.), but it is never remotely poetic. *Elizabeth the Queen* (1930), on Elizabeth and Essex, was the first modern blank-verse play to pay at the box-office. *Both Your Houses* (1933) attacked political corruption. Probably Anderson's most famous play was *Winterset* (1935), his second attempt to deal with the truly tragic material of the Sacco-Vanzetti case. It was a success at the time, but a total failure in literary terms: as Edmund Wilson wrote, 'in the text I could not discover anything that seemed to me in the least authentic as emotion, idea or characterization'. He rated Anderson more highly as a prose playwright. Anderson's best is in fact the relaxed musical comedy *Knickerbocker Holiday* (1938), which had the inestimable advantage of a score by Kurt Weill. Anderson came off in his lifetime, and deserved to; it seems unlikely that any of his plays will survive.

Sidney Howard (1891–1939), a Californian who died prematurely in an accident with a tractor on his farm, was as skilful as Anderson (q.v.), but more orthodox. He was a member of Baker's '47 Workshop'. His first play, in verse, flopped; he took the hint and did not return to this medium. Howard went on to do fine, conscientious work of all kinds – translations (Vildrac's *S.S. Tenacity*, q.v.), adaptations (*The Late Christopher Bean*, 1932), documentaries (*Yellow Jack*, with Paul de Kruif, 1934) as well as original plays. *They Knew What They Wanted* (1924), which was granted a second lease of life in 1957 as the musical *The Most Happy Fella*, was a lively comedy about a Californian grapegrower and his mail-order bride, and immediately established Howard. In the same year

Howard collaborated with Edward Sheldon (q.v.) on *Bewitched*. *The Silver Cord* (1926) was an unsentimental and psychologically accurate portrayal of a possessive mother, and would stand revival. *Paths of Glory* (1935), adapted from a novel by Humphrey Cobb, was an excellent anti-war play, and was made into a moving film with real and effective bitterness against war. Howard listened carefully to common speech and reported it accurately. He is an example of the man who does the best he can – rather than compromise himself – with a limited imagination: a really good second-class playwright.

Robert Sherwood (1896–1955), a forthright radical who was gassed in the First World War, and put much of his energy into anti-totalitarian activities, was perhaps as skilful – but more trivial. *The Petrified Forest* (1935), although its theme is ostensibly the disintegration of the artist in modern society, suffers from technical slickness and sentimentality, though the movie gave Humphrey Bogart his first important part. The 'continental' comedy *Reunion in Vienna* (1931) is not as intellectually ambitious, and is Sherwood's best play. A psychiatrist thinks that a love-affair his wife is conducting with Prince Maximilian Rudolph, whose mistress she has been, will cure her of an obsession; his complacency is shattered. Apart from this and *Tovarich* (1936), which he adapted, Sherwood is probably better regarded as an admirable journalist than as an imaginative writer. He wrote some of Roosevelt's speeches.

Elmer Rice (ps. **Elmer Reizenstein**, 1892–1967), a worthy man of the theatre, may be described as an experimentalist of abundant gifts but no genius. Rice, like Sherwood (q.v.), is a radical, and has on several occasions taken a stand against censorship and witch-hunting by the authorities. His first play, *On Trial* (1914), a thriller, used the movie technique of flashback. *The Adding Machine* (1923) depicts Mr. Zero, executed for the murder of his boss, dissatisfied in the Elysian Fields and returning to the earth to become a perfect slave of the machine age. This is wholly expressionistic in technique, and a fine satire, which Rice has not bettered. Unfortunately Rice has no capacity for psychological penetration or characterization – even of the workmanlike sort practised by Howard (q.v.) – and this has tended to impoverish his drama. His best plays after *The Adding Machine* are the realistic *Street Scene* (1929), *Dream Girl* (1945) and *Cue for Passion* (1958).

Philip Barry (1896–1949), another of Baker's pupils, collaborated with Rice (q.v.) in *Cock Robin* (1928). Barry was another prolific, intelligent and workmanlike playwright. Many of his plays are comedies with a serious note; the others tend to be his best. *You and I* (1923) is a poignant study of a father who discovers his own frustrations when he tries to turn his son into an artist. *Hotel Universe* (1930) was perhaps unfortunate: this drama of an old man who helps people to find themselves was rather too well made and contrived, but some of the individual portraits – including a man who has lost his faith and a girl whose love is unrequited – are excellent. He realized his potential most fully in *Here Come the Clowns* (1938), an odd and disturbing play about the effects of a magician's hypnotic powers on a vaudeville troupe. Barry was also responsible for the smooth and entertaining *The Philadelphia Story* (1939).

S.N. Behrman (1893), yet another of Baker's pupils, tried to combine comedy with social drama, and dealt, in *No Time for Comedy* (1939), with his own predicament. Once again, too much skill at entertainment vitiated seriousness. He adapted, with Joshua Logan, Pagnol's *Fanny* (q.v.) as a musical comedy in 1945.

George S. Kaufman (1889–1961) and **Marc Connelly** (1890) began in collaboration, with several plays, the most successful of which was *Beggar on Horseback* (1924), an expressionist satire on the oppression of the artist (here, a composer) by bourgeois society. Kaufman went on to write several smooth farces, some with **Moss Hart** (1904–61), including the famous and deftly written portrait of Alexander Woollcott, *The Man Who Came to Dinner* (1939). Connelly's Negro play, *The Green Pastures*, has a little more weight; but this well-meant picture – based on a well-known book of sketches – of the Negro conception of the Old Testament is at heart both folksy and patronizing rather than dignified and poetic.

The Thirties saw the rise of a more aggressive social theatre, whose white hope was **Clifford Odets** (1906–63). Odets was a protégé of the important Group Theatre, founded by Harold Clurman, Lee Strasberg and Cheryl Crawford in 1931. The actor and director Elia Kazan was early associated with this venture, which devoted itself to Stanislavsky's (q.v.) principles of group acting. (Kazan later, 1947, founded the influential Actors' Studio, which taught the Method, a technique in which the actor is exhorted to 'become' the part he is playing. The Method is less different from other methods of training actors than some have thought, since every actor should in one way or another 'become' the stage-person he is representing – provided he does not forget the audience.) Odets began with *Waiting for Lefty* (1935), an effective and bitter piece, without characterization, about a taxicab strike. *Awake and Sing* (1935), ecstatic, well made, at times funny, established him as the leading playwright of his generation. *Golden Boy* (1937) is so well done that its central character, a musician who turns under economic pressure to professional boxing, is made almost credible. By the time of *The Big Knife* (1948) Odets, while he retained all his skill, had become affected by the pressures involved in producing big, successful plays: this indictment of Hollywood seems to come right out of Hollywood itself.

Sidney Kingsley (1906) was another competent social dramatist, responsible for the originals of the movies *Dead End* and *Detective Story*. His first play, *Men in White* (1933) about a young doctor's indecisions, is among his best. *They Shall Not Die* (1934) by **John Wesley** (1902) and *Stevedore* (1934) by **Paul Peters** (1908) were more strident: written with the leftist fervour of Odets (q.v.), they lacked his passionateness and concern for character.

John Howard Lawson (1895) preceded all these left-wing or Marxist playwrights. Lawson began with expressionist plays, such as *Roger Bloomer* (1923) and *Processional* (1925), all of which harped on class distinction. In 1936 he wrote a Marxist textbook of proletarian theatre. Once again, although he is a very skilful writer, he is best considered as a journalist and a propagandist for social change. Really only Odets (q.v.), of the social and Marxist dramatists, achieved anything beyond the journalistic – and he did not altogether fulfil his promise.

Lillian Hellman (1905–85), who was born in New Orleans, is as radical as any of these, but is less ideological and more interested in characterization. Her one attempt at a proletarian piece, *Days to Come* (1936), about a strike, failed. She is one of the most able and effective of modern dramatists in the old 'well-made' technique. Her first play, *The Children's Hour* (1934), about a schoolgirl who maliciously accuses her two headmistresses of being lesbian, is skilful but ambiguous in that it leaves the audience in doubt as to whether the greater vileness in the play is the child's false accusation or lesbianism itself. *The Little Foxes* (1939) is an excellent study of greed and unpleasantness: a Southern family seizes its opportunities as industrialism rises there. Her next two plays, *Watch on the Rhine* (1941) and *The Searching Wind* (1944), were finely made propaganda against fascism and opportunistic appeasement respectively. Then came her best play: *Another Part of the Forest* (1946), a comic study, rightly described as Jonsonian, of hateful people cheating each other. *Toys in the Attic* (1960) embodies Lillian Hellman's most memorable portrait of an evil person, and her most hopeful (if defeated) one. Charges of misanthropy against Miss Hellman are frivolous, and come from those whose optimism is flabby. But the 'well-madeness' of her plays does tend to vitiate them, even though one recognizes that she cannot proceed except in this way. *Another Part of the Forest* is a picaresque comedy, and is freer from the limitations of 'sardoodledom' (q.v.) than any other of her plays. (*The Little Foxes*, written earlier, is its sequel in time.)

William Saroyan (1908), born of Armenian parents in California, had exuberance, energy and tenderness; he might have been a major writer, and as it is he is now an undervalued one; unfortunately he was seldom able to control his sentimentality, or force himself into moods in the least discriminatory. For this naïve (q.v.), all that matters is the glory of the dream. 'He puts everything in', one critic has said, 'in case he misses anything important'. He never went beyond his fictional début, *The Daring Young Man on the Flying Trapeze* (1934), short stories written with a strikingly innocent eye and a direct, appealing lyricism. Saroyan went on to produce much more fiction of the same sort, but the good bits become harder to find. He made his début as a playwright with *My Heart's in the Highlands* (1939) and *The Time of Your Life* (1939), the curious opposite of O'Neill's *The Iceman Cometh* (q.v.) since the somewhat similar central character dispenses happiness, not despair. For a time it looked to many people as though Saroyan might become an important figure in the theatre, but he lacked craftsmanship and discipline, and all his promise petered out into showy, patchy, sentimental drama such as *The Beautiful People* (1941) or improvisations such as his more recent *Sam the Highest Jumper of them All* (1960). One play stands out among all the others: *Hello Out There* (1942), a genuinely tragic one-act piece about the lynching of a tramp. Saroyan can be silly ('I am so innately great by comparison others who believe they are great ... seem to me to be only pathetic, although occasionally charming'), and he has produced masses of rubbish; but his best is worth looking for.

Thornton Wilder (1897–1975), born at Madison, Wisconsin, novelist and playwright, has certainly been an odd man out throughout his career; his work, unquestionably skilful, intelligent and technically resourceful, has been the subject of much controversy: is he at heart a middlebrow charlatan exploiting the discoveries and procedures of his betters, or is he an original writer with something of his own to say? The truth is that Wilder seems pretentious because (as he himself has come near to admitting) he can never answer the huge questions he asks. He is by no means a middlebrow in intention, and he has specifically stated that one of the problems of the modern dramatist is to create a theatre that will be genuinely disturbing to its audience. But in actually dealing with this problem he has succeeded in pleasing rather than worrying them: they can think they are worried, but are not really. He lacks an inner core of imaginative resilience, or passion, and consequently too quickly falls back on mere cleverness, laced with folksiness and sentimentality. In other words, his unconventionality resides in his daring technique rather than in his somewhat unoriginal content. The impact of his plays (and novels, with one exception) is perfectly middlebrow in that it provokes superficial 'discussion' rather than meditation or wonder. *Our Town* (1938) gives the intimate history of a New Hampshire town by means of a bare stage (a shrewd reaction against the theatre's obsession at this time with décor) and a choric stage manager, who describes the characters and talks casually to the audience. It is a dazzling performance, but all it ultimately offers is the rather mundane thought that there is 'something way down deep that's eternal about a human being': a Yankee inarticulateness underlies the high articulateness of the bright presentation. In *The Skin of Our Teeth* (1942) the Antrobus family represent humanity and the escape, by the proverbial skin, from most of the terrors that are known to have beset the race. This is again brilliant; but an arch folksiness precludes real warmth.

Wilder's first popular success was the novel *The Bridge of San Luis Rey* (1927), which traces the fortunes of a number of people killed when a South American bridge collapses. But this was meretricious compared with his first novel, *The Cabala* (1926), or with the most solid of all his works, *Heaven's My Destination* (1935), about a book salesman called

George Brush, a foolish saint, who reminds one of Duhamel's Salavin (q.v.). In this comic story Wilder found his own voice, and although his plays have their moving moments, they never measure up to this (he did not come back to fiction until 1967, with *The Eighth Day*; this has all the old brilliance of technique, but is otherwise sadly disappointing), which is a major work.

*

Since the Second World War the theatre almost everywhere has got increasingly into the hands of the directors; in certain cases the public are even more interested in the producers of plays than their authors. Americans have reacted to this by going 'off Broadway', and now this is where most of the dramatic energy lies. Great Britain is beginning to follow suit. The development is a healthy one, because it means that playwrights, writing for tiny audiences, are able to get away from commercial demands to fulfil artistic ones. This kind of theatre sees as much rubbish as the commercial theatre; but the good writers have more chance. However, the playwrights who dominated the immediate postwar scene – Tennessee Williams, Arthur Miller and, to a lesser extent, William Inge (qq.v.) – had to fight for recognition in the commercial theatre. This is an artistically dangerous business – not everyone is Shakespeare, who was, of course, a commercial success.

Tennessee Williams (ps. **Thomas Lanier Williams**, 1911–83) was born in Mississippi. His father was a salesman who was probably (according to a gossipy book Williams' mother wrote) a mean drunk; at all events in his childhood he knew more anger and alienation than love. After much struggle to establish himself, Williams found an agent who believed in him, and in 1945, with *The Glass Menagerie*, he became accepted. His persistent theme is the agonized, even shrieking alienation of violent and crippled eccentrics: homosexuals, madmen, sex-driven women. The air his characters naturally breathe is that of romantic hysteria; without it they would wilt and die immediately. He combines lush vulgarity with lyrical despair, to produce plays of undeniable power. But their language is not enduring, and they fade in the mind. He is adept at presenting nerve-shot situations, but has never written a successful play of reconciliation. His characters are happiest at not being happy, and when his plots contrive to satisfy them they protest by being totally unconvincing: a tribute to the power of his depiction of despair. Williams shows sensitive people as being ravished by the brutal and materialistic demands of society. But this is not genuine social comment: his sensitives are too often hopeless and irremediably crippled neurotics, and 'society' is represented by persons whose greed or lust or dishonesty is pathological. He loves the grotesque, and in effect he pays tribute to it by lyrically depicting hells on earth. But he could move convincingly.

His first success, *The Glass Menagerie* – his twelfth play – is his tenderest and best: this account of a slightly crippled girl's coming briefly out of the world of dreams she lives in – symbolized by a menagerie of glass animals – is moving within a non-pathological realm. The rest of Williams' plays are set in a pathological world that does not often allow the spectator to visualize his own world – equally tragic – that is not entirely peopled by freaks. *A Streetcar Named Desire* (1947) almost succeeds, but Blanche, its heroine, destroyed and driven into madness by the hideous Stanley, is herself too impossible to gain full sympathy. *The Rose Tattoo* (1951), about Gulf-coast Sicilians, declines into sentimentality and a false vitality. *Camino Real* (1953), a fantasy, is another failure: it has theatre-life, as a clever rhetoric, but a cool reading exposes its pretensions – and reveals the meagreness of linguistic resource which is Williams' basic weakness. The more realistic *Cat on a Hot Tin Roof* (1955), dealing with the frustrations and anguishes of a Southern family, contains some marvellously evocative individual portraits – Big Daddy, his alcoholic son Brick who cannot face up to the homosexual component in himself, his wife Maggie – but does not altogether succeed in setting them against each other. This is a play in which Williams, not dishonestly, tries to suggest the possibility of future happiness (for Maggie and the too detached Brick); but it remains unconvincing. In the Gothic *Suddenly Last Summer* (1958) the homosexual 'poet' Edward, the unseen hero, is eaten by the boys he has used (a characteristically vague allusion to Orpheus being devoured by furies). His mother, in order to inherit his fortune, is glad to submit her daughter-in-law to a lobotomy. The language here is particularly thin, and the intentions confused; but there are moments of power. More recently Williams wrote *Sweet Bird of Youth* (1959), the factitious *The Night of the Iguana* (1961) and *The Eccentricities of a Nightingale* (1965). Williams, gifted as a realist, has chosen – and on balance the choice is probably a correct one – to work in more or less expressionist modes. This leads him into some difficulties with language; but he does gain poetic, and sometimes heartrending, effects from his juxtapositions of characters and settings. He is a writer as flawed as any of his heroes; but more of a genius, too, than any of them. In 1969 he joined the Roman Catholic Church, perhaps as a substitute for the writing of plays, which had served (he has said) as 'therapy' to reduce tension. He is the author of a not outstanding novel, *The Roman Spring of Mrs. Stone* (1950), another later one no better, many short stories (*One Arm*, 1948; *Hard Candy*, 1954; *It Happened the Day the Sun Rose*, 1982) and some fuzzy, mystical verse that is collected in *In the Winter of Cities* (1956 rev. 1964). He has not really, as a writer, faced up to the problem that obsesses him: homosexual anguish.

Arthur Miller (1915), who was born in New York City, has by contrast more of the journalist and social reformer than of the poet in him, but is as important as Williams (q.v.). Miller began to write plays while at the University of Michigan, won prizes, and after graduation (1938) worked for the Federal Theatre Project. (This, which lasted from the autumn of 1935 to the summer of 1939, was the first American state-sponsored theatre project, a typically New Deal enterprise which invented such devices as the Living Newspaper, and encouraged Negro theatre; it was suppressed by reactionary elements in Congress.) *Situation Normal* (1944) was a rather flat and starry-eyed piece of reportage about military life; *Focus* (1955) is an ironic novel about anti-semitism: the protagonist is an anti-semitic Gentile who gets demoted when a new pair of spectacles makes him appear Jewish; but he is slow to learn the lesson, and when he finally does his transformed character is unconvincing.

In 1947, with the strong drama of *All My Sons* (1947), Miller established himself as, with Tennessee Williams, America's leading young dramatist. This is a straightforward, traditional play, which shows the strong influence of Ibsen (q.v.), whose *Enemy of the People* Miller adapted in 1951. Joe Keller has in the war allowed some faulty engine parts to be sent to the air force, which has meant the deaths of some pilots; his partner has been wrongly blamed and imprisoned, while he was exonerated. Now, after the war, his son discovers his guilt – and that his own elder brother, having realized their father's guilt, has allowed himself to be killed as a kind of expiation. Joe, after trying to wriggle out of his responsibility in every way, kills himself when he realizes that those dead pilots were all his sons. ... This is a good, well constructed play, but nothing out of the ordinary. Far superior is *Death of a Salesman* (1949), which was directed by Elia Kazan (q.v.) and had the excellent Lee J. Cobb in the leading role. Willy Loman, who is presented with great compassion, is perhaps still the most vivid example on the modern stage of the 'other directed' man of modern industrial societies that David Riesman postulated in his (and collaborators') *The Lonely Crowd*: the social character who is controlled by the expectations of other people, the 'marketing character' of Erich Fromm (who has influenced Riesman), who becomes anxious when he 'lapses' from the standards of selling himself to other people. Like all his kind, Willy preaches the bourgeois virtues to his family; but in reality he accepts dishonesty. But Miller shows him as possessing a humanity that, deep down, recognizes this. His suicide is genuinely tragic.

The Crucible (1953), about the notorious Salem witch trials, was performed at a time when witch-hunting for communists was prevalent in the United States. This is a play about commitment, and the French movie script was written by Sartre (q.v.): condemned to die for witchcraft, John Proctor confesses to it to save his life – but then refuses to live, and thus triumphs.

In 1956 Miller married the film-actress Marilyn Monroe, and became the object of a good deal of publicity which did not help his creative life. He wrote a film for her, *The Misfits* (1961), which is presented in its published form as a kind of novel; this is interesting, but its attempt to show how innocence (Miller had seen Marilyn Monroe as innocent) is destroyed was vitiated by the nature of the medium itself. The ending is sentimental – and Miller does not really suffer from sentimentality. He and Marilyn Monroe were divorced in 1960.

After the Fall (1964) is overtly autobiographical, though Miller later denied this: Maggie is clearly a representation of Marilyn Monroe (who had recently died) and Quentin is the 'intellectual' Miller. It is as good as any of Miller's previous plays, and is most notable for its maturity – a maturity beyond that of any commercial audience – and its refusal to find easy or glib solutions. In *Incident at Vichy* (1964), a semi-documentary, about the Nazis' treatment of various Frenchmen, he seemed to be marking time, but the play is workmanlike and more than mere entertainment. He has not written anything very substantial since.

It is in Miller that 'social realism', in the most intelligent, Ibsenian sense, has found its best and most compassionate playwright.

William Inge (1913–73), who was born in Kansas, is more conventional in technique than either Williams or Miller (qq.v.); his plays are not as ambitious, but he has successfully portrayed midwest people, intelligently revealing them as they are beneath the public surface. *Come Back, Little Sheba* (1950) is one of the best of modern plays on the subject of alcoholism. *Picnic* (1953) and *Bus Stop* (1955) became famous in movie versions; in the latter the old technical device of bringing strangers fortuitously together is given new life by fine characterization and convincing dialogue. *The Dark at the Top of the Stairs* (1958) is that darkness into which both the child of a family and its parents dare not – whatever they pretend – climb up to. *A Loss of Roses* (1960) was a disappointment: the relationship between a mother and her son clearly springs from a psychiatric textbook rather than from a human situation. Inge is perhaps not more than a useful playwright (in the sense that Telemann and Hindemith are useful composers) – but this is something considerable in its own right.

The off-Broadway movement has not yet brought many playwrights to prominence; but that sort of prominence may not be what the real theatre needs. However, three dramatists who have graduated from this milieu to some commercial success should be mentioned. The best known, **Edward Albee** (1928), is not necessarily superior, although his *Who's Afraid of Virginia Woolf?* (1963) is more substantial than anything so far written by **Jack Gelber** (1932) or **Jack Richardson** (1934). Albee is unusual in that he seems to have nothing in him of American optimism, and actually began – with *The Zoo Story* (1959) – with an example of the Theatre of the Absurd (q.v.). Even so, this brilliant dialogue does end both violently and sentimentally: a gesture, it seems, to the American insistence on one or the other (in the absence of actual Utopian choruses). Its theme – a young homosexual inveigles an ordinary bourgeois into killing him – foreshadowed that of its successors, except for *The Death of Bessie Smith* (1959) and *The American Dream* (1960). The adventure into realism of the former has a shocking subject: the real reasons for the refusal of a hospital for whites to admit the injured blues singer, whom they could have saved. But it is no more than a dreary and uninteresting protest piece. *The American Dream* abandons realism, and is better. This is a send-up of America in terms of its clichés, beautifully heard and reproduced, that resembles Karl Kraus (q.v.) even more than Ionesco (q.v.), upon whose techniques it greatly depends.

Who's Afraid of Virginia Woolf? (1963) is superbly inventive theatre, but is ultimately sterile, inasmuch as it amounts to an alyrical assault not merely on marriage but on all heterosexuality. Or that is how I read it. But its dialogue is masterly in its capture – or deadly parody – of a certain kind of upper middle-class Americanese; and throughout there is a yearning for understanding. *Tiny Alice* (1965) is a kind of disguised well-made play. A story of the richest woman in the world who seduces, marries and destroys a Catholic lay-brother, it works well on the stage, but reads badly except to critics set on interpreting its incredibly complicated symbolism. Once again, the real theme is the horror any man lays in store for himself by having truck with the evil trickster Woman. But for some the mood and language raise the play above this. In *A Delicate Balance* (1966) Albee returns to more realistic family horrors, but the message is similar. Albee does not of course load the dice against women, or make his men paragons – he is too intelligent; it is simply that one gets a strong sense, from his plays, that for him femininity is the ultimate destroyer and spoiler of happiness. But the greatly inferior William Burroughs (q.v.) is completely (and stupidly) explicit on this point, whereas it would certainly be doing Albee an injustice to suggest that this is his rational view. Albee has made excellent adaptations of Carson McCullers' *The Ballad of the Sad Café* (q.v., 1963) and *Malcolm* (1965), James Purdy's (q.v.) novel. Albee alternates adaptations with original plays, and, while the adaptations remain excellent, the language of the original plays has become coarser and more rhetorical; but in the theatre Albee remains compelling.

Jack Gelber's *The Connection* (1960) vacillates too uncertainly between realism and expressionism – Gelber is not sure whether he wants to protest against the drug laws or to depict a group of junkies waiting for their fix – but is nevertheless a vivid and accurate presentation of people who simply don't want anything to do with society. Its form is interesting: a jazz quartet improvises on the stage, two film cameramen become involved in the action; the aimless dialogue is authentic. *The Apple* (1961), an improvisation, departs more radically from the conventional theatre, but is less successful. *On Ice* (1965), a novel about a hipster called Manny, is surprisingly low in energy and humour. Gelber has continued to write plays – *Starters* (1980) – and he also works in the theatre; but he has never equalled his first play.

Jack Richardson's *The Prodigal* (1960), an acerb and witty treatment of the Orestes theme, came from off Broadway; so did his *Gallows Humour* (1961). *The Prison Life of Harris Philmore* (1961) is a novel. Richardson has for some reason written no plays since 1968: he does not much like the theatre.

Another American dramatist who has attracted attention by serious work is **Paddy Chayefsky** (1923). He began as a television playwright, and became famous when *Marty* (1953) was filmed, with Ernest Borgnine. *The Bachelor Party* (1954), a touching but not quite unsentimental play, was also filmed. Chayefsky was attacked for his 'tape recorder' realism, and has unwisely tried in his stage plays for symbolic effects which do not really suit him. For *The Tenth Man*, his best play, he combined an authentic Bronx setting with the Jewish legend of the Dybbuk.

However, despite the vitality and proper irreverence of the off-Broadway drama, the American theatre is in decline. Critics have tried to compare Albee to O'Neill (qq.v.), but this is foolish, especially when it is suggested that the former is 'more articulate' (Leonard Ashley). It is significant that Richardson has remained silent so far as the theatre is concerned. But mention should be made of one fine playwright who died young. **Lorraine Hansberry** (1930–65) called herself a 'playwright who happened to be black', and this was a sensible self-characterization. She began as a painter, but found that she was not good enough to satisfy her high standards. In *A Raisin in the Sun* (1959), rightly called the best American play of the Fifties, she depicted an episode in the life of a black family in Chicago (she came from that city): the family suddenly obtain some money and decide to buy a house in a white neighbourhood (as the author's father had done). This was deservedly very successful, and was filmed from Lorraine Hansberry's script in 1961. *The Sign in Sydney Brustein's Window* (1964) was about a New York Jewish intellectual. It was tragic that this warm, intelligent and vigorous talent, capable of giving so much more, was cut short by cancer.

IV

Gertrude Stein (1874–1946), born of a wealthy family near Pittsburgh, was not altogether modern – she has even been put forward as one who belonged essentially to the 'sunset phase' of the nineteenth century – but she understood the importance of modernity. Her writings were not, as Sherwood Anderson (q.v.) saw, necessarily very important in themselves; but they provided incomparable signposts for others more imaginatively gifted. Gertrude Stein studied at Radcliffe under, among others, Santayana and Moody (qq.v.); the most important influence on her there, however, was William James. She planned to become a psychologist, and so began medicine, including brain anatomy, at Johns Hopkins. In 1903 she went abroad, learnt about art from her brother Leo, who – though he kept in the background – was always a better art critic than she, and set about establishing herself as an expatriate queen and patron of artists. She bought the work of Picasso, Braque, Matisse and others, and amassed a famous collection. She lived with her secretary and companion Alice B. Toklas in Paris for the rest of her life (except for a period during the war, when they lived in Vichy), returning to America only once – for a lecture tour in 1934. Her early books appeared so difficult that she had to publish or guarantee them herself. But when she had acquired fame as a personality, through both her salon and her assumption of the headship of the avant garde of the Twenties, she was able to write a popular book: *The Autobiography of Alice B. Toklas* (1933), which purported to be her life as told by her friend. She repeated this with *Everybody's Autobiography* (1937). Gertrude Stein encouraged Anderson, Hemingway, Wilder, Fitzgerald (qq.v.) and others gifted, talented – and mediocre. No poet gained anything from her example. But she was certainly regarded as the most influential English-speaking writer in Paris in the early Twenties – Pound ('Gertrude Stein liked him', said Miss Stein in *Toklas*, 'but did not find him amusing. She said he was a village explainer, excellent if you were a village, but if you were not, not') and Ford Madox Ford (qq.v.) were also there. In her last years she and Miss Toklas entertained many American soldiers; she had known the Americans of two wars, and wrote of them in the popular *Wars I Have Seen* (1944) and in *Brewsie and Willie* (1946). This latter was her last; it reconstructed the language of the GI Joes of 1944–5 with brilliance and affection as well as sentimentality.

Apart from her popular works, which are not only witty and readable but also sometimes egocentric and surprisingly arch, *Three Lives* (1909), and some posthumously printed earlier writings, Gertrude Stein's books are hard to read: child-like but repetitious, monotonous and not always justifiably inscrutable. It was after *Three Lives* (her best work) that she began to evolve the style for which she is known. By that time she had come to understand what Pablo Picasso and his friends were trying to do in painting: to elevate the picture itself over its 'subject'. Thus, for her, words became objects-in-themselves. Meaning became an overtone. Picasso and the others concentrated on the paintings; she concentrated on the writing. (This offered, perhaps, a convenient enough way of evading the issue of self-appraisal.) Her teacher William James had 'discovered' the 'stream of consciousness' (q.v.); as a psychologist he was interested in the flux itself – whereas she was more interested in the moment of 'the complete actual present': in the capturing of instants. One of the intentions of her repetitions is to convey an illusion like that of a motion picture: each sentence is a 'frame', and differs only slightly from its predecessor. Once the novelty has worn off, this tends, of course, to be as boring as exposing each frame of a movie not for a fraction of a second but for several minutes. But perhaps it had to be done. Gertrude Stein had the effrontery and self-confidence to do it.

She was also against the 'objective' or transcendent self: the self of which James claimed psychology could give no account. In that hopeful, Utopian manner common to many Americans she believed in the present – and thought the future was a rosy one. Perhaps such optimism requires to ignore sequence, structure and what I have called, in relation to Dreiser, the grain of life. The substantial, or transcendent, or objective self – what Wyndham Lewis (q.v.) thought of as 'the eye of the artist' – did not interest her any more than 'realism': she was peculiarly modern in this concentration on the qualities of objects, and in her opposition to 'stories'. She tried to get rid of narrative and put into its place a technique of extracting the essential quality of a thing or person. For example, this piece called 'A Cloth' from *Tender Buttons* (1914): 'Enough cloth is plenty and more, more is almost enough for that and besides if there is no more spreading is there plenty of room for it. Any occasion shows the best way'. Witty, intelligent – but trivial, and when in bulk, tiresome. ... This was the trap into which she fell. Not perhaps wishing her imagination to be free to investigate her lesbian – and masochistic – personality, she allowed herself to create abstractions that were inexorably separated from life or anything like it. *Ida, a Novel* (1941), for example, is really 'about' all that is least important in its protagonist's life – or at any rate it tells us nothing that is significant. The mimetic or representational was for Gertrude Stein a vulgarity and a sentimentality. Her writing tried to be 'abstract' in the sense that painting is abstract. It is curious that of her modern non-representational or would-be non-representational successors (Olsen, Creeley, qq.v. etc., etc.) only the American poet Robert Duncan has shown any real interest in her; but he is an 'intellectual', and very well read, as she was; the others cannot really be described as such. She also influenced Laura Riding (q.v.), but there were complications in this because Riding refuses to admit to having been influenced by anyone – impossible though that is.

Gertrude Stein was in her own way, from her 'home town' of Paris, an American pioneer. She saw how American procedures – indecorous and adventurous – differed from English, which are neat and traditional because 'Nothing is perplexing if there is an island. The special sign of this is in dusting'. In other words, she saw the right direction for American literature. But she became increasingly megalomanic and remote, and it is not strange that she early turned from novelist to critic (demonstrator of how things ought to be done). *Things As They Are* (1950), a straightforward (though not 'obscene') treatment of a lesbian theme, written in 1903, gives us some clue as to why she chose the course she did. It is fortunate that she wrote *Three Lives* (1909) before she made this choice, for it is a masterpiece – as well as being the most accessible of all her writings. There are hints of the future manner, but it has not degenerated into a method and become tiresome. The book consists of three stories of women, all of whom are defeated by life. Outstanding is 'Melanctha', about the daughter of a Mulatto mother and a Negro father who hates her: this, as has many times been pointed out, is almost the first American fiction to treat a Negro as a human being. The vigour and scope of this book make it clear that Gertrude Stein abandoned imaginative for critical fiction for reasons other than experiential capacity. *Three Lives* owes much to Flaubert. One wonders what effective literature does not. . . .

Elizabeth Madox Roberts (1886–1941), born in Kentucky, is unlucky not to be as well remembered as Stein (q.v.): she was more imaginatively gifted – though not as obviously historically important. Her first novel, about Kentucky hill-dwellers, *The Time of Man* (1926), immediately established her reputation, and led Wescott (q.v.) to remark, justly, that 'no other author will ever have the right to call his place Kentucky'. Although somewhat laboured in its attempt to parallel Homer, this first novel demonstrated the huge grasp of Roberts' imagination, as well as her acute intelligence. It is most successful in its depiction of the individual struggles of its migrant-farmer's-wife protagonist's struggles against malign fate and the cyclical nature of the life of poor white Kentuckians – in part she accepts this with serenity, but she also revolts against it within herself, and in a way peculiar to herself. The material of this book is reworked and refined in her best novel, *The Great Meadow* (1930), which is set in the eighteenth century – and is surprisingly, but successfully, sensational in some of its incidents (which include scalpings). It is the most achieved of all the versions of the settling of Kentucky. Elizabeth Madox Roberts was also a poet (her poems are still seen in children's anthologies); this side of her came out in two mystical novels which ultimately fail, but of which the first is nonetheless very interesting. (The poems themselves are neither here nor there.) This is *My Heart and My Flesh* (1927), a sort of sequel to *The Time of Man*, but entirely different from it in style and intent. Here the protagonist begins in more privileged circumstances, but suffers a series of savage blows. In many ways the novel anticipates Faulkner (q.v.) in its raw violence. Particularly interesting is the episode in which Theodosia, the heroine, finds herself compelled to share the company of Negroes and to share, as well, their hatred of their white oppressors. What fails in this unusual, and in certain respects pioneering, novel is the form in which the dialogue is presented: as in a play. This simply does not work – it seldom does in novels, which are, after all, not plays. *He Sent Forth a Raven* (1935) is also allegorical and experimental: it possesses great power in parts, but lacks control and coherence. Elizabeth Madox Roberts is a novelist who urgently requires reappraisal. Her style at its best is lyrical, her symbolism quite unforced; and she is greatly superior to many male novelists (Hemingway, q.v., is one example) who are much better known. As a portrayer of feminine sensibility and a regionalist who transcended regionalism with ease, she is undoubtedly a classic. She wrote two volumes of excellent short stories.

No fiction could have been further from Gertrude Stein's (q.v.), or for that matter Elizabeth Madox Roberts' (q.v.), than that of Sinclair Lewis (1885–1951); if they were super-literary, he was never more than super-journalistic. He is one of the worst writers to win a Nobel Prize (he was the first American to do so, 1930), and the worst American writer to achieve fame on a more than merely popular level. Yet although he was in no way as serious as Gertrude Stein, he was in a certain sense as historically important as her. The son of a doctor of Sauk City, Minnesota, he went to Yale, became a journalist, and fell under the influence of the journalist and sometimes acute critic **H.L. Mencken** (1880–1956), an important debunker and satirist who, despite his crudities, was an often effective destroyer of hypocrisy, cant and pretentiousness. Mencken's trouble was his inconsistency and tendency to take the cheap, easy way out when 'demolishing' someone he disliked. However, the assertion, recently made, that he was a proto-fascist is absurd. It is simply that he had an unpleasant side to his nature. But there is much to enjoy in *Prejudices* and its successors.

Lewis wrote a number of realistic and partially satirical novels, but did not achieve recognition until *Main Street* (1920). This attacks Sauk City (here called Gopher Prairie) and every similar town in America on very much the same lines as Mencken and the critic George Jean Nathan (1882–1958) were currently doing in their magazine *The Smart Set* – but rather more ambiguously. For Lewis makes his symbol of freedom, Carol Kennicott, return to the dull doctor husband she has walked out on; not only that, but we can now see very easily that Carol Kennicott herself is an extremely sentimental and middlebrow creature – she is merely a bit smarter than the others. Lewis followed this with *Babbitt* (1922), a portrait of an average American business man which its readers took as satirical at the time, but which may now be seen as loving as well as critical. Still, this added a new word to the language. *Arrowsmith* (1925) is about a scientist, and *Elmer Gantry* (1927), by far his best novel, is an almost Dickensian extravaganza about the attractions of phoney religion and a fake preacher who takes advantage of them. *Dodsworth* (1929) is a sentimental novel on the obligatory theme of the American being educated in Europe. The books of Lewis' last twenty years are more overtly in favour of what he began by satirizing; but the tendency was always there.

Lewis appealed to so vast a readership because he was 'safe'. As he finally confessed, he had written of Babbitt with love and not with hate. He could oppose nothing to the materialism of the small towns he portrayed. He was intellectually feeble. His powers of characterization were nil. What, then, were his virtues? First, he had a masterly journalistic grasp of his material: he really knew about the society of which he wrote. And if he did not really hate it, he none the less depicted it with vitality. He owed something to Wells (q.v.), but most of all to Dickens. For essentially he was a caricaturist of great energy and zest. His readers were easily able to kid themselves that they were not like Babbitt; but the accuracy of his fine detail still fascinates – and in Elmer Gantry he has created a monster of Dickensian proportions and of some complexity. There was a true novelist in him, and his writing career is important in the development of American fiction.

*

William Faulkner (1897–1962), born in New Albany, Mississippi, and raised in Oxford in the same State, won the Nobel Prize nineteen years after Lewis (q.v.), and was the fourth American to do so (if Eliot, q.v., is regarded as British); he was incomparably the better writer; he is regarded by some, in fact, as the greatest of all American novelists. The claim is by no means absurd, though towards the end of his life he lost power and tended towards the production of punk. Faulkner joined the Royal Canadian Air Force in 1918, after the American Air Force had rejected him because of his smallness (5 feet 5 inches); he did not see any active service, but was able to enter the University of Mississippi, for which he could not qualify academically, as a veteran. He stayed there for just over a year, and then took a variety of jobs. He worked on a newspaper and in 1924 published a book of poor, imitative verse called *The Marble Faun*. His first novel, *Soldiers Pay* (1926), published with the help of his friend Sherwood Anderson (q.v.), *fin de siècle* in style, is about a dying soldier's return. *Mosquitoes* (1927) is a mannered satirical book; no one would notice it now if it had not been Faulkner's second novel. In 1929 he published his first important novel, *Sartoris*. For this he drew on his family history (his great grand-father's colourful life was ended by a bullet fired by a rival only eight years before Faulkner's birth), and created the domain for which he became famous: Yoknapatawpha County, county seat Jefferson. This place has a relation to Lafayette County, and Jefferson has a relation to Oxford (and other towns, such as Faulkner's birthplace, New Albany). It is also Faulkner's 'world': a world as untidy as the real one as we actually have it in our minds, with geographical and historical exactitudes distorted – and as vivid as any created by a novelist in this century. Within this world, with certain inconsistencies that make it more rather than less convincing, Faulkner traced the decline of certain families (the Compson, Sartoris, Benbow and McCaslin families) and the rise of the Snopes. The scheme is a vast map of Faulkner's imagination: it blurs somewhat at the edges, and there are undefined areas – but, again, that is how we ourselves grasp history and hard unimagined fact; much is illuminated and illuminating.

Faulkner is an example of a writer who managed, for a period – of about twelve or fourteen years – to keep his powerful imagination dominant and under control. His genealogies and complex accounts of the 'history' of his region were essential parts of this process. He had to bring his internal world into line with the external world. In the end, and understandably, he gave way under the strain of maintaining his gloomy but not life-denying vision: his speech of acceptance of the Nobel Prize is dutiful, a series of clichés almost worthy of a politician, unworthy of the creative writer. The view implied in Faulkner's works is not the view expressed by the winner of the Nobel Prize: '... man will not merely endure: he will prevail ... because he has a soul, a spirit capable of compassion and sacrifice and endurance'. That may be true; but the way it is stated is empty because derivative and meaningless: the words are not Faulkner's own. The view of the best work is more sombre. It has been well summed up as follows: '... the Faulkner novel is designedly a silo of compressed sin, from which life emerges as fermentation'. Faulkner believed in no system; he was at his best when he tried to discover the patterns of his internal world – this is of course, in part, a result of the impact the external world made on him. The values of Christianity will do for him; but there is no evidence that he believed that God had ever intervened in human affairs. His late novel *A Fable* (1954), an attempt to re-enact Christ's Passion against the background of the First World War, is imaginatively an atrocious failure: laboured, its bitterness misplaced, its use of the Christ-theme palpably erroneous because of Faulkner's clear lack of belief in it.

His first wholly characteristic novel was *The Sound and the Fury* (1929). Here the Compson family are shown degenerating, fallen from their former gentility, leading a doomed life. The story is told through the consciousnesses of three members of this family: Benjy the idiot, the sensitive Quentin and the twisted, mean Jason. Quentin kills himself through shame at his incestuous desire for his sister Candace; Jason's is a tale of pettiness and greed. A final section centres on the Negro servant, Dilsey, whose goodness and wholesomeness contrast with the horror of the Compsons' decline. Caldwell (q.v.) can convey a mild sense of the lowness and crudity into which oppressed people can decline; Faulkner can show why they decline – and without oppression. But his vision of evil is rich in the affirmation of the qualities which foil it, which produce guilt – which rise above it.

Faulkner made the interior monologue his chief technical device. He enters too bodily – and with a rare creative courage which cost him much – into his characters (white, black, successful, defeated) ever to speak confidently of men prevailing. His world is infinitely more complicated than the platitudinous one in which such utterances can be made.

Faulkner's best work was written between *The Sound and the Fury* and *Intruder in the Dust* (1948), the story of how a Negro is saved from lynching by a white boy who has grown into understanding and humanity. After this – which is itself seriously vitiated by the introduction of a character who will insist on interpolating his unconvincing theories about race relations into the narrative – although none of his books is without some virtue, Faulkner tended to make optimistic intellectual inferences from his earlier works and elevate those into a kind of moral system. The three finest novels of all came early in Faulkner's career: *The Sound and the Fury*, *As I Lay Dying* (1930) and *Light in August* (1932). *As I Lay Dying* deals with the last journey of Addie Bundren: in her coffin as her family – her husband, her three legitimate sons, her bastard and a pregnant daughter – carry her to Jefferson. When there her husband finds himself new teeth and a new wife. This is a great novel because it reads perfectly as a realistic novel, and yet its symbolic possibilities are infinite. *Light in August* sets the bastard Joe Christmas, who may be half Negro, but in any case feels and behaves as if he were, amongst a strict Calvinist community. This book touches, more closely than any of its predecessors, on one of Faulkner's main themes: that the doom and decline of the white man springs from his insane and self-defeating, and irrational, inability to treat the Negro as a fellow human being. This conviction – that all people should treat others as human beings – is one of the mainsprings of Faulkner's creative impulse. It is not 'political', but merely human. But there are characters as primitive and evil, in Faulkner's books, as some Southern demagogues with whom we are familiar: he penetrates their minds with his understanding, too. His job is not to satirize or to make judgements: he presents people as they are, and he can do so. Although *Light in August* is a grim book, it is a positive one because it is made clear, from the beginning to the end, that Joe Christmas' tragedy is his refusal to take or give love, and that he got into this condition – from which he cannot escape – because he was originally denied love.

Absalom, Absalom! (1936) brings back Quentin Compson, who is preparing for suicide in *The Sound and the Fury*, but only as narrator. The story is of Thomas Sutpen, the 'demon' poor white who has ambitions to achieve aristocracy and destroys everyone who gets in his way. Sutpen marries a planter's daughter and they have a son (Charles), but he abandons them when he discovers they have Negro blood. He goes to Yoknapatawpha County, obtains land by dishonest means, marries again, and has a son and a daughter. Later his son Henry goes to the University of Mississippi and meets and admires Charles, not knowing who he is. Charles falls in love with his own half-sister, Judith – and it is Henry who kills him when he learns about his Negro blood. Then Henry disappears. Sutpen is obsessed with begetting a male heir, and when he abandons a poor white girl on his land because she bears him a daughter, her grandfather kills him with a scythe. Ultimately it is only Sutpen's Negro heirs who live on his land; in the end, finding the aged Henry come back and hidden in his own house, one of them burns it down. Thus Faulkner gives his most complete version of the doom of the South. Once again he spells out the message: the fatal flaw is its refusal to accept the Negro on equal terms. This working out of the flaw is presented with passion, for Faulkner truthfully shows it to come of a horrible innocence. A doctrinaire Marxist explanation of the South simply will not do – and it is Faulkner who shows this most clearly. It would be more comforting if it would do. To have to report that this attitude to other human beings arises from an innocence is agonizing; but Faulkner, himself a Southerner, found the courage to tell the truth. There is a sense in which he had earned the clichés of his Nobel Prize acceptance. What else could he have said but read *Absalom, Absalom!*? *The Unvanquished* (1938) linked episodes previously published as short stories into a novel about the fortunes of the Sartoris family in the Civil War. There are many more short stories, collected in *These Thirteen* (1931), *Doctor Martino* (1934), *Go Down Moses* (1942), *Knight's Gambit* (1949) and then in *Collected Stories* (1950), in which there is at least one masterpiece, 'Burn Burning' – though the story form was not Faulkner's great strength. *The Wild Palms* (1939) relates the defeat, through love, of a New Orleans doctor who performs an abortion on his mistress. This is counterpointed with what seems to be a totally unconnected one: but the reson- ance between the two shows Faulkner at his technically most assured. There is also a revealing account of pulp writing – which Faulkner was himself forced to do.

The Hamlet (1940), *The Town* (1957) and *The Mansion* (1960) are a trilogy on the Snopes family; the first part is the best, but the second two contain the most humorous writing of Faulkner's latter years.

Faulkner is a very difficult, even forbidding writer. He is also, perhaps largely because of the strain and responsibility imposed upon him by his concern with the nature of evil, the most uneven of all the major writers of our time. His metaphors and similes can seem forced, and even jejune. He can be pretentiously complex. He can be portentous and confused. But his best work is not more difficult than it has to be. Those long and intricate sentences are not too long and intricate when they are describing the processes of a mind. Few techniques more effective in doing so have been evolved. The subject of the beauty and innocence contained in evil is a difficult and paradoxical one, which can lead to misunderstandings. The sheer energy of Faulkner's stories of perversion, horror and despair gives the lie to those who would accuse him of doing the dirty on life itself, for his own creative ends. He was forced to write scripts for Hollywood (one, *The Blue Dahlia*, with Raymond Chandler, q.v., is famous), and he was subject to fearful bouts of alcoholic dissipation. It is no wonder.

*

F. Scott Fitzgerald (1896–1940), born at St. Paul, Minnesota, was the laureate of the Jazz Age, of what Gertrude Stein (q.v.) called 'the lost generation'. These were people who were 'so deliberately and determinedly cynical that [they] became naïve'. Fitzgerald belonged to this age, and at times he indulged himself in it to the hilt, but he knew that it was all wrong. In *The Great Gatsby* (1925), he achieved a balance between empathy and analysis, and produced the most memorable and accurate description of the American Twenties – a devastating criticism that is none the less rich and romantic, for Fitzgerald was an out-and-out romantic, and it was in large measure his violently offended romanticism that produced his disgust.

He began as very much one of his age. His family was prosperous and when he went to Princeton in 1913 he was anxious to distinguish himself in every field including foot- ball; in 1920 he published his first successful novel, *This Side of Paradise*, which is about Princeton. Here Fitzgerald romantically sets his (immature) notion of true love against the corrupting power of money; the novel's strength, apart from its brilliant descriptive passages, lies in Fitzgerald's convincing grasp of what is unselfish in his initially snobbish and hedonistic hero. Fitzgerald had married a beautiful girl, Zelda, and he now began to live it up in one plush hotel after another, going from party to party, consuming himself rapidly but of course, in his twenties, imperceptibly. Zelda wanted to be a ballet dancer – she was very good, but she had started too late, and was not mentally stable – and she insisted on competing with Fitzgerald, which upset him, tearing him in two directions. Eventually she entered an institution; she was in one – in America – when she was burned to death in an accidental fire in 1947. She did write one novel, which has recently been published; it is no good, though of course interesting. Fitzgerald, earning a lot of money but increasingly in debt, wrote two volumes of short stories, a novel – *The Beautiful and Damned* (1922) – and a play before his first masterpiece, *The Great Gatsby*. The action takes place in the valley of ashes, beneath the huge eyes of Doctor T.J. Eckleburg (an advertisement). The story is told by Nick Carroway, a device that gives Fitzgerald the precise distance he needs between himself and his material. Poor Jay Gatz from Dakota quickly becomes one of the rich ('They are different from you and me. They possess and enjoy early, and it does something to them, makes them soft where we are hard, and cynical where we are trustful, in a way that, unless you were born rich, it is very difficult to understand') because he wants to win back Daisy Buchanan, Nick's cousin. After an affair with Jay when he was an army lieutenant, she had married the brutal, materialistic proto-fascist, Tom Buchanan – a marvellously prophetic portrait of an evil, ill-willed, vulnerable, vicious man. Through Nick Gatsby he meets Daisy again, and is able to make her his mistress. Tom takes a garage proprietor's wife for his mistress; her jealous husband locks her up, she runs out into the road – and is killed by Daisy, who does not stop. Gatsby takes the responsibility and Tom tells his own mistress's husband, Wilson, that it was Gatsby who killed her, and drove on. Wilson shoots Gatsby in his swimming-pool, and then turns the gun on himself.

The Great Gatsby is another of those seminal books – one of the most perfect of the century, and absolutely right-hearted – that manage to exist simultaneously and convincingly on both the realistic and the symbolic plane. Fitzgerald depicts the rich society into which Gatsby hoists himself as empty of all but putridity; the object of his simple romantic dreams, Daisy, is no more than a treacherous whore without the discrimination or inclination to diagnose the evil in her cruel and stupid husband. But Gatsby, as is often and rightly pointed out, comes, 'divided between power and dream', to represent America itself, and he (Nick says) 'turned out all right at the end; it is what preyed on Gatsby, what foul dust floated in the wake of his dreams that temporarily closed out my interest in the abortive sorrows and short-winded elations of men'. Fitzgerald is able to see Gatsby as both an ex-criminal, vulgar member of the *nouveau riche*, and a dreamer: as the man who had believed in Daisy's (as it turns out corrupt) kiss so fervently that he had dedicated his whole being to what he thought it represented. In this way Gatsby embodies the famous – or notorious – 'American dream', which will (Fitzgerald implies) founder on its preference of appearance to reality.

Tender is the Night (1934; rev. 1951) is the love story of Dick Diver, psychiatrist, and his rich patient Nicole Warren. This is a more personal, more autobiographical book (for Nicole's mental illness he obviously drew on his experience of Zelda's); it does not have the universality of *The Great Gatsby*. It is none the less a masterpiece. The manner in which sick Nicole attracted Dick, and how she then corrupts him, is truly tragic. He loses his sense of vocation and becomes merely charming, a corrupted healer. Even though mentally ill and utterly dependent when she is sick, Nicole is somehow superior, the victor: she destroys her husband because in their marriage there is a tacit understanding that he is being paid for staying with her. In the end Dick returns to America, to – it is implied – rot away and waste his substance. Unlike Gatsby, he survives to some sort of infamy and defeat.

The Thirties were bad years for Fitzgerald. He worked in Hollywood, drank too much, behaved in such a manner as to give inferior men the opportunity to pity him, and almost stopped writing. At thirty-nine, in 1936, he experienced what he himself called a crack-up: Edmund Wilson (q.v.) edited the interesting notebooks, papers and essays describing this nervous breakdown in the volume *The Crack-up* (1945): why, Fitzgerald asked himself, had he gone so far as to have become identified with all he loathed and pitied? He had a daughter by Zelda, and it is clear that he desperately wanted to appear to her as a good and decent father – and that he felt he could not do so. Luckily for his personal happiness he met a journalist, Sheilah Graham, who sweetened his difficult final years, and helped him to get himself into a fit state to attempt his last novel, *The Last Tycoon* (1941). Fitzgerald died, after two heart attacks, before he could finish it. Essentially it is a self-portrait: Monroe Stahr, a film-producer at the end of his rope, tries to struggle on although he no longer believes in life. It is clear that Fitzgerald's alcoholism and involvement with commerce had not weakened his powers, and if this had been finished it might be safe to agree with those critics who find it his best novel. Fitzgerald wrote many short stories, of varying merit; there is a selection of eighteen of the best of them in *The Stories of F. Scott Fitzgerald* (1951).

Ernest Hemingway (1898–1961) also came from the Midwest – he was the son of an Illinois doctor – and, as Fitzgerald had done, but to much greater point, he sat at the feet of Gertrude Stein (q.v.) in Paris. As a young man he made many hunting and fishing expeditions; his descriptions of these activities were one of the high points of his writing. Hemingway was a reporter in Kansas City, volunteered as an ambulance driver and was wounded in Italy in 1917. He served with the Italian infantry until the Armistice. In Paris he came to know Gertrude Stein, Ford Madox Ford and Ezra Pound (qq.v.), all of whom encouraged him. (His memoirs of his Paris years were published posthumously in *A Moveable Feast*, 1964. This is an example of Hemingway at his worst: self-parodic, arch, vicious, envious, unfair about others and untruthful.) His early short stories were collected in *In Our Time* (1925). The tedious *The Torrents of Spring* (1926) parodied (or tried to parody) Sherwood Anderson's (q.v.) style – a style from which Hemingway had already appropriated what he wanted. *The Sun Also Rises* (1926), called *Fiesta* in Great Britain, his first novel, is his best. This was followed by the short stories *Men Without Women* (1927) and the novel *A Farewell to Arms* (1929); the short story collection *Winner Takes Nothing* (1933) was Hemingway's last book of account.

Hemingway was famous for his style, his four marriages (only the final one, lasting from 1944 until his death, took), and his various sporting exploits. The record is not very clear on his prowess as a sportsman. It seems that he was not always as good as he said or thought he was. When he went to the front in the Spanish Civil War he nearly killed someone with a grenade, and was regarded as a nuisance. But he could fish and he had enthusiasm for (though not a very good knowledge of) bullfighting. During most of the Thirties Hemingway lived in Key West in Florida. After the Second World War, during which he was a correspondent with the Fourth Division of the First Army, he lived on an estate near Havana, Cuba, until the Castro revolution. After this he settled in Idaho. But he was already mentally and physically ill, and in 1961 he shot himself in a fit of depression for which he preferred not to be treated. After 1933 his main publications were: *To Have and Have Not* (1937), *For Whom the Bell Tolls* (1940), on the Spanish Civil War, the badly received *Across the River and into the Trees* (1950), *The Old Man and the Sea* (1952), all novels, and *The Green Hills of Africa* (1935), on big game hunting. *The Fifth Column*, a hollow and cliché-ridden play about a newspaperman in Spain, was included in his collected short stories: *The Fifth Column and the First Forty-nine Stories* (1938). A posthumously issued, excruciating novel, *Islands in the Stream* (1970), is best ignored. There may be more to come.

Hemingway, especially the late Hemingway, has been a vastly overrated writer; but this does not mean that he was not in some ways a good one. The earliest influence on him, **Ring Lardner** (1885–1933), whose style he was imitating at school, deserves a paragraph to himself.

Lardner was better known as a sports columnist than as a short-story writer. He did not fully realize his genius, but he was the first to listen properly to and carefully reproduce the speech of the lower classes, the speech of people who went to prize fights and baseball matches. He refrained from judgement, and his idea of what was comic was also very often (as he knew) tragic; he missed greatness because there was just a shade too much of the casual about his misanthropy. His lunatic short plays anticipate the Theatre of the Absurd, although they did not influence it. But Lardner had a greater and more secure sense of the decent than Hemingway. Lardner suffered from tuberculosis, and he drank himself more or less to death: he allowed himself to rot. But he knew it, and always there was a detached observer there. He is one of the finest purveyors of awfulness of our time, and he is this because, although he can never portray goodness, he can throw it into relief by his descriptions of awfulness: vulgarity, lovelessness, the sort of bad taste that really is bad (not innocent or ignorant), ruthlessness. He thought he was drawing desperate self-portraits; but he kept himself above this, in fact.

The mature Hemingway of the Twenties owed the authenticity of his dialogue and his toughness to Lardner's example; in the latter the toughness was unassumed, in Hemingway it functioned laconically and truthfully as a guard against sentimentality.

Hemingway's style was self-conscious and carefully worked out, but it arose from a simplicity of feeling – one that he gradually lost. Apart from Lardner, its sources are in the economy of the newspaper report, the purity of Gertrude Stein, the honesty and lyricism of Anderson, the innocence of Huckleberry Finn, the simplicity of Stephen Crane (qq.v.). The Hemingway of the Twenties is complex; but he has not yet fallen prey to cliché or to noisy exhibitionism about 'action'. He is not as much of a 'man' as he would like to be: the hero of *The Sun Also Rises* has been emasculated by the war. But he lives to a code – the famous Hemingway code of 'grace under pressure'. For Jake Barnes there can be no meaning in life except to live gracefully. He cannot have the girl he loves, Brett; but she returns to him at the end because the novelist Robert Cohn, to whom she has briefly given herself, has nothing to offer – he is the victim of mere words and fine sentiments – and because she fears she will injure the bullfighter she loves if she stays with him. This is Hemingway's most moving novel, fine in characterization, pellucid in style, and contrasting without sentimentality the anguish of futility with the dignity of a few people's graciousness. As he himself would then have conceded, it is not much because it is not enough; but it is very real and very poignant. *A Farewell to Arms* is poignant, too, but the English nurse, Catherine Barkley, is quite unreal. Aside from Brett in *The Sun Also Rises*, whom he observes but upon whose qualities he does not comment, Hemingway could not create women. There was, it seems, a homosexual component in his nature which led him both to want to establish himself as masculine (i.e. not 'feminine'), and to make up soft, yielding, sweet women – too obviously the ideal complement for strong and hairy warriors. Catherine is the beginning of this line of girls, who get younger and more improbable as his heroes age along with him. But apart from this, *A Farewell to Arms* – with its implied comments on the futility of war, its descriptions of battles, and its depiction of the state of mind of the hero – runs *The Sun Also Rises* very close.

The best short stories are in the first three collections. In them Hemingway was getting nineteenth-century culture out of his system, and saluting a primitivistic, non-industrial kind of life in which males (the females are out except for purposes of comfort, and as something a man 'needs') must learn to live and die with courage and grace: people must behave well. The best stories, particularly those about Nick Adams, are laconic and as pure as spring water. Hemingway's fascination with death (he chose it rather than life at the end) was genuine, and he is especially good in describing encounters with death.

But in many ways he never grew up. He lacked anything but the most temporary generosity. The kind of badness of his posthumous novel reveals him to have been capable of fantasies of action so puerile that it is hard to believe the author of *Fiesta* could have perpetrated them. His longest novel, *For Whom the Bell Tolls*, has good passages, but is flawed as a novel by its meaningless and sentimental love affair. The symbolism of *The Old Man and the Sea* is portentous, its simplicity false. It is, it is true, a skilful performance, and – the Christian symbolism apart – a sincere one. It conveys Hemingway's message: life is futile, but we must still live it nobly and with courage. However, it is not fresh, but lucubrated; the words have not been drawn up from a deep well, but pondered and put together by the legendary image: 'Papa Hemingway'.

The message itself is not and never was much, of course. Hemingway will be valued, surely, for the discovery of a style that enabled him to make vivid, lyrical and piercingly accurate descriptions of graciousness and male companionship (as in the fishing trip in *The Sun Also Rises*). He is a moving writer, but it is an error to go to him for 'philosophy'.

Thomas Wolfe (1900–38) was less gifted than Hemingway (q.v.), and his failure to grow up was more comprehensive. But he cannot be ignored. He was born in Asheville, North Carolina, where his father made grave masonry and his mother ran a small hotel. A giant in height – he was six feet six inches tall – he poured out a gigantic torrent of thinly fictionalized autobiography which his publishers, first Maxwell Perkins of Scribners and then Edward C. Aswell of Harpers, edited into four books (themselves massive novels). He had graduated from the University of North Carolina and then gone to Harvard to try George Pierce Baker's (q.v.) course in playwriting. He took his first novel to Perkins in 1923, and between them they put it into shape – meanwhile Wolfe was an instructor of English at New York University. *Look Homeward Angel*, in which he appears as Eugene Gant, was published in 1929, and was immediately successful; it was followed by *Of Time and the River* (1935). In his next two novels, both posthumously published, Gant becomes George Webber. Shortly after delivering the Webber manuscript Wolfe caught pneumonia; he died of a brain infection. Aswell edited and published the material Wolfe had left as *The Web and the Rock* (1939) and *You Can't Go Home Again* (1940). Since his death Wolfe's reputation has somewhat declined – no competent critic recommends him wholeheartedly – but he is still read. Clearly, for all his lack of self-discipline and failure to consider any phenomenon or person except in the light of his own interests, he is a writer of some importance.

He is most important to the young. Go back to him after thirty and you will find yourself selecting; before thirty you take it all in. In the first novel Gant tells the story of his father and mother. Even as edited by Perkins it is badly, inflatedly written; but this does not seem to matter, because Wolfe does create an unforgettably vivid picture of a savagely quarrelling, mutually recriminative family. Probably he could not have done it in any other way. The continuation, and the unsuccessful attempt to cover the same ground more objectively in the Webber novels, tells his own story: of the search for success (rather than meaning), for a father (found in his editor Maxwell Perkins) and for a mother (found and finally repudiated in the stage designer Aileen Bernstein, almost twenty years older than himself). And yet through all the inchoateness something does emerge: the ghost of man trying to find, fumbling with, sometimes finding and using, his own self-expression. Wolfe is a romantic rather than a novelist: the author of a vast body of work that seeks to define the myth of the American artist. But he failed – except as a writer of fragments – because he could not altogether discipline Wolfe into the artist, could not sensitively enough separate the ego from the creativity. But for all Wolfe's adolescence, for all the egoism that he drags into his fiction, much of what his prose recreates – his childhood, his tortured romance with Mrs. Bernstein (whose Jewishness he attacked in the most repulsive terms), his relationship with the homosexual Francis Starwick – is as vividly evoked as anywhere in the fiction of our century. It is often as paranoiac, adolescent and unpleasantly egocentric as Wolfe himself was; but it is of legendary proportions, and we do not forget it, even if sometimes we should prefer to.

*

Not much of the proletarian literature that flourished during the depression of the early Thirties, which subsided only with the Stalinist purges, the Nazi-Soviet pact, and then (ironically) the alliance with Russia, has survived or deserves to. But there were important writers who sympathized with the proletarians without subscribing rigidly to their Marxist point of view. No writing that subscribes rigidly to any dogma (Christian, Marxist or whatever), where there is a choice, survives for long: this kind of writing is, after all, criticism, or propaganda in which the work of the resolutely non-dogmatic imagination may take only second place.

Chicago-born **John Dos Passos** (1896–1971), whose grandfather was a Portuguese immigrant, had gained fame and flourished before the Depression, but his important work fits most appropriately in with, and even influenced, proletarian literature. He had grave faults; his retreat into conservatism after the Second World War is unconvincing and adds nothing to his literary stature – and he is most important as a technician. But whatever may spoil his work, of whatever period, it is never dogmatism or rigidity.

After graduating from Harvard (1916) Dos Passos saw service in France. His first book was an autobiographical novel about an ambulance driver: *One Man's Initiation – 1917* (1920; rev. as *First Encounter*, 1945). His next, *Three Soldiers* (1921), was more characteristic, and although it does not incorporate his later technical innovations it does conveniently illustrate his strengths, weaknesses, and chief preoccupations. During the Twenties Dos Passos wrote plays incorporating 'movie' techniques, and he translated Blaise Cendrars (q.v.), whose panoramic methods of composition were to influence him considerably. He also made translations from the Brazilian and the Spanish.

Three Soldiers takes three different men and traces the impact of war upon them: the optical worker Fuselli, who wants promotion; the farm-labourer Chrisfield who wants only to go home; and the educated musician, Andrews. All are destroyed. Fuselli gets not promotion but syphilis. Chrisfield kills a sergeant and deserts. Andrews is unjustly sent to a labour battalion, escapes, is let down by his girl, and is eventually recaptured. He faces a bleak future (death or years of imprisonment), and the sheets of music he has composed blow away.

This is the real, gloomy Dos Passos. *Three Soldiers* was one of the first novels to describe the war as it really did affect people; those who thought it a fine thing, and patriotism meaningful, upbraided Dos Passos; but he manfully defended himself. The novel is vivid, and it manifests the nihilism from which Dos Passos guiltily suffered all his life: he feared anarchy for the obvious reasons, and was not an anarchist; but even more he feared the society for whose portrayal he became so famous: he feared for the survival of the individual. In *Three Soldiers* he shows the destruction of three men by society; this he really, and reasonably, believed to be the fate of individual man in the twentieth century. But naturally enough he wanted to offer some hope, and so he turned to the portrayal of society itself, in the hope of reforming it. Whether he had read Romains' *Death of a Nobody* (q.v.) is not clear; but from *Manhattan Transfer* (1925) onwards his thinking had – or tried to have – something in common with unanimism (q.v.). He knew French literature well. But he could never make up his mind whether his entities with a life of their own were good or bad. However, one suspects that society itself was for Dos Passos an evil entity; he never, for all his reformist zeal and his active leftism of the Thirties, caught a sense of that authentic corporate life that is explored by the sociologist Durkheim. And, as *Three Soldiers* already makes clear, he could not create character: even his leading figures are types, and they are portrayed without psychological richness.

However, the naturalism of *Manhattan Transfer* and the trilogy *U.S.A.* (1938) escapes drabness for three reasons: his technique is lively as well as skilful; he is responsive to poesy, and had been exposed to imagism (q.v.) and other colourful new developments while at Harvard, so that his writing, too, is often gay and fresh; and although his creative imagination was deficient he was driven by real passions: passion against the injustices caused by the social and economic conditions between wars, and passion against the bigger injustice of life itself. For Dos Passos the naturalist gloom was all-pervading because he had no real imaginative life to set against it. His counterweight was provided by travel; and his travel books, particularly *Orient Express* (1927), are superb – at a time when his novels are, understandably enough, more known about than read, these travel books ought to be reissued.

The technique Dos Passos invented is very fine indeed, and I think it is still useful and valid. It has been utilized, notably, by Döblin and Sartre (qq.v.), both much superior as novelists to Dos Passos – but both fertilized considerably by his method. Dos Passos himself derived it mainly from Joyce (q.v.), but he added much of his own, and his approach, although lyrical, was realistic rather than introspective. He was not interested in language – his language is flat and unexciting – but social reality; Joyce's books are increasingly an investigation into language itself.

Dos Passos first used this technique in *Manhattan Transfer*, which deals mainly with the teeming life of New York City over a period of some years, and in particular with certain defeated individual lives. Dos Passos takes a number of characters and deals with the rise and fall of their fortunes in parallel (sometimes converging) episodes. These episodes are combined with three other devices: brief 'biographies' of important people (giving opportunities for irony when contrasted with those of poor people); the 'newsreel', a collage of headlines, phrases from popular songs, and so on, that define the general atmosphere; and 'the camera eye', in which the author himself enters the field, mixing prose poetry with impressionistic and stream-of-consciousness (q.v.) passages. These, with some exceptions, are the weakest passages in *Manhattan Transfer* and *U.S.A.*, which consists of *The 42nd Parallel* (1930), *1919* (1932) and *The Big Money* (1936), with a new prologue and epilogue. *U.S.A.* takes twelve characters and treats them with what Marcus Cunliffe well calls 'circumstantial unloving competence'. Each one is supposed to be subordinate to the life of the city; but Dos Passos does not succeed in concealing his despair – a rather sterile despair. His later books – among them the trilogy *District of Columbia* (1952), *Chosen Country* (1951) and the very poor *Most Likely to Succeed* (1954) – collapsed, doubtless from exhaustion, into facile phoney patriotism, flat reportage and a nearly whining self-indulgence. It would certainly be unfair to judge Dos Passos' earlier work by them. He began as a pessimistic individualist and in fact remained one all his life. But in his best works his commitment to collectivism is sincere, arising from that streak of Utopian idealism that runs through most American consciousnesses. Nor does he falsify his sense of doom: both *Manhattan Transfer* and *U.S.A.* are ultimately depressing books. What the novel really owes Dos Passos is a still viable method; it was a considerable achievement.

Of Irish-Catholic background, **James T. Farrell** (1904–79), who was born in the South Side section of Chicago that provides the background for his works, set out his literary principles in *A Note on Literary Criticism* (1936), which is Marxist but never in a crude or oversimplified sense: it opposed the official communist literary line. In *The League of Frightened Philistines* (1945) he defends realism sensibly; some of his arguments are reminiscent of those of the French 'populists' (q.v.). Farrell owes debts to his Catholic upbringing, to Marx, to Sherwood Anderson, to Proust, and, especially, to Joyce (for his use of stream-of-consciousness) and Dreiser (qq.v.). He resembles Dreiser in being, at bottom, a true naturalist, with little hope for the poor or the ill-fashioned, but much pity; his prose style is not distinguished. Because Farrell's later prose and many short stories are the products of a comparatively exhausted talent, his *Studs Lonigan* trilogy has been undervalued since the Thirties. Studs is his doomed character; Danny O'Neill makes it, but the pentalogy through which he does so is not more than competent; in the Bernard Carr trilogy, in which Farrell traces his own literary aspirations, the energy is even more dissipated, although the Carr books are always readable and intelligent. But *Studs Lonigan – Young Lonigan: A Boyhood in Chicago Streets* (1932), *The Young Manhood of Studs Lonigan* (1934) and *Judgement Day* (1935) – is different. This at least is worthy of Dreiser. Studs comes from a poisoned place – Chicago's South Side – and his fundamental decency is shown as stifled by it. He has the usual adventures; he wants to be a real human being; but the desire to appear like his gang companions – tough, unsentimental, ruthless – prevails. When he grows up he becomes a crook and torturer, and learns to drink unwisely; his girl rejects him. Finally he marries and tries to make it; but his weak heart, his lack of real or wholesome experience, the indifference of society – these conspire to defeat him. He dies at twenty-nine. This reveals, as it sets out to do, the 'concrete facts' of 'spiritual poverty'. It has force and passion. It is the most powerful work of naturalism in a post-naturalist era.

Although he won the Nobel Prize in 1962, **John Steinbeck** (1902–68), who was born of German-Irish parentage in Salinas, centre of the Californian lettuce industry, never produced a single work nearly as rawly effective and moving as *Studs Lonigan*; but he was a gifted novelist, who has written many novels of interest. Steinbeck did not share the natural pessimism of Dos Passos or Farrell (qq.v.), but – although evidently a sturdy rationalist, and just as indignant an enemy of injustice – substituted for it something very like the unanimism of Romains (q.v.). But in some of his better books (they all belong to the Thirties), such as *Tortilla Flat* (1935), he seems to have grasped a sense of that 'Durkheimian' (q.v.) corporateness the lack of which has been noted in Dos Passos. *Tortilla Flat* consists of tales about the *paisanos* of Tortilla Flat, on the outskirts of Monterey: people who do not share the 'values' of society and have opted out from it, so that they are idle and thieving but untainted by commerce and generous to those in need. There is a strong vein of sentimentality running through *Tortilla Flat*, but it does not quite spoil the freshness and liveliness of the conception.

Steinbeck got his unanimism from the eccentric biologist Edward Ricketts, whose interest was in groups of marine creatures functioning as one organism. Writers and others began to get interested in unanimism in this century when the corporateness of

behaviour of human groups became less evident (especially in the religious and philosophical spheres). That this interest is fruitful we have seen from the sociology of Durkheim and the novels of Romains, to name only two writers; Steinbeck did add something
of his own, in his insistence on bestowing a loving consideration upon all living things,
even freaks – an attitude he opposed to morality. This produced the best of his novels,
really a novella, *Of Mice and Men* (1937). Some of the characters are wooden, the symbolism is lucubrated, Lennie's hallucinations at the end are wildly unconvincing; but the
theme of the animal-child, the giant who does not know his own strength, protected by
the little, intelligent, physically weak man, is not sentimental even though it is fundamentally homosexual (Lennie is led from 'good' non-sexual friendship to murder by vile
uncomprehending women) – though unconsciously so.

Unfortunately Steinbeck did not realize the contradictions in which his unanimistic
ideas involved him: why be sorry for the individual if the individual does not matter? Of
course Steinbeck cared about the plight of individuals, and about injustice, and with *In
Dubious Battle* (1936), the story of a strike of fruit-pickers, he aligned himself with the
proletarian school. *The Grapes of Wrath* (1939), about the Joad family which with
thousands of others came to California to find work, is epic in proportion and gripping as
narrative; the coming of the sharecroppers from the Oklahoma dustbowl to California is
convincingly seen as a vast instinctive migration. Again, brilliant impressionistic writing
is mixed in with some intolerably folksy sentimentality. But the novel's chief fault is that it
does not cohere: Steinbeck makes it clear that he believes the behaviour of the profiteers
in California is humanly inadequate, but he cannot show why; there is a conflict in him
between the philosophical unanimist and the humane socialist. The book's message, that
everything that lives 'is holy', is vitiated by its philosophy – and in any case it conveys this
message not in imaginative but only in sentimental terms. Steinbeck's later books do
nothing to resolve this paradox, and the ambitious *East of Eden* (1952), although it
contains a few passages of good writing, is pretentiously symbolic.

Erskine Caldwell (1903), from Georgia, no less gifted, is too easily dismissed by critics
today. Like Steinbeck (q.v.), Caldwell tends to deal in inarticulate or simple characters
not only because he wants to depict people depressed by economic and social circumstances but also because he cannot create complex or articulate ones. However, his early
work illuminated the lives of Southern poor whites in the Thirties – the backwoodsmen
and sharecroppers, whose lives he knew well – in a way that they had never been illuminated before. In *Tobacco Road* (1932), a dramatization of which ran in New York for eight
years, and *God's Little Acre* (1933), all these wretched and degraded creatures possess is
sex. They have been so reduced by circumstances that they are only parodies of human
beings – and Caldwell writes of them forcefully. That what he writes is sometimes very
funny is (perhaps) sometimes beyond his own intention, but has a savagely ironic effect.
Caldwell should not be judged by his later and frequently sensationalist and self-parodic
novels, but by the two novels already mentioned and by *Journeyman* (1935), *Georgia Boy*
(1943), *Trouble in July* (1940), about a lynching, and, an exception, the more recent *Miss
Mamma Aimee* (1967). A few of his stories are excellent – they were collected in *Complete
Stories* (1953) – especially 'Kneel to the Rising Sun' (1935), a tale of racism that has classic
stature and ought to be better known than it is. The best of Caldwell will survive, and
deserves to do so.

Nelson Algren (1909–81), once the lover of Simone de Beauvoir (q.v.), and written
about by her in *The Mandarins*, was born in Detroit and reared in poverty in Chicago, his
home for most of his life, and the scene of most of his novels. He was connected with the
proletarian movement and its predecessor, naturalism, because his immature first novel,
Somebody in Boots (1935), which sold only 758 copies, was deliberately Marxist – and

because his fiction seems to resemble Dreiser's or Farrell's (qq.v.) in its relentless build-up of detail. Actually his mature work is highly original in its effect. He was, one might say, a naturalist without a philosophy, or even an interest in a philosophy – he stuck to his own vision of life. Caldwell's subjects were the dregs of a rural, Algren's those of an urban, society – usually from the slums of Chicago's West Side. He soon lost his political interests, and was honest in doing so – for he was properly the laureate of these doomed dregs: content to perform this minor function, his novels and stories are remarkably successful within their limitations. Algren really wasn't trying to say anything at all: just, by implication, to claim a proper human interest for his people, who are tramps, petty criminals with grandiose dreams, hustlers, prostitutes, bar-flies. *Never Come Morning* (1942) is about the Polish immigrants in Chicago, and in particular about Bruno Bicek, whose dream is to be heavyweight champion of the world. He ends by committing murder. In *The Man with the Golden Arm* (1949) Frankie Machine (Majcinek), another Pole, has genius at gambling – and heroin. He could escape: but the poetry of his environment as well as its hellishness, which he recognizes, drags him back: he fails, and kills himself. *A Walk on the Wild Side* (1956) is set on the way to, and in, New Orleans, and records the self-destruction of an innocent strong man, Dave Linkhorn. This is probably Algren's most powerful novel; he never wrote a substantial book again. *The Neon Wilderness* (1947) contains memorable short stories. Algren, though he faded out early, is too often ignored; but he was one of the most consistent of American novelists, and while the fact that he does not try to see further than his characters' world limits him, it also gives him purity and power.

The wholly undisciplined **Edward Dahlberg** (1900–77), born in Boston and a friend of Herbert Read, D.H. Lawrence (qq.v.), and many others, cannot be put into any category. His literary criticism is mystical, his indictment of civilization both constructively Jewish and destructively vituperative, his philosophy intermittently learned; but he began as a novelist of the proletariat even if not as a proletarian novelist, as a realist if not as a naturalist. *Bottom Dogs* (1929) is to a certain extent his own story: Lorry Lewis is the bastard of an itinerant woman-barber of Kansas City; he goes to an orphanage and then drifts. This is interesting because, although its material is similar to that of Farrell (q.v.), Dahlberg's method is impressionistic. *From Flushing to Calvary* (1932) less convincingly treats of similar material. Dahlberg, whose *Bottom Dogs* was introduced by D.H. Lawrence, did not fulfil his promise although he retained a certain small following.

Farrell and Algren (q.v.) were often bracketed together, as 'Chicago realists', with a third: the Negro writer **Richard Wright** (1908–60). Wright was born in Mississippi and migrated to Chicago on the eve of the Depression. He was a communist from 1932 until 1944. He educated himself during the late Twenties and Thirties, studied sociology, whose compilations of facts, together with his experiences in dozens of jobs, gave him the background for *Native Son* (1940). This, which is often described as 'a Negro *American Tragedy*', tells the story of the Chicago Negro boy Bigger Thomas. Although Wright had already written the four novellas collected in *Uncle Tom's Children* (1938; rev. 1940), this is still the work of a prentice writer. But for all the crudities of its writing, and the structural collapse of Book III (the long speech by Bigger's lawyer which ought to have been expunged from later editions) owing to confusions between Marxist and creative imperatives, it remains a powerful and seminal book. In essence this novel is as critical of communists as of everyone else; where it isn't, as in the long speech of Bigger's communist lawyer – a Marxist plea that society has made Bigger what he is – the material is extraneous. And it must be admitted that at the heart of *Native Son* is a savage and demonic nihilism. Bigger, as underprivileged and conspired against as Studs Lonigan (q.v.), but black into the bargain, becomes reluctantly involved with the communist friends of the daughter of his white employer. In a moment of panic he accidentally kills her. While in flight he kills his own girl. He is captured, tried and, after rejecting both Christianity and communism, is executed. What is interesting about *Native Son* is that its power comes, not from its revelation of society's responsibility for Bigger Thomas, but from its nihilism: clearly society is not altogether responsible for him, because he is shown as vicious even amongst his own equally underprivileged contemporaries. The power comes from his violent assertion of himself, his defiance of the whole city of Chicago, his final and terrible affirmation of his murderous self.

Wright followed this with *Black Boy* (1945), an autobiography, and his best and least confused book. This gives a clue to his nihilistic attitude, for in it he confesses to the extent of his horror of the Negro's collaboration with the white man to keep himself down. Since Wright had been brought up by a strict mother, a Seventh Day Adventist, he had felt doubly alienated in his childhood; when he grew up he was able to sublimate his self-hatred – usual in all creative people – in a generally critical attitude towards his people as a whole. He underestimated Negro culture; tended, in fact, if only by impli- cation, to see the Negro as actually inferior because of his lack of self-assertion. Yet *Black Boy* is a masterpiece, a series of episodes that demonstrate with a terrible dramatic exacti- tude the predicament not only of the Negro, but of the artist who sees the ills in his society, is punished for it, and yet is of it.

After the Second World War, partly at the behest of Gertrude Stein (q.v.), who had liked a review, Wright settled in Paris. He remained in France until his premature death, at only fifty-two, from a heart attack. Wright was by then a famous man; much of his time was taken up entertaining visitors, travelling and lecturing. The books he wrote in these years did not fulfil the promise of *Native Son* and *Black Boy*. Robert Bone has summed him up admirably: he cannot, he points out, 'convincingly exorcise his demon. His sense of self is too deeply rooted in revolt. To opt for love is to give up his identity as a picaresque saint, metaphysical rebel, lonely outsider'. This explains the failure of his long novel *The Outsider*, which betrays his imagination because it is contrived, stilted, pompous – ultimately, egocentric and insensitive. Because industrialization had freed him from the stultifying traditions of the South, he came to invest too much in it – to ignore the evils inherent in it. But in the posthumous *Eight Today* (1963) there is one novella, dating from the early Forties, in which Wright wholly succeeded. It is called 'The Man Who Lived Underground', and it bears some close resemblances to Ralph Ellison's almost classic *The Invisible Man* (q.v.). Here Wright more or less abandons a painstakingly realistic surface, and concentrates on the sensations and consequences of being driven under- ground. His hero, Fred Daniels, resembles Bigger Thomas in that he breaks the laws of the white masters and defies them. Furthermore, unlike Bigger, he penetrates to the absurd centre of their inauthentic world, based as it is on exploitation and falsehoods. Here Wright's indignation goes well beyond the Marxist line: it reaches beyond the political. But Fred Daniels wants to integrate himself (as the expression goes): he tries to return, from the sewer where he has been living, to the world. But that white world does not know him, even when he confesses to the crimes he has committed. Eventually he is murdered by policemen, determined not to accept his reality, in his own sewer. On account of this story alone Wright must be given a place in the front ranks of modern American writers of fiction. But the first two books of *Native Son*, and parts of the third, and *Black Boy* also entitle him to this position.

Ralph Ellison (1914) was born in Oklahoma City, the son of a construction worker and tradesman who died when he was three, leaving his mother to support him, which she did by working as a domestic cleaner. Ellison was and has always been as interested in jazz as in literature. He played the trumpet in his school band, knew Hot Lips Page, is a lifelong friend of Jimmy Rushing. He chose first to study music. Then in 1936 he went to New York, met Richard Wright (q.v.) and **Langston Hughes** (1902–67), another Negro writer, mainly a poet with a fine ear for colloquial speech, but also a novelist (*Not Without Laughter*, 1930), playwright and influential and intelligent leader of Negro culture – and began writing. After war service in the Merchant Marine he worked on *Invisible Man* (1952). Ellison's high reputation is unusual since it is based on this novel alone; in the thirty-odd years that have elapsed since its publication he has added to it only a disappointing volume of essays, *Shadow and Act* (1964), and fragments from his novel in progress, printed in periodicals.

The style and method of *Invisible Man*, a novel whose prophecies have been realized in its own time, have as many antecedents as those of other highly original novels. The one that is most often pointed to is Kafka (q.v.): the hero is not named, and is manipulated in ways mysterious to him. But this resemblance to Kafka, while it does exist, is somewhat misleading. So is the oft-made comparison with surrealism (q.v.). For the Negro's consciousness of his predicament – and *Invisible Man* is first and foremost about that – is prophesied, so to speak, by Kafka. And Ellison can hardly be said to be indebted to Kafka for that. As for surrealism: 'reality is surreal', as Ellison himself has said. (The Czechs read Kafka as a comic realist, and are right to do so – even if this is only one aspect of his genius.) Joyce (q.v.) is a more certain influence: Ellison has learned much from Joyce's use of modern methods, including stream-of-consciousness and the introduction of comedy. An even greater debt – or is it a resemblance? – is owed to Nathanael West (q.v.). It is often held to be essentially a 'backward-looking-novel'; but this is where the Kafka comparison is misleading. After all, *Invisible Man* is the first Negro novel to transcend its genre. This even led Philip Larkin (q.v.) to insult Ellison (inadvertently) by calling him 'a writer who *happens* to be an American Negro'. That this is wrong is clear from Ellison's proposition that 'we view the whole of American life as a drama acted out upon the body of a Negro giant, who, lying trussed up like Gulliver, forms the stage and the scene upon which and within which the action unfolds'.

Invisible Man uses symbolism, allegory, myth and any other modernist device to hand, but never to the detriment of the 'mad' narrator's account of his alienated and 'invisible' state. He begins as an idealist, studying at a college for Negroes in the South run by an 'Uncle Tom' called Dr. Bledsoe. His rejection by the South is redolent with irony: through the 'accident' of being no more than he precisely is, the narrator brings the school into disrepute. He travels North and, like Fred Daniels in Wright's 'The Man Who Lived Underground', holes up in a Harlem basement: 'invisibility' is for the time being the only endurable condition. His ultimate wisdom – reached after working in a nightmare paint factory, and becoming a noted member of an underground liberal party whose policy, he comes to see, is betrayal and totalitarianism – is disillusionment. The end of the book, describing a Harlem race riot, might have been a piece of impressionistic reporting of events that took place more than ten years after it was written. The narrator ends by asking: 'Who knows but that, on the lower frequencies, I speak for you?'

The most impressive of the fragments from his work in progress (if it still is in progress) that Ellison has published is called 'And Hickman Arrives'. It concerns a small boy acting out, in a coffin, 'the meaning of resurrection'; but it seems likely that the novel as a whole is now beyond Ellison's powers.

The truly ideological representatives of the proletarian movement – **Robert Cantwell** (1908), who wrote only two novels, *Laugh and Lie Down* (1931) and *The Land of Plenty* (1934), and **Mary Heaton Vorse**, author of *Strike – A Novel of Gastonia* (1930), and so on – did not leave any important fiction behind them. And even the more enduring work of Richard Wright (q.v.) (but not of Ellison, q.v., who was six years younger and in any case waited until he was thirty-eight before publishing his novel) is flawed by political conviction rather than otherwise. Steinbeck's (q.v.) view was confused; Farrell's (q.v.) was limited, enabling him to complete only the one satisfactory book, the Lonigan trilogy. However, there are three novelists of the Thirties, all Jews, whose fiction goes beyond politics to, as Walter Allen has rightly claimed, confront 'the human condition in its naked terror'. That is not to say that these men were not affronted by the hideous injustices of the Thirties. They certainly all were. But in their books they went straight to the reasons for them; they did not see the reasons as primarily political or economic. And the general superiority of Roth and West (qq.v.) perhaps proves that it is not at any rate the writer's business to see things in economic terms – but rather to examine the human disease that produces the economic symptoms, and which perpetuates capitalism (or its alternatives).

Daniel Fuchs (1909), the least gifted of these writers, but nevertheless a substantial talent, was born in New York City; he long ago turned to the writing of movie scripts as a way of life; his three novels of the Thirties, *Summer in Williamsburg* (1934), *Homage to Blenholt* (1936) and *Low Company* (1937), attracted no attention until they were reissued in 1961 as *Three Novels* (*The Williamsburg Trilogy*, 1972), when they were immediately acclaimed. Fuchs' apparently lightweight, Jewish humour, his good-natured irony, anticipated the manner of the 'Jewish novel' with which we have become perhaps too familiar in the last decade. He seems to stand squarely behind Bellow and Malamud (qq.v.). And yet he was writing like this – about Jews in New York's Lower East Side during the Depression – long before either of these writers began. Fuchs is a comic novelist; his characters inevitably fail, usually comically; they are incapable of inspiring any reader with a sense of tragedy. They are knowing, but their knowledge gets them nowhere: they are innocently without innocence, and some of them intuitively realize their futility. There is no tragic resonance in Fuchs' work, but his comedy is the genuine article. Above all he is truthful and never gratuitously unpleasant. He is detached from his characters, but he understands them. His stories are in *The Apathetic Bookie Joint* (1979). The later novel *West of the Rockies* (1971) demonstrates that Fuchs has not changed his attitudes – but that movie-script writing has affected his style, to its detriment: it is careless when compared to the earlier trilogy.

Henry Roth (1906) is the author of one indisputable masterpiece, *Call it Sleep* (1934), one of the most beautiful books of the century. He found himself unable to complete a second novel, and he has never been able to return to writing again – apart from nine uncollected stories. This has been a real loss. Essentially *Call it Sleep* is the story of the anguish of a small boy, David Schearl, the son of European Jewish immigrants to America in 1907. His father is a withdrawn paranoiac who is useless to this sensitive son; so the boy goes to his mother, who is herself in a state of perpetual culture-shock: alienated from her surroundings by language and custom. The boy haunts the streets learning about sex, crime and cruelty, all the time in an abject terror of something his irritable Rabbi teacher calls God. At last he finds a way to unify his disparate fears into something meaningful and divine. His teacher has spoken of the coal of fire with which God cleansed the mouth of his prophet, Isaiah. And two young toughs have forced him to drop a piece of metal into the crack between the two electrified streetcar rails. The resultant flash has struck him as something fearful but divine. One day he is forced to fly from his father's sick rage. This phantasmagoric flight through the streets, and its outcome, is one of the most intensely related episodes in American fiction. The boy thrusts a metal ladle into the electrified crack, and is shocked into an insensibility which purges him of the horrors he has endured. As he recovers he has a reconciling vision. He does not know how to describe this unconsciousness: 'call it sleep'.

Nathanael West (originally Nathanael Weinstein, 1903–40), who lost his own and his wife's life when he failed to stop for an oncoming car in California, was a close friend of many writers, including Farrell, William Carlos Williams and Fitzgerald (qq.v.), but his four novels were not greatly appreciated until the early Fifties. He drifted around in the late Twenties in such jobs as sub-managing or managing hotels; and for a time he edited the magazine *Contact* with Williams. He had spent some time in Paris in the mid-Twenties, and he thoroughly absorbed surrealism (q.v.) – but hardly ever reproduced it. He spent the last six or seven years of his life in Hollywood, a sexually solitary and perhaps tormented man. Then he met Eileen McKenney, the heroine of the silly book *My Sister Eileen* by Ruth McKenney; he married her and they had a few months of great happiness before they died in the car accident.

West was not a more powerful or poetic writer than Henry Roth, but he developed a wider range. His first book, *The Dream Life of Balso Snell* (1931), entirely ignored when it appeared, is nothing much in itself, although brilliant in promise. It is a fantasy inspired by surrealism, in which Balso Snell discovers, 'while walking in the tall grass that has sprung up around the city of Troy', Homer's 'ancient song'; he decides to enter the wooden horse, and discovers the 'posterior opening of the alimentary canal', by which he enters it, 'O Anus Mirabilis!'

West was not only original in his own right, but he was the original black comedian (and with a surer touch than any of his successors) – after all, *Miss Lonelyhearts* (1933) preceded Fuchs' (q.v.) first novel by a year. This is not his best book – *The Day of the Locust* (1939) is that – but because in it he discovered the procedures most suitable to his genius, it does sometimes reasonably seem to be. It is certainly a very good, and a very grim, book. The journalist hero is given the job of answering the 'lonely hearts' letters on a popular newspaper. He collapses under the pressure of the job and of the cynicism of his colleague Shrike ('Why don't you give them something new and hopeful? Tell them about art'). He needs to become nothing less than Jesus Christ; and he means it. But he perishes (crucified?), the accidental victim of a cripple whose wife he has seduced and whom he (too sentimentally?) wants to save.

The irony and terror of this was already beyond anything a specifically modern America had yet produced; and it was written from the centre of it. It is instructive to compare West's response to that of Fitzgerald (q.v.): the former was hardly an inferior writer – though he lacked Fitzgerald's psychological penetration, he compensated for this with his crackling energy. West's next novel, *A Cool Million, or The Dismantling of Lemuel Pitkin* (1934), was a departure from the realistic surface of *Miss Lonelyhearts*. It has been criticized, and probably underrated, because it adopts a parody of a woman's magazine style. It is sometimes a little jejune, but also very funny – and in the end horrific. There are still few more effective exposures of naïve 'Americanism' and capitalist optimism than this story of the honourable, trusting and parodically innocent Lemuel Pitkin, who loses an eye, his teeth, his scalp and his leg, and after being jailed and used as a tool for both communist and fascist conspiracies, is killed and becomes a martyr in the fascist cause. It disappoints only because it fails to transcend its immediate object – the Horatio Alger legend of the rise to fame and fortune of the honest poor boy – and become a major work of the imagination. It may have been influenced by Ransom's (q.v.) famous poem 'Captain Carpenter'. The same cannot be said of West's last novel, *The Day of the Locust* (1939). This was composed in a straightforwardly realistic style, and with the great economy West had by then achieved. Despite its refusal to compromise facts or situation or character with sentiment or, indeed, with emotion of any kind and despite the despair which pervades it, *The Day of the Locust* is redolent with pity and understanding as well as the terror of the previous books. The events he depicts are outrageous – he knew and lived in Hollywood, which is enough – but he nurses their vitality, celebrating it sadly.

West's decade was that of Jean Harlow, who initiated a line of sex-symbols that culminated in Marilyn Monroe. Both girls died young. In the character of Faye Greener, West displays a more perfect understanding of the type, and what it represents, than any writer since. What would his wry, intellectually cruel and yet compassionate genius have made of the Miller-Monroe (q.v.) marriage, in which the intellectual, however briefly, 'caught' the dream girl? His description of the relationship between his intelligent hero, the painter Tod Hackett, and Faye Greener suggests an answer. Tod knows what Faye is, but she nevertheless captivates him. He feels that if he can possess her honourably, every-thing may change. ... He has qualms about approaching her as a client while she is working in a brothel. He travels hundreds of miles in order to see her misperform brief scenes in movies she has made. 'Her invitation wasn't to pleasure', West memorably writes. The truth of such books as this often has to wait years before it is heeded. 'It is hard to laugh at the need for beauty and romance', West wrote in it, 'no matter how tasteless, how horrible, the results of that need are. But it is easy to sigh. Few things are sadder than the truly monstrous.' West's work relentlessly depicts the truly monstrous, but also expresses the exact and human quality of its sadness.

Jerome Weidman (1913), another New York Jewish novelist, is unlucky to be given no credit at all by critics. Certainly he is slick and sentimental in his later work (which is nevertheless readable and amusing light reading), but few novelists have been as good at portraying repulsively ruthless (Jewish) characters. His first three books are his best: *I Can Get It for You Wholesale* (1937), *What's in It for Me?* (1938) and the short stories col-lected in *The Horse That Could Whistle 'Dixie'* (1939). Here, as in none of his succeeding work, Weidman displays a cynicism so shocking that, whatever its motives, it is really fascinatingly effective, even if in a thoroughly minor way. Weidman cannot be considered on a level with Daniel Fuchs, let alone West (qq.v.); but he has his tiny niche as carica-turist of Jewish go-getters.

John O'Hara (1905–70), born in Pennsylvania, is another novelist famous for his portraits of heels and for his brutal realism. He had more merit than Weidman (q.v.), especially as a craftsman, albeit somewhat glib, in the short story. After the Thirties O'Hara's work grew increasingly pretentious, vulgar and lurid; little of it needs to be taken into account, although some of the short stories of his final decade are finely observed and compressed. His best novel is his first: *Appointment in Samarra* (1934). This tells of the events leading up to the suicide of Julian English, of Gibbsville, Pennsylvania. While drunk at the country club English throws a highball into the face of a man who could help him in business. It leads to his self-destruction. For although he promises his wife that he will try to make it up the next evening, events conspire to make him drunk again; he goes off to a roadhouse and dances with the mistress of a powerful local boot-legger; then later gets into a fight and finds himself ostracized on all sides. English's motives are not clear, but presumably the throwing of the drink into his potential business friend's face is seen as a decent (anti-materialistic) gesture that he has not the resilience, the decent substance, to sustain. The analysis of Gibbsville and its mores is masterly and fascinating, and on a higher level than anything achieved by Sinclair Lewis (q.v.). But one feels even here that O'Hara is an excellent journalist and sociologist rather than novelist. He has little insight into human character, and his accounts of it resemble good newspaper reporting rather than fiction. All his skill and readability cannot save him from his obtuseness about individuals. The best of his later novels was *Ourselves to Know* (1960), about the life of a successful murderer; but this is none the less rather prolix in the later-Cozzens (q.v.) style.

Very different from O'Hara, superior but less well known and prolific, is the Wisconsin novelist **Glenway Wescott** (1901), who was encouraged but then disliked by Gertrude Stein (q.v.) ('... Glenway Wescott at no time interested Gertrude Stein. He has a certain syrup but it does not pour'). Wescott, though an expatriate for many years, has remained obsessed by Wisconsin, and might even be described as its reluctant laureate. Wescott found the repressive puritanism of his native region restricting and oppressive; but it fascinated him, as did the history of his tough pioneering forebears. He began as a poet (*The Bitterns*, 1920), and his best fiction tries to recapture the bitter poetry of Wisconsin. *The Grandmothers* (1927) is, in its quiet way, of classic status. Although very American it is a highly original novel; the only discernible influence, that of Proust (q.v.), has been thoroughly assimilated. Alwyn Tower, a young man living on the French Mediterranean coast, recreates the lives of his relatives: his three grandmothers (for one grandfather had two wives), his parents, and others. This sometimes painfully nostalgic book recreates the American past with the accuracy and love of a Willa Cather (q.v.). The short stories in *Goodbye Wisconsin* (1928) have similar power. Later novels – *Pilgrim Hawk* (1940), set in Paris, and *Apartment in Athens* (1945) – are of similar high quality. But the lapidary Wescott dried up as a creative writer after 1945. But for what he has achieved he deserves to be classed as an exquisite minor.

High claims have occasionally been made for **John P. Marquand** (1893–1960), but they can hardly be sustained. At its very best, his writing is that of a bland, shrewd and gentlemanly journalist. He began as a journalist, popular romancer and detective-story writer, but then graduated to a higher-middlebrow comedian of manners. He at once satirizes and indulges New England society, but never so as to offend. On the other hand, he is observant and writes smoothly and amusingly. Some of his well known, smug (but pleasantly readable) books are *The Late George Apley* (1937), *Wickford Point* (1939), *H.M. Pulham, Esq.* (1941). His two best are *So Little Time* (1943) and *Sincerely, Willis Wayde* (1955). The first expresses his own regrets at his creative mediocrity in the form of a story about a New York play editor who would like to have done something serious; the second is a knowledgeable study of a business man's rise to power.

Extravagant claims have been made for the Chicago-born **James Gould Cozzens** (1903–78), even by serious critics – one of whom has compared him to C.P. Snow (q.v.), perhaps not without unwitting point. For Cozzens, a crude elitist, is an arch-middlebrow, although by no means an inoffensive one. The book that rocketed him to fame, *By Love Possessed* (1957), is perhaps the most repulsive of all the pretentious novels of the twentieth century. Its successor, *Morning Noon and Night* (1969), is almost deliriously bad in the pretentiousness of its language. However, few critics take these books seriously; attempts to put Cozzens forward as a serious writer have mainly centred on *Men and Brethren* (1936), *The Just and the Unjust* (1942) and, in particular, *Guard of Honour* (1948). What can be said for him? The last book is a fairly meticulous account of three days at a United States Air Force training field in Florida in 1943; but it lacks characterization, and the attitude behind it is reactionary and simplistic. It is one thing to dislike change, another to refuse to acknowledge it. In other words, Cozzens has nothing whatever to say. He was a man with a commonplace temperament who, with happy results for himself, strayed into the field of literature. Cozzens, as *By Love Possessed* shows, has gathered no wisdom, and never had warmth – all one can discern is an extraordinarily virulent hatred of sex – although this did not prevent this anti-semite from selling his wares by including 'explicit sex' passages. Cozzens hides his coldness and civil servant's smugness behind what his admirers take to be a stoical irony. The combination in him, of sly authoritarianism, unwisdom and iciness, is unique. One must grant him, especially in *Guard of Honour*, a certain technical skill. But his 'objectivity', much vaunted by admirers, is simply insensitivity – a human stupidity of remarkable dimensions. A world that grants Cozzens a place in literature is on a long, steep slide into indifference. But he will be rapidly forgotten.

*

Henry Miller (1891–1980) is probably best regarded as an educationist. His reputation has been distorted because some of his books were for years banned in Great Britain and the United States. He has been thought of variously as a writer of dirty books, mage, mystic, daddy of the beats. . . . Miller was born in New York City and worked in a variety of jobs, eventually becoming employment manager for Western Union. He was nearly forty when he went to Paris and took up a literary and bohemian life. He has told the story of his early life in a series of autobiographical books, including *Black Spring* (1936) and *The Rosy Crucifixion* trilogy, consisting of *Sexus* (1949), *Plexus* (1953) and *Nexus* (1960). His tender and straightforward writing about his family and his earlier life is his best, and is run a close second only by the account of his travels in Greece, *The Colossus of Marousi* (1941), and by his account of Conrad Moricand, an astrologer he had known in Paris and unwisely invited to Big Sur, in the section of *Big Sur and the Oranges of Hieronymus Bosch* (1957) called *A Devil in Paradise*, which appeared as a separate volume in 1956. For the last years of his life Miller lived in Big Sur, California.

Miller resists classification inasmuch as he cannot be called critic, poet, novelist, essayist – or even all of these things together. He had no imagination, and his attempts to write 'poetically' (in imitation of Rimbaud, q.v., whom he did not understand and about whom he wrote very poorly) are disastrous. But this gives no cause for puzzlement once it is realized that Miller is a simple-minded, and literal, heir of American nineteenth-century romanticism. Since he lived in the twentieth century, his romanticism developed a defensive, nihilist edge: he is famous for his denunciations of America (*The Air Conditioned Nightmare*, 1945). But it is wrong to call this side of him satirical: it is merely vituperative.

Miller is a true naïve (q.v.), as his embarrassing compilation called *The Books in My Life* (1952) demonstrates: here Rider Haggard rubs shoulders with Mary Baker Eddy and Shakespeare in one of the most haphazard lists ever made. The sage of Big Sur, the Whitmanesque celebrator of the body and the enemy of literature, became for the most part a highly 'literary' writer. It was a sad end to the career of the man who tried harder than any other twentieth-century American writer to realize the specifically American dream of absolute Edenesque freedom. However, Miller had his intrinsic importance as an autobiographer, and his historical importance as a kind of educator of the beat generation. Leslie Fiedler is quite correct in saying that the years of Depression, unemployment and appeasement produced no 'brand of apocalyptic hysteria . . . so eccentric or so heartless as Miller's', and that, deliberately hilarious at his best and undeliberately so at his worst, he was the 'first important . . . anti-tragic writer in America'. But in freeing himself entirely from morality and responsibility – this involved 'being a swine' in the sense of sleeping with his benefactors' wives or stealing the car-fare home from the bag of a woman while laying her – he played a significant role. He carried 'innocence' and candour as far as they could be carried in this century; those who want to study the results need look no further. He thought living more important than writing, and we can judge him as liver as well as writer from his prose. In *Sexus* he tells us: 'I was approaching my thirty-third year, the age of Christ crucified. A wholly new life lay before me, had I the courage to risk all'. This, one might say, is bad life but good writing: good writing because it is true, as true as Miller's lifelong devotions to pseudo-religions and phoney prophets.

Miller is certainly not important for his contributions to the sexual life of the twentieth century. Sex unsettled him so much that a good deal of his writing about it is fairly describable as a way of filling in time (and not much time at that) between orgasms. In his writings about sex Miller proceeds frantically from one encounter to another, a gentle person desperately trying to brutalize his sexual role, not knowing what he is looking for beyond a conscious need to degrade woman, make her comic, not to be tender towards her. Simultaneously he is seeking for a proto-Reichian 'total release'. He can be compassionate about anyone unless it is a woman in a sexual role; but he tries to push all his women into sexual roles. ... He is the less likely to represent a woman as already degraded (simply by the fact of her being physically capable of fulfilling his mindless pleasure) the more she genuinely puzzles him or reminds him of his mother. Thus his second wife, Mona, lesbian, taxi-driver, whore and pathological liar, fascinated him more than any other woman in his writings: his sexual use of her does not exhaust her meaning. Somewhere behind all this, it seems, there is a Whitmanesque homosexual impulse that not even the so much vaunted innocence of total freedom can erase.

Miller is the authentic non-intelligent, natural, 'anti-tragic', free man. One can rightly call him 'eccentric and heartless'. But in him, one might also say, mankind has come some way – from employment manager to lucid autobiographer and clown. His despair, if he had any, had no quality; and his writings about sex are disappointingly pornographic. But can one say more of the silence of employment managers?

Another odd man out of American letters, although in almost every respect at the other end of the scale, is **Vladimir Nabokov** (1899–1977). Miller (q.v.) was odd because he was so representative; Nabokov was so odd because he was, of course, not. One might treat him as Russian, since he was born of a noble Russian family in St. Petersburg (now Leningrad), and he wrote in Russian until 1940. But Nabokov was educated at Cambridge, was an exile all his adult life, was an American citizen, and wrote his more important books in an expert and confident though none the less desperately alienated English, and wrote them about America. Nabokov taught Russian literature at Stanford and Cornell in the United States before his literary success enabled him to retire. He was a distinguished entomologist.

Nabokov's Russian books, most of which have now appeared in English, deal coldly with the anguishes of exile, which none the less come through strongly. They are brilliant, but only one or two of the short stories show feeling towards the characters. The best is *Laughter in the Dark* (*Camera Obscura*, 1933; tr. 1936), about a man's fatal infatuation for a cinema usherette; the worst – foreshadowing the ignominious depths plumbed by *Ada* (1969) – is *King Queen Knave* (1928; tr. 1968). Nabokov's best books came in his second, American phase, when he decided to accept exile and to become – so far as he could – American. Then he began to analyse, with the so far genuinely innocent eye of the foreigner, his surroundings. *Pnin* (1957) tells of a Russian professor of entomology at a college in New York State. *Lolita* (1955), banned for a time, is probably Nabokov's best book. Humbert Humbert becomes obsessed with a twelve-year-old 'nymphet', and in order to gain possession of her marries her mother. After a flight across the United States, as vivid a description of it as has ever been made by a non-American, Lolita is seduced by a playwright, whom Humbert kills.

Nabokov might have been a major writer, but self-congratulatory cleverness and envy killed the intensity in him. His stylistic tricks – punning, anagrams – have energy but very soon become monotonous; they do not add anything fundamental. His style is so hard that it is sometimes brittle, and that brittleness indicates that his aristocratic sensibility – early battered beyond repair by exile – is accompanied by an innate romanticism. Nabokov's course as a writer has been to challenge, combat, even at times to deny this romanticism, acknowledging it only as a sort of baroque nostalgia for St. Petersburg. However, in *Lolita* Nabokov was able, by means of a detachment he had cultivated with care and skill, convincingly to describe the enslaving effect of a certain kind of sexual passion – perhaps one of the things he 'means' by Humbert's passion is romantic love – and the opportunities for evil that it opens up. It is not the novel it might have been because it fails to examine the nature of Humbert's sexual pathology, and because Nabokov pretended that he himself was not fascinated by 'nymphets'. Nabokov's lack of interest in the psychological content is a positive defect, but the book is none the less glitteringly horrible. The clue to Nabokov's deficiencies lies in the atrocious *Ada*, where his delight in himself is anything but aristocratic. The only interest in this book partakes of the nature of the solution to a crossword puzzle.

*

Mary McCarthy (1912), born in Seattle, was orphaned when both her parents died in the influenza epidemic of 1918; she has recorded her experiences at the hands of various relatives in one of her best books, *Memories of a Catholic Girlhood* (1957). For a time she was the wife of **Edmund Wilson** (1895–1972), one of the best of American literary journalists and, with Geoffrey Grigson (q.v.) and one or two others, the last representative of a dying race of literate and informed periodical critics. Wilson, notable for his generosity and his shrewd judgements as a reviewer, also wrote some moderately good fiction, including *I Thought of Daisy* (1929) and *Memoirs of Hecate County* (1946). Like her ex-husband, Mary McCarthy has always remained a journalist; in recent years she has written persuasive criticism of the American involvement in Viet Nam, which she visited. She is a readable, successful and intelligent novelist, often described as 'scathing'. Her subject is usually the unwisdom of those who in our time regard themselves as wise: the cultured and the intellectual. She has little love for her own kind, and this may be the reason why she appeals to a middlebrow readership (she has stooped to its level only twice, in her two books about Venice and Florence); but it must be said that her characters tend to be manipulated for the benefit of her sometimes cheap wit, and that she has little warmth. Her best novels are *The Oasis* (1949), about a modern would-be Utopia; *A Charmed Life* (1955), in which the artistic are castigated; *The Groves of Academe* (1952) and *The Group* (1963), a novel about the fates of eight girls who graduated from Vassar at the same time as Miss McCarthy. This is not psychologically profound, and like all Mary McCarthy's work lacks grace and charity; but it is a useful and readable piece of social history.

The output of **Jean Stafford** (1915), who was born in California and grew up in Colorado, was slender. From 1940 until 1948 – eight difficult years for her – she was married to Robert Lowell (q.v.), and later, after a second marriage, she had a short (1959–63) marriage to the late A.J. Liebling, journalist and sports writer. Her perceptive and sharp first novel, *Boston Adventure* (1944), subjects Boston society to the scrutiny of Sonia Marburg, the daughter of an immigrant chambermaid; Sonia works as secretary to the wealthy spinster Miss Peabody. *The Mountain Lion* (1947) is one of those rare novels that can penetrate the world of children without shattering or sentimentalizing it. *Children Are Bored on Sunday* (1953) and *Bad Characters* (1965) are collections of short stories. Her final novel *The Catherine Wheel* (1952) was a failure; but the *Collected Stories* of 1969, though not complete, showed her at her best.

The South is a violent place, and a conservative one. It is not an easy place for its sensitive or liberal inhabitants, who, like Faulkner (q.v.), form part of its tradition and yet oppose it – thus opposing a part of themselves. Perhaps the painfulness of living in the South is one of the reasons why the New Criticism – essentially an attempt to evolve an objective criticism – came from there. Following the period of reconstruction after the Civil War the South, given the best will in the world, had nearly insoluble problems. Where, above all, was it to deploy the mass of freed slaves? The problem is not, of course, solved; the South-eastern United States throws up Faulkners, and it also throws up Wallaces. Literature often flourishes under difficult conditions; the Southern renaissance has added greatly to the literature of modern America, even if its contribution has been markedly pessimistic. This has been a defeated area, not one of hope; but it is also a perfect microcosm of crazy modern man as he ruins his world. Faulkner towers above everyone else in this renaissance of letters, both in scope and depth; if in his life he had to hit the bottle, and if he ended in self-parody, in his best works he still sums up the South: its aspirations, its despairs, above all its doomed sense of itself. But there were others besides Faulkner. Some writers, although Southerners, contributed little to Southern literature as such: Thomas Wolfe (q.v.) is one; Erskine Caldwell (q.v.) is another. The first of these is an individualist (or an egocentric); the second is excellent on poor whites, but does not even try to see them in their context. They certainly do not build on the foundations laid by Kate Chopin and Ellen Glasgow (qq.v.).

In 1962 **Katherine Anne Porter** (1890–1980), born at Indian Creek in Texas, published a long novel, which had become a legend, having been announced as imminent over a period of twenty years. This was *Ship of Fools*. An 'appallingly obvious and dull' (Leslie Fiedler) 'moral allegory' about a voyage, it is a surprising middlebrow negation of her previous work, which consists of short stories and novellas. In these earlier works – *Flowering Judas* (1930), stories, *Pale Horse, Pale Rider* (1939), three novellas and *The Leaning Tower* (1944), stories – she studies the effects of the changes in the South on the personalities of individuals; many of the stories deal with a girl called Miranda – into whose figure Katherine Anne Porter doubtless projected some of her own history – at various stages of her life. However, she became embroiled in the fanciful lies she told about herself and her origins (more humble than she admitted), and probably she quite early lost the ability to distinguish between fact and fiction. But this does not detract from her best work.

Although Katherine Anne Porter travelled all over Europe, and lived in many parts of America (New Orleans, Chicago, Denver, Mexico City, New York, and elsewhere), the central concern of her writing is her Southern heritage – not the actual one, but the one she made up for herself. Her life was dedicated to the subsidization of her creative writing, a vocation she once said she would not herself have chosen; in her earlier days she had to perform many unwelcome journalistic chores. She spoke of herself (1933) as 'a woman who goes with her mind permanently absent from the place where she is'. Her aim was 'to tell a straight story and to give true testimony'. But the testimony was not to the truth of fact but of her imagination. One might describe her best writings as imaginatively in quest of the meaning of herself and of her peculiar heritage, even though she romanticized this. She revealed her awareness by means of 'epiphanies' (q.v.), moments of sudden illumination: for example the child Miranda, curiously alienated from the tradition of which she is a part, even a kind of freak, understands her situation through seeing a circus performance. It is interesting that her Miranda is, potentially at least, the kind of liar Porter was. But then fiction is lying. Almost always the moments of revelation indicate a tragic situation, meticulously and exquisitely set forth. The nearest to such illuminations is to be found in some of Emily Dickinson's (q.v.) poems. Few writers have been able to suggest such vast accumulations of fact, such complex histories, in so short a compass. *Noon Wine* (1937), included in *Pale Horse, Pale Rider*, is characteristic. It works perfectly on the realistic level, but sets up extraordinary resonances, both parabolic and symbolic. Mr. Thompson, married to an invalid, unhappily and inefficiently runs a Texas dairy farm. Then the work of an enigmatic new hired man, Mr. Helton, puts things right. After nearly a decade Homer T. Hatch turns up: he claims that Mr. Helton is an escaped lunatic, and tries to capture him for profit. Thompson kills him, but is acquitted of murder; however, Hatch posthumously succeeds in ruining his life, for he cannot bear his guilt, and kills himself. What really happened? The question forms itself as naturally as it does when we seek explanations in the non-fictional world.

Since most of the members of the Southern Agrarian movement were poets, it is dealt with in the following section. One of the leading spirits was Allen Tate (q.v.), who for over a quarter of a century was married to the Southern novelist **Caroline Gordon** (1895–1981). Caroline Gordon was born in Kentucky; her people on both sides had been tobacco-planters 'since the weed was first cultivated by white men'. Her novels are exceptionally skilful, but their austerity has prevented them from having a wide effect. They were constructed with great deliberation on principles derived mainly from Flaubert and Henry James (qq.v.); in particular Gordon prized the Jamesian 'central intelligence'. *Penhally* (1931), her first novel, set the tone for its successors. An account of a Kentucky family over several generations, it demonstrated the author's grasp of the details of Southern history. Only Caroline Gordon remained truly faithful to the original aims of the Southern Agrarians (q.v.). She accepted the destruction of the South, but demanded a return to a new order based as far as possible on the old one. Thus she is hardly a realist, and one does not go to her for her political ideas. She would not write about the sort of people who interfered with her moral plans. *None Shall Look Back* (1937), a study of the Confederate general, Nathan Bedford Forrest, is her most severe novel. It gives her picture of the old South: gracious, heroic, feudal but benevolent to its slaves (who are represented as ungrateful!), and yet is, as Walter Allen has said, somehow 'abstract ... static': has life ever actually been lived like this? But this is nevertheless an important novel, even if an obviously limited one: it gives, at a serious level of intelligence (however its sensitivity is to be judged), the picture of the old South that so many still hold – and have great nostalgia for. Unfortunately *None Shall Look Back* appeared in the shadow of Margaret Mitchell's *Gone With the Wind* (1936), a piece of unauthentic though skilful trash about the South that made history as a best seller, and then as a movie. The best of Caroline Gordon's later novels is *The Malefactor* (1956), which puts to good use her extensive knowledge of literary people, including the essentially shifty, selfish, inflated Tate. Caroline Gordon's over-deliberate craftsmanship and Roman Catholic dogmatism vitiate her fiction; but she remains readable within a highly conservative tradition.

Another close associate of the Agrarians, although somewhat younger than the rest of the group, was the Kentuckian **Robert Penn Warren** (1905), who is a critic, poet and academic as well as a novelist. It was Warren, who cannot now be described as other than a liberal, who first saw that Faulkner (q.v.) was being misjudged, in the Thirties, for 'having the wrong politics'; who saw that Faulkner's work went well beyond any kind of politics. A considerable but never wholly satisfactory writer in every genre that he has attempted, Warren has some affinities with Faulkner, in particular his tendency to treat of violence and evil. But Warren's approach is more cerebral, and rhetorical at points of stress, and thus loses power. He has a colloquial liveliness that is rare in a 'new critic' of his generation; certainly, reading some of his criticism, one would not imagine him to be the kind of novelist he in fact is. As a poet Warren is consistently interesting; but he has not succeeded in discovering a voice that is distinctively his own, and he lacks concentration. His and Cleanth Brooks' *Understanding Poetry* (1938), a text book of the New Criticism, revolutionized the teaching of poetry in American universities, and its effects are still felt; it is possible that Warren's critical self-consciousness has weakened or dispersed his poetic impulse. *Selected Poems 1923–1975* (1976).

He is a self-conscious novelist, too; and again, whatever weaknesses his fiction has may be traced to this (he and Brooks wrote an *Understanding Fiction*, 1943, as well . . .). For example, might not his surprisingly crude and often middlebrow (i.e. empty) rhetoric (something, however, to which many American writers are prone) be an attempt to escape from his over-intellectualism? His fiction has rightly been seen as developing straight out of Faulkner; one senses that he would sacrifice much of his critical intellect in order to attain to Faulkner's power. Certainly one sometimes gets the notion that Warren hates being a thinker, and wants to escape from it. And yet this is to judge by the highest standards. Warren is a serious writer, of undeniable quality; it is this that makes his failure to reconcile his strong creative impulses with his intellectual processes a serious and disappointing one. In his most famous novel, *All the King's Men* (1946), a study of a Huey-Long-style Southern politician, there is an imbalance that results from Warren's attempt to escape his critical self-consciousness. This is a pity, because few more gifted novelists have tackled a more fascinating theme: that of the problem of how, when or why doing good by corrupt means is wrong, or ultimately destructive. Willie Stark does good (as well as evil) ruthlessly, and one of Warren's intended messages is perfectly clear: that nothing, even reform and justice and a square deal, is worse than totalitarianism. But Warren chooses as narrator a newspaperman called Jack Burden, a history graduate. Burden begins by accepting Stark at face value, and idealistically supports him. He even causes the suicide of a respected judge by digging something discreditable from his past – only to discover that this judge was his own father. Eventually, when Stark is assassinated by an idealistic doctor – but not for political reasons – Burden is supposed 'to understand'. However, he is an unconvincing figure, and the novel as a whole leaves one with a strong impression that Willie Stark is, after all, a hero – that had he not become personally (sexually) corrupted by power, he might have survived to do even more good. Burden is supposed to understand, by the end, that Willie has been corrupted by power; but Burden is an intellectual, a representative of Warren, and he is not convincing. *All the King's Men* therefore fails to demonstrate how power does corrupt. It simply shows power corrupting.

Warren has written some notable short stories, collected in *The Circus in the Attic* (1947). His 'tale in verse and voices', *Brother to Dragons* (1953), is his most formidable effort to recapture the horror of the Jacobean era; much more successful than the lurid and theatrical novel *World Enough and Time* (1950); *Brother to Dragons* tells the story of the axe-killing of a Negro by the sons of President Jefferson's sister; the author introduces himself as 'R.P.W.', an interlocutor of the twentieth century. This is, again, a powerful work, and yet it is a little too calculated, for all its concentration on evil and the deliberateness of its melodrama, to quite come off.

Claims have been made for Warren's later fiction, especially for *Flood* (1964). But it is likely that posterity will endorse Walter Allen's view that Warren's best novel is his first: *Night Rider* (1939). This is, in a way, on the same theme as the more ambitious *All the King's Men*: Percy Munn joins the Night Riders, an illicit organization formed to destroy a tobacco-buyer's ring that threatens the small growers of Kentucky, out of idealism; but the nature of its activity, which he helps to direct, corrupts him. The scenes of violence here are superbly described, and reinforce the suggestion that the full expression of a tragic vision of life has been prevented by too zealous an adherence to a critical theory, and by too violent attempts to escape from this.

A lesser novelist, but an interesting one, is **T.S. Stribling** (1881–1965), who was born in Tennessee. He is interesting because his obvious starting-point, his inspiration, was

Sinclair Lewis (q.v.), a considerably inferior writer: his first significant novel, *Birthright* (1922), appeared just two years after *Main Street* (q.v.). This applies Lewis' methods to a different kind of problem: not one of mere smugness but one of savage injustice. An educated mulatto returns to a Tennessee town to try, as is his just and human due, to make his way. He fails horribly. The novel has more point than Lewis', although it is worse written by any standards, and much less journalistically clever; and Stribling, who had practised law in the South and knew his rogues as well as the others, displays as much knowledge as Lewis – which makes this and some of its successors rather neglected novels (two years after his death not a single book by him was listed as in print). *Teeftallow* (1926) is an even more Lewisian study, this time of a confidence-trickster, a small-time Southern politician, Railroad Jones, who climbs to wealth and influence by exploitation of the vileness of the people of his Tennessee mountain town. The couple who love each other and fail to conform are destroyed. Again, this is a novel whose corrosive bitterness is not forced. But better was to come from Stribling: a trilogy consisting of *The Forge* (1931), *The Store* (1932) and *Unfinished Cathedral* (1934). This traces the history of a family, the Vaidens, in Florence, Alabama. It is not a major work of the imagination, nor is it well-written; but it is none the less a truthful novel. Jimmy Vaiden rises from poor white to a position of dominance in the region; but he loses his slaves after the Civil War, and gets into debt to the local storekeeper. His son Miltiades, Klansman and ex-colonel, unscrupulously and dishonestly acquires the store. Finally we see him in his power, president of the local bank, feared and 'loved'. He is building a cathedral as his monument. Stribling is crude and his satire is laboured. But he was a pioneer. We meet the Vaidens again, after all, in the Snopes. Faulkner (q.v.) purchased the Vaiden trilogy as it appeared and kept it until his death. He owed much to it.

Eudora Welty (1909) was born in Mississippi, yet in one important sense she chose to be Southern, for her father was from Ohio and her mother from West Virginia – which does not count, culturally, as a Southern state. Although she has written good novels, Eudora Welty is plainly at her best as a writer of short stories and novellas. She is an original, even an idiosyncratic writer, who was admired and encouraged by, among others, Ford Madox Ford, Katherine Anne Porter and Robert Penn Warren (qq.v.). A writer who has influenced her is Henry Green (q.v.), about whom she has written interestingly.

Eudora Welty is at her strongest in the short forms of fiction probably because she is best of all at compressed portraits of eccentrics. These are often called caricatures, but this is not the right word: Miss Welty seizes an individual at a self-revelatory moment, and the resultant portrait often appears as a caricature. In fact it is more often a truthful account of the person. She has the capacity to create characters that puzzle as much as those from everyday life. Is the postmistress of China Grove, Mississippi, in 'Why I Live at the P.O.' – in the collection *A Curtain of Green* (1941) – schizophrenic or merely eccentric? That the story generates arguments on the point is tribute to Miss Welty's powers of characterization. It is true that the characters in the stories are frequently neurotics, eccentrics or in a few cases psychotics; but they are nevertheless seen as they are, and if they provide comedy, they provide quite as much pathos. Of course, dealing with such material invariably produces risks, and when Miss Welty tries consciously for symbolic effects she fails. But when she concentrates on the small-town Mississippi life that she has observed so carefully and understands so well, she frequently makes more universal statements. Besides *A Curtain of Green*, her story collections include *The Wide Net* (1943), *The Golden Apples* (1949) and *The Bride of the Innisfallen* (1955). *The Shoe Bird* (1964) is for children. *Delta Wedding* (1946) and *The Ponder Heart* (1954) are two of her five novels. *Collected Stories* (1980) was followed by another collection, *Moon Lake* (1980). It has been suggested that Eudora Welty is not essentially Southern. The answer is to imagine her fiction without the South. The strangeness of her characters is a Southern strangeness.

Two important Southern woman novelists are **Carson McCullers** (1917–67) and Flannery O'Connor (q.v.). Carson McCullers was born Lula Carson Smith in Georgia. She studied in New York, and married Reeves McCullers when she was just twenty. She published *The Heart is a Lonely Hunter* in 1940, at just about the time when she and her husband had agreed to divorce. For the next five years she lived mostly in New York, publishing *Reflections in a Golden Eye* (1941) and a number of short stories. She remarried Reeves McCullers, who had been wounded in the war, in 1945; this broke up in 1951, for Reeves had turned into a drug- and alcohol-addict – he killed himself in Paris soon after Carson McCullers left him. She herself suffered intermittently from heart disease, paralytic strokes, and pneumonia; when she died from a stroke she was also suffering from breast cancer. Her health had been deteriorating since her marriage in 1937. She managed, however, to produce several more books: *The Member of the Wedding* (1946), which she dramatized (1950), *The Ballad of the Sad Café* (1951), an omnibus volume containing her first three novels as well as collecting most of the stories, the play *The Square Root of Wonderful* (1958) and the final novel, *Clock Without Hands* (1961). Edward Albee (q.v.) successfully dramatized her short story *The Ballad of the Sad Café* in 1963. Although her last years were such a struggle against illness and incapacity, Carson McCullers published in 1964 a charming book of children's poetry: *Sweet as a Pickle and Clean as a Pig*.

Like the other Southern woman writers of fiction (Katherine Anne Porter, Eudora Welty, Flannery O'Connor, qq.v.) Carson McCullers deals in eccentrics and grotesques. This is an effect that the South has upon the minor writer. (It may well be that in trying to meet the challenge with major fiction, such a writer as Warren, q.v., has fallen short of the achievement of this quartet; certainly Wolfe, q.v., failed so abjectly, so far as the South is concerned, that his fiction has scarcely any relevance to it.)

Carson McCullers is essentially a minor writer, and she has strengthened her best work by keeping strictly to her limitations. She has been misunderstood when critics have judged her analyses of crippled individuals as dissections of poisoned cultures. Miss McCullers was enough of a medical freak to be able to feel sympathy for more drastically maimed persons. But there is no sense, in her books, of horror at physical or mental deformity. She is in one important sense an affirmative writer, for she shows the world of her crippled characters to be beautiful and loving rather than horrible; true, her sense of the whole world is not an altogether beautiful one – but she does show, as few other modern writers have done, that what seems or is taken to be ugly is not necessarily so.

Her best work is in *The Heart is a Lonely Hunter*, the short story, almost a novella, 'The Ballad of the Sad Café', and *The Member of the Wedding*. *Reflections in a Golden Eye*, set in a pre-war army camp in the South, was a disastrous experiment in the macabre and is a thoroughly bad and, by its author's standards, pretentious piece of Gothic. *The Heart is a Lonely Hunter*, set in a small Georgian mill town, is concerned with an intelligent deaf-mute called John Singer and his effect on four people. He lives with the feeble-minded Spiros Antonapoulos, whom he loves. (There is no hint of homosexuality.) When Antonapoulos becomes ill and anti-social and has to be taken to a mental hospital, Singer enters into the lives of four other people, none of whom has an inkling of the grief he is feeling. Most beautifully drawn of these is the twelve-year-old girl Mick, who wants to be a composer. Finally Antonapoulos dies, and Singer kills himself; his disciples are puzzled – for they have never understood or cared about him personally. But each of them, too, is defeated. This book is flawed by over-writing, by a too conscious use of allegory that sometimes ruins the action on a realistic level, and by some too consciously taken – and contradictory – decisions about what Singer represents (Christ? Satan?). But it remains an important and beautiful book; the enigmatic, ambiguous nature of Singer, which is really the point of the novel, is maintained despite such details as his age at death (thirty-three) and his 'look of peace'.

'The Ballad of the Sad Café' is the most perfect of Carson McCullers' fiction. In this grotesque tale of Miss Amelia Evans, grasping merchant and generous healer, her imagination found its real shape; simultaneously she discovered her true voice. In all her other books, even *The Member of the Wedding*, her language is uncertain: she is given to ineffective comparisons and has a penchant for lofty pseudo-poeticisms. *The Member of the Wedding* is Carson McCullers' most realistic book, and her best full-length work. It tells the story of the entry of Frankie Addams into adolescence, and introduces the most straightforwardly sympathetic of all the author's characters, the four-times married, black cook, Berenice Sadie Brown. This is a lyrical, comic and hardly ever sentimental novel, moving and refreshing. *Clock Without Hands* never comes up to this level; its chief weaknesses are linguistic slackness and, again, unfulfilled symbolic pretensions. However, it is at least evident that had its author not been so seriously incapacitated (mainly by paralytic strokes) she could have gone on to write the major novel of which *The Heart is a Lonely Hunter* had shown her capable.

Flannery O'Connor (1925–64), another Georgian, was also the victim of painful and crippling ill health: she inherited disseminated lupus from her father, and became progressively crippled by the complications the necessary treatment set up; she must have known that she would die prematurely. Flannery O'Connor was born a Roman Catholic and remained one all her life. She began by trying to become a cartoonist, but soon changed over to fiction. Her fiction is quite clearly related to cartoon – but to a very sophisticated and extended form of it. Despite her illness and the discomfort it caused her Flannery O'Connor was a gay and wisecracking woman, who accepted as many invitations as she could to lecture and to appear in public. She found time to write two novels, *Wise Blood* (1952) and *The Violent Bear it Away* (1960), and two collections of short stories, *A Good Man is Hard to Find* (1955) and the posthumous *Everything that Rises Must Converge* (1965).

Flannery O'Connor is a difficult writer, who mixes Southern Gothic (but in a more controlled form than Carson McCullers, q.v.), grotesque humour and an extremely complex and sometimes over-complicated and therefore self-defeating symbolism. Once again, her characters are grotesque. But her Catholicism (her religious 'position' seems to have approximated to, or at least to have been sympathetic towards, that of Teilhard de Chardin) gives her a completely different perspective from any other Southern writer. Her first remarkable novel is about an anti-Christ, one Haze Motes who loses his (Protestant) faith while in the army and thereafter tries to establish a Church Without Christ, 'the church that the blood of Jesus don't foul with redemption', in the Tennessee mountains where he lives. Haze believes his blood is wise because it is natural; his blood actually is wise, since he is, despite himself, the voice of the living God: even if he preaches an anti-Church, his preachings are more authentic than those of the secular contemporary Church: he is holy. Haze, in a book whose symbolism becomes more and more complex and theological, finally blinds himself with lime. Although herself of the Catholic faith, Flannery O'Connor sees Southern Protestant primitivism as an authentic Christianity – as hideously authentic as the truth (to her) of God's love and Christ's redemption. (It is only fair to add that her theme has also been interpreted as 'the spiritual distortions that are the consequence of Protestant primitivism'.) The symbolism of *Wise Blood*, which is very theological, tends to show Haze's life as comic – and distorted – but as a comic and distorted parallel to Christ's. Its fault is that, because of the bizarre and comic elements, no sense of anguish is allowed to come across. The things the author writes about (wearing barbed wire next to the skin, blinding oneself with quicklime) are so painful, so Grand Guignol, that they defeat their own ends: this gospel is ultimately eccentric rather than authentic. However, the manner in which Flannery O'Connor has set up an anti-Christianity is subtle and intelligent, even if, finally, a kind of sermon lies at the very back of it all.

The Violent Bear it Away (1960) has more imagination and less ingenuity, and is the better book. Francis Marion Tarwater's great-uncle, a mad prophet and illicit whisky-distiller, dies; but he has instructed his great-nephew to become a prophet, and to begin his ministry by baptizing his cousin Bishop Rayber. Tarwater, who does not wish to be a prophet, carries out this order – but also drowns him, as directed by Satan, previously only a voice in his head. He does all he can to avoid his calling. But ultimately, drugged and sodomized by Satan, he is driven into madness and authentic prophecy. Tarwater is certainly representative of the true Church, which must become itself – lose reason – to save the world. Clearly Flannery O'Connor, like so many other contemporary Catholics, was desperately unhappy about the present Church, which she saw as betraying itself.

It is possible that posterity will see the best of Flannery O'Connor's short stories – such stories as 'The Artificial Nigger', 'The Lame Shall Enter First' and 'Parker's Back' – as her most enduring work. On the whole these are easier to read in the sense that, while they possess as formidable a symbology, it is not as relentlessly calculated a one. But this view has been challenged, on the grounds that she put everything that was really important to her into the novels. The answer to that might be that she put in everything that she thought most important to her into the novels. ... Certainly she is the most unusual of the Southern woman writers. As Stanley Edgar Hyman has pointed out, she goes back not to Faulkner but to Mark Twain (qq.v.), as her brilliant use of dialect shows; further, the writer by whom she was most influenced (this again was Hyman's discovery) was Nathanael West (q.v.). She also resembles certain French Catholic writers such as Bernanos and, even more, Bloy (qq.v.): for example, racial integration is for her a senti-mentality: what is important is beyond life. And yet, for all her important differences from her fellow Southern writers, it is impossible to consider her as anything but a Southern novelist: 'I have found that any fiction that comes out of the South,' she said, 'is going to be considered grotesque by the Northern critic, unless it is grotesque, in which case it is going to be considered realistic'. To a certain extent she dealt with material that was necessarily beyond her experience; and to that exact extent her material is over-distorted. But she saw very deeply into the actual distortion which the South is – and into its peculiar violence.

James Agee (1909–55), born in Tennessee, was almost the only one of all the serious writers who went to Hollywood to script movies that were above average: *The African Queen* is a real improvement on its original. Agee was a good film critic, one of the best; but he destroyed himself in the interests of the cinema industry – even though he was trying to improve it. He first attained fame with *Let Us Now Praise Famous Men* (1941), superb chronicles of the daily lives of Alabama sharecroppers with photographs by Walker Evans. He wrote some poetry of quality, though not of genius, and took to fiction only towards the end of his life. *A Death in the Family* (1955), which is an unfinished, partly autobiographical, novel, is one of the few positive novels to come out of the South. It tells of the shattering effect on a happy Tennessee family of the father's death in a car accident (Agee's own father died in one when he was six years old). It is important for its picture of decency in Tennessee – not a thing much celebrated in fiction. Agee dispersed his gifts, but his novels – the first was *The Morning Watch* (1951), about a young student at a religious school who gradually loses his faith – achieved enough to ensure his survival.

The Virginian **William Styron** (1925) is a most gifted writer who has become progressively the victim of an ambition to write the great Southern novel. He has finally settled down to writing vulgar blockbusters which become 'important films' and which are wholly irrelevant to literature. This became apparent with the overblown, over-rhetorical *Sophie's Choice* (1979). *Lie Down in Darkness* (1951) was acclaimed. Since then, with the exception of the novella *The Long March* (1953), he succumbed to the temptation to try to contain the whole Southern story between the two covers of one book. His only complete failure, however, was *The Confessions of Nat Turner* (1969), the story of the slave insurrection of 1831 and its leader, in which he simply took on more than he could handle. This novel is of course interesting, but Styron, consciously a liberal and consciously a subtle and sophisticated novelist, left his invention and his imagination too little room. *Lie Down in Darkness*, for all its debts to Joyce and Faulkner (qq.v.) and its lofty and highly unimpressive rhetoric, is, like its successor *Set This House on Fire*, an impressive book, with passages of first-class quality. The latter has the courage to try to take a leaf out of Dostoevski's book; at least it does not make itself look foolish. One can certainly say that Styron's novels do not cohere, and that the Nat Turner book was a mistake, an attempt to take on too much; but one must concede that his first two books are both readable and continuously intelligent.

The admirers of Nebraska-born **Wright Morris** (1910) invariably complain that he is neglected. To the extent that he does not enjoy huge sales and that not one of his novels has been a total critical success, this is true. But he is very much an intellectuals' writer: he makes no concessions. (And yet there are many snobs and fools among his admirers.) Wright Morris is an off-beat, original writer, whose sardonic approach to life – which he regards as absurd without making any fuss about it whatever – has not attracted the 'general reader'. His books have not been kept in print, and not one of the near-score he has written since 1961 has found a British publisher. Morris' outlook is neither comforting nor discomforting; he is, rather, acutely sophisticated. He is, apart from his fans (many of whom cannot read him), awaiting discovery. His first novel, *My Uncle Dudley* (1942), is about a long trip and a successful confidence man. Morris is a professional photographer, and two of his books are illustrated with his own photographs. *The Inhabitants* (1946) set out to show 'what it is to be an American', and failed; but the photographs are interesting. *The Home Place* (1948) is a novel about a writer who returns to Nebraska with his wife and children to live; *The World in the Attic* (1949), without the nostalgic photographs, is its sequel. These combine an aching love for the past, felt to be pointless, with a horror of the present that spends itself as nervous comedy. His first substantial, and his most moving, novel was *The Works of Love* (1952), about a Midwest egg-farmer who is successful in business but comically unsuccessful with women. This is a subtle variation on the 'holy fool' theme, as exploited in Wilder's *Heaven's My Destination* (q.v.). Wright Morris is a most peculiar and unusual writer in that he expects nothing good whatever from life – but this is none the less a bitter book in effect, since no one to whom the egg-farmer offers his love even recognizes it for what it is. *The Huge Season* (1954) is about money and its corrupting effects. *Love Among the Cannibals* (1957), his most sheerly comic novel, deals with two bad song-writers and the girls they pick up on their way to Acapulco. *What a Way to Go* (1962) is a relentless but wayward study of the marriage of a middle-aged small-college professor to a very young girl. Morris is often an over-subtle and too self-conscious writer; he has not always succeeded in being simply the 'photographer' he wanted to be in the sense he meant when he said 'The windmill, the single plough, the grain elevator, the receding horizon, are both signs and symbols at the same time. They speak for themselves. They would rather talk than be talked about.

The man who loves these things ... is a photographer.' He also suffers from an archness and an involuteness, a lack of straightforwardness. But he is serious and sensitive, and his peculiar methods force his readers to see things from new angles. However, he is a minor writer because of his wild unevenness: no serious novelist can write so sheerly badly. He is also capable of being very silly. Probably his first two books of 'photo-texts', inspired by *Let Us Now Praise Famous Men* (q.v.), though flawed, are his best: *The Inhabitants* and *The Home Place* (1948).

Wallace Stegner (1909), born in Iowa, is, in truth, more neglected than Morris (q.v.), for he has achieved more, though his ideas are intrinsically less interesting. He writes from the conviction that men cannot be defined except in forms of the groups that formed them. So that, while (as he says) he resists the more rigid aspects of social mores, he is essentially a conservative and traditional writer, standing in sharp contrast to someone like Bellow (q.v.) – though these remarks have no relevance to political stance. There is something of the unanimist (q.v.) about Stegner, the unifying theme of whose consider- able body of work is the American West, the trek towards it, and its continuing traditions, and, increasingly, the betrayal of those traditions. Into the nature of this betrayal Stegner does not see too clearly.

Stegner, a 'solid' minor writer rather than a sensationalist one, is less of a psychologist than an observer of the fates of groups as they move from place to place in search of a satisfactory life. But in *On a Darkling Plain* (1940) he wrote convincingly and movingly of a young First World War veteran who tries to isolate himself from the modern ways, which, like his creator, he essentially rejects (Stegner hates the urban and everything about it, and can deal with it only as a huge menace to civilization). Stegner has written a useful history of the Mormons, *The Gathering of Zion* (1964) – he graduated from the University of Utah – and a biography of the explorer John Wesley Powell, *Beyond the Hundredth Meridian* (1954), which is as much about the 'Second Opening of the West' (its sub-title) as it is about Powell. Stegner is not a profound writer, but he is a meticulous realist who makes a very considerable use of a limited imagination. His later works are over-bitter and angry. Notable novels are *The Big Rock Candy Mountain* (1943), about the wanderings of a family in Western lands, and the very unusual and uncharacteristic *Angle of Repose* (1971), a cripple's re-creation of the past of his grandmother. This is his best novel, for in it he is able to deal with his own bitterness objectively. There are many more novels and two collections of stories.

Saul Bellow (1915), who won the 1976 Nobel Prize, spent his first nine years in his birthplace, Canada. His parents were Latvian Jews who had emigrated two years pre- viously. The family moved to Chicago in 1924, and Bellow went to Chicago and then to Northwestern University, graduating (1937) in anthropology and sociology.

Bellow was America's first major writer to shift, decisively, the central concern of his fiction from the social and political to the existential, or, if that is too fashionable a word nowadays, the experiential. Although one of the most intellectual of all American novelists, he has discouraged critical examination of his work; his admiration for Dreiser and Hardy (qq.v.), not intellectual writers, is significant. For all his wit and brilliance, Bellow's subject is ultimately what a critic has called 'the porous quotidian texture which is squeezed between the accidents of birth and the fatal sicknesses which end in death'. He is a realist (emphatically not a 'new novelist') armed with a formidable, vigorous poetry: his style. Bellow is above all an individualist, a man concerned to demonstrate that, although society has become so gigantic, individual human beings have not become smaller. He has tended to show Kafkaesque, put-upon man in his absurdity but also in his glory. It is mistaken to miss this essential simplicity in Bellow. One must remember that he has said, of Dreiser, 'I often think criticism of Dreiser as a stylist at times betrays a resistance to the feelings he causes readers to suffer. If they can say he can't write, they need not experience these feelings'. This unfashionable statement tells us much about the novelist who made it; fashionable interpretation of him does not always take it into account.

Although Bellow has developed, by widening his scope and his style accordingly, he sees all his protagonists as 'victims' of life in search of a cure in the Godless twentieth century. In his first novel, *Dangling Man* (1944), he introduces the first version of his hero, Joseph (not Joseph K; but he has no surname), who is 'dangling' because he has given up his job and is waiting to be called up. The form is a journal. Joseph is passive, resigned, but hypersensitive about life; finally he begs for defeat by asking to be called up as soon as possible. *Dangling Man* shows modern man burdened, bored, by his very liberty – and yet alienated from those around him by his passionate concern. *The Victim* (1947) goes more deeply into the question of Jewishness. Asa Leventhal, a journalist, worries about his position; he is picked up by a mad, drunken anti-semite who accuses him of having once done him a wrong. Leventhal becomes aware, through being persecuted by this creature, that he needs something to hate: that he too carries within him an anti-human virus. There is a marvellous scene, characteristic of Bellow at his most powerful and moving, in which the two men come into physical contact – to blows; Leventhal is suddenly aware of his complicity, with his antagonist and torturer, in life itself. The two men are thus 'brothers'. This novel ends on a serene note, and one of the characters makes a remark that might serve for an epigraph to all Bellow's fiction: 'Choose dignity. Nobody knows enough to turn it down'.

In the picaresque, technically unambitious, loose *The Adventures of Augie March* (1953) Bellow presents what has been called his first 'above ground' hero, Augie, who refuses to accept defeat although he recognizes that 'everyone got bitterness in his chosen thing'. Augie is different from Joseph or Leventhal: although still a victim, he affirms rather than questions everything. He becomes a gangster, a kind of gigolo, a husband: he accepts it all.

But this (*Henderson the Rain King*, *Herzog*, *Mr. Sammler's Planet* and *Humboldt's Gift* are its successors) is the first of Bellow's 'big' books, of which only *Herzog* and *Humboldt's Gift* really come off. There is a sense of strain here. The novel does not cohere: it is a series of episodes, some superb, where its predecessors clearly were not. The novella *Seize the Day* (1956), which (as originally published) appeared with a play and another shorter story, accomplishes more in a tenth of the length. This is about a failure – as a breadwinner, as a husband, as a son: the most clearly defined of all Bellow's victims. He knows he is unworthy and a fool to do it, and yet he must hand his money over to a crooked psychiatrist, Tamkin, to be 'multiplied on the stock exchange'. He can fulfil himself only as the dupe of a confidence man; must sit and watch as his money is lost. In the end, defeated, stripped of money, turned away by his rich, valetudinarian old father whom he merely embarrasses, Tommy Wilhelm bursts into tears in a chapel at the funeral of a complete stranger ('It must be somebody real close to carry on so', someone says). The music plays: 'He heard it and sank deeper into sorrow, through torn sobs and cries towards the consummation of his heart's ultimate need'. This is, curiously or otherwise (as one looks at it), one of the most moving endings to any work in twentieth-century literature.

Henderson the Rain King (1959) is a comparative failure. This story of a (non-Jewish) millionaire who goes to Africa in quest of wisdom incorporates Bellow's anthropological interests (anthropology, it should be remembered, is a science, an art and an imaginative activity without some knowledge or intuition of which no one can properly discuss anything of social, political or even individual significance) and, despite its exuberance, is ultimately bogged down in intellectuality. *Herzog* (1961) is, however, a successful long study of a middle-aged Jewish intellectual, a kind of Tommy Wilhelm but without the final masochistic need to submit to fate. Herzog is, of course, another victim; he is betrayed by his friends and wives and even his doctor, and he is forever writing letters of carefully reasoned complaint. These letters are really to God, the architect of his misery, in whom he continues to believe, 'Though never admitting it'. The greatest challenge to Herzog has been the one who makes him suffer most acutely, his second wife, who is unfaithful to him with the repulsive Valentine Gersbach. Without her choice treachery and her themselves insane charges that he is insane, he feels nothing: she makes him remarkable. The vigour of this novel is the shrill vigour of nervous exhaustion; and yet Bellow succeeds in portraying an intellectual (a brilliant one) more convincingly than any other novelist of his time. *Mr. Sammler's Planet* (1970) is another exercise in the picaresque. Since Bellow's is a major talent, it has exquisite passages. But it hardly coheres around its central character as *Herzog* does. It is largely a vehicle for Bellow's (counter-revolutionary) philosophy. This philosophy, 'old-fashioned' in terms of today's youngest university rebels, but in no way reactionary, seems wise and mellow to many of Bellow's readers; unfortunately this does not make his novel more than a series of episodes, a product of thought rather than imagination. With *Humboldt's Gift* (1975) Bellow triumphantly returned to his highest level. Loosely based on the life and death of Delmore Schwarz (q.v.), it movingly tells the story of a gifted but obstinate man who descends into self-destructive paranoia. Bellow's insight into abnormal states in this book is almost uncanny in its accuracy. The central character, however, is a successful writer called Citrine, who has been himself almost destroyed by the results of his success; this is in part a comment on Bellow himself, and on his own weariness with the kind of world (and people) who are attracted to the sort of writer who is successful but who happens, too, to be serious. This kind of writer is rare – though the sales of Saul Bellow are in no way to be compared to those of such a perpetrator of cruel manipulative trash as, say, Harold Robbins.

Bellow has written a play, *The Last Analysis* (1965), which was produced in 1964, and a volume of short stories, *Mosby's Memoirs* (1969).

Bernard Malamud (1914–86), born in New York, is, like Bellow (q.v.), the son of parents who had emigrated from Russia not long before his birth. It is Malamud who made the famous remark (which, however, does not bear too much repetition, since despite its metaphorical truth it contains a patent untruth), 'All men are Jews', by which he meant that all men are at heart sensitive, alienated – 'chosen'. His first novel, *The Natural* (1952), was a comic masterpiece, a treatment of baseball in terms of the American hero. This contained the germ of Malamud's method – a marriage of realism and fable that has been called 'magic realism' (q.v.) – as well as exploiting his pride in being a Brooklyn baseball aficionado. His next novel, *The Assistant* (1957), a work of rare beauty and affirmation, is on his theme of 'All men are Jews'. Nothing he wrote after it is even half as good. It remains his best novel. *The Assistant* is about nothing less than goodness. Frankie Alpine is a Gentile hoodlum who robs a poor Jewish shopkeeper. Out of a pity he tries to resist – one is reminded of Flannery O'Connor's (q.v.) heroes demonically resisting their vocation, though Malamud is more realistic and humanistic – he goes to work for him, and gradually becomes involved in his defeated and unsuccessful life. He falls in love with the grocer's daughter, Helen, and accepts her criticisms of him. In the end he actually becomes the grocer (who dies): running the store and grumblingly performing the same acts of charity. He has himself circumcised and becomes a Jew.

A New Life (1961) is a campus novel, tracing the progress of Seymour Levi from rock bottom to a realization that life is holy. This, although occasionally richly comic, is not altogether free from sentimentality. *The Fixer* (1967) is Malamud's most ambitious novel. It is not as good as *The Assistant* because its effects have been strained for too hard: it is an attempt to rival Bellow with a 'big' novel, and an attempt to write the great 'All men are Jews' novel. Considering this – the sense of strain is apparent – it is quite successful. It is loosely based on the case of Mendel Beiliss, an innocent Jewish workman who was tried in Tsarist Russia for the 'ritual' murder of a boy – and acquitted in spite of the conspiracy against him. *The Fixer* (handyman) describes the ordeal of Yakov Bok; the result of his trial, however, is left open. *Pictures of Fidelman* (1969) is a picaresque novel set in Italy. This was Malamud's weakest work to date, in which he experiments unsuccessfully with surrealism, and where his invention often seems less comic than farcical. Much better are his short stories, collected in *The Magic Barrel* (1958) and *Idiots First* (1963). The Jewish stories in the first collection remind one of the Yiddish-American author, Isaac Bashevis Singer (q.v.); the later stories try to get away from Brooklyn, as if in preparation for *The Fixer* and *Pictures of Fidelman*. Later work has moments, but is of a comparatively low quality.

We get another and very different version of American Jewish fiction in the work of **Norman Mailer** (1923), who was also raised in Brooklyn. The accent here has been increasingly on performance; the fiction deteriorated as the journalism improved. Then the journalism suddenly became careless rubbish; and the most recent novel, *Ancient Evenings* (1983), is naïve trash and was for the most part condemned as such – it does not merit serious discussion, and may be taken as Mailer's punishment for an egoism as intense as Keroac's (q.v.). The radical sociologist turned into the white Negro hipster. Mailer was the most vivid figure on the American literary scene; decidedly not a playboy, he was always a manic exhibitionist – and he eventually fragmented himself. However, he is contemptuous of any kind of official literary criticism, and with some justification; and he has to be saluted for his past courage in trying, by every means in his power, to capture and bring up out of himself what is unconscious and mysterious. His seeing of himself as a performer, his unabashed self-appraisal in *Advertisements for Myself* (1959), where he tells of his vanities and aspirations, may irritate some. But they should look into their own minds. He is often silly; but it would not be possible for him to fulfil his existential project in any other way. But that is to speak only of the Mailer who preceded the author of the books about Monroe and the Utah criminal Gary Gilmore – this last, *The Executioner's Song* (1979), was a banal, conceited disaster, and would have been a disgrace to a young journalist; yet his script for the movie was excellent.

His first novel, *The Naked and the Dead* (1948), one of the best of the American Second World War books, was in the realist tradition; but it foreshadowed the rest of his work. It concerns two different kinds of proto-fascist, a general and a sergeant, and an ineffective liberal lieutenant – in retrospect one can see that this figure is Mailer himself, unhappy in the role of a traditional radical writing a war book in conventional terms. This is a good book, containing in particular shrewd analyses of the motivations of the authoritarian types. But it has little characterization and, curiously enough, little compassion.

In *Barbary Shore* (1951) and *The Deer Park* (1955) we see Mailer making more effort to put himself meaningfully into his fictions. He goes into first-person singular narration and drops pretence of strict realism; the prose is messy, but some of the portraits, such as that of Eitel the radical film director, are unforgettable. However, these are based on real people. They are not invented: they are very good journalism. As one reads on in Mailer's fiction, coming to *An American Dream* (1965) and the appalling – perhaps desperate – *Why Are We in Vietnam?* (1967), one begins to suspect that he does not have an inventive imagination at all. Certainly he has evolved a 'position', one that is derived in large part from the psychoanalyst Wilhelm Reich, and resembles D.H. Lawrence's (q.v.).

Reich (originally, at least, a characterologist of genius, whose *Character Analysis*, tr. 1949, is well nigh indispensable) preached the necessity of full, creative orgasm, and towards the end of his life could detect the 'orgone energy' in the universe (it gave off a blueish light). Mailer is not quite so set on the orgasm, or at least not on its blueish light; but the central theme of his later work is the necessity of living life according to instinct. The 'White Negro' or hipster is distinguished from the passive Beat by his active, energetic quest for pleasure. Rojack in *An American Dream* is simply an embodiment of this new kind of overman – and if his story is not biblical in its import, then one has to take it as being very silly and, worse, dangerous in its implications. We have to applaud Mailer for his courage (as he wants us to do); but we are also entitled to ask how much, in fact, he cares about anything but the quality of each of his particular performances. The generalization 'love', which comes easily to the lips of his disciples, is unconvincing in the absence of an answer. Commitment to Reich is one form that current American Utopianism takes. (Another, following Norman O. Brown, is against Reich's 'full genitality', and insists on a return to bisexual 'polymorphous perversity' and play without orgasm.) Bellow (q.v.) has been said to be committed to Reich; but the truth is that he believes that there is 'something in' Reich, which is a very different matter. Bellow has self-respect.

Mailer is a public man, and he functions as such – like a boxer always forced to put on a performance. The question is whether in this way, without solitude, with public pressures upon him, he can properly function as a writer. The answer is that he has sunk into confusion, and fashionably hip reportage – as his report on the 1970 American moonshot, *A Fire on the Moon* (1970), suggested. The energy that drives him is phenomenal; but it now drives a husk. His most recent journalism is pathetic punk.

*

I have omitted almost all writers who have devoted themselves exclusively to crime from this book. But there are four exceptions, three of whom are American – the other is Simenon (q.v.). It would be impossible to ignore **Dashiell Hammett** (1894–1961), **Raymond Chandler** (1888–1969), or their only heir, **Ross Macdonald** (ps. **Kenneth Millar**, 1915–83). The first two exercised an enormous influence on American fiction as a whole (quite apart from American crime fiction, which is not considered here); Hammett employed crime as a metaphor for much more than what is mere crime in 'police' terms (Chandler in fact did not, and has been overrated – but to omit him would be to beg the question); Macdonald, though inferior to Hammett (he was superior to Chandler), did the same thing, although in a rather different way; but without Hammett he could not have written as he did – and it could be argued that he needed Chandler, if only to improve on.

Dashiell Hammett was a professional Pinkerton detective from 1908 to 1922 (with a year off for war service), from which he derived much of his material, which was more authentic than that of either Chandler or Macdonald. As well as being a detective, Hammett had worked as a clerk, a stevedore and as an advertising manager. He knew a good deal about the rough side of life, though when he came to literature (and it was literature, though at first he did not realize this), he knew little about that. It was an advantage in his case. He was probably a member of the American Communist Party, but he would never tell even his companion of very long standing, Lillian Hellman (q.v.), whether he was or not. Eventually he fell a victim to alcoholism; but he pulled himself out of that, and had a daily drink only when he was dying – and so lived his last years in sobriety. He was respected by almost everyone as an honourable and dignified man: when he went to prison for displeasing the Macarthy inquisition, his warders called him 'sir'. Communist or not, he was a member of the Advisory Board of *Russia Today*, and was president of the Civil Congress of New York (1946–7). However, we do know that the Stalinist purges worried him greatly, and that he disliked the idea of revolution, though he felt a revolution might be needed. Hammett was plainly worried about being a communist, but felt that he could not pull out. This is why he was reticent about it – this and the fact that if he talked at all he felt he might 'incriminate' his friends, a thing he never could bring himself to do. These attitudes lie squarely behind his more important books. He wrote at least seventeen (far more than most readers are aware of); but certainly the most important ones are *The Dain Curse* (1929), *Red Harvest* (1929), *The Maltese Falcon* and *The Glass Key* (1931). Then drink got a hold on him for a long time: *The Thin Man* (1934) was inferior and almost twee, though very cleverly written (it was made into a highly successful movie) – and when towards the end of his life he tried to write an autobiographical novel (the fragment that survives, called 'Tulip', is in *The Big Knockover*, 1969, first published in 1966 as *The Dashiell Hammett Omnibus*) it was clear that his powers had failed.

Hammett changed crime writing, even though his first stories, about the Continental Op, appeared in pulp magazines. He showed that detective work was dirty and banal and corrupt – and not ratiocinative at all, or hardly so. But what was most important was that he exposed corruption without making any comment about it. His attitude might have seemed cynical; but it was not, for we know how he felt about society. There are incidents in which a sense of honour is evoked – but, unlike Hemingway (q.v.), he laid no emphasis on it. He left it, so to say, to his readers' own consciences. Enough of them noticed. Also, unlike Chandler or Macdonald (who did not even try), Hammett's use of criminal argot was almost perfect.

Yet his world is not the real world: his art is not mimetic. The four major novels are, in a sense, parabolic. The achievement of Hammett has been exquisitely summed up by John M. Reilly: '[His detectives] are what Huck Finn would have been when he found the Territory where he hoped to escape civilisation dotted with cities, and in adulthood converted his sense of complicity in events beyond his control into a principle of behaviour'. Hammett's urban world is a cartoon of the real urban world: an uncannily accurate one. He demonstrated, at least, that there is something wrong at the heart of capitalism (this implied a Marxian answer for him, it seems, though clearly an uneasy one; but it does not have to for anyone else, and especially not now), and that corruption causes rottenness of heart. His novels are very carefully, if often bizarrely (and for good reason), constructed.

Chandler's novels are not well constructed: they move from incident to incident, with a skilful aimlessness. He, too, started as a pulp writer; and he fully and generously admitted a debt to Hammett. But he is only a shadow of him. His best work was done as a movie script writer: *The Blue Dahlia, Double Indemnity, Strangers on a Train* – and others. His stories, of which there are some six volumes, are crude. His use of criminal slang is weak. He is a clumsy writer. His detective Philip Marlowe is supposed to be a mixture of idealism and cynicism but, although the illusion is skilfully perpetrated, Marlowe is not convincingly this at all. He is a masochistic persona of the author's: a sort of fantasy figure. What authenticity he has is derived from Hammett; but even this is uneasy. But he does provide an excellent read, and there is sensitivity in many passages of the better books (*The Big Sleep*, 1939; *The High Window*, 1942; *The Long Goodbye*, 1953), despite their meandering plots. He also wrote very well about crime fiction: especially about

Hammett, most of whose virtues he saw clearly, and about the shortcomings of conventional crime fiction. He wrote well about Los Angeles as a seedy, sleezy place. But the sense of effort is too apparent, and the claims that have been made to the effect that he is now (posthumously) recognized as one of America's most 'important novelists' cannot be sustained. He is of high quality as a crime writer; as a writer he only just merits notice.

Ross Macdonald began by simply trying to improve on Hammett and Chandler, and even called his first novel (his first four were published under his own name; the fifth under that of John Macdonald – this may have been dropped because of the skilful hack, John D. Macdonald; the rest under his familiar name) 'Chandler with onions'. His mature books did not really resemble those of Hammett and Chandler; and they showed less acquaintance with the criminal world. He did resemble Hammett, though, in his tacit exposure of the corruption which exists in the lavish world of wealthy California. His detective (in almost all the later books) is Lew Archer, whom Macdonald pointedly caused to be non-literary (he has not heard of Kafka, for example); Archer does derive from Hammett's detectives (not from Marlowe, though, who is more of a fantasy figure), in that he is intelligent, non-committal, cynical. Macdonald makes him an unfit living companion, and there are continual hints at his selfishness as a husband (brought out more clearly in the movies, in which he is played by Paul Newman – here he is called 'Harper', for contractual reasons). Always in the Macdonald novels the real causes of the present troubles lie deep in the twisted recesses of the past: always there are skeletons in cupboards; these are the author's true themes. The writing, in particular the epithets used to describe dumb types, is often brilliant, witty and imaginative. Macdonald is usually classed as one of the 'hard-boiled' school. This was associated with the magazine *Black Mask* (founded 1919), in which Hammett's stories appeared, and with its editor Joseph T. Shaw. But that style eventually degenerated into the pornographic sensationalism of the lay-preacher Mickey Spillane – who wrote stories which seemed like the products of an extremely neurotic and sadistic, as well as commonplace, imagination; Macdonald can hardly be called 'hard-boiled' at all, since his writing – even the earliest – is not truly laconic in that style (for the best of 'hard-boiled' fiction one should read Hammett's 'Fly Paper', which appeared in *Black Mask* in 1929). All his eleven novels, from *The Galton Case* (1959) to *The Blue Hammer* (1976), his last, give a dark picture of a rotted culture haunted by ghosts; they lack any suggestion of a too professional gloss – which disfigures so many crime novels that might be something more – and are clearly the work of a serious and deeply troubled man. Macdonald is not 'the truest of any [novelist] of his time', as one critic has foolishly asserted; but his work will survive both for its sociological and its artistic value. He worked very hard to detach himself from the bad habits of most crime novelists, and he succeeded. Eudora Welty (q.v.) is one of those who early recognized his worth.

*

When one considers the critical attention directed to footling (and already, some of them, forgotten) novelists, the neglect of **Kay Boyle** (1903) is puzzling indeed. There are but two indifferent articles in periodicals about her work, and she seldom appears in surveys of the American novel. Thrice married, she did live in Europe for thirty years; but she has lived in America since the death of her third husband (a Baron) in 1963, and in 1977 she was admitted to the American Academy. She has written fourteen novels, nine books of short stories, *Three Short Novels* (1958), five books of verse (not her natural medium – but a useful guide to themes, and to her presentation of them, in her fiction) and seven other books. Her name is well known, her work not.

Boyle thinks of herself, she has said, primarily as a poet. Although her verse is over-effusive and uncontrolled (one can admire it as almost anything except poetry), as is frequently the case with prose-writers (Cary, Patrick White, Maurras, Graham Greene, qq.v., are merely a few well known examples), what she is saying, and trying to say, in her verse provides an invaluable clue to the tenor of her work. She is lyrical and extremely personal in her poems, but also socially committed (she has been openly although not always stridently left-wing for the whole of her life, and she did a few days in gaol over Viet Nam). She likes to tell a story, but quite often – she was first influenced by transition (q.v.) and the group around it, so is no stranger to at least the trappings of aggressive modernism – she simply assumes it as having been told, and so does not give the reader any of its details. The poem 'A Complaint for Mary and Marcel' is thus constructed, and, although it is a failure as poetry, it is an interesting one. Some passages in it have a power which suggests that had Boyle developed her capacity to concentrate in this direction, she might have achieved more. As it is, she has brought the qualities only latent in her poetry to her fiction, both short and long. *Collected Poems* (1962) was followed by one other volume of verse.

Boyle's later novels are marred, as has been admitted even by her admirers, by her tendency to simplify character in the interests of her notions of good and bad. Thus, the 'good' (humane, just, socially aware) characters are too often presented as capable only of good behaviour, whereas the 'bad' are bad all through. But Boyle's notions of good and bad are anything but simplistic, this tendency was a comparatively late development in her fiction – and there is always something else, rather more interesting, going on. This is not didactic, but imaginative, and frequently cuts across Boyle's conscious intentions powerfully enough to capture the main impetus of the novel or story. *Plagued by the Nightingale* (1931), her first book, is an intense study of a French family in which closeness becomes destructive; it is characterized by an irony of situation (one daughter accepts the family, but dies; the rest desperately await escape). Boyle has been a didactic writer for most of her life, and her moralistic attitudes have sometimes vitiated her work. But hers is a fluid and humane didacticism, so that while her idealization of some characters is a mistake (because she is manipulating them), her fervency can often function unimpaired. *Generation Without Farewell* (1960) is the best of her later novels; in it the characters are too wilfully manipulated into plain good and plain bad, but her attempt to portray occupied Germany in a fair and balanced light is still remarkably successful. However, it is in the short story that she is at her strongest: the language of these has more life, and she uses metaphors (particularly animals) to gain her highly intense effects. Outstanding among her many collections is *The Smoking Mountain* (1951): all the stories are about occupied Germany, and all search out both humanity and inhumanity, contrasting them relentlessly. *Fifty Stories* (1980). Boyle is a writer whose work would repay much closer attention than it has so far received: she is more versatile than has been recognized, and her humane point of view – if at times distorted by an admirable passion for justice – has remained remarkably consistent, and is by no means unsubtle. Her qualities are those of an original writer, however wildly uneven her output may be.

Hortense Calisher (1911) has always deliberately defied being categorized, perhaps a little wilfully and at her own expense: she is brilliant, but lacks confidence at sometimes crucial points, and so becomes aimless or (suddenly and surprisingly) sentimental. She was born in New York City of Jewish parents, who had an unusual and rich history, upon which she drew in her earlier work and – more obliquely – in her later. She began with short stories, *In the Absence of Angels* (1951), in which the stories about Hester Elkin are autobiographical accounts of her growing up; the rest, more disconcerting, deal with people's failure to communicate, and with unhappy blurred memories. Proust was an obvious, sometimes obtrusive, influence. The sudden descents into sentimentality which unhappily characterize all her work – this is reminiscent of both Moore and Bishop (qq.v.), who both lapsed into it in a different way – begins here. *False Entry* (1962), her first novel, a series of episodes about identity problems, is strangely mixed: it is full of brilliant and disturbing passages, but is not coherent as a novel. Neither is its very loosely connected sequel *The New Yorkers* (1970). *Journal from Ellipsia* (1966) is an odd, SF-like fantasy of great cleverness, but is prolix and uncertain; it deals with life on other planets, and with an alternative to male-female relationships – it is written in too precious a style to quite come off, and the author's stated confidence in what she is trying to do clearly conceals a sense of insecurity. Calisher is best in shorter forms, as *Collected Stories* (1975) immediately demonstrates. This is a truly distinguished volume. She is, as a novelist, a minor writer after bigger successes than she can sustain; in the stories she is less tempted. *The Railway Police* (1966), which is a novella, but appeared under that title with another short work, is about a woman who abandons her wigs and faces the world in her bald-ness. It is her most powerful and individual work. Her stories are precise and very varied: they can be comic and bizarre, or simple and moving. She does not have time to stray. *Herself* (1972) is a memoir which gives (mostly) her rather aggressive views about art, and is disappointing. She is very much a cultivated taste; but her short fiction is among the best in America of her time, for its range, its amiable oddness, and its intelligence: this is an intelligence which works conspicuously well in the presence of the imagination, much less well in its absence.

Another, but much more overt, odd-woman-out, a genuine eccentric, is **Marguerite Young** (1909). She is a scholar who has an odd-angled vision of life but no other (this is to say, she gives no signs of awareness of what is called the normal view). Born in Indiana, she went to university and studied Milton, esoteric seventeenth-century lore, and, later, philosophy. She came to love William James (q.v.), whom she preferred to his brother, who, however (she characteristically says), 'often visits me in my dreams and talks of the literary arts'. She has written only three volumes of creative work: two indifferent books of verse, and an astonishing and irritating long novel, seventeen years in the making, called *Miss MacIntosh, My Darling* (1965). This is 1197 pages long. It is about Vera Cartwheel's search for her nurse, who for her embodies reality; Vera's mother embodies uncertainty; everyone else is deluded. When Vera discovers reality in the form of her old nurse (presumed drowned), she finds her to be hairless, incomplete and false: life is nothing but imagination. This book is one of the genuine curiosities of the age, and, although it has *longueurs* – it lacks the robustness of mundane experience – it simply cannot be ignored. Those who feel they enjoy Bainbridge (q.v.) ought to read this: Young is intelligent, learned, where Bainbridge dons the persona of a twee droll trying to imitate what she thinks (wrongly) Stevie Smith (q.v.) was like. Her original insight, that life is mostly (or all?) deception, does drive the book; but it also almost destroys it. It is redeemed by energy, and by some acute mythological observations. Its main interest, really, lies in its view of life as a series of concentric myths. More like such a book as *The Anatomy of Melancholy* than a true novel, it is at least serviceable as an eccentric anthology strung on an intellectually interesting string.

Eleanor Clark (1913), since 1952 the wife of Robert Penn Warren (q.v.), seldom gets her due, possibly because almost a quarter of a century separated her first and second novels. Apart from *Dr Heart* (1974), a novella with stories, she has written *The Bitter Box* (1946), *Baldur's Gate* (1970) and *Gloria Mundi* (1979). The first book was prentice work, about a bank clerk who rejects both capitalism and communism. Something like the same theme was exploited with greater power and pathos in Gabrielle Roy's *Alexandre Chenevert* (qq.v.). But *Baldur's Gate* is a mature novel of unusual merit. The book teems with rhetoric, rather in the style of Penn Warren, but this is not an empty rhetoric; one would merely prefer it to be somewhat subdued. However, the minor American novel increasingly thrives on rhetoric – and this is a better example than most. *Baldur's Gate* is Jacobean in its complexity, and the several layers of symbolism, often over-self-conscious, tend to obtrude. But the theme, which is essentially that although there seems to be no hope for a better world, it is necessary and perhaps even natural to assume such hope (the last scene concerns a rubbish dump, standing not only for waste but also for renewal), is handled with delicacy and power, and is deeply felt. The majority of the characters fail to make quite the required impact, but the central one – an old sculptor who arises from despair to confront and challenge the world anew – is wholly convincing. This is all the more impressive in that such figures are too often encountered, and are usually embarrassing – good examples are Iris Murdoch's (q.v.) chokingly sentimental 'beautiful characters', the product of an inability to create character, and the outcome of trying to illustrate a rather tawdry moral philosophy by means of fiction. Clark's philosophy, really an imaginative view of life rather than an abstract construct, arises from the fictional situation, which, despite the novel's weaknesses, remains dominant throughout.

Toni Morrison (1931) is not an easy writer; but she is arguably the most important black novelist in America since Ellison (q.v.), and she adds something upon which he does not touch. She was born (*née* Wofford) in Ohio, and did not publish her first book until she was almost forty. Although she has faults – an at times over-obtrusive use of symbolism being the most serious – she has never succumbed to any easy or simply cerebral way out: her vision is not that of anyone else, but her imagination's own. If she is 'political', then that is simply because such fiction, which more or less excludes whites (until *Tar Baby*, q.v.), is bound to be seen as political – the world, and the American world in particular, being what it is. She is too intelligent to be 'against whites', or 'against men' in any stridently generalized manner; indeed, of all living woman writers, her portraits of men are among the fullest, most sympathetic and penetrating.

Her first novel, *The Bluest Eye* (1970), is centred on a young girl, Pecola Breedlove (this aptronym was ill-advised), who is raped by her father: the ironic premiss is that she desperately needs love, and gets it only from her father, before he rapes her. She becomes mad, develops a need for blue eyes, and finally believes that she has acquired them. The narrator of the novel escapes this fate – of agonized schizophrenic withdrawal – by having grown up in a much more 'ordinary' family, which knew how to 'breed love' (though that love is not real or full love, it is ironically seen as just about as much love as human beings can take), and by directing hatred at her Shirley Temple doll (the persona adopted by the young Temple being a paradigm of cute pseudo-infantile horror in any decent American eye). *Sula* (1974) is bleaker, and recalls Faulkner (q.v.) in its quasi-nihilist despair. It contrasts, against a rich backcloth of characters, a woman and her grandmother: Sula is wilful and selfish, and ends as a witch whose pestilential example shocks the lives of those around her into a kind of improvement, while her grandmother is savage (she burns her drug-addicted son) but compassionate. But sympathy is never held back: the origins (environmental and genetic) of Sula's disruptiveness are traced with meticulous accuracy, and her final function as a witch is given its full weight in what is essentially a mythopoeic work.

Song of Solomon (1977) is on a more massive scale. Here the aptronymic technique works perfectly, and Morrison reaches full maturity as a novelist. The book is concerned with a 'genteel' black family of the name of Dead. Their son, Milkman, truly dead, returns to Virginia to rediscover life in song and flight. His friend Guitar is the finest study yet of the extremist black racist attitude – an attitude that is presented with an objectivity which embraces the whole spectrum of feeling, from repulsion to love and understanding. Doubtless Morrison could be accused of the 'wrong' attitudes by various political groups; but in fact she serves the purpose of truth and of dignity (for all human beings) by her eschewal of the political in its foul and familiar sense: as that which is practised by the person who trades his or her principles for power. The justification usually given ('the art of the possible') is that there have to be politicians. But that is not true, and novels such as Morrison's incidentally show it.

Tar Baby (1981) is a new departure, inasmuch as it brings in white characters – among them, a millionaire – and deals with Carribean expatriates. Because of this, symbolism once again sometimes becomes over-obtrusive (a black man's real name is Son); but the novel more than compensates in its convincing – and perhaps unwelcome to some – demonstration that there is in truth more to human dissension than the colour of skin, although differences in these colours are the ironic subject of the novel. What Morrison shows, with a now almost elegant and deadly panache, is that other issues become horribly attached to these differences, which are here graded into a bizarre hierarchy. She is a dense novelist, one of the really important writers to emerge in the Seventies. Her work is rich in allusions both to literature and to myth; and although difficult, it is rewarding always, and of as high a quality as that of any of her contemporaries.

Joan Didion (1934), born in Sacramento, California, has distinct talents (rather than gifts) which she has never been able to weld together into a satisfactory book. Her travelogue on El Salvador of 1982 was a perhaps revealing failure: she managed to say nothing at all, and her famous 'seriousness' was exposed as a total insensitivity. She uses traditional methods and plots, is intelligent though never imaginative, and seems to preach a conservative philosophy of self-reliance. She might be described as the middle-brow 'concerned person's', portable Ayn Rand. Like Cozzens' (q.v.), her 'philosophy' may be seen to collapse in the face of the situations she manages to invent for herself in her novels (but, unlike Cozzens, she is not malevolent). Her use of dialogue and of some of the techniques associated with Dos Passos (q.v.) is intelligent; and she has a partial understanding of sexual disruptiveness. But she can solve this only by her inadequate 'philosophy': she lacks heart, and is at her best when she is doing journalism, her true métier (there are two books of essays as well as the disastrous El Salvador volume). Hers is essentially the world of *Vogue* (for which she worked for several years): fashionable, shallow, cold, merciless in its superficiality. Such a writer, as novelist, could only be a pseudo-moralistic advocate of an unreal 'order'. There is no understanding of what has caused chaos, only the irritation of a mind flashily brilliant but fundamentally fearful, defensive and suburban. Her fiction is bright, depthless; but has a journalistic appearance of depth. *Run River* (1964) traces the collapse of a marriage, gives a hysterically earnest picture of 'evil' in California, and presents a Mephistopheles character worthy of *Gone with the Wind*. One needs, perhaps, to look at Macdonald's (q.v.) depiction of evil in California to see just how fashionable and un-evil this seemingly persuasive stuff is. *Play It As It Lays* (1970) tries to improve on Nathanael West's *Day of the Locust* (q.v.), but is dead at the centre and is about a dead person: a person who could not possibly exist. The central figure is, it is true, supposed to be spiritually dead. But her state of deadness is not given that sense of life with which novelists must endow such characters – that terrible sense of not being dead that those who will not take their own lives do feel. Martha Wyeth is in fact a concatenation of a West Coast lady's glib complaints about 'lack of seriousness' and not an imagined character at all. Her daughter is brain-damaged, she faces an abortion – isn't it terrible? As Alfred Kazin has observed, it's all 'so mod, empty, American. ...' Certainly Joan Didion is afraid, frightened: often she has written about her 'panics'. Evil, she has said, is 'the absence of seriousness'. Not much good here, then. *A Book of Common Prayer* (1977) is more ambitious: it takes place, in part, in a banana republic with no history – that is, of course, California. The book is sick in its ambivalence towards the young and the frightened older ones: sentimental, its men unreal, its morality professional, its glitter cold and miserly. A better answer would be the Simbianese Liberation Army – or the *Ayn Rand Newsletter*. It makes no difference. But these aren't really very 'nice'.

Joyce Carol Oates (1938), born in New York, is, by contrast, serious in a true sense – but consumed, it has been appropriately suggested, by self-hatred. Her chief faults are that she is mainly humourless, and that she writes far too much. It would be well if she had to do this in order to strike substantial sparks from the stone; but as it happens she disperses her gifts so as, it sometimes seems, to evade what she imagines they would reveal. She has not fulfilled herself as a writer; but her relentlessness and prolificity conceal a real gift and a valuable desperation. She has tried to concentrate her abundant unhappy energies into at least eight volumes of verse, and these offer some clue to her essential dissatisfaction: she cannot find a form of words which calms her into even temporary acceptance of her generously self-infuriated state. Intelligent, she cannot discover an imaginative objective correlative that is less than frenetic.

Most of her books borrow from other writers – Faulkner (q.v.) in particular – and some try to do more than even those writers could. *Bellefleur* (1980) is the most ambitious and unconvincing of her books: it tries to combine history and the Gothic supernatural into a family saga that will be popular but never kitsch; despite the intelligence with which it is put together, it ends up by being merely tedious. *Them* (1969) is in part an attempt to recreate *The Great Gatsby* (q.v.), an exercise which hardly seems worthwhile, though the reconstruction amounts to good literary criticism. In its other aspect *Them* treats of mindless violence in a mindless manner, almost as if it had been taken by the author as one big manifestation without origin. What Oates had tried to do in this book is quite near what **Harriette Arnow** (1908) actually had done in *The Dollmaker* (1954). Oates herself has generously admired and praised the novel, and helped to make it more widely available. *The Dollmaker* contrasts rural with urban life in Detroit and Appalachia, to the latter's disadvantage. A woman whose only skill is in carving wood – hence the title – has to go into Detroit in the war; there her family and herself are destroyed by commerce, vulgarity and standardization. This is a very powerful study of one woman, whose artistic nature is meticulously conveyed. Oates simply cannot achieve this in her own novels, despite her generosity towards those who can. Her characters (and this is a little surprising in one who can be so keen a critic) are mindlessly driven. *Unholy Loves* (1979) is her least characteristic and most successful novel to date: set in a university, it is more controlled than anything else she has written, and is actually comic in its exposé of the stupidities of academic life. If Oates could proceed in this more analytical direction she could yet become a more than competent novelist. Her honesty and good will have always been evident.

Anne Tyler (1941) is a very original novelist who is only just now getting some of the recognition she has so long deserved. She was born in Minneapolis, but writes principally about Baltimore (where she now lives) and Southern towns – the latter to an extent that she could be considered almost as a 'southern writer'. She is a pessimistic writer who will not affirm more than half-hearted relationships – because she cannot see that there is anything better. Her early novels, *If Morning Ever Comes* (1964), *The Tin Can Tree* (1965), are not so much concerned, however, with presenting this as a 'philosophy of life' as with demonstrating that it is the case. This she does with consummate psychological skill and wisdom. These people she depicts are lacking; and one gets to feel, with her, that all human beings may well be similarly lacking – that there is a gap of deadly emptiness between everyone, that the half-gesture is better than the deluded one offering a complete relationship. It is a point of view with which one cannot quarrel; one can only point to the sorts of people she chooses to depict, and suggest that they may not be the only sorts of human beings. But she is as good as this: she makes one wonder continually how right she may be. Her writing is precise and lucid, and relieved by humour and warmth. Of her nine novels the best are perhaps the first two, and *Celestial Navigation* (1974) and *Morgan's Passing* (1980). There are a score or so of as yet uncollected stories. So far she has limited herself, probably deliberately, by refusing to consider that the dreams and imaginations of some people demonstrate yearnings which transcend – however transitorily – the absolute necessity of separateness; but she is excellent in not going beyond what she can herself feel. She never manipulates her material to make a case.

*

William Burroughs (1914), born in St. Louis, for much of his life an expatriate, is part of an American sociological phenomenon. The Beat (exhaustion, but also beatification) movement began spontaneously in San Francisco in the Fifties, and was at first entirely sociological. People who were dissatisfied with bourgeois society reacted against it not by rebellion but simply by dropping out. The original Beats had no leaders; their aims were passive. They were influenced by, but did not properly understand, Zen Buddhism, and they sought private illumination by means of drugs and/or drink. Their spiritual fathers included Whitman and Henry Miller (q.v.); and the good-natured, unconsciously adept business man who put them on the map, and invented several reputations – including that of Burroughs – was the poet Allen Ginsberg (q.v.). Burroughs' best book was his first, published in 1953 under the pseudonym of William Lee: *Junkie*. This is an account of his life as a drug addict. He had held a number of jobs in New York (private detective, factory-worker, barman); then in 1944 he became addicted to heroin and moved to New Orleans and Mexico, where he shot his wife in an accident. *Junkie* was a relatively straightforward book. In 1957 he flew from Tangier to London for the apomorphine treatment, and apart from two relapses immediately afterwards has not touched the drug since. Nowadays Burroughs, having delivered himself of his main works – *The Naked Lunch* (1959), *The Soft Machine* (1961), *Nova Express* (1964), and others – is mainly a prophet-interviewer and, latterly, public reader from these and other sketchier, later works. What is perhaps most impressive about him is his monumental stupidity and naïvety. He discovered Reich late, and refreshes himself in one of those boxes – to gather orgone energy – that earned their inventor a prison sentence he did not survive. He is (or was) a 'scientologist'. He postulates, with apparent seriousness, an all-male community in which reproduction would be confined to test tubes. He said he admired China's Red Guards not because he could understand anything about them, but because (like Hitler?) 'they feel they have something important to do'.

His creative work is unoriginal, but none the less looks different. His techniques consist of: the use of various aleatory devices to produce associations that arise from illogic, especially the illogic of dreams; these are superimposed on pulp type plots, bad SF or gangster books. His 'cut-out' and 'fold-in' techniques, consisting of certain semi-aleatory ways of manipulating existing material, are merely variations of old surrealist games: but the technique goes back at least to the sixth century – there is nothing new about it. *The Naked Lunch* counterpoints a realist account of a junkie's life with the subjective horrors he experiences; it is supposed to have been given what little coherence it has by the shrewd Ginsberg, whose own incoherence is voluntary. The real subject, which is what a junkie experiences in withdrawal, is nausea. The organization of *The Naked Lunch* is naïve in the extreme. The themes are addiction, control (leading to more control), power and means of cure. His other works do not radically depart from this scheme. Burroughs submits his original material (which is probably bathetic and ill written) to his various techniques, spicing it up with clippings from his 'favourite' cut-in sources, such as the novels of William Golding (q.v.). But his chief obsessions emerge: the erections of hanged men, anal rape. . . .

What is pitiful is that Burroughs, an essentially simple-minded man, and one perhaps less unintelligent on than off narcotics, has been treated by some critics (including, amazingly, Mary McCarthy, q.v.) as an innovator. He is historically important; but his importance is as, in Leslie Fiedler's words, a 'pioneer mutant', pledged to become a child. But his own prose perhaps has a talent which is conspicuously absent from his 'critical' pronouncements.

Jack Kerouac (ps. Jean-Louis Kerouac, 1922–69), who 'died of drink and angry sicknesses', had a grotesquely inflated reputation; but as a latter-day Thomas Wolfe (q.v.), though a vastly inferior writer, he has historical importance. Kerouac was always a wanderer, and was thrice married and twice divorced, both times in less than a year. Originally he was a drunken drifter who managed to commit to paper a bad Wolfeian novel called *The Town and the City* (1950). It contains in embryo his stale message: ignorance, incoherence and illiteracy are beatific, crime is lovely, do as you want, get stoned, learn to be naïve, attain sweetness and light. But it took the astute Ginsberg (q.v.) to launch him as a legend. *On the Road* (1957), typewritten on a continuous roll of art paper in three weeks flat, has distinction as being the most non-structured book of its decade. In writing it Kerouac simply followed his own nose. It is in no sense fiction, but a record of the wanderings of three bums: Sal Paradise (Kerouac), Carlo Marx (Ginsberg), and Dean Moriarty (a friend of theirs called Neil Cassady). *The Dharma Bums* (1958) is similar, but puts emphasis on Kerouac's search for realization through some kind of Zen Buddhism. If anyone doubts Kerouac's pretentiousness, and the self-delusion in which he existed, he should read *Satori in Paris* (1966), in which he humourlessly describes a journey to Paris in search of his French ancestry, drinking bouts, and a final Buddhist illumination – as convincing as the meaning of his meaningless death through abuse and self-neglect. Kerouac wrote many books, and in all of them he splashed, a critic rightly said, 'everything energetically with his own boisterous, messy ego'.

*

Truman Capote (1924–85), who was born in New Orleans, is close to Tennessee Williams (q.v.) in atmosphere; all his books up to *In Cold Blood* (1966) sugar and prettify the same kind of Gothic-invert world. Leslie Fiedler calls Capote a respresentative of the 'Effete Dandies or ... Decadents' school, which he sees, not very convincingly in this case, as deriving from Faulkner (q.v.). Certainly Capote is flip and his 'amusement' at evil is tiresome and even irresponsible – he can give a sense of a perverse boy liking to annoy his reader by being sick and crippled; but that is only one side of the picture. Capote is a consummate artist, a writer very serious about his craft, who, no matter whether his reader likes it or not, does create a world of his own. Things are seen by Capote not with an innocent but with the goblin eye of a self-retarded soul. In his first book, *Other Voices, Other Rooms* (1948), the boy Joel Knox sinks into a decadent homosexual relationship with the transvestite Randolph in just the same way as his paralysed father's rotting house sinks gradually into the swamp on which it is built. As John A. Aldridge has said, Capote here achieves a purity, of 'the sort that can be attained only in the isolation of a mind which life has never violated, in which the image of art has developed to a flowerlike perfection because it has developed alone'. Capote is no surrealist; but his world is more dream than real. He does not like to call himself a Southern writer, but there is no doubt that his dream is a Southern one. Its inner coherence is admirable; but its relationship with anybody else's world is problematical. If Joel Knox's pilgrimage is for the father or the Holy Grail then these are fathers and grails few others would know anything about. *The Grass Harp* (1951) is about an eleven-year-old orphan who, with one of his elderly aunts and three others, is driven, by the nastiness of the world, to live in a tree-house. This little community is presented as innocent and even improved in its efficacy to deal with reality; there are allusions to Noah's ark and to Huck's raft. There is much sharply perceptive, fresh writing; but the pretty vision is corrupted by Capote's lack of interest in people as people. With *Breakfast at Tiffany's* (1958) Capote tipped his talent in the direction of the middlebrow: this traced the adventures of a playgirl, Holly Golightly, against the background of modern Manhattan. The book may well have achieved its popularity because Holly is utterly superficial, flip, all phoney; the book has a kind of false vitality, but is quite without warmth. And yet the writing is on an altogether higher level than the cult of the child which the book is advocating. Still, Capote scarcely deserved the glamour with which at this time he was invested by the media. *In Cold Blood* (1966) is a piece of gripping and highly intelligent journalism reconstructing a peculiarly brutal murder; Capote investigated the case in depth. This marked a complete break with the first three, narcissistic novels; but *In Cold Blood*, in spite of its author's claim to have invented a new form, 'the documentary novel', is no more than very good journalism. *Tree of Night* (1949) collects short stories. Since 1966 Capote has written nothing substantial, but has continued as public figure – projecting himself variously as nervous wreck, aesthete, and so forth; but this belongs to the history of boulevard entertainment.

Mark Twain was the first American to see the Noble Savage as a child (Huck), and writers have not stopped imitating him, or sharing in his vision, ever since. Truman Capote is a good example. Another is **J.D. Salinger** (1919), whose *The Catcher in the Rye* (1951) achieved heights of popularity denied to any other 'quality' novel since the war. Salinger had studied at various establishments before the war without getting a degree; he ended up at Columbia in a short-story class taught by Whit Burnett, founder and editor of *Story* – not to be confused with the writer of superior gangster fiction **W.R. Burnett** (1899), author of *Little Caesar* (1929) – a magazine which published his first story in 1940. He entered the army in 1942, and took part in five campaigns. It has been suggested that his military experiences brought his nausea with modern existence to the surface.

Salinger became so popular, a star *New Yorker* writer, because in *The Catcher in the Rye* he discovered the exact tone and flavour of post-war middle-class adolescent alienation. The use of the vernacular owes much to Ring Lardner (q.v.); but it is Salinger's own (and greatest) achievement. The book is about Holden Caulfield, who flunks school and must go home to tell his parents about it. He spends a weekend in New York failing to connect, being nauseated by everybody, finding everything phoney. Only two nuns he meets at breakfast strike him as genuine. After an experience of feeling 'damn happy', which anticipates the kitsch Zen of the later stories, Holden goes home, falls psychiatrically ill, and is psychoanalysed. The monologue that is *The Catcher in the Rye* is (presumably) part of a healthful therapy. But to what purpose? The book ends: 'don't ever tell anybody anything. If you do, you start missing everybody'. This message has been more fruitfully explored by Anne Tyler (q.v.) than by Salinger in his later fiction. *The Catcher in the Rye* is limited by its failure to go beyond Holden: it catches a style, and one must concede that it does so marvellously; but it has no wisdom, can imply no alternative either to the phoney world or the, ultimately, tiresome Holden. Here lies another reason for its popularity (although Salinger should not be blamed for this): the young do not want alternatives, or to acknowledge the necessity of compromise with the adult world they reject; so they seized on Holden Caulfield. As Walter Allen has said, Salinger's is the *New Yorker* version of the Beats and hipsters. For his older readers, whose notion of the ultimate in intelligence is to be found in the pages of the *New Yorker*, he had a comforting message: junior has been sick like you once were, but next week he will be coming home and he will go back to school. ... I do not think this was the intention, but Salinger would have been a really important writer only if he could have written of the defeat (or victory?) of an adult Holden Caulfield; and if he could then have peopled his world not with cliché-shams (that is what the 'phonies' of *The Catcher in the Rye* are) but with real people – shams, yes; but shams with the varyingly concealed humanity that they do have. But the successors to *The Catcher in the Rye*, all short fictions, skilful though they are, do not suggest this possibility; and it is significant that except for a single story published by the *New Yorker* in 1965 Salinger has, since the Sixties, dried up. *Nine Stories* (1953), *Franny and Zooey* (1961) and *Raise High the Roof Beam, Carpenters*; and *Seymour: An Introduction* (1963) form a chronicle of the eccentric Glass family, including Buddy Glass, who is a representation of Salinger himself. Even by the side of *The Catcher in the Rye*, these tend to be cute and to fall back not on any kind of mellowness or comprehension of the real nature of the world, but on pseudo-religiosity. It is only fair to add that Salinger claims that he is still writing – but not publishing. He is extremely sensitive to criticism.

John Updike (1932) worked for the *New Yorker* after leaving Harvard, and is now the brightest, funniest, most intelligent and entertaining from that depressingly glittering stable. His first novel, *The Poorhouse Fair* (1959), is about a revolt of the old people in an institution against their liberal director. *Bech* (1970) tells the story of a successful middle-aged Jewish writer who can do everything except write well. It is clearly Updike's effort to justify his own middlebrow success, which has led Leslie Fiedler to say of him that he provides 'the illusion of vision and fantasy without surrendering the kind of reassurance provided by slick writing at its most professionally *all right*'. It fails to explain Bech at all; but Updike does manage to convey a sympathy for this husk, who is presented not as a bad writer but a victim of the middlebrow public. ...

But Updike went on interestingly. *Buchanan Dying* (1974), a closet play about an American president neglected by historians. is a remarkable *tour de force*. He explores ideas that have become kitsch – notably the union of man and woman in the sexual act, as one, before a Christian God – with a brittle and disenchanted intelligence. In *The Coup* (1978) he brilliantly attempts to demonstrate that myth is meaningless in a commercial, electronic age – and he does reveal the crassness of the age, but at the same time his own limitations: demonstrator of sterility, he displays no robustness of his own; one can only recall that other writers possess it.

James Baldwin (1924) was born in Harlem. He never knew his real father, to whom his mother was not married; but his stepfather, a preacher, rejected him and told him he was ugly – all against a background of bigotry and religious fanaticism. At fourteen Baldwin, in competition with his stepfather and wanting to draw bigger audiences than he did, became a preacher, a Holy Roller in the Fireside Pentecostal Church in Harlem. Except for the few years in which he wrote his two first (and best) novels, Baldwin has been a preacher ever since. His first novel, *Go Tell it on the Mountain* (1953), describes the conversion of a fourteen-year-old; this is a vision of ecstasy brought about by the guilts and stresses of initiation into puberty, by the hatred of his father, and by the desire to escape altogether to a new world. *Giovanni's Room* (1956) is set in Paris and deals with a conflict between homosexual and heterosexual love. *Another Country* (1962) mixes fine fiction with homosexual preaching. As Leslie Fiedler has been most articulate in pointing out, in America Jew, Negro and homosexual have become to some extent identified – because, of course, all are discriminated against. In Baldwin's third novel ('precisely because he is a homosexual as well as a Negro', claims Fiedler) one of the messages – the most important message, to Baldwin – is that hate between white and black is exacerbated by male-female relationships but healed by homosexual ones. Now the predicament of Negroes and homosexuals (how long before we write this word with an initial capital?) is similar (although the most potent enemies of homosexuality are themselves homosexuals, but repressed); but, unless one takes negritude to be a disorder, the nature of the Negro and the homosexual *may* not be similar. At all events, Baldwin has to manipulate his people and his situations to elevate homosexuality into a panacea for the racial human illness. This approach does not really help to resolve the tension between the two ideas which Baldwin has recognized that any writer – but most particularly a Negro writer – 'must hold ... forever in his mind': '... the acceptance, totally without rancour, of life as it is ... [and the idea] that one must never ... accept ... injustices as commonplace. ...' Eric Jones, the bisexual actor who dominates the second part of *Another Country*, is an unreal figure. *Tell Me How Long the Train's Been Gone* (1968) deals with Baldwin in his role of publicist in the person of Leo Proudhammer; it seems to have been thrown hurriedly together, and shows a marked deterioration. What follows it is feeble and of little interest.

There are at least a score of American novelists under fifty who have some fair claims to importance. Some, like Philip Roth (q.v.), have gained commercial success; others, like John Hawkes (q.v.), have not. The greatest *succès d'estime* has been **John Barth** (1930), though so far critical enthusiasm tends to be expressed around publication time. The immensely ambitious *Giles Goat-Boy* (1967) is one of those novels that is either a masterpiece, albeit a flawed one – or something very much smaller. Barth is an academic and has been one ever since he graduated from Johns Hopkins. His novels, however, are as anti-academic as they are academic. He is amusing, inventive of situations, a trained philosopher, a polymath. His work is by a large number of people (including Nabokov, Kafka, Borges, Beckett, qq.v., Bunyan, Lewis Carroll) out of James Joyce (q.v.). He relies on puns, slang of all sorts, pastiche and parody. His own ability to write prose has so far been concealed by these intellectual pyrotechnics (his use of slang is photographic). Barth is an author of 'in-books'; that so astute a critic as Leslie Fiedler can admire them is evidence that they contain in-jokes about academe that are good jokes; but a number of reviewers have knowingly saluted the achievement without, however, understanding it in the least.

Giles Goat-Boy is the ultimate in the *Bildungsroman* (q.v.); like Barth's preceding three novels – *The Floating Opera* (1956, rev. 1967), *The End of the Road* (1958, rev. 1968) and *The Sot-Weed Factor* (1960, rev. 1967), only more specifically and ironically, it deals in 'education'. Here the universe is a university, into which are launched a false Messiah – and a counter-claimant, Giles Goat-Boy, a 'horned human student'. This is dazzlingly clever, and I suppose some of those who combine crossword-puzzle mentalities with philosophical inclinations might have got through its 700-odd pages. The fact is that *Giles Goat-Boy* is a prototype for a certain kind of book: the new, scholastic, inturned Joycean epic. The justification comes out of Borges: the novelist is to re-invent the universe, but adding the coherence 'God' lacks. The self-caressing, 'fiendish' ingenuity comes from Nabokov, the Nabokov of such books as *Pale Fire* (1962) and, alas, *Ada*, with its whiff of exalted kitsch. Barth is serious, a comedian, a man with marvellous ideas – but his own language offers no clue to the presence of a creative imagination. *Lost in the Funhouse* (1968) is simply a decline into a sort of literary criticism, and its bright moments are lost in tedium.

The enormous success of the 'masturbation novel', *Portnoy's Complaint* (1969) by **Philip Roth** (1933), who was born in New Jersey, makes it difficult to assess him. It is an amusing comic book, an eminently worthwhile variation on the American Jewish novel; but it is not in the top flight. Roth belongs, as a critic puts it, in the tradition of American writers 'which examines the individual's posture of optimistic wilfulness and finds it wanting'. Thus, the compassionate sensibility of the hero of *Letting Go* (1962), Gabe Wallach, is crippled by his sentimentality and his weakness. But this book was ill organized, and its author's flipness drowned his delicacy of insight. *When She Was Good* (1967) is his best book. Lucy Nelson revenges herself for her inadequate childhood by turning herself into a castrator, a possessor of men-objects; and yet the vitality that throbs in her, tragic substitute for humanity, is vividly conveyed. *Portnoy's Complaint* is intelligent black Jewish comedy; but sheer professionalism, a facility for skating over the difficult explanations, spoils it. Alexander Portnoy cannot learn that his feelings of imprisonment arise from his failure to relate to others; but masturbation is not an adequate symbol for this. The successors to this novel have all been lively but over-self-conscious; the best is *The Ghost Writer* (1979), which has moments of great humour, even though it collapses beneath its ingenious and complex plot.

American critics are mostly hostile to **James Purdy** (1923), who was born in Ohio. One can see why: his homosexual Gothic is unmitigated and his control of it is doubtful, and, in any case, inelegant. But he has unquestionable power. He experienced fierce rejection until Edith Sitwell (q.v.), doubtless in a receptive mood, since she possessed small judgement in her last monomanic years, found him an English publisher. In America he was eventually, and predictably, taken up by **Carl Van Vechten** (1880–1964), a dilettante old critic who was born out of his time and whose pussy predilections Purdy fulfilled with suitable modern garishness. In Van Vechten's decadent, well written novels – *Peter Whiffle* (1922), *The Tattooed Countess* (1924) and the excellent *Nigger Heaven* (1926) – we may find foreshadowed not only Purdy's anguished quest for love in violence but also a source (or anticipation) of much American fiction concerned with homosexuality. The early fiction of Purdy gets less attention than that of many inferior writers because, although he has humour, he does not pretend that his view of life is other than despairing. It was unacceptable to the *New Yorker* public because his misogyny was not comfortingly conveyed: not smuggled in, so to speak, between cocktails. *63: Dream Palace* (1956), the novella that made Purdy's name when it was published with other stories in *Colour of Darkness* (1957), portrays a man, lost and misused in a small town, who kills the brother he loves. He is seen as a victim of urban technology; but the author's Calvinist ancestry is more obvious than any desire to criticize modern society. .... *Malcolm* (1959) projects homosexual anxiety onto a fifteen-year-old boy who wanders through a world of depravity in search of his lost father, only to be destroyed by ugly and evil forces. This, written in terms of bitter comedy, is a horrifying story, but it illuminates the urban indifference to evil with a real poetry. *The Nephew* (1960), a more integrated novel, and the high point in Purdy's writing, describes a spinster's search for the personality of the nephew, missing in Korea, whom she brought up; she does not find what she seeks – predictably, this nephew was among other things homosexual. The author cleverly and with surprising gentleness reveals the mainsprings of her own personality as she puzzles over her discoveries. If *Cabot Brown Begins* (1965), whose central character makes contact with others by means of rape ('at the rate of about $1\frac{1}{2}$ per diem'), is Grand Guignol then *Eustace Chisholm and the Works* (1968), set in the Chicago of the Depression, is fashionable Gothic. The eponymous hero writes 'the Works' in charcoal on old pages of the *Chicago Tribune*. Another character is able to express his true homosexual bent only when sleep-walking; he is disembowelled by a mad Captain, also – it need hardly be added – homosexual. It was sad to see so eloquent a writer reduced to this; but much worse was to come: two parts of an uncompleted trilogy called *Sleepers in Moon-Crowded Valleys*, and four more separate novels. All these books are characterized by a tiredness of style (once Purdy had caught the speech of Ohio with unerring accuracy), a resort to windy rhetoric which wholly obscures whatever the writer thinks he may have to say. Yet Purdy remains bitter, saying that the literary establishment can 'promote only lies' and that were he in a position to do so, he would never publish anything commercial again. All that emerges from his recent novels is an unremitting, generalized bitterness – though a few critics have seen this later prose as 'poetic' and full of love for humanity. One hopes that this is a temporary lapse, for at his best Purdy – whether the literary establishment was hostile to him or not – wrote fine and compassionate novels.

John Hawkes (1925), born in Connecticut, has a number of faults, the main one being a tendency to very heavy rhetoric; all his work, too, is uneven. But he is that very rare article: a genuine experimental writer. This is something for which a price usually has to be paid. Hawkes, like Barth (q.v.), is concerned with the creation of fictional worlds, not with the transcription of events. But his approach is quite different; and less intellectual. Whatever the faults of his prose, it is always evident that an imagination of great power is struggling to express itself – with Barth one does not feel that the great energy arises from more than ingenuity. Hawkes' books are something like dreams, and so is their logic. He has been called a fabulist and a surrealist, but neither term really helps to describe him. The fact is that, for all the suddenly emerging rhetorical crudities and fallings-back on brutality when his own procedures break down, Hawkes is one of the most original writers of his time. It is true that his peculiar methods resemble those of Djuna Barnes (q.v.); but he seems to me, although not to all critics, superior. Still, the comparison (originally Fiedler's, who called one of Hawkes' novels '*Brighton Rock* rewritten by Djuna Barnes') is useful.

Djuna Barnes (1892–1982), born in New York, for long a member of the between-the-wars Paris expatriates, is a minor Gothic decadent – who was somewhat irresponsibly commended by T.S. Eliot (q.v.), with the predictable effect that she became a cult-object. Eliot wrote that her *Nightwood* (1936) had a quality 'very nearly related to that of Eliza-bethan tragedy'. This was, quite simply, wrong: the quality of this surrealist study in psychopathology (mostly sexual) is actually related to the French decadence of the Nineties. Djuna Barnes has also written *The Book of Repulsive Women* (1915), *A Book* (1923; rev. as *A Night Among the Horses*, 1929), the stream-of-consciousness novel *Ryder* (1928), and *The Antiphon* (1958), a tedious play in blank verse written perhaps under the in-fluence of Eliot's linking of her with the Elizabethans. Her *Selected Works* were published in 1962. Djuna Barnes undoubtedly possesses originality; she adds to it an element of pretentiousness; and when all else fails her she retreats into irresponsible surrealism; attempts to demonstrate how her images cohere have not been convincing.

Hawkes' work resembles Djuna Barnes' in the integrity of its peculiar atmosphere. *Nightwood* is too long and too full of forced Gothic to be a major book; but it does have its own extraordinary atmosphere. Hawkes' *The Cannibal* (1949), his first novel, has a similar integrity but is less spoilt. It is no more about the horrors of devastated Germany than Robbe-Grillet's *The House of Assignation* (q.v.) is 'about' Hong Kong. Hawkes' post-war

Germany is, however, as valid as any other: such fiction implies the question, Whose Germany can be viable? *The Lime Twig* (1961) is possibly based on Greene's *Brighton Rock* (q.v.) in the way Golding's *Lord of the Flies* (q.v.) is based on Ballantyne's *Coral Island*. It takes place in what Hawkes calls the London blitz. But this is only his surrender to a certain image he has (uncorrected by any historical investigation) of this event. *The Beetle Leg* (1951), perhaps his most successful novel, is about a worker buried alive while building a dam. It is certainly not realistic, but it is not symbolic either. One might better say that Hawkes' world here illuminates the reader's. ... Of course he can be merely quaint; one of the stories collected in *Lunar Landscapes* (1970) begins: 'Early in the morning in a town famous for the growing of some grape; I arose from my bed in the inn and stepped outside alone to the automobile'. But that was perhaps to get a start. As is always apparent, the influence of Sir Thomas Browne, the English seventeenth-century writer, is as potent as that of Barnes. But after *Second Skin* (1964) Hawkes, knowing himself to be almost too original, very sensibly worked into his novels some semblance of 'conventionality'. *The Blood Oranges* (1971), about 'wife swapping', is a genuinely comic (as well as ironic) novel. Hawkes explicitly, in a manner reminiscent of Nabokov (q.v., to whom he has a debt), rejects the notion that his novels are autobiographical; while all fiction is of necessity autobiographical – it could not be otherwise – it is clear that Hawkes' struggle not to base his books on his own actual experiences or even views has been productive and interesting. He wants only his imagination to work, almost as if it were separate from him. It is a genuine try for the objective, even though Hawkes – as a gifted critic – knows that objectivity is not attainable. But his deliberate pretence of it, not a disingenuous one, is valuable – as is his insistence on basing his fictions, its *données*, on his visions and dreams (which are of course subjective, but which become extremely fascinating when treated as objects or events separated from the man who experienced them).

Death, Sleep and the Traveller* (1974) followed on *The Blood Oranges*, but was slighter. Then came *Travesty* (1976), perhaps Hawkes' most powerful and coherent work: it is a monologue by a man who is driving to a murder and a suicide, but it is also Hawkes speculating imaginatively and often inspiredly about the meaning of life (the car travelling towards death). It is the only book to draw from *The Fall* (q.v.) and to be worthy of that masterpiece. In *The Passion Artist* (1979) Hawkes returns from the conventional world to that of his first novel, *The Cannibal*. Hawkes has said that sexuality is destroyed by every possible means, and in saying so seemed to be echoing the message (if not the entire viewpoint) of Wilhelm Reich. In *The Passion Artist* he seems to be examining his own contribution to this destruction, for he gives the misogyny in him (and there is misogynous fear in every man) full imaginative reign. The occasion of the novel is a revolt in a woman's prison and the violence it generates. One suspects that the male fears and misogyny in it point to some of the reasons for which women, or femininity, are imprisoned. Hawkes has written a number of effective, well-constructed plays; *The Universal Fears* (1978) collects stories.

Evan S. Connell** (1924) is one of the most accomplished of American novelists. He is always professional, but this never obtrudes into his work; he does not make concessions to gain entertainment value. He is not a loud novelist, but the way he distances himself from his material should not lead any reader to suppose that he lacks feeling. His less good novels (for example, *Diary of a Rapist*, 1966) do, it is true, strain after effect at the expense of feeling; but *Mr. Bridge* (1969) amply demonstrates that this is not lacking. At his worst Connell writes too tastefully well; but his mastery of technique stands him in good stead in *Mr. Bridge*, in which he portrays a modern Babbitt more skilfully and unambiguously than Sinclair Lewis (q.v.) – but not with the same raw power. Here he composes in vignettes, some not more than a page long; the cumulative effect is remarkable, and conveys the picture of a whole man. Connell is not a major writer; but within the limits he sets himself he is an excellent minor one. His other novels include *Mrs. Bridge* (1959); *The Anatomy Lesson* (1957) and *At the Crossroads* (1965) collect short stories. *Notes From a Bottle Found on the Beach at Carmel* (1963), a long poem in the manner of Pound's *Cantos* (q.v.), is not poetry but is interesting, intelligent and readable.

Having dealt with the Bridges, Connell passed on to Muhlbach (this name is common in Kansas City), a New York insurance man. Now the author becomes more comic, although *The Connoisseur* (1974) seemed to be more an opportunity for Connell to exhibit his own knowledge of pre-Columbian art (with which Muhlbach becomes obsessed) than to study his insurance man. *Double Honeymoon* (1976), employing the montage effect of *Mr. Bridge*, but not as successfully, is more about a girl called Lambeth – who eventually kills herself – than about Muhlbach. These last two books are so fragmented that they scarcely warrant the description of novels: they are more of a series of erudite notes, giving a more or less *pointillist* effect. *St Augustine's Pigeon* (1980) is a selection from all Connell's short stories. His best novels remain the two about the Bridge family; *Diary of a Rapist* is a fascinating failure, sometimes brilliant in its depiction (it is narrated by the rapist) of a paranoid personality – but it was an opportunity missed, since Connell gives us no reality against which to test the narrator's beliefs.

Hubert Selby (1928) achieved notoriety through *Last Exit to Brooklyn* (1964). It is a book of short stories, essentially in the realist tradition, about homosexuals and trans-vestites in Brooklyn. Few have written so vividly about the miseries of the extreme forms of homosexuality. It is ironic that Selby should have been selected for prosecution, because his attitude towards his material is somewhat puritanical. Doubtless it was his truthfulness and starkness that offended: he is one of the few writers of his generation to prove the continuing viability of realism. *The Room* (1972), describing the sexual fantasies of an imprisoned psychotic, is at once a terrifying and a deeply compassionate novel. Although the protagonist is undoubtedly mad, and although his sadistic fantasies of hate against the policemen who arrested him are repulsive in the extreme, an irony permeates the whole book: there is a metaphorical sense in which these policemen, who are unjust and bestial, actually are what the madmen imagines them to be. Humanly, they are as mad and as unjust as he. But – and this is horrific – they did not 'need help'. He does; but he gets none.

The Demon (1977) is more uneven. Harry White's insane womanizing is well depicted; but what it leads up to (murder) is too obviously just a device – Selby for once fails to connect sex and violence in a meaningful way, as he had intended to do. Harry is so obsessed by his demon, his need to obtain gratification, that the rest of him is psycho-logically obscured. In *Requiem for a Dream* (1978) Selby quite exhausts his hatred of the modern world, which begins to lose its valid edge. In the first two books he demonstrated sympathy with his obsessed characters, and saw them as much as victims as moral criminals (in *The Room* the 'criminal' is not even morally condemned). In *Requiem* the description of addiction – real and metaphorical – becomes almost mechanical, and the people mere puppets. But this may herald the end of a phase and the beginning of a new and more fruitful one. Selby is a writer of no mean capacities: the terrifying density of his first novel demonstrates this.

Successors to Selby do not exhibit his raw power, and for the most part are more evidently literary and even academic. Certainly most are slighter, even though Toni Morrison (q.v.), who started writing later, towers above even him. Only **Gloria Naylor** (1950), in *The Women of Brewster Place* (1983), seems to come near to equalling him in range and scope. This novel, her first, deals with seven women living in a slum tenement in New York City (where she was born): the technique is realistic, although much intelligent use is made of interior monologue – and of interspersed Blues lyrics. This non-didactic novel impresses by its psychological depth and the subdued passion of its feeling for its characters. It promises major works to come.

Robert Coover (1932), from Iowa, although more imaginative and more entertaining than Barth (q.v.), is singularly self-limiting. His turning away from realism has been accomplished at the cost of his inventive abilities, even though it was done for reasons that are philosophically intelligible. So many over-cerebral novelists, particularly in America, choose to forget that no one has questioned the novel and its validity more than Cervantes. Yet Cervantes was able to become a genuinely popular classic. This will never happen to Coover, let alone Barth and his like. Although there is something in contemporary life which tends to cripple and destroy true creativity, there always ought, one might fairly claim, to be a chance that an author's work might one day (if not now) reach the public imagination. One is not to say that the common reader does not 'understand' *Don Quixote* as well as the 'advanced critic': he may respond to it more completely, despite his lack of detailed knowledge. It depends on the advanced critic, and on the degree of his humility. Detailed knowledge often acts as a smokescreen. There is much intimidation of readers, as well as much unnecessary sense of inferiority. If there is something wrong with most of modern literature, if modernism as an idea has been carried too far, then Coover is an example, if not a very bad one, of how and why it has gone wrong. Here is a writer who could be quite different – wholly more creative, more secure in his possession of his imagination's gifts – had he not chosen criticism instead of fiction. Even the questions he poses about the status of fiction would have emerged in a more tangible manner had he made that choice. *Pricksongs and Descants* (1971), his earliest work although not published until after his first two novels, tries to 'convince' the reader that fiction is merely a Borgesian (q.v.) affair: that the author is the only creator, and that there is no reality, no order, no meaning, except that which the writer imposes. What he succeeds in doing is to demonstrate that such abstractions function very weakly when they are imposed – and that they undermine the imaginations of minor writers. What is happening is that Coover is trying to eschew mystery because he is afraid of it. He is like a conventional modern physicist who cannot allow himself to admit that everything will not be explained by what he thinks of as 'science'. Borges is certainly a master; but posterity will show him to be himself a minor writer, brilliantly inventive, but empty-hearted and possessed of trivial passions. The notion of the author as God can have very distressing consequences if it is carried too far. It may also even be hubristic if the imaginative material 'given' has its own life. We are bound to ask: how godlike is that author who begins from the premise that he is God? His work is going to be pretty thin when it is compared with that of, say, a Dreiser (q.v.), a no doubt clumsy and simple-minded realist who did not bother his intellectually undistinguished head with such stuff. ... The point is that such ultra-modern criticism of fiction as essentially hermetic ignores the dynamics of the relationship – perceived by the reader – between fiction and life. If the element of life, the sense of life as she is lived by the millions (the thing that makes substantial fiction breathe), exists in a work, then it may after all exist as itself: there may be something essentially humble and ungodlike in the author of that work. We find that element in Bellow (q.v.), intellectually more distinguished than Dreiser, but his humble admirer.

The Public Burning (1977), Coover's third and altogether most ambitious novel, consists of language-games and every modernist device (almost) except an original one. Language is supposed to be an end in itself, and to do all the creative work. But language is not an end in itself in what persists in seeming to be life to the vast majority, who are not linguistic philosophers. It is one (but one) of the devices by which human beings attempt to communicate with one another. Coover seems entirely to forget this. Joyce (q.v.), in

Finnegans Wake, even though that is ultimately a failure – he wrote it, in my estimation, because his daughter Lucia withdrew into uncommunicativeness (schizophrenia) and he desperately needed to make sense of this – never forgets it. One gets a sense of the tragedy of withdrawal. In Coover it is assumed that tragedy is 'an adolescent response'. That is philosophical poppycock.

Yet, apart from the amateurish impudence and, of course, adolescentness of all this, Coover in his first two novels might have done well – had he been able to resist his ideas in favour of his inventiveness. *The Origin of the Brunists* (1967), about a 'new religion', could have been excellent comedy; it is spoiled by the author's didactic purpose of 'showing' that religion is 'meaningless'. Any anthropologist, atheist or otherwise, could inform Coover that this is simply not the case, and that to try to demolish it in such simplistic terms is a waste of time. Coover sets out to show how a 'meaningless' myth is made. But his account tells us nothing. However, in terms of comedy and sometimes of character it is occasionally inventive: something else is going on besides silly and ill informed thinking. *The Universal Baseball Association* (1968), again, has all the ingredients of a fine comic novel; but it is undermined by the author's dogmatic purpose yet again, inasmuch as Coover is trying to present an alternative reality which is 'better' than 'ours'. For obvious reasons, this does not make philosophical sense. In *The Public Burning* what could have been visionary is undermined by slickness and the itself meaningless conviction (meaningless because wholly cerebral: in, say, Beckett, q.v., the conviction is emotional) that everything is meaningless. Nixon, the mean, revengeful, mad (and at one point sodomized) narrator of much of the book, would suggest to many of its readers that Coover really believes that the disgraced politician was all of those things. But how could that mean anything? Nixon in Coover's terms must be unreal. That Coover knows very well that there is some awful connection between Nixon and reality, an apprehensible reality, makes his own enterprise look rather foolish – and, if one were to choose to make an issue of it, disingenuous.

Coover himself is not worth the space I have devoted to him. But the tendency he represents is worth that space. However, I should add that he is one of the least unentertaining of his sort of novelist. There is always a novel struggling to escape from the by now trite philosophy.

William H. Gass (1924), born in North Dakota, is Coover's senior by eight years – and he is often coupled with him in discussions. Unlike Coover, he is a professional philosopher – that is to say, he teaches the subject at a university – and he clearly values the discipline over literature. Gass says that Plato's objection to poets was justified at least in as much as poets are not special sources of knowledge. 'There are no events but words in fiction.' This latter remark is or at least seems true, and provides a challenge that must be answered. Nor does Gass ignore the issue of how or when words themselves are actually 'events', and whether or not the associations they generate in the brains of those who read them could be called other events, not verbal. Unlike Coover, he is a formidable thinker. But it may be that his provocative critical book *Fiction and the Figures of Life* (1970) is superior to his fiction. ... As a novelist and short-story writer (one true novel, *Omensetter's Luck*, 1966, one 'essay-novella', *Willie Masters' Lonesome Wife*, 1971, and two collections of stories) Gass tries to be a sort of Mallarmé (q.v.) in prose. His notion of Mallarmé, though, is novel. He does not try to create character or tell stories (things the misguided world enjoys, even now), and he says that he is 'principally interested in the problems of style'. It sounds a grim prospect, despite the stimulating criticism (a mixture of Barthes, Borges, Wittgenstein, Lévi-Strauss which seems too sharply stated to be much like the magma it may well be). It unhappily is a rather grim prospect, though few might admit it.

Omensetter's Luck, despite the author's desire to destroy narrative and to set up 'language as all', is in essence a treatment of two sorts of men: Omensetter who is 'lucky' because he is simply natural, and Jethro Furber who thinks, and is obsessed: it is the latter who is presented to us as the 'saved character'. But it is hard to disentangle the somewhat tedious philosophical jargon about make-believe, from the imaginative core of the novel. Gass was using something that looked like a novel in order to demolish the novel. Theory was taking over from fiction. *Willie Masters' Lonesome Wife* is even more recondite: it is supposed to clear the ground for the free use of the imagination (it has been asserted); but if it does that by pretending to dispense with character and narrative and so forth, then really it is undermining the imagination. These illusions persist, and nothing so thoroughgoingly philosophical is going to dislodge them. Gass has said that he tries to write poetry, but that he cannot do it: 'I am a rotten poet and have absolutely no talent for it'. His experiment, to use *symboliste* methods ('working in the tradition of the Symbolist poets') in prose, demonstrates that verse is the correct medium for such experiments. But Gass has also said that he would like people to read his books as though they were listening to music. It seems, therefore, that he ought to be a composer. The problem set by his enterprise is this: the function of language is a universal puzzle, and you cannot really solve it by limiting it to the novel. In 'life' language seems to lead to 'extra-linguistic' results. Therefore the novel above all (except for poetry) might be expected to lead to such results. Language is not 'all' in it.

Donald Barthelme (1931), born in Philadelphia, belongs to the Gass-Coover (qq.v.) stable, but theorizes less and writes rather more. The most powerful influences on him have been Borges and Calvino (qq.v.). He seems to be content with a minor role, and achieves a good deal more than either Gass or Coover. There is an element of cartoon in his work, which reminds one of what was not sentimental in Disney (that was not much, but was important for an understanding of American literature, as John Gardner, q.v., recognized). Barthelme, who is much more successful in the story than in the novel, is a wildly uneven writer; but few pieces by him contain nothing that does not scintillate or amuse or stop the reader short. He is not so much a celebrator of meaninglessness (and apostle of the word-in-itself: all that really belongs to the history of poetry, not of prose) as a man writing from an assumption of it. So he is content to make his whimsical points, based on the frustrating minutiae of life: *City Life* (1971), perhaps his best book, is really bleakness relieved by humour; occasionally the author does give away the meagreness of his basic vision, though: 'that muck of mucks, human consciousness'. One cannot expect anyone who writes like that to provide more than light relief. But this Barthelme does, though his satirical attention to cliché and the absurd manner in which people employ language has gradually undermined his readability. His story collections include *Come Back, Dr. Caligari* (1964) and *Amateurs* (1976).

Richard Brautigan (1933–85) provides a menu – this word is used advisedly – of somewhat tedious understatement which for some reason has caught on among a number of readers. He has written some ten novels, a book of stories, and a dozen or so volumes of verse which do not sell like his fiction, but which have a mindless 'underground' following. His poem about the pill runs:

> When you take your pill
> it's like a mine disaster.
> I think of all the people
> lost inside of you

This is trite, and the author clearly does not mean what he says. Brautigan would not like to be committed to thinking or feeling at all, so far as one can tell from his odd, un-interesting fiction. His characters (though they are as cardboard as is possible) are floppy and idly cunning, posing as naïves or innocents. After his fourth novel *The Abortion* (1973) Brautigan, perhaps amazed that anyone could be enthusiastic about his work at all, began to 'experiment', so we got such titles as: *The Hawkline Monster: A Gothic Western* (1974), and *Sombrero Fallout: A Japanese Novel* (1977). No body of fiction in our time that purports to be serious is so irritatingly depthless; but the author is no doubt gambling that he may be right, after all. Well, if he were, we should have to invent something more interesting. Yet his readers seem to delve into him as though they were fishing for some-thing wise.

John Gardner (1933–82), from Batavia, New York, built up a substantial reputation before dying prematurely in a motor-cycle accident. He was a medieval scholar, and relied greatly (as he admitted) on Chaucer for his technique. There was not, perhaps, a natural novelist in Gardner as there is in Gass and Coover (qq.v): rather, he was an intel-ligent and lively man who wanted to write novels, and found a means of pretending to do so. He wrote some scholarly books about Chaucer and Old English poetry. As he said in an interview, he borrowed heavily in his fictions: too heavily, as it happens, because it seems as if there was never an imaginative core in his work, without which even the most allusive writer cannot hope to achieve real creative life. Gardner's admirable quest was to affirm 'positive moral values' ('as long as these aren't oversimplified – like don't commit adultery, nonsense like that'), which he saw as a 'life-affirmation'. And his ten novels are full of affirmation, fine writing and intelligent observation. But they are, ultimately, artificial – manufactured. They fail to take on a life of their own.

The first mature work was *Grendel* (1971), 'the other side of the story' of the *Beowulf* epic, in the scholarship of which Gardner was well up. Grendel is mostly a voice, and, legendary monster, is made to seem 'good': he will kill the human unless it takes know-ledge of him. The conception is superb, but the language cannot rise to it, and the notion of 'monstrousness' is confused. *The Sunlight Dialogues* (1972) is set in Gardner's native Batavia in modern times; here the 'monster' Grendel is represented by the Sunlight Man, who intrudes into the realism of the book as a mythical being. Again, it is a mag-nificent conception, but again, the book does not work – one has only to read Hamsun's *Mysteries* (qq.v.) and consider the figure of the midget to see why: Hamsun's book does all, and more, than Gardner's, but its realism is far more convincing, it is more con-densed, and its perhaps (who really knows?) 'supernatural' creature comes across as eerily natural, simply emphasizing to us that our own lives are not as 'ordinary' as we think. The rest of Gardner's work falls off gradually: he tries again and again to bring to life an enigmatic 'monster' or mythical being or force who is not as baleful as humankind would have him, and he fails more and more dismally. Yet his view that nihilism (of the sort practised by Gass or Coover or many of their other, inferior, imitators) is merely fashionable was right-hearted and right-headed. *Grendel* and *The Sunlight Dialogues* come very near to being important books; but both are too long and too ambitious – and, alas, too thin in vision. His greatest achievement is *On Moral Fiction* (1978), in which he lashes Mailer (q.v.), Coover and others, for the falsity of their despair; but this was not popular at the time, as it attacked fashionable writers when their star had not finally fallen (as Mailer's now has) – soon it will be taken up again. It is tragic that it should not have been supported by a more substantial creative achievement.

Two Black writers who have achieved a great deal more than Coover, Gass, or even Gardner are **Ishmael Reed** (1938) and Charles Wright (q.v.). Reed is an Afro-American who was born in Tennessee. His fiction has been attacked as 'mindless' and 'insane', and he has been the despair of such newspaper critics as will warily and uncomprehendingly welcome Coover (q.v.). But he has said that storytelling will always be with us, and in that he is right. Much is wrong with the world, and the novels of those who want to destroy story on feeble philosophical grounds have not yet remedied a single one of these wrongs; they probably add to them. Reed and others have recently started a revolt against the novel-as-criticism, and they now seem the livelier for it. His first novel, *The Free-Lance Pallbearers* (1967), is zany satire on that world which is hostile to 'foreigners', and the attack is mounted from a 'foreigner's' viewpoint. In *Yellow-Back Radio Broke-Down* (1969) Reed weaves his Negro tapestry with more skill and control, though the whole reads as 'crazily' as ever. He shows the energy and the coherence (though it does not look like coherence to all readers) of the Afro-American tradition as perhaps no other writer has. *Mumbo-Jumbo* (1972) was written from the notion that, as Reed puts it, the 'black writer lies in the guts of old America, making readings about the future'. *Mumbo-Jumbo*, a wholly ironic title, is a mock 'classical detective story', although most of its critics failed to notice this. Reed was of course poking fun. In essence this book, with its photographs and collages, describes the struggle between the always living Black culture with the American conventional tradition, which is synthetic and denies its own roots – it is about as 'American' as kilts are truly Scottish. But one could not take this as being a political book, any more than one takes Morrison's (q.v.) books as political. Reed bases his technique largely on television, although this does not obtrude, and it is probable that he uses it simply as an available and appropriate means. He takes up a position very different from that taken by Baldwin (q.v.), although he admires the older writer. He is critical of, although not rude about, 'white liberals' such as Irving Howe (q.v.), and he is outspoken about what he called the 'fascism' not only of the American government but also of *Playboy* millionaire Hugh Hefner. However, to satirize these people, he prefers to be funny rather than strident; and he can be very funny indeed. *The Last Days of Louisiana Red* (1974) and *Flight to Canada* (1976) consolidated Reed's position as the leading Black comic writer of America.

   Charles Wright (1932) is 'out on his own', as Reed (q.v.) himself has observed. He is extremely critical of his own people, and has veered away from the Baldwin-like (q.v.) frenzy and rage which characterized much Black thinking in the Sixties. The writer from whom Wright has learned most is undoubtedly Nathanael West (q.v.), although he is more explicit about the hideous and treacherous sleaziness of the world he depicts than West ever felt like being; and he is much concerned with homosexuality, which West was not. Wright sees the American Blacks, one might think, as slowly killing themselves. But his settings, unlike Morrison's (q.v.), are almost exclusively urban. *The Messenger* (1963) is an autobiographical novel about a writer, Charles Stevenson (the latter is Wright's second name; in *Absolutely Nothing to Get Alarmed About*, 1973, the protagonist is called Charles Wright), who moves from the south (Wright was born in Missouri), then into the army (Wright served in Korea), and finally to New York. *The Wig* (1966) is about a Black who turns his Afro hair into a white 'wig' and tries unsuccessfully to enter white society. *Absolutely Nothing to Get Alarmed About*, set in the Bowery, is altogether more serious – and more strained – but in many ways it is an improvement: the surface is more realistic, and for that reason more vivid – Wright is less keen to corrugate the surface of his prose with high satirical jinks, and more concerned to concentrate on psychological issues. But since the writing of this book he has found it hard to do what he wants, and has admitted to a 'creative block'.

*

There was of course a reaction to the novel disguised as criticism, even though that reaction took account of the questioning of the status of fiction. The most interesting results often looked no less 'modernistic' than do the novels of Gass or Coover (qq.v.). They may have been stimulated, too, by the work of a distinctly odd man out, **Thomas Pynchon** (1937), who cannot be categorized – and whose impact is by now fast diminishing. *V* (1963) was greeted as a classic example of 'black humour', and has even become enshrined as one; but essentially it and its two successors are explorations of the 'dustbin' (as it has often been called since Freud (and others independently of him such as Groddeck) put it on the map) of the 'id'. Pynchon also owes much to the 'surrealistic' (as Koestler, q.v., described them) discoveries of modern physics about the behaviour of 'waves', and 'particles', and (at least in *V*) to Graves' (q.v.) concept of the White Goddess. Pynchon is a highly literate Henry Miller (q.v.), whose penchant it is to explore the modern nightmare. His three books (*The Crying of Lot 49*, 1966, and *Gravity's Rainbow*, 1973, followed *V*; and there is a story called *Mortality and Mercy in Vienna* of 1976 and two more stories of 1978 and 1981) are immensely and deliberately complex and allusive, and are weak in at least the sense that they are susceptible to no one certain outline of an interpretation: that is to say, they lack emotional power, and all feeling is bogged down in intricate cerebral detail. Many readers find them tedious and unreadable. On the other hand, they were very highly praised.

They consist of interludes of mad narrative, slabs of erudition which the author might have copied out or might have absorbed (who knows?), and a huge variety of pastiche of various styles ranging from pop horror to that favourite of contemporary Americans, Sir Thomas Brown. They were very much cult books, though the cult was quite wide, and a great deal that was said about them ('Pynchon's heroism') had to be taken on trust if taken at all. Certain it is that no writer could have gone on in this manner, an almost entirely literary one, without his bluff being eventually called: without someone coming out and saying, well, yes, this is all very well, but is it fiction, and isn't it boring? Gobbets of what look like undigested knowledge hang about and clutter up the flow of Pynchon's undoubtedly manic inventiveness; his writing in itself is not all that exciting. ... *Gravity's Rainbow* rests, really, for all its complexity, on the fact that a man's erections coincide with the sites of rocket explosions in London. It takes a better novel than this to make something out of that not unobvious ploy, and it hardly helps when a critic says simultaneously that this is one of the century's great novels and that it is 'disappointing ... maddening'. Of course Pynchon is not 'great' or even almost great: he is not in that category. Pynchon is a fanatically private man, and one who might well have become engulfed by the paranoia he has depicted in his books. He has been compared to Céline (q.v.) and Swift, but such comparisons are premature: he shows neither the essential lucidity of the one, nor the satiric genius of the other. Negativity of vision he does demonstrate, powerfully; but so far there is nothing with which to counter it – not even the assumption, implicit in all effective satire, that somewhere some light illumines the darkness (otherwise why attack, except for unhealthy motives of pure hate?).

Two other writers whose attitudes have something in common with that of Pynchon are more readily accessible, and both have written best sellers. **Joseph Heller** (1923), from Brooklyn, served in the USAAF throughout the Second World War. But it took him until 1961 to write the legendary *Catch-22*, which did for that war what Graves' *Goodbye to All That* (qq.v.), with which it has much in common, did for the earlier one. *Catch-22* was a brilliant and seminal book, and Heller paid the price for its excellence: it successors, two novels and two plays, are not remotely on the same level, and need not be discussed here. It is a fair judgement that in *Catch-22* Heller wrote the 'definitive novel of modern warfare': Heller's book contains almost everything that is in Hašek (q.v.) or in Graves about war; but he steals from neither, although the techniques of both are evident, as is that of Ben Jonson. 'Catch-22' is a crazy bureaucratic formula: if you are mad then you can get out of the war, but you must ask; and if you ask, you can't be mad. This has endless implications, and they have not been missed. *Catch-22* is humane as well as a masterpiece of comic improvisation (based on the uncomic and life-denying aspirations of 'rational' bureaucrats), and is a classic about which refreshingly little need be said. Its successors have the touch, but not the inspiration or the substance. But isn't one classic sufficient?

Kurt Vonnegut (1922) has as great a reputation amongst readers who stray seldom into serious realms as he has amongst critics and discerning readers. And his work has declined. He has, quite simply, become less serious. He has come to depend more and more on too simplistic Science Fiction frameworks, and he has repeated himself too easily in his self-proclaimed role as 'total pessimist'. Pynchon (q.v.) might actually have become a total pessimist, sunk beneath the horror of the enormities he has perpetrated (although this is a condition from which a person can emerge); but Vonnegut's work has never seemed totally pessimistic. *Player Piano* (1952), about the dehumanization of the already dehumanized, really did have a touch of Swift, in demonstrating the pointlessness of revolution on the grounds that people are too stupid to take advantage of them. There were several fine stories in *Canary in a Cat House* (1961). Vonnegut then reached his apogee, after four more novels, with *Slaughterhouse-Five* (1969). This deals with the author himself and a protagonist, both of whom can discern the horrors of modern life (here epitomized by the destruction of Dresden by British bombs), and even diagnose some of the reasons for them, but who cannot bring about any change. The ending, in which the protagonist is transported to another planet, is contrived and sentimental – but at least it showed Vonnegut attempting to exercise the compassion he had possessed up to this time in his writing career. Its successors are clownish and hollow. The first novels are the best, but *Slaughterhouse-Five* contains passages of greater power, even if it fails overall. The rest merely take advantage of cleverness about horrors which still engage the minds and hearts of other people: tomfoolery.

Ronald Sukenick (1932), from New York, is increasingly talked about by American critics, but so far has failed to find a British publisher. The only comment that he will make about his work is: 'My fiction is not "experimental"' – and in the present circumstances this is an admirably laconic and intelligent response. The earlier novels *Up* (1968) and *Out* (1973) did look very experimental – but no more so than the verse of Cummings (q.v.) had looked in the Twenties; and he, of course, was anything but experimental. The chief influence behind these playful and fairly superficial books, with their typographical innovations and their refusal to accept anything as reliable, was a pervasive one: Sterne. *Up*, however, which is about a man called Ronald Sukenick who is (guess), was highly amusing. *Long Talking Bad Condition Blues* (1979) is a modest exercise in total incoherence, and was published by Fiction Collective (a possible last resort): it does not have the promise of Sukenick's remark to the effect that his fiction is not experimental. Yet this book, essentially a self-analysis of a man who wants (for some undefined reason) to write a novel, but who has no idea whatever what he wants it to be about, does have some fascination: it is the ultimate in pointlessness, and is of interest because it shows the direction in which those who regard writing as process (and no more) are heading. There is a desperate sort of instability here which points to a collapse into a willed schizophreniform withdrawal – or, and this is what is interesting, a possible desperate reaching towards a new form.

Jerzy Kosinski (1933) has become in recent years so much of a star that several critics have tried to demonstrate that there is no substance to him at all. I include him among the American novelists, rather than the Polish, only because he is a naturalized Ameri-

can, and because he has written his more important books in English. He was born in
Łódź and educated (as a sociologist) at the university there; but he emigrated to the
States in 1957 and became a citizen in 1965, the year in which his first novel, *The Painted
Bird*, appeared. His imagination is a distinctively Polish one; but, instead of allowing his
dark and melancholy vision to degenerate wholly into mere petulance (this happens with
more than a few Poles, especially exiles), he sharpened it; but he has not escaped the
temptation to flavour his later books with more than a touch of fashionable 'sick kitsch',
and it now looks as though he is in sad decline. When Kosinski first came to the USA he
did many manual jobs, teaching himself English all the while. Eventually he gained a
Ph.D from Columbia (1964). He says that mastery of English 'freed me from what I had
been. I was acquiring a new tradition and a new relationship not only with the external
world but with my old Russian-Polish self [his parents were Russians, who left in 1918].'

Kosinski's first novel (1965, rev. 1970, with new intro. 1975), *The Painted Bird*, features
himself as 'The Boy' in Poland during the Second World War and just after it. This dark
boy is taken to be a 'painted bird' among sparrows, and is not only despised but feared
for his strangeness. He discovers that he can survive only by means of an imaginative
hatred and sense of vengeance. 'Disagreeables' seldom entirely evaporate in 'black' Polish
fiction (this predates the so-called 'black humour' by very many years: one has only to
think of Conrad, q.v.), and they don't here. Kosinski's method, he declared, had been
'Jungian' – and that is seldom encouraging, for Jung has exercised a profoundly bad
influence on pretentious literature of the second-class sort, and Kosinski, though first-
class in some respects, is essentially second class, as his more recent novels have shown.
We don't, as Kosinski claimed we could, discover the 'simple keys to the European
culture of the mid-twentieth century' – nor are these as simple as in Jungian theory,
which is 'irrefutable' in the worst manner. *Steps* (1968), to which Kosinski provided a
further book of 'notes' (also 1968: *The Art of the Self*), relapses into clever brutality: the
sense of abomination is there, certainly, and with it a sense of power – it is not merely
puerile as in the paradigmatically overrated Ted Hughes (q.v.). But it is suspiciously
intellectual and clinical and cold, and the critic who found it to be no more than a series
of 'leaps of self-indulgence' may have been near to the truth. Horrors are being exploited
for personal purposes. For so abominable a theme, the text was too slick, glossy, professional, plain nasty. *Being There* (1971), Kosinski's gentlest and probably best novel – it
was successfully filmed – is a satire which contains within it almost all Kosinki's better
feelings. A retarded gardener called Chance can only echo his interlocutors' remarks, or
make comments based on television chat, which has been his only contact with the real
world. He is taken as a profoundly wise man, especially when he gives out gardening tips,
and is even considered as a popular candidate for the Vice-Presidency of the United
States. Kosinski's later novels, such as *Blind Date* (1977), take an easier way out: they are
relentlessly unpleasant, and their author claims for them a Nabokov (q.v.)-like omnisci-
ence, which is repellently immodest. It is true that they are both intelligent and readable,
because their prose is undoubtedly lucid in a compelling manner. But they are narrow in
range, because the author has found an increasingly facile formula consisting of certain
patterns of unpleasantness, and these patterns are becoming wearisomely predictable.

V

The general tendency in American poetry in the past forty years, at least until very
recently, with the advent of the 'continental' Ashbery (q.v.), might be said to be towards

Williams and away from Frost and Ransom (qq.v.), with the figure of Pound (q.v.) in the middle. Such figures as Lowell and Berryman (qq.v.) certainly did not turn entirely away from Frost, or even Ransom; whether or to what extent they turned towards Pound or Williams, or to another so-called 'confessional' kind of practice, is an arguable matter. But in their self-conscious modernism they were certainly 'left of centre', whereas such a poet as Marianne Moore (q.v.), despite her eccentric and quasi-modernist use of form, is right of centre; Roethke (q.v.), like Lowell and Berryman, is to the left of it.

But this is no more than a useful initial generalization. It would be pointless in any case to try to classify the verse of Lowell or Berryman except in its own individual terms. The 'Beats' (q.v.), entirely 'redskin' (q.v.), did not like, or ignored, Berryman and Lowell. Whether they were worthy of it or not, they were trying (inspired by Miller, q.v., and their times) to return to the tradition of Whitman, the paradigmatic redskin with his 'barbaric yawp'. Until quite recently, however, two schools did exist side by side, and for the most part sullenly ignored each other. On the one hand there were such 'Black Mountain' (q.v.) poets as Creeley (q.v.), Edward Dorn, Gary Snyder (q.v.) – the sort collected by Donald Allen and Creeley in their *New Writing in the U.S.A.* (1967); on the other there was an academic group, more traditional: this included Lowell, Wilbur, Snodgrass (qq.v.); James Wright, Robert Bly (qq.v.); and some others occupied a middle position – or, perhaps it is fairer to say, a more independent one. There were also the 'New York' school (q.v.) and the 'San Francisco' school, which embraced some Beats and also Duncan (q.v.).

But the 'Black Mountain' (q.v.) movement has fragmented during the Seventies, its members going their own ways – which is no way at all. And the 'Fifties', 'Sixties', 'Seventies' School of Bly and others has also lost its cohesion as a movement. Figures such as Ashbery have become more dominant. American poetry is for the moment a more confused and disparate affair. It is not very inspiring as a whole. The last serious conservative, traditionalist movement in American poetry was promulgated by the Southern group of poets who called themselves the Fugitives. *The Fugitive*, a bi-monthly 'little magazine', appeared between 1922 and 1925. The contributors were mostly associated with Vanderbilt University; their leader was **John Crowe Ransom** (1888–1974), the son of a Tennessee Methodist minister. After studying (as a Rhodes scholar) at Vanderbilt and Oxford, England, Ransom went back to Vanderbilt as an instructor in English. He stayed there for a quarter of a century and played a leading part in the Southern renaissance – that 'renaissance' which was in fact preceded by nothing.

'Southern Agrarianism' was conservative, but the individuals who propounded it were not illiberal. The Agrarian programme is set forth in the 1930 symposium *I'll Take My Stand*, to which Ransom, Warren, Tate (qq.v.) and other Southerners contributed. One could make out a case for this programme being crypto-fascist, especially since its philosophy flowed from Plato; or a case for its being over-scholarly and, in politics, naïve – which in some aspects it is. Its importance, however, is not as a political programme – whatever its proponents may have thought at the time – but as the matrix for some important creative writing. The programme itself is essentially nostalgic; but being intellectual and scholarly it was carefully non-populist. The Agrarians advocated a non-industrialized, Agrarian South, and thus one not exploited by the North: they wanted culture to take the place of politics, in an aristocracy. Their version of the Civil War is, of course, a complicated one; but we may be forgiven for interpreting it as a fight between culture (the South) and politics (the North). Agrarianism was not, however, obscurantist: regarded as something to be re-created. It would have to grow up as the men of the South learned to mould their lives to the natural geography of their region. Politically this was doomed from the start. But then the Southern Agrarians were not politically ambitious:

all they wanted was a programme which they found congenial. Then they could write.

What all this actually represented was the last intelligent traditionalist movement in American (or British) poetry. A poetry that is for the most part content to work within the limits of what has gone before it needs to be attached to a set of real beliefs. (The trouble with the routine Georgians, q.v., in England, or, indeed, with any set of routine middle-brow versifiers, is that they have only a set of pseudo-beliefs, and slackly sentimental ones at that.) For a short time Agrarianism provided a set of politically absurd but simultaneously intelligible beliefs. Not all people will wholly condemn a movement – even if it virtually ignores the Negro problem – that referred to science and technology as new barbarisms 'controlled and directed by the modern power state'. And when it was clear that Agrarianism was no longer viable the same group, the Fugitives, turned to the development of the 'new criticism'. This term had been used as early as 1910 by the critic Joel E. Spingarn to describe his own methods, which involved various comparatively objective ways of examining texts; but what Ransom meant by it – in his book *The New Criticism* (1941) – was different. Taking into account all the critics who have been described as new critics one can fairly say no more than that the new criticism, as generally understood (Ransom's text of 1941 has had a considerable effect on that understanding), introduced higher and more responsible standards into criticism, and put it onto a more, but not of course a wholly, scientific basis. Eventually the movement petered out into the sometimes apparently half-hysterical pseudo-science of such critics as W.K. Wimsatt ('The Structure of Romantic Nature Imagery'). But in its heyday, for all its excesses, and in particular its tendency to artificially isolate works of literature from their contexts (this had begun as an admirable redirection of attentions that had wandered from texts), the new criticism represented a renaissance of sense and sensibility after a period marked mainly by sentimentality and soft thinking.

Ransom's own criticism is ingenious and important, but somewhat frigid and inhibited. Its frigidity, at any rate, confirms the truth of Dryden's remark that 'the corruption of a poet is the generation of a critic'; although 'corruption' is perhaps in this case too strong a word. If we do not (as he does not) count the crude, commonplace and often clumsy *Poems About God* (1919), then Ransom's fecund period – there are only four poems dating from the Thirties – lasted for only four years, from the beginning of 1922 until the end of 1925. In this time, in a series of remarkable and very highly original poems, he held the balance between an archaic, mannered and ornate conservatism and his own personal, emotional concerns. Invariably these poems are cast in the form of elaborate fictions, sometimes learnedly historical and sometimes ironically idyllic. Direct utterance is carefully avoided; but a dark passionateness, usually locked up in powerful and often difficult language, imbues almost every poem.

For Ransom the thinker (not necessarily the poet), man was once whole, and able to perceive the world as it really is; now he is split into reason and sensibility, body and soul. Science, for Ransom, is materialism; it gratifies rational impulses. His kind of poetry, 'metaphysical', 'miraculist', is theoretically made up of structure (the logical sense, the syntax, the metre), and texture (tone, imagery, sound, subject). The texture needs to be supported to a certain extent by the structure, but the two may nevertheless be almost independent of each other: in any case the resultant poem is independent of either a rational or a 'platonic' (this is the kind of poetry Ransom, for all his Southern Agrarianism, dislikes) impulse. Essentially, it will be noted, the poem, in this theory, is a strategy; and as a critic Ransom has undoubtedly enjoyed isolating it – to that extent – from its author, for one of the oblique themes of his poetry is how a passionate man might viably attempt to live at a distance from himself.

Ransom's criticism is important and has deserved its wide influence. It is important, incidentally, because based on the experience of being a poet – not because it is good theory. But it is essential to recognize that the criticism, including the over-meticulous account of Ransom's own four years of poetic life, is a transformation of the poetic function into a series of the very abstractions the poet hates: for it is less criticism of specific poetry, illumination of texts, than a theory. In other words, we have to sit patiently on the banks of a pond of theory to trick the secret fish of poetic intuition into biting. The poet Ransom, the anti-abstractionist, is one of those who think of a theory as what someone has called 'a structure of interrelated empirical propositions'; the critic Ransom, who all but renounced real poetry (many poets do in one way or another) because it began to bring him too uncomfortably close to himself, is a theorist, a pre-scriber of rules upon which poetry should be written and read. And by now, forty years after he could not continue with poetry, Ransom (in the definitive *Selected Poems*, third edition, 1969) ruins his earlier poems, 'pairing' the original texts of eight poems with 1968 versions, and adding commentaries in most cases longer than the poems themselves.

> Conrad, Conrad, aren't you old
> To sit so late in a mouldy garden

becomes the intolerable, arch

> Evening comes early, and soon discovers
> Exchange between two conjugate lovers.

> 'Conrad! dear man, surprise! aren't you bold
> To be sitting so late in your sodden garden?'

The critic has sat in judgement on the poetry. There could be no more decisive demon-stration of which possesses the vital ty.

In one sense the critic Ransom is a strategist leading us away from one of the main features of the poetry: that the poet got more into his poems than their rigorous composer had planned. In his smaller poems, such as 'Janet Waking', Ransom does get the effects he plans: here he shocks the reader out of sentimentality into a realization of what the death of Janet's hen, her first experience of death, really means to her. In the justly famous *Captain Carpenter* he goes beyond himself, achieving a major poetry. The personal price paid is great. As he said in his poem about what the poets ate and drank:

> God have mercy on the sinner
> Who must write with no dinner. . . .

Poetry comes out of experience, and there are points at which it becomes intolerable to question experience, and especially what it tells the undefended heart, too deeply. Yet the best of Ransom, for all its indisputable archaic quaintness, is among the best of our times.

Allen Tate (1899–1980), born in Kentucky, was a critic, historical biographer (of Stonewall Jackson and Jefferson Davis) and the author of a novel, *The Fathers* (1938, rev. 1960), as well as a poet. He was Ransom's (q.v.) pupil, and was the first undergraduate to be invited to join the Fugitives (q.v.). Tate's poems were from the beginning brilliantly phrased; he was always an adept at sustaining one manner or another: a brilliant student. All his work is elegant and accomplished, and yet there is a curious neutrality about it: not a lack of distinction, but the lack of a voice distinctive enough to suggest any personal unifying view. A large minority of literary people in America disliked him intensely, and even marked him down as a treacherous and deceitful careerist. That may have been unfair; but there was certainly something distinctly unappealing about him. His poem 'Ode to the Confederate Dead' (1936) does sum up an ethos – roughly, the ethos of a typical Southern Agrarian (q.v.) – but even this, for so sheerly accomplished a poem, lacks personality. Almost always Tate's poetry seems to be trying to discover a literary language to define a position; but one has to persuade oneself that it is his position. Thus, although he has seldom been criticized (by the Williams-Olson-Black Mountain School, q.v., he has been ignored, like Ransom, simply as an antique) or attacked, Tate has also seldom been warmly praised. There is not often either warmth or passion – or the notion of such feelings being suppressed – in his poetry. He attracts praise, but it is seldom enthusiastic. Conrad Aiken, who had some personal regard for Tate, was forced – in defending him against a severe appraisal – to resort to the word 'useful', hardly a compliment. Is he no more than a model of what a good 'twentieth-century metaphysical' should be? Usually Tate has simply taken too much thought ('So many fine things have a way of coming out all the better without the strain to sum up the whole universe in one impressive pellet' Hart Crane, q.v., once wrote to him); and for all his insistence on tension ('Tension in Poetry' is the title of his best known critical essay), the intellectual ingenuity of his poems tends to rob them of that very quality. (Though Tate over-ingeniously meant by 'tension' the clash between abstract and concrete, denotation and connotation – but it comes to the same thing.) But in such a poem as 'The Swimmers', where the poet remembers the lynching of a black man and a swim he shared with some other boys, he achieves a personal note of indignation and sadness – as in one of his sonnets, where he tells of how he got a Negro beaten unjustly. In the long meditative 'Seasons of the Soul' Tate is at his weakest: the poet is at all times clothing his thinking in suitable linguistic terms – the language is not arising of its own volition. This language has, somehow, a second-hand flavour: 'The living wound of love', 'the mother of silences', 'Irritable spring': a very good model of what modern metaphysical poetry ought to be like, but it fails to convince.

Tate's single novel, *The Fathers* (1938), is a greater achievement than anything in his poetry – not because it is anything very different, but because if you are as clever as Tate is then you can get away with more in fiction than you can in poetry. *The Fathers* is about the old South, the time the months during which the Civil War broke out. It is narrated by an old man, but its central character is really Major Buchan, the narrator's father, a feudal gentleman and an anti-secessionist who has no defences against the commercial, materialistic North. His son-in-law, George Posey, represents man uprooted from tradition. This is beautifully done, and the character of Major Buchan is movingly conveyed. And even if one is left wondering if Tate's old South is not idealized, and his vision of it deliberately blinkered, one accepts it as his legitimate view of the way in which the good life has disintegrated.

Merrill Moore (1903–57), born in Tennessee, was another member of the Fugitives (q.v.). For most of his life he practised psychiatry in Boston (he was able to give valuable help to Edwin Arlington Robinson, q.v., and he was brought in, unsuccessfully, to help Frost's, q.v., son, who killed himself); his immense poetic output consisted entirely of sonnets. He did not, eventually, take literature seriously; but if his comic verse were better known it would perhaps rival that of **Ogden Nash** (1902–71), who though himself inexorably middlebrow, and writing comfortingly for middlebrows, did smuggle a few half-truths into his deliberately banal and mostly irritating verse. Nash's great achievement was in fact to console people who could not write poetry by parodying the bathos of their efforts and so making them laugh.

Laura Riding (ps. **Laura Reichenthal**, 1901) was born in New York. Her father was an

Austrian tailor, a naturalized American, and a lifelong socialist. She attended Cornell University, and there married a history instructor, Louis Gottschalk. Her first poems were signed Laura Riding Gottschalk. From her divorce in 1925 she was known as Laura Riding; since she married Schuyler B. Jackson (died 1968) in 1941, her published works have been signed 'Laura (Riding) Jackson'. From 1926 until 1941, in England, Mallorca, Rennes (France) and finally America, she was associated with Robert Graves (q.v.), with whom she published a number of books and pamphlets. The Fugitives (q.v.) awarded her a poetry prize and made her an honorary member of their group; she was highly enthusiastic, and devised schemes to publicize their work, although she has subsequently denied programmatic association with them. Soon after she published her *Collected Poems* (1938) she came to the conclusion 'that poetry had no provision in it for ultimate practical attainment of that rightness of word that *is* truth, but led on ever only to a temporizing less-than-truth (the lack eked out with illusions of truth produced by physical word effects)'. It has been suggested, however, that her true reasons for rejecting poetry were based in her very evident hatred of Robert Graves and in her husband's insistence. She worked with her husband, a failed writer, on a project 'that would help to dissipate the confusion existing in the knowledge of word-meanings', and she has now completed it alone. In the magazine *Chelsea* (12 and 14, 1962, 1964) she has detailed her reasons for rejecting poetry, and told 'the story of human beings in the universe' (*The Telling*, 1972). In 1970 her *Selected Poems* appeared in Great Britain, with a Preface explaining why she considers even her own poetry an inadequate approach to her function of truth-telling. She knows, she says, of 'no one besides myself and my husband ... who has put feet beyond the margin on the further ground – the margin being the knowledge that truth begins where poetry ends. ...' Her *Collected Poems* were reprinted in Great Britain in 1981, but met with no better reception than they had in 1938.

The notion of poetry – and, indeed, all writing – as humanly inadequate is not new. Rilke, Broch and Thomas Mann (qq.v.) all had similar forebodings, and so have many others. In a century in which everything is questioned, it is unlikely that art would not have been, too. But Laura Riding has been more specific about it than anyone else. She calls the vanity of 'artistically perfect word-use' 'a parasitic partner in the poetic enterprise'. How simply American this is! And how interesting that where she, in her own word, '*stopped*', such writers as Charles Olson (q.v.) simply tried to make a new sort of poetry. But, her extreme personal peculiarities apart (they involve her in continual complaints that everyone has ill-treated her and stolen their styles and ideas from her, and have been said to constitute a 'Jehovah complex'), she has drawn attention to a crisis of poetry in our time – and she has done so whether, with her, we abandon poetry, or whether we go on trying to make it. Her main weakness is that she always has been, as her first husband declared, 'under educated': this gives her less weight than she believes she has when engaged in intellectual argumentation. Much of her later thought consists of variations on Platonism. Her post-1940 writings have generally been considered to be unreadable, and have not attracted the attention of a single distinguished mind.

Laura Riding's own poetry, which has interested only a minority, but a distinguished one – the Fugitives, Graves, Auden, Cameron, Larkin, Bottrall (qq.v.) – is difficult but, at its best, as in her first collection, *The Close Chaplet* (1926), astonishing: almost a definition of sense of the poetic, though not in any familiar form. To what extent it is astonishing because it is simply strange – the utterances of a human being who wants to be God, or of a person who feels herself God but tainted by humanness – is arguable. Here, anyway, good or bad, is the kind of absolute dedication to poetry of a Rilke: all experience is continuously subjected to the heroically objective scrutiny of a truthful heart. Her quality is as well illustrated in 'The Mask' as in any other short poem:

Cover up,
Oh, quickly cover up
All the new spotted places,
All the unbeautifuls,
The insufficiently beloved.

With what? with what?
With the uncovering of the lovelies,
With the patches that transformed
The more previous corruptions.

Is there no pure then?
The eternal taint wears beauty like a mask.
But a mask eternal.

Even if the rejection of the poetry that came in 1940 was forced upon her by her husband, it is in a way already there, in the poems: 'if poetry', she often seems to imply, 'won't get me further in my quest for the perfect and the pure, then poetry will have to go'. Or of course this can be put: 'If poetry doesn't further my needs, then it will have to go' – she had quite vulgar ambitions (property deals; influencing world affairs; slowing up the civil rights programme) along with her huge spiritual ones. Her assertions of her knowledge of the direction of truth do not make for her best poetry; the best lies in her descriptions of the sufferings of a woman of genius, with aspirations towards goodness: 'Nor is it written that you may not grieve./There is no rule of joy ...' is a notable example. This is a poetry that either makes no appeal or deeply fascinates; the full, important and fascinating story of it, and of its aftermath, has yet to be told. She is a notoriously difficult woman, and it will not be told until after her death.

*

Hart Crane (1899–1932), born in Ohio, failed to escape the demons that drove him to drink and compulsive homosexual encounters; he died when he jumped from a ship after a bad night gambling with some sailors, who had beaten him up. He was travelling with a woman with whom he had had a satisfactory heterosexual relationship in the previous months; but she came too late into his life to help him to achieve stability and the heterosexuality he craved for. He published *White Buildings* (1926), short poems, and the American epic, *The Bridge* (1930), in his lifetime. *Collected Poems* (1933) incorporates a last group of shorter poems. His *Letters* (1952) – there are editorially imposed ellipses in these which are singularly ill-judged – are full of acute and generous critical insights into his own and his contemporaries' poetry. An excellent example is his summing-up of Tate's (q.v.) problem, quoted above. Crane, who was patchily self-educated and who was, in an academic sense, unfamiliar with the history of his own country, was quintessentially American and poetically enormously gifted; he is the subject of an increasing number of contradictory monographs, certain of which reach the fantastic in their projections of their authors' involved symbolisms onto Crane's often historically confused conceptions.

Crane was not, it should be emphasized, naïve (q.v.) in the modified Schillerian sense in which I have used it in this book. He was just badly educated, and too frenetic to do anything about it. His parents were unhappily married, and both seem to have been thoroughly unpleasant people (his father made bad chocolate, which might be considered to be a particularly rotten action). He was a classic victim; and when he emerged from adolescence he was dangerously mother-attached, ambisexual (though for years it looked as if he were a pure homosexual – only his poems make it clear that he was not) with a ritual emphasis on the homosexual side, and an alcoholic. But Crane's letters make it perfectly clear that his intelligence, when allowed to function unimpeded, was powerful. He has been compared, inevitably, with Dylan Thomas (q.v.); but – as a comparison of the letters demonstrates – Crane was by far the more intelligent of the two (and infinitely the better and more important poet). His letters, indeed, despite his terrible problems and frequent descents into horrendous behaviour, bear some comparison with Keats'.

The more academic the approach to Crane – that is to say, the more his poetry is approached as an entity separate from his drunken and hell-driven self – the more emphasis is put on *The Bridge* as a more or less successful American epic. But Crane is particularly badly served by an exclusively academic approach. His poetry embodies the drives of his own frenetic personality. The tragedy of Crane's authority as a poet in conflict with his lack of confidence in it is a painful one.

No really aware critic considers *The Bridge* a success. He conceived this epic in a state of desperation in order to get money from a business man patron, Otto Kahn (whose $2,000 he soon spent in drink and debauchery, as well he might – perhaps Wallace Stevens, by then fairly well-heeled, should have advanced the cash). Crane told Kahn that the poem was supposed to represent the American past by showing the present in its 'vital substance'; but it is good only when Crane is doing other than that; it can only be judged as a ragbag of fragments, some sentimental and forced, others beautiful. Nothing in *The Bridge* coheres. The concept of it belongs to the semi-literate side of Crane: his conscious Americanism is exceedingly laboured. He was not, at twenty-five, equipped to write any kind of epic. Nor, in this century, has any successful epic been written. But at least *The Bridge* is the last important failed one – Williams' *Paterson* (qq.v.) is not in this class at all.

Crane had a number of mediocre and, worse, pretentious friends and acquaintances; he had very little more than his superb intuition to distinguish between the fake and the real. Yet he was not himself pretentious: rather, he overwrote, putting out hot gusts of rhetoric to the sound of jazz and the glug-glug of his throat as he poured alcohol down it. He would interrupt his bouts of drink-writing to indulge in equally heroic bouts of homosex. It was demeaning, disgusting and wasteful. But he passionately knew it – and the usually banal remorse of the alcoholic was in some way, in his case, informed by a quality which demands mercy.

Yet after all this has been said, Crane is one of this century's major poets. In some dozen or so poems – they include the 'Voyages' sequence and several other poems from *White Buildings*, and the late 'The Broken Tower' – he found a language as suitable to his time as to himself. It cost him immense pain; the real reason for his death, apart from the local remorse that occasioned it, was that he believed his powers were failing. Crane has much to tell us: of the nature of romantic love; of gentleness, for he was gentle; of sexuality; of the anguish of homosexuality; of poetry and of being a poet. No twentieth-century poet has written more moving poetry. 'The Broken Tower', the poem he believed had failed, is perhaps more moving than any other. This combines the themes of his ambisexuality and his capacity as a poet in a complex image of bell-ringing at dawn (which he had helped to do in a Mexican town). Its strength and poetic confidence make a tragic contrast with his state of mind a few weeks after he had written it. These are its last six stanzas:

And so it was I entered the broken world
To trace the visionary company of love, its voice
An instant in the wind (I know not whither hurled)
But not for long to hold each desperate choice.

My word I poured. But was it cognate, scored
Of that tribunal monarch of the air
Whose thigh embronzes earth, strikes crystal Word
In wounds pledged once to hope – cleft to despair?

The steep encroachments of my blood left me
No answer (could blood hold such a lofty tower
As flings the question true?) – or is it she
Whose sweet mortality stirs latent power? –

And through whose pulse I hear, counting the strokes
My veins recall and add, revived and sure
The angelus of wars my chest evokes:
What I hold healed, original now, and pure ...

And builds, within, a tower that is not stone
(No stone can jacket heaven) – but slip
Of pebbles – visible wings of silence sown
In azure circles, widening as they dip

The matrix of the heart, lift down the eye
That shrines the quiet lake and swells a tower ...
The commodious, tall decorum of that sky
Unseals her earth, and lifts love in its shower.

Like Rilke's, Crane's poetry in its very different way nakedly poses the dangerous question of just what poetry itself is. A surprisingly large number of his poems stand up, after fifty years, astonishingly well.

*

Yvor Winters (1900–68), born in Chicago, was much better known as critic than poet. He taught at Stanford University from 1928 onwards. He began as an experimental imagist poet, recording life as a series of ecstatic perceptions in an ineffective free verse. Then he became, or tried to become, the moral and classical spokesman of his generation: the upholder of rationality. Since Winters could really think, it is probably fair to call him an exponent of the new criticism (which was never really a school); but his criticism does not otherwise resemble that of other well-known 'new critics' such as Warren or Ransom (qq.v.). He was ill-tempered, racked with envy and frustration, and pompous; at its frequent worst his criticism is grotesque (as when he claims that Bridges', q.v., verse drama is the best in English since Shakespeare, a judgement with which no one at all agrees, and which he must have formed in a dream of rage). But at his best, as when he attacks Hopkins and Yeats and Crane (qq.v.), he demands an answer, and is thus provocative. His own poetry, however, tells us why he became the enemy of romantic self-discovery and expressionism. First, there are the early 'modernist' poems. These are commonplace and affected. Then come the 'restrained' models for his contemporaries (almost the only ones he wholly applauded were Elizabeth Daryush, Bridges' daughter, and T. Sturge Moore, q.v., who served him as model). These are restrained because there has been no feeling to restrain. This enemy of romanticism does not understand what he hates. Many of the poems, such as 'On the Death of Senator Thomas J. Walsh', are disguised tributes to himself:

> An old man more is gathered to the great,
> Singly, for conscience' sake he bent his brow. . . .

What one objects to here is that what is stated is so over-stated as to be untrue in the manner of an encomium for a dead politician. Why did he become so famous as well as unpopular? Because, I think, the deliquescent hatred, product of envy and inner emptiness, that informs his criticism does give it an energy, and when that energy is harnessed to logical argument the results are interesting and stimulating. Here egocentricity shrieks contortedly in the name of 'reason' and 'classicism'. And his passionate exhortations to young poets towards restraint did occasionally have useful results, particularly in the case of J.V. Cunningham (q.v.). It is considered bad form to attack him. Yet few agree with his positive judgements, and fewer have wanted to recognize that his original motivation for hating romanticism was his own inability to write in a romantic manner – or to feel in it. Why did he reprint his early 'irrational' exercises? Because he desperately wanted them to be applauded. This was inconsistent to an intolerable degree. He does have his uses – but he is a very minor critic.

J.V. Cunningham (1911) was born in Maryland and studied at Stanford. He has interestingly transformed Winters' (q.v.) aim; and his motive is not to lead an impoverished emotional life or to make an inability to create an energetic language into poetic virtue. Therefore his project, at least, is of great interest – particularly to those who are concerned with what I have termed *Künstlerschuld* (q.v.). Poetry, and his own poetic impulse, Cunningham wants humbly to reduce to the level of other 'ordinary' activities: poetry 'is a concern of the ordinary human self. . . . Its virtues are the civic virtues. If it lacks much, what it does have is ascertainable and can be judged'. This was very much the ostensible view of W.H. Auden (q.v.) (dealt with as an English poet), who believed that poetry changes nothing and regarded it as an entertainment (and yet continually acted as a public man who believed in the civilizing virtues of art). Thus Cunningham writes a good deal of 'light' verse – much of it highly accomplished and amusing. His more serious poetry, in such volumes as *The Judge is Fury* (1947), *To What Strangers, What Welcome* (1964), is difficult but of great integrity. He is a neglected poet – but probably not one who would appeal to upholders of the civic virtues of the average American town – a fact perhaps ironic. *Selected Poems* appeared in 1971, *Collected Poems and Epigrams* in the same year.

Delmore Schwartz (1913–66), born in Brooklyn, was an extremely brilliant man who perished under the burden of his gifts. In him were uneasily combined two traditions: the Brooklyn Jewish (he planned a baseball novel before he was thirty, but it was Malamud, q.v., who wrote *The Natural*) and the intelligent academic. When he died he was a mental and physical wreck, whose gift had long ago choked on itself. Schwartz's Marxist inclinations (he was at various times concerned with editing *Partisan Review* and *The New Republic*) often clashed with those of his imagination; this may have been one of the reasons why he failed, in poetry, to discover his own voice for more than a few lines at a time. A trained philosopher with an intellect too clear for his own good, he wanted simply to observe, pessimistically; but his acute Jewish conscience would not allow him to do this. Hence the title of his first book, *In Dreams Begin Responsibilities* (1938). He is forever philosophizing against the horrors his imagination involuntarily reveals. Towards the end he became too consciously 'symbolic': the bright heart of his work had entered into a tunnel of gloom. In his poetry the language that his self-consciousness, his guilt, struggles to produce is expected – but never comes. But the Jewish stories of *The World is a Wedding* (1948), the acute criticism – and the so nearly successful poetry, much of which is collected in *Summer Knowledge* (1959) – gave him an important place in modern American literature, as a writer of high quality destroyed, to an alarming and poignant degree, by his predicament and his honesty. *The Last and Lost Poems* (1979) followed a useful *Selected Poems* of 1976.

The poetry of **Muriel Rukeyser** (1913–80), born in New York, was more specifically directed towards socialism than Schwartz's (q.v.); what was not tended to the too exuberantly and self-consciously feminine. It is not that the sense of it is embarrassing; but the poet wrote too much in the 'open' tradition of Sandburg (q.v.) and never discovered her own voice. She translated a good deal of the poetry of Paz (q.v.). Her *Collected Poems* appeared in the year before her death. She was influenced by **Horace Gregory** (1898), from Wisconsin, a distinguished translator who has not found his own voice, either – because of too easy philosophical and Marxist predilections. Both these poets have floundered intelligently about, but have been too much at the service of simplistic ideas. Better, because resolutely minor, was **Kenneth Fearing** (1902–61), born in Chicago, who in his fiction – notably *The Big Clock* (1946) – achieved a level of intelligence seldom seen in the thriller: he influenced the Englishman Julian Symons, who never, however, quite achieved the distinction of his master. His poetry (*New and Selected Poems*, 1956), in free verse, is funny and sometimes compassionate: a readable and sarcastic rebuke to the pretentious excesses of others more ambitious, and still worth reading.

Minnesota-born **Richard Eberhart** (1904), who has been both director of a polish company and an academic, has experimented with too many forms; he has diffused his considerable gift into a too rambling poetry, which ranges from the metaphysical through the allegorical to the descriptive-romantic. He protests against the deadly anonymity of the 'system' that pseudo-orders life, but cannot often enough seem to set against it anything personal enough to convince us of more than his own, rather than his poems', excellence. He has published *Selected Poems* (1965), *Collected Poems 1930–1976* (1976) and more volumes since then. No clearly serious poet is, perhaps, so uneven. His 'philosophy' shifts between a pessimism that he will not sufficiently explore and a mild religiosity that is unconvincing. One of his best known poems begins:

> You would think the fury of aerial bombardment
> Would arouse God to relent. . . .

This seems slack, careless, undistinguished writing: too generalized even to call forth a personal rhythm. And yet when the poet becomes personal, his poetry leaps into life and the apparent banality of the opening is miraculously redeemed: that same poem ends with these four magnificent and moving lines:

> Of Van Wettering I speak, and Averill,
> Names on a list, whose names I do not recall

But they are gone to early death, who late in school
Distinguished the belt feed lever from the belt holding pawl.

The long quarry into the vague, always sweet mud of his poetry yields similar jewels, and is worthwhile. He has worked long and devotedly in the verse theatre, and was the first president of Poets' Theatre at Cambridge (Mass.). *Collected Verse Plays* (1962). Whatever his failings, Eberhart has always been a credit to literature and humaneness, and an example for others to follow.

Stanley Kunitz (1905), born in Massachusetts, is one of the most skilled poets of his generation. His achievement stands, like Eberhart's (q.v.), but more solidly, behind the poetry of Lowell (q.v.) and others; but this is not yet fully acknowledged. His first book, *Intellectual Things* (1930), appeared when Lowell was twelve years old. His is one of the earliest poetries to concern itself exclusively with the naked, solipsist self, unconsoled, in a hostile world. There is in the earlier poems too much dependence on Yeats, and a corresponding rhetoric; but personal suffering and a refining of style has modified this to a spareness of diction in the later work. He has made many translations from Russian poets. He is not a major poet, but his achievement is more solid, less spectacular, less ambitious, than that of Lowell. He was praised by some because for many years he edited the H.W. Wilson series *Twentieth Century Authors* and its predecessors and successors. But he has not had his due.

*

American poetry since the war has divided itself into two diverging streams. Some of the more or less traditionalist poets – such as Lowell, Jarrell, Roethke, Elizabeth Bishop, Snodgrass, Hecht (qq.v.) – have been influenced by, or at least enjoy, the poetry of William Carlos Williams (q.v.), who is the real twentieth-century father of the anti-traditionalists: Olson, Creeley, Duncan, Snyder (qq.v.). But these latter will have no truck with the Fugitives ('antiques'), Frost (qq.v.), or Lowell himself.

The exception is **Robert Duncan** (1919), who although he has connection with the Beats and the Black Mountain (qq.v.) poets is a genuine eclectic, and who is far more informed about literature than most of his 'redskin' contemporaries. He has learned much from Stein (q.v.). Unfortunately the complex of ideologies behind his work is more interesting than the work itself, which, although intelligent, lacks attack or any clear emotional drive. *The First Decade* (1968) and *Derivations* (1968) contain most of the work of this interesting poet. The one figure to which nearly all acknowledge allegiance is Pound (q.v.). It is the Black Mountain poets and their disciples, however, who have most decisively broken away; and their immediate prophet is Charles Olson. To be fully aware of what they have broken away from it is necessary to look, first, at the continuers of the tradition: those who, whether in fact avant garde (as Lowell is or, rather, wanted to be) or not, have not been self-consciously, programmatically so. Mostly they are poets of self-revelation, who have written 'confessionally' in the belief that by exploiting their verbal gifts in the interests of self-analysis they may create a world comprehending enough to allow the realization of all individual values. The danger, as one soon sees, is that under the strain of confession they become self-publicists, cultural film-stars: that their imagination may be robbed of authority, so that they themselves subscribe to sentimental photographs of themselves as middlebrow poet-heroes. Thus society pulls them into the very life-impoverishing system they set out to destroy: gives them a glossy place, reports on their pain, panders to their ideals.

Thus, **Robert Lowell** (1917–77), scion of a great family, ended as a public figure whose poetry degenerated into a sterile, exhibitionist journalism: the confessionalist put himself on show, inserting into an account of his selected private and public activities such odd striking lines as he could compose. Thus isolated, they lacked power or meaning, and looked what they were: embellishments to a monument of egocentricity. This is *Notebook 1967–8* (1969, rev. 1969, rev. 1970). No mistake should be made about this: it is rank bad, and its successors *For Lizzie and Harriet* (1973), *History* (1973) and *The Dolphin* (1973) were worse.

Lowell's early poems, the best of which are to be found in *Poems 1938–49* (1950) and *The Mills of the Kavanaughs* (1951), were metrically tight and invariably rhymed. Lowell had learned about prosody from Bridges (q.v.) – that master technician who had nothing of poetic importance to say – as Auden had, and these early poems show him as the leading technician of his time. These youthful, livid, melodramatic poems look rather like a magnified, violent revision of Allen Tate (Tate and Ransom, qq.v., were Lowell's first masters):

> Wallowing in this bloody sty
> I cast for fish that pleased my eye
> (Truly Jehovah's bow suspends
> No pots of gold to weight its ends);
> Only the blood-mouthed rainbow trout
> Rose to my bait. . . .

The tone has been well described as one of 'baroque exaltation'. But the poems, because they were written by a man more anxious to excel than to tell the truth, are more full of 'promise' than of youthful achievement, as they should have been. During the war Lowell ('a fire-breathing Catholic C.O.') was a conscientious objector and went to prison; the themes of the early poems are generally speaking Jansenist (he left the Catholic Church in the Fifties), and harp on the punishment that man must resign himself to for his failure to fulfil his obligation to God. Their mood, if nothing else, is not unlike that of the earlier novels of Mauriac (q.v.). It probably derived from it, since there is some doubt as to whether Lowell, who was above all a narcissist of the first order, ever felt anything more than superficially. From the beginning Lowell carried within him a consciousness of a certain regality; he studied, so to speak, to assume the regal duties of appraising Boston and, in due course, his family. He had evaded his background at first; but during the Fifties, experiencing divorce (from the novelist Jean Stafford), remarriage and madness, he went back to it: the result was *Life Studies* (1959). The fuller edition of this (1968) contains a prose autobiography and autobiographical poems – the method of which, Lowell has acknowledged, he borrowed from his pupil W.D. Snodgrass. This collection included the famous 'Skunk Hour', with the lines:

> One dark night
> My Tudor Ford climbed the hill's skull;
> I watched for love cars. Lights turned down,
> they lay together, hull to hull,
> where the graveyard shelves on the town. . . .
> My mind's not right.

These are the poems, cleverly accomplished, for which Lowell is most celebrated. His

Imitations (1961), often deliberate distortions or alterations of European poets, are also admired – and arouse interest as part of the education of an allegedly major poet. But some have preferred the crabbed, tightly restrained energy of the earlier Lowell, seeing in *Life Studies* the beginnings of the process that leads through *For the Union Dead* (1964) and *Near the Ocean* (1967) – some original poems and more translations – to the self-vulgarizing disaster of the *Notebooks*, which read, says Donald Hall cruelly but justly, 'like prayers to Stockholm'. The poems of *Life Studies*, and some of those that come after them, seem masterly in technique; but the autobiographical ones often seem less good than the prose. Lowell never achieved a truly personal rhythm, even though his technique was so highly accomplished. He always needed to impress. He was seldom haunted by that sense of failure which characterizes the true poet. Comparison establishes that the poem is often a fiercely worked up version of the prose: often nothing has come up from the well of the unconscious – rather, the poet has manufactured a poem out of his raw material, tricking it up and making it rhetorical. The best poems, the ones to Ford, Schwartz and Santayana (qq.v.), 'Skunk Hour' and others, are minor rather than major: the distinction is nearly all in the manner in which style manipulates tone and feeling. The poetry is impressive, fashionable, superbly appropriate for treatment in approved critical modes. One can see why Lowell got into a state of mind in which he felt obliged to imitate his friend John Berryman (q.v.) – to the extent of even copying the form of the *Dream Songs*. *Notebooks* often looks like what it is: a rival to *Dream Songs*. The career of Lowell, and the embarrassing impasse into which it has led him, exemplifies the difficulties of poetry in our time. The poet is transformed into politician; he has to justify himself, get glass eyes; his imagination is threatened.

Lowell suffered throughout his life from manic-depressive psychosis; but he was also a bad character and a hysteric. One has little sympathy for his histrionic sufferings. He provided the supreme example of the overrated poet, who sacrifices love of truth to his lust for fame – but whose verse provided the perfect vehicle for the predilections of academic critics. At least in him, though, intelligence and an awareness of poetic obligations did exist. So did a knowledge of technique. In Hughes (q.v.), in whom the nadir of modern criticism is reached, few or perhaps none of these are even present. However, lilies that fester. ... Madness can and indeed does 'excuse' bouts of apparently 'bad behaviour'. It does not excuse consistent manipulativeness and hysterical egocentricity; nor does it usually co-exist with it. These defects characterize Lowell's poetry increasingly: he was much more of a histrionic exhibitionist than a minor poet.

Another poet who suffered from bouts of madness throughout his difficult life was **Theodore Roethke** (1908–63), the Michigan-born son of the Prussian owner of a huge and well-known nursery business, the details of which figure greatly in his poetry. Roethke's subject is the state of his being as it comes into contact with reality. He is not 'confessional', is not, like Lowell (q.v.), interested in making his subject his own awareness of his behaviour. He presents his biography in lyrical, semi-mystical terms that were notably influenced, at various times, by Blake, Yeats, Eliot, Auden, Dylan Thomas and Léonie Adams (qq.v.). His first poems, published in *Open House* (1941), were in strict forms; but those of *The Lost Son* (1948) are in a freer verse. They consist of interior monologues, in which Roethke incorporates microscopic descriptions of plants that are not in fact scientific or even very carefully observed – rather they remind one of Graham Sutherland's close-up paintings, which try to define the nature of their subjects by pictorial metaphor. *Praise to the End* (1951), which contains much pastiche of Yeats (q.v.) and mimicry of Dylan Thomas (q.v.), is at once less original and more self-consciously visionary.

Roethke's poems were collected in *The Waking* (1953), again in *Words for the Wind*

(1958), and finally and posthumously in *Collected Poems* (1968). He was an insecure poet, and his most serious fault is his compulsion to parody or mimic other poets. It makes most of what he has to say unconvincing: it is not in his own voice. Such tender poetry as 'The Meadow Mouse' is spoiled because, in it, all that is not imitated from John Clare is petty moralizing. Eliot is drawn upon not only for manner but for a whole symbolic method that Roethke himself – like Lowell a hysterical egomaniac – was not close to.

What is left, and may survive, is a small body of unhysterical minor love poetry, such poems as 'The Apparition', 'Her Reticence' and 'The Happy Three' – all of these from his posthumous collection *The Far Field* (1964).

Roethke often looks very good indeed. His poetry nearly always has a most attractive surface. His technique seldom lets him down. But close investigation usually shows the poetry to be second-rate and second-hand, the ecstatic voice something the poet frenetically jollied himself into. The long para-surrealist poems about greenhouses and plants have a certain value, but ultimately they fail to take us beyond the experiences of mental disintegration and regression to childhood which they record. Again, the purely physical love poetry, which is not as plagiaristic as most of the rest of his work, is of little value because, when one comes down to it, it does no more than find various ingenious ways of describing (rather than illuminating) physical desire. Roethke's 'mystical vision' consists of nothing at all. But his breathless, lyrical manner (often, in him, trite – as in 'The Geranium', with its banal ending) had a wide and probably beneficial because releasing influence. It is often stated authoritatively that he killed himself: he did not. An alcoholic, he exhausted himself and died of a heart attack.

A poet admired by Lowell (q.v.) and others of his group is **Elizabeth Bishop** (1911–79), whose *Complete Poems* appeared in 1983. If this quiet and fastidious poet, who was born in Massachusetts and spent much of her life in South America, has a model then it is Marianne Moore (q.v.). She is not immune from awfulness ('Invitation to Miss Marianne Moore' begins 'From Brooklyn, over the Brooklyn Bridge, on this fine morning,/please come flying' and continues in that vein), but in general she is more discriminating in what she publishes than most. Although she has written competent ballads and done some translations from the Portuguese of some Brazilian poets, she is mainly a poet of description so accurate and skilful that she suggests something beyond her subject, although this remains imprecise and vague – some impression of obscure psycho-sexual processes, pure in its apprehension but singularly undefined. She owes part of the curiosity of her style to Marianne Moore, and her method is rooted in imagism – but a Bishop poem has its own unmistakable stamp. When she tries anything other than this she is liable to sentimentality and tweeness, as in 'Cootchie'. But, with a group of some twenty-five poems, such as 'The Fish' and 'The Weed', she has made a special place for herself in modern American poetry. Her lesbian love poetry is unsuccessful but interesting and physically descriptive in an intense manner. Her achievement is a mainly impressionistic one: she had little to say.

There can be no more purely technical skilful poet living than **Richard Wilbur** (1921), who was born in New York. Wilbur is graceful, learned, civilized – but he cannot allow himself to mean as much to his readers as they would like. He cannot be wild. His discretion, his control, insists on decorum. He observes well, writes beautifully, translates exquisitely; but it is all just a little too good to be true. No one really important, alas, could be that fastidiously perfect. And yet. ... One finds oneself lamenting that Wilbur, so intelligent and decent, lacks 'attack'. Even 'Beasts', one of his finest poems, lacks a really cutting edge. Yet *Poems 1943–56* (1957), published in England and collecting the best of three American volumes, contains many pleasurable poems, as do his next three books, the most recent of which is *The Mind Reader* (1976). Perhaps a British critic put his finger on the trouble when he suggested that Wilbur's poetry may not cost him enough. Much bad verse doubtless costs dear; but all good poetry must do so. Wilbur's diction has remained resolutely academic; and he himself belongs to a tradition of very highly competent conventionality.

Sylvia Plath (1932–63), who was born in Boston and died in London, was the exact opposite of Wilbur: at the end of her life, her marriage to the English poet Ted Hughes (q.v.) broken up, the surface of her life was, quite literally, poetry, or what seemed to her to be poetry. She had had a nervous breakdown in America in 1951, when she had tried to commit suicide. She wrote about this time of her life in her novel *The Bell Jar*, which was first published in 1963 under the pseudonym Victoria Lucas. When she became seriously ill in London in 1963 she had no one to look after her, and she finally gassed herself. She had published *The Colossus* in 1960; but it is generally agreed that it is the poems of the posthumous *Ariel* (1965) that are her most important. More has been and will be issued; but none of this appears to have much intrinsic value, as *Collected Poems* (1981), with an inane introduction by Hughes, confirms.

Most people are dedicated to the surface of their lives, and this protects them from the stresses of poetic thinking: from caring intensely about what does not, in material terms, matter – but which does really matter in terms of the whole personality. Because for a few months Sylvia Plath made all her existence into poetry (her children were her only distraction), critics have too confidently assumed that her ostensible subject matter, of concentration camps and the plight of Jewishness, is their real subject matter. One, calling her a 'minor poet of great intensity', yet states that 'the last, greatest poems culminate in an act of identification, of total communion with those tortured and massacred'. This is mystical. Another critic (no doctor) assumes that her illness was schizophrenic and pronounces that her poetry 'defines the age as schizophrenic'. But her illness was a form of manic-depression – a form in which euphoria and depression may sometimes mysteriously co-exist (cf. Campana, Bacovia, qq.v.): the so-called 'mixed state', different for each sufferer, occasionally schizophreniform in appearance, but never schizophrenic – mania and depression mixing into a sinister compound. That, certainly, is the mood of the last poems.

These are minor poems – although they may in an age of increasing urban stress and consequent madness be historically prophetic, especially in the Great Britain of post-1979 – because their subject is never really more than her own illness. So 'minor poet of great intensity' is right. But that is enough. For they tell us much of the nature of her mental and therefore of human illness. But fashionable criticism has been wrong in emphasizing 'the contemporary predicament' in her poems. They should read the French diarist and essayist Simone Weil to find this: she really writes about the contemporary predicament. Sylvia Plath was writing about herself. The comparison is a revealing one.

When A. Alvarez, an able critic and, to a point, good on Sylvia Plath, says that she 'gambled ... and lost', implying she 'did it' for poetry, he is projecting his own poker-playing preoccupations onto her. For it evades the issue. Her predicament was not to gamble but to remain truthful while she suffered madness; and the best of her poems do remain truthful, if only to her condition of a suicidal depression shot through with ambitious euphoria. They tell us about this condition – not about 'the schizophrenic world', a critic's ambitious and rhetorical abstraction. As I have already pointed out in my introduction, schizophrenics produce word-salads. These poems are not word-salads. They record a 'mixed state'.

However, Sylvia Plath did find apt words to describe her condition as she waited to die. In 'Death & Co.' she imagines death as two business men calling, one of whom 'exhibits'

> The birthmarks that are his trademark –
> The scald scar of water,
> The nude
> Verdigris of the condor.
> I am red meat. His beak
>
> Claps sidewise: I am not his yet
> He tells me how badly I photograph. ....
>
> The other ...
> His hair long and plausive.
> Bastard
> Masturbating a glitter,
> He wants to be loved. ....

The tone of this aggressive (if oblique) caricature of whatever person she felt was betraying her comes straight out of Roethke's (q.v.) greenhouse poems, but it is sharpened by knowledge of self-inflicted death: a suicide-as-revenge, as suicide sometimes is. These are suicide poems. They are not at all, and cannot be, about any kind of love. Nor are they in any way about Jews or concentration camps. They are about an internal horror. But however much this diminishes their stature, they will remain important for the chilling accuracy of their descriptions of psychological terror.

Anne Sexton (1928–74) was usually described as of the 'confessional' school, although she preferred to be classed as 'an imagist who deals with reality and its hard facts'. She wrote, inevitably, in the shadow of Sylvia Plath (q.v.), since some of her poems are about mental breakdown. The title of her first book was *To Bedlam and Part Way Back* (1960), and this dealt with, among other things, a suicide attempt. She published her *Selected Poems* in 1964. Two more collections followed: *Live or Die* (1967) and *Love Poems* (1969). The poems written preceding her suicide were collected in *The Death Notebooks* (1974) and *The Awful Rowing Towards God* (1975). Anne Sexton was a sometimes excellent although diffuse writer of lyrical autobiography. She wrote of her own experiences – illness, motherhood, love – descriptively, not moralistically or squeamishly. Her poems set up few resonances, are autobiographically 'regional'. Her love poems, for example, are splendidly physical, and extremely feminine inasmuch as they make no attempts to extrapolate 'meanings' from the pleasures they record. The last poems are over-influenced by Plath, and, rather than describing states of suicidal depression, intersperse such descriptions with an over-conscious symbolism and with a somewhat facile exploitation of concentration-camp horror. They are only very occasionally successful, and seldom cohere. She seems – though it may be unkind to put it in this way – to have been a depressive who leaned, in her last years, on the example of Plath, and who wrongly believed Plath to have transcended in her poetry the barriers of insanity. *The Heart of Anne Sexton's Poetry* (1977) is co-edited by her daughter, and is a representative selection.

John Berryman (1914–72), who was born of Roman Catholic parents in Oklahoma, and whose father shot himself, could well be described as the confessional poet *par excellence*. His style is frequently cryptic, mannered, convoluted; but the subject (beginning with his *Sonnets*, which he wrote in the Forties but did not publish until 1967) of his poetry has increasingly been himself: his mental instability, his adultery, his friends, his general agony. Obviously Berryman is in the *Dream Songs* – *77 Dream Songs* (1964), *His Toy, His Dream, His Rest* (1968) – frequently a very bad poet indeed: impenetrably obscure, ruthlessly making use of private references, crabbed, pointlessly archaic (where

Ransom, q.v., was not), over-dramatic. ... This is hardly denied unless by the kind of uncritical reader whom no one wants. The question, in the *Dream Songs* as much as in the *Sonnets*, is whether by taking these risks Berryman achieved a new, more lucid, better poetry. Well, he has achieved a very fascinating and different kind of poetry, which demands to be studied. Berryman does not pretend that he does not lust for fame:

> He can advance no claim,
> save that he studied thy Word and grew afraid,
> work & fear be the basis for his terrible cry
> not to forget his name.

And yet he said (in an interview on British TV) that he had only six readers who really understood what he was doing. ... Did he mean this? The number of private references in his poems suggests that in one sense he did – but it is unfortunately not a question he chose to answer, perhaps because he remained Roman Catholic enough to leave such matters to God. Berryman, an alcoholic, killed himself during a spell of depression partly caused by his going off drink. Towards the end of his life he became almost wholly insane, even at one point comparing himself to Jesus Christ. But he had periods when he was unhysterically lucid and truly self-critical; and he was never the obvious skunk his friend Lowell (q.v.) undoubtedly was.

Berryman began as an almost academic poet, writing in tight stanzas; Dudley Fitts found in them 'an aura of academic contrivance'. He collected together such of his early poems as he wished to preserve in *Short Poems* (1967); but these are quite different from the three later sequences. *Homage to Mistress Bradstreet* (1956) is a poem-sequence based on the twin conceits that the Puritan Anne Bradstreet, America's first poet, is his mistress – and that she is his alter ego. By participating in her life – into which Berryman made research – the poet illuminates his discovery of his own country. But the whole poem, and its difficulties, is somewhat corrupt: it reads as though Berryman was forced to be recondite and 'obscure' not because he was breaking ground that could not be broken in any more coherent way, but because he wanted to look original. Academic contrivance? Perhaps Fitts was not so far off the mark after all.

The organization of *Dream Songs* is calculated to allow the writer to explore himself and his world in as free a manner as possible. Each poem consists of eighteen lines divided into three stanzas of six lines each; but lengths and stress of line, and rhyme pattern, vary. Berryman projects himself into several voices: Henry, a white man in black face, who speaks like a nigger minstrel (Berryman says the poem is 'essentially about' him), an unnamed friend who calls him Mr. Bones, and some other not definitely iden-tified voices. This Henry and his friend are not more than acknowledgements on his part that no poet can himself be the 'I' of any poem; he can only pretend it. This pretence is not necessarily reprehensible; but it will not do for so long and ambitious an epic – a rival to the *Cantos* (q.v.)? – as Berryman planned. The poem has rightly been called artificial, uneven and pretentious. The question is: How much more artificial, uneven and preten-tious than its author (or its readers)? Could one get such comic effects as Berryman gets in the following stanza by not being 'quirky'?:

> Henry sits in de plane & was gay.
> Careful Henry nothing said aloud
> but where a Virgin out of cloud
> to her Mountain dropt in light,

> his thought made pockets & the plane buckt.
> 'Parm me, lady.' 'Orright.'

This, which is certainly not important even if it fascinates, shows a poet being himself (in just the way Wilbur will not be himself) with a vengeance. It has attendant risks, and it can lead to an egocentric and even offensive verse. Someone who cared about the past of poetry, and for the notion of effort in making it, had to take some kind of plunge, but was this the right kind of plunge? Berryman, quite unlike Lowell – who never displayed signs of critical intelligence – had been a useful and illuminating critic; he viewed his decline into alcoholism with real horror, if not with the agonized edge of Hart Crane (q.v.). But he became swept away on its tide. He did tremblingly reach for comfort, and hope for virtue – where Lowell could do little more than look into a mirror and still applaud himself – but ultimately he lacked the patience to wait for poems to turn up: he manu-factured them, wilfully, and to impress. The true poet does not know where the next poem is coming from ... *Love and Fame* (1970 rev. 1972); *Delusions Etc* (1972); *Henry's Fate* (1977).

Randall Jarrell (1914–65), who was born in Tennessee, threw himself under a truck at the age of fifty-one. He was a leading member of the gifted generation of Schwartz, Lowell and Berryman (qq.v.), and like them he taught in universities. In the Second World War he served in the United States Air Force. He was a critic of genius (*Poetry and the Age*, 1953), being particularly funny at the expense of the wholly academic critics; and he wrote a good novel satirizing small college life, *Pictures from an Institution* (1954). Jarrell was a poet of, above all, sensibility: sensibility about man's doomed quest for decency and goodness. He wrote much about childhood because innocence was what interested him. He was a very friendly poet – the friendliest of all of his generation. But he fell into sentimentality, his obvious temptation, less often than Schwartz did into windy abstrac-tion, Lowell into regal exhibitionism, Roethke into pastiche, Berryman into private and idiosyncratic muttering. ... He will no doubt be called a minor poet; he is not as am-bitious as Lowell (although history will see him as far more effective and true), and does not try for so much as Berryman; Robert Fitzgerald was possibly justified in his stricture that we 'admire' Jarrell's poetry, but are 'unrelieved; we miss the great exhilarations of art'. Or was he? The latter phrase has an artificial ring, especially when we think of Lowell and his struggles to achieve something that looks like those great exhilarations – we are thankful for the more modest Jarrell. But then Jarrell was more sceptical and less personally ambitious; he might even, at his best, have avoided the phrase 'the great exhilarations of art'. One is above all grateful for him when thinking of the gush that has gathered around such apocalyptics as Dylan Thomas (q.v.): like Thomas, Jarrell stood for poetry, and was against its impoverishment by the sort of criticism he called 'nearly autonomous'; but unlike Thomas he resisted the fake-Bardic in himself.

His war poetry, *qua* war poetry, is probably the best to come out of the Second World War. It has some of the bitter irony of Owen (q.v.), and great compassion. Reading it one really does wonder about those 'great exhilarations': doesn't he have here, at least, what Fitzgerald meant?

> In bombers named for girls, we burned
> The cities we had learned about in school. ...
>
> The soldier simply wishes for his name. ...
>
> Strapped at the centre of the blazing wheel,

His flesh ice-white against the shattered mask
He tears at the easy clasp, his sobbing breaths
Misting the fresh blood lightening to flame,
Darkening to smoke. . . .

The best of these, with others, were included in *Selected Poems* (1955). The post-war Jarrell, with his love of Grimm and the *Märchen*, could not always keep away from the whimsical. And such poems as 'Nollekens', based on the famous book, are a little too wide-eyed ('All that my poem says he did, he did . . .'). Then, in his last years, Jarrell found a more suitable style. Although it was not Browning's, Browning, with his dramatic monologues, pointed the way. The poems, most of them dramatic monologues spoken by women, are in the posthumous *The Lost World* (1966). At their best these have the exact quality of the nostalgia of his admired Proust. 'Thinking of the Lost World' begins:

This spoonful of chocolate tapioca
Tastes like – like peanut butter, like the vanilla
Extract Mama told me not to drink.
Swallowing the spoonful, I have already travelled
Through time to my childhood. It puzzles me
That age is like it. . . .

and later occur the lines:

All of them are gone
Except for me; and for me nothing is gone –
The chicken's body is still going round
And round in widening circles. . . .
Mama and Pop and Dandeen are still there
In the Gay Twenties.

It ends

I hold in my own hands, in happiness,
Nothing: the nothing for which there's no reward.

It is by no means great poetry, and parts of it verge on sentimentality; but it is purely felt: in an age of pretence, it has been given to few American poets to write so beautifully and so simply – and to avoid the exploitations of the psychopathic, the abnormal, the terrible, at the same time.

W.D. Snodgrass (1926), who was born in Pennsylvania, first wrote on very personal subjects; since he tried to widen his range, and deliberately made his language, once straightforward, more complex, he has been notably less good. But this might happen to any poet who has run low on inspiration. His best poetry is collected in two books: *Heart's Needle* (1958) and *After Experience. . . .* (1969). Essentially, when one has ruthlessly cut out the over-mawkish, the complacent and sentimental, Snodgrass is another quite good autobiographical poet like Anne Sexton. The later volumes – *Remains* (1970), as by S.S. Gardons, *The Führer Builds a Bunker* (1977) and *If Birds Build With Your Hair* (1979) – display a remarkable falling off, and have been deservedly neglected.

New York-born **Anthony Hecht** (1923) has sometimes been associated – misleadingly – with the 'confessional' school. Actually he is a factitious poet, wholly traditional, who would not dream of letting slip a confession that had been undoctored with wit or irony. Behind all this care, though, lurks an Old Testament Jewish voice, sometimes very angry; Hecht mutes it, but its prophetic bray is still there. *The Hard Hours* (1967) selects from the earlier *A Summoning of Stones* (1954). Hecht has written some of the best authentically Jewish poems – he believes in God, as well as in the Devil – in the English language, and always has much to say: he has never been at the mercy of abstractions. *Millions of Strange Shadows* (1977); *The Venetian Vespers* (1979).

W.S. Merwin (1927), also born in New York, is a skilful constructor of poetic surface. He began by writing poems, of excellent technique, that looked as though they were meant to satisfy all the requirements of the new critics. They analysed beautifully, one might say; but they lacked a distinctive voice, and they were not moving or convincing. The experience they reflected was that of thinking about being an acceptable poet. Since then Merwin has gone through a Williams (q.v.) phase, and is now writing in the style of the French poetry that stems from Reverdy (q.v.). He is a good craftsman, and is evidently sincere – he least of all needed to switch from traditional to unrhymed and free modes – but his new poetry looks too much like translation. And he is of course a notable translator from Spanish and from French: he translated Jean Follain (q.v.) in 1969, in a volume called *Transparence of the World*, and the French poet's influence is evident. Merwin's first verse was collected in *A Mask for Janus* (1952); recent books include *The Moving Target* (1967), *The Lice* (1967), *The First Four Books of Poems* (1975) and *Feathers from the Hill* (1978). He is useful to critics who can only utter meaningless platitudes ('Given a world of cosmic indifference'; 'Merwin's persona is drawn to this world and would "ride awhile the mortal air"'); but, alas, nothing in his output can mean much to the dedicated reader. 'Cold as hell' (in the words of one of his more robust contemporaries), he is a lost soul, paying heartless but devoted homage to the 'exhilarations' of love; but he can find no personal voice to express his loneliness, and is never more than 'interesting'. He is wholly alyrical.

*

There are probably more than a thousand published Beat (q.v.) poets. We need consider only one: **Allen Ginsberg** (1926). Ginsberg is a socio-anthropological phenomenon, a shrewd business man, and now, ironically, a part of the way of American life. He was educated at Columbia University, after which he went on the hoof. Then in 1955 he published the long poem *Howl*, and he was made: the Beat Generation was accepted. And Ginsberg cannot rebel again; so he boasts 'I ... achieved the introduction of the word *fuck* into texts inevitably studied by schoolboys'. This is again ironic (if, of course, we accept that he alone did it): for this genuinely amiable pseudo-Zen droll is by no means a propagandist for heterosexuality. His poetry, he says, is 'Angelical Ravings'; but he is too comfortable to do more now than worry about his influence – and, it must be added, to give considerable help to the needy, even if most of them lack talent or even gifts. He is a truly kind and possibly good man; he is also usually rather silly. But that is

not all there is to it. His poetry is actually simply the manifestation of the eclectic, syn-
cretic, 'redskin' American tradition.

It is appropriate at this point, because still highly relevant to American literature, to
discuss the paleface/redskin dichotomy: this was first posited by the critic Philip Rahv
(1908–73), in an essay which was eventually published in his collection *Literature and the
Sixth Sense* (1969). The essay, 'Paleface and Redskin', has been called 'one of his weakest':
the two terms 'seem to be saying something important but in effect offer an excuse for not
having to make finer discriminations and distinctions'. But the writer who said this,
Elmer Borklund, is himself quite incapable of making any 'fine distinction' at all (his
responses are inevitably what Dr. Leavis, q.v., used to call 'stock', and he has never
written an original sentence in his life), and this opinion is worthless. There is a very well
recognised limit to the usefulness of any such polarizing terms (classical/romantic; naïve/
sentimentive, qq.v., and so forth): it is well understood, if not by Borklund, that there is a
danger of reductionism implicit in the reckless employment of them. There are very few
and perhaps no examples of 'pure' romantics, 'pure' classicists, or 'pure' anything. But it
is necessary to generalize in life, even though we know we are asses to do it – and Rahv's
paleface and redskin have come to stay. It was a brilliant insight by a critic who began as
a convinced Marxist and ended by preaching an interesting modification of Marxism,
based actually on what Marx wrote and felt, and not on the results he is supposed to have
caused. And through this line of thinking, which he developed, he was able to discover or
help to discover (and publish) Jarrell, Malamud, Berryman (qq.v.) and many others.
Rahv's distinction derives from, or at least parallels, Nietzsche's one between Apollonian
and Dionysian (qq.v.) – one which is, unfortunately, all too often – as with most of the
ideas of Nietzsche – seriously misunderstood. For Rahv, American literature was 'fragmented' because the palefaces such as James (q.v.), Hawthorne and Melville are
educated and self-conscious, but 'estranged from reality', whereas the redskins, who
enjoy raw reality, are crude (as Dreiser, q.v., could be). 'For the process of polarization
has produced a dichotomy between experience and consciousness – a dislocation
between energy and sensibility, between conduct and theories of conduct, between life
conceived as an opportunity and life conceived as a discipline'. Rahv wanted a 'rich
balance' between mind and energy, and he found this in, for example, Bellow (q.v.).

This is of course an over-simplification. But it is one well worth bearing in mind –
especially if we can dissociate ourselves from Rahv's own approvals and disapprovals,
which were partly based on his Marxist predilections. The distinction could be summed
up as being very similar to the one between the raw and the cooked, which has been
made famous by Lévi-Strauss in other connections. It is useful. Wilbur's (q.v.) poetry
really is much too over-cooked. Trilling's morally horrendous attacks on Dreiser and
Anderson (qq.v.), and indeed the whole attenuated cast of his frightened mind, really is
also far too over-cooked – in that case, it is burnt, but the burntness is covered over with
superior academic syrup. Whitman (q.v.), though a paradigmatic redskin (he could think
no better than a Bernard Levin or some other similarly egregious columnist), achieved in
Song of Myself a perfection of form which can only be described as palefaced – but it arose
from relaxed receptiveness to his feelings at a time when they were uninflamed. . . . Once
we see the use that can be made of this dichotomy, we can appreciate the insight it
contains. I do not think we can dispose of it – with regard to American literature – any
more easily than we can dispose of classical/romantic. It supplies very valuable terms of
reference: starting points. Ginsberg, as pretty nearly redskin a writer as you can get,
supplied a verve to American poetry in which it had been deficient. That he did not do it
with a poetry of real quality (one has simply to compare *Howl* to *Song of Myself* to see this:
the two poems are on entirely different levels, the one being half-punk and the other great

literature, if 'great' is to mean anything at all) is beside the point. Foolish, unscholarly and ill-informed though his critical remarks have been, he was sincere. Thus Grigson (q.v.) has said that he would rather have one Ginsberg (of whom his opinion is about the same as mine) than a thousand Lowells (q.v.). One sees what he means. Ginsberg is a shrewd business man (this has been demonstrated); but not on his own account. He was angry, when he wrote *Howl*, and he did his best. There was at least no failure of nerve here. His first poems, although incoherent, had a pressure of indignation behind them. Their 'literary' badness was deliberate. The poet 'simply followed his Angel in the course of compositions'. There was just a very tiny bit of Blake in all this: the poet meant it. It expressed the drop-out's attitude to organized society, which is in all 'civilized' societies quite as bad, and possibly worse, than any of those who drop out from it. Ginsberg did have something that Lowell did not. But all this became corrupted, a way of life in itself; and life has not changed. Ginsberg's latest verse is publicly performed, chopped-up prose, incoherent and self-indulgent. It is preferable to the antics of politicians; preferable even to most of what passes for literature in the 'literary world'; but if it is indeed the 'new poetry', then a poetry in which thought, care and effort play a part is dead. And that is false to gods Ginsberg himself appeals to: Blake, Smart, Shelley. Ginsberg's is a way of life. And so far we have not had a poetry that went along with any accepted way of life – certainly not ones that are sponsored by (now) national institutions like Ginsberg. Whatever Ginsberg does, he is trapped: society has tamed him. It is pathetic that by 1970 he should have been worrying about the effect he had had with his ideas about the values of drugs. *Selected Gay Poems and Correspondence* (1979), in collaboration with his lover Peter Orlovsky, is tedious stuff indeed.

The Black Mountain school of poets, of whom I shall here discuss Olson and Creeley, did not arise from the Beat movement, although Creeley welcomed Ginsberg, who had previously been endorsed by Williams (who endorsed, in fact, pretty well anyone, including Lowell). Black Mountain College began in the Thirties and finally collapsed in the late Fifties. The emphasis was at first on the visual arts, on the art-object as thing-in-itself, and the tradition was that of American pragmatism. So far as literature is concerned, with the exception of Olson's doctrines (to be outlined below), the preoccupations were those of the objectivists (q.v.).

Charles Olson (1910–70), who was born in Worcester, Massachusetts, was fifty before he became well known; and when he did it was in an atmosphere partly created by the Beat (q.v.) generation. At the end of Williams' (q.v.) life almost all American poets admired or at least respected him – as they did and do Pound (q.v.). But Olson, who drew on Williams and Pound, knew only the admiration of disciples. He represents an apostle of a certain sort of Americanness: another step in the voyage of American self-discovery. He published many small volumes; but his main work is to be found in *Selected Writings* (1967), *The Maximus Poems* (1953; 1956; 1968); collected poetry is in the posthumous *Archeologist of Morning* (1970). He was a prime example of that 'intelligent philistinism' from which G.S. Frazer (q.v.) thought much of American literature sprang. But his intelligence was badly distorted by bellicosity and a mania for over-simplified diagrams of the history of you-name-it. He lacked a proper knowledge of the background of culture – and if you are going to question culture, you ought to know about it fairly thoroughly even if you hate what you know.

Olson's doctrines are to be found in the now famous (it should be infamous) essay 'Projective Verse'. They too spring directly from the American pragmatic tradition: verse is to be of 'essential use', must reflect the breathing of the poet. Energy must be immediately transferred from writer (speaker) to reader (listener). This is 'kinetic': 'composition by field'. The old method ('closed verse ... which print bred') interposes the ego of the writer between himself and his audience; Olson claimed, contentiously – in fact certainly wrongly – that this was what Keats meant by 'the Egotistical Sublime' (rather as if Keats had been born in Massachusetts in 1910: neither Olson nor his disciples are very strong on the past, except in their own deliberately ignorant terms of 'essential use'). The new poetry Olson demanded in his essay, which was published in 1950, was to put rhyme and metre in the background, and let 'the syllable . . . lead the harmony on'.

All this, written in sometimes old-fashioned professorial slang ('And the joker? that it is in the 1st half of the proposition that, in composing, one lets-it-rip. . . . Consider the best minds you know in this here business . . .' and so on), was interesting as a theory: it was just one more, rather dogmatic and slapdash, way of looking at the problem of prosody, about which no one has ever been able to agree beyond the most elementary points. It was also a plea, of course, for more poetry readings – but would, in the course of these, the ego of the poet still not obtrude? Olson's own poetry does not seem less ego-centric, or 'egotistically sublime', than anyone else's; in fact it is a very noisy, blustering, bullying, empty poetry. And his theory wholly ignores the fact of a form (selected or invented by the poet: not necessarily failing to 'extend the content', one of Olson's pre-requisites, which, given his instructions to poets to let their breathing determine their lines, are excessively rigid) and a content acting as two poles to generate a poetic tension. It also ignores the ritual element in poem-making, which leads to the creation of forms. All men live within a recognizable bodily pattern: two ears, two eyes, a nose, and so on. And yet all bodies are different. . . . One way of approaching the problem is, of course, Olson's. What is distressing is his insistence that only his own way is valid . . . His own poetry noisily insists, too: is as inefficiently philosophical as his criticism. It is so American that it can have no more than historical interest to British readers; it looks unlikely to survive long. It was as though a redskin (q.v.) disguised as a jocose paleface (q.v.) were dragooning everyone into being mindlessly redskin. It never discussed the illusory effects of rhetoric on hyped-up audiences, or the importance of reading poems on pages. It bred pretence and exhibitionism: hundreds of atrocious poetasters who roared – imagining that they were 'honouring their breathing' – their chopped-up prose at audiences, but were seldom read.

Robert Creeley (1926), also born in Massachusetts, began as an avowed disciple of Olson's (q.v.) although his lines have always been short where Olson's were long. It is ironic that when he writes at his best, as in 'Kore':

> As I was walking
> I came upon
> chance walking
> the same road upon.
> As I sat down
> by chance to move
> later
> if and as I might,
>
> light the wood was,
> light and green,
> and what I saw
> before I had not seen.
>
> It was a lady
> accompanied

by goat men
   leading her.

Her hair held earth.
   Her eyes were dark.
A double flute
   made her move.

'Oh love,
   where are you
leading
   me now?'

his rhythms are idiosyncratic rather than a fulfilment of any theory: the inversions (influenced by early Pound?) are in contradiction of Olson's instructions. This is a fair lyric in a distinctive manner, and before about 1960 Creeley wrote a number of similar poems – candid in their self-appraisal, attractive, and very much his own. His later poems are commonplace and often trite. Where the ballad-like clumsiness and archaism of the early poem, above, added something essential to it, the form of the later indicates the writer's tiredness. It is very like bad conversation. It – like Olson's theory and indeed any other theory if a poet has nothing to say – leads to the production of work that lacks tension.

Creeley's tightly held even if simplistic dogmas are, of course, a way of life. His novel *The Island* (1963), although autobiographical, and dealing with a hard time in his life, resolutely concentrates upon its author's perceptions (except when it slips); he thus misses much he might achieve, by denying himself the results of his imagination. He is a didactic poet because he needs to 'prove' that his own way of perceiving the world is the only right one. But does he not dream? And does he reject his dreams? In 'Kore' he did not. In the past twenty years he has. He cannot, or refuses to, say of what use making poetry is. Now that is a difficult, a primitive, even a philistine, position to be in, if you are a poet. 'Things continue, but my sense is that I have, at best, simply taken place with that fact. ... Words will not say more than they do. ...' It is not enough to arouse interest outside the hall where the poem is being performed. He has said that he 'hates the metaphors'. But he does not understand the pervasiveness of metaphor, or, perhaps, its nature. 'Words will not say more than they do. ...' The question is, though, how much they 'do' (itself a metaphor). ... Creeley's poetry is in *Collected Poems* (1983).

Gary Snyder (1930), who has studied Zen Buddhism in Japan and has been regarded as a Beat (q.v.), is a good deal less intransigent about learning from the tradition. His poetry actually works by means of images (in Olson's or Creeley's, qq.v., theory, 'interpositions of the ego'), and it has developed in a manner reminiscent of poets working in the tradition. Yet Snyder has learned something from Ginsberg (q.v.) and from Olson and Creeley, for he eschews any kind of literary style. His sense of the world as he records it in his poetry is relaxed, pleasurable and without exhibitionism; but it was never very interesting. Much of his best work is contained in *A Range of Poems* (1966), *The Back Country* (1967) and *Regarding Wave* (1970). His later poems are flaccid and tedious, and Snyder seems to have deserted poetry for 'teaching Zen' and publicity.

The emergence of **James Dickey** (1923), 'star college athlete (football, hurdles); night fighter pilot with over one hundred missions in World War Two and Korea; a hunter and woodsman; and a successful advertising executive in New York and Atlanta [Georgia, where he was born]', has not been as extraordinary as many irritated critics have assumed. He is that genuine article (at last, as some well-heeled readers might say), the

poet as Horatio Alger, the Yankee all-male who has put poetry into its place by con-
quering it with the tools of straightforward and simple striving for Success and Winning
Friends and Influencing People. Like Ronald Reagan, he really does, though as macho
as a man can be, hate war. But his sensibilities, if increasingly like battering rams
attached to his own noisy ego, can appeal to an audience Reagan cannot reach: naturally,
being a National Poet (he is the nearest since Frost, q.v., or was until recently when
people began to be bored with him), he condemns 'heavy industry and finance and the
volume turnover system'.

He began writing poetry at twenty-four, and was loosely associated with the group
around Robert Bly (q.v.) – who at the beginning of the Seventies wrote a devastating and
memorable attack on him and what he had become.

As he has written, he began without much knowledge of poetry; much of what he
gained was through the examples set by Bly and Wright (q.v.) and the many poets they
translated (Vallejo, Huidobro, Trakl, qq.v., and a multitude of others of this calibre). But
he wanted to be like Blake, too: a visionary. (This is inevitably disastrous and inevitably
indicative of grandiosity.) And he drew on his own experiences as athlete, business man,
hunter and pilot. His use of war experiences was rather different from that of others:
while of course he did and does deprecate war, he also seemed, if not consciously, to treat
it as a form of athletics or youthfully daring motorcycle exploits. His model was clearly
Hemingway (q.v.), but he did not share Hemingway's sensitivity, and could never have
written of war as Hemingway did in *A Farewell to Arms*: he had nothing of Hemingway's
involuntary sensitivity and feminine sense of outrage at war (that this was later wholly
suppressed is neither here nor there). James Dean was obviously another influence. . . .
What energy there is in his accounts of his bombing exploits comes from his sense of
exhilaration; in attempting to modify this the sense of horror is wooden, unfelt, manufactured. He is unquestionably America's brave boy; but he has always hated the weak
(his notion of strength, however, is a crude and stereotyped one) and has always arbit-
rarily condemned them – as finally becomes apparent in his loathsome novel, *Deliverance*
(1970), an ill-written celebration of social-Darwinist (q.v.) 'fitness' which reached the best-
seller lists and was made into a nasty and silly film with appropriately macho stars.

His poetry was never in the least delicate, and concealed its technical inadequacies
(which were so considerable as to transform what he thought was verse into a sort of
rhetorical prose) beneath a surface of crude, thoughtless but undoubtedly powerful
energy. He soon became the laureate of the 'common', not 'man', but 'American'. As
Michael Mesic has put it in his shrewd demolition of this writer: 'Dickey is proud to be
an American and often proud of himself, but I do not think he would be quite as proud to
be a writer, had he not been a celebrated one'. Of course men and women feel a certain
pride in being whatever, ethnically, they happen to be. But some of them also feel a
concomitant shame (the greater the degree of 'civilization', or whatever passes for it, the
greater, usually, the degree of shame). Dickey knows about the shame, all right; he even
knows about the virtues of the so-called 'uncivilized', though in no accomplished
anthropological sense. What is bad about him is that he pays a lip service to these qualities without feeling anything about them at all. Had he not received an education he
might have been some kind of 'natural'. As it was, Dickey made use of a 'split line' in
order, he hoped, to enhance his rhythmical effects. This involved inserting a space
between words instead of any punctuation (sometimes he put in a raised dot): it looked
like an original technical device, but in fact demonstrated his lack of sense of what a
poetic line is. He received the National Book Award (1965), and other honours, and was
praised in terms such as that he possessed 'seemingly endless imaginative resources and
capacity for extending the range of his feelings' and did things so 'beautifully and

amazingly'. These kinds of judgement were not supported by quotations except by the most incautious of criticasters. The only true sense one can get from his huge output is that he possesses the true American 'paranoid style': he feels himself threatened on all sides, and so has to 'win'. He wins not by writing poetry at all, but by being regarded as a poet: this is his *Deliverance. Poems 1957–1967* (1967); *The Strength of Fields* (1979). The title of 'A Comprehensive Selection of His Poems', edited by Laurence Lieberman in 1968, *The Achievement of James Dickey*, was not intentionally ironic.

A.R. Ammons (1926), who was born in North Carolina and now teaches English at Cornell University, has been increasingly celebrated as an American romantic who has expressed the transcendentalist ideas of Emerson (q.v.) in suitable modernized forms. The title of an essay on him by the not unpretentious if intelligent critic Harold Bloom is 'A.R. Ammons: When You Consider the Radiance'. This essay – like Bloom's on Ashbery (q.v.), 'The Charity of the Hard Moments' – contains much more of the Bloomian poetic aspirations than it does of the Ammons achievements, which are sincerely intended but inconsiderable and disappointing. Although Ammons is plainly inspired by Emerson, he would clearly like his roots to be in Wordsworth, though the methodology he has borrowed is usually that of Whitman (q.v.). This is a dangerous procedure. To be at all like Whitman, were that possible or desirable, you would have to lack a certain kind of critical intelligence, and Ammons does not lack it. Therefore he actually looks as though he is trying to look like Whitman, and of course falls short by a long distance. The imitations are transparent and embarrassing. There is nothing memorable in his diluted and diffused pantheistic verse, which sometimes runs to inordinate length (especially *Tape for the Turn of the Year*, 1965, which was written in short lines on a roll of adding machine tape), although there are plenty of worthy emotions and diffused, tedious philosophizing. When a contemporary poet can write 'I know them, I love them, I am theirs' you know that he has gone seriously astray: this is straightforward pastiche of Whitman, and tends to suggest to the bored reader that Ammons does not 'know' 'the weak, disoriented, sick, hurt, the castaways, the needful useless' at all, that he does not 'love' them (a tall order, however worthy), and that he is certainly in no sense whatever 'theirs'. Why should he be? There is nothing in his poetry to tell us why. In Whitman himself there is plenty that makes sense of that notion of possession by others; but Whitman was the poet of democracy, the one who gave that word a meaning beyond its increasingly spurious political one. . . .

John Ashbery (1927) was born in New York and has been hailed by an impressive number of readers as the authentic voice of America's new poetry. As Marjorie Perloff put it: 'the outstanding poet of his generation'. But is he? That would mean he is now taking over from Creeley, Bly, Wright (qq.v.) and a large number of erstwhile heroes, one of whom might even be Dickey himself, although he is five years older (I should explain that there are at least two more Dickeys, **R.P. Dickey**, 1936, and **William Dickey**, 1928: the extent of the former's luck, Dale Doepke tells us, 'is to have escaped being nailed "to that well-built cross on which the stricken and hopeless hang"', while the latter, says Charles Molesworth, is 'set adrift', and in 'mid-stride', and once wrote 'A wild deer burst into the office & bled to death/Kicking the files to mush', which is 'ironic' but does not bring 'things to focus').

Ashbery, who teaches English at Brooklyn College, is an intelligent and well read man; he has written a number of plays, and one novel in collaboration with James Schuyler called *A Nest of Ninnies* (1969). The readers whom he still worries are those who are said to 'long nostalgically' for a 'poetry of statement' – and a critic shrewdly wrote of him (1978) that he 'eliminates meaning without achieving any special intensity'. Perhaps what we all truly long for is a poetry of coherence, rather than meaning. For we all know that there is a poetry 'direct and oblique', and that such as Trakl and Vallejo (qq.v.) certainly achieve coherence (in their best work) without always being direct in the way 'poetry of statement' implies. Bly (q.v.), in America, can do this too. But it is fair, though both unfashionable and possibly simplistic, to ask what a poem 'means', if by this question we are really asking: what does this poem, or this poetry, convey that is illuminating to our minds, feelings or imaginations? Are we the victims of a confidence trick, if even a moderately sincere one? Is a poet apparently incoherent, as sometimes Vallejo was, because he is expressing a sense of inner and outer coherence in such a way as to illuminate that sense, i.e. to be coherent about his confusions – or is he being incoherent because he feels he can't achieve clarity, but still would like to be regarded as a 'good poet'? These are the sorts of question Ashbery's poetry inevitably raises. In defending Ashbery from the rude directness of the 1978 attack (by Robert Boyers) Perloff accuses the critic of regarding '*meaning* as some sort of fixed quantity' and claims that Ashbery's poetry celebrates a 'magic world' that 'really does exist'. But this defence begs the question, and her critique of Ashbery never goes into the question of the nature of his language: is that vital, energetic – like Vallejo's – and does it contain within it a sense of what Ashbery himself has said is 'unknowable': does it contain suggestions of the sort of experience of the 'unknowable' in which one feels simultaneously very far and yet very near to it, a suggestion of the apprehension of the mysterious nature of connections between disparate things, of the extraordinary sense that pervades a person when he or she knows that for a moment he or she loves another? Or is it synthetic, disingenuous, manufactured, lazy, irresponsibly surreal?

Ashbery's roots, or at least his preferences, are diverse. They have been said to lie mainly in Stevens (q.v.), but that is more of an accident. He has made increasing use of Stevens – the more irritating and mechanically 'aesthetic' Stevens – when he has been tired or not known what he wanted to do; but he learned most from Roussel (q.v.) and the French 'cubist' poets such as Reverdy (q.v.). He thought that in Roussel he had found a pointer to what he called the 'republic of dreams'. But one must remember that we go to Roussel (most of us, anyway) because he is interesting and crazy, not because we have much idea of what he is telling us, or even of what he is trying to tell us. In any case, you cannot lay a valid foundation for a whole poetry on any set of poetics, especially French ones, when you happen to be a New Yorker. Ashbery certainly did not like symbolism as Eliot (q.v.) practised it, and he said so early. He did not think it good for American poetry, and he was probably right (though a true poet might find his beginnings in anything). Perloff does not disapprove of the fact that Ashbery liked to employ a language that was 'on the point of revealing its secret without ever actually doing so'; indeed, she praises him for it. But this seems to be concentrating too much on language simply as language: to be playing games with it. We are reminded of Gass, Coover (qq.v.) and others. Worse, it could be an evasion of two things: first, of experience which is feared, and of the feeling implicit in it which is also feared – and secondly it might simply evade a sense of inadequacy in the medium of poetry, which is not easy to write, and which, while it must come like the leaves to a tree, needs a great deal more than natural growth. Nowadays we see much synthetically produced, apparently 'given' verse – stuff that means nothing at all, and is nothing like the leaves springing from any tree, but just the inane jottings of people taking advantage of climate which is either simply uncritical or on the lookout for work which can accommodate a critic's projections. We need to take Ashbery's considerable volume of verse (nearly twenty collections, beginning with *Turandot*, 1953; three plays; the novel) apart from his various and numerous philosophical pronouncements.

Bloom (q.v.) calls Ashbery (along with Ammons) 'superb' (where would this leave

Crane, Ransom, qq.v., and others?). He also writes that Ammons and Ashbery have in common only their 'authentic difficulty'. That is a clever phrase, and indeed, Bloom makes out a case for the superiority of parts of Ashbery's verse over other parts of it. It sounds convincing; but it is in reality an example of a man both arguing with himself and making a pretence of being critical. ... Auden (q.v.) called Ashbery a seer 'of sacred images and ritual acts'. Looking about in Ashbery criticism, of which there is now quite a lot, one finds many similar pronouncements; it is hard to see what they really mean. Such words as 'sacred' and 'ritual' are difficult, and should not be employed by those without at least an elementary knowledge of anthropology, in which half scientific, half poetic discipline they achieve something at least approaching a definition. But Auden knew nothing whatever of anthropology, and although Bloom's novel *The Flight to Lucifer* purports to be about gnosticism, it does not illuminate it at all (as Anita Mason's *The Illusionist*, qq.v., a much less pretentious and more deeply felt novel, does). All this amounts to is that people are saying very vague things about Ashbery in the hope that no one will notice that their comments, and most of Ashbery's poetry, do – as Boyers (q.v.) suggested – miss out what he understandably if perhaps a little imprecisely calls meaning to very little purpose.

Yet something interesting is happening, from time to time, in Ashbery's poetry. More than ever happens in Ammons, for example. However, it is the kind of thing that ought to happen (if we cut out the sophistication and vast number of literary allusions) in the poetry of a person in his teens, not in that of a man of fifty-six. There are, as I have mentioned, oblique poets; but their obliqueness nonetheless holds a kind of directness within itself. In one way or another they speak to us immediately. There are, too, poets who are by no means explicit about the nature of their sexuality. Yet, because the nature of the sexuality is an issue in the personality (and because the personality of the poet is an issue in poetry), their sexuality becomes evident. This is because poetry is about life (though how much of Ashbery's is?), and in life sexuality, even the apparent lack of it, is an unavoidable issue. Andrew Young (q.v.), a poet who spoke almost exclusively in metaphors, makes the nature of his sexuality almost immediately apparent to those who read him well; the revelation is rewarding. The slender best of Stevens (q.v.) is by no means explicit; yet there his delicacy and obliqueness from raw experience tell us all we need to know: and what we need to know is not his demonstration of how poetry ought to be written nor his 'philosophy' (which was pretty shabby, as we have seen).

Ashbery's poems in *Some Trees* (1956) were more conventional than his later ones; and they were failures, both rhythmically and as vehicles of the 'meaning' which the writer had not yet quite decided to 'eliminate'. The title poem begins:

> These are amazing: each
> Joining a neighbour, as though speech
> Were a still performance.
> Arranging by chance
>
> To meet as far as this morning
> From the world as agreeing
> With it, you and I
> Are suddenly what the trees try
>
> To tell us we are:
> That their merely being there
> Means something; that soon
> We may touch, love, explain. ...

It is the last line of the third stanza (it has two more stanzas, which slide off into a sort of pastiche of Stevens) that this poem wants to be about: the rest is 'philosophy' because it does not convey a real sense, at all, of the paradoxical feeling we experience of being both separated from and yet a part of nature (the trees, here): it conveys only an idea of that, and it is used as framework by the poet because he wants to evade – but without seeming to evade – any explicit statement that might arise from the to him frightening line about touching, loving and explaining. Who is the shadow to whom he is speaking? If Ashbery had anyone in mind here (and perhaps he had) then he gives us no sense of his warmth to him/her/it, and, above all, no sense of the other. So these are poems that would like to be love poems, but are instead pieces in which little terrified nodules of faint-heartedly expressed love-feelings are embedded in meshes of sophistication: cubist techniques, the procedures of Stevens, action painters, and the mad methods of Roussel. It would be polite to call this a world of 'sacred images' and 'rituals' and so forth; but the psychological facts relentlessly expose the academic collage of praise as a fiction: they speak for themselves. Nonetheless, something interesting is going on: the rhythms have a certain life and a certain nagging energy, there is a longing to express the forbidden meaning, and occasionally there is a line which stands out as authentic, the voice of experience and not some idea of it to be imposed upon the reader. But Ashbery did not go on to fulfil this slender promise.

In *The Tennis Court Oath* (1962) Ashbery conceals everything, and even Bloom calls it a 'fearful disaster', writing that it joins 'bland truisms ... of almost total disjunctiveness'. It has been called exasperating, but it is also claimed – by the same critic, A. Poulin Jr. – that the 'atmosphere remains charged with elusive emotional impact'. Ashbery and his admirers, taking Stein (q.v.) as a model, defend this procedure by giving this sort of elusive poetry a kind of status: you must not disclose too much, for this would lead to 'contrivance' (the force of this is much weakened by the facts that Ashbery is in any case highly contrived, though in a woefully disorganized way, and that the critics are using 'contrivance' not as a near-synonym for 'manufactured', but to denote the process by which a poet 'cleans up' and makes intelligible the raw 'given' material); but they admit that excessive concealment leads to boredom and lack of intelligibility. The general consensus seems to be that in *The Tennis Court Oath* Ashbery did conceal too much, but that in later years he became successfully 'Proustian'. He had asked that poems be hymns to possibility: he was writing about Stein's 'Stanzas in Meditation', but really about his own procedures, and he praised the Stein exercise, by implication, by stating that 'it would be difficult to say precisely what is going on' – '... it is not usually events which interest Miss Stein, rather it is their "way of happening". ...' The story of these 'Stanzas', he said – and Harold Bloom would do well to note it – 'is a general, all-purpose model which each reader can adapt to his own set of particulars. The poem is a hymn to possibility'. One is bound to ask: possibility of what? And one may also add that anyone who says he or she is not interested in events is something of a liar. Stein, we know, was forced to conceal her lesbianism – though she made it perfectly obvious to initiated readers. All the jargon about 'possibility' is a cover for an act of evasion: Ashbery cannot generate feeling, and is presumably unwilling to allow his feelings to surface in his poems. One of his most admired lines, a sort of modernized Shakespeare pastiche, is 'In service stairs the sweet corruption thrives'. And what Perloff calls his first great 'dream song' is 'These Lacustrine Cities'. This came after experiments in collage, 'cut-out' (q.v.) and so forth; 'These Lacustrine Cities' is in *Rivers and Mountains* (1966); its virtue is supposed to be that it is just on the point of revealing the secret of language and of the unknowable; but to some readers it is all very abstract. It does not read as though the writer frequently experienced feeling on the verge of discovery; nor does Ashbery ever make clear what he means by the 'republic of dreams' of which he speaks so frequently. He writes a perfect mix: a poetry that will please academic critics through its accommodatingness, and one disjunct enough not to anger the very powerful (sometimes) 'intelligently Philistine' set of American readers, who normally gravitate to the Beats, the Black Mountain group (or its remnants) or even to Dickey (q.v.). 'These Lacustrine Cities' is a delicate exercise (I use this word advisedly), and, whatever critics may say, it is firmly based in Stevens' manner, though it builds on it. It is a poem that wants to be about loneliness, perhaps even about sexual loneliness of a certain sort; but instead it makes a series of statements which are every bit as disjunct as the earlier frankly surreal poems, but which do not look as fragmented as they do (they are quite abjectly 'meaningless', e.g. 'Leaving the Atocha Station', which anyone could write):

> These lacustrine cities grew out of loathing
> Into something forgetful, although angry with history.
> They are the product of an idea: that man is horrible, for instance,
> Though this is only one example.

This, like the rest of the poem, is muddled, a subdued rhetoric, an attempt to catch a mood in words, but not to make sense of it.

I have spent much space on Ashbery, because at the present time he is widely regarded as the chief representative of American poetry as it ought to be. This is an unhappy state of affairs. He wants to embody, in this poetry, the unknowable. But this poetry comes nowhere near to resolving the paradox (as Stevens at times did). Instead he uses a not very interesting aesthetic philosophical framework to dissipate in himself both robustness and feeling. He talks about experience without conveying it. He embodies nothing. Yet he has bred a host of imitators, none of whom seems to understand even what Ashbery himself is trying (and failing) to do. *Selected Poems* (1967); *Houseboat Days* (1977); *As We Know* (1979); *Three Plays* (1978).

Ultimately Ashbery did not achieve more than did the frivolous, if sincere and in its way quite readable, verse of his friend **Frank O'Hara** (1926–66), who was one of the so-called 'New York' school of poets – of whom Ashbery was regarded as a member. O'Hara is still read, although his poetry consists of little more than a series of arhythmical urban jottings shot through with musical and artistic allusions. As a personality (he knew almost everyone) with his verse attached to him, so to say, O'Hara had his distinct uses. But, in the posthumous *Collected Poems of Frank O'Hara* (1971) and successive collections, one can see why only certain sorts of Americans still read him: partly for nostalgia's sake, and partly because they remember with affection how he seemed to break down every convention that was in the air in the Fifties and Sixties. He could be lightheartedly spontaneous, and does have historical importance. Other members of this 'school' such as **Kenneth Koch** (1925) and **Ted Berrigan** (1934) have nothing at all but post-Dadaist (q.v.) frivolity to offer, and are simply trite. Lines by O'Hara which are still admired include these:

> oh oh god how I'd love to dream let alone sleep it's night
> the soft air wraps me like a swarm it's raining and I have
> a cold I am a real human being with real ascendancies
> and a certain amount of rapture what do you do with a kid
> like me if you don't eat me I'll have to eat myself

which has been described as demonstrating how 'self-discovery dominates all other impulses'. One must decide if this kind of verse provides an exemplum for younger poets or whether it does not.

Robert Bly (1926), who was born in Minnesota, made many important translations (of Vallejo, Huidobro, Trakl, Jimenez (qq.v.) and others) long before anyone else in America had heard of European and Latin American poetry. Bly bitterly attacked the whole concept of the new criticism – and the poetry of Robert Lowell (q.v.). His ideal poet is probably Trakl; which means that he eschews rhetoric, and is a poet who dislikes 'talk' in poems: as he has said of Trakl, the images speak for themselves. His own procedures resemble those of Trakl. But in his first book, *Silence in the Snowy Fields* (1962), he introduced a bareness, an austerity. He wants to allow the things of Minnesota to speak for themselves. Later, in *The Light Around the Body* (1967), he finds he cannot: they are too spoiled by the world. He therefore took to the writing of a poetry of protest, chiefly against America's involvement in the Far East. He was the most prominent amongst those who gave public readings against American foreign policy, and he continues to make his living by giving public readings – and by translation (Ekelöf, Neruda, Tranströmer, Rilke, Aleixandre, Hamsun, qq.v.). He has more recently arrived at a position akin to that of Graves (q.v.): that society must return to a 'matriarchal order' – whether he believes that there were or are 'matriarchies' (there were not) is not clear; but this is scarcely relevant. He is one of America's boldest poets, one who employs what looks like a surrealist (q.v.) methodology, but one which in fact depends on the 'given image', which he believes arises from a non-logical faculty of the brain. His strange poetry is both original and coherent. *The Teeth Mother Naked At Last* (1970); *This Tree Will Be Here for a Thousand Years* (1979). His thinking is best exemplified in his anthology *News of the Universe: Poems of Twofold Consciousness* (1979). If more Americans looked to Bly rather than to Ashbery (q.v.), it would be a heartening sign.

James Wright (1927–81) was much influenced by Bly (q.v.) and was closely associated with him in the formation of the Fifties (later Sixties and Seventies) Press. He began as a disciple of Frost and Robinson (qq.v.), and had been a pupil of Ransom and Roethke (qq.v.). But he was affected by Bly's war against rhetoric, and the poems of his third book, *The Branch Will Not Break* (1963) – the first two were *The Green Wall* (1957) and *Saint Judas* (1959) – are in free verse, and are almost Japanese in their spontaneity and freshness. Later poems, in similar style, are collected in *Shall We Gather at the River?* (1968). *Collected Poems* appeared in 1971. He felt it appropriate to change his style, so that his whole ouevre appears to lack consistency – and certainly all his mature work is marred by instances of looseness and even hysteria. He became too confessional (though not in the self-conscious Lowell, q.v., style) and too self-analytical – and was afraid that his powers were failing. Nonetheless, in his last books, including *Two Citizens* (1974), *Moments of an Italian Summer* (1976) and *To a Blossoming Pear Tree* (1977), there are a number of tremulously moving poems, which are apt testament to the genuineness of his compassion.

Although **Louis Simpson** (1923), who was born in Jamaica, was associated with friends of Bly (q.v.) as an anthologist, he cannot be regarded as one of the 'Sixties' school. His best poetry is in his *Selected Poems* (1965). Simpson, who believes that poetry 'arises from the inner life of the poet, and is expressed in original images and rhythms', is a lyrical poet of great power who, perhaps unusually, is also an accomplished ironist. He has absorbed enough of the native American schools, without sacrificing his notion of the uses of knowledge, to suggest that he may be a pioneer of style. He is an excellent critic, and has drawn perceptive attention to the failings of a much overrated writer, Lionel Trilling (q.v.).

Arabic Literature

The literature of the Arabs has its own magnificent tradition. But its contact with modernism, as this is understood in the West, has been comparatively slight and small-scale. Moreover, much that is traditional in Arabic literature – for example, the panegyric habit – is and always will be unpalatable to that vast majority of Western readers who are not scholars of Arabic. Understandably, the demands of Arab nationalism have continually conflicted with those of literary modernism, which is European. The great debate in Middle Eastern literature at the turn of the century revolved about the question of what a writer's subject ought to be. It was a Syro-Lebanese faction living in the United States who, at about the beginning of the First World War, took over the leadership of a school, modern at least in that it advocated the assimilation of the European literatures. These Syro-Lebanese originally left their countries owing to Turkish oppression (the Albanians, q.v., suffered similarly); first they went to Egypt – where they helped to create an Arab press – and then to Brazil and North America. These writers were nationalist, but urged their compatriots not to reject European discoveries and methods but, on the contrary, to employ them. The forces of conservatism are so strong in the Middle Eastern countries, however, that this group did not at first make a strong or general impact. Later Egyptian literary activity became dominant; but this, too, had its roots in the Syro-Lebanese movement of the Eighties and after. The debate between the conservative and cosmopolitan factions goes on to this day in Arab letters, confused only by such essentially modernist concepts as 'arabism' (cf. negritude, q.v.).

The difficulties facing the Arab novelists in the later nineteenth century were almost unsurmountable. The potential readership – the educated classes – were more or less anti-European and regarded story-telling as a disgusting and vulgar activity. Literary Arabic was unsuitable for modern narrative and sounded ridiculous when used as dialogue. The earliest important novelist, the Egyptian **Jirji Zaydan** (1861–1914), the self-educated son of a poor Christian family, tried to solve the problem by writing historical novels. He became a noted scholar, writing a standard history of Islamic literature. His twenty-two novels are imitations of Scott (cf. the development of the Japanese novel, q.v.), and have no literary value; but they did in their modest way begin something. Their chief purpose was educational, but they were also sensationalist. **Yaqub Sarruf** (1852–1927), a Lebanese who eventually established himself in Egypt (which had just then come under British rule), devoted much of his life to the popularization of science. His novels, which include *Egypt's Daughter* (1905) and *The Prince of Lebanon* (1907), are poor – and, of course, deal with the past. But they do attempt some description of society. In *The Story of Isa Ibn Hisham* (1907) the Egyptian **Muhammad Muwaylihi** (1858–1930) cleverly and sensitively preserved the old form of the *maquama* (a usually picaresque tale told in an ornate way in

180

rhymed and rhythmic prose) but introduced a cautious note of social criticism. An early nineteenth-century Pasha dreams of Cairene everyday life in 1900 – thus giving Muwaylihi the chance to compare the old with the new. In Lebanon the art of the short story was cultivated with some success. But in general, fiction lagged far behind the essay: it was clumsy, sentimental and lacking in interest. The chief writers of the Syro-Lebanese diaspora (*mahjar*) added little or nothing to the development of fiction. **Mikhail Nuayma** (1894) wrote some competent but not innovatory short stories; his friend **Gabran Khalil Gabran** (1883–1931), subject of a still thriving Western cult, was a master of the modern prose poem, but his novels are rhetorical and sentimental; **Amin Rayhani** (1876–1940) initiated the Arabic prose poem, but, like Nuayma (q.v.), has not written novels. All three of these authors wrote in English as well as Arabic.

The first true modern novelist in Arabic is the Egyptian **Muhammad Husayn Haykal** (1888–1956) who, significantly, studied in Paris. His *Zaynab* (1913), published anonymously, was a study of a village girl of the Delta, and introduced colloquial dialogue for the first time. It is not a good novel by Western standards, but is a pioneer Arab work. Haykal, who was in the Egyptian cabinet in the late Thirties, exercised a powerful influence by his advocacy of modern usage. His last novel, *She Was Created Thus, She Is Like That* (1955), is cast in the form of an Egyptian woman's biography. **Muhammad Taymur** (1892–1921) introduced, under the influence of Maupassant (q.v.), realistic vignettes of everyday life, in which his brother, **Mahmud Taymur** (1894), followed him with even greater success. His *The Call of the Unknown* has been translated by H. Haren (1964). These two between them helped considerably to rid serious fiction of the moralizing element.

There was a flurry of literary activity in Egypt in the Twenties and Thirties dominated by **Taha Husayn** (1889–1973), who went blind at a very early age. His autobiographical trilogy, consisting of *An Egyptian Childhood* (1925; tr. 1932), *The Stream of Days* (1939; tr. 1948) and *A Passage to France* (1967; tr. 1976), exercised an enormous influence: its style broke with formalism, and affected the attitudes of his successors. His novel *The Sufferers on Earth* (1949) helped pave the way for the 1952 revolution, which he supported. He was regarded as the leading Arabic writer of his time.

By 1945 the way was prepared for better and longer regional and social fiction. **Nagib Mahfuz** (1912) covered the years in Cairo between the European wars in a comprehensive and lucidly written trilogy: *Bayn al-Qasrayn* (1956), *Qasr ash-Shawq* (1957), *as-Sukkariyya* (1957). (Each is the name of a suburb of Cairo.) This trilogy marks the beginning of the urban Egyptian novel, and has not been equalled in its genre. He continued to write novels, which have become increasingly experimental. **Abd Al-Rahman Ash-Sharqawi** wrote, soon after the socialist revolution that toppled King Farouk's corrupt regime, *The Earth* (1957), a well-written novel about the landowners. His novels remain committed to a peasant point of view.

Ehsan Abdel Kuddous moved from journalism to the novel, of which he is an extremely popular expositor. He has long been associated with all the progressive movements in Egypt. His best novel is *Something Inside Me*, which deals with the life of a millionaire. *Don't Shut Off the Sun* is an intelligent treatment of the 1956 Suez scandal.

Kamil Husayn (1901), an eminent Cairo osteopath, wrote about the trial of Jesus in *City of Wrong* (1954; tr. 1959; 1966). **Yusuf Idris** (1927), a doctor, was the leading socialist realist, but later turned to more modernistic styles. Technically he is the best of the short story writers, as he shows in *Night of the Unloved* (1954). With **Sonallah Ibrahim** (1935) the Egyptian novel comes of age: *The Smell Of It* (1968; tr. 1971), a novella of a young man's sexual and social frustrations in Cairo, was banned in 1968, and was allowed to appear only when substantial cuts had been made. The leading woman author is **Andrée**

Chédid (1921), who writes in French. She has written plays, poems and novels. Her novel *The Sixth Day* was translated in 1962; *From Sleep Unbound* in 1984.

Good writers have now begun to appear in other Middle Eastern countries. **Layla Balabakki** (1936), from the Lebanon, has published two novels of sexual and social revolt in *I Live* (1958), of which there is a French translation (1958), and *The Monstrous Gods* (1960). The Iraqui **Abd Al-Malik Nuri** (1914), in *The Song of the Earth* (1954), is gloomy and nihilistic. **Dhu N-Nun Ayyub** (1908), his countryman, a professor of physics and chemistry, is a 'committed' writer. His best work is about his years of exile (1954–8) in Vienna: *Stories of Vienna* (1957).

Apart from Mahmud Taymur (q.v.), who has written some excellent comedies rather in the style of his short stories, there are only two outstanding Arabic dramatists of this century: **Ahmad Shawqi** (1868–1932), who was of noble birth, was close to the court and, although an ardent nationalist, never made any serious attempt to face the grave social problems of his time. But he was a man of wide learning and humanity. His lyrical poems are in the strict classical tradition. His plays – the fruit of his last four years – are important because in them Shawqi, who had had a European education, imported the spirit of the European and English classical theatre, in particular that of Corneille. *The Death of Cleopatra* (1929) is, in fact, Corneille done over into Arabic; pastiche perhaps, but the pastiche of an educated man and not of a charlatan.

Tewfiq-Al-Hakim (1902), who was born in Alexandria (possibly four years earlier than he admits), and lived in Paris for many years, is a sharp, realistic novelist as well as a poetic dramatist. He is still Egypt's most cosmopolitan and sophisticated writer – as at home in France as in Cairo. His novels include *The Return of the Spirit* (1933), of which there is a French translation (1937), about ancient Egypt, and a Simenon (q.v.)-like mystery story – in the form of a journal by the investigating officer – about murder in a Delta village: *The Maze of Justice* (1937; tr. 1947). Tewfiq-al-Hakim is a versatile playwright ranging from the fantastic and symbolic – *The Cavern of Dreams* (1939 tr. as *The People of the Cave*, 1971), *Scheherazade* (1934), a masterpiece of exoticism – to the modern. Many of his plays are difficult or even impossible to perform, and he has himself described them as 'closet plays'. A translation, *Plays, Prefaces and Postscripts*, appeared in 1981. *The Treeclimber* (1962), an 'absurdist' (q.v.) play, was translated in 1966. *The Bank of Anxiety* (1967) was an experimental play which made some bold criticism of Egypt in the Sixties.

*

Arabic poetry has changed in form over the past hundred years; its content has remained almost consistently dull. The leading poet, the Egyptian **Hafiz Ibrahim** (1871–1932), is a case in point. Skilled in technique, he had nothing to say, and concentrated on conservative social pronouncements and obituary poetry for notables (for example, Queen Victoria and himself). The poets of Egypt remained neo-classical in style and spirit for some years; but the Syro-Lebanese broke with the past (mainly represented by the *quasida*, the sanctified traditional form), and initiated freer forms. This had its effect in the

Arab world itself only after the Second World War. Meanwhile, in Baghdad the poet **Maruf Rusafi** (1875–1945) remained faithful to the classical forms, but was able to produce a less indifferent content because of his awareness of modern life and the changes that had come over it.

The great exception in this era was the Lebanese Gabran (q.v.), who lived outside his native country from the age of twenty. Gabran was a traditionalist, but one with an acute awareness of the West and of the changes that were taking place there. Eventually he became more of a Western mage from the East than a true Arabic writer, though his popular works are by no means absolutely worthless.

After 1945 Arab poetry came under the direct influence of contemporary European writing. It is not hard to explain why the modern poet found most congenial was Lorca (q.v.). There is much experimentation with form, usually resulting in modifications of blank verse; the most substantial poet to emerge so far has been Syria's **Adonis** (ps. **Ali Ahmed Said**, 1930), a selection of whose poetry has appeared in an English translation by S. Hazo: *The Blood of Adonis* (1971). In 1960 Adonis became a citizen of the Lebanon, where he has been active in literary affairs. Here he has run two magazines and edited an important anthology of Arabic poetry. His poetry reflects French influences, but remains Arabic in character. Notable contemporary poets of his include the Iraquians **Jalil Haidar, Moayad El-Rawdi**, the Egyptian **François Bassily** and the Syrian **Mahmud Adwan**.

Australian Literature

Twenty-five years ago it was widely held, even by academic critics of repute, that there was no Australian literature worth mentioning outside Australia itself. Today that is an untenable view. Patrick White (q.v.) won the 1973 Nobel Prize and the work of at least three Australian poets (Slessor, Judith Wright, Hope, qq.v.) is well known throughout the world; that of some others deserves to be. Australian woman prose writers have been especially notable.

Australian literature developed along familiar colonial patterns. There was poetry before (creative) prose, and this was uninhibitedly based on that of England. Thus an anonymous poet of the late eighteenth century wrote: 'And none will doubt but that our emigration/Has proved most useful to the British nation'. The work of the three leading poets of the colonial period – Harpur, Kendall and Gordon, none of them good except in flashes – must be judged mainly in terms of the late romantic or decadent literature into which their Australian experience happened to fit. More truly native writing, whether superior or otherwise, is to be found in such fugitive writing as J.F. Mortlock's *Experiences of a Convict*, which was not published (ed. A.G. Mitchell and G.A. Wilkes) until 1965.

The foundation of the *Bulletin* in Sydney in 1880 established the nationalist movement, which lasted until after the Second World War, and which still exercises a certain influence – though not at a high level. That this movement has been shown to embody a tradition which is largely non-existent is not surprising; most movements are susceptible to similar retrospective reassessments. Not all the Australian writers of the early part of the modern period can be fitted into it, and the best certainly cannot. But it is useful to define the 'myth', if only to see it fall apart as we consider individual writers – and, indeed, as we consider some aspects of Australia itself. For the glowing, American kind of optimism could never have existed in Australia; the earliest settlers were convicts, the interior was vast and hostile and apparently unconquerable. There were criminal heroes in plenty, but no 'great men' who struggled for and gained independence – which did not have to be fought for. Sin and the melancholy loneliness of the individual in vast and mysterious places lie at the heart of the true Australian consciousness. This new world was never very brave. And, last but not least, the early development of the economy depended upon corporate rather than individual effort – which has had its oblique effect. We can learn more about nineteenth-century Australia from Trollope's neglected novels about it than from the official records of the time.

The nationalist movement tried to ignore this darker side. It was chauvinistic, democratic (in the early, broad, populist American sense of setting the ordinary man up against the privileged), and in that sense 'left-wing', Utopian, and anti-literary (in that it opposed aristocratic 'polish' as genteel). The main literary figures were **Henry Lawson** (1867–1922), **Tom Collins** (ps. **Joseph Furphy**, 1843–1912) and **Andrew Barton ('Banjo') Paterson** (1864–1941). After the heyday of these men, themselves in some ways exceptions, most major Australian writers are to be found outside nationalist tradition.

Lawson, the laureate of 'mateship' (the sense of corporateness that keeps Australians going in the face of hardship) and the outback, had a hard time on his father's farm in his youth – but spent most of his life in Sydney. His bush ballads were popular in his lifetime, but it is his short stories that will survive. Lawson is a sardonic realist, writing of the bush and its inhabitants with naturalistic resignation, but also with humour and energy. Early reading of Dickens encouraged his capacity for taking pleasure in eccentric or roguish characters, whom he describes with brilliant zest. His best prose is admirably simple and sharp. It is seldom vague and its observation is keen and exact. Despite lapses into sentimentality, repetitiveness and unevenness, Lawson's genius for selecting what details are significant is not in question. After the turn of the century the quality of his work fell off, and he sought refuge in drink, unhappily divided in mind between outback and city. *Best Stories* (1966); there are many editions of his *Prose Works*.

The writing of Tom Collins, now usually referred to by his real name because he became well known only some thirty years after his death, is more sustained. Furphy was born in Victoria, and had a harder life than Lawson. After he married, a farm he had taken failed, and he became a bullock-driver for some seven years before going to work in a factory. By 1897 he had finished 'a full-sized novel'; this is lost. But it was published in an abridged, revised form as *Such is Life* (1903); some of the material rejected for it appeared in shorter works. *Such is Life* was the first Australian novel to break with the English tradition. It made no attempt at a plot, and satirized effete British gentlemen (understandably but possibly in certain respects unfairly). Furphy described the book, famously, as in 'temper, democratic; bias, offensively Australian'. He was a semi-naturalist, fascinated by the notion of ineluctable destiny stemming from choices made in a moment (thus, because at one point he does not fill his pipe, the narrator, Tom Collins, gets involved in a series of mishaps). *Such is Life* is crude, but crude in an authentically Australian manner; it is also comic and impolite in a way that (in book form) would have shattered a true Britisher of the time. The title is in itself a criticism of the carefully plotted Victorian novel; and I have called Furphy a semi-naturalist because, while he acknowledges destiny as a force, his experience had taught him a measure of scepticism about all aspects of life.

Banjo Paterson, author of *Waltzing Matilda*, is a literary balladeer who reflected native Australian, rather than colonial, experience; his poems read best aloud. At his least inventive he tends to collapse into components of patronization (he was, unlike the people he wrote about, an educated man), chauvinism and populism. But there is an authentic note: 'Clancy's gone to Queensland droving, and we don't know where he are'; and the magical 'There was movement at the station for the word had passed around/That the colt from Old Regret had got away. ...' (PBAV). At his authentic best Paterson is inimitable and marvellously good. He acquired his nickname from a racehorse he fancied. This vein of popular poetry was continued, but to less good effect, in the work of **Clarence James Dennis** (1876–1938), in *Songs of a Sentimental Bloke*.

The Victorian **Bernard O'Dowd** (1866–1953) will survive only as a figure of historical interest. He corresponded with, and to a certain extent imitated, Walt Whitman, whose subtleties and complexities he lacked. His manifesto is *Poetry Militant* (1909), which is contained in his *Collected Poems* of 1941: this postulates a poet who understands history and can therefore contribute to the building of the future. O'Dowd was a clever versifier of a conventional kind, but his work is overloaded with rhetoric – and suspiciously free of personal concerns – to be of any but historical interest today. (BAV; PBAV) A better poet is **Furnley Maurice** (ps. **Frank Wilmot**, 1881–1942). He can be both archaic, but with a Housmanesque edge, and – at times – extraordinarily direct. (PBAV)

Shaw Neilson (1872–1942), born at Penola in South Australia, was a poorly educated manual worker who suffered for most of his life from bad eyesight. He used to compose his poetry in his head and then wait for a suitable amanuensis; many poems, he himself said, were lost in this process. Neilson is a minor poet, at his very best slightly resembling

Blake (whom he never read); he was the first unselfconsciously Australian poet, in whose simplicities lie just a few jewels of insight and genuine ecstasy. He modelled himself on Thomas Hood, and often his insufferably 'poetical' language ('Plague me no more') spoils his effects. But occasionally his poetry comes through breathtakingly, as in 'The Orange Tree'. *The Poems of Shaw Neilson* (1965; rev. 1973). (BAV; PBAV)

Neilson's was a delightful and touching achievement, and greater than that of the over-sophisticated and learned **Christopher John Brennan** (1870–1932), who went to Sydney University (where he was later a professor), travelled in Europe, and was deeply conscious of the European poetic tradition. To put it briefly, the gifted Brennan went adrift on that notorious sandbank for the poets of his generation: sex. He felt he had to deal with his own failure to find sexual fulfilment in marriage, but he did so – as James McAuley (q.v.) has pointed out – pretentiously. An evader of the true nature of his experience – a central feature of which was that the hopefulness contained in his innocent, overforcefully applied wedding-night lustiness was shattered by his virginal wife's shuddering revulsion – he posed as a 'confessional' poet. He had waited, Victorian-like, for some years for the ecstasy of sexual fulfilment – and when it came he found it not only a let-down but also a focal point for every kind of guilt. He drew on French symbolism (q.v.), German romanticism and Pre-Raphaelite womanology in order to construct an edifice that would look like sexual wisdom. But for all his failings he was the first Australian poet to be intelligently aware of a poetry outside the Anglo-Australian tradition, and is important for this reason. His ultimate ambition, in conscious terms, was to create a complete symbolist myth; in unconscious terms to erect a Platonic paradise that would compensate him for his sexual disappointment. And his poetry is interesting and skilful, even though it is hardly ever fully satisfying. He came under the influence of most of the important poets of his time – Verhaeren and George (notably) as well as the early French symbolists (qq.v.) – and he never indulged in pastiche. As a minor poet Neilson does sometimes come off; but Brennan had to come off as major – or not at all. And he fails because his impressive structure of intellect, scholarship and literary awareness cannot subsume his personal experience. He was eventually sacked from his post at Sydney University when his wife divorced him and he began to drink too heavily. The definitive edition of his poetry is *Verse* (1960). (BAV; PBAV).

Hugh McCrae (1876–1958) has been important to almost every Australian poet. This seems curious to the outsider, because his poetry is not only very limited, but tiresome. The commonplaceness of McCrae's vitality is hardly compensated for by its abundance; his 'paganism' (satyrs, fauns and so on) is irritatingly simplistic, and is inadequate as a poetic response to his times. He was the hero of the *Vision* group that gathered round Norman Lindsay (q.v.) in the Twenties – Australia's first clearly defined literary group. They, like other Australians, chose McCrae as a hero because he seemed so energetically anti-bourgeois. He was the obvious alternative to the new middle-class smugness; and in that he really was, he was genuine. The poet R.D. Fitzgerald (q.v.) edited and selected his lively *Letters* (1970). Of his poetry one can now say little; like Lindsay's work and persona it became one of the weekend treasures of the very class whose values it set out to challenge. *Best Poems* (1961). (BAV; PBAV)

Mary Gilmore (1865–1962) declined into what James McAuley (q.v.) calls 'a repulsive example of a formidable will, cannily sucking homage indiscriminately out of the environment' some years before this attitude was properly rewarded by the DBE (1937). But earlier in the century she had successfully avoided, in her unpretentious short lyrics, most of the vices of inflated diction and the poeticizing that disfigured the poetry even of Neilson (q.v.). She was a pioneer feminist, and a devotee of Aboriginal culture. (BAV; PBAV)

The next stage in Australian poetry came after the First World War, with the publication of the magazine *Vision* (1923). Its inspirer, **Norman Lindsay** (1879–1969), has to be considered both as an influence (in Australian terms, immense) and as a novelist (minor). He was primarily an illustrator. Like his friend McCrae (q.v.), Lindsay had boundless energy as mannered draughtsman and crude philosopher of 'vitalism' or 'biologism'.

His 'philosophy' is expressed in *Creative Effort* (1920), an inconsistent mish-mash of pseudo-Nietzschean vitalism, Godless immortality and heavy-handed amorous innuendo. The obvious message of this book, as of *Vision*, is pseudo-Rabelaisian 'vitality, vigour', of any sort – and not necessarily Australian. And this was what the writers in a more settled Australia wanted; they could thus evade their melancholy destiny (a thing we all wish to do) and yet seem to oppose bourgeois complacency. The members of this group did their best work after leaving it; but it did nearly all of them harm. For it was essentially a backwards-looking movement, which avowedly preferred 'being alive' to being modern – and this was inadequate to the inner needs of the best Australian poets. *Vision*, of which only four numbers appeared, vanished from Australia and reappeared in London (briefly) as *The London Aphrodite* (1928), edited by Norman's son **Jack Lindsay** (1900), who remained in England, became a Marxist, and poured out an immense amount of lively Marxist historical fiction, translation, often valuable biography and interesting reminiscence.

The best of Norman Lindsay's books is his children's novel *The Magic Pudding* (1918), because here the sheer thoughtlessness of his exuberance cannot offend. As he himself said, its basic themes are 'eating and fighting'. It is said by some to be a children's classic. His adult fiction, although stylistically offensive, is not negligible. It is probably a testimony to the accuracy of *Redheap* (1930), about life in the Australian Nineties, that it was for over twenty years banned by the Australian government. Perhaps his best novel is *Saturdee* (1933), which helps to explode the myth of boys as angels.

The most gifted member of the *Vision* group was **Kenneth Slessor** (1901–71), with whom many critics feel modern Australian poetry began. But his early poetry consists of little more than energetic and linguistically promising literary inventiveness – sophistications of the subject-matter of McCrae (q.v.). He is descriptively brilliant, playful (often archly so) and has no content beyond a generally bristling sexuality and materialism. Slessor later became a more interesting poet; but it is only in a few individual poems, mostly noted by critics, that he has wholly succeeded. 'Gulliver' appropriately shows what sort of experience his uneasy later poems can explore with success (although even here the exasperated tone of the monologue is somewhat forced):

> I'll kick your walls to bits, I'll die scratching a tunnel,
> If you'll give me a wall, if you'll give me simple stone,
> If you'll do me the honour of a dungeon –
> Anything but this tyranny of sinews.
> Lashed with a hundred ropes of nerve and bone
> I lie, poor helpless Gulliver,
> In a twopenny dock for the want of a penny,
> Tied up with stuff too cheap, and strings too many.
> One chain is usually sufficient for a cur.
>
> Hair over hair, I pick my cables loose,
> But still the ridiculous manacles confine me.
> I snap them, swollen with sobbing. What's the use?
> One hair I break, ten thousand hairs entwine me.

Love, hunger, drunkenness, neuralgia, debt,
Cold weather, hot weather, sleep and age –
If I could only unloose their spongy fingers.
I'd have a chance yet, slip through the cage.
But who ever heard of a cage of hairs?
You can't scrape tunnels in a net.

If you'd give me a chain, if you'd give me honest iron,
If you'd graciously give me a turnkey,
I could break my teeth on a chain, I could bite through metal,
But what can you do with hairs?
For God's sake, call the hangman.

Clearly McCrae's vitalism is too simplistic for him, and yet he resents a universe in which this should be so: the giant trapped by 'hairs' therefore wants to die. To McCrae himself he said (most Australian poets have written poems to McCrae): 'We live by ... your masks and images/ ... But you take passage on the ruffian seas/And you are vanished in the dark already'. One continually feels, reading the poetry of Slessor, that one is just about to encounter a linguistic revelation; but it seldom really comes. 'Five Visions of Captain Cook' is an interesting and genuinely Australian poem, with some good passages; but as a whole it is not *réussi*: the thought and the language fall together only sporadically. However, 'Five Bells', a meditation on the death of a friend by drowning, is an impressive poem of despair: here at last Slessor is able to see the unhappy nihilism that his vitalism and sensuality papers over, and to respond with words that haunt the mind. Slessor frequently revised his poems in the course of his life; the definitive edition is *Poems* (1957). He wrote no more than three or four poems after 1940. (BAV; PBAV)

The poet **Rex Ingamells'** (1913–55) Jindyworobak school of the late Thirties, with its emphasis on the importance of the Aboriginal culture, produced no important poetry, even though it hit the (literary) headlines. The *Jindyworobak Review* ran from 1938 until 1948. However, its attempt to bring Aboriginal culture, with its highly poetic central concept of 'dream time' (*altijira*), into the mainstream of Australian poetry may yet have its effect; that this was premature and that Ingamells (who died in a car accident) was himself a poor poet should not distract us from appreciation of his admirable project.

The only poetically gifted member of this abortive movement was **William Hart-Smith** (1911), whose extreme concentration and economy are remarkable in that they so seldom pull him down into the trivial or whimsical. Born in England, he left there at twelve, and lived in New Zealand for a while (being at one time represented as a New Zealand poet), but he is now permanently in Australia. He has been influenced by Sufic ideas and the teachings of Gurdieff, but these seldom obtrude. There is no collected edition. Representative volumes are *The Talking Clothes* (1966) and *Minipoems* (1974). (PBAV)

R.D. Fitzgerald (1902) contributed to *Vision* but was not associated with Lindsay's group as closely as Slessor (qq.v.). Some see Fitzgerald as Australia's major poet of the century: the writer who succeeded where Brennan (q.v.) failed. Certainly he has been as aware as Brennan of European poetry, and his goal has been ambitiously philosophical. An intellectual poet, he also suffers from a brash optimism ('I regret I shall not be around/to stand on Mars') that may either attract or repel; but he is in any case honest. He is to be seen at his best in such poems as 'The Wind at your Door' (AWT), a sensitive and skilful meditation on an ancestor, a doctor, 'caught in the system', which broadens out into a lyrical and humane exploration of the original sin that lies at the back of the

Australian experience (a nation of convicts and, as bad, their no less criminal oppressors). 'I find I lack/the hateful paint to daub him wholly black' Fitzgerald says of this ancestor: 'Perhaps my life replies to his too much/through veiling generations dropped between'. The language of the poem is simple almost to clumsiness; but retrospectively one sees that it suits the awkward and agonized honesty – and makes the poet's vain wish to be a descendant of the flogged man who (under the medical supervision of Fitzgerald's forebear) guiltily haunts the poem. Fitzgerald has probably received most praise for his collection of 1938, *Moonlight Acre*; but these philosophical poems are less spontaneous than *Between Two Tides* (1952), an epic of eighteenth-century Tonga, and the lyrics of *This Night's Orbit* (1953). Fitzgerald has often been called 'profound', but no one has demonstrated how. But like Slessor, Hope and the younger McAuley (qq.v.) Fitzgerald has never really been able to achieve an authentic Australian voice more than sporadically; it has been left to Patrick White (q.v.) to do this, in prose; and to Kenneth Mackenzie (q.v.) to come very near to, and sometimes attain, it in poetry. *Forty Years' Poems* (1965) (BAV; PBAV; AWT)

A.D. Hope (1907) did not publish his first collection, *The Wandering Islands* (1955), until he was nearly fifty. Since then he has exercised an increasing influence on Australian poetry. He is a ferocious conservative; but his apparent conservatism and rejection of modernism (including that of Eliot, q.v.) may appear on closer examination to be an expression of Swiftian disgust at all developments in human history since about 1750. Hope is a sexual romantic, highly energetic (again in a familiar Australian way), operating in severely classical modes of his own choosing. The sex-fun, however, is basically McCraen (q.v.). A similarly gifted poet, James McAuley (q.v.), a witty and astringent critic, displayed a similarly intelligent but unhappier conservatism. Like the New Zealand poet James K. Baxter (q.v.), he became a Catholic; but his poetry hotly limited his own faith, rather than affirmed it. Australians bitterly attack their own 'way of life', but, watching the developments in the outside world (of which they are acutely aware: they are not 'cut off'), are not happy about letting in pop-culture.

A.D. Hope has been a 'literary nuisance' on the Australian scene, sometimes silly but always amusing; he is at his best when caught between the nervous tension of his deliberately Augustan formalism and his sexual wildness. And yet even here one wonders if the Australian predicament itself is not responsible for a refusal to allow rhythms to develop in their own idiosyncratic way: the traditional forms seem to trap Hope, at his most personal, in poeticisms that the term 'irony' cannot quite accommodate:

> She does not tire of the pattern of a rose,
> Her oldest tricks still catch us by surprise.
> She cannot recall how long ago she chose
> The streamlined hulls of fish, the snail's long eyes.

His has been the most skilful and versatile means of defeating both hatred of Australian philistinism (a very brash phenomenon) and his failure to discover his own voice. But the over-celebrated 'Ode on the Death of Pius the Twelfth' reveals not only his accomplishment but his pomposity and degree of artificiality. Frequently described as 'beautiful', it is in fact a very bad poem, and its view of Pius XII is a disturbingly conventional one. Not many intelligent Catholics can possibly think of him as a 'great pope', and his successor certainly did not. Neo-Augustinism is not an adequate response to any modern predicament, let alone an Australian one, and though Hope's performances in this vein are superior to those of Winters (q.v.), they do not ring at all true. He has published *Collected Poems* (1972) and other volumes since. He is a writer of fine exercises in verse, but has no voice of his own and is not really a poet at all. **James McAuley** (1912–81), who has criticized Brennan's (q.v.) inadequacies in no mean terms, has brought the influence of Rilke (q.v.) into Australian poetry – something Brennan could not have done. It was after his first book, *Under Aldebaran* (1946), and after the Ern Malley hoax – in which he and another poet, Harold Stewart, faked a Dylan Thomas-like poet and successfully put him across on Australian letters – that McAuley became a Roman Catholic and defined his anti-sceptical position: the danger, as he reasonably saw it, was that everyone was being encouraged to be uncommitted, 'without fixed principles or certainties'. Considering the self-limiting nature of his own faith, one is bound to consider that McAuley may merely have been urging himself to take arms against the sea of his own troubled scepticism. His own later poetry, as in 'A Letter to John Dryden', is less celebratory of the joys of understanding the true God than shot through with hatred of scepticism. It seems a highly provincial kind of position for so gifted a critic and poet. The lyrics of McAuley's first book were his best work: he made the mistake of taking up a critical position in his poetry – afraid, perhaps, of what he might find if he did otherwise. His *Collected Poems 1936–1970* appeared in 1971. He failed to do justice to himself; but his criticism is full of incidental insights. (BAV; PBAV)

The third force in Australian poetry (as she might be called) is **Judith Wright** (1915), who published her first book, *The Moving Image*, in 1946. She has written intelligently on her contemporaries, and in poetry has been less ambitious and perhaps more healthily stark in her use of language. But she is better on her non-sexual experience than on her position as wife and mother: here, while she is translucently sincere, a puritanically bourgeois attitude becomes too apparent; a typically Australian, frozenly ineffectual resistance to what is happening in the world causes her to cast a rosily sentimental glow over 'family life'. One's own experience is one thing; lack of understanding through a dogged refusal to understand is another – and there is a residue of the latter in her over-fragrant attitude. She has rightly emphasized that poetry must finally depend upon emotion; but she has tended to diminish the role of that hard thought which must so often precede the statement of emotion. Her early despair at loneliness relieved only by sexual contact, which produced her best and most limpid poems, has given way to a less self-explorative assertion of 'old-fashioned' values. She has by far the highest reputation of any Australian woman poet, but is not half as interesting or original as Gwen Harwood (q.v.). (AW; BAV; PBAV)

Two other women poets have been less influential. **Rosemary Dobson** (1920) probably has no more to say than Wright, but she has found a decidedly less self-consciously 'feminine' way of saying it. Her usually tight forms effectively and unarchaically contain and control her strongly felt sense of erotic and religious dismay, but the influence of Lowell (q.v.) has hardly helped her to achieve a less metrically strict, more rhythmically free form; yet when she achieves it she will be found to have much more to say than, for example, Anne Sexton (q.v.). A *Selected Poems* appeared in 1963. (BAV; AWT; PBAV) **Gwen Harwood** (1920) is an oddity, and an extremely good one; she is certainly Australia's best living woman poet. She owes much to Morgenstern (q.v.), but has an entirely original and powerful lyrical capacity. She is as strange as Stevie Smith, but less hit-or-miss, more intelligent and more controlled: a very greatly superior poet, but a less ambitious one. Her rewarding work may be found in *Poems I* (1963) and *Poems II* (1968). (AWT; PBAV) Her two main sequences concern Professor Eisenhart and Kröte, a musician. Both these men bring European culture to Australian philistinism, but neither is treated very flatteringly. More than any other poet, Harwood is concerned with music. Both she and Rosemary Dobson (q.v.) should be more widely read in Great Britain and America.

Douglas Stewart (1913) was born in New Zealand, where he learned to write nature poetry. He belongs to the still flourishing Antipodean tradition of conservative formalism; by not forcing himself into an intellectual stocktaking he has managed to continue writing poetry and vigorous, though conventional, verse drama. 'The Sunflowers' demonstrates his strength and his limitations:

> 'Bring me a long sharp knife for we are in danger;
> I see a tall man standing in the foggy corn
> And his high, shadowy companions' – 'But that is no stranger,
> That is your company of sunflowers; and at night they turn
> Their dark heads crowned with gold to the earth and the dew
>
> So that indeed at daybreak, shrouded and silent,
> Filled with a quietness such as we never knew,
> They look like invaders down from another planet.
> And now at the touch of light from the sun they love –'
> 'Give me the knife. They move.'

This is in certain respects poor: no one can say that the clichés of observation and language are exploited, either ironically or otherwise – and yet it was worth doing. (BAV; AW; PBAV)

Conservatism of the kind practised by Hope and McAuley (qq.v.) has always been very strong in Australia. It seemed for some time as if all Australians writing in Australia were trapped in a straitjacket of a traditionalism that was almost Georgian (q.v.) in its refusal to face up to the times. One wonders, really, what Hope would say about Eliot's (q.v.) remark to the effect that true 'free verse' is not really 'free' at all – that it is difficult to write. That has given many poor poets the excuse to write in what is in effect chopped-up prose. But that there is no free verse that is poetically viable simply is not true. Riding (q.v.), as an example, wrote in what was in effect free verse. *Prufrock* is free verse; but who could say it lacked form? So of course are many of the best poems of our age in other languages. However, the conservative tradition has been continued by another Roman Catholic, **Vincent Buckley** (1925), a critic and poet whose performance has always been vitiated by a certain rigidity and dogmatism; Buckley has tried to absorb more modernistic influences, but has failed. It was, of these three ultra conservative poets, only McAuley who could occasionally be touching. Hope, as I have remarked, was really everything except a poet: all he did smelled of the lamp, and in all his poems he strained too hard for effect. There was no ease, no personal rhythm. The test piece is the Pius XII ode (q.v.), and astute readers will immediately note how it is desperately trying to be 'beautiful', to be 'exquisite' – they will note that it is unoriginal, even insincere – far too 'manufactured' to be real poetry. This tendency held Australian poetry in its grip for many years – in a sense it still does – though the best modern Australian poet, the late Francis Webb (q.v.) was not at all influenced by it.

Another effective and outstanding poet who wrote determinedly in his own style is **Bruce Beaver** (1928), whose work began to be noticed only in the Seventies. His verse is more rhythmically alive than Hope's (q.v.), and he cannot share Hope's conservatism. *Letters to Live Poets* (1969), his first mature book, expresses feelings of genuine horror and disgust at what is perpetrated by those who hold political power. But there is still a certain stranglehold: Beaver seems unable to express personal feeling – and it is personal feeling in poetry, however expressed, that is unique. We expect it from a poet of Beaver's energy. So far he has restricted himself to generalizations about how he feels in general, and that means his poetry now begins to disappoint.

Les A. Murray (1938) has a similar energy and independence of spirit. But he is still writing less as himself than as he feels an Australian poet of his age ought to write. His energy is largely wasted. One wants to hear what the poet himself has to say. *Lunch & Counter-Lunch* (1974).

Chris Wallace-Crabbe (1934) is, to quote a line from one of his own poems, 'Not warm, not cold (in all things moderate)'. He has felt, as so many Australians did, the influence of Dylan Thomas (q.v.), but has wanted to retain coherence. He has a good command of technique, and writes intelligent poems (they are now being increasingly read in Great Britain); but ultimately he is a frustrating and frustrated poet, strangled – as so many Australians seem to be – by his intellect. **Peter Porter** (1929), who went early to England, and has become to all intents and purposes an English poet, is in similar case; but he has no technique and no mind, as his criticism (displayed from time to time in the columns of newspapers) shows all too clearly. He has conducted his own education in public, but this has been less of an educational than a merely touching process. Porter now uses 'difficult' foreign words, and poses as a boulevard (q.v.) thinker and 'philosophical' poet. The results are embarrassing.

The great exception in Australian poetry was **Francis Webb** (1925–74), whose poetry was being praised by Herbert Read (q.v.) in the Sixties. Webb, who suffered much from mental illness, served in the war in Canada, and then went back there to work for a publisher. He may thus have escaped the conservative stranglehold out of which so many Australians seem to have found it hard to break. His poetry is hardly ever quite *réussi*, but from the start it was extraordinarily original: it was clear that he had something very different and personal to say. His poetry is largely a record of his own struggles against his compulsion to write it. The chief influence on his early work was Browning, but only in the sense that Webb learned from him how to construct and sustain dramatic monologues: *A Drum for Ben Boyd* (1948), *Leichhardt in Theatre* (1952). It was White (q.v.) who later celebrated Leichhardt in *Voss*; Webb sees this semi-charlatan, semi-visionary, as the man who cannot make art without being a fraud, madman and clown. Both the long poems are somewhat inchoate; but of their power there can be no doubt. Webb was always clumsy:

> Because the wise world has for ever and ever rejected
> Him and because your children would scream at the sight
> Of his mongol mouth stained with food, he has resurrected
> The spontaneous though retarded and infantile light.

> ('Harry')

This, about the Christ figure who looms larger and larger in Webb's poetry (*Collected Poems*, 1969), is confused – and yet it is obvious what it 'means'. Read (q.v.) thought Webb as good as Rilke (q.v.), which is wildly extravagant. Webb did not possess Rilke's awful ashamed sanity. But there are passages of great power scattered throughout his work; and the control he managed to exert over it, since he was an absolutely genuinely tortured visionary, is remarkable. So long as he maintained that control, he could live. His poetry is ultimately, perhaps, a disappointment – if only by the highest standards; but no Australian in post-war poetry wrote as powerful a poem as 'Harry', about the idiot, the 'pudgy Christ' who is writing a letter from an institution (Webb spent part of his life in mental hospitals, including one in Great Britain):

> Consider the sick
> Convulsions of movement, and the featureless baldy sun

Insensible – sparing that compulsive nervous tic.
Before life, the fantastic succession,
An imbecile makes his confession,
Is filled with the Word unwritten, has almost genuflected.

Australian poetry would look very thin and sick without Webb.

*

Australian dramatists have been few. Douglas Stewart's (q.v.) verse plays have vigour, but their language – read over – is prosy. His best known and most successful play is *Ned Kelly* (1943). The one authentic Australian play that has so far been written is by the actor **Ray Lawler** (1913): *The Summer of the Seventeenth Doll* (1955). This deserved its success. It is an examination of the legend of the tough Australian outdoor man and his innate superiority; the notion it gave non-Australians of Australia was both truthful and moving. It was not flawless – sentimental box-office concessions were made – but its final departures from psychological accuracy do not challenge the basic conceptions of the play. *The Piccadilly Bushman* (1959) was not as successful, and later plays by Lawler have settings other than Australia. There have been good plays by Patrick White and Hal Porter (qq.v.), but so far no Australian of Lawler's calibre has emerged, even though younger dramatists eschewed the 'well-made play'.

Alan Seymour (1927) now lives in England, but his most important and popular play, which was almost as successful as Lawler's (q.v.) *The Summer of the Seventeenth Doll*, though less deservedly so, was specifically Australian. This was *The One Day of the Year* (1962). The day in question is Anzac Day (25 April), when the Australians mourn their war dead. This was attacked and even refused a performance (at first): it presented a disenchanted view of 'glory'. But it is finally sentimental, and the rest of Seymour's work, though enjoyable as entertainment, is not more than competent.

Dorothy Hewett (1923) did not begin to write plays until the mid-Sixties. Before becoming a playwright she had written fiction and verse, but most notably left-wing journalism. *This Old Man Comes Rolling Home* (1976), which was produced in 1966 and then revised for a new performance in Perth in 1968, deals with the foolish attempt of Menzies to ban the communist party. It is good fierce stuff about activists (who are idealized), and remains her best – perhaps one should say most vital – play.

Australian drama is now lively, especially in the smaller theatres, but has not yet produced an outstanding playwright.

*

The first Australian novelist of importance was **Henry Handel Richardson** (ps. **Ethel Florence Richardson**, 1870–1946). She was in Europe studying music until 1903, and her first essays into literature were translations from the Scandinavian; Jacobsen's *Niels Lyhne* (q.v.), so important to Rilke (q.v.) and others, she acknowledged as a formative influence – her anonymous translation of it appeared in 1896. *Maurice Guest* (1908), autobiographical in many diverse ways, none of them quite direct, is naturalistic, Freudian and 'amoral'. Although Henry Handel Richardson revisited Australia only briefly – she lived in England, where her husband was a professor of German literature, and she died at Hastings in Sussex – she is still to be considered an Australian novelist, for the main subject of her most important novel, *The Fortunes of Richard Mahony* trilogy (1929), is wholly Australian. It is a brilliantly intelligent work, a late flowering of naturalism; its theme, of an English Victorian doctor's emigration to Australia and the crushing of himself and his decent qualities by fate, in the form of his own characteristics and circumstances, is never forced. The societies of Australia and England (to which Mahony at one point returns) are acutely described, and Mahony's defeat and moral collapse are observed with feline attention to detail. Pity is withheld; but not understanding.

Naturalism has flourished longer in Australian writing than elsewhere (except perhaps in Canada): the fatalistic habit of mind has not yet been dispelled. Even the best poets tend to insist on retreating into conservatism (or, like Slessor, give up after a final nihilistic fling); the novelists can cling on to naturalism, which after all – with its insistences on exact mimesis and cruel destiny – is a kind of faith. A novelist who has had his due neither in his native Australia nor outside it is **Leonard Mann** (1895), a bleak and clumsy writer whose best fiction approaches the power of Dreiser's (q.v.). Mann tries to irradiate the darkness he sees over the world with socialistic hope, but gloom dims his effort; the glow in his novels is one not of hope but of courage in adversity. *Flesh in Armour* (1932) is one of the best of the First World War books, and has been unduly neglected. The ex-schoolmaster Frank Jeffreys is the typical Mann victim: he tries to make himself into a soldier with the AEF, but cannot manage it; he shoots himself in the hour of the Allied victory. Mann presents this early anti-hero, the man who could not kill, as in one sense superior to his companions – but doomed. After *Human Drift* (1935) came *A Murder in Sydney* (1937), a gloomy metropolitan study of crime and redemption (through the agency of a Dostoevskian maimed lover), which is set in the years of the Depression. *The Go-Getter* (1942) is Mann's tensest and finest book: Chris Gibbons is redeemed from cheapness by his tough challenge to fate. His heartless project to seduce a girl turns into love. Mann then wrote a very long novel about Australia in the Second World War, but publishers found it too 'leftist' and outspoken, and it has not yet appeared. *Andrea Caslin* (1959) and *Venus Half-Caste* (1963) maintain the high standards of this powerful and too unheeded novelist. The key to Mann's fiction may be found in his minor but not undistinguished poetry. (BAV)

Frederic Manning (1882–1935) produced one classic; it appeared anonymously in Paris in 1929 under the title *The Middle Parts of Fortune*, but is better known under its English title of *Her Privates We* (1930) – the author called himself 'Private 19022'. This is a contrast to Mann's pacifistic *Flesh in Armour* (q.v.), than which it is a more artistically successful – but not more powerful – work: Manning treats the war as a test of character. Where Mann is deliberately anti-heroic Manning is heroic – but not by choice. It is simply that his Bourne can what Mann's Jeffreys cannot. But there is as much irony in *Her Privates We*: Bourne is, in effect, murdered (by being forced to go on a suicidal sortie) by an officer who fears and envies his qualities. Manning, who wrote other graceful minor prose, suffered from asthma even while serving in Flanders; he died in Italy. His book was much admired by T.E. Lawrence.

Vance Palmer (1885–1959), a competent author, was a better writer of short stories than novels; he could deal well with the apparently trivial, but whatever struck him as important seemed to inhibit him. But his novels contain much excellent work. His best books are *Separate Lives* (1931), *Sea and Spinifex* (1934) and *Let the Birds Fly* (1955), all collections of stories, and the novel *The Passage* (1930), in which he fails with the love relationships but succeeds with the description of the stresses and strains experienced within a family. His big trilogy about a socialist politician, *Golconda* (1948), *Seedtime* (1957) and *The Big Fellow* (1959), is honest and informative but psychologically mediocre.

Katherine Susannah Prichard (1884–1969), although she played some part in the formation of a specifically Australian novel, never produced a masterpiece. Her first efforts were feeble, and almost all her books are flawed by too great a reliance upon a crude Marxism. She was a simple-minded and sincere socialist; but it did not do her writing much good. She is at her best in *Haxby's Circus* (1930), a humorous and vivid account of circus life which contains no manipulation of character in the interests of theory, and no preaching. *Coonardoo* (1929), reckoned by most to be her best book, is a moving story (based on what used to be called 'real life') of a black Australian's romance with a white man. It is flawed by the poor handling of its melodramatic plot, and its inept attempt to emulate D.H. Lawrence's (q.v.) manner of dealing with 'elemental' sex ('deep inexplicable currents of his being flowed towards her'); but the author makes Coonardoo herself understandable. Later books, particularly the goldfield trilogy – *The Roaring Nineties* (1946), *Golden Miles* (1948) and *Winged Seeds* (1950) – are worthy: always worth reading for their author's mastery of the facts of her material, and her honest treatment of it.

For Katherine Prichard the naturalistic gloom of imagination was replaced by Marxist socialism; **Kylie Tennant** (1912) is a more thoroughgoing naturalist who has written several vivid novels of city life. *Tiburon* (1935) is about unemployed relief-workers in the country during the Depression; *Foveaux* (1939) is a vivid picture of Sydney slum-life in the years 1912–35. She is a documentary novelist, but is not without psychological penetration, as is evidenced in her massive *Tell Morning This* (1968), about prison life (she got herself locked up in gaol during her research).

Of the expatriates since Henry Handel Richardson (q.v.), **Christina Stead** (1902–83) was the most distinguished. She went to London in 1928, and settled in America in 1937. She was mainly a 'critic's author' until the reprint in America, in 1965, of *The Man Who Loved Children* (1940). Her first book was a collection of stories, *The Salzburg Tales* (1934): this was followed by *Seven Poor Men of Sydney* (1934), about young revolutionaries in Sydney in the Twenties, remarkable for its realistic picture of the Sydney docks. *The Man Who Loved Children* is her masterpiece: a study of the savage warfare between a wild but intelligent woman and her neurotic, proto-fascistic husband, and of their seven children's varying means of evading permanent damage. This is set in America, and it is hard to see anything Australian about it: Christina Stead is a cosmopolitan novelist, nominally left-wing (but without party), and she has studied French fiction – particularly that of Louis Guilloux (q.v.), whose influence she has acknowledged. But *The Man Who Loved Children* is entirely original; sovereign among its many qualities, perhaps, is the detachment of its portrayal of Sam Politt, the husband who drives his wife to suicide and 'never thought she meant it'. Other books by Christina Stead include *For Love Alone* (1944), the earlier part of which is set in Australia, *Letty Fox, Her Luck* (1946), *A Little Tea, A Little Chat* (1948), *Cotter's England* (1966) and the four superb novellas in *A Puzzleheaded Girl* (1967). One can at least see the fascination that Guilloux had for Christina Stead: like him, she horrifiedly and fascinatedly dwells on the tiny details of obsessions. *For Love Alone* thus dwells on the behaviour of an Australian girl who falls in love with a student and follows him to London. *Cotter's England*, set in England, looks at the lives of a couple somewhat reminiscent of Sam and Henrietta in *The Man Who Loved Children*. Nell, an unsuccessful left-wing journalist, 'collects' women and fills her house with them; her husband George is more important in the world, less neurotic and cares less about other people. Christina Stead was one of the most gifted novelists of her generation, a master of significant detail. Certainly *The Man Who Loved Children* is one of the dozen or so finest novels in English of this century. Stead returned to London in the Forties, but spent her last years in her native Australia.

Martin Boyd (1893–1972) improved on his expatriate fiction after he returned to Australia in 1948. In England he had been a monk for a time. Boyd is not a sensational novelist, and although generally readable his books have their *longueurs*; but he is an intelligent and gifted analyst of the Australian past, who deserves more attention than he has had. *The Montforts* (1928), written under the pseudonym of Martin Mills, traces the history of his mother's family over five generations; *Lucinda Brayford* (1946), however, which deals with the same subject-matter, is superior. It traces the fortunes of the Vanes from William Vane's emigration to Australia after being sent down from Cambridge for cheating at cards until the death of his great-grandson in England in the Second World War. This is an intelligent and sensitive 'family saga' novel, and avoids the sentimentalities and dishonesties into which Galsworthy (q.v.) fell. The 'Langton' tetralogy – *The Cardboard Crown* (1952), *A Difficult Young Man* (1955), *Outbreak of Love* (1957) and *When Blackbirds Sing* (1962) – is more substantial and is his best work. For the whole of his life – he never settled permanently anywhere – Boyd was tormented by the dual pulls of scepticism and religious faith; but he put much more of this into his fiction than he himself believed (he was legendarily modest). Now much more attention is being paid to his achievement, and this is as it should be.

Seaforth Mackenzie (ps. **Kenneth Mackenzie**, 1913–55), whose novels but not poetry collections were published under the name of Seaforth (because his publisher had another Kenneth Mackenzie on their list), could well have been treated as poet, for he was equally – perhaps more – distinguished in this field. He has been compared with Dylan Thomas (q.v.): he was Australia's latter-day *poète maudit*: alcoholic (meths drinker sometimes), an isolate, always poor, usually desperate, died young (by drowning, although this seems to have been a 'deliberate accident'). But in his shrugging, complex, sardonic despair he resembles Malcolm Lowry (q.v.) rather than Thomas. He is certainly an odd man out of Australian letters – and an important one. Not one of his four novels is an absolute success, but each achieves something. *The Young Desire It* (1937) and *Chosen People* (1938) are sometimes marred by pastiche of Lawrence's (q.v.) vitalism, or by youthful awkwardnesses. But both introduce something new into Australian fiction. The most successful feature of the first is its sympathetic portrait of an unhappy homosexual schoolmaster. (Clearly Mackenzie had had some adolescent trouble with homosexuality, though he seems to have emerged as a fully fledged heterosexual at adulthood.) There is also some excellent observation of the narcissism natural to certain types of adolescent. One critic, Evan Jones, has most unfairly confused his dislike of the manifestation with Mackenzie's portrayal of it. *Chosen People* is a vile story told with hideous conviction and power: a beautiful woman gives up her young paramour – already sucked dry by her – and grooms her equally beautiful daughter for marriage to him. *Dead Men Rising* (1951) is disappointing; but Mackenzie's last novel, *The Refugee* (1954), shows a return to the form of *Chosen People*, and is his best-written book. This is the story of a love affair ending in murder; it reads straightforwardly on a realist level, but has unmistakable symbolic overtones. Lloyd Fitzherbert falls in love with a young woman, a double agent who has renounced both her employers; he renounces her offer of herself to him. Later, however, they marry secretly; the girl takes his beloved son (whose mother died in giving birth to him) as lover; Fitzherbert kills her, with, it seems, her consent. This has mythological and incestuous overtones; it is also about isolation and the tragedies this can lead to: in a diary Mackenzie wrote: 'Perfect moonlight – absolute, utter silence of windless night, cold'. This is the spiritual atmosphere of *The Refuge*.

Mackenzie's poetry, at last properly edited in *Poems* (1972), is at its best as good as any

Australian's of the century, and perhaps suggestive of greater gifts. That includes even Webb (q.v.). From his personal hell Mackenzie seems to have been unique in breaking free of that stultifying kind of traditionalism which even the most brilliant of Australian male poets seem to oblige themselves, in one way or another, with varying reluctance, to cling to (the exceptions are Hart-Smith, q.v., but he is not fully Australian, and Webb, who spent many years outside his own country). Mackenzie at his best has a voice more unmistakably his own than any of his contemporaries; you can never confuse it, as you can even McAuley's and Hope's (qq.v.), with that of a dead age:

> Blackness rises. Am I now to die
> and feel the steps no more and not see day
> break out its answering smile of hail all's well
> from east full round to east and hear the bird
> whistle all creatures that on earth do dwell?

Mackenzie did not always write well, but we now have the measure of his complete work: he almost (although not quite) alone of contemporary Australians was prepared to risk himself in the quest for an adequate response to his time.

Hal Porter (1917–85) has, after Patrick White (q.v.), been the most versatile and vigorous talent of all Australian contemporary writers. His best prose is in his magnificent autobiography, *The Watcher on the Cast-Iron Balcony* (1963 pt. AWT), which has extraordinary control and detachment, as well as a Proustian (q.v.) sense of the past. This is one of the most quintessentially Australian books to be published since 1945 – because Porter's experience has been Australian and because his book remains true to it. Its exuberant manner owes something to Dylan Thomas' (q.v.) Welsh idylls, but transcends their meretriciousness. A sequel volume, *The Paper Chase*, followed in 1966. Much influenced by Katherine Mansfield (q.v.), Porter writes well, in short stories, of innocence betrayed by maturity: *A Bachelor's Children* (1962) and *The Cats of Venice* (1965). In his novel *The Tilted Cross* (1961), set in mid-nineteenth-century Tasmania, Porter seemed to be going out of his depth in trying to follow Patrick White, and in *The Right Thing* (1971) he seemed still to be taking the wrong direction. So far his best fiction has been in short stories.

Patrick White (1912), born of Australian parents in London, educated at Cambridge, returned to Australia permanently only after serving in the Second World War. He began with a book of poems, *The Ploughman* (1935) – though this was preceded by the very rare, privately printed *Thirteen Poems* (c 1929) – which has considerable value as an index to his later works. His first important book was *The Aunt's Story* (1948). This dealt with what is really his central theme, the Nietzschean (q.v.) one of the lonely atheist's agonized capacity for insight into the nature of existence. Comparisons with Dostoevski and other such writers are not, in White's case, foolish, although he continually experiences difficulty in sorting out wild and pretentious rhetoric from what is a kind of truly mantic utterance. *The Aunt's Story* is concerned with Theodora, who in her desire to lose personal identity – she rejects love as a threat to this process – becomes mad, but possibly feels at peace. In *The Tree of Man* (1955) White tried to resolve this problem of solitude by anchoring his characters – husband and wife who build up a large farm from a smallholding – in everyday life; but one can see his obstinate and guilt-ridden obsession with the necessity of loneliness even in this most realistically conceived of his novels. *Voss* (1957) goes entirely the other way: its hero's project is, by making an expedition into the Australian interior, to become God: to turn himself into what is not. Although this profound and beautiful book has sources in the journeys of actual explorers – mainly the half-mad Leichhardt (q.v.) – the most instructive general background to it is undoubtedly the thought of Nietzsche. Voss has to transcend his sense of beauty (one is reminded of Hopkins, q.v., punishing himself for having taken too much pleasure from the landscape) in order to achieve his project: he must not yield to the sensuous. Perhaps he loves his dog: he kills it. He is also a clown, a liar, a charlatan and a buffoon. . . . Yet of course he stands for all of us in our half-pathetic, yet half-noble, explorations into ourselves. White did achieve this metaphor. In *Riders in the Chariot* (1961) White achieves on a major level, with alienated freaks, what Carson McCullers (q.v.) could only hint at. This takes place in Sarsaparilla, the Sydney suburb that White has made as real as Faulkner (q.v.) made Yoknapatawpha County. All the freaks are in quest of a loss of identity that is not a suicide or an escape. *The Solid Mandala* (1966) is about twins, one apparently simple, the other clever, who are brought to Sarsaparilla by their English parents when young. First we see life from Waldo's point of view: he is 'superior', but he fails and ends his life hating his twin Arthur because he knows that Arthur is his only contact with life. Then we see the same events from Arthur's point of view: Arthur is a 'holy fool', a wise man who from childhood has wanted to climb to 'the red gold disc of the sun' – but he is judged by all but a neighbour, Mrs. Poulter, as a madman. The apparently sordid *dénouement* is seen through her eyes. This is a difficult but immensely powerful novel, another milestone in a strange and poetic journey. *The Vivisector* (1970) is about a painter, and, astonishingly, maintains the classic level of the earlier novels – as, indeed, does *The Eye of the Storm* (1973), which was misunderstood by reviewers. White has written short stories (*The Burnt Ones*, 1964) and four plays of varying dramatic effectiveness but extreme significance in the context of his fiction. He won the Nobel Prize in 1973. Since then he has continued to write novels, most particularly *The Twyborn Affair* (1979), which he felt everybody would 'hate'. In fact this book is one of his most successful: it treats of its author's homosexuality (diagnosed and explained in the autobiography *Flaws in the Glass*, 1981) in imaginative terms which transcend personal problems. This is one of the most illuminating books on a difficult subject ever written, and is good enough to be beyond description. One can only direct readers' attention to it.

The novelist and poet **Randolph Stow** (1935) is a follower of White. He leans too heavily on him; but it is hard to see how a still young man who genuinely shares White's predisposition to the symbolic could fail to do so. His first two novels were powerful but melodramatic; only in the third, *To the Islands* (1958), about a sixty-eight-year-old Antipodean Lear, did he really begin to find himself. Heriot, a missionary, loses his faith and goes off on a voyage of exploration, accompanied by an old aborigine, to the islands of the dead. *Tourmaline* (1963) is about a ghost-town stricken by drought; a water-diviner who comes there persuades the inhabitants of his magic qualities, but proves to be a fake. This intended fable of man's capacity for self-deceit does not come off: Stow is dealing in fact with his own religious feelings, but tries to rationalize these into generalized comment. In *The Merry-go-Round in the Sea* (1965) he abandons conscious symbolism for a vein of tender realism, and does much better. He falters only at the end, when he tries to contrast the old world of childhood with the new one of adult reality. In his poetry Stow expresses a vision much akin to that of Sydney Nolan (who has illustrated one of his collections); he speaks of his 'sad-coloured country/bitterly admired'. What James McAuley (q.v.), in a lecture on Australian poetry, has called 'the personal element' has so far been missing or ineptly expressed; but of his seriousness there is no doubt. He has recently come to live in England, but his novels written there, while competent, do not measure up to his earlier promise.

Australian fiction since Stow has not been impressive, although prizes have been awarded. **Thomas Keneally** (1935) is not really more than a middlebrow White (q.v.) in disguise – at least Stow has not tried to be this. Nobody has come up to the level of Hal Porter (q.v.) in the short story or the novel, although some competent novels have appeared. Perhaps fiction needs the inspiration of a man such as Webb (q.v.) – but White, like Goethe in Germany, has (unintentionally) made it difficult for Australians to write good fiction. Either they want to better him, which they can certainly not do – or they want to differ from him: but they still have him too firmly in mind. Perhaps they ought to start learning from Christina Stead (q.v.).

Baltic Literature

Although both Swedish and Finnish literatures could with reason be called Baltic, and although Finnish is very close to Estonian, there are by common consent only three so-called Baltic Literatures: Estonian, Latvian and Lithuanian. All three of these countries have been grabbed by and incorporated into Soviet Russia, whereas Sweden and Finland have escaped that fate; the grouping is therefore appropriate, despite the very close cultural links between Estonia and Finland.

I

The development of the literature of Estonia was abruptly checked when Soviet Russia occupied it in 1940. (The Germans subsequently entered the country; the Russians returned in 1944, and cruel mass-deportations followed over the next five years.) From 1918 Estonia had been an independent state; today it remains the fifteenth state of the USSR, although not officially recognized as such by certain countries. Its ruling communist party has been permeated by Russians; but the Estonians themselves are a Finno-Ugric people whose literature is related to Finnish. They have preserved their own literature throughout a difficult history, and although the policy of the Soviet Union has hardly encouraged them to continue doing so, there is a fairly vigorous expatriate literature (mostly in Sweden, but also in the USA, and Canada). Since the nineteenth century there has been no illiteracy in the country, which has meant that (proportionately) huge editions of books are issued.

In Estonia, as elsewhere, mid-nineteenth-century romanticism gave way, towards the end of the century, to a more realistic approach. The first considerable figures in modern Estonian literature were the novelist **Eduard Vilde** (1865–1933), the playwright August Kitsberg and the lyrical poet and short-story writer Juhan Liliv (qq.v.). Vilde began as a journalist and popular light novelist; rather unusually, he graduated to serious literature, and wrote his best novels in the last years of his life. He knew German well, travelled in the USA, and for a time during the First World War was the Estonian minister in Berlin. He made his first impact on Estonian literature in the Nineties, with pointedly realistic stories and novels that were almost naturalistic in mood. *A Cup Full of Poison* (1893), a description of the miseries of the poor, is typical. Just before the beginning of the First World War he refined and improved his language considerably, wholly purging it of its journalistic elements. Between 1902 and 1906 he had written a long trilogy on mid-nineteenth-century Estonian life: *The War at Mahtra, When the Peasants of Anija Visited Tallinn* and *The Prophet Maltsver*. This is sociologically valuable, but the novels and plays of his final twenty years are psychologically and artistically superior. The best is perhaps *The Dairyman of Mäeküla* (1916); this is about an aristocrat's lust for his dairyman's wife, and ranks with the best novels of social realism of its time. Vilde, who took part in the 1905 Revolution and was for a time forced to live in Finland, fiercely resisted later manifestations of modernism, but was nevertheless one of the three writers to bring Estonian literature into our century.

Juhan Liliv (this is sometimes spelt **Liiv**) (1864–1913), who died of consumption, and who was mentally ill – but with periods of coherence – for the last twenty years of his life, was a pioneer realist in his earlier poetry and fiction; but in the disturbed verse of his last period he reverted to romanticism, and was influenced by symbolism (q.v.). (AMEP)

Estonia's second and more decisive modernist stage is associated with the Young Estonia (*Noor Eesti*) movement, which lasted from 1905 until the middle of the First World War. Liliv, in his last poetry, had anticipated the attachment of this group to French symbolism; now the emphasis was on Western literature and on artistic autonomy. Most of the leading writers in the group were inclined to the left in politics; but all insisted on the independence of the writer as a first requirement for successful literature. Linguistic reform, involving a new flexibility and an approximation to common speech, gave the movement impetus. The leader of the group was the poet and scholar **Gustav Suits** (1883–1956), who went to Sweden in 1944. Suits was a scholar deeply versed in nineteenth- and early twentieth-century French literature; his poetry is emotionally insubstantial but in his search for Parnassian (q.v.) perfection of form he has unquestionably widened the range of modern Estonian poetry. His ideal was George (q.v.). 'We want more culture!' he cried: 'Let us remain Estonians, but let us also become Europeans.' (AMEP) His schoolfellow **Friedebert Tuglas** (ps. **Friedebert Mihkelson**, 1886–1971), who remained in Soviet Estonia and even took over Suits' old university post for a while, combines a basic realism with a strong and occasionally irritating *fin de siècle* colouring; his short stories contain much of his best work, although his novel *Felix Ormusson* (1915), the diary of an artist who entirely rejects reality, is more than a mere period piece, and deserves translation.

It may be that, of this generation, despite the huge and deserved extrinsic influence of Suits, the most original of all the choate poets (Oks, q.v., can hardly be called choate) was **Villem Ridala** (ps. **Villem Grünthal**, 1885–1942), whose shorter poems have a peculiar softness of language and perfection of rhythm which is unmatched in anyone else's work in Estonian. He translated Carducci (q.v.). His melancholy evocations of the Estonian islands in *Songs* (1908) are quite important in European poetry; Suits was important only in Estonian poetry. (AMEP)

Largely independent of the Young Estonia group, with which he is nevertheless usually associated, is the poet **Ernst Enno** (1875–1934), to whom symbolist techniques came more easily and naturally than to any preceding Estonian poet. Although his mystical orientalism is shallow and dated, his poetry – sometimes reminiscent of Ady's (q.v.) in its combination of modern with folklorist themes and preoccupations – remains one of the most original, after Ridala's, to come out of modern Estonia. (AMEP)

The Young Estonia group was succeeded by a new one, calling itself *Siuru* (a fabulous fire-bird in Estonian folk-lore); this wished to carry the individualism and modernism of its predecessor further than Suits and Tuglas were prepared to take them. The poet they followed was the expressionistic (q.v.) **Jaan Oks** (1884–1918), whose intense work – in prose as well as poetry – has not yet received its critical due. Oks is not the equal of Strindberg (q.v.), as has been suggested, but his often pathological imagination deserves more examination than it has so far had. *Siuru*'s most gifted member was the poet **Marie Under** (1883–1977). Marie Under – another of the eminent Estonian writers who fled to Sweden at the time of the second Soviet annexation – began as a lush, self-absorbed neo-romantic; the influence of the German expressionist poets (q.v.), some of whom she translated, transformed her into a more original and interesting poet. She is now justly regarded as the leading Estonian poet of the period of independence, though Estonian critics writing in English probably tend to overrate her. Her first book, *Sonnets* (1917), showed mastery of form and energy; but its eroticism was conventional, and so of course it shocked conventional people. Her best collections were published in the Twenties and early Thirties. *The Bleeding Wound* (1920) and *The Heritage* (1923) represented her efforts to restore a mind suddenly shattered by conflict between personal and social pre-occupations. Her poetry did not regain its intensity until her old age. *On the Brink* (1963), published in her eightieth year, contains poetry that is nearer to that of her years of crisis. The magnificent title poem, translated by Ants Oras – one of the most distinguished Estonian scholars and writers of the century, now in America – sums up its grave mood:

> Times rushed. Times whirled and whirred.
> Their breath stays, rank and eerie.
> A second time, a third.
> Brief lies of smoothing years.
> Time to untime all times. ...
>
> What was the last bird's query?
> I've rhymed my answering rhymes.
> Blind silence stares and sneers.

Child of Man (1955) is a selection of Marie Under's work in an archaic English translation by W.K. Matthews that is only just better than no translation at all. Ants Oras' excellent translations have not been collected. Marie Under is herself a distinguished translator into Estonian – she has translated *Doctor Zhivago* (q.v.), many of Rilke's poems (q.v.) and other works. (AMEP)

A.H. Tammsaare (ps. Anton Hansen, 1878–1940) was associated with Young Estonia and then, loosely, with *Siuru*, but his vigorous and versatile art transcends the limitations of both. He is the only modern Estonian novelist whose work has the kind of epic sweep possessed by such writers as Andric (q.v.), and, to a lesser degree, Kazantzakis (q.v.), than whom he is superior. He is the most important Estonian prose writer of the century. After naturalist beginnings, he came to maturity with his drama, *Judith* (1921), an exciting re-telling of the Biblical story; but his masterpiece is the mammoth novel about Estonian peasant life in the latter part of the nineteenth century and the first few years of this: *Truth and Justice* (1926–36). No single work expresses with such accuracy and pathos the nature of Estonian society in this crucial period. The chief influences upon Tammsaare were Dostoevski and Hamsun (q.v.); Shaw (q.v.), whom he translated, helped him to develop a hard-headed and quizzical manner, which became apparent in the (understandably) pessimistic work of his last years. *Old Nick of Hell Valley* (1939) is a deeply melancholy allegory which Tammsaare casts in a folkloristic framework. His masterpiece remains untranslated, but other novels and plays have been put into French and German. Obviously *Truth and Justice* awaits translation into English.

Other gifted writers in the *Siuru* group included Henrik Visnapuu (1890–1951) and August Gailit (1891–1960). Visnapuu's life was cut short by his sufferings in German Displaced Person Camps after he had fled from Soviet Estonia (he died in the USA soon after he arrived). His first collection, *Amores* (1917), lush and sensual love poems, is his best; his later patriotic poetry is ineffective. Gailit, whose family was half Latvian, wrote fantastic tales, of which the most famous is the story-sequence *Toomas Nipernaadi* (1928), about a writer who wanders about the countryside and is taken for a beggar. In exile Gailit wrote a worthy novel on the theme of the flight of those Estonians who decided to escape from the Russians by crossing the Baltic Sea: *Across the Restless Sea* (1951). But his imaginative powers had left him.

In the Thirties there was a violent, mainly leftist reaction against what appeared to some – in those politically uncertain and economically disturbed times – to be a dangerously insular attitude. But few of the writers in this Literary Orbit group – as it was called – were particularly gifted. In purely literary terms, the movement represented a reversion to the realism and naturalism of the Nineties. The many naturalistic novels of **August Jakobson** (1904–63) read like what they are: clumsy and inferior imitations of Zola (q.v.). Better writers than Jakobson supported the Literary Orbit for a time, but left it when they perceived its crude dogmatism and lack of interest in literature except as an instrument of propaganda.

The plays of **August Kitzberg** (1856–1927), important in the modernization of Estonian literature, gained a new popularity at this difficult time: these (both naturalist dramas and comedies) are well made, witty and realistic, and deserve their status as classics of the Estonian theatre. Another successful Estonian playwright is **Hugo Raudsepp** (1883–1951), whose cynical and grotesque comedies – *The Demobilized Father* (1923), *The Idler* (1935) – became exceedingly popular. Raudsepp tried to please the Soviet authorities after 1944 by writing socialist realist (q.v.) comedies; but they put him in prison, where he died.

Mait Metsanurk (ps. **Eduard Hubel**, 1879–1957) was a critic of society, but in a more imaginative and psychologically viable manner than Jakobson (q.v.) managed in his naïve fiction. Metsanurk wrote a number of vivid novels about war, the best on the subject in Estonian. **Karl August Hindrey** (1875–1947), who studied in Russia, Germany and Paris, stands somewhat apart. He was a brilliant writer of children's fiction and of stories about animals; but his most seriously intended novels deal with the Estonian upper middle-classes. Hindrey's point of view is undisguisedly conservative, but his portraiture is not less accurate for that. His conservatism was not of the reactionary sort: it combined eccentricity with a certain gay cynicism. He wrote good historical fiction. Two more leading Estonian realists who established their reputations in the period of independence went into exile to Sweden: **August Mälk** (1900) and **Karl Ristikivi** (1912–77). Mälk, like many Estonians, was first influenced by Hamsun (q.v.); his earlier fiction deals with the lives of fishermen and dwellers by the sea; in exile he has written a more complicated and psychologically subtle kind of novel, of which *The Vernal Soil* (1963) is outstanding. Ristikivi was a realist turned magic realist (q.v.): his earliest work is in the tradition of Vilde (q.v.), but *All Soul's Night* (1953) is more in the style of Hesse (q.v.). He wrote a number of successful historical novels. His best novel, though, was in his more realistic style: *Fire and Iron* (1938). There was always something uneasy about his later experimentalism.

One of the most gifted poets of a generation younger than that of Marie Under (q.v.) is **Betti Alver** (ps. **Elisabet Lepik**, 1906), wife of **Heiti Talvik** (1914–45), also a poet. Talvik was removed to Siberia and there died. Betti Alver was a leading member of the 'Magicians' (*Arbujad*) circle, which had sought in 1938 to revive a lyrical and ideologically independent poetry – most of all, perhaps, in order to have something to oppose to the meaningless chaos which, with every justification, they sensed as coming. She has remained in her own country, but was silent for twenty years; then, in the mid-Sixties, she was able to publish a retrospective selection and a volume of new poetry. The Soviets disapproved, but Betti Alver was 'rehabilitated' nevertheless; her books sold out overnight. Her most recent collection is *Flying City* (1979). She is still influential, and has criticized the Soviet tyranny with great boldness. As a poet she has been compared to H.D. (q.v.). She is unexciting, but a worthy writer and a courageous woman. (AMEP) But it had been the younger **Jean Kross** (1920) who broke the monotony of socialist realism (q.v.); he writes interesting if somewhat over-selfconscious novels employing techniques such as interior monologue (q.v.). He attempts to puncture all the Estonian historical misconceptions: both the nineteenth-century 'National Awakening' and the twentieth-century Soviet 'ideal life'.

Bernard Kangro (1910) lives in Sweden, and in recent years has turned to the novel. In the Thirties he wrote nature poetry under the *Arbujad* (q.v.) influence; his six-volume novel *Tartu* (1950–62) is a vivid and valuable account of Estonian city life in the inter-war period. (AMEP) Other poets include **Arno Vihalemm** (1911), **Alexis Rannit** (1914) – now in the USA – **Ukv Masing** (1903), characterized by the Estonian poet, critic and translator **Ivar Ivask** (1927) as a 'Blakean mystic surrealist', **Kalju Lepik** (1920) and **Ilmar Laaban** (1921) – both now in exile. Vilhalemm is a satirical mocking poet; Rannit is a skilful but self-conscious heir to the symbolists (q.v.). Lepik, who has been influential in the Sixties in Estonia, seems to have gained something from Enno (q.v.), and has successfully integrated folkloric elements with surrealism. Estonia's only real surrealist, however, has been Laaban, a genuinely experimental if rather trivial poet. Ivar Ivask is perhaps the most attractive of all the modern Estonian poets in exile: he writes a poetry of wonder and gratitude that comes from deep within him, and successfully avoids the inconsequential. But he owes rather too much to Guillén (q.v.). Some of his poetry has been written in German. Unfortunately all of this Estonian poetry is synthetic, much of it a sort of cross between Seferis and Ungaretti (qq.v.).

Young Estonian writers of the Sixties and Seventies have produced some of the most interesting, courageous and exciting writing in the entire Soviet Union – which has not itself done anything to encourage them. Ivask has gone so far as to claim that **Paul-Eerik Rummo** (1942) and **Jaan Kaplinski** (1941) are of the calibre of Voznesensky (q.v.). Both are anti-dogmatic, intelligent and exuberant poets, and both typify the accelerating vitality of Estonian literature within the USSR and outside it amongst the 70,000 exiles. Another manifestation of this development is the Estonian theatre of the absurd (q.v.), which flourishes. Rummo's *Cinderella Game* (1969) is the most famous example of this.

II

The languages of Latvia and Lithuania, the other two Soviet Baltic states, are related to one another but not to Estonian and Finnish: with Old Prussian and Curonian, both extinct, they form the Baltic branch of the Indo-European languages. Modern Latvian literature – which coincided with political emancipation – begins with the first realistic portrayal of peasant life, and the first Latvian novel, *The Times of the Surveyors* (1879), by the brothers **Reinis Kaudzīte** (1839–1920) and **Matīss Kaudzīte** (1848–1926). This is still regarded as a classic. A spate of fiction influenced by naturalism (q.v.) followed; but at the same time work was begun on a gigantic collection of Latvian folklore. Of all contemporary Western literatures, Latvian is the most imbued with folklore and myth. The socialistic New Current (*Jaunā Strāva*) combined in the Nineties with a tendency to neo-romanticism to supplant the nineteenth-century 'National Awakening', of which *The Times of the Surveyors* had been the finest blossom. The chief representative of this period is the poet, dramatist and translator **Jānis Rainis** (ps. **Jānis Pliekšāns**, 1865–1929). Rainis, whose work was supplemented by that of his talented wife, the poet **Aspazija** (ps. **Elzā Rozenberga-Pleikšāns**, 1868–1943), had to leave Latvia in 1905 (he had been embroiled in the affairs of that year), and did not return until after independence in 1918; thereafter he held such positions as Minister of Education, and was a leading liberal. Rainis was undoubtedly a romantic at heart; but he wore no blinkers. The main theme of his plays and poetry is hatred of oppression. He was as hated by the Tsarist Russians (who arrested him in 1897) as by the Latvian supporters of Stalin. His tragedy *Fire and Night* (1905) remains one of the most eloquent of statements of the Latvian spirit. But his best writing is to be found in his most personal poetic work, as in the charmingly entitled collection *Distant Feeling in a Blue Evening* (1903) in which he explores his nostalgia and loneliness: 'Year after year your solitude will become stronger,/For friends will quit and you must climb alone. ...' Rainis is regarded by some as Latvia's greatest poet; this is an exaggeration, for his genuine nobility of mind too usually manifests itself in pompous and dated language, and in too self-consciously 'philosophical' poetry. But his technique is unsurpassed; and in the drama *The Sons of Jacob* (1919; tr. 1924) he contributed a memorable expression of his own dilemma: whether to devote himself to art or to politics. No Latvian writer has greater historical importance. Not the least important aspect of Rainis' work is his use of folkloristic themes. His political preoccupations have to some extent vitiated his achievement; but his realization that a viable literature must come to terms with its time (as well as have roots in the authentic past) gives him an immense importance. (CLP) The early poetry of his wife, Aspazija (*Crimson Flowers*, 1897), puts emphasis on social justice and the rights of women, but at heart it is as romantic as her later work (*A Soul's Journey*, 1933). She also wrote drama, but less successfully than her husband. He wrote his best work in exile.

Jānis Poruks (1871–1911), who studied in Germany, wrote introspective and melancholy lyrics, and was a symbolist and a dreamer. Yet in his novella *Pearl Fisher* (1895) and in other works he introduced psychological realism (as distinct from social realism) into Latvian literature. He began as a pallid Christian idealist, but ended as an almost authentic Nietzschean (q.v.). Poruks died mad. Rūdolfs Blaumanis (1863–1908), originally a business man, began writing fiction in German, but at the age of thirty abandoned it for Latvian. At the time of his early death he was the leading prose author. Blaumanis, whose delicate sensibility abhorred naturalism, was a most versatile writer: his few poems are memorable, his dramas and comedies of peasant life excellent, his novellas exquisitely sensitive and shrewd. He belongs by the side of Rainis (q.v.) as a pioneer; his literary achievement is probably greater. He rejected naturalism in favour of deft psychological realism. He died of tuberculosis in a Finnish sanatorium.

It will be noted that all the outstanding Latvian writers of the first modernist phase had their roots firmly in the past. This applies, too, to Kārlis Skalbe (1879–1945), a unique allegorical writer who has quite properly been compared to Hans Andersen. He wrote much poetry, some short stories and seventy-six exquisite fairy tales. Unfortunately only a few of these last have been translated into English: *Pussy's Water Mill* (tr. 1952). Skalbe's language is limpid, lucid and delicate; he hardly puts a foot wrong. To some critics his achievement, despite his modest aims, is as great as that of any Latvian writer. His world, though a fairy one, is as Latvian as that of any other writer. To a lesser extent Anna Brigadere (1861–1933) shared his gift of making ancient themes meaningful in modern contexts.

Latvia's graduation to independence after the First World War inaugurated a new phase of international modernism. Those communists who went to Russia perished in Stalin's purges; those who stayed behind survived. Jānis Ezeriņš (1891–1924) was one of the first expressionists, although in his later and better fiction he combined realism with 'decadence' in a series of effective tales: *The Bard and the Devil* (1920), *The Street-Organ* (1923–5). This style, although less overtly based on French models, was successfully developed in the fiction of Kārlis Zariņš (1899–1947).

Aleksandrs Čaks (ps. Aleksandrs Čadarainis, 1901–50) certainly has some claims to be regarded as Latvia's most considerable modern poet. He was deeply influenced by Mayakovsky (q.v.), and is regarded as seminal by all his younger contemporaries. He remained in Soviet Latvia. Čaks, who served in the Latvian Red Guards in 1917, is an impassioned, urban poet (the city of his poetry is Riga): he has enormous gifts but is sometimes prone to diffuse them into prosy chaos. However, he remains the great naïve (q.v.) Latvian poet of his generation. Outstanding among his voluminous work is the long poem 'Life', in which he sees himself as an Orpheus-figure, a priest-poet. Čaks is the first thoroughgoing Latvian modernist, and it is entirely logical that new Latvian poets in exile should claim him as their ancestor. Politically, he was an opportunist, since he did not oppose the German occupation of 1941–4, but then began to praise the Soviets again in dreary public verse. But his best poetry, published outside Latvia, is like that of Mayakovsky: non-political. It deals with urban things in a lyrical and excited manner. Esenin (q.v.) influenced Čaks, too; but the latter is a wholly urban poet. *Let Us Get Acquainted* (tr. 1973); *Selected Poems* (tr. 1979).

Freedom for Latvia was effectually ended by the fascist coup d'état of 1934. Most writers found it expedient to abandon modern techniques and concentrate on patriotic themes; such novelists as Kārlis Zariņš (q.v.) turned to historical fiction. Since the Soviet annexation Latvian literature has mainly flourished in exile: although there is no lack of talent in Latvia itself, the desire for free expression of such poets as Ojārs Vācietis (1933) and Imants Ziedonis (1933) is largely frustrated, although the latter's collection *I Go Into Myself* (1968) shows signs of development. Zenta Maurina (1897), who now lives, like a number of other Latvian writers, in West Germany, made her reputation as a critic in Latvia itself: most of her novels have appeared since she went into exile. The best of these is the autobiographical trilogy consisting of *The Far Journey* (1951), *To Venture is Beautiful* (1953) and *The Iron Bolts Break* (1957). Zenta Maurina is a conventional but meticulous and humanitarian writer. She has been paralysed since an attack of polio in childhood. She now writes mainly in the German language, and has been officially honoured by West Germany.

Latvia's leading living playwright, Mārtiņs Ziverts (1903), now lives in Sweden. He is a skilful and over-productive author, a facile symbolist whose plays, were they more widely translated, would prove popular in almost every Western capital. When Stoppard hears of Latvia and of Ziverts, he will 'adapt' him. His early comedies, such as *The Jester* (1938), about Shakespeare, are his best work.

Many of the leading Latvian novelists of the generation born in the first decade of the century went to the USA. There is a selection from the excellent short stories of Knuts Lasiņš (1909): *The Wine of Eternity* (tr. 1957); he has also written novels. Anšlavs Eglītis (1906) is one of the most versatile and gifted of living Latvian writers of fiction; he is also a poet. His best novels sympathetically satirize the world of artists and students: *The Hunters of Brides* (1940) and *Homo Novus* (1943), set in inter-war Latvia, are picaresque novels in the manner of the early work of Iris Murdoch or John Wain (qq.v.), but are less pretentious than the former and better executed than the latter.

Poets in exile include Velta Sniķere (1920), a woman poet of surrealist tendencies now living in London, and Veronika Stēlerte (1912), in Sweden, whose poetry is finely written although hardly unconventional in content. Linards Tauns (ps. Alfrēds Bērzs, 1922–63) and Gunars Saliņš (1924), the leaders of an American school of Latvian poets calling themselves 'Hell's Kitchen' (from the district of Manhattan so named), looked back to Čaks (q.v.) as their master. Tauns is a visionary, urban poet with flashes of Baudelairian (q.v.) power. Saliņš possesses the same intensity of style, although so far he has confined himself to less sensational themes. Latvian poetry now being written is on the whole more impressive than Estonian or even Lithuanian. This is evident from *No Such Place Lasts Summerlong* (tr. 1974), in which Velta Sniķere translates poems by herself and her friend Eglītis (q.v.). This is one of the most interesting volumes of translation of poetry from any language into English to be published in the Seventies.   .

Really modern techniques have found their way into Latvian prose through the autobiographical fiction of the late **Guntis Zariņš** (1922–65) and **Benita Veisberga**. Zariņš' early work was quasi-surrealist; his last, best work is simpler but absorbs the tragic lessons of modernism. *Heroism's Song of Songs* (1962) and *Exile's Song of Songs* (1967) explore the history of Pudikis: his passivity in face of Nazi evil, and then his gradual reawakening, in exile, to his human responsibilities. Zariņš, cut off from his own people, killed himself in exile. Benita Veisberga, also in exile, has from the beginning experimented with the vernacular. *I, Your Gentle Lamb* (1968) is a remarkable first novel, an exploration of the kind of alienation that led to Zariņš' suicide.

Perhaps the most important novel to come out of Latvia in recent years, however, has been *Mayor's Son Kurbads* (1970), by **Jānis Turbads** (ps. **Valdis Zeps**, 1932). Fragments of this novel, whose title could be translated *Mare's Son Kurbads*, appeared in the Soviet-sponsored Latvian magazine *Jaunā Gaita* in 1959 – and created a scandal. This 'fairy tale' was part of an inevitable 'demythologization' process: it boldly broke with the whole folklore tradition – yet very cunningly employed it, in a modernized and non-static form, to do so. .... The scandal was caused not in the minds of the communists, but in those of the numerous American Latvian exiles, who saw it as an attack on their 'aims and morality'. This was reactionary and humourless, and eventually the whole novel appeared, not in Latvia, but in America. It was seen that this wild and witty work was attacking the conservative view of Latvian myth as static and nineteenth-century – not the myth itself, which was utilized throughout. Essentially this extraordinary book tells of how a person becomes so embroiled in the myths that he is 'sentenced to live', and is pushed into the world of reality, which for Turbads seems to be more Freudian than Marxist.

Ilze Škipsna (1928) is an American exile who explores what is perhaps too often described as 'interior space'. Her novels do suffer in fact from lack of roots: the 'real' world is made not to seem to matter, whereas we know that it does matter, since it infringes upon us. There is no lack of observed landscape in Kafka (q.v.), although the way it is observed is quite another matter. And in Kafka reality certainly exists – even though it is menacingly ambiguous. Yet *Beyond the Seventh Bridge* (1965) and *The Unpromised Lands* (1970) do possess a certain sombre power, because the author is dealing with the problem of exile, and is struggling to express her genuine sense of alienation. She would have been more successful in these novels if she had written them without previous literary experimentation in mind, but rather as exercises in realism. The end result would not have been 'realistic', but it would have been more original, and so more authentic.

Alberts Bels (1938) lives in Latvia, and, perhaps not altogether surprisingly, is somewhat more successful – although just as ready to experiment when he has to. He seems not to have been affected by pseudo-Marxist literary demands. *The Investigator* (1967) reads like a realist novel, but its content is hardly realistic in any conventional sense: the 'crime' which it investigates proves only to have been thought of, not committed. *The Cage* (1972) is a fairly open criticism of the world of the 'socialist dream', in which the theoretical benefits and assumptions of Marxist-Leninism are mere illusions which, all together, form a prison.

III

The Tsarist policy of 'Russification' in the latter half of the nineteenth century, which included the banning of all books in Lithuanian (1865–1904), virtually determined the strong nationalist trend of Lithuanian literature in the period. Like Estonia and Latvia, Lithuania knew a brief inter-war independence; now it, too, is one of the states of the USSR. The Roman Catholic clergy, following the example of one of their bishops, began the practice of smuggling books into the country during the period of Russian oppression; this was fortunate for the development of Lithuanian literature, although it was indulged in by clergy not because of any love of freedom but because of their fears for the future of their religion.

Written Lithuanian literature did not begin before the mid-eighteenth century: pressure from neighbours had given little time to develop one. One of the first important nationalistic poems was written by **Antanas Baranauskas** (1835–1902), yet another Catholic priest: his charming but insubstantial *The Grove of Anykščiu* (1858–9) consists of variations on the subject of a pine grove.

Baranauskas virtually gave up the writing of poetry after he took orders; his fellow-priest **Maironis** (ps. **Jonas Mačiulevičius-Mačiulis**, 1862–1932), later a professor of theology at Kaunas University, dominated Lithuanian poetry for two generations: his technique (he introduced accentual verse) laid the foundations of modern Lithuanian poetry; his subject-matter – the Lithuanian past and character – played a part in creating the short-lived independent Lithuania. He wrote heroic dramas. Perhaps inevitably, his work now seems dated; but his historical importance is unquestioned.

A writer of similar historical stature but much greater intrinsic importance is the scholar **Vincas Krėvė-Mickievičius** (1882–1954), usually known simply as Krėvė. He began as a poet, but his best work is in drama and, more particularly, fiction. Krėvė became Foreign Minister in 1940, but went into hiding in the same year, when he learned of Stalin's duplicity. Eventually he settled in the USA. His outstanding early works are *The Legends of the Old Folks of Dainava* (1912), a classic exploitation of Lithuanian folk-lore, the short-story collection *Under a Thatched Roof* (1921) and several dramas. Unfortunately, of these works only the earlier and less mature *Gilshe* (1909; tr. 1947) has been translated. But later stories are in *The Herdsman and the Linden Tree* (tr. 1964). His finest work, the epic novel *The Sons of Heaven and Earth* (1907–63), planned in the early years of this century, is unfinished; this is one of the few modern works about the life of Christ (it contains much else) that possesses true literary quality. Krėvė's account of communist duplicity, a revealing and sharply satirical novel, *The Temptation* (1950), was translated in 1965.

Of the Baltic literatures, it was the Lithuanian and the Finnish that were most susceptible to the ultra-modernistic movements such as Russian futurism (q.v.) and German expressionism (q.v.). Nothing in Estonia or Latvia was as avant garde as the poet **Kazys Binkis'** (1893–1932) magazine *Four Winds*, after which a Lithuanian movement was named. Unfortunately it produced no writer of major talents. Distinct from this, and longer lasting, was the leftist 'Third Front' circle, the 'generation of independence'.

The most important members of this group were the woman poet **Salomėja Neris** (ps. **Salomėja Bačinskaitė**, 1904–45), who turned from a tender lyricism (she was called 'the nightingale') to become a strident communist propagandist, and the novelist **Petras Cvirka** (1909–47), an honest social realist with a genuine satiric edge. Other writers were more loosely associated with it. **Bernardas Brazdžionis** (1907) continued the symbolist tradition developed by the mystical **Vydūnas** (ps. **Vilius Storasta**, 1868–1953), whose most popular work was the tragic drama *The World on Fire* (1928), and by **Jurgis Baltrušaitis** (1873–1944), who began by writing in Russian but whose poems in Lithuanian, dating from 1930, attain quite an impressive technical level. Brazdžionis was an even more thoroughgoing symbolist, nominally a Christian but fundamentally a Platonist yearning for a lush world of ideals. **Jonas Aistis** (ps. **Kossu Alexandravičius**, 1904–73), who went into exile to the USA, was one of the most original modern Lithuanian poets: he devoted himself to personal themes (and signally failed when he tried his hand at patriotic verse, as he understandably did while witnessing, from America, the assimilation of his country into the USSR), and had a style and manner entirely his own. His first book appeared in 1933; much of his best poetry is collected in *Poetry* (1961).

Antanas Vaičulaitis (1906), also now in America, is the leading Lithuanian prose writer of his generation. He made his name with the novel *Valentina* (1936), a sensitive study of a girl who is too emotionally delicate to choose between the man she loves and the man to whom she is indebted. Vaičulaitis has since concentrated on delicate and evanescent short stories. Some of these are fantasies, others are about animals; in the best, nominally realistic tales of country life, an autonomous world of nature almost takes precedence over the human world.

The native Lithuanian genius has of course suffered under Soviet dictation – as any writer suffers under any dictation – but it has done so possibly less than that of any of the other recently created states of the USSR. The versatile **Juozas Grūsas** (1901) has quietly lived at Kaunas since 1944, writing almost as he likes. Dramatist, novelist and story writer, Grūsas does not interest Lithuanian critics in exile as much as he should, despite the fact that he has written distinctly modernist plays and surrealistic (q.v.) prose. Perhaps this is because he is modernistic only when he feels he needs to be. His outstanding and somewhat Dostoevskian stories, as in *The Light of Anger* (1969) and *The Luckiest of all – Myself* (1973), explore the inner world of victims and cripples with subtlety and, above all, compassion. All his drama is excellent: realistic 'problem plays', historical dramas such as *Herkus Mantas* (1957) – and, above all, his 'absurdist' (q.v.) plays such as *Love, Jazz and the Devil* (1967), which paved the way for his important absurdist successor **Kasys Saja** (1932), Lithuania's leading modern dramatist. *The Holy Lake* (1971) is typical: behind its 'absurdity' lie both savage satire of Sovietism and a folklorist structure. **Kostas Ostrauskas** (1926) has written more superficial absurdist drama.

Socialist realism (q.v.) has not prevented Lithuanian poets from looking back to the example of **Vytautas Mačernis** (1920–45), whose attitudes were profoundly modernistic, even to the point of justifying the frequent description of him as an 'existentialist' (q.v.). The most talented poet in Soviet Lithuania is **Eduardas Mieželaitis** (1919) whose communist verse is sincere but embarrassing; his descriptive poetry is superior. Two more important Lithuanian writers who went to America are the novelist and playwright **Algirdas Landsbergis** (1924) and the poet Henrikas Radauskas (q.v.), regarded by most critics as Lithuania's finest poet yet. Landsbergis made his name with *The Journey* (1955), a subtle and satirical study of a Lithuanian immigrant to the United States, for which he drew upon much autobiographical material. In his plays, which have been performed throughout the USA, Landsbergis has dealt with the situation of Lithuanians both in their own country and in America. **Henrikas Radauskas'** (1910–70) first book was published in 1935; but it was after his exile that his poetry developed. He was born in Poland. Although indisputably a modernist, he is certainly the odd man out of modern Lithuanian poetry, since he cannot be assigned to any main trend. The comparison with Mandelstahm (q.v.) that is often made is apt; but Radauskas was a minor poet. He tried to devote himself to that aspect of poetry that is art; but life and its anguish make themselves ironically present. He did not quite achieve the aesthetic ideal he set himself. Many of his best poems have the quality of a series of paintings:

> In a room which has been dead for twenty years
> An old woman's shadow is yawning, turning an empty
> Coffee mill, the clock shows Sunday,
> The cuckoo fell silent, the guest was stabbed in the tavern.

It is not surprising that some of Radauskas' poems attracted Randell Jarrell (q.v.), and were translated by him. He might have been a great poet – there are flashes – but became a victim of Western influences which were abstract to him: he lacks Mandelstahm's warmth and rootedness in life.

British Literature

I

Although no country had more good novelists than Great Britain at the beginning of this century, the European naturalist movement (q.v.) had little direct effect on British fiction. It did, however, influence the work of **George Gissing** (1857–1903), who in turn has exercised a strong, although largely subterranean, influence on later writers (particularly on Orwell, q.v.). Gissing, an unhappy and unhealthy man, led a life of almost unrelieved misery. At college he stole to help a prostitute he had befriended; after serving a prison sentence he went to America for a year; he failed to support himself there, returned – and married the same woman. She was a nagging psychopath, and Gissing's life was for ten years a nightmare. Then she died, and he went out and picked up and married a similarly impossible woman. When she became insane Gissing found a Frenchwoman who understood him and with whom he was happy. He never achieved financial stability, and kept his head above water only by constant overwork – which subsequently weakened his constitution and led to his early death. His close friend H.G. Wells (q.v.), who was with him at his death, wrote of him with great acumen: he called him 'an extraordinary blend of a damaged joy-loving human being hampered by inherited gentility and a classical education'.

There is something a little repulsive about Gissing: a genteel defensiveness and a not always wholly repressed whining self-pity. Yet at his best, as in *Born in Exile* (1892), Gissing is not merely a good but a major novelist – perhaps as great in achievement as his older, more sophisticated and more obviously gifted contemporary George Meredith (q.v.). Some of Gissing's twenty-two novels are poor and thin, and the writing is cliché-ridden and weary. But at least in *Born in Exile*, the bitter tale of a free-thinker who destroys himself by pretending (against his principles) to be a Christian in order to gain love and position, Gissing wrote a major novel – and one of Dostoevskian overtones.

His original model had been the Dickens who recorded the seamy side of life; he wrote of this with sourness and no humour – but managed to add something. Personally doomed by his own foolish propensity to 'redeem' and 'genteelize' lower-class women, he was a naturalist in spite of himself: his characters are often driven – sometimes one must read between the lines – by their anguished sexual preoccupations, as he was. There is much worth reading in him beside *Born in Exile*, his masterpiece: *Demos* (1886), in which he expresses his distrust of the people en masse, *A Life's Morning* (1888), *New Grub Street* (1891), *The Private Papers of Henry Ryecroft* (1903), and more. He still requires his critical due. He was particularly adept at describing genteel poverty and its wretchedness.

George Meredith (1828–1909), although nearly thirty years older than Gissing (q.v.), is a modernist *manqué*. He deserves credit for his intentions; and if he must ultimately be said to have failed – and this is by no means a foregone conclusion – then his was a very notable failure. The spirit of naturalism also influenced Meredith, although in a different

211

and even less direct way than in the case of Gissing: he retained a somewhat obstinate conviction that everything may be explained mechanically – this is at the heart of both his (uninteresting and unconvincing) optimism and his (interesting) sense of the comic, which in some respects anticipates that of Wyndham Lewis (q.v.), and which is not really as well understood as it ought to be. He had a hard time establishing a reputation – even at the height of his Victorian fame there were influential cliques who had no use for him – and he had not long been dead before he became widely unread. And yet he was a tireless experimenter; and he will never quite lie down. He is simply too good and too substantial for that ever to happen. No one's novels sound more interesting in detailed summary. He would have liked to have been an ironic comedian in the manner of the Brazilian Machado de Assis (q.v.), whose work he did not know; but his subtle and intelligent novels too often tend to become victim to his meretriciousness, his false philosophical optimism and the puzzling manner in which he transforms his huge imaginative energy into something merely whimsical or even plain crazy. And yet, as Henry James (q.v.) carefully said, he did 'the best things best'. He has his magnificent moments, and these are prophetic of what was to come in the modern novel.

Meredith was badly hamstrung by the Victorian necessity for sexual reticence: his realistic view of women, and of sexual matters in general, cut sharply across the Victorian fantasy, which enshrined women only to patronize them and neutralize their (in anthropological terms) magical qualities. His imaginative sympathy really was with women – as victims of this male distortion – and it involved him in the kind of extreme difficulties with which we, in turn, must sympathize. Meredith's sympathy with women and his understanding of sexual problems led to some inspired passages (such as the scene, in *The Egoist*, where Clare watches Vernon Whitford asleep under the cherry tree; or earlier, the masturbation scenes in *The Ordeal of Richard Feverel*) but never, alas, to a completely successful novel. The only book in which the notorious Meredithian difficulties are wholly absent is the comparatively early and simple *Rhoda Fleming* (1865). However, despite the existence during his lifetime of a band of loyal (but not all comprehending) 'Meredithians', he has not had his due even for what he attempted. He is, after all, as V.S. Pritchett has said in an excellent study of him, 'a storehouse of ways and means' and 'rather hard and intelligently merciless – which is refreshing in the nineteenth century'. And the best of his poetry, despite his unfortunate penchant for trying to sound – and sometimes sounding – Shakespearean, is at the least interesting, and sometimes more. He awaits an inspired study.

George Moore (1852–1933) deserves to be considered both as a nineteenth- and a twentieth-century writer. He is the most seriously neglected major novelist of the past century: too many critics have confused his best work with his frequently sloppy and foolish persona (even if he was ultimately, in Sherard Vines' oddly apt words, 'a dear good soul'). He was a pioneer, as the 'English naturalist' – a category he may be said to have invented for himself, in order to get a real start as a novelist – as autobiographer and as post-realist novelist; he is one of the best writers of short stories in the English language (yet, in a recent survey of this form by a reputable critic, he gets exactly one sentence). Moore is a remarkable illustration of the fact that great writing frequently springs from personal humiliation: the sources of his energy certainly include his foolish boastfulness and his sexual voyeurism. He turned both these exceptionally humiliating characteristics to creative account.

His first important book was the autobiographical *Confessions of a Young Man* (1886 rev. 1926): he needed to satirize what he had been as a very young man in Paris. This book conveys an accurate sense of the genuine (as distinct from the theatrical) element in his immature 'paganism' of those early days – by isolating it and thus keeping it at a proper comic distance. As early, then, as 1886, Moore had abandoned any serious attempt to present himself in conventionally realist terms. This is so incongruous as coming from the later self-styled champion of Zolaesque naturalism (q.v.) that it has been overlooked. By the time he came to write the autobiographical trilogy *Hail and Farewell* (1911–14) he had perfected the process. By then he knew, as he put it in a letter (1913) to Robert Ross, that a 'man only seems natural when he is speaking aside or to himself: he seems quite mechanical when he is uttering little phrases to people standing. . . .'

But his first undoubted masterpiece was a work avowedly naturalist, and certainly realist: *Esther Waters* (1894). This is a tender study of a servant betrayed and left pregnant, and of her fight for her son. Grudgingly acknowledged as a classic, it has nevertheless been consistently underrated. It is too moving, perhaps, and too beautifully simple without being sentimental, for the average professional critic. Virginia Woolf (q.v.) claimed that Moore 'had not the strength to project Esther from himself'; but she merely put a finger on a weakness of her own. All Zola's naturalism did for Moore was to give him a method to get started. *Esther Waters* is naturalist in intention, but its effect is, eventually, anti-naturalist: the 'message' is that compassion is all, not that character or environment is destiny. However, naturalism taught Moore not to be reticent about sexual matters, and it purged him of the gentility that even today bedevils English literature and most of the criticism of it.

Moore went on to produce at least three more major novels. The first was *The Lake* (1905); later came *The Brook Kerith* (1916), the story of Paul's betrayal of a Christ who, rescued from the cross, has come to reject his earlier fanaticism; *Héloise and Abelard* (1921) is hardly read now, and is not in print – but it is another masterpiece. These later novels (the new manner began with *The Lake*, but was not developed until *The Brook Kerith*) demand to be read aloud if the reader is fully to appreciate how so lyrical and uninterrupted (but varied) a 'seamless' flow can contain so much complex material. There is, after all, a part of ourselves that perceives our experience as an unstitched and seamless whole (cf. Bergson, q.v.); Moore seized on this aspect of perception and made himself its master.

And yet his greatest achievement of all is in the realm of the short story: from the relatively early *Celibates* (1895), through *The Untilled Field* (1903) and *A Story Teller's Holiday* (1918) to the perfection of *Celibate Lives* (1927), which is the final revision of *In Single Strictness* (1922). 'Albert Nobbs', originally from *A Story Teller's Holiday* but included in *Celibate Lives*, is the greatest comic short story of the century in any language: magnificently told, psychologically immaculate, absolutely original. *The Untilled Field* (as Graham Hough has observed) precedes Joyce's *Dubliners* (q.v.) just as *Confessions of a Young Man* precedes his *Portrait of the Artist as a Young Man*.

There were once excuses for not looking at Moore; in his famous quarrel with Yeats (q.v.) he made himself look foolish; his disciples (they included Charles Morgan, q.v.) were the most mediocre any great writer has gathered around him. These excuses are no longer viable. Moore is a very important – and modern – writer indeed, both extrinsically and intrinsically: far from ever having left him behind, there is a whole readership that has yet to catch up with him.

W.H. Hudson (1841–1922) was born of American parents who emigrated to Argentina; he went to England in 1870 and became an English citizen in 1900. Although he gained wide recognition with *Green Mansions* (1915), he is now a rather neglected writer. Conrad said of him to Ford (qq.v.): 'He writes as the grass grows. The Good God makes it be there . . .' He was a brilliant and unusual observer of countless small natural things; his observations fly, like richly coloured birds, across the bleakness of his recollections of Spanish-American savagery and of his own poverty and neglect. *Green Mansions*, the story of a bird woman, is still insufficiently acknowledged as a classic; that it was derived from an earlier and inferior novel (Lady Morgan's *The Missionary*) makes little difference, since it transforms and improves it.

R.B. Cunninghame Graham (1852–1936), once the toast of many distinguished authors (including the impeccably generous and perceptive Ford, q.v.), is now buried in oblivion. This is not wholly undeserved. Three-quarters Scottish and the rest Spanish, he was a fierce and flamboyant personality, who lived an adventurous life: as a young man he pioneered in South America and America; later, in England, he got himself jailed for championing the then unpopular cause of justice for working men. He should be revived in selection. He was at one time an MP and later helped found the Scottish Nationalist Party. Conrad (q.v.) valued him greatly. He was at heart an anarchist – and a not unintelligent one. Edward Garnett's selection, *Thirty Tales and Sketches* (1929, and *Rodeo* (1936), edited by A.F. Tschiffely, reveal an original minor writer, one of the few British masters of *costumbrismo* (q.v.), a portraitist of wild places, whose lawless bohemianism has – despite its occasional over-dependence on rhetoric – a fine and genuine quality. Cunninghame Graham is a Kipling-in-reverse: he suffers from the same violent anarchic passions, but channels them into socialism instead of imperialism. He shamelessly indulged himself in both his Scottish-dour and Spanish *hidalgo* aspects, but had a clear sense of the places he wrote about, and his uncompromisingly shame- (as distinct from guilt-) directed approach is sincere – more sincere, less puerile, than that of, say, the unhappily ambisexual Roy Campbell (q.v.).

Joseph Conrad (originally **Teodor Jozef Konrad Kornzeniowski**, 1851–1924), a Pole, was the son of a literary man who was sent into political exile; he went to sea, and soon began serving in English ships – he passed for master in 1880, and took up British citizenship in 1886. He began writing while still at sea. His first novel, *Almayer's Folly*, was published in 1895, and gained critical success; but he did not get public recognition and the relative (it was only ever relative for him) financial independence that flows from it until *Chance* (1913), which is not one of his best novels. He wrote English much better than he spoke it; and each of his novels cost him an inordinate amount of nervous energy. The influence and help of Ford Madox Ford (q.v.) has been deliberately underestimated by critics; it was, however, vital in his development. Conrad and Ford wrote three novels in collaboration: *The Inheritors* (1901), *Romance* (1903), which was a kind of rehearsal for *Nostromo*, and *The Nature of a Crime* (1924), which was written in 1906–7 and first published by Ford in his *English Review*. Ford also wrote a small part of *Nostromo* and other larger parts of other works.

The best of Conrad's fiction has been the subject of an exorbitant amount of critical exegesis, in both Great Britain and the United States. Recognition of his supremacy as a novelist was a cornerstone of the ultra-dogmatic school of the critic F.R. Leavis (q.v.) at Downing College, Cambridge, which was influential between 1930 and 1960 (Leavis has written well on him). There have been remarkably few dissentients from the basic assumption of his greatness; his position as a great novelist remains secure and undisturbed. The case for the prosecution (if there is one) has never really been presented. And at the very least this does pay tribute to Conrad's massive seriousness, his great struggle with himself, his wide range – and his extraordinary mastery of written English. Henry James (q.v.), it seems, could turn his sexual deficiency into a triumph of art; Conrad, likewise, turned both a clumsy incapacity for full human relationships (perhaps this culminates in the partial portrait of his wife Jessie as Winnie Verloc in *The Secret Agent*), and a difficulty with the English language, into a triumph. He was by nature a chronic depressive, of pathological proportions, who positively needed misery and penury to goad him into his best work. Here is another sceptic, anxiously probing at heroic and moral truisms, masterfully avoiding what he hardly understood, though personally yearned for: friendship, love, communion. It so happened that Conrad's genius coincided in certain respects with that of the English language, which (as is natural in a Pole) he approached for its Latin rather than its Anglo-Saxon qualities. But he worked desperately hard to achieve the coincidence.

Conrad's unquestioned masterpieces are *Typhoon* (1902), *Heart of Darkness* (1902), *Nostromo* (1904), *The Secret Agent* (1907) and *Under Western Eyes* (1911). *Heart of Darkness*, which contains the quintessence of his art, is set in the Congo – where Conrad himself, in difficult circumstances, discovered his true vocation. This is Conrad's exploration of his narrator Marlow's recollections (on the Thames in London) of a nightmare journey into the interior. It demonstrates the firmness of his control, through style and tone, over his material; agonizedly, it shows human sympathy existing where an 'official' view would allow of none. It is marred by rhetoric – 'purple passages' – as Leavis was the first to point out; but this is understandable, the story remains intact, and Conrad later rid himself of the habit – in *The Secret Agent* he has almost perfected his English style.

Conrad's chief subjects include revolution – its causes, its excesses and its betrayal; and the evils of acquisitiveness. His concern is always imaginative rather than political. There lies at the heart of Conrad's best fiction a horrified awareness of evil, a scepticism about the validity of human attitudes, and a terrified recognition of human solitude. In *The Nigger of the 'Narcissus'* (1897) he shows how sympathy itself can threaten survival; in *Lord Jim* (1900), again narrated by Marlow, he demonstrates how imagination and idealism can corrupt and lead to cowardice – and also how impossible non-intuitive moral judgement (the prerogative of establishments and the systems they perpetuate) is to achieve (in *Heart of Darkness* we find two moral opposites in profound kinship. ...). In *The Secret Agent* Conrad found a sardonic objective correlative (q.v.) – Ford provided some of the material – for his uneasiness over his marriage (which was, at bottom, an unhappy one – but any marriage Conrad made would have been thus: he both required a family and could not endure it, and his lack of endurance of it sparked off his imagination) and over the role of the writer (his treatment of the *Künstlerschuld*, q.v., theme), whom he projects into the morally insensitive dealer in pornography, Verloc, who gets more involved in the game of spying and terrorism than he had intended (he thought he could play with evil); but the characters transcend their origins in the author's mind. It is probably true to say, as a critic has, that Conrad does not 'explore human relationships'; but he does use this incapacity to show how they can fail to exist; at other times he can imply them very cleverly. The lack of love between the comically sinister Verloc and his wife is one of the most chilling things in the whole of his work. There is often a ponderousness about Conrad's style that not everyone finds to their taste (he is sometimes a bit too much the Polish 'master of English prose'); but of his stature, his subtlety, his seriousness, there can be no doubt whatsoever. His persona was that of an 'English' Tory country gentleman; but as *Nostromo* and *The Secret Agent* demonstrate, he was at bottom a profound pessimist, with a strong sense of justice, who saw society as a thoroughly rotten fabric. And in Mrs Gould of *Nostromo* he showed that, like all great writers, he knew the heart of rottenness to lie in the trampling down of the feminine.

Rudyard Kipling (1865–1936) is a strange case indeed. He is certainly not less than a major writer of fiction (though only a minor poet) and yet, more than any writer of his stature, he seems to suffer, not simply from ignorance or lack of education, but from an advanced philistinism and, at times, an insensitive proto-fascism. His attitudes, taken simply as attitudes, form an offensive constellation: racist, blindly imperialist, British 'public school' in the worst sense, feudal. ... But actually, of course, his thought is confused. The real man does not hold these views at all: unlike his actually philistine counterpart, the stupid British Tory (not the intelligent Johnsonian one, of whom Ford's Tietjens, q.v., was the last), Kipling has an imagination. A good deal of Victorian imperialistic sentiment (which was not of course as 'offensive' then as it is now) undoubtedly released repressed sexual energies: Elgar's symphonies, for example, are as much 'about' a series of sexual climaxes and sexual guilts as they are 'about' anything else. But Elgar was a robust and relatively uncomplicated Roman Catholic. The evidence suggests that Kipling – and here lies the secret of his creative strength – was a sado-masochistic ambisexual. His rationalizations of his (in his own Victorian terms) 'hideous' impulses took two forms: one was what he thought were his political doctrines; but the other was often a true objective correlative, a creative resolution of his severe emotional and sexual problems. And in many of Kipling's stories and one or two of his novels we find instinctive wisdom, love, kindness – and, sometimes, terror. As a writer he was, after all, at his best, very good – his Nobel Prize of 1907 is not incongruous, as is, say, Galsworthy's – and that is what is really important. He is one of the best of the immensely popular writers of the twentieth century.

Kipling was born in Bombay; after some unhappy years in England with a relative and then four years at school in Westward Ho! in Devon, he returned to India. W.E. Henley, who among other better things was a chauvinist, enthused about his early *Barrack-Room Ballads*, and printed them in the *National Observer*. Kipling collected his first stories in *Plain Tales from the Hills* (1888) and *Soldiers Three* (1888). *Barrack-Room Ballads* were collected in book form in 1890 and 1892. In the latter years Kipling married the sister of an American journalist, Wolcot Balestier; he seems to have been in love with both brother and sister, and he lived in Vermont until 1896, when a quarrel with Wolcot caused him to leave. After this he settled in Sussex, eventually purchasing a large house, Batemans, from which august headquarters he continued to issue prose and verse until the end of his life.

Kipling's tales are at their best when their sheer realism becomes independent of the code of 'honour' that he consciously built up – and which was largely responsible for his immense popularity. Kipling, when he was not trying to think, possessed an uncanny insight into the minds of the common soldiers and officers about whom he wrote so vividly. Kipling's code consists of 'fair play' (approximating rather to the 'fairness ethic' that Erich Fromm has wryly distinguished as a capitalist contribution to society), British public school solidarity and loyalty (this was partly fantasy on Kipling's part, as he showed in *Stalky and Co.*, 1899, where he transformed his own timid role at a rather enlightened non-public school into that of a rebellious hero playing the game against the game), self-reliance and paternalism. He applies this, in the course of his fiction, to many situations, in particular to animals (*The Jungle Books*, 1894, 1895) and to simple masculine situations – military, engineering and so on. As C.S. Lewis (q.v.) pointed out, Kipling longed to be in on all masculine mysteries, to be 'one of the boys'. This was one of the channels his homosexual impulses took. Max Beerbohm (q.v.) put his finger on Kipling's motivations when he wrote: 'Mr Kipling is so far masculine that he has never displayed a knowledge of women as they are; but the unreality of his male creatures, with his worship of them, makes his name ring quaintly like a pseudonym. ... Strange that these heroes ... were not ... created out of the inner consciousness of a lady novelist ...' This is malicious but just. Eliot (q.v.) tried to defend Kipling from the charge of fascism by calling him a Tory (Eliot was insensitive, however, to fascism, and was at heart a benign anti-semite: he was unfit to pass those kinds of judgement). But Kipling was not a Tory: he was a Tory-anarchist – a passionate, confused man – whose confusions, however, passionately appealed to the thousands of Englishmen like him. Ford's Edward Ashburnham, from *The Good Soldier* (q.v.), would have read and admired Kipling; but he would not have seen that Kipling projected his own 'cheap cynicism about the female sex', his own propensity and 'relish' for 'the ugly word, the ugly action, the ugly atmosphere' (Beerbohm) into his characters. He has, too, a pathic slyness and cunning that give his tales, with their pristine and lyrical feelings, not only technical mastery but also great power. His best novel is *Kim* (1901): here the writer took over entirely, and the British and Indian characters are seen with equal imaginative sympathy.

In verse Kipling is what Orwell (q.v.) called 'a good bad' poet. 'Danny Deever' has an authentic *frisson*, but the conflict in Kipling's mind between his false code ('a sneakin' shootin' hound': ''e shot a comrade sleeping') and his sexual and sadistic fascination with hanging is too nastily apparent, and the poem doesn't have the strength to resolve it. His poems, whether ballads or nostalgic lyrics, seldom get beyond the bounds of self-indulgence. But they are much more odd and sometimes appealing than over-sophisticated readers think: he is very interesting to re-read, and not at all what he is taken to be.

Kipling's best work arose out of confusion and even viciousness; it also has a strange beauty, something not altogether definable – a gentleness and childlikeness – which functions as a soother and a neutralizer of the violence of the 'Freudian' elements. He was ungenerous in his views; but it would be ungenerous of us to take these at face value, and to refuse to judge him from his best books. His collected works were published in thirty-one volumes (1913–38), and are still available.

If **Arthur Conan Doyle** (1859–1930) will eventually be forgotten as a historical novelist, he will be immortal for his creation of Sherlock Holmes. His historical romances are excellent, and some remain in print; but they are romances. His photograph of his fantasy-self as Sherlock Holmes, however, is an offbeat literary achievement: a Victorian portrait of an eccentric, with innumerable implications, and embellished with a splendid and absorbing ingenuity. Conan Doyle's Holmes is the dream-paradigm of the brilliant decadent, cunningly written from a non-decadent point of view; it transcends most of the decadent literature of its time. Holmes, really a dope-fiend, is his own great enemy Moriarty: he is the supreme criminal in the eyes of his time, but politely presented, and that is why people loved him. There is no emphasis on virtue in these essentially dia-bolical tales. But Conan Doyle did not know that.

H.G. Wells (1866–1946), despite his huge and continuing popularity with all sections of the public, is with critics a persistently underrated and misunderstood writer. He himself disclaimed interest in his literary reputation and stated, in a mock-obituary of 1936, that he was 'much more the scientific man than the artist, though he dealt in literary forms'. But he was a major novelist, praised fulsomely by Henry James (q.v.), and told (1920), by Ford (q.v.), one of the most perceptive men of his time, that he was a 'genius' who wasted too much of his time on 'social speculation'. The reasons why Wells the propagandist, the inconsistent and irascible generalizer, was led to betray – at least in part – the creative writer in himself, and the ways in which he unconsciously rapped himself over the knuckles for this betrayal, are exceptionally interesting.

The most destructive criticism of Wells the 'thinker', the 'Utopian', is Max Beerbohm's (q.v.) deadly parody 'Perkins and Mankind', in which he has Wells writing an account of an old man happily going to the 'Municipal Lethal Chamber' on 'General Cessation Day', 'walking with a firm step in the midst of his progeny. ... He will not be thinking of himself. ... He will be filled with joy at the thought that he is about to die for the good of the race ... for the beautiful young breed of men and women who, in simple, antiseptic garments, are disporting themselves so gladly on this day of days. ...'

But Wells the Utopian, the public figure with 'brains but no tact' (his uncle said this of Wells when he was fourteen), is only the least important part of a story that is more complicated than is generally acknowledged. The popular idea of Wells – publicist, novelist, pioneer of science (better called speculative) fiction – seems to be that he betrayed the glowing optimism of a lifetime only in his gloomy last work, *Mind at the End of its Tether* (1945). Nothing could be further from the truth. The root of the false view lies in the notion that Wells was an optimist. He was nothing of the sort. He was, it is true, a cheeky satyr, full of good humour and tactlessness, who thoroughly enjoyed gatecrashing a high society that he despised; but his continuous sexual curiosity (he was exceptionally good to his many cast-off mistresses) and his ebullience hid a gloomy dreamer: a man of profound imaginative capabilities, who read Blake as well as science text-books. Allying itself to this pessimistic streak was Wells' feeling of social inferiority, which never really left him, and which he exploited to superb comic effect in his early straight novels. It was the submerged poetic, subversive elements in Wells, working through the scientifically trained exterior, that led him to make his most startling prophecies and anticipations. For besides the better known scientific prophecies, some of which we cannot yet assess, Wells made many astute sociological guesses; all of these are negative, satirical, gloomy.

The cannibals of Rampole Island (in the neglected dystopia *Mr. Blettsworthy on Rampole Island*, 1928) who call their enemies 'cannibals' are as good an example of doublethink as anything in Orwell's *Animal Farm* (q.v.); their failure to refer to un-pleasant manifestations of state authority by their proper names (criminals are 'reproached', not punished) is worthy of Swift. Compare this morbid side of Wells – the far future envisaged in *The Time Machine* (1895), the death of Griffin in *The Invisible Man* (1897) – with the antiseptic, imagination-free, laboured naïvety of a *Modern Utopia* (1905) or the lecture on the World Encyclopaedia project (1936). ... In all the fiction in which Wells tried to creat a Utopia he never quite knew what to do with it: he did not believe in Utopias. But he felt guilty about the pessimism which his imagination generated.

Wells' range is very wide. As a writer of speculative fiction he has not been equalled for versatility, ingenuity or credibility; the atmosphere of those early tales is unfor-gettable, unrepeatable, poetic. He is a great comic novelist: *Kipps* (1905), *Tono Bungay* (1909), *The History of Mr. Polly* (1909). His later and more complex fiction has been unjustly neglected. *Mr. Blettsworthy on Rampole Island*, although flawed, is one of the most memorable of modern dystopias; *The Bulpington of Blup* (1933), in part a portrait of Ford, is a notable psychological study. Wells' work as would-be shaper of human destiny and popularizer of science did partly undermine his creativity: he never, after *Mr. Polly*, reached the point at which his imagination could function positively. But his earlier work deserves the praise James conferred on it ('You are a very swagger performer indeed' who 'makes even dear old Dickens turn ... in his grave'); the best of his later work demands responsible reconsideration. There is as yet no truly perceptive study of him.

By contrast the talent of **John Galsworthy** (1867–1933) is drab. He cannot hope to achieve more than his recent enshrinement as author of the original script (so to speak) of the television soap opera of *The Forsyte Saga*. His best work, which is very modest in achievement, is in the drama and the earlier part of the *Saga*. He won the Nobel Prize in 1932. Easy as it is to sneer at him, D.H. Lawrence's (q.v.) attack on him as a 'sneaking old cynic' cannot really be countered: we find ourselves apologizing rather than pointing to positive virtues.

Galsworthy wrote nothing of account before *The Island Pharisees* (1904) and the first of the *Forsyte Saga: The Man of Property* (1906). The latter remains the best of his novels, and even Lawrence conceded that its satire on the upper crust of society 'really had a certain noble touch'. But even this and its successors, *The Country House* (1908) and *Fraternity* (1909), can hardly be described as important books. One has only to think of Ford's *The Good Soldier* (q.v.) to realize just how ordinary they are. The characters are flat and lifeless;

the redeeming factor is the author's genuine but over-cautious social indignation, which expresses itself in the form of satire. By 1922, introducing the first Forsyte trilogy (*The Man of Property*; *In Chancery*, 1920; *To Let*, 1921), he was able to say: 'Human Nature, under its changing pretensions ... is and ever will be very much of a Forsyte, and might, after all, be a much worse animal'. He remained a courteous, considerate, conscientious man; but as a serious writer he was finished. The Forsytes who had been the villains of the early novel now became the heroes; nor in the later volumes (the trilogy is called *A Modern Comedy*, 1929) did Galsworthy display the least understanding of the post-war generation. And in all these later novels Galsworthy indulges himself in the middlebrow habit of manipulating his characters according to his emotions, which became progressively more sentimental and conservatively 'worthy'. He was not at any time a major writer. His dramas, notably *The Silver Box* (1903), *Strife* (1909) and *Justice* (1910), are well made, restrained, and display a modulated passion for social justice. They represent Galsworthy at his most skilful and agreeable. But his undeservedly high reputation justifies the harshness of D.H. Lawrence's verdict: 'Vulgarity pays, and cheap cynicism smothered in sentimentality pays better than anything else'.

   Arnold Bennett (1867–1931) is both very much more gifted and more puzzling. To many readers of modern poetry he is no more than a footnote to Ezra Pound's (q.v.) unkind poem 'Mr. Nixon':

> ...'Consider
> Carefully the reviewer.
>
> I was as poor as you are;
> When I began I got, of course,
> Advance on royalties, fifty at first,' said Mr. Nixon,
> 'Follow me, and take a column,
> Even if you have to work free. ...
> I never mentioned a man but with the view
> of selling my own works. ...
>
> And give up verse, my boy,
> There's nothing in it.'...

This goes well enough with 'I write for as much money as I can get' and the admonition by Bennett to those 'parasites' (poets) to try to understand that nothing matters so much as cash and the preservation of 'decency'. Galsworthy (q.v.), possibly to his credit, would never even have considered such philistine sentiments; the irony is that Bennett was, incomparably, the better novelist. Even in the late Twenties, when rising critics such as Edwin Muir (q.v.) found it necessary to dismiss Bennett, they would admit that in *The Old Wives' Tale* (1908) he had 'beautifully and profoundly expressed the passing away of human delight in possessions'.

   The truth is that Bennett's 'philistinism', while tactless and reprehensible in itself, was part of an ironic self-defence. He could not quite understand how his ambition had driven him into being a writer: there must have been something wrong there: he had been a cocky, self-confident law-clerk and prentice-journalist down from Hanley (one of the Five Towns) to escape from a puritanical atmosphere and his father's domination: a man with an eye on the brass should have been able to do better than that. The puritan in him felt guilty, too, about the self-indulgence (he was a famed sybarite) that success in letters had allowed him. As a popular recommender of books to a middlebrow audience (in his capacity as critic of *The New Age* and *The Evening Standard*) he did much to push his fellow authors, displayed as consistently high standards as any such columnist ever has, and was remarkably unspiteful and unpretentious. 'Mr. Nixon' is a fair comment on the value of certain of Bennett's pronouncements, many of which were as absurd as George Moore's (q.v.); it is not a fair comment on the man himself – who was generous, sensitive and vulnerable – or on his best work.

Bennett is a strange case. Throughout his life he issued a stream of pot-boiling novels, instructive handbooks on *Self-Help* lines and popular 'philosophies of life'; yet this did not corrupt his creativity. As late as 1923, when he was fifty-six, he produced a novel whose flaws of style and presentation cannot prevent its being a masterpiece – in creation of atmosphere, in psychological acuteness and, above all, in warmth of feeling: *Riceyman Steps*. His really important books are: *The Old Wives' Tale*, the *Clayhanger* trilogy (*Clayhanger*, 1910; *Hilda Lessways*, 1911; *These Twain*, 1915); *The Card* (1911); *Riceyman Steps* (1923); *Lord Raingo* (1924). His last novel, *Imperial Palace* (1930), is as sceptical about great hotels as it is awe-inspired; and is a lively and amusing performance. He knew nothing whatever about poetry, and was silly when he talked about it (hence Pound's justified satire); but although he regarded literature as a business, his imagination never became corrupt; the quality of *Riceyman Steps* is as high as that of anything he ever wrote.

Bennett's first models were the 'French' George Moore (q.v.) and the later French nineteenth-century novel. He was always more at home in French than in English literature. Although influenced by naturalism, Bennett was a realist without (in his novels) any philosophy; however, the grim puritanism and drab ugliness of the Five Towns affected him deeply, and are reflected in the best books. *The Old Wives' Tale* (1908) is his greatest achievement: its people, as Frank Swinnerton has said, 'are within his heart as well as his head'; he is at his best here because he is 'both humorous and humane'. This is a great unsophisticated classic. *The Card* (1911, called *Dendry the Audacious* in America), a kind of delightedly objective self-study, did something that had not previously been done in English fiction, even by Wells – the thread was taken up again by the less gifted William Cooper (q.v.) forty years later; but *The Card* has not been bettered. For all his lapses, his spasmodic puritanism, his unevenness, Bennett succeeded in achieving the 'all-embracing compassion' that he believed to be the 'essential characteristic of the really good novelist'. His *Journals* (1932–3; abr. 1954) help to give an insight into his underrated sensibilities. Of his other more notable books the Clayhanger trilogy is especially worth mentioning: *Clayhanger* (1910), *Hilda Lessways* (1911), *These Twain* (1915). There is an almost unknown sequel to *The Card*: *The Old Adam* (1913).

Stephen Hudson (ps. **Sidney Schiff**, 1868–1944) presents a complete contrast: a member of the so-called Bloomsbury Group (centred in Cambridge and the Bloomsbury district of London, and including Leonard and Virginia Woolf, q.v., the art-critics Clive Bell and Roger Fry, the painter Duncan Grant, the writers Lytton Strachey and E.M. Forster, qq.v., the economist John Maynard Keynes, and many others; chief common or overlapping interests were Fabianism, beautiful young men – such as Rupert Brooke, q.v. – and humanism), he was self-consciously literary. He completed Scott Moncrieff's famous translation of Proust – notoriously badly. But his fiction deserves to be remembered. His best book is *A True Story* (1930; rev. 1949), which is a revision and condensation of three earlier novels and part of a fourth: *Richard Kurt* (1919), *Elinor Colhouse* (1921), *Prince Hempseed* (1922) and *Myrtle* (1925). This, the story of Richard Kurt, is an original and economically written study of motivation – and of, as Walter Allen has pointed out, 'the Oedipus Complex working its doom throughout a man's life'. Hudson was aware of the discoveries of psychoanalysis, and his unobtrusive use of them was both intelligent and pioneering. The beginning of *A True Story* is the best part: the account of

Kurt's adolescence and of his life in America. I agree with Walter Allen (who has been largely responsible for drawing attention to Hudson's distinction) that the succeeding parts, in which Kurt's relationships with two women are explored, are less satisfactory: Hudson was weak when dealing with women, and he cannot disguise this. But when he deals with Kurt's own motivations he remains impressive. His technique consists of selecting certain incidents in his hero's life, and concentrating upon them with great psychological intensity. *Tony* (1924), a portrait of Kurt through his brother's eyes, is more interesting than the modest and over-sophisticated Hudson himself would allow.

The Powys brothers – **John Cowper Powys** (1872–1963), **T.F. Powys** (1875–1953) and **Llewellyn Powys** (1884–1939) – sons of a Church of England parson, were a remarkable trio of eccentric writers; the first two have become the subjects of cults. John Cowper's virtues, and in particular his sexual philosophy, have been urged by the critic G. Wilson Knight; and T.F. Powys is or was compulsory diet for budding Leavisites (q.v.). The least unconventional of the three was Llewellyn, who spent most of his life struggling with tuberculosis, to which he finally succumbed. He wrote well of this struggle (*Skin for Skin*, 1925) and of his travels (*Ebony and Ivory*, 1924); he was also a competent biographer. But he was hardly a creative writer, and his two novels are negligible.

John Cowper is a writer on a huge – deliberately cosmic – scale; Theodore Francis is usually a miniaturist. But both brothers see the universe – as do Bernanos and Jouhandeau (qq.v.) – as a battleground for the forces of good and evil. Both writers have been overrated by their admirers; both had genius; both too rapidly become bores by harping on their particular obsessions. Of the two, T.F. Powys is more likely to survive: he used shorter forms.

John Cowper Powys' best book, by far and away, is his *Autobiography* (1934); this should be read in conjunction with the American edition, *The Art of Happiness* (1935), which differs considerably. Powys' self-insight and honesty are here displayed at their best. His more massive novels tend to be both boring and pretentious; there is an element of charlatanism in them. The imagination of the author is less in evidence than the grandiose schemes suggest: there is usually more of his philosophical world-view than of invention: he tells us about his characters' conflicts, but cannot convince us of their existence. The 'imaginative power' with which he is so often credited consists in large measure of a vulgarly 'cosmic', pseudo-mystical approach to life, which ignores individuality and concentrates on mere largeness of conception. *A Glastonbury Romance* (1933), a modern treatment of the Grail legend, is unreadable except by those who want to escape from themselves into a vague pantheism. *Wolf Solent* (1929) is better, but suffers from the same grandiosity. And yet there was a grand obstinacy here, and an occasional achievement of colloquial style (when Powys tried to be archaic he was excruciating; but his vernacular is often excellent). At the heart of all this high intention and self-inflation is a minor writer of distinction, best savoured in short passages. Like his brother Theodore Francis, John Cowper Powys was a miniaturist; but he would not accept this limitation. Yet he is a writer who cannot be ignored – the cult should be – and certain of his less grandiose novels deserve and are now receiving (through reissues) attention: *Rodmoor* (1916), *Weymouth Sands* (1934) – perhaps his best novel – and *Mortal Strife* (1941). When he was depicting character rather than constructing romances on a grand scale, he frequently achieved insights of genius, as in his early *Rodmoor*.

T.F. Powys is superior. Certainly his sadistic morbidity becomes absurd when taken in quantity. The perverseness and cruelty of his rustic characters are too easily caricatured. It is not that he had an exaggerated picture of the beastliness inherent in human beings; it is rather that he usually (he wrote eight novels and more than twenty collections of short stories) fails to place this beastliness (often sexual) in a convincing context. It becomes *grand guignol*, too much of a joke, but not meant as a joke. In *Mr. Tasker's Gods* (1925), a notorious example, a rapist feeds his father to the pigs, who are his Gods. Despite the power and the conviction, it does not come off. Powys is not, in H. Coombes' words, a 'great and extraordinary writer' who has 'the terrifying honesty of genius'. He is an extraordinary writer and he sometimes has genius; but even he is neither great nor quite terrifying. One can see (this has often been pointed out), in Dylan Thomas' (q.v.) early short stories in *The Map of Love* (1939), how this kind of semi-surrealist perversity can spill over into a sick and ill-accomplished nastiness. From the difference between Thomas and Powys one may discern that whereas Thomas (in this aspect at least) was a dirty little boy playing with immature ideas of evil, Powys was genuinely and more maturely obsessed; he might, indeed, have been a great writer if he could have got things into better balance. But he fails (unlike another similarly obsessed writer, Céline, q.v.) to reveal his charity. One needs at least one 'normal' rustic, as a foil for the others. His best novel, *Mr. Weston's Good Wine* (1927), an allegory in which God appears in Dorset, has a lightness of touch and a gentleness that neutralize his usual concentration on the bestial side of man; but one must resist, as grotesque, the comparisons with Shakespeare that have been made. However, for this, for the novel *Black Bryony* (1923), and for a handful of the short stories, Powys has his place as an original minor writer.

C.E. Montague (1867–1928), one of the last of the great journalists, wrote four competent but now dated novels, of which the best is *Rough Justice* (1926), and one masterpiece of non-fiction: *Disenchantment* (1922), a description of the Western Front, and one of the earliest and fiercest denunciations of the cruelty and stupidity of militarism. *Fiery Particles* (1923) contains some good short stories.

Norman Douglas (1868–1952) is possibly more memorable as a personality than as a writer. But at least *South Wind* (1917), *Old Calabria* (1915) and his two books of auto-biography – *Looking Back* (1933) and *Late Harvest* (1946) – will survive. These books contain many exquisite, deeply felt and shrewd appraisals of Douglas' contemporaries, and are invaluable. *South Wind* is a unique light satirical novel, a study of a group of expatriated English on Capri (an island which he made, so to speak, his own). Nothing is as harmless and tolerant as Douglas' 'hedonism', although his own sex-life, which included the purchase of children from their Italian parents, is unattractive.

Max Beerbohm (1872–1956) is just about as substantial as a minor writer can become – and a warning to those who regard minor writers as mere *repetiteurs* of their elders and betters. Beerbohm was, in fact, minor entirely by choice: he preferred to wound with arrows shot from the periphery. He is distinguished as an essayist, as a parodist and a short-story writer ('Enoch Soames' is a masterpiece). He was also a notable caricaturist. He understood more than his deliberately lightweight style suggests – as the superb parodies in *A Christmas Garland* clearly demonstrate. These amount to highly valid criticism.

G.K. Chesterton (1874–1936) could never be uninteresting, as man or writer. It has been said that he is a 'master who left no masterpiece'; and this seems just – or does some masterpiece-like quality inform at least the conception of Father Brown? ... The vitality of Chesterton's best writing is not a consequence of his Roman Catholicism, the intellectual content of which may now be seen as accidental. Chesterton spent his creative life indulging his nihilism, but rendering it powerless with brilliant final twists. Terror is the father of his ingenuity. His ostensible message – bluff, matter-of-fact, 'jolly', beery, genial – is 'Everything's all right really; see how harmless I render these fascinating horrors'. But a little examination reveals a profound unease: a spirit wrestling with the notion of absurdity as far as it dared without madness. The wonderfully ingenious *The Man who was Thursday* (1908), the best of his novels, reveals all evil as non-existent: six of the anarchists are really detectives, and the seventh is God. But the figure of Sunday (God behind the mask of Nature) is ambiguous and ill-defined: a confession of 'faith' but a failure of the imagination. His poetry is cheery and beery; but he did not put much of himself into it.

Hilaire Belloc (1870–1953) never achieved the creative level of his friend Chesterton (q.v.), but he did certain small things well. He is most distinguished of all as a writer of comic verse: here he was relaxed; his essential decency and gaiety found their best and purest form in parodying smug, false Victorian didacticism. *The Verse of Hilaire Belloc* (1954).

Saki (ps. **Hector Hugh Monro**, 1870–1916), who was killed in the First World War, was born in Burma; but at the age of two he was sent home to Devon in the care of two sadistic maiden aunts. This experience formed him as a writer. He first became known as a journalist, but before his death he had established a reputation for his grotesque short stories about Reginald and Clovis, those clever young assailants of the pretentious, the fake-adult and the orthodox. His short stories were collected in 1930; he wrote one novel, *The Unbearable Bassington* (1912). Saki could be as cruel and sick as those maiden aunts: they prompted in him (and in his sister) a desire for revenge that lasted all his life. His standard procedure is original: the gruesome or sinister is wrapped up in a farcical package. The novel is an exception: here Saki seriously tries to account for his hero's sadism; there is evidence that he took this book more seriously than his short stories. It was on an unusual theme for its time, and psychologically it is penetratingly accurate; it suggests that, had he not been killed (by a sniper), he might have developed into a major novelist. He has been compared with Beerbohm, Wilde and Firbank (qq.v.); a more telling comparison, allowing for nationality, might be with Wedekind (q.v.): Saki has the same gay grimness, the same hatred of gentility and of its life-denying emptiness.

Oliver Onions (1873–1961) is now a somewhat neglected writer who wrote one minor masterpiece: *In Accordance with the Evidence* (1912), the first of a trilogy, about a clerk who murders a rival and gets away with it by tricking him into writing a suicide note. This is a powerfully unpleasant novel, with an uncanny and oppressive air of reality about it. Its two successors (*The Debit Account*, 1913; *The Story of Louie*, 1913) are not quite as good. The whole trilogy was issued as a single volume in 1925. There are some very effective stories in the *Collected Ghost Stories* (1935). The best of his later fiction is *The Story of Ragged Robyn* (1945).

Ford Madox Ford (originally **Ford Madox Hueffer**, 1873–1939), if only for five novels (he wrote, counting collaborations, thirty-two, plus scores of other books of criticism, travel, history and belles lettres), is one of the dozen greatest novelists of the century. The most generous of men – only Pound (q.v.), himself conspicuously loyal to Ford, has been as generous and helpful to other writers – Ford was a boastful and often grotesquely silly liar and, like Coleridge, made a mess of his life; yet, like Coleridge, he was a better human being than most of those who denigrated him. Stella Bowen, who lived with him for many years and bore him a daughter, said: 'Ford's weakness of character, unfairness, disregard of truth and vanity *must* be accepted. ... On the other hand, his tenderness, understanding, wisdom (about anything that didn't apply to himself!) and the tremendous attraction of his gorgeous mind, must make him always regretted. ...' England, to its eternal discredit, more or less rejected him; in recent years Graham Greene (q.v.) has crusaded for him almost alone; all the substantial studies of him, as well as the standard biography by Arthur Mizener (1971), are American. When he is praised by English critics the praise always grudgingly displays a meanness of spirit and a refusal to recognize genius unless it be accompanied by conventional morality which are unfortunately still characteristics of English criticism. Ford did lie – but less than he is supposed to have done. No man was more persecuted by women – Ford suffered unreasonably from his wife, but more from the woman he left her for, Violet Hunt – and he was lucky to find some happiness with Stella Bowen and then even more, in the last nine years of his life, with Janice Biala.

Ford's five great novels are *The Good Soldier* (1915) and the Tietjens tetralogy, consisting of *Some Do Not ...* (1924), *No More Parades* (1925), *A Man Could Stand Up* (1926) and *Last Post* (1928). His good, if flawed, novels include the *Fifth Queen* trilogy (1906–8), on Henry VIII's Katherine Howard, and *When the Wicked Man* (1931). Throughout his life he wrote charming minor poetry; the series of poems he wrote in the Thirties to Janice Biala, *Buckshee*, are rather more than charming, and deserve revival: they convey a sense of the absolute – and holy – sweetness at the heart of Ford the bumbling, romantic, self-deceiving, vain man. That wise sweetness glows at the heart of all his best work.

Pound, Joyce, Wyndham Lewis, Eliot (qq.v) and Ford are sometimes, because of their pioneering spirit and innovations, known as 'the men of 1914'. Pound, Joyce and Eliot have had their due (and more); Lewis and Ford have not. And yet in terms of intrinsic importance Lewis' and Ford's achievements are greater: their best prose is of higher quality than Pound's or Eliot's poetry.

Ford, thrust by his parents into the Roman Catholic Church when a youth, remained a nominal Catholic all his life; when it suited him, as his biographer Arthur Mizener has said, he could be very Catholic indeed. But he was never a believing Catholic. Considering the impartiality of his treatment of Roman Catholics in his novels, particularly in *The Good Soldier*, Ford cannot other than disingenuously be claimed as a real member of the fold. (Nor, to be fair, has the claim been made: few groups, to their shame, have wanted Ford among them.) By 1914 he had painted a picture of himself – as an honourable, radical, romantic Tory. This Toryism was of the old-fashioned sort (as George Orwell, q.v., said in 1946, and it applies particularly to the early Eighties, there are now no Tories: only 'liberals, fascists and the accomplices of fascists'). He was always thoroughly humanitarian in his political opinions, which seldom showed any of the silliness of which he was so capable. His sense of history and of current political situations was excellent. There is an important sense in which Christopher Tietjens, although a character in a book and not a real man, really is the 'last Tory'. Much has been written about Ford's personal involvement in the characters of *The Good Soldier*; but while it is of course true that there are elements of both his wife and Violet Hunt in the two chief woman characters, and of himself in Dowell, the narrator, and in Edward Ashburnham, he here entirely transcended his own difficulties. No better novel in the realist mode has appeared in this century in any language. The story is simple enough: of the American narrator's unconsummated marriage to a shallow but lustful and deceitful woman, and of their apparently placid but actually fatal relationship with an English couple: a 'good soldier', an honourable and brave man who is corrupted into a liar and a betrayer by his compulsive womanizing, and his Irish Catholic wife. There is disagreement about the narrator: is he a sexual and moral idiot, or a sensitive man? The first view, which depends on a Lawrentian (or Reichian) view of men as undeveloped unless fulfilled sexually, of course reads more irony into the novel as a whole. It is, I believe, untenable: nothing in the text suggests that Dowell would be 'better' as a sexual he-man. There is enough irony in the fact that these four people are 'well behaved': Edward Ashburnham is stupid, but he is a conscientious magistrate and a benevolent and humane landlord. And there is irony in Dowell's well-bred failure to get sexual possession of his wife (and evidence that he wants her); but he is by no means an idiot. *The Good Soldier* is the complex and ironic presentation of an Edwardian tragedy. The novelist is always in perfect control. There is no more formally perfect novel in the language.

Ford became dissatisfied with *Last Post*, the final novel of the tetralogy *Parade's End*; but as Arthur Mizener says, 'it cannot be made to disappear': it was undoubtedly a mistake to reprint the series, as was done in recent years, without it. Fundamentally *Parade's End* is the story of how the Edwardian Tory Christopher Tietjens transforms himself into a modern man: the story of endurance (of war, of a fearsome bitch, of mis-understandings) and finally of survival and love. Christopher's brother Mark, by contrast, chooses to die rather than live in a new age. No books, fiction or non-fiction, reflect more exactly or more profoundly the radical changes that British society underwent between 1910 and 1925. Walter Allen has suggested that the 'Tory Christian' character of Christopher Tietjens is laid on a little too thickly: that it is difficult not to see him as a sentimental creation. This is not a frivolous charge – little that Allen says is less than sensible and carefully considered – but I think it misses one of the central ironies of the book as a whole: whatever Ford's conscious intentions, Tietjens does not come across simply as the wholly 'good man', who will not break his code. There is an element of caricature in him – of self-criticism. Ford's picture of him hovers, throughout the book, between these two views – as a piece of music may hover between a major and a minor key. He is too good to be true. ... But is he? This adds to, rather than detracts from, the excellence of *Parade's End*.

Much else might be said of Ford: as a critic, as a writer of travel books, as an editor (the most impractical, but the best of the century), as a man. Arthur Mizener's fat biography is sound, sensible and sensitive, and should do much to gain Ford his rightful place – even if it tends to underestimate him. There has been no English novelist like Ford; it is time he had some of the praise that has been so willingly lavished on his contemporaries.

W. Somerset Maugham (1874–1965) wrote many skilful but now mostly dated (though still playable) dramas and farces; his fiction cannot be so easily dismissed. With the exception of Franz Werfel (q.v.), he is the most serious popular writer of this century; if he wrote nothing as good as Werfel's earliest poetry, he wrote nothing as nauseating as *The Song of Bernadette* (q.v.). His fiction, even at its slightest, was always intelligent and craftsmanlike, and although he appealed to a middlebrow (q.v.) public he was neither pretentious nor did he manipulate his characters in accordance to set formulas. Maugham is neither brilliant nor profound; he is a sardonic, or sometimes merely wondering, observer of human nature. Even at his tritest he serves up an interesting assemblage of odd facts about human nature. In his best work he is not as limited as some critics have made him out to be. His first novel, *Liza of Lambeth* (1897), written out of his experiences as a medical student, is a warmly indignant book, influenced by Zola (q.v.) but not much resembling him. He wrote a number of other goodish but not spectacular realistic novels, conquered the London stage (*Lady Frederick*, 1912, ran for over a year) and then, in the second year of the First World War, produced his finest although not his best written novel: *Of Human Bondage* (1915). This is a fine realistic novel, and it is not a minor one. It is largely autobiographical, although in it, because of the time at which it was written, Maugham was unable to face his problem of ambi-sexuality. The waitress to whom Philip Carey becomes enslaved may well have been (in Maugham's own life) a vicious and beautiful young man; but the transformation is in any case entirely successful. The 'bondage' in which Philip feels himself to be is not only that of the waitress with whom he is infatuated, but also the whole constellation of beliefs that he has inherited; finally he succeeds in casting them off. But the world of the book is nevertheless an exceedingly bleak and hostile one. This is a novel to which one returns gratefully: for the account of Philip's schooldays, of his years as an art student in Paris (this is particularly vivid and well-realized), above all of his fatal infatuation. What prevents Maugham from being a major writer, the mundane (although beautifully styled) quality of his point of view, is, paradoxically, one of his strengths: he is never pretentious. At his most lightweight, as in *Theatre* (1937), he is simply trivial – but even here he manages to be entertaining. The rest of Maugham's best work is to be found in various short stories and in one more novel, *Cakes and Ale* (1930), a malicious and subtly observed tale about writers; it contains an uproariously funny caricature of Hugh Walpole (q.v.) as Alroy Kear. (Hardy, q.v., sometimes taken to be portrayed in it, is not in fact present at all.)

E.M. Forster (1879–1970) is Great Britain's chief representative of humanism. He published five novels in his lifetime – *Where Angels Fear to Tread* (1905), *The Longest Journey* (1907), *A Room with a View* (1908), *Howards End* (1910) and *A Passage to India* (1924) – a number of short stories (collected in 1948), criticism, essays and biographies; *Maurice* (1971), a weak novel dealing with his own problem of homosexuality, is posthumous. His finest achievement is, without doubt, *A Passage to India*; after it he wrote no more creative work of significance. Forster's stature as a major novelist undoubtedly depends on this novel: his earlier books are seriously flawed and over-contrived, and in them his blandly old-fashioned technique is usually a hindrance. In *A Passage to India* Forster's creative impulse was strong enough to generate an organic plot, hinging on an ambiguity (what happened in the Marabar Caves between Adela Quest and Aziz? Aziz is tried for attempted rape; but we never know). He conveys a unique sense of the tragedy of the gap that lies between Indians and Englishmen, even if they do not desire it. Further, while this novel works perfectly on a realistic and psychological level, it also functions on a symbolic level – with the Marabar Caves themselves, and the strange figure of Mrs. Moore, as the two central symbols.

In an excellent (because intelligent and provocative) book of criticism, *Aspects of the Novel* (1927), Forster very interestingly examined and then rejected Henry James' (q.v.) notion that the writer of fiction must above all avoid giving his own point of view; and in his own fiction he is very much the omniscient narrator. And yet, apart from Jane Austen and Samuel Butler, he felt his master to be Proust (q.v.). ... His technique was deliberately old-fashioned, then; but his practice in the last and best of his novels was authentically 'twentieth-century'. The wisdom of Mrs. Moore, although it consists of no more than an understanding of the necessity of good will in every kind of situation, is thoroughly 'modern' in its function, and it is still as valid as it was in 1924.

The formative influences on Forster were his life at Cambridge at the turn of the century, his extensive travels – and Cavafy (q.v.), whom he knew. He might well have achieved more had he been able – which he was not – to come to terms publicly (as a novelist) with his homosexuality. The posthumous *Maurice* is sensitive, but it shows how far off he was from facing up to the aspect of himself which so disturbed him.

Compton Mackenzie (1883–1972) wrote two excellent novels, *Sinister Street* (1913–14) and the less well known *Guy and Pauline* (1915), many good minor ones – and a number of light novels that are among the funniest of their time (*Buttercups and Daisies*, in America *For Sale*, 1931, is perhaps the funniest of all). As late as 1956 he turned out a first-class tale of a homosexual politician who becomes the victim of blackmail. Like Maugham (q.v.), Mackenzie expresses no higher aim than to 'entertain'; in his comic novels that is just what he does, and without offence; the earlier novels – and to some extent *The Four Winds of Love* (1937–45) – possess a lyricism, a keenness of observation and a psychological insight that go beyond entertainment. Most of his other fiction is spoiled by over-indulgence in sentimental romanticism or deliberate Gaelic eccentricity; but *Sinister Street* at least is genuinely realist throughout.

Hugh Walpole (1884–1941), talented, promising, immensely successful, never achieved much more than competence. The best of his many readable novels is his third, *Mr. Perrin and Mr. Traill* (1911), a psychologically acute study of two schoolmasters. Walpole was intelligent – so much so that Henry James (q.v.) admired him, and not for wholly extra-literary reasons – and he had feeling; when he did not try to do too much he could be highly effective. But he preferred keeping his name in front of the public to cultivating his craft; consequently he produced some atrocious work, such as the pseudo-historical *Rogue Herries* (1930) and its sequels. One of the reasons for this may well have been that he was a (notorious) paedophile with sadistic inclinations (the flogging scene in *Jeremy at Crale*, 1927, clearly shows this) – but he could hardly work out this theme in public. When he tried to do so, as in *Portrait of a Man with Red Hair* (1925), he was near his best. There is a sympathetic biography of him, but omitting details of his homosexuality, by Rupert Hart-Davis (1952).

P.G. **Wodehouse** (1881–1975) began by writing conventional school stories; but before the First World War he had turned to the books for which he is famous. These are farcical fantasies, unconnected with any kind of reality, featuring (most notably) the drone Bertie Wooster and his man Jeeves. The Jeeves books, his best, are set in an upper-class world, nominally Edwardian (later Georgian), but essentially timeless. Wodehouse wrote the same book scores of times (he was still working when he died) but his skilful use of upper-class slang and his highly professional skill at handling plot give many of them what Orwell (q.v.), who wrote well on him, called a dated and nostalgic charm. Unfortunately there is a cult of Wodehouse which takes him to be a great writer: a master of style, creator of a convincing and 'truly imagined' world. This is not so. Wodehouse's style is limited (if delightful), he can become boring, and his world is one of escape. True, he is one of the great escapist writers of the century; but no escapist writer, no novelist who cannot convey a sense of the real, can be major. It is foolish to try to make an occasionally gorgeous entertainer into a great writer.

II

Victorianism and its last burst of (fatigued) vigour, Pre-Raphaelitism, survived into this century as Georgianism. This was an actual movement, named after Edward Marsh's anthology *Georgian Poetry 1911–12* (1912), which was the first of five similar collections. The movement itself is unimportant, because Marsh was (by literary standards) a conservative dilettante. It was his love for Rupert Brooke (q.v.), and for Brooke's youthful enthusiasm for some of his contemporaries, that first set him off. (Brooke is Georgian, but, for reasons of contrast, is dealt with as a war poet.) Not all those represented in *Georgian Poetry* were in fact Georgians: D.H. Lawrence and James Stephens (qq.v.), for example, certainly were not. The word 'Georgian' has come to have a pejorative meaning, and understandably so. One's sympathy must be historical or sociological. As a literary movement it has no redeeming features, simply because although it did try to break with Victorian conventions, it failed to do so in a convincing manner. It was a movement of gentlemen conservatives in literature, who really succeeded only in present-ing a slightly updated version of Victorian optimism: it took no account of the changes in the world. It was really a commercial venture (only Marsh's pleasant sentimentality conceals this); and it cannot really be said to have succeeded in its aim of creating a large reading public for poetry (the volumes were to sell very well, as of course verse does in wartime) because what it actually created was a large reading public for verse (with a bit of poetry accidentally thrown in). Georgianism – appearances aside – even as war-clouds gathered, insensitively aimed to perpetuate Victorian values at a time when Victorian standards, procedures and practice were no longer adequate. What may fairly be described as Georgian poetry continues to be written today, in both Great Britain and America: it is escapist in the worst sense (rural fantasies set in a countryside both unthreatened by technology and commerce, and inhabited by servile dream-peasants), flatly traditionalist and uninventive in form, sentimental in attitude, crudely mechanistic in its assumptions about human nature.

Of the Victorians Robert Bridges, Thomas Hardy (qq.v.) and **Algernon Charles Swinburne** (1837–1909) survived into this century. Little need be said of Swinburne, who was a spent force long before the turn of the century. It is impossible to say what kind of poet – with his enormous metrical facility, his vigour and his learning – Swinburne might have been had he possessed emotional maturity. Unfortunately he never grew up sexually, and this seriously affected his intellect. It was natural enough for the poets of this century to react against the rhetoric of even his earlier, better poetry; the imitation of Swinburne's lush and imprecise manner (at its most reprehensible in Gilbert Murray's translations of Greek drama, as Eliot, q.v., observed) would have been fatal to a viable new poetry.

Robert Bridges (1844–1930), the Poet Laureate (1913), was a conservative innovator (in matters of technique), but wrote not one single good poem. He lacks the energy necessary to a poet. Attempts have been made to rehabilitate him (notably by Yvor Winters, q.v.), but they are unconvincing. He is at his least conventional in the conversational 'Poor Poll' (in its least attractive aspect an envious and ineffective parody of Eliot's polylingual montage in *The Waste Land*, q.v.), but this is not incisive enough, and is too labouredly and exasperatedly eccentric (in place of the modernism Bridges knew he could not achieve) in manner to be of much appeal today. All his poetry, especially the long philosophical *The Testament of Beauty* (1929), is marred by artificiality, lack of feeling (once called restraint but now recognized as frigidity) and unintelligent conservatism. He shrank too much from life – nor could he examine his reasons for doing so. The age still allowed such lack of robustness to be 'good form'. The last long poem, which purports to prove that the natural order is 'good', does not do so in spite of its length. His friend Gerard Manley Hopkins (q.v.) praised Bridges' poetry in general but criticized it in particular. The critic Sir Walter Raleigh, his contemporary, summed up Bridges best: 'Just a shade too little of a blackguard. ...' Bridges' experiments with classical, quantitative metres have some importance, and doubtless he deserves credit for dimly recognizing the genius of Hopkins – and for eventually giving his poems to the world.

Thomas Hardy (1840–1928) wrote all his novels in the nineteenth century; I shall not discuss them here, since they are essentially of their century. He continued to write poetry, however, until his death. Although he was a traditionalist in both conscious attitude and technique, his poetry has been influential in this century. He is a major poet, and the sheer bulk of his best work continues to surprise. Nor is the good easily separable from the bad. Hardy's poetry springs from a tension between overpowering feelings (for people, for landscape, for justice and for women – whom he saw as instruments of men, whose function in this respect he equated with careless or malign fate) and a courageous and toughly held conviction that life is purposeless or even subject to the dictates of a wanton or malevolent God:

> Let me enjoy the earth no less
> Because the all-enacting Might
> That fashioned forth its loveliness
> Had other aims than my delight.

Hardy represents the tragic and imaginatively articulate side of Victorian unbelief; but he was not an intellectual, though as one of his critics has pointed out, he was essentially gnostic (q.v.) in his attitudes. He had simplicity. But what continually buoys him up above his faults (they would have been faults, at least, in other writers) – clumsiness of diction, reliance on the poetical rather than the poetic expression ('all-enacting Might'), the simplistic polemicism of his naturalism (for this can be seen as a version of naturalism, q.v., even though Hardy believed in fate rather than character or environment as destiny) when it is functioning unimaginatively – is, quite simply, beauty of spirit. To state that a man means what he says is to make no claim at all for him creatively; but to say that he means it when he says such things as Hardy said is to make a very large claim. And Hardy is, indeed, the last indisputably great naïve writer in the English language. He is also the most accomplished portrayer of women in English literature since Shakespeare. Like all naïve writers, he was content to be a part of his times – but he imaginatively transformed the drab rationalism of the late nineteenth century, with its various humanistic consolations: at the heart of his work, as at the heart of Shakespeare's, is a vision of absurdity quite as complete as Camus' (q.v.) – but more robustly tragic. That is why Hardy is 'modern'. He is intrinsically of more importance than any British or Irish poet of the twentieth century, if only because his poetry is validly accessible to a greater audience without playing down to that audience; and his range is wider. And, as Ford (q.v.) wrote in 1925, it was 'first Browning and then ... Hardy' who 'showed the way for' the imagists (q.v.); '... his power to excite – is that ... he simply takes his lines by the throat and squeezes them until they become as it were mutinously obedient. ...' Hardy has not attracted the same volume of academic criticism as Eliot and Yeats (qq.v.), but he has been as much read and assimilated. He is an infinitely greater writer than either. Michael Millgate's *Thomas Hardy* (1982) is an invaluable corrective to earlier malicious and insensitive criticism of him.

A.E. **Housman** (1859–1936) published his first collection of poems, *A Shropshire Lad*, in 1896; within a few years he was one of the best selling of all twentieth-century poets. He issued *Last Poems* in 1922, and *More Poems* appeared in the year of his death. The best collected edition is *Complete Poems* (1960). While at Oxford Housman fell in love with a fellow-student, Moses Jackson. The exact nature and extent of their relationship is not known, but it affected Housman so much that, a gifted classical scholar, he failed his finals. To make up for this he turned himself into one of the most formidable classical scholars of his day, ending up at Cambridge, 'the other place'. As a poet he worked within the limits of a narrow epigrammatic tradition. Much of his poetry is trite and speciously pessimistic; and it is hardly 'classical', as its admirers used to claim. One of Housman's models is Heine, another is the Greek Anthology; a third, less happily, is Kipling (q.v.) – and his imperialistic ideas. However, despite his frequently poetical triteness, he is at his best an exquisite and moving poet. His poetry arose from the conflict between strong homosexual feeling and a genuinely acute horror of this, reinforced by convention. He remained emotionally immature, as possibly many homosexuals do; but within his limits he did something no one else has done. His 1933 address *The Name and Nature of Poetry*, published separately and then in *Selected Prose* (1961), is wrong-headed in places (as when it equates 'nonsense' with 'ravishing poetry') but contains an understanding of poetry greater than that of the critics who deplore it. His best poetry is not pessimistic – as he glacially intended – but heartrendingly gloomy and yet tender. His brother **Laurence Housman** (1865–1959) was an efficient minor essayist, novelist and illustrator; he is most famous for his dramatic biography of Queen Victoria, collected in *Victoria Regina* (1934); this is skilful but sentimental.

No account of modern British poetry is complete without mention of Gerard Manley

Hopkins (1844–89). Hopkins, although he was an innovator, was a Victorian poet and a Jesuit priest, and he needs to be considered in those contexts if he is to be properly understood. But (with the exception of a few poems that appeared in an anthology published after his death) his poetry did not become available until 1918. Within a decade he had become a major influence.

Hopkins was caught between his duties as a priest (one of the factors in his decision to enter the Society of Jesus two years after his conversion must have been his discovery of his homosexual leanings) and his intense and sensuous joy in the details of nature. His observation of these details was so sharp that he was impelled to invent an ecstatic language to match it. He also expressed his negative moods in violent and vivid language. Hopkins succeeded in his aim of rejuvenating poetic language; he showed the way for the poets of the twentieth century who were trying to break away from the stale Victorian conventions. His 'sprung rhythm' is, essentially, a more flexible, musical way of looking at poetic technique than the metrical one. It is an accentual system, taking into account rising and falling movement; the poet is in effect freer and has more equipment at his command. Attempts to imitate Hopkins' own extreme use of his technique are invariably grotesque: it is too much his own. But the example he set had enormous influence on both the development of 'free' (or irregular) verse and the amount of license poets allowed themselves. It was Hopkins, too, who first turned back to the seventeenth century and the 'metaphysical' tradition of deliberate exploitation of the ambiguities inherent in language. Clearly his concepts of inscape and instress anticipate expressionism (q.v.) in its general sense.

A rather better and more interesting poet than Bridges (q.v.) was **Thomas Sturge Moore** (1870–1944), a classicist of some skill who 'made' poems rather than dealt with any strong pressure to do so, but whose work is executed with taste and precision – and in an awareness of the exhausted state of fashionable Victorian diction. His poems were collected in four volumes (1931–3); the 1934 *Selected Poems* is still a useful introduction. His correspondence with Yeats (q.v.) is interesting (1953).

Thirteen years older, and considerably less well adjusted to the world, **John Davidson** (1857–1909), a Scot, was a more gifted and incisive poet who became a victim of what Hugh MacDiarmid (q.v.) admiringly calls 'giantism': the disease of attempting to create a grandiose system, a 'philosophy of life'. When he killed himself a journalist said of him that he had been murdered by Nietzsche (q.v.), of whom he was one of the earliest English explicators. What he was murdered by, however, was what might be called a misunderstanding of Nietzsche, who as himself, and not in other versions, gives courage and not suicidal despair. He was a prolific writer: the author of fiction, criticism, translations, epic poems and plays. ... His philosophy was that 'Man is but the Universe grown conscious'. It is a pity he did not leave it at that. Davidson was right in seeing the need to destroy the pseudo-values of his environment and (this he did learn from Nietzsche) the 'Christianity' that it had erected as a defence against the terrors of self-knowledge. But he expressed this more effectively as a lyrical poet than as an epic poet and dramatist – although there are good things buried in the five *Testaments* (*The Testament of a Vivisector*, 1901; *The Testament of a Man Forbid*, 1901; *The Testament of an Empire-Builder*, 1902; *The Testament of a Prime Minister*, 1904; *The Testament of John Davidson*, 1908). His best poetry, which was popular at the time but then went out of fashion, was published in the Nineties. *John Davidson: A Selection of his Poems* (1961) is an excellent introduction. Among the best of his ballads are 'Thirty Bob a Week', 'A Ballad of a Nun', 'A Ballad of Hell'. Davidson began as a Pre-Raphaelite and decadent, but soon developed out of this manner, discovering his true voice in the ballad-form, in which he has a strength most of the Pre-Raphaelites lack. At his best he was a fine urban poet. And few of his contemporaries could equal 'The Runnable Stag' as a lyric.

W.E. Henley (1849–1903) was an invalid (a tuberculous disease brought about the eventual amputation of a foot), and he consequently worshipped not only health, and the feelings of strength that stem from its possession, but also imperialism. His politics were, in fact, offensively jingoist; and one has to say that the spirit of the too famous 'Invictus', rousing at first, is specious. But Henley had another and preferable manner: light, impressionistic, sensitive, delicate. He is at his best in the 'Hospital Sketches', graceful and vivid impressions, in an almost free verse, of his ordeal in hospital.

The unhappy career of **Francis Thompson** (1859–1907) is a monument to the failure of more or less traditional methods to express the complex and neo-baroque. One has only to compare Thompson's poetry, particularly the famous 'The Hound of Heaven', with that of Hopkins (q.v.) to see its shortcomings. Thompson was a passionate Roman Catholic (his parents were converts) who tried, first, to become a priest, but was refused as unsuitable, and, secondly, to enter his father's profession of physician – he failed in this, too. He took to opium and the streets, and for a while lived off the earnings of prostitutes. By the time he was discovered and rescued by a magazine editor, Wilfred Meynell, his health was ruined. Thompson, though gifted, was weak, lazy and without inner resource. 'The Hound of Heaven', influenced by the seventeenth-century poet Richard Crashaw, has some academic virtues (speed, shape, high style), but does not achieve real poetic success: Thompson tries for tough, metaphysical paradox but lapses into semi-hysterical self-indulgence. Hopkins, who dealt with his tendencies towards hysteria and self-indulgence by embracing a strict monkhood, never found the way to God so easily. However, there is something touching about Thompson's work, which is not quite at its best in 'The Hound of Heaven': he manages, at times, to convey both his observation of nature and his profound suffering. His weakness is that he lacks originality of style, and falls back on earlier manners: he is not strong enough to transmute Crashaw's baroque ecstasy, and depends too much on that vague, 'Shelleyan' style which vitiates so much Victorian verse.

Ernest Dowson (1867–1900) was similarly weak, but a few of his poems are more effective than anything of Thompson's (q.v.), because he had less grandiose aspirations. He, too, embraced that brand of Roman Catholicism peculiar to the decadents of the late nineteenth century. As a member of the Rhymers' Club he knew Lionel Johnson, Oscar Wilde and W.B. Yeats (qq.v.), its co-founders. The famous 'Non Sum Qualis Eram Bonae Sub Regno Cynarae' ('I have been faithful to thee, Cynara! in my fashion') is limited, so to speak, only by its innate decadence: it perfectly sums up the attenuatedly romantic attitudes of the Nineties poets; it is well done, and, as Eliot (q.v.) observed, it escapes the traditional metres of the time 'by a slight shift'. Better and even more original, however, is 'Spleen'.

The most gifted of the Rhymers' Club poets was **Lionel Johnson** (1867–1902), a brilliant classical scholar who, although English, identified himself with his Irish contemporaries: Yeats (q.v.) was his close friend. Johnson had much more to offer, in the way of learning, intelligence, skill and inner poetic resource, than Thompson or Dowson (qq.v.). His critical book on Thomas Hardy (1894) remains even today one of the best. He became a Roman Catholic in 1891; when he fell off a bar stool (he drank heavily) eleven years later he cracked his skull and killed himself. Johnson looked intelligently to the Caroline poets of the seventeenth century for inspiration; through this he was able to achieve a more austere poetry than that of others in his group. He had assimilated Greek and Latin poetry, and unlike most of his contemporaries he designed his poems with some consciousness of the nature of true design; even his over-ornamentation (which we can now see as a fault) has elegance. Johnson was not a major poet: his mystical outlook is too vague; his hard-headedness comes out in style but not enough in irony (this was needed to slash sarcastically across the too inebriating God-yearnings). But he was a distinguished minor poet, and there is an interesting conflict in him between a genuine classicism and a decadent romanticism (qq.v.).

John Masefield (1878–1967), who became Poet Laureate on the death of Bridges (q..v.), is now a little undervalued. True he never quite realized his poetic gifts; but he achieved something vivid and vigorous in the difficult realm of narrative verse (*The Everlasting Mercy*, 1911, and *Reynard the Fox*, 1919, are his best), and he was a competent novelist in the vein of Robert Louis Stevenson (*Lost Endeavour*, 1910; *Sard Harker*, 1924). None of his later verse, or his verse plays, is of account. The forthrightness of the earlier narrative poetry, which shocked some people at the time, is not absolute, and seems tame enough now; but it did introduce a new anti-genteel element (Masefield went to sea and knocked about a great deal before settling down to a literary career); the story of the poacher Saul Kane's conversion in *The Everlasting Mercy* is by no means wholly specious, though when it came to it Masefield could never face up to the full implications of the non-respectability that he implied. One of the most intelligent general comments on Masefield's poetry was made by the critic John Middleton Murry: 'He is seeking always to be that which he is not, to lash himself into the illusion of a certainty which he knows he can never possess. . . .' The illusion was that he could ever be wholly free of that stifling gentility which he seemed, to his first admirers, to be so effectively challenging. But all his prose remained vigorous; and *William Shakespeare* (1911 rev. 1955), although unscholarly, is stimulating where many more sophisticated or learned performances are not.

Charlotte Mew (1869–1928), an eccentric figure, wrote a few memorable poems in an idiom that she forged for herself out of an extremely unhappy life that ended in insanity and suicide. Her talent was recognized by Monro, Hardy, Masefield and De la Mare (qq.v.). Charlotte Mew had something of the gnarled wisdom of W.H. Davies (q.v.); she wrote not of a fanciful world, as she might be expected to have done, but of the unhappy real world that she observed, bird-like, from her sad, shabby-genteel experience: of prostitutes and sailors, in a dramatic verse that is from time to time remarkably effective and moving. Her poetry was collected in 1953.

A younger woman poet of similarly eccentric and lonely demeanour, Anna Wickham (1884–1947) may conveniently be classed with Charlotte Mew (q.v.). She hanged herself when the Chancellor of the Exchequer increased the tax on cigarettes, of which (like Charlotte Mew) she was an inveterate consumer: she lived the latter part of her life in poverty and neglect. She had begun with marriage and hope. Anna Wickham's poetry, which has never been collected, lacks Emily Dickinson's linguistic power, but has something of her epigrammatic quality, and is distinctly individual and, at its best, wisely sardonic. She published three books: *The Contemplative Quarry* (1915), *The Man with a Hammer* (1916) and *The Little Old House* (1921). The contents of the first two books were gathered together in America under the title of the first (1921).

J.C. Squire (1884–1958) was a typically Georgian figure: he was critically obtuse, being all for 'straightforwardness' and over-prejudiced against poetry he could not understand; he usually stifled his genuine poetic impulses with a blanket of bluff Englishness. In his parodies (*Collected Parodies*, 1921), however, he was often brilliantly funny; for he had the parodist's knack of intuitively catching his victim's manner and then caricaturing it. He was a highly influential editor, and champion of Georgianism, and was knighted in 1933. He ended his days as a forgotten, agreeable drunk, occasionally giving lectures to schools for small fees (he would frequently turn up on the wrong day, or on the right day of the wrong week). He was a kind and generous man, and a better poet than many who now enjoy temporary reputations and have not heard of him. His *Collected Poems* appeared in the year following his death.

Edward Thomas (1878–1917), who was killed in France, is sometimes classified as a Georgian (q.v.), but he did not appear in Marsh's anthology; nor is he really one of the 'war poets' (Rosenberg, Sorley, Graves, Sassoon, Owen, Gurney, qq.v.). Though claimed by the Georgians, he does not deserve the epithet except in a few isolated instances. He spent most of his life as a hack critic and editor, under conditions of great poverty (asked for his address, he retorted: 'Ask any publisher in London'); he wrote one novel, *The Happy-Go-Lucky Morgans* (1913). His work in prose is discerning but not distinguished, although his nature essays contain descriptions that anticipate his poetry. He did not begin to write in verse, in his adult life, until persuaded to do so by Robert Frost (q.v.), who was visiting England (1912–14). His first collection, *Poems* (1917), appeared under the pseudonym 'Edward Eastaway'; he was dead before he acquired fame. His *Collected Poems* (1920 rev. 1949) represents, there is no doubt of it, a major achievement. Norman Douglas (q.v.) said of his years as a hack writer (three books a year) that 'the lyrical love of his mind was submerged, imprisoned, encysted in an impenetrable capsule'. But in the last four years of his life this capsule exploded. His range is wider than the frequent label, 'nature poet', implies. He is not a merely descriptive poet: although his observation of the English countryside is exact, he is almost all the time probing the core of sexual melancholy, of solitude, of nostalgia. He used only the technical equipment available to him, but was plainer, less rhetorical, freer, than any true Georgian – and as a whole Georgian editors did not much respond to him. They could not find enough metre or full rhyme; the poems are too conversational; there is an originality that would have disturbed a Georgian.

Thomas often falls into what looks like cliché ('The glory of the beauty of the morning') but then successfully invests the tired phrases with life (he can do it because he means it) as he illustrates them with the beautifully observed particular ('The cuckoo crying over the untouched dew;/The blackbird that has found it, and the dove/That tempts me on to something sweeter than love ...'). He knew that he could not penetrate to the heart of what he felt as beauty ('I cannot bite the day to the core'), but in his poetry he strove for a language that would do so. Miraculously he avoided, but without ever evading, the ugly and the urban; his is the last body of work to seek to define a rural concept of beauty that was finally invalidated by the First World War, by the growth of technology – and by that complex process whereby the anti-human has crystallized, or is still crystallizing, into the political, even the apparently 'liberal' political. Given the hideous context of today, the kind of solitude Thomas' poetry explores – as a man he had wandered through it for his nearly twenty years as a hack writer – no longer exists. But it still functions as a metaphor for solitude and for solitudes relieved and/or threatened by love. One of his most remarkable poems is 'The Other', in which he follows a phantom of himself, and tries to come to terms with it; this beautifully illustrates his quality of toughness, by which he refuses to depend on any body or thing to arrive at his answers. Although widely read, he remains relatively unexplored by critics.

Harold Monro (1879–1932) hardly realized his considerable poetic gifts. Ezra Pound (q.v.) summed it up in a letter to him (of about 1922): 'only HELL – you never had a programme – you've always dragged in Aberbubble and Siphon. ... One always suspects you of having (and knows you have had) sympathy with a lot of lopp ...' Monro did weakly succumb to Georgianism (q.v.), and as generous proprietor of the Poetry Bookshop he did sympathize with far too much 'second-rate lopp'. None of his own verse is as bad, as flaccid and uninventive, as really bad Georgian; but some of it is undeniably Georgian. Monro compromised with his own standards, as the unevenness of his book

Some Contemporary Poets (1920) clearly shows. And yet Eliot's (q.v.) generous tribute to him is justified: 'His poetry ... is more nearly the real right thing than any of the poetry of a somewhat older generation than mine except ... Yeats's ... like every other good poet, he has ... done something that no one else has done at all'. Monro's achievement rests on about a dozen poems, nearly all of them written towards the end of his life. In at least two of these poems ('Friendship', 'The One, Faithful ...') Monro went further towards a resolution of his ambisexual problems than most English-language poets of the twentieth century in similar predicaments have been able to do:

> But, probing, I discovered, with what pain,
> Wine more essential in the end than you,
> And boon-companionship left me again
> Less than I had been, with no more to do
> Than drop pale hands towards their hips and keep
> Friendship for speculation or for sleep.

Even if Monro did dissipate his poetic energy by giving aid to inferior talents, this arose from a generosity that is apparent in the best poems, the most famous of which is 'Bitter Sanctuary', a poem surprisingly far, in manner, from the escapist sonnet-sequence 'Weekend', or the much anthologized 'Milk for the Cat'. What he did in this poem is indeed 'something that no one else has done at all'. There is a valuable (and painful) portrait of the man Monro, as Arnault, in Conrad Aiken's (q.v.) *Ushant.*

W.H. Davies (1871–1940) was self-educated; he had been a tramp and pimp in America and England, and wrote lucidly of this in *Autobiography of a Super-Tramp* (1908), a minor classic that has remained in print. Before that he had hawked an ill-printed collection of his poems – *The Soul's Destroyer* (1905) – from house to house. It was through the encouragement of Shaw (q.v.) that he became established. His *Complete Poems* (in texts by no means impeccable) appeared in 1963. Most of Davies' later poetry is bad: artfully simple, deliberately appealing, slyly mock-innocent (Davies was nothing like as 'simple' as he liked to make out), banal, insipid. But, when not trying, he wrote some highly original lyrics – charmingly whimsical, blackly melancholic, mysteriously impudent (as in the famous 'The Inquest'), or, very occasionally, of a genuinely Blakeian simplicity. Davies has been neglected because the bulk of his output is poor and because there is nothing in him for academics; but the reader who does not take the trouble to pick out the jewels from the rubble of imitation stones is missing an exquisite minor poet. The critic Jonathan Barker has rectified this in a sensitive selection (1984).

Walter De la Mare (1873–1956), undoubtedly in certain respects a Georgian (q.v.), is a very difficult case; he has not had the serious critical attention he deserves, although there is a general awareness of his worth. The best study of him (1929) is by Forrest Reid; later criticism has been poor. He is distinguished not only as a poet but also as a children's poet (indisputably the greatest of his time), novelist, anthologist and short-story writer. At his weakest De la Mare is lush, excessively romantic and imprecise (as in 'Arabia'); at his best he is unique: quite certainly a poet of major proportions. He has often been described as an 'evader of reality', even by his admirers; this seems obtuse. What is woodenly called unreality was, for De la Mare, a reality. It is of no use to try to judge the achievement of his finest work by the values propounded in his more self-consciously poetical verse, where he is often thoughtlessly romantic. But although he did so often make what H. Coombes has well called 'a routine use of the properties [of] verbal magic and romantic symbol', De la Mare was a master of the world of childhood. Such lines as:

> 'Grill me some bones,' said the cobbler,
>   'Some bones, my pretty Sue;
> I'm tired of my lonesome with heels and soles,
> Springsides and uppers too;
> A mouse in the wainscot is nibbling;
> A wind in the keyhole drones;
> And a sheet webbed over my candle, Susie.
>   Grill me some bones!'

from the (ostensibly) child's poem 'At the Keyhole' make his mastery perfectly clear. He is rhythmically inventive; and he can enter into the world of children – sinister and cruel as well as innocent – with uncanny ease. 'The Song of the Mad Prince' is unthinkable outside the context of childhood, but it is not simply a children's poem: it is unusual in that it is for both child and adult. This poem, in which De la Mare takes on the mask of the 'mad' Hamlet, is one of the subtlest, most dramatic, and most beautiful that he ever wrote; it shows him at strength: rooted in literature, but not in the literature of escape:

> Who said, 'Peacock Pie'?
>   The old King to the sparrow:
> Who said, 'Crops are ripe'?
>   Rust to the harrow:
> Who said, 'Where sleeps she now?
>   Where rests she now her head,
> Bathed in Eve's loveliness'?
>   That's what I said.

> Who said, 'Ay, mum's the word'?
>   Sexton to willow:
> Who said, 'Green dusk for dreams,
>   Moss for a pillow'?
> Who said, 'All Time's delight
>   Hath she for narrow bed,
> Life's troubled bubble broken'?
>   That's what I said.

There is rather more of this calibre in De la Mare than has usually been allowed, as his *Complete Poems* (1969) made apparent. A reading of the whole of this strengthens the impression that De la Mare is a major poet. What he alone does, he does so well. It has been something to have, in this country, so exquisite a ponderer on the various mysteries that life offers (even such simple ones as described in the haunting 'The Railway Junction'); after all, the crasser scientists and the least creative critics have, between them, attempted to remove all element of mystery from life. De la Mare unfashionably affirms it.

De la Mare's fiction is uneven, but at its best it, like the poetry, does what no one else has done. The novel *Memoirs of a Midget* (1921) is a sinister *tour de force* that would long ago have been seen as genuinely expressionistic if it were not for its unashamedly archaic manner. It is a strange and degenerate book: attempts to neutralize its undoubted power and originality by attributing 'unsound' opinions to De la Mare have failed. As to the short stories: as Graham Greene (q.v.) has written, here 'we have a prose unequalled in its richness since ... Robert Louis Stevenson'. It is, of course, a certain kind of richness

('Stevenson', says Greene, 'comes particularly to mind because he played with so wide a vocabulary – the colloquial and the literary phrase'), and it has its obvious limitations; but as the investigator of what is odd or spectral or puzzlingly 'lost' in experience De la Mare has no peer. Such stories as 'Seaton's Aunt', and there are many of them, show up the modern cult of pulp 'horror', with its cynical and inhumane reliance on the conventionally 'disgusting', as the puerile and commercial exercise it undoubtedly is. This trash would remain unread if its readers were aware of De la Mare and a few others like him. The fault lies more with the purveyors of this *merde* than with those who read it. De la Mare is not above the head of any literate person – and in his stories of horror the details correlate with true horrors. His total achievement is undoubtedly an important one.

Lascelles Abercrombie (1881–1938) stands out from amongst the Georgians (q.v.) for his intelligence and excellent criticism. He showed a greater awareness of the seventeenth century than any of his Georgian contemporaries; his *Colloquial Language in Literature* (1931) shows that he wanted to transcend the Georgian limitations. But he was, as one might fairly put it, 'no poet'. His imagery is sometimes interesting and original, but its source seems to be Abercrombie's interest in the metaphysical poets rather than in his own poetic impulse. His language as a whole, notwithstanding his imagery, continually lapses, just as his theme is becoming interesting, into Victorian bathos. He is at his best in his plays (the best are included in *Collected Poems*, 1930), where his psychology is powerful and his plots subtle; but once again it is his language that lets him down. Had he employed prose in them he might have been a major dramatist. His *A Plea for the Liberty of Interpreting* (1930) has some marginal importance in the history of Shakespearean bibliography.

Ralph Hodgson (?1871–1962), who may have been even older than he gave out, was a tough eccentric who from 1940 lived in Ohio (USA), where he owned a farm. Before that he had worked on newspapers in America and as a graphic artist – and had bred and judged bull-terriers; he was a dedicated spectator of boxing. He is most famous for his poems condemning cruelty to animals (boxing is a mutually agreed means of inflicting cruelty). Such a poem as 'The Birdcatcher' not only categorizes the malevolent hunter himself but also, by extension, a certain kind of frigid intellectual. Hodgson, a man of steadfast integrity and strong personality, possessed true distinction; the following famous short poem, 'Reason', displays his epigrammatic and lyrical power:

> Reason has moons, but moons not hers
> Lie mirrored on her sea,
> Confusing her astronomers,
> But O! delighting me.

Hodgson (like Andrew Young, q.v.) is an excellent example of the man who can write really good and relevant poetry strictly within the tradition (De la Mare, q.v., who has seemed so much part of it, has unwittingly strained and distorted it to a point where, paradoxically, he is considerably more 'modern' than, say, Cummings, q.v.). His *Collected Poems* appeared in 1961, and is an essential book for real connoisseurs. In both 'Song of Honour', an ecstatic meditative poem reminiscent of Smart, and 'The Bull', which comes as near to Clare's unsentimental sympathy with animals as any poet ever has, Hodgson achieved convincing poetry.

James Elroy Flecker (1884–1915), whom tuberculosis early killed off, was regarded as one of the central figures of the Georgian (q.v.) movement. And he was, it is true, low in vitality, firmly anti-realistic and a somewhat pallid pursuer of 'beauty'. However, his poetry is stylistically more distinguished than that of a mere Georgian: he was intelligently aware of foreign literature – particularly that of France – and he learned from the Parnassian (q.v.) poets, whom he tried to emulate in English. His poetry has a fastidiousness, a deliberate and studied lack of diffuseness, that is alien to the vague Georgian ideal – and for this he should be remembered. Flecker spent most of his adult life in the East, in diplomatic posts. He wrote a good deal, including some readable fiction and the verse dramas *Don Juan* (1925) and the more famous, lush, dated but not entirely ineffective *Hassan* (1922).

W.J. Turner (1889–1946) was born in Australia; but he came to England as a very young man and remained there until his death. He was a well known music critic, a novelist – and a notable playwright in *The Man who Ate the Popomack* (1922). Turner seldom succeeded in reconciling his wild romanticism (so wild that it sometimes ran over into irresponsibility and irascibility) with his satirical impulses; but he was an interesting although uneven poet, who sought for subtler and profounder themes than he was able to cope with. His passion for music led him to treat his poetry as a sort of music; this spoiled much of it. But at his best he is memorable and deceptively simple. There is a *Selected Poems* (1939); his last collection, *Fossils of a Future Time?* (1946), is as interesting as anything he did. Yeats and Raine (qq.v.) admired his poetry.

*

Some poets of the Georgian (q.v.) generation remain entirely immune. For all that the poetry of the Scottish parson (he changed from nonconformist to Church of England, and was vicar of a parish in Sussex for many years until his retirement) Andrew Young (1885–1971) is firmly traditional in form; it is never tainted with the poetical, and it always has acuteness of observation and fine sharpness of style. Furthermore, Young remained a minority taste until after the Second World War – his first collections were pamphlets issued somewhat late in life; his first trade collection *The White Blackbird* (1935) was issued when he was fifty. His poetry has no Georgian affinities, and he, a fastidious user of words, could never have tolerated the slack and styleless meandering that generally characterizes Georgian verse. Young is a tough, precise, even dour poet who says almost all that he has to say through a rapt contemplation of nature. Watching birds through binoculars, he feels his shoulders prick as though he himself were sprouting wings. He has much – if only incidentally – to say about the phenomenon of anthropomorphization. Above all, because of his remarkable sensibility, he is a describer of the natural world of Great Britain that no discerning reader could do without. His *Collected Poems* appeared in 1950. This includes all his lyrics; a later, narrative poem, *Into Hades* (1952), which begins with the poet's funeral, is lively and interesting but less successful. *Nicodemus* (1937), included in the *Collected Poems*, is a straightforward and effective verse play, quite as good as most essays in this, in the twentieth century, impossible genre. *Complete Poems* (1974) omits the play, but has all the poems he wrote.

Charles Williams (1886–1945), poet, dramatist and novelist, had his admirers – including such critics as C.S. Lewis (q.v.). But his work raises grave doubts. His 'cosmic thrillers' are frankly middlebrow, written to raise money: he disowned them. In them the 'belief in the supernatural' is insincere and vulgar: he so patently disbelieves in their action. They are nearer to the crudely written occult romances of Dennis Wheatley than to literature, yet they do make much better reading. He was a confused, unsatisfactory critic: an obscurantist without even the resources of a C.S. Lewis. His early poetry is a semi-Chestertonian (q.v.) attempt to revive a Victorian style. His most highly praised poetry is in *Taliesin through Logres* (1938) and *The Region of the Summer Stars* (1944), a sequence on the Arthurian legend. No critic, however, has made out a satisfactory case for it: C.S. Lewis could only call it 'gorgeous', with 'profound wisdom'. In fact it is muddy work; what looks like originality is simply disguised archaism; the 'grand style' proceeds to nothing. Behind all Williams' work – particularly the novels – there seems to be something thoroughly unpleasant: the orthodox Christian apologetics conceal a human rather than a merely Christian heresy: one senses Williams hanging masturbatorily over his nasty, middlebrow images of evil, even though he is remembered kindly by those who knew him.

Arthur Waley (1889–1966) has exercised a considerable influence on the development of English poetry through his brilliant and poetic translations from the Chinese. These, admired by Pound (q.v.) (and superior to Pound's essays in the genre – Pound did not know Chinese, and purported to read a Chinese text while holding it upside down) and Yeats (q.v.), represent a remarkable achievement, and are a substantial contribution to modern poetry. The translations – *170 Chinese Poems* (1919), *The Book of Songs* (1937), *Chinese Poems* (1946) – are done into a sensitive, rhythmically impeccable free verse; the sense is not really Chinese (how could it be?), but it introduced into English poetry as many new attitudes as new procedures. Waley's translations helped English poets to regain something of the spontaneity and lyricism that are so difficult to attain in twentieth-century poetry without resort to cliché. Again, in his less direct way, Waley has influenced the use of imagery in English poetry almost as much as Pound: the Chinese poems he translated employed concentrated images in place of mere description. His influence has been subterranean but (almost) all-pervasive.

*

The burst of creative activity that took place in Ireland at the turn of the century is sometimes called the Irish literary renaissance. It was not, however, a movement, but rather the result of the sudden diversion of national energy from politics to literature after the Parnell scandal (1892). The main activity was in the drama (this is discussed in the appropriate section), but there was also a Gaelic revival (and some translations out of the language of Ireland's only wholly native culture) and a resurgence of poetry. **Padraic Colum** (1881–1972), dramatist (he helped to found the Irish National Theatre), autobiographer and folklorist, wrote attractive poetry (it was seldom verse) for almost the whole of his long life. (He came to America at the beginning of the First World War and remained there until his death.) Colum's poetry, though minor, has a quality with which, as L.A.G. Strong said, 'literary criticism has little to do': 'simplicity', which 'cannot be analysed'. Colum's plays, discussed elsewhere, are historically important; but so is his poetry, which ought to be better known. Some of it has passed back into the folk tradition from which it came. ... It is remarkable that Colum never spoiled the purity of his gift in his near sixty years of exile in America (and Hawaii); his fairly frequent visits to Ireland seem to have protected him from sentimentality and feyness. His *Collected Poems* (1953) – other volumes followed it – is an essential part of any comprehensive library of twentieth-century poetry in English. Although his poetry always has a lilt, it is not a monotonous one – he has an exquisite and original ear, as the deservedly famous 'She Moved through the Fair' demonstrates. Colum, 'whose goodness and poetic innocence speak at once to all that is good and innocent in his audience' (L.A.G. Strong), is one of the very few English-language poets to draw his strength from tradition throughout his career. *Poet's*

Circuits (1960), a collection of poems published in his eightieth year, is as pure and strong as ever.

Æ (ps. **George William Russell**, 1867–1935) – he wrote an early article under the pseudonym 'Aeon'; the printer dropped the last two letters, and he stuck to the result – was a prolific and active member of the Irish revival: in fact, he and his close friend Yeats (q.v.) dominated it. He was an interesting man, helplessly divided between active social idealism (half his time was given up to founding co-operatives and trying to persuade the farmers to abandon their wasteful and inefficient methods) and a mysticism that he acquired from the reading of oriental literature. His activities are often described as political. This is unfair: Russell was no purveyor of clichés or seeker after power, but was honest, meant what he said, and was a competent economist and, far from being an 'expert' (in the meaningless manner of politicians), was actually an authority on agricultural matters such as soil conditioning; he retained his sympathy for the poor. Furthermore, Russell so disliked Irish politics after the First World War that he spent his last years in England, where he died of cancer. One may learn much about the personality of Russell from his *Letters* (1961), which have been well edited and annotated by Alan Denson. So far as his poetry is concerned (there is a *Collected Poems* of 1926; *Selected Poems*, 1935, contains much of his best poetry) Æ (he kept this name for his 'mystical' and poetic identity) is essentially an Irish Platonist: this world is unreal, and our only clues to that real world, of which it is the shadow, are dreams and visions of beauty. Yeats said, brilliantly, that his poems had 'a mind of scented flame consuming them from within'. At their best they faithfully describe their author's trance-like mood – for Æ was not a vague dreamer: he had experienced what he tried to convey. But whereas Yeats, who shared his combination of interests, was able to evolve his own style, Æ had to fall back on a diction and manner not quite his own: he could only talk of 'the breath of Beauty', where Yeats could eventually supply some of the actual particulars of beauty. . . . But as a minor Celtic twilight poet Æ is delicate, sincere, with a subdued glow.

One of Æ's most valuable books, which deserves revival, is about his own poetry and how it came to be written: *Song and its Fountains* (1932). His religious thought, which contains some cogent criticisms of Christianity, is interesting and original; as thought – although not as a vehicle for poetry – it is superior to Yeats' elaborate system. There have been few kinder literary men in this century.

It was Russell (q.v.) who rescued **James Stephens** (1882–1950) from life in an office, and introduced him to the literary world. A few years afterwards, with the generosity and shrewdness characteristic of him, he spoke of him as 'a poet without a formula', 'perplexed' but moving 'down to earth'. Russell was referring to the division in Stephens between comic, faun-like, impudent elf – and poet-as-angel; this conflict was resolved in his best poetry. In his prose Stephens succeeded admirably both as realist and as fantasist. Joyce (q.v.) regarded him very highly. His first success was the novel *The Crock of Gold* (1912), one of the best of modern fairy stories. The stories in *Etched in Moonlight* (1928) show him in more realist vein: he is in debt to Moore (q.v.) for his material, but introduces a lyrical quality that is his own. As a poet he is most attractive: more sophisticated than Colum (q.v.), he is nevertheless simple and innocent without guile. His Irish charm (of the best variety) is revealed in the celebrated 'The Centaurs'; occasionally he strikes a deeper, almost Blakean note, as in 'The Shell' and 'What Thomas An Buile Said in a Pub': here God is going to strike the unsatisfactory earth, but Thomas (he claims) tells him:

> Stay,
> You must not strike it, God; I'm in the way:

And I will never move from where I stand.'
He said, 'Dear child, I feared that you were dead,'
And stayed his hand.

'Little Things', too, strikes exactly the right sweet and simple note. Some of the poems in *Strict Joy* (1931) and *Kings and the Moon* (1938) are as good as anything in the *Collected Poems* (1926); Lloyd Frankenberg's *A James Stephens Reader* (1962) is an excellent job – but a more substantial selection from the poetry is still urgently needed.

The poetry of **William Butler Yeats** (1865–1939) has attracted much criticism and exegesis, a high proportion of which consists of wilful projection (of the critics' own predilections) or frigid abstractions. Considering his intrinsic and extrinsic importance he has, in fact, attracted surprisingly little really good, lucid criticism – although a few of the straightforwardly explanatory guides and handbooks collect facts that are indispensable to an understanding of his poetry. Yeats is clearly a major poet; but the high reverence in which he is held frequently conceals an inability to come to terms with him. The 'philosophical' system which he developed is, in fact, one about which it is impossible not to have reservations.

He was the son of J.B. Yeats, a lawyer turned painter, whose family originally came from England – but had been in Ireland since the seventeenth century; his mother's family, also English, had been in Ireland for a considerably shorter period. Yeats began as a vaguely Pre-Raphaelite poet; but from the beginning his manner was different from that of his friends Dowson and Johnson (qq.v.) because he had Sligo folklore to fall back on: this acted as an effective antidote to his Pre-Raphaelite vagueness and dreaminess. Of the poems of this first period, much of it spent in London, the Irish ones are the strongest: they are the most down to earth, precise, natural, unforced. That Yeats was likely to develop into a poet of genius was already apparent in 1889, when he wrote 'Down by the Salley Gardens', 'an attempt to reconstruct an old song from three lines imperfectly remembered by an old peasant woman' in Sligo. Clearly the author of this beautiful song understood how real poetry sounded. During the Nineties Yeats wrote plays, and was active with Lady Gregory (q.v.) and Douglas Hyde in founding the Abbey Theatre (1900).

As he matured Yeats sought to purge his language of excessive romanticism (the extent to which he succeeded may be seen in the *Variorum Edition* of his poems, 1957; the fullest, definitive *Collected Poems* appeared in 1956). He clung to the poetically formal (he never really abandoned it) as his expression of the high, aristocratic calling of the poet, and as an appropriate response to the mysteriousness and magic of the natural – as distinct from the 'ordinary', sordid, commercialized – world. But he laced his formal language with colloquialese, to achieve an effect unique in English poetry. The style he wanted to create eschewed abstraction and cliché, and yet it was based in Irish tradition. Yeats, although he fell early under the influence of Blake, Shelley and neo-Platonic ideas in general, could not remain immune to Irish aspirations. The conflict between the ethereal, the immaterial, and the concreteness of Irish nationalism produced, in fact, some of his best poetry. During the Nineties he was associated with the Socialist League; but in the first ten years of this century, under the influence of visits to Lady Gregory's country house, Coole Park, and of his convictions of the poet's high calling, he began to evolve his feudal idea. This, which involved a total rejection of middle-class materialism, an enlightened aristocracy and a partly idealized peasantry (which knew how to keep its place), was both unrealistic and politically naïve; but it did not prevent Yeats writing meaningful poems in the important collections *The Green Helmet* (1910) and *Responsibilities* (1914). It was in this period that Yeats was in love with the actress and patriot Maud

Gonne, who refused to marry him and caused him much sexual frustration and despair. In 1917 he married.

By this time his poetry had entered into a third phase: in response to Pound (q.v., whom he knew well) and imagism (q.v.) he began to evolve a laconic, even epigrammatic manner; at the same time, more independently, he had become increasingly concerned with mysticism (oriental and neo-Platonic) and with the 'occult'. His wife claimed mediumistic powers, and she faked (with the best of intentions: to help him) 'automatic writing', which he used as raw material for his poetry. Yeats believed that this writing was dictated by spirits, and it helped him to evolve the symbolic system he outlined in *A Vision* (1925 rev. 1937), the astrology of which is particularly ill-informed. The poetry of *The Wild Swans at Coole* (1919), for all its conversational quality, is technically finer than anything preceding it. It is rhythmically more subtle, and it plays an important part in freeing English verse from metrical (i.e. iambic) monotony.

From here on Yeats proceeded into his penultimate phase. This is the period of his richest poetry, in which he combines a number of themes: the conflicts between the spirit and the flesh, 'madness' and cool reason, permanence and change. In 1934 he underwent the Steinach 'monkey gland' operations – for sexual 'rejuvenation' – and this ushered in the poetry of his final phase: wild, lustfully romantic once again – and yet conscious of 'sin' and 'the foul rag-and-bone shop of the heart'. Yeats won the Nobel Prize in 1923. Since his death he has been almost universally regarded as the greatest English-language poet of this century. However, the viewing of him from a position of over-reverence has not helped towards an understanding of him – any more than it has helped in the case of Shakespeare. ... A good deal of nonsense has been written about Yeats by academic critics who know nothing of poetry's roots in real life. It has become exceedingly difficult to tell the truth about him – to criticize him at all – without heaping abuse upon one's head. Thus, when Conor Cruise O'Brien, who admires him, asked the question, 'How can those of us who loathe [Yeats'] politics continue ... to love the poetry ...?', he brought coals of fire upon his head. However, he convincingly proved that Yeats' politics, *qua* politics, were naïve, disagreeable and opportunistic (his record as a Senator in the Twenties, when he supported Protestant landed interests, is not good by humane standards); and critics do have the right to ask the question. The relationship between poetry and virtue is hardly an irrelevant one, although it is extremely tenuous; and Yeats' politics, naïve or not, are humanly reprehensible. Auden (q.v.) has asked a similar question of the 'occult' beliefs: 'How on earth ... could a man of Yeats' gifts take such nonsense seriously?' And he goes on to point out, further, that since Yeats was a 'snob' (it is a fair word, and it fits in with his politics), it is all the more remarkable that he believed in 'mediums, spells, the Mysterious Orient'.

The problem is this: Yeats' politics are stupid or humanly disgraceful, or both; his 'philosophical' system, as outlined in *A Vision*, is a synthesis of vulgar rubbish, bad astrology, intellectually ill-digested lore from neo-Platonism and what Auden calls the 'Mysterious East', and Ancient Greece and elsewhere – and of insensitive, authoritarian politics, too; and yet the poetry is admired – and is almost always interpreted in the terms of *A Vision* by critics who would not dream of associating themselves with anything 'occult'. ...

The short answer is that it does not matter in the least what Yeats' ideas actually mean – but what, in his poetry, he meant by them. By no means all the elements in his system are specious in themselves; one may argue, without granting intellectual or philosophical respectability to the system itself (it simply doesn't have it), that Yeats responded intuitively to what was important in it, and that his responses are contained in his poems rather than in his obscure and difficult expository prose. Or one might agree with L.C.

Knights: 'Measured by potentiality, by aspiration, and by the achievement of a few poems, it is as a heroic failure that one is forced to consider Yeats' poetic career as a whole'. For, as Knights goes on to say, Yeats thought that 'Unity of Being' is impossible without 'Unity of Culture'; and yet he realized that 'Unity of Culture', in the face of a mechanized society drifting towards cultureless technocracy, is itself increasingly impossible.

The fundamental symbolism of the poems in the two books regarded by the majority of critics as Yeats' greatest – *The Tower* (1928) and *The Winding Stair* (1929) – and of the later poems, is fairly simple: our life is a walk up a spiral staircase in a tower; we keep covering the same ground, but at a different height; because we travel in a 'gyre' (Yeats' word for a spiral), we both go round in a circle and yet make progress; the point, of final understanding, the tip of the spiral, where we are 'above' every place we have been before, is also the point of death; thus the summit of the tower is ruined. History, too, is for Yeats composed of gyres (cycles), as he makes most clear in 'The Second Coming', which he wrote in 1920 and published in 1921:

> Turning and turning in the widening gyre
> The falcon cannot hear the falconer;
> Things fall apart; the centre cannot hold;
> Mere anarchy is loosed upon the world,
> The blood-dimmed tide is loosed, and everywhere
> The ceremony of innocence is drowned;
> The best lack all conviction, while the worst
> Are full of passionate intensity.
>
> Surely some revelation is at hand;
> Surely the Second Coming is at hand.
> The Second Coming! Hardly are those words out
> When a vast image out of *Spiritus Mundi*
> Troubles my sight: somewhere on sands of the desert
> A shape with lion body and the head of a man,
> A gaze blank and pitiless as the sun,
> Is moving its slow thighs, while all about it
> Reel shadows of the indignant desert birds.
> The darkness drops again; but now I know
> That twenty centuries of stony sleep
> Were vexed to nightmare by a rocking cradle,
> And what rough beast, its hour come round at last,
> Slouches towards Bethlehem to be born?

This is an example of Yeats at his most powerful; it embodies both his rejection of Christianity as a system, and his religious sense. Furthermore, it does not really depend for its full poetic effect on a knowledge of the system of thought behind it; the opening image of the first two lines is self-evident: the falcon breaks free, goes out of control.

It is often asserted that the two famous Byzantium poems, 'Sailing to Byzantium' and 'Byzantium' (they appear, respectively, in the 1928 and 1929 volumes), written some years later, exercise their power before any knowledge of their symbolic patterns has been gained by the reader; this is true, but perhaps to a more limited extent than has been realized or admitted. These and other poems of the late Twenties and early Thirties contain magnificent lines, but they also contain elements as pretentious as the 'system' upon which they are too carefully and calculatedly based; either the spontaneity of the original impulse has been eliminated (Yeats first wrote them out in prose, which is somewhat suspect because parts of any poem are invariably 'given': the prose version suggests a wholly rhetorical 'working up'), or there never was a true impulse; after they have been fully examined, they shrink into something less profound than their grand surface suggests. Perhaps the poems in *The Wild Swans at Coole*, however, have had less consideration than they deserve: are not these more central to humanity, less concerned with the poet himself, than the more spectacular ones of the late Twenties and early Thirties?

In any case, Yeats is not on the level of Rilke, Vallejo, Valéry, Mandelshtam, Montale (qq.v.). ... He failed because his sophistication failed. Being sensitive to and monumentally aware of the demands of this century, he tried to transform himself from a naïve to a sentimentive poet (q.v.); his effort appeared to be much more successful than that of (say) Gerhardt Hauptmann (q.v.); but ultimately it was not successful. He possessed consummate technical skill and epigrammatic mastery – but his intellect was not strong, and he sought refuge in the over-factitious. His skilful rhetoric cannot wholly disguise his lack of an intellect. The metaphysical complexity of the Byzantium poems, for example, is ultimately a factitious rather than a poetic element in them. The much vaunted 'intellectual power' of these poems has been exaggerated; whatever qualities they may have, real intellectual power is not one of them. Passion is. But, despite the public air, it is an egotistic passion. The incredible richness – but it is too often an over-richness as well – of most of these poems has been bought at a price; the comparative simplicity of the poems in *The Wild Swans at Coole* suggests this. And yet they, too, can attain a majestic simplicity:

> When such as I cast out remorse
> So great a sweetness flows into the breast
> We must laugh and we must sing,
> We are blest by everything,
> Everything we look upon is blest.

*

T.S. Eliot (q.v.), although not officially one of the imagist poets, stated (1953) that the London imagist group of 1910 is 'usually and conveniently taken, as the starting-point of modern poetry' in the English language. Ezra Pound (q.v.) was the moving spirit behind this group; but others in it were important. Imagism was never clearly enough delineated to allow of precise definitions; however, one can fairly say of it that it represented 'British-American expressionism'. It was, however, less violent and aggressive, generally less self-confident and extensive in its aims, and more limited in its results, than German expressionism (q.v.). Its poets were on the whole less gifted. The intrinsic importance of every self-consciously 'imagist' poem is minor – or even trivial. But to claim that 'apart from Pound, and also Lawrence, ...' the imagists 'have no importance' (John Holloway) is plainly wrong: Eliot's statement that modern Anglo-American poetry has its starting-point in imagism is authoritative. The actual poetry of the imagist anthologies was trivial, theoretical. But it was not historically unimportant.

Apart from the effervescent and ever-active Pound, the chief figure in the imagist group was the philosopher **T.E. Hulme** (1883–1917), a victim of the First World War.

Hulme did not have time to mature, but he is none the less an important and prophetic thinker. The work he left was collected by his friend Herbert Read (q.v.) in *Speculations* (1924; 1960) and *Notes on Language and Style* (1929); *Further Speculations* was edited in 1955 by Sam Hynes. Five of his poems were printed by Pound at the end of his own *Ripostes* (1912) as 'The Complete Poetical Works'; further poems were added by Alun Jones in his useful *The Life and Opinions of T.E. Hulme* (1960). Hulme's poems, delicate, elegant, beautifully phrased, are the best produced by the actual imagist movement; we have tended to take them for granted. His thinking was confused: he preferred, as Read wrote, 'to see things in the emotional light of a metaphor rather than to reach reality through scientific analysis', and this led him to some foolishly extreme conclusions, such as that all romantic poetry was sloppy, or that 'fancy' is to be preferred to 'imagination' (his argument on this point is peculiarly confused and inane). However, it is unfair to call him a 'premature fascist'. He was perceptive about the faults of democracy and made noises about authoritarian or monarchist regimes – but he was never exposed to the reality of fascism, and actually put to the test; there is much in the fragments he left behind that could be taken as 'proto-anti-fascist'. ... He studied for a time under Bergson (q.v.), and from him he gained his predilection for the concrete and for the notion of qualitative, 'real time'. Bergsonism hardly chimes in with authoritarianism. ... He is said to have been a particularly 'lewd' man, whatever this may mean; I cannot for myself take this as pejorative.

However, this is not the place to examine the inconsistencies of Hulme's thought; the main point is that he was prophetically aware of the fact that the twentieth century would see a drastic break away from types of thinking that had been traditional since the late fifteenth century. He misdiagnosed the nature of this revolution, confusing it with his own brash neoclassicism, and he was guilty of over-simplifications (as when he claimed that blank verse, being new, had alone been responsible for the Elizabethan efflorescence); he wrongly thought of all romantics as Pelagian optimists. But his programme for poetry – and for intellectual life and art in general – was, although confused, symptomatic: neoclassical, abstract (non-representational), 'royalist', 'hard' (as against 'romantic', 'softness' or sloppiness), intellectual (not emotional), precise (not vague), 'religious' (in the broad, public sense), pessimistic (man is seen as a limited and sinful creature; only his art raises him above the status of an animal). We can see many of these lines of thought converging in the positions taken up by Eliot and Wyndham Lewis (qq.v.) – but also by the anarchist Herbert Read. Yet Hulme's own poetry, instructive in intention, is by no means, of course, non-romantic:

> Three birds flew over the red wall into the pit of the setting sun.
> O daring, doomed birds that pass from my sight.

The actual starting-point of imagism may be traced back to Hulme's formation of a 'Poets' Club' at Cambridge in 1908; he wrote and published one of his most famous poems, 'Autumn', in that year. Soon afterwards he got into a fight in a pub and was expelled from the university, whereupon he appeared in London. Here he met F.S. Flint (q.v.) and Pound. In 1909 a group of poets, including Hulme, Pound and Flint, began meeting in a Soho restaurant. Out of these meetings, the subject of which centred on poetic technique and French and Japanese poetry, was eventually evolved the following credo (published by Flint in 1913): '1. Direct treatment of the "thing" whether subjective or objective. 2. To use absolutely no word that does not contribute to the presentation. 3. As regarding rhythm: to compose in the sequence of the musical phrase, not in sequence of a metronome'. And Pound added a note in the course of which he referred to an image as 'that which presents an intellectual and emotional complex in an instant of time'.

By 1913 Pound, as was his wont, had taken over: the group he now called 'Les Imagistes' (active in 1912–14 and rightly regarded as the true imagists), which did not include Hulme but acknowledged his influence, was organized and publicized by him. The chief members, besides Pound and Flint, were the American H.D. (q.v.) and the Englishman who became her husband for a time: Richard Aldington (q.v.). The first anthology of imagism, *Des Imagistes*, appeared in 1914. The British poets included, besides Aldington and Flint, were Ford and Joyce (qq.v.). Soon after this the American poetastress Amy Lowell gained control of the imagist group – and imagism quickly turned into what Pound called 'Amygism'. (This is a part of literary history – several good poets, including Lawrence, q.v., and some of the original imagists, were represented in Amy Lowell's anthologies – but it is not important.)

Many of the attitudes subsumed under the term imagism are peculiar to Pound, or were initiated by him, and have been discussed in the section devoted to him. The imagist poems themselves were, as has been mentioned, small or trivial affairs; but the state of mind which produced them was modernist. The actual imagist poem concentrates so hard on being visually exact and vivid that it hardly has time, in its brief life, to demonstrate the anti-logical direction of its origins. But both Hulme (through Bergson) and Pound rejected ordinary logic as an acceptable surface for poetry: Hulme spoke (1908) of a new impressionism, and of an introspective (rather than heroic) poetry which would deal 'with expression and communication of momentary phases in the poet's mind'; Pound resorted to the Chinese ideogram, or to his incorrect, excited understanding of it – which was entirely alogical. It was the imagists – again, chiefly Hulme and Pound – who put forward 'free verse' as the most appropriate vehicle for poetry. This, then, was what was most modernist, most expressionist, about imagism: its assumption that poetry communicated metaphorically rather than logically.

Milton and, in the nineteenth century, Arnold had written 'free verse': verse in irregular lines. Whitman had not obeyed metrical laws – although his verse is by no means 'free' – and neither had a number of other nineteenth-century poets after him. But imagist free verse is not really 'free' at all; rather, as Pound wrote, it is 'a rhythm ... which corresponds exactly to the motion or shade of emotion to be expressed'. This left the poets themselves free of rules; it did not mean that poetry was now to become a kind of chopped up prose.

Whenever English poetry has radically changed its direction (in, for example, the sixteenth and twentieth centuries) it has turned to foreign poetries. Surrey and Wyatt and their minor contemporaries turned to Italy for the sonnet and blank verse; Pound and his contemporaries turned to the poetry of China and Japan – or to their understanding of them – and of the French symbolists. Directly and indirectly, then, English-language poetry of this century has taken some of its sustenance from elsewhere.

F.S. Flint (1885–1960), an important figure in the history of imagism, but possessed of an 'almost imbecile modesty' (Aldington, q.v.), was a civil servant (Chief of the Overseas Section, Statistics Division); he translated Verhaeren (*Love Poems*, 1916; *Plays*, 1920) and others, and published three volumes of original poetry – the last of these appeared as long ago as 1920. Flint, whom Ford (q.v.) called 'one of the most beautiful spirits of the country' (did he suggest some aspects of Tietjens, also in the Statistics Division?), had an exquisite gift; unfortunately it was too slight – or perhaps fragile is the apter word – to fully convey the acuteness of his sensitivity. He too frequently fell back on visual preciosity: 'Under the lily shadow/and the gold/and the blue and mauve/that the whin and the lilac/pour down on the water,/the fishes quiver. ...' (Flint) is not of the quality of the briefer 'Green arsenic smeared on an egg-white cloth. ...' (Pound, q.v.). Nor do

Flint's longer poems ('Hats', 'Otherworld') quite come off. 'Hats', an attack on the complacent bourgeoisie very much in the manner of Richard Aldington, lacks originality and linguistic edge. However, a few of his shorter poems, such as 'Eau Forte', have the vivid sharpness of good etchings.

Richard Aldington (1892–1962), poet, novelist, translator, critic and biographer, never realized his potentialities. A man of learning, sensibility and even some genius, he turned into an exhausted hack. His last works, critical and biographical, are worth reading; but they are enervated and frequently exasperated in tone (especially the biography of T.E. Lawrence). Aldington, who fought in the First World War, suffered from a tendency to incoherence and bitter, convulsive rage; it is most apparent in his novel *Death of a Hero* (1929) – about war and its prelude and aftermath – which has passages of power but which is written in too headlong a style. When Aldington had his emotions under control he was interesting; too often he is either debilitated or hysterical; he seldom does justice to his intelligence. His *Complete Poems* appeared in 1948. One of his best and most self-revealing books is the autobiographical *Life for Life's Sake* (1941).

As a poet, Aldington was seldom self-confident enough even to search for his own voice. From elegant imagist he moved (perhaps under Pound's, q.v., influence) to pastiche of the styles of previous centuries (in his 1923 collection, *Exile*). The phantasmagoric *A Fool i' the Forest* (1925), one of the long poems of disillusion written as a response to Eliot's *The Waste Land* (q.v.) (Aiken's, q.v., *Senlin* is another), is his most original work, and the one that most nearly pinpoints the nature of his disabling pain – an alarming combination of cynicism, sense of failure, blurred emotionalism, hysteria, frustration and satirical indignation. As a whole Aldington's poetry fails to throw off sufficiently the mere posture of romanticism; surprisingly, a good deal is taken for granted, and this operates as a sort of background of cliché. Aldington knew ancient Greek poetry well, but did not learn enough from it. His violently anti-bourgeois attitude is unsubtle and over-romanticized.

The poetry of Eliot, which to a large extent developed out of imagism and the poetic mood in which that movement originated, was one of the factors that led to the clear emergence of a 'modern' style in the Thirties. Another, less immediately obvious, factor was the poetry of some of the men who fought in the trenches in the First World War; their work originated in an ambience more or less Georgian – but the exigencies of the war jerked them out of this complacency.

The Sitwells offered a third, minor but lively challenge to Georgianism. The comment that this trio belong 'more to the history of publicity than to the history of poetry' (Leavis) is manifestly unfair in the case of Sacheverell Sitwell (1897), and both Edith Sitwell (1887–1964) and Osbert Sitwell (1892–1969) did many things that transcended mere publicity. Undoubtedly the Sitwells, especially Edith, were frequently tiresome and exhibitionistic; the 'progressive' anthology *Wheels* (1916), edited by Edith, contained mostly mediocre work; there was a strident egocentric note about most of Edith's public statements and critical pronouncements; her fiction (*I Live Under a Black Sun*, 1937, on Swift), criticism and biography are spoiled by a jarring, sometimes hysterical note that is, in fact, not confidence or certainty, but spinsterish self-love. None the less, although she became a bore, Edith's earlier poetry has seldom, since her death, had its due.

Osbert Sitwell was an amusing, accomplished and clever satirist (*England Reclaimed*, 1927, 1949; *Wreck at Tidesend*, 1952; *On the Continent*, 1958); but, as Conrad Aiken (q.v.) said in 1928, he 'never disturbs us, he never reveals'. As an essayist and critic he is pompous but often shrewd and informative. His best book, and this really is 'revealing', is his five-part autobiography: *Left Hand, Right Hand* (1944), *The Scarlet Tree* (1946), *Great Morning* (1947), *Laughter in the Next Room* (1948) and *Noble Essences* (1950). The autobiography is good because it does not take up a defensive position ('I belonged by birth, education, nature, outlook, and period to the pre-war era'), but simply records. Not the least excellent passages deal with the eccentric Sitwell father, Sir George, who, among other things, invented a toothbrush that played 'Annie Laurie' as it brushed the teeth and a 'small revolver for shooting wasps'. Osbert Sitwell also wrote one perceptive novel about the provincial England of 1914, before the First World War hit it: *Before the Bombardment* (1926).

Sacheverell Sitwell is a more limited writer. His many travel books are self-consciously aesthetic, and evade seriousness; his writings on baroque art and architecture are learned but curiously neutral in their effect. His poetry, notably *Canons of Giant Art* (1933), is eccentric, accomplished, artificial; it has unmistakable quality, but the most diligent investigation fails to yield an answer to the question, 'What quality?' What Sacheverell Sitwell has is a manner; but this, elegant and assured, conceals a lack of poetic conviction and self-confidence – the sad emptiness of a man born into the wrong time.

Edith was at once the most eccentric and most poetically gifted of her family. She was never more than a minor poet; but her verbal virtuosity and dexterity have hardly been equalled, within traditional limits, in this century. She chose not to draw upon her personal experience, but instead to construct an aristocratic-surrealist world that owed much to her interest in painting. (She was occasionally surrealist in spite of herself: the movement itself never really interested her, and she failed to register it.) The value of this lies in its style and its arch pseudo-innocence; resolutely avoiding the serious, the grotesqueness of Edith Sitwell's play-world reflects the grimness of the sexual experience (itself a narcissistic indulgence, or even celebration, of lack of sexual contact) she eschewed. 'Colonel Fantock', one of the more revealing of her poems, is haunted by the shadow of incest and degeneration, but this shadow is only an idea – which robs the poem of any robustness. The most successful of her poems is undoubtedly *Gold Coast Customs* (1930), a rhythmical *tour de force*.

With the advent of the Second World War Edith Sitwell adopted a new, earnest, apocalyptic manner, which culminated in her (surely too triumphal) entry into the Roman Catholic Church in 1954. This new style, cruelly referred to by James Reeves (q.v.) as 'death-bed repentance', was disastrous. Edith Sitwell attempted to fuse the richness of Yeats (q.v.), a grand high style, and the seventeenth-century complexity of such poets as Crashaw and Vaughan. The result is pretentious, vacuous, rhetorical, as at the beginning of 'Dirge for the New Sunrise', which has the solemn epigraph 'Fifteen minutes past eight o'clock, on the morning of Monday, the 6th of August, 1945':

> Bound to my heart as Ixion to the wheel,
> Nailed to my heart as the thief upon the cross,
> I hang between our Christ and the gap where the
> world was lost. ....

Rhapsodies of praise flowed from certain knighted cultural entrepreneurs, but not from critics. These later effusions of Edith Sitwell – Dr. Leavis, having been read one of them in a suitably lugubrious manner by an enthusiastic pupil, is supposed to have asked 'What do I do now? Ejaculate?' – are now for the most part unread. But the vigour of her early poetry, for all its emotional emptiness, should never be forgotten. Edith Sitwell's *Collected Poems* appeared in 1957; this is supplemented by *The Outcasts* (1962).

*

Rupert Brooke (1887–1915), a dazzlingly good-looking young man who held Henry James (he 'took for *his* own the whole of the poetic consciousness he was born to, and moved about in it as a stripped young swimmer. ... Rupert expressed us *all.* ...') as well as Edward Marsh spellbound, was in many ways the epitome of Georgianism (q.v.). But he is best treated as a war-, or rather a 'pre-war-', poet, because here he provides the clearest example of the limitations of Georgianism. He wrote some pleasant (and grace-ful) light verse, but was not a substantial poet and could never have been one. His rebel-liousness is schoolboy – his father was a master at Rugby School, which he attended and apparently enjoyed; nothing he wrote is ever in bad taste, nothing is profound. The excitement he caused in his male contemporaries was largely sentimental and homo-sexual in origin, although he himself was heterosexual. Because of his energy, his skill and his accomplishment, he seemed more original to his contemporaries than he actually was. Had he not died of blood-poisoning (at Skyros) while on his way to Gallipoli he would not have continued to write verse – his proficiency at it was but one of his accomplishments: there is no pressure behind his work – but would have become a publisher, or, most likely, a moderately reformist politician and then a peer. His famous sonnet 'The Soldier' sums up a mood that was almost universal among young people in the autumn of 1914; one can hardly blame Brooke himself for it. But it is bad poetry: under the guise of specious patriotism the poet celebrates a racial and therefore personal superiority ('a richer dust') that he has in no sense earned: God ('the eternal mind') is coolly equated with all things English. Now Brooke could hardly have known what the First World War was going to be like; but this sonnet is none the less non-poetry, a piece of inadequate traditionalism that sets out to supply what its public desires. It is still better known and more widely read than any single poem by any of the genuine poets of the First World War. Brooke's fundamental unoriginality is shown in one of his better poems, 'Dust': this, we realize, is all he can do with the new and exciting influence of Donne: all that comes through is a self-consciously bluff, 'young' tone. Nevertheless, he wrote some useful early criticism of the Jacobean poets and playwrights who were soon to be re-discovered in earnest, and the prevalent image of him as wholly sentimental and wrong-headed is unfair.

The first poet – and an incomparably more important one than Brooke (q.v.) – to realize the true nature of war in this century was **Charles Hamilton Sorley** (1895–1915), killed before he had time to develop his remarkable poetic gifts. His *Letters* (1919) are, for their time, extraordinary; they anticipate attitudes not taken up until after his death. In one of them he condemns Brooke for his 'fine words' and sentimentality. 'There is no such thing as a just war', he wrote, 'England – I am sick of the sound of the word. In training to fight for England, I am training to fight for that deliberate hypocrisy, that terrible middle-class sloth of outlook ... after the war all brave men will renounce their country and confess that they are strangers and pilgrims on the earth'. Before writing this he had diagnosed the hypocrisy underlying the British public school system (he experi-enced it at Marlborough); there is enough here to make it clear that the loss to English literature and life occasioned by his death is incalculable. His poetry is, for the most part, no more than immensely promising. But its eloquence, studiedly unrhetorical, already points to an astonishing integrity of purpose. *Marlborough* (1916), which collects most of his poetry, is eminently worth studying: the poems are not precocious, and so few are entirely memorable – but the promise is enormous.

Isaac Rosenberg (1890–1918), a Bristol Jew who began as an art-student, is not often given his due. The usual verdict is 'greater in promise than achievement'. His *Collected Works* (1979) clearly demonstrates that this is an unfair and ill-considered verdict. He is patronized for his 'imperfect education', but this did not in fact 'obscure his genius' any more than the more 'perfect' education of other aspiring poets illumined theirs. ... On the whole critics have failed to understand that his poems, far from being 'unfinished', are rhythmically original – and they have failed to recognize the intense Jewishness that underlies everything he wrote. Sorley (q.v., who was not twenty-one when he died) apart, Rosenberg was the most naturally gifted of all those who fell in the First World War (and I include Owen, q.v.): although of course war drew poetry from him (he suffered greatly at the front, as his health was poor: he was not in fact medically fit for service), it was not a decisive factor – as it was in the case of Owen. There is a complexity (sometimes wrongly referred to as 'verbal awkwardness') in Rosenberg's poetry that is absent from that of any of his contemporaries. Siegfried Sassoon (q.v.) saw it as a fusion of British and Hebrew culture, 'a strenuous effort for impassioned expression ... he saw things in terms of sculpture ... a poet of movement ... Words which express movement ... are essential to his natural utterance'. The most substantial and sensitive critical accounts of him so far are in C.H. Sisson's (q.v.) *English Poetry 1900–1950* (1971), and in Joseph Cohen's excellent *Journey to the Trenches* (1975), an exemplary study by one of the most intelligent of modern critics.

'Expression' illustrates the intensity of Rosenberg's poetic awareness – and his courage in not limiting the complex sense of what he is trying to say:

> Call – call – and bruise the air:
> Shatter dumb space!
> Yea! We will fling this passion
>   everywhere;
> Leaving no place
>
> For the superb and grave
> Magnificent throng,
> The pregnant queens of quietness
>   that brave
> And edge our song
>
> Of wonder at the light
> (Our life-leased home),
> Of greeting to our housemates.
>   And in might
> Our song shall roam
>
> Life's heat, a blossoming fire
> Blown bright by thought,
> While gleams and fades the infinite
>   desire,
> Phantasmed naught.
>
> Can this be caught and caged?
> Wings can be clipt
> Of eagles, the sun's gaudy measure
>   gauged,
> But no sense dipt

> In the mystery of sense.
> The troubled throng
> Of words break out like smothered
>   fire through dense
> And smouldering wrong.

The 'wit' (in the metaphysical sense) of this poem works: here – in a poem written in 1914 or 1915, before Rosenberg enlisted – is 'modern' writing apparently arising from nowhere. Actually Rosenberg sensed the 'seventeenth-century' aspirations in the poetry of the intelligent Lascelles Abercrombie (q.v.) – one is tempted to say that he admired it because of what it tried to do rather than for what it did – and put these to work. ... Rosenberg's view of the war that destroyed him was extraordinarily objective and comprehensive (more so than Owen's): he realized that the hideous destructiveness of 'shrieking iron and flame/Hurled through still heavens' nevertheless called forth, from men, what D.W. Harding (one of Rosenberg's early editors) calls 'a simplified greatness which they could never have reached before'. Rosenberg is quite as 'modern' as Eliot (q.v.), but he has more experience – and much more to say. The neglect in which he has been held is puzzling; probably the main reason for it lies in the difficulties his poems present. He is unique in English-language poetry inasmuch as, like Vallejo (q.v.), he passionately seeks to turn his poems into actual things, spells; too often this differentness has been dismissed as 'immaturity', for it terrifies the 'regular critic'. For the ex-painter Rosenberg, however – he did not finally decide to devote himself solely to poetry until 1915, when he was staying with a married sister in Capetown, South Africa – words had a magical value: they existed for him, as they do for some contemporary writers in Spanish, as the actual mysterious doubles of the things or qualities they denote (cf. Vallejo). He sees, in 'On Receiving News of the War' (1914), the ill tidings as 'Snow', 'a strange white word'. In 'Dead Man's Dump' a 'choked soul stretched weak hands/To reach the living word'; the dead lie in 'great sunk silences'. Rosenberg's poetry requires only close attention to be more widely recognized as the greatest to come from any soldier poet in this century. No contemporary English-language poet has had greater potentiality.

Wilfred Owen (1893–1918), who was killed only a week before the Armistice, was unknown to the public in his lifetime; he saw only four of his poems in print. Owen was the son of a Shropshire railway clerk. The account of him by his brother **Harold Owen** (1897–1972) in his memoirs, *Journey from Obscurity* (1963–5) – itself a masterpiece of reluctant, doggedly honest (except in the one obstinate denial he made of his brother's homosexuality) self-revelation – suggests that he was in many ways a prissy and self-absorbed youth. His earliest poems are Keatsian exercises – without anything very special about them. His parents could not afford to keep him at London University, where he matriculated in 1910; instead he was forced to take up a post as assistant to a vicar; he was supposed to decide whether to take orders. This exposure to the Church itself led him to a mental crisis: naturally enough, he lost the simple Christian faith of his childhood. Between 1913 and 1915, when he enlisted, he was a private tutor near Bordeaux. In September 1914 he wrote from France to his brother Harold (Owen's *Collected Letters* appeared in 1967) about a visit he had made, in the company of a doctor, to a hospital where some of the earliest casualties of the war were being cared for. Considering that Owen was the man who, less than four years later, was prepared to sacrifice the poetry ('Above all I am not concerned with Poetry' he wrote in the famous preface he drafted to a future volume) for the pity ('The Poetry is in the pity'), this is an odd letter: ostensibly written to 'educate' Harold 'to the actualities of war', it gives a clinical account, with illustrations, of the wounded. 'I was not much upset', Owen told his brother. But nearly all the poems of pity by which he is now remembered were written in the last eighteen months of his life. Owen's 'pity' is in fact a sort of homosexual love. It is not less poignant for that, but it is limited by its lack of naturalness. However, Owen almost broke over those limits by his passion for justice at the very end.

Now that we have Owen's letters and his brother's remarkable reminiscences we are able to see more clearly that his rather frozen and forbidding manner as a young man arose largely from sexual confusions. Joseph Cohen has shown in his *Owen Agonistes* (1967) that Owen was in fact a passive homosexual and what he aptly calls an 'injustice collector'. It seems that he fully discovered this fact about himself when he was in hospital in Craiglockhart after his first spell of active service (1916–17). While there he met Siegfried Sassoon (q.v.) – who was also a homosexual; one letter to Sassoon settles the matter deyond dispute. (There is, furthermore, a well-founded suggestion that he was buggered by C.K. Scott-Moncrieff, the translator of Proust; he could not accept the experience, and it quickened him into his most moving poetry. Genteel critics refuse to accept these facts, but they are not really beyond dispute.) All that we know about Owen tends to support this view: there is sometimes a certain morbidity in him which, despite the indignation and the anger which undoubtedly seared him, is not even, perhaps, primarily compassionate. This is particularly apparent in 'The Show', whose subject is not only the 'pity of war' but also an undiagnosed sickness in Owen's mind:

> My soul looked down from a vague height with Death,
> As unremembering how I rose or why,
> And saw a sad land, weak with sweats of dearth,
> Gray, cratered like the moon with hollow woe,
> And fitted with great pocks and scabs of plagues.
>
> Across its beard, that horror of harsh wire,
> There moved thin caterpillars, slowly uncoiled.
> It seemed they pushed themselves to be as plugs
> Of ditches, where they writhed and shrivelled, killed.
>
> By them had slimy paths been trailed and scraped
> Round myriad warts that might be little hills.
> From gloom's last dregs these long-strung creatures crept,
> And vanished out of dawn down hidden holes.
>
> (And smell came up from those foul openings
> As out of mouths, or deep wounds deepening.)
>
> On dithering feet upgathered, more and more,
> Brown strings towards strings of gray, with bristling spines,
> All migrants from green fields, intent on mire.
> Those that were gray, of more abundant spawns,
> Ramped on the rest and ate them and were eaten.
> I saw their bitten backs curve, loop, and straighten,
> I watched those agonies curl, lift, and flatten.
>
> Whereat, in terror what that sight might mean,
> I reeled and shivered earthward like a feather.
> And Death fell with me, like a deepening moan.

> And He, picking a manner of worm, which half had hid
> Its bruises in the earth, but crawled no further,
> Showed me its feet, the feet of many men,
> And the fresh-severed head of it, my head.

This is one of Owen's most powerful and self-revealing poems: often he himself remains curiously uninvolved in the 'pity' he describes – it is a legitimate criticism of the body of his later anti-war poems – but here he is a part of the horrible murder-process he is describing. Almost all of the anti-war poems are, of course, effective and deeply moving. However, we have, I think, to look again at Vallejo's (q.v.) poetry to see clearly that in Owen there is something morbid – something that actually enjoys the suffering that is being described, something nearly self-indulgent. (This is to judge by the high standards that the poems themselves demand.) Further, the poems do not altogether avoid a note of personal resentment: 'Miners' ('... they will not dream of us poor lads/Lost in the ground') does read like the poem of an 'injustice collector' – it has that note. Sassoon was wrong when he said 'he did not pity himself'; had he said it of Rosenberg (q.v.) he would have been nearer the mark. There is a sullen, homosexually oriented resentment of women that, every so often, surfaces in the poems ('all women, without exception, *annoy* me', he had written in 1914).

But this is only to redress a balance: Owen has long been slightly overrated, Rosenberg miserably underrated. Owen at his best is a poet of great power, who discovered, in his complex response to the war, new poetic procedures that were to influence the next generation of poets. His experiments with half-rhyme and what Edmund Blunden (q.v.) called 'para-rhyme' – most effective in the famous 'Strange Meeting', where he meets the man he has killed – were extensive and intelligent. His blend of irony and pity, too, was new in English poetry. Certainly his finest poems bring any decent reader to tears.

Siegfried Sassoon (1886–1967) was the most satirical of the war poets. He had started (in his anonymous *Poems*, 1906, *Hyacinth*, 1912, and other collections of pre-war poetry) as a conventional post-Pre-Raphaelite; his originality first made itself evident, not in his war poems of *The Old Huntsman* (1917) and *Counter-Attack* (1918), but in *The Daffodil Murderer* (1913), published under the pseudonym of Saul Kain: this was intended as a parody of Masefield's *The Everlasting Mercy* (q.v.), but it ended as an almost serious poem. Sassoon's attitude to the war was at first orthodox ('war has made us wise/And, fighting for our freedom, we are free'); experience of it soon changed this, and he became perhaps the most savage satirist of war that has ever been known. A captain in the Royal Welch Fusiliers, he was a close friend of Robert Graves (q.v., who held the same rank in the same regiment) and, later, in hospital at Craiglockhart, of Wilfred Owen (q.v.) – upon whom he exercised a decisive influence both sexually and poetically. *The Daffodil Murderer* revealed what can only be described as a strange inner twistedness: a kind of half-crazy, delirious pathic decadence, mixed in with strong feelings of guilt, lyrical compassion (expressed in the justly famous 'Everyone Sang') and whatever love for the 'wholesome', aristocratic, distracting 'sport' of fox-hunting represents. ... Sassoon, a confused man, never succeeded in solving his problems; but the horrors of war – which turned him into a lifelong pacifist – brought out in him a satirical ferocity and power: paradoxically, he found a kind of valid spiritual peace in the hellish sufferings of war. The war poems are unique in their crude and raw power: lack of control in them, because it is humaneness gone wild, becomes an actual virtue. His poetry went off at the end of the war, and after the Second World War he reverted to facile patriotism – a kind of 'dash ... of Winston Churchill in an ocean of water', as a critic has put it. He ended in the Roman Catholic

Church (he entered it at 70). His many volumes of fictionalized autobiography, such as *The Complete Memoirs of George Sherston* (1937) and *Siegfried's Journey* (1945), have been much admired, although they are very artificial books. He could not tell the truth about his private life, and his diaries are only just now being published for the first time. *The Old Century and Seven More Years* (1938) is the least contrived, the most lucid and touching and informative, of these. But for the essence of Sassoon, a good minor satirical poet, one must go back to those angry poems of the war which he so hated and in which he fought with such courage.

Although he saw longer service, and was badly wounded, the war did not prompt such powerful work from **Robert Graves** (1895–1985), who matured considerably later. His poetry may, allowing for anticipation and regressions, be divided into four main phases: from his schoolboy beginnings in 1906 until his discovery of the poetry of the American poet Laura Riding (q.v.) in 1926; the duration of his literary and personal association with her (1926–39); the period of his war-time sojourn in a South Devon farmhouse and of the first years of his return to Mallorca (1939–56); and what may be called the years in which he has emerged into world fame. He stopped writing in 1975, when he published the last of his oft-revised, updated, *Collected Poems.* The two main events in his poetic life have been the impact upon him of two years' trench warfare in the First World War, and his response to the poetry and personality of Laura Riding (q.v.). While the effect of Graves' war experiences has been adequately appreciated by his critics, the influence of Laura Riding has been very seriously underestimated – owing, one feels, to failure to understand her poetry.

Graves' faith in the poem he has to write – although not attended by careless arrogance about his capacities to write it – has been as great as that of any English poet, perhaps greater. In this sense the poem, for Graves, is a thing outside himself, a task of truth-telling – and not a thing to be invented or 'composed'. Poem-writing is a matter of absolute truthfulness to the mood of self-revelation. Graves is not the kind of craftsman who invents shapes in stone, to his own desires; but one who seeks, by means of intuition, to discover the exact shape in the middle of the stone, in which he has absolute faith. These fundamental beliefs are set forth in his earliest critical writings, which are, however, confused: he knew what he was looking for only when Riding came into his life.

If one of the signs of a major as distinct from a minor poet is development, then Graves is certainly a major poet. Yet his technical experiments have always been within the limits of tradition. As a schoolboy he worked on hosts of complicated rhyme-schemes and verse-forms, including the Welsh *englyn*, as well as with assonance and dissonance. For his subject-matter he drew on the worlds of chivalry, romance and nursery rhyme. Much of his technical facility and his capacity to use folk-themes without parodying them he owed to his father, **Alfred Perceval Graves** (1846–1931), himself a graceful minor Irish poet.

Graves has rejected not only nearly all his war poetry but also much of his immediately post-war poetry, written under the twin (and opposing) influences of war-trauma and pastoral marriage. This is technically accomplished, charming, and with an underlying complexity that is by no means as typically Georgian (q.v.) as its surface. Graves was at this time working – under the influence of W.H.R. Rivers, the anthropologist – on the Freudian theory that poetry was therapeutic, a view he largely abandoned in the later Twenties. The poems of the earlier Twenties tell a different story, however.

Little of the poetry of Graves' first period has been preserved in his *Collected Poems*; but its main positive features – delight in nonsense, preoccupation with terror, the nature of his love for women – have survived into his later poetry. What was purged was softness and cloying over-sweetness. Yet it was not Laura Riding's procedures that influenced him, but the content of her poems – and the personality that went with this. The poems of his maturity are in no sense at all imitations of hers; but her remarkably complicated view of life (and therefore the work in which she expressed this) is relevant to them: he shared, or rather, attempted devotedly to learn, this view, and the material of the poems is his struggle to accommodate himself lovingly to it and to her. The process proved impossible in the end, as he foresaw in 'Sick Love', written in the late Twenties: 'O Love, be fed with apples while you may', this begins; and it ends:

> Take your delight in momentariness,
> Walk between dark and dark – a shining space
> With the grave's narrowness, though not its peace.

The poems Graves wrote in his second period record, with great directness and in a diction of deliberate hardness and strength, the nerve-strains of impossible love ('To the galleys, thief, and sweat your soul out', one begins) and his attempt to achieve an existence that accorded with the goodness that Graves and (at that time) Laura Riding saw as residing in poetry above every other human activity. These are therefore 'existential' poems, and to be understood they must be read in this way: they are at once an account of the condition of romanticized devotedness, of a search for perfection (always tempered with ironic realism and earthy masculine robustness) and of human failures. Poems such as 'The Legs' describe the distractions that Graves saw as tempting him from the concentration his single-minded quest for poetic wisdom required. His 'historical grammar of poetic myth', *The White Goddess* (1947 rev. 1952), is essentially a generalization from his experiences of these years of devoted struggle to serve a savagely demanding muse, whom in 'On Portents' he had seen as a vast propeller, a 'bladed mind' strongly pulling through the 'ever-reluctant element' of Time. These poems, by which – together with those of the succeeding phase – Graves will probably be chiefly remembered, provide what will almost certainly become the classic latter-day record of romantic love; this is so not least because of their unsentimentality, their tough and unidealistic acceptance of the author's strong masculine recalcitrance. Thus, his mood changes from confidence –

> We tell no lies now, at last cannot be
> The rogues we were – so evilly linked in sense
> With what we scrutinized that lion or tiger
> Could leap from every copse, strike and devour us.

to zestful gloom –

> Yet why does she
> Come never as longed-for-beauty
> Slender and cool, with limbs lovely to see ...?

As he wrote in 1965, 'My theme was always the practical impossibility, transcended only by miracle, of absolute love continuing between man and woman.' It is the tension between 'practical impossibility' and 'miracle' that gives Graves' poetry its power.

The poems of Graves' third phase, written when he had abandoned his prodigious enterprise of creating – with Laura Riding – an existence in which poetry and what it represents would be a natural way of life, reflect upon the meaning of his experience:

> her image
> Warped in the weather, turned beldamish.
> Then back came winter on me at a bound,
> The pallid sky heaved with a moon-quake.
>
> Dangerous had it been with love-notes
> To serenade Queen Famine ...

They also discover new love, in some of the most beautiful love lyrics in English:

> Have you not read
> The words in my head,
> And I made part
> Of your own heart?

Finally, they humorously state his position and accept that fame has caught up with him, as in 'From the Embassy', where he refers to himself as 'ambassador of Otherwhere/To the unfederated States of Here and There'.

The poetry of Graves' most recent phase lacks the tension of the earlier work. It owes a good deal to the Sufic ideas by which Graves has been influenced in recent years; it discovers, but unconvincingly, the peaceful figure of the Black Goddess who lies behind the crueller one of the White Goddess. Love, to Graves in these new poems, walks 'on a knife edge between two different fates': one fate is to consort with the White Goddess, and is physical; the other, more difficult yet more rewarding, is to find peace in the domains of the Black Goddess. Frequently the poems are so lapidary as to remind the reader of Landor; but they reach a greater power than Landor usually achieved when they envisage the hell of a world made dead by a too great reliance upon physical passion. Of one who is trapped in this hell, who in departing too casually has said, 'I will write', he says in a poem of the same title:

> Long letters written and mailed in her own head –
> There are no mails in a city of the dead.

These late poems provide, in their explorations of the possibilities of a world purged of what he calls 'the blood sports of desire', and of the agonies of alienation from such a world, a sequel to those of his earlier years. But they are seldom as tense, or as moving, as they are written for the most part to the formula he provided for himself (unknowingly) in *The White Goddess*. He will be, perhaps, the last romantic poet to operate within traditional limits. His mastery of these is not in question.

Graves has also written some important prose. The best of his many historical novels are the two Claudius books: *I, Claudius* (1934) and *Claudius the God* (1934); *Wife to Mr. Milton* (1943) – an account of the first marriage that has been called 'distorted', but never on evidence – and *The Golden Fleece* (1944). His autobiography, *Good-bye to All That* (1929), is rightly regarded as a classic. *The Nazarene Gospel Restored* (1953), which he wrote in collaboration with Joshua Podro, is a remarkable reconstruction of the Gospel story; it was damned out of hand by orthodox theologians, but has gained wide currency – and was highly praised by Reinhold Niebuhr.

For **Edmund Blunden** (1896–1973) too, the war (in which he was gassed) was a devastating experience; but for the most part he reacted to it in a very different way: in a pastoral, although gnarled and highly original poetry. Blunden, a self-effacing and modest but on occasions privately vituperative man, has been a useful although not a trenchant critic – he has been absurdly although touchingly over-generous to some of his feebler contemporaries; carrying on where Norman Gale and Arthur Symons left off, he became the pioneer of the major eighteenth-century poet John Clare. *Undertones of War* (1928), though somewhat archly written, is one of the better prose books to come out of the First World War.

Nearly all Blunden's best poetry was written between about 1914 and 1929; it may be found in *The Poems of Edmund Blunden 1914–1930* (1930); the most substantial later collection is *Poems of Many Years* (1957), which is supplemented by *A Hong Kong House* (1961). The best of the poems, with a very few notable exceptions such as 'Report on Experience' – a major poem of great pathos – come into the category perhaps unfortunately called 'nature poetry'. Blunden's poems about nature combine accuracy of observation with an odd (and by no means always 'pleasant', in the sense that this word in understood by devotees of the pastoral and the bucolic) imaginative malice. This is when he is at his best and most disturbing. At other times he is artificial and literary. 'The Midnight Skaters' shows him at his best:

> The hop-poles stand in cones,
>   The icy pond lurks under,
> The pole-tops touch the star-gods' thrones
>   And sound the gulfs of wonder,
> But not the tallest there, 'tis said,
> Could fathom to this pond's black bed.
>
> Then is not Death at watch
>   Within those secret waters?
> What wants he but to catch
>   Earth's heedless sons and daughters,
> With but a crystal parapet.
> Between, he has his engines set.
>
> Then on, blood shouts, on, on,
>   Twirl, wheel and whip above him,
> Dance on this ball-floor thin and wan,
>   Use him as though you love him;
> Court him, elude him, reel and pass,
> And let him hate you through the glass.

Blunden edited a selection, *Poems* (1954), of his friend, the Gloucestershire man **Ivor Gurney** (1890–1937), who was a gifted composer of songs as well as a poet. For many years he was unaccountably neglected – it was in part the fault of his friend, Marion Scott, who, although his loyal supporter in life, continually frustrated the efforts of his friends to issue substantial collections of his work. At last, in 1982, a *Collected Poems* was issued. This is incomplete, but does give the reader enough to judge Gurney's extraordinary and unique achievement. *War Letters* (1983) is another valuable volume. *The Ordeal of Ivor Gurney* (1978) is a useful biography by a musician who makes no claim to assess the poetry. It is sometimes inconsistent (Gurney fell in love but had no definable sexuality) and is not a profound psychological study – this must come later – but is sensible and sound.

Gurney published two books in his lifetime: *Severn and Somme* (1917), and *War's Embers* (1919). They did not get the attention they deserved, and this was a vital factor in

Gurney's life, for he spent much of the last years of it in mental institutions – and at a time when there was virtually no treatment, except kindness, for any severe mental disturbance. It is usually said that shell-shock sent Gurney mad. This is misleading. It is true that his war experiences uncovered and perhaps helped to trigger his illness, even possible that he would not have collapsed so dramatically had he not been in the war. But the cause of his mental condition was not war experience, even though war experience played a part in the psychosis which he developed. His letters from France do not give a picture of a man cracking up, and Gurney was not – any more than, say, Graves (q.v.) was. He has been called by his biographer a 'paranoid schizophrenic'; but he was not (paranoia is by no means necessarily schizophrenic). Rather he suffered from what is variously called manic-depression, 'affective illness' or, perhaps most appropriately, 'bipolar illness' (see my introduction for a longer discussion of writers and mental illness). Certainly he suffered from 'mixed states' (q.v.). But one of the most striking features of his illness was, undoubtedly, what is called 'acute disappointment reaction' – which can be a component of affective illness. The nineteenth-century poet John Clare, read by Gurney, certainly suffered from this, among other illnesses.

Gurney was a gifted boy in an ungifted family. He did very well before the war, obtaining a scholarship to the Royal College of Music and the praise of Charles Villiers Stanford, a fine composer and an excellent judge. But, undoubtedly owing to some kind of chemical or electro-chemical derangement in his brain – through which he lost touch with reality for much of the time – after he had been through the war, he developed a terrible bitterness: he had not got, his whole being decided, what he deserved. It was an irrational feeling, and he would write to the police complaining about his treatment; yet his notion of fame was not in the least like that of Berryman (q.v.) – it was not corruptive. That Walter De la Mare, and others as distinguished as poets, rallied round him made no difference to his feelings of bitterness. He felt himself to be 'unclean', and developed an obsession with enemas. His earlier poems had been well constructed and often 'Georgian' (q.v.) in diction; but they were never conventional. Lines that ought not to work somehow do work:

> One comes across the strangest things in walks:
> Fragments of Abbey tithe-barns fixed in modern
> And Dutch-sort houses where the water baulks
> Weired up, and brick kilns broken among fern,
> Old troughs, great stone cisterns bishops might have blessed
> Ceremonially. . . .

and the poem ends:

> Birdlip climbs bold and treeless to a bend,
> Portway to dim wood-lengths without end,
> And Crickley goes to cliffs are the crown of days.

That is not one of his most successful poems. But it demonstrates that he had something peculiar, something peculiarly original, to say: the apparent lapses in grammar are partly just that, but not altogether that, as the astute and sensitive reader will have noticed. Those suffering from affective disorders frequently have the most piercing (if temporary) insights, and here we catch glimpses of such insights: of what is extraordinary in the apparently ordinary. His apprehensions of nature are as strange as those of Edward Thomas (q.v.), although they are not always as choate or controlled: much of his so-called (and it is a disgraceful term: one might better say poetry written in undeserved mental torture) 'asylum poetry' does lack control. However, whereas the genteel critic will sigh and shake his head and mutter 'such a waste of talent in such bitterness!', the reader of poetry will recognize that even in his alienation from reason, Gurney found a valid poetry of despair. And he will understand what the tormented Nietzsche (q.v.) meant when he said that all art was joy. ... For what Gurney's later and most mature poetry is about is not at all Gurney's own sense of bitterness and hatred of the world for taking away his 'fame': it is about the way the modern world, that world which began definitively with the First World War, robs almost all men and women of their honour. Late on Gurney wrote:

> I would not rest till work came from my hand
> And then as the thing grew, till fame came,
> (But only in honour) ... and then, O, how the grand
> Divination of ages grew to faith's flame.
> Great were our fathers and beautiful in all name,
> Happy their days, lovely in considered grain all their wood,
> Their days were kindness, growth, happiness, mindless.
>
> I would not rest until my county were
> Thronged with the Halls of Music; and until clear
> Hospitality for love were e'er possible ...
> And any for honour might come, or prayer, to certain
> Fondness and long nights' talking till all's known.
>
> Madness my enemy, cunning extreme my friend,
> Prayer my safeguard. (Ashes my reward at end.)
> Secrecy fervid my honour, soldier-courage my aid.
> (Promise and evil threatening my soul ever-afraid.)
> Now, with the work long done, to the witchcraft I bend
> And crouch – that knows nothing good, Hell uncaring
> Hell undismayed.

We discover from Gurney's other poems what he meant by 'honour'; and we know too that, near the very end, he was still reminded of 'poetry's truth'. Nor does that statement fail to find its justification in its context. There is much more than enough that is original in diction, and linguistically powerful, to indicate that Gurney finally triumphs, for us, as the recorder of the fate of the man or woman who tries to tell the exact truth (not truth with a capital T: this is the realm, perhaps, of the truly mad, and by no means all of these are confined in hospitals, as Gurney had to be from 1922 until his death), and can find the means only in poetry. Those who suffer from illness such as Gurney suffered do not totally withdraw from reality, as untreated schizophrenics tend to do: they cannot live in the world (though now Gurney would have been able to, with the aid of drugs), but they can and do, with extreme suffering, inhabit the world of the imagination – and in particular the world in which crass materialism, the greed of infantile and anti-feminine impulses which lead to war, evasion of facts as well of the search for the truth – the world in which all these and other evil matters thrive. 'Hell undismayed' (the politician sending the task force, the general ordering the invasion, the newspaperman lying, the public man pretending to do good, the criticaster wondering what he ought to say rather than what he feels), as he called it, defeats honour:

> Evil bitterly persisted in
> Keeps gods and devils fatally set on sin ...
> And sorcery-torture gives never any grace
> But evil acknowledgement, nets for claims, Hell-sent:
> Messages of thieves that broke her treasuries in.

Gurney awaits his enthusiastic critic (though P.J. Kavanagh's introduction to the *Collected Poems* – necessarily short – sounds the right note; the job has been done with proper humility and love) and expositor. There is much to be found in him. And if herein he has seemed to be given more space than he warrants, then that is because it is only now that we can begin to discover the rewards and insights he offers us: he achieved more than Sassoon (q.v.), perhaps much more – more even than Owen (q.v.): he is a genuine new discovery kept from us (in large part) by unfortunate accidents.

Herbert Read (1893–1968), who also fought in the First World War, was unquestionably an important, though by no means unconfused, eclectic critic. He was also an influential art critic. Probably his finest creative work is the novel *The Green Child* (1935). His poetry (*Collected Poems*, 1966) is very seldom as successful as it could have been. He was a man of great sincerity and exquisite sensibility – over-tolerant towards bad art because of his generous assumption that others shared his qualities – but, like Bridges (q.v.), 'just a shade too little of a blackguard'. He was, of course, a stronger poet than Bridges (who appears to have influenced him at one point); but he failed to achieve a consistent manner of his own. Ultimately he acknowledged this, quoting Yeats' (q.v.) remark to the effect that 'perfection' is to be found in the 'life' *or* in the 'work', but not (presumably) in both. However, his acknowledgement of the fundamental problem of *Künstlerschuld* (q.v.) made him into an important creative critic, and *The Green Child* is a masterpiece.

*

Hugh MacDiarmid (ps. **Christopher Murray Grieve**, 1892–1978) is – as he would have wished it – unclassifiable. He has been overrated by Scottish critics, who tend, as David Daiches does, to confuse his extrinsic importance to Scots literature with his intrinsic value as a poet; but he was undoubtedly a true poet, even though the accidentals which seem to obscure this are in his case multitudinous. Until the Sixties he was unjustly neglected outside his own country; since then there has been a good deal of irrelevant hullabaloo; there is still no proper collected poems (the book of that title, 1962, is not nearly what it purports to be, and is only partially supplemented by its successors; the decently edited retrospective collection, so badly needed, is only now in progress). MacDiarmid's achievement is uneven. His egotism (he could seldom write about anyone else without concentrating upon himself – although he was never ungenerous) and much of his militant communism often seem frustratingly irrelevant to his poetry. His endorsement of the Russian invasion of Czechoslovakia (1968) – 'fraternal entry' – as of Hungary twelve years earlier has raised doubts about his decency and, indeed, his historical judgement. These were grave lapses – not political lapses, but lapses into inhumanity. He was obstinate and refused to yield even to his better impulses over the matter of his communism. But he was never really a thinker – there is much more of the naïve than of the sentimentive (qq.v.) about him. For half a century he waged war against philistinism and

against the tendency of the vast majority of his fellow Scots to affect an unnatural Englishness – thus emasculating themselves and undermining their native genius, of which they
are as timidly afraid as a law-clerk of a cut lily (to adapt Pablo Neruda's, q.v., phrase).
The strain, accompanied by neglect and hostility, eventually told. MacDiarmid's external
persona was not wholly attractive: he thought too much of himself too solemnly, and his
grandiosity was too often tedious and irrelevant.

MacDiarmid is the pioneer of, and the most gifted figure in, the Scottish literary
renaissance (which came twenty-five years later than the Irish); he provided its
'programme ... focus, and ... models' (David Daiches).

He has done more than any other Scottish writer to develop Lallans, a synthetic
language that draws upon Middle Scots, English and modern local dialects. Lallans has
unique vitality in the right hands; in the hands of inferior poets it is laboured and tedious.
As Daiches has pointed out, Lallans is in fact no more 'synthetic' than the language of
Dunbar or Burns; it has closer links with Anglo-Saxon than modern English; it preserves
English words that English has lost. ... Here, in a well-known poem, 'Lourd on my
Hert', is MacDiarmid using it as it should be used:

> Lourd on my hert as winter lies
> The state that Scotland's in the day.
> Spring to the north has aye come slow
> But noo dour winter's like to stay
>   For guid
>   And no for guid.
>
> O wae's me on the weary days
> When it is scarce grey licht at noon;
> It maun be a' the stupid folk
> Diffusin' their dullness roon and roon
>   Like soot
>   That keeps the sunlicht oot.
>
> Nae wonder if I think I see
> A lichter shadow than the reist
> I'm fain to cry 'the dawn, the dawn!
> I see it brackin' in the East.'
>   But ah
>   – It's just mair snaw!

MacDiarmid's concern for Scotland is better shown here than in his many cantankerous
utterances on the subject. Practically all his best work was done by the mid-Thirties,
including the long poem-sequence *A Drunk Man Looks at the Thistle* (1926), a linguistic
tour de force of immense vitality, in which satirical verve exists side by side with self-
contemplation. Here Lallans is triumphantly appropriate: it functions as the poet's pure
voice. MacDiarmid never reached this level again, although some of his short Scots lyrics
are arresting in their freshness and depth of emotion. Much of MacDiarmid's later verse
is in English: long poems (such as *In Memoriam James Joyce*, 1955, and 'A Raised Beach')
setting forth arguments. Most of this resembles dull prose: MacDiarmid is not impressive
as a thinker (there is something distinctly ingenuous about his possibly only apparently
polymathic enterprises), and he lacks an ear for English rhythms. Intelligent critics speak
of 'the cumulative pattern of meaning' (much of this English verse consists of mere

catalogues of facts), but this is over-charitable. The claim that MacDiarmid is the best Scottish poet since Burns is a just one; but this is on the strength of his earlier Scots poetry. Eventually, a heavy drinker, he burned himself out in an orgy of ineffectual self-importance – although his closer friends saw another and gentler side to him.

Of poets born in the nineteenth century, the most distinguished successor to MacDiarmid was **William Soutar** (1898–1943), who was a bedridden invalid for almost a quarter of a century. Soutar's Scots poems (his English are negligible) are narrow in range of subject and feeling, but none the less exquisite in tone, style and execution. His *Collected Poems* appeared posthumously, in 1948; *Poems in Scots and English* (1961) adds more good poems. Soutar's moving and perceptive journal, *Diaries of a Dying Man* (1954), deserves to be better known.

The most eminent Scots poet to write in English was **Edwin Muir** (1887–1959), one of the most modest and self-effacing of contemporary writers. Muir, who came from the Orkneys, had a bitter struggle to establish himself: for nearly twenty years he lived a grim and miserable life in Glasgow. His first book, of literary criticism, appeared under the pseudonym of 'E. Moore' in 1918, when he was already past thirty. Muir and his wife Willa Muir made many translations from contemporary German writers; the most important were from Kafka (q.v.). The translations from Kafka have now outlived their usefulness: they need replacing, and are being replaced. But they were not bad versions, and they played a crucial part in establishing some understanding of Kafka. Muir was one of the better critics of his time (the book-reviewing he did towards the end of his life is his least important criticism: the best is in *The Structure of the Novel*, 1928, comparable in importance to Lubbock's *The Craft of Fiction* and Forster's, q.v., *Aspects of the Novel*). His three novels – *The Marionette* (1927), *The Three Brothers* (1931) and *Poor Tom* (1932) – are of a high standard as well as being important guides to the nature of his complex sensibility. Muir's unambitious and diffident nature gives his poetry a unique quality; unfortunately these qualities were also responsible for his too frequent lack of linguistic distinctiveness and energy. He could rarely develop a rhythm of his own: his poetry, traditional in form, relies too much on metrical norms; he often evades, one might say, the sound of his own voice. And yet he is a remarkably original poet, who avoided both the Scottish and the English traditions. There is nothing of the Georgians and little of Eliot (qq.v.) in his work. He took his inspiration from fable and myth, and from his observation of the natural world of animals. He was not a major poet only because he lacked procedures adequate to fully express that combination of the visionary and the metaphysical which characterizes his attitude. And yet he is a rewarding and often beautiful poet, in whom there is no fatal failure in humour (see 'Suburban Idyll'); one is prepared to accept his faintly stilted, strained diction and his awkwardness – arising from the fact that his poetic impulses usually fail, very oddly, to find their complete verbal counterparts: there is little verbal excitement in Muir – because one has such faith in his integrity, sweetness of disposition and wisdom. He is not a sensuous poet – this means that he lacks the force and conviction of a Yeats or a Graves (qq.v.) – and he is sometimes given to a kind of too obviously symbolic, abstract writing that lacks experiential reference; but his best poems, such as 'The Horses', have their own substance. Muir's first book of poetry appeared in 1925; the definitive *Collected Poems* was published in 1965. His *An Autobiography* (1954; originally *The Story and the Fable*, 1940) is revealing and rewarding.

*

Two woman poets born in the Nineties stand out above others: **Ruth Pitter** (1897) and **Sylvia Townsend Warner** (1893–1978). The latter is a distinguished novelist, and her fiction is mentioned elsewhere; but her poetry has been unduly and strangely neglected. Ruth Pitter is less resourceful and less interesting linguistically, but she is a graceful craftsman, and her quiet manner can be attractive. She is one of those rare woman poets who, like Marianne Moore (q.v.), can make a poetic virtue out of an apparently genteel and orthodox respectability. Often her themes are Christian; her gentle optimism functions pleasantly, as a kind of innocence. She has written just a handful of truly distinguished and original verse or poems which, beneath an unruffled surface, combine pastoral charm with emotional vitality.

Sylvia Townsend Warner was a musician learned in the church music of the fourteenth, fifteenth and sixteenth centuries. Her prose achieves what T.F. Powys (q.v.) – an admirer – tried but so seldom succeeded in achieving. Her poetry needs only to be better known to be more widely acclaimed. She never had her due; perhaps this is because she knew her limitations too well. 'Nellie Trim' is one of the most effective of modern literary ballads, and conveys an authentic poetic *frisson* in a way that many more ambitious poems do not. She has an epigrammatic style, a fine technique, and the capacity to employ traditional diction without distorting her meaning. Her best poetry is to be found in longer works, such as the extraordinary *Opus 7* (1931).

Sylvia Townsend Warner did not stop writing poetry, and 'Gloriana Dying' from *Twelve Poems* (1980) is perhaps her most remarkable poem: a moving and profound meditation on death and on the decline of England.

*

T.S. Eliot (1888–1965) – who, although loosely associated with the imagists (q.v.), requires separate treatment – was born in St. Louis, Missouri, and educated at Harvard. After study in Paris and Germany, and a short period as an assistant in the department of philosophy at Harvard, he settled permanently in England. He gained his living as an editorial director of the publishing firm of Faber and Faber (originally Faber and Gwyer). He married an Englishwoman (who subsequently became insane) in 1915. In 1927 he became an English citizen; it was in the following year that he issued his famous statement (influenced by *Action Française*, q.v.) that he was 'Anglo-Catholic in religion ... classicist in literature, and royalist in politics.' He won the Nobel Prize in 1948. He made a second marriage in the Fifties.

Eliot's enormous extrinsic importance is undoubted. It is so great that Geoffrey Grigson's (q.v.) comparison of him with Cowley, the minor late seventeenth-century poet who in his lifetime was regarded as a major figure, is hardly appropriate: Grigson is certainly correct to draw attention to Eliot's extremely limited intrinsic achievement – but he was very much more influential, and accomplished, than even Cowley – and he knew more about poetry, even if he wilfully blinded himself to his knowledge, than Cowley ever did.

Eliot poses a formidable problem: the distance between his remarkable critical sensibility and perceptiveness and his poetic achievement is so great as at first to seem impossible; furthermore, he possessed the technical accomplishment – if not the rhythmical energy – of a major poet. Eliot was one of the first to see that, as he put it in his tribute to John Davidson (q.v.), it was necessary for a poet to 'free himself completely from the poetic diction of English verse of his time. ... ' Eliot saw this more clearly than any one else of his generation (he owed much to Pound, q.v., who established him; but his mind was always clearer than Pound's); he had the capacity to demonstrate it in a practical form – in 'The Love Song of J. Alfred Prufrock' (written while Eliot was at Harvard and published, with other poems, in *Prufrock and Other Observations*, in 1917). This poem, like most of its successors, is full of technical excellencies: the control of tone and the juxtaposition of the literary and the colloquial are perhaps the main ones. However, it owes much to Robinson (q.v.), and even more to Italian crepuscular poets (q.v.). At all times Eliot demonstrates a superior intelligence – in fact, when one thinks of the English-language poets who dominated the scene at the time Eliot was actually writing the poem, this intelligence is not short of astonishing.

But it is primarily a critical intelligence. 'Prufrock', like the best of its successors (the 'Sweeney' poems are the best), is a minor poem. Eliot is a minor poet: he cannot write about love; he lacks real sympathy, or empathy; he is frigid. ... Skill, accomplishment, sensibility – even these are not enough to make a major poet. Emotional substance is needed. 'Prufrock' is the best as well as the earliest of Eliot's important poems: it is the only one that tries to deal, fully, with his own problem – his lack of feeling. That is to say, it states his predicament and it laments it; ultimately it is thin stuff, for all the delicacy of manipulation and the cleverness and the sensitivity. Eliot's use of Laforgue and other French poets is masterly, as is his pastiche – no weaker word will do – of Gozzano (q.v.); his importation of French symbolist techniques into English poetry has been valuable; but even as early as 'Prufrock' his procedures tend to function as a substitute for an original poetic impulse. This he never really has. That is why, in later poems, his technique of montage becomes poetically reprehensible: the reason for it is that he cannot make his own poetry, and so – with the exquisite sensibility that can so beautifully discern poetry – he uses other people's. It amounts to a splendid and judicious patchwork; but it is critical, anthological – not, in the final analysis, poetic. Yet in all the poetry up to *The Waste Land* there is a strong feeling for and towards poetry.

The fact is that Eliot, although extremely sophisticated in literary matters, was sexually and poetically naïve to a quite extraordinary degree. His inability to write about love is illustrated by the disastrous 'A Dedication to my Wife', written to his second wife: however touching this may seem in everyday terms, it amounts to a confession of total poetic failure in an area that is surely important. Again, Eliot's political position – although not actually 'fascist' as has often been urged – is simply naïve, insensitive, somewhat inhumane, and humanly ignorant. The celebrated disdainful contempt for humanity that emerges in Eliot's plays, particularly in the final comedies (*The Cocktail Party*, 1950; *The Confidential Clerk*, 1954; *The Elder Statesman*, 1959), is not the product of suffering or bitterness, but of a near-giggling frigidity and an ultra-conservative insensitivity. The crucifixion, on an ant hill, of his character Celia – in *The Cocktail Party* – is the supreme, atrocious example of this element in his attitude: of his failure to see ideas in terms of their human results. His attitude was not 'fascist', but it was insensitive; thus he could subscribe, at the end of his life, to a lunatic-fringe right-wing newspaper (I should add that there are also lunatic-fringe left-wing newspapers). Eliot's notion of the England he adopted as his own country was as simplistic as that of one of its military servants in the last century, and it had less justification. The contrast between that fantasy and his literary judgement – when this operated freely and autonomously – is extraordinary, as is his undoubted anti-semitism.

The Waste Land (1922) coincided with a universal mood of disillusion and despair. Its near-nihilism is more dignified than that of the icy and sneering little commercial verse-comedies of the Fifties – for in the early Twenties Eliot had no sustaining orthodoxy to cling to. The notion that *The Waste Land* is a unity, however, is incorrect: it is a ragbag of satirical and pseudo-lyrical and sensitively dramatic pieces, all on the general theme of present decay and past beauty. The satirical feeling is poetic, but the carpentry is obtrusive – and already the positive element, the beauty of the past, is factitiously presented, and is unconvincing. The sense of present degradation is well conveyed; there are scenes of genuine comedy; but the non-satirical sections (especially at the end) are pretentious. As a satirical poem – or, rather, a series of satirical poems – *The Waste Land* is successful. As a poem it fails: all traces of the experience that prompted it have been carefully removed. The critic John Peter implied, in an essay that was withdrawn (out of courtesy) when Eliot's solicitors threatened to take action, that it is (in part) an elegy for a young man who was killed at Gallipoli. ... Whether this is so or not, there is little doubt that, at a personal level, it examined the problems of 'the waist land'; the fact of sexual as well as spiritual loss and frustration. Eliot did have a mental breakdown coinciding with his wife's collapse, and there is little doubt that his homosexual feelings played some part in this – for ever after he over-concealed the nature of his sexuality, and at some cost to his poetry.

Eliot's poetry after his conversion to the Anglican religion becomes empty. E.M. Forster, writing in 1929, put his finger on the reasons for this conversion: 'if it [religious emotion] exists [in Eliot's books], it cannot be relegated. He has not got it; what he seeks is not revelation, but stability. ... Most writers ... ask the reader in, to co-operate or to look. ... Mr. Eliot does not want us in. He feels we shall increase the barrenness. ..., He is difficult because he has seen something terrible, and (underestimating ... the general decency of his audience) has declined to say so plainly'. Eliot saw not one but two 'terrible' things: he saw not only the repellently commercial and mechanized nature of modern life – but also the arid nature of his own heart. The *Four Quartets* (1936–42) consist of theological and philosophical abstractions piled up on one another in a skilful and sometimes entrancing but almost always 'Parnassian', over-self-conscious manner. They represent an evasion of experience, a failure to examine an incapacity for experience. For all the many ambitious exegeses that have been made of them, it is safe to predict that they will not survive as major poetry.

Eliot, then, is a vitally important influence; but the enormous edifice of his authority stands on a pin-point of actual poetic achievement. It remains to say that in his public life he was courteous, scrupulous, modest and generous. It will be difficult to sort out the psychological details of his poetic collapse since his widow, while a most excellent guardian of his memory, is by no means a literary critic (she was his secretary) and is over-sensitive to descriptions of him which seem, in her eyes if not in those of others more intelligent, to be discreditable to him. *Complete Poetry and Plays* (1969).

III

The drama in Great Britain in the Nineties was in just such an attenuated and totally exhausted state as it was in Europe. Although Ibsen (q.v.) had been known to a devoted few since about 1880, London audiences refused to accept him. He did not pay, and what he had to say was unpalatable to regular – twice-a-week – theatregoers, who are now and always have been (with, of course, exceptions) paradigmatic exponents of boulevard culture (q.v.): shallow, easily persuaded by rhetoric, entranced by the star-system, empty-headed and full of cackle signifying nothing. Oscar Wilde's (q.v.) comedies, particularly *The Importance of Being Ernest* (1895), represented the very best that could be commercially viable. **Arthur Wing Pinero** (1855–1934), of Portuguese-Jewish ancestry, represents the best of the popular theatre outside Wilde and Shaw (q.v.). Like many playwrights Pinero began as an actor (with Irving's company); his many plays show a mastery of the technical side of the theatre. He made his reputation with *The Second Mrs Tanqueray* (1894), a social tragedy which still plays entertainingly. Pinero manipulated his characters; they do not develop; they are two-dimensional. But he lacked the innate vulgarity of his German contemporary Sudermann, and within his limitations he is an effective, extraordinarily skilful and sometimes witty dramatist.

George Bernard Shaw (1856–1950) is a part of history; he made the world of his intellectual or enlightened contemporaries a more lively place; he was a skilful technician; he was on the whole a humane and generous, although certainly shallow, man; he had a most engaging personality. But he was a superficial thinker and a third-rate creative writer. His career as a whole is a monument to the failure of reason alone to solve human problems. His importance in the history of the theatre, as an Ibsenite (q.v.) revolutionary, has been exaggerated. Shaw is an excellent dramatist of ideas; few can go to the theatre and fail – in the theatre itself – to respond to the lively entertainment he usually offers. He is a man of almost infinite theatrical skill. But his drama is not literate, and his characters are not alive – actually they don't even pretend to be so. His portraits of real creative writers (the 'poet' Marchbanks in *Candida*, 1894, is the chief one) show no understanding whatever of the creative process, or the creative character: they are, in fact, hopelessly conventional. Shaw was brilliant and he was lucid; but he entirely misunderstood the nature of the imagination. He thought himself to be in the tradition of Molière, and was seriously disturbed because no one would agree with his own estimate of himself as superior to Shakespeare. He really believed he was. ... And he was immensely persuasive. But he never uttered a wise sentence in his long life. And he was a stranger to passion, as his deplorable letters to the actress Mrs. Patrick Campbell demonstrate. His attempt to write an imaginative, a 'great', play, which deals with emotion, is *St. Joan* (1924): when it tries to be moving it is execrable – as embarrassingly false as the 'passion' expressed in his letters to Mrs. Campbell (published in their *Correspondence*, 1952). Shaw's lack of emotion, which was not accompanied by any sort of unkindness, enabled him to be acute on occasions, as well as obtuse (as in his failure to see anything wrong with Mussolini's 'castor oil treatment' of his political opponents, or his sentimental worship of 'great' men, or his 'philosophy of life' – a cheap version of Bergsonianism, q.v.). Shaw undoubtedly belongs to the history of the theatre; his place in literature, however, is a very minor one. One may say, indeed, that the place of the 'drama of ideas' itself – when it is no more than that – in literature is a very minor one. But he is indispensable to dramatists because of his technique. Shaw won the Nobel Prize in 1925.

In attacking the complacency of the Nineties theatrical audience – *The Quintessence of Ibsenism* (1891) – Shaw concentrated on the reforming, didactic element in Ibsen, entirely ignoring the imaginative; his own plays, while full of outrageous (rather than genuinely vital) dialogue were structurally conventional. With his long and elaborate stage directions he helped to create the anti-linguistic, 'director's' theatre that still dominates the English and American stages, and stifles real drama. He did help to initiate a theatre with more life in it; but, as has now been recognized by some critics, it was in no sense really new.

The most important and enduring work of **Harley Granville-Barker** (1877–1946) is contained in his *Prefaces to Shakespeare* (5 volumes, 1958); but, a man of quite exceptional intelligence, he was also a more than competent playwright. Long, Shaw's (q.v.) protegé, was one of the earliest pioneers for the British National Theatre. In 1911 he published his 'paraphrase' of Schnitzler's *Anatol* (q.v.). He also translated plays by Romains and the Quintero Brothers (qq.v.). His best plays, *The Voysey Inheritance* and *Waste* (published, with *The Madras House*, as *Three Plays*, 1909), are reminiscent of Galsworthy (q.v.); but Granville-Barker is better at the creation of character, and lacks Galsworthy's smarmy cautiousness.

The failure of **James Barrie** (1860–1937) to fulfil his high potential has most usually been attributed to his over-attachment to his mother. Certainly this played a part in his life and work: his best play and his greatest success, *Peter Pan* (1904), about the boy who wouldn't grow up, is clearly related to his maternal problems. But Barrie's unresolved Oedipus complex was by no means as crippling to him as has been supposed; he failed to fulfil his gifts because he wilfully and slyly chose to indulge his sentimentality (and the sadism that went with it) – and he refused to remain in Scotland and become a Scottish instead of a popular British writer ... It was Edwin Muir (q.v.) who first pointed out that he was really tough, not soft at all; but Beerbohm (q.v.) had hinted at it when he said, apropos of the newly produced *Peter Pan*: '[Barrie's preoccupation with children] forces me to suppose that Mr. Barrie has, after all, to some extent, grown up. For children are the last thing with which a child concerns itself'.

Barrie began as a journalist, then succeeded as a novelist in the 'kailyard' (q.v.) tradition, which exploited Scottish humour and peculiarities in a manner that combines whimsicality, sentimentality and acute observation. His best book was *My Lady Nicotine* (1890), about his journalistic experiences; this is delightful. After that he sank into a cunning utilization of his audiences' most immature and crude instincts: a hard, subtle little Scot almost cynically purveying the cult of the child. *Peter Pan*, like the later *Mary Rose* (1924), is a masterpiece of polymorphous perversity, a Freudian joy-ride whose whole existence furiously denies the efficacy of beastly Freud. ... It is as irresistible and as horrible as a nasty day-dream, or poisoned sweetmeats.

More important than Shaw (q.v.) or anyone operating in England or Scotland was the group of playwrights associated with the Abbey Theatre in Dublin. This came into being in 1903. It gathered its inspiration from a desire to treat Ireland and her problems in an honest manner (the recalcitrance of the censor was thus a negative stimulus) and from the austere style of acting just then initiated in Paris by Antoine (q.v.). Because of the cosmopolitan policy of Edward Martyn (1859–1924), Moore's (q.v.) cousin, the Abbey Theatre became more than a mere platform for Irish peasant plays: it looked beyond England, to the continent. Yeats (dealt with here in his capacity as a verse dramatist), George Moore, Colum, Joyce and Æ (qq.v.) were among those who were concerned with the venture; the most gifted playwright of the first period was **J.M. Synge** (1871–1909), one of the five or six great playwrights of our century (cf. Brecht, O'Neill, Pirandello, Lorca, qq.v.). Synge trained as a musician, but became interested in literature while in Germany. In Paris he met Yeats, who encouraged him and sent him off to the Aran Islands to express 'a life that has never found expression'. Synge was a naïve (q.v.) writer who never had time to ruin his work with 'thought'. Yeats said to Moore of him: 'Synge has always the better of you, for you have brief but ghastly moments during which you admit the existence of other writers; Synge never has'. And he added that he did not think that Synge 'disliked other writers': 'they did not exist'. And Moore himself spoke (1914) of Synge's strangeness and solitariness; he 'was interested in things rather than ideas' (what a boon for a creative writer!). Moore also suggested that Yeats 'could not keep himself from putting rouge on Synge's face and touching up his eyebrows'. What Synge, second only to O'Neill in the English-speaking theatre of this century, gave to an enervated drama was the vitality of non-literary, country people and their speech. Hence he got close to real theatre: theatre played by wandering players, none of whom is a 'star', who remain attuned to their audiences. But he rejected realism: his greatest play, *The Playboy of the Western World* (1907), is poetic in all but its actual prose form. Synge, even though his greatest achievement lies in the theatre, was primarily a poet. An excellent linguist, he made some fine translations (many of them in prose) from the Gaelic, Hebrew, French, Italian and German (his *Translations* were collected in 1961). In the Aran Islands he spoke Irish and listened to the English that the Irish spoke – the English of which Yeats said: it 'takes its vocabulary from the time of Malory and of the translators of the Bible, but its idiom and vivid metaphor from Irish'. His own poem 'In Kerry' reflects this linguistic experience – and Synge's own fear of death:

> We heard the thrushes by the shore and sea,
> And saw the golden stars' nativity.
> Then round we went the lane by Thomas Flynn,
> Across the church where bones lie out and in;
> And there I asked beneath a lonely cloud
> Of strange delight, with one bird singing loud,
> What change you'd wrought in graveyard, rock and sea,
> To wake this new wild paradise for me. . . .
> Yet knew no more than knew those merry sins
> Had built this stack of thigh-bones, jaws and shins.

Synge died of cancer in 1909 just as he was beginning to achieve fame. His plays deal with and draw their energy from the untamed wildness of Ireland; the greatest, *The Playboy of the Western World*, functions at a number of levels. The language is as fresh as Jacobean English (it is interesting and significant that, like O'Neill, Synge knew better than to employ verse): exuberant, extravagant, tender, beautiful. It is splendidly primitive – its first audiences were profoundly shocked because it cut sharply and neatly across their pseudo-sophisticated gentility and false patriotism – with its roots deep in the true Irish tradition. Its theme, that a man can become what people think of him, anticipates the contemporary drama of Europe rather than that of Ireland or Great Britain. A properly edited *Collected Works* began to appear in 1962. Synge, a truly poetic dramatist, has never really been understood or accepted by the Irish urban audience, to whom he is superior. As a critic has said, 'his plays demand that kind of attention from ear and brain and heart, which appears to have been lost to the English-speaking theatre three centuries ago'. He stands almost alone in a century in which most theatre has belonged to managers and directors – almost all of them intellectually callow, emotionally crippled playboys.

None of the other Irish playwrights of the first decade of this century (with the exception of Yeats) was near Synge's stature; but many vigorous plays were written. Padraic Colum's (q.v.) *The Saxon Shillin'* (1903) was effective both as nationalist propaganda (it protested the enlistment of Irishmen in the British army) and as drama; his *Thomas Muskerry* (1910), set in a rural community, recalls both Ibsen (in its social awareness) and Synge (in its language). **Isabelle Gregory** (1852–1932), Lady Gregory, manager of the Abbey, was a graceful minor dramatist whose *The Rising of the Moon* (1907) and *The Gaol Gate* (1908) deserve to survive. **Lennox Robinson** (1886–1958), who also ran the Abbey Theatre for many years, produced a number of workmanlike realist plays; he lacked Synge's or even Colum's (qq.v.) power over language, but he remained faithful to Irish experience. *The Lost Leader* (1918) is about Parnell; his best play, *The White-Headed Boy* (1920), is a shrewd comedy of peasant life. Later, in *Church Street* (1934), he successfully attempted a Pirandellian (q.v.) experiment. English audiences should know more of his work.

Lord Dunsany (Edward Dray Plunkett, 1878–1957), an isolated figure, cannot be ignored. Dunsany developed a highly individual style as a writer of fiction as well as of one-act plays. He was educated at Eton and Sandhurst, and saw service with the British army in the Boer War, and the First World War – he had, in fact, a sardonic persona as a 'correct', cricketing, Englishman; but, as Ernest Boyd shrewdly pointed out, he failed 'in some slight … details to conform exactly to type'. It is easy to see why Dunsany is one of Borges' (q.v.) favourite authors: he is a thoroughgoing fantasist, one of the few who succeeds in this form. As the marvellously perceptive Ford (q.v.) put it, 'Says he: "I am sick of this world. … I will build up a world that shall be the unreal world of before the fall of Babylon. …" And all [his] effects … are got by the methods of sheerest realism'. One need add little more. He was a master of the one-act play and the short story (his verse has dated); one who builds his own worlds, and adventures in them – rather than indulging himself in them. Yeats (q.v.) introduced a *Selection* from his earliest work in 1912; there are a number of collections of the plays and stories. These are only occasionally strained. Dunsany created a world of his own, and a strange and fascinating one it is. He makes almost all contemporary 'fantasists' look tawdry.

The next major Irish dramatist to emerge after Synge (q.v.) was **Sean O'Casey** (originally **John Casey**, 1880–1964), whose best plays are his first three: *Shadow of a Gunman* (1925), *Juno and the Paycock* (1925) and *The Plough and the Stars* (1926). O'Casey came from the slums of Dublin and educated himself. He early joined the Irish Republican Brotherhood, and even Gaelicized his name. Later he turned away from this, and became a follower of the Labour movement, led by Jim Larkin. He worked at various manual jobs, and, although he finally turned to the theatre, he remained left-wing for the whole of his life. His first published books were satirical ballads and pamphlets. O'Casey's three great plays are set against the background of the Irish revolution and civil war. O'Casey, too, rejected that kind of realism of which Yeats (q.v.) had said that it 'cannot become impassioned, that is to say vital, without making somebody gushing and sentimental'. He chose highly melodramatic plots, but these were no more obtrusive than Shakespeare's. O'Casey, in these early plays, was able – as Synge had done before him – to create something that was so intensely Irish as to transcend it. These will continue to be played as long as the theatre lasts; they bring out the best in their audiences. By the time O'Casey arrived, the true genius of the Irish theatre had been almost stifled; but at first the Dublin audience accepted him, if only because his tragedy is screened by an inspired, savage farce. His vision is pessimistic, but tempered by comic irony; in *Juno and the Paycock* the violence and the horror are continuously redeemed by ebullience and vitality. O'Casey's indignation and hatred of priestly bigotry later got the better of him: where once his sense of the comic had operated lovingly and affirmatively, as an organizing and controlling factor, his later work tends to be either frozen into too consciously expressionist modes or merely chaotic (as in the case of his six nonetheless invaluable volumes of autobiography, 1939–54). But in *The Plough and the Stars*, which caused so much anger that he left Ireland for England, O'Casey was still at the height of his powers. No play, even *Juno*, so successfully describes and defines the peculiar tragedy of Ireland – a tragedy that continues into our own times. Of course O'Casey's later plays contain much excellent work. Some critics have even seen *The Silver Tassie* (1929) – rejected by the Abbey, although he had earlier saved it from bankruptcy – which is certainly one of the fiercest and most moving anti-war plays ever written, as his finest. And his expressionist experiments, influenced by film techniques, are valuable. But it is a pity that O'Casey's hatred of the capitalist system led him to embrace the dogma of communism: the imagination – so far as any dogma is concerned – is a sceptical instrument. Too much of the language of the later plays is factitious; too many of the targets are objects set up by the author simply to indulge his rage. O'Casey began as an eloquent, compassionate and comic diagnostician of the Irish tragedy – of both the beauty and the terror in the Irish soul. He ended as a victim of violence and hatred, sustained only by the lyricism of his sense of justice and love of humanity. He failed (as, after all, even Marx did not) to see that individual members of an oppressive class may be as, or even more, 'human' than individual members of an oppressed class. ... His plays were collected in four volumes (1949–51); *The Bishop's Bonfire* (1955), *The Drums of Father Ned* (1960) and three shorter plays, collected under the title of *Behind the Green Curtains* (1961), followed.

The only Irish dramatist of real stature since O'Casey (q.v.) is **Denis Johnston** (1901), who has been living in America since 1960. Johnston was a co-director of the Gate Theatre (which became a rival of the Abbey when the latter became state subsidized and respectable) for a number of years before joining the British Broadcasting Corporation. He lacks the sheer power and wildness of O'Casey, but has more control and perhaps more intelligence. He is one of the few English-language dramatists who has thoroughly absorbed and understood expressionist (q.v.) techniques. His first two plays are his best: *The Old Lady Says 'No'* and *The Moon in the Yellow River* (published together in 1932 under the latter title, and included in *Collected Plays*, 1960 – now superseded by *Dramatic Works*, 1977–9). The first explores both sides of the myth of Ireland. The second, Johnston's simplest play in terms of technique, contrasts the reality of an independent Ireland with the dream: a German engineer comes to Ireland to supervise an electrical power project. The time is the Twenties, when the Irish had newly won their independence. Johnston, while characteristically refraining from actually making judgements (this is one of his strengths), shows that the impact of technology on a rural society is not a happy one – it must be remembered that when the play was first performed the notion of 'progress' was more respectable among intellectuals than it now is. In 1936 Johnston adapted a play by Ernst Toller (q.v.) with the author's co-operation, as *Blind Man's Buff*. Johnston has continued to produce highly intelligent plays, including *The Dreaming Dust* (1940), about Swift, and *The Scythe and the Sunset*, which is set in Dublin in 1916. He has never had his due outside his own country, and this is puzzling. One of his most outstanding plays is *Strange Occurrence on Ireland's Eye* (1960) which was produced at the Abbey in 1956. This is perhaps the most gripping of all the many courtroom plays – it is based on a nineteenth-century trial, but is updated.

Another Irish playwright who deserves mention is **Brendan Behan** (1922–64). He was a diabetic alcoholic and that dangerous combination killed him early. He had little skill of any kind, but his enormous energy partly compensated for this. Wilful egocentricity and self-adoration drowned his gift, and before he died he had become a pitiful and tiresome self-publicist; but he produced three memorable works: the plays *The Quare Fella* (1954) and *The Hostage* (1958), and his memoirs, *Borstal Boy* (1958). *The Quare Fella* is a fine, moving, indignant exposure of the villainy of capital punishment and of the cruel hypocrites who believe in and operate it. *The Hostage* is a lively, if formless, depiction of the Dublin underworld. *Borstal Boy*, an account of authoritarian and official infamy and stupidity, is sharp, amoral, objective.

Brian Friel (1929) is a more thoughtful dramatist than Behan (q.v.), but on the whole less effective. He is best known for *Translations* (1981), which was produced first in Londonderry and then at the National Theatre – those who had not heard of Friel at that time, soon heard of him then. But he has written (counting adaptations) at least sixteen other plays. He has also published four volumes of indifferent short stories. Friel is very much a man of the theatre, which is to say that he is ultimately concerned with effects rather than with whatever he has to say. *Faith Healer* (1981) is highly promising, since Friel does half-convince us of his character, who cannot understand his own powers – but in the interests of stage-business he spoiled the construction, and the four monologues into which the play is broken up disturb, fatally, the story he has to tell. *Translations* was at first hailed by a theatre columnist as a 'masterpiece'. It is by no means that. Though less spoiled than *Faith Healer*, it is none the less spoiled. An allegory of the situation in Ulster today, though never a clear enough one, it is set in the earlier part of the last century: a group of Royal Engineers engaged in making an ordnance survey turns up in a 'hedge-school', where people learn Gaelic but no English. All the characters speak in English on the stage, but we always know who is speaking in what tongue. The play collapses at the end: once again Friel prefers to create an effect (the great temptation for playwrights, and one into which all but a very few fall) rather than to clarify his meaning. Thus the play ends up by saying nothing at all, and all the beauty of the linguistic effects is lost. To retain the attention of the audience without cheating on, or betraying, the imagination is extremely difficult in the prose play – but this is a century of prose plays; verse drama seems to be impossible to achieve.

Unlike James Barrie (q.v.), **James Bridie** (ps. **O.H. Mavor**, 1888–1951) remained in Scotland: for most of his adult life he practised as a doctor in his native Glasgow. But his star, once thought to be rising, fell into the sea with a hissing plop: he simply could not be serious enough. He could write superb scenes, but never managed to produce a single satisfactory play. His weakness springs not only from lack of imaginative self-confidence but also from a feyness that archly replaced creative recklessness. Like Shaw (q.v.), whom he resembles, Bridie lacks emotional substance and tries to make up for it by ingenuity. And yet he has enormous energy and inventiveness, and his best work (*The Anatomist*, 1931; *Jonah and the Whale*, 1932; *The Black Eye*, 1933; *Dr. Angelus*, 1950) reveals what is best and worst in the middlebrow Scottish audience – and that is one way of being superior to it. But he disappointed many serious Scots by his failure to initiate a revival in the theatre that would match the one begun by MacDiarmid (q.v.) in poetry.

Noël Coward (1899–1973) was middlebrow in all but one respect: he was never pretentious. His sophisticated comedies of modern life (the best are *Hay Fever*, 1925, *Private Lives*, 1930, and *Blithe Spirit*, 1941) are, within their admittedly – but unashamedly – extremely narrow limits, accurate, truthful, cynical and funny. He also had a sentimental, semi-jingoist, 'patriotic' vein (*Cavalcade*, 1932; *This Happy Breed*, 1942), which is surprisingly inoffensive: one has never been asked to take him seriously, and one accepts this as part of him. Shaw (q.v.) was never in fact more serious, although he would like to have been. Coward's wit and language are extremely accurate, and he had a sound notion of good and bad character. His books of autobiography – *Present Indicative* (1937), *Future Indefinite* (1954) – are well written and shrewd. Coward's fault is brittleness; but when one considers his work as a whole one is impressed by the tolerance and decency that – I use the word advisedly – shine through. This is particularly apparent in the short stories, collected in 1962. Coward was the most successful of all the non-'profound' writers in the theatre because he had a generous heart as well as being a professional to his finger-tips.

Frederic Lonsdale (1881–1954), though less gifted, was similarly professional. His greatest success was *The Last of Mrs. Cheney* (1925), a clever post-Wildean comedy with a melodramatic plot. He wrote for the moment. 'He delighted the millions', wrote W. Bridges-Adams, and 'the party over, his mirror reflects an empty mask'.

Some other successful playwrights who emerged in the pre-1956 (that is, pre-*Look Back in Anger*, q.v.) period are **Terence Rattigan** (1911), an excellent technician, the comedian and actor **Peter Ustinov** (1921) and **Rodney Ackland** (1908). All of these, and some others, have provided intelligent and skilful fare for London's theatregoers, though none wrote a truly serious play. But their technique, and with it the whole notion of the 'well-made play', has been repudiated by the post-Osborne dramatists. In the long term, however, this has made little difference – one might as well have the well-made play after all.

*

As Eugene O'Neill (q.v.) realized, great drama needs 'great language' – which is usually in verse rather than prose. Has any English-language dramatist of the twentieth century been capable of great language? Only Synge (q.v.), perhaps. ... Certainly the contemporary attempt to revive verse drama has been an almost unrelieved failure. The most poetic verse play of this century, Hardy's (q.v.) *The Dynasts* (1903–8), was not designed or written for the theatre. There has been no audience for real, contemporary poetry in the English theatre (and there is no sign of one developing). Hardy saw this, and in *The Dynasts* he anticipated the technique of both radio and cinema. It is not free from faults, but it is considerably more profound than its sometimes portentous surface suggests. When one compares it to Bridges' (q.v.) attempts at verse drama ('I spake too roughly, Margaret; I was angry:/I knew not what I said. Margaret, I am sorry. ... My God, oh, if I have killed her! Margaret, Margaret!' – this sad trash sent the unfortunate Winters, q.v., into paroxysms of ecstasy) one realizes its strengths. *The Dynasts* has not yet been subjected to really intelligent, extensive, critical examination. Its stage directions alone represent a high point of English prose – and once it is realized that no verse at that time could have come much nearer than Hardy's to success in dealing with so comprehensive and vast a theme, the magnitude of his achievement may be grasped. Kenneth Muir's verdict that he writes in a 'strange jargon', an understandable enough response, is not, however, a fair one. This 'jargon' expresses a remarkable complexity of thought.

The century's best verse dramatist in the theatre itself is certainly Yeats (q.v.). But (and surely this is as significant as O'Neill's conscious eschewal of 'great language' and Hardy's refusal to write for the actual theatre) his finest play, *The Words Upon the Window Pane* (1934), written in the last years of his life, is in prose. ... In the verse play Yeats very nearly, in the words of his compatriot Frank O'Connor, 'made good': he, almost alone, came to understand that no verse play in which the verse is merely ornamental to the action (the fault of, e.g., Fry, Maxwell Anderson, qq.v.) can be poetic. His very early *The*

Countess Kathleen (1891) has some good (minor) poetry in it – but this has no relevance to the action. Later Yeats came to realize that his drama could appeal only to a minority; this minority did not constitute the kind of audience that could have prompted a real revival of poetic drama – but it enabled Yeats to do almost as well as anyone could have done. The best of his verse plays are in one act. He had a good sense of theatre (he learned this while trying to run an actual theatre), but was poor in characterization. However, since most of his plays are on mythological themes, this hardly matters. His plays were collected in 1952.

The history of the verse drama since Yeats is uninspiring. Masefield (his best play is *The Tragedy of Nan*, 1909, which is in dialect) and Binyon (qq.v.) made serious efforts, but they have dated. Abercrombie (q.v.), as already noted, failed as a playwright actually because he chose to write in verse instead of prose. ... Eliot's (q.v.) verse drama, which lay very near to his heart, was a disastrous affair that would not have attracted attention but for his fame in other fields. When *Murder in the Cathedral* (1935) is stripped of its Christian pretensions it is revealed as an empty, pseudo-liturgical affair, devoid of psychological interest; skilfully executed though it is, it can only be of real interest to churchgoers. *The Family Reunion* (1939) has dated, and its verse is prosy and tired. The comedies of the Fifties have already been mentioned. In his plays Eliot betrayed poetry by trying to make it unobtrusive: his fashion-conscious audiences believed they had been watching drawing-room comedies – and so, as it happens, they had. Many were unaware that these plays were 'in verse'.

Gordon Bottomley (1874–1948) wrote accomplished verse; but not one of his plays, which include glosses on *Macbeth* and *King Lear*, really hits the mark. He was always devoid of dramatic sense, and as he grew older he tried to turn his plays into rhetorical performances. His verse is better than that of most Georgians (q.v.), and for this reason one searches in it for something more than mere verbal beauty – but, alas, in vain. His gift consisted of little more than a capacity for concealing clichés.

Auden, Spender and MacNeice (qq.v.) all wrote verse plays during the Thirties. Three of Auden's were written in collaboration with Isherwood (q.v.), who supplied the plots. *The Ascent of F6* (1936) and *On the Frontier* (1938) are no more than lively reflections of fashionable preoccupations; *The Dog Beneath the Skin* (1935) anticipates the later interest in Brecht (q.v.) and in the 'musical'. Verse is not an essential element in any of these. MacNeice made a good verse translation of *Agamemnon*, but his original verse play, *Out of the Picture* (1937), is weak. His plays for radio are excellent, but ephemeral. The best of the Thirties verse plays, although it is gravely flawed, is Spender's *Trial of a Judge* (1938): this is more mature than anything comparable of its time, and has at least the virtue of trying to make use of poetry to express an agonizing situation – that of a liberal judge trapped between extremes. The language fails, and *Trial of a Judge* would not be playable now; but the attempt is testimony to Spender's political and critical awareness.

After the Second World War there was a revival of Eliotian (q.v.) 'Christian' drama; some of this was moderately successful in the theatre, but none has survived. Andrew Young's *Nicodemus* (q.v.), written earlier, is superior to all these productions. Then **Christopher Fry** (1907) burst on the scene. Fry began as an imitator of Eliot, but soon switched to comedy with *A Phoenix too Frequent* (1946) and *The Lady's Not for Burning* (1949). Later he did *Venus Observed* (1950). Soon after this he began to go out of fashion, although he has tried to make several comebacks. Fortunately for himself he was able to earn money writing kitsch scripts for Hollywood (*Ben Hur* is the most impressive). Fry's verse is perhaps most clearly defined by the adjective 'non-poetic': his language is inorganic, over-confident, slick, pseudo-effervescent, grovelling for the superficial response of an inattentive audience. His verse has no life in it, as is exemplified in the following characteristic passage, presumably composed for suburban theatregoers in search of uplift:

> We reach an obstacle, and learn to overcome it;
> our thoughts or emotions become knotted, and we
> increase ourselves in order to unknot them; a
> state of being becomes intolerable, and, drawing
> upon a hidden reserve of spirit, we transform it.

Among the obstacles Fry never even reached are verse composition or a notion of what vulgarity is. Fry's sense of 'wonder' and 'delight' is as meretricious as his sense of character. One feels sorry for him as a victim of fashion (the fickleness of the middlebrow audience is one of its chief characteristics) – but on the other hand he has perpetrated an offensive pretentiousness (thus a newspaper critic once spoke of his 'great hymns to living'): a smug prosiness snuggles cosily at the heart-cavity of the false vivacity: '... in the heart/Of all right causes is a cause that cannot lose. ... ' His skill works most effectively in translation, where he is controlled by meanings outside the area of his own self-indulgent fancy, and only his ingenuity is engaged.

*

The English theatrical revolution – if it can really be called that – is usually dated from 8 May 1956, when **John Osborne**'s (1929) play *Look Back in Anger* (1956) was staged. This was certainly an important date in the history of the theatre: theatrical impresarios – who are seldom intelligent in a literary sense – became interested in the work of young authors, and the theatre became more lively: the age of the drawing-room comedy was past. A journalist and theatrical historian, John Russell Taylor, has claimed that, now, 'there is a hard core of exciting new writing in the theatre'. This is partly justified, although the influence of Osborne's play (which has already begun to date) is limited to its effect on the mentality of the people who run the theatre – as Taylor himself remarks, there was no 'School of Osborne'. The 'core' has grown steadily softer and less 'exciting'. Taylor's term 'exciting' should not be taken to imply that there has been a genuine theatrical revival: there has not. This would have required an audience, and it could not take place in the commercial theatre – or under the present star system. The general, slight improvement of the British theatre in the third quarter of this century is largely due to the belated influence of Brecht (q.v.) – and of other continental playwrights. The theatre of an essentially conventional playwright such as **Robert Bolt** (1924), for example, is probably rather more lively for its cautious assimilation of Brechtian and other innovations; but Bolt writes for stars and for audiences who want to pretend they have been 'disturbed', and so never strays over the boundary of the generally acceptable. The other beneficial influence on the new British theatre has been that of the music hall. **N.F. Simpson** (1919), for example, is too confidently treated as an absurdist by Martin Esslin in his book *The Theatre of the Absurd*: he is (as Taylor, again, has pointed out) much nearer to the wartime radio show *Itma (It's That Man Again)* and the Goons than to Ionesco (q.v.). *One Way Pendulum* (1960) is theatrically excellent – 'it plays itself', as one experienced member of the original cast, the late John Laurie, put it – but its nonsense is that of the old variety comic rather than that of a Lear or a Carroll or a Morgenstern (q.v.). ... When Simpson has tried to be allegorical or 'significant' the result has been disastrous.

Osborne's own progress since *Look Back in Anger* has been disappointing. *Look Back in Anger* was a muddled but passionate play which caught the muddled and passionate mood of young people in the Fifties, and provided a younger generation with a portrait of itself in Jimmy Porter. Plays written earlier than *Look Back in Anger* include *Personal Enemy* (produced 1955) and *Epitaph for George Dillon* – both in collaboration with Anthony Creighton. Both these, although derivative, showed promise. In *The Entertainer* (1957) Osborne's confusions vitiate the play; nor does he successfully convey the spirit of the old Edwardian music hall which he so admires. *Luther* (1961) is simply pseudo-Brechtian documentary; the words (mostly Luther's) are effective, but the dramatist's selection of his material is oddly uncreative. *Inadmissible Evidence* (1965), although admired by some, and certainly the best of Osborne's plays since 1956, is basically a rehash of *Look Back in Anger*. *West of Suez* (1971), an attempt to make a major comeback, is a failure. It has turned out that Osborne never really had anything to say: he was just bloody-minded. At his best Osborne is, in Raymond Williams' words, 'uncontrolled, unresolved but directly powerful'. A major playwright needs more than that. When Osborne takes control he becomes a writer of (perfectly good) commercial documentary; and he loses power. The worst of his faults is his inability to rid himself of trivial obsessions. He is now a damp squib, although the recent publication of his autobiography attracted attention.

John Arden (1930) is more original than Osborne (q.v.), but has not achieved comparable commercial success. Arden uses verse in parts of some of his plays, but this is not poetic – or, I think, intended to be so. Arden, though himself what would be described in newspapers as a 'radical', used not to write 'committed' plays. In fact it is this that upset his audiences, who expected him to take sides. Actually he is an individualist, a man more in love with vigour or personality and vitality than with morality. He has more control over language than Osborne, and more complexity. His first substantial play, *Serjeant Musgrave's Dance* (1959), met with a fairly hostile reception because, although 'about' pacifism, it had no comforting message. It showed instead a man of semi-pathological personality spearheading a confused pacifist movement in a provincial town in the North of England. This is 'about' Arden's own confusions, and it resolves them in human terms: Serjeant Musgrave, the central figure, is as splendidly puzzling as Brecht's Mother Courage (q.v.), with whom he has often been compared. The language is the richest in the modern British theatre. It ran for twenty-eight performances, but was later presented as a television play. *The Workhouse Donkey* (1963) is a comedy: a caricature of local politics in a northern town, and it does not favour the left. *Armstrong's Last Goodnight* (1964), set in sixteenth-century Scotland, fails because Arden has invented an unsuccessful and pointless equivalent for the Scottish speech of the time; but in other respects it is an impressive and subtle play. Since then he has tried to write 'committed' plays, and these have been disastrous, which seems to have had a bad effect on him.

It has been said that his wife, Margaretta D'Arcy, with whom he has written most of his plays since *Friday's Hiding* (1967), has exercised a 'baleful influence' upon him: led him from a liberal-pacifist stance to a 'revolutionary' one. Certainly something has led him from the one to the other stance, and as certainly his plays have become progressively less effective. The row over the *The Island of the Mighty* (1972), which led to its authors themselves picketing the theatre (it was produced by the Royal Shakespeare Company), may have obscured the fact that this is not an effective play. They complained that the production of their play was 'imperialistic' whereas the play itself was 'anti-imperialistic'. They were probably right; but that a play is anti-imperialistic does not make it a good play – if anti-imperialism is the motivation of any work, rather than an assumption simply built into it, then it is likely to be polemic rather than literature. Yet the struggle Arden and D'Arcy have made against the 'director's theatre' and its comforting assumptions has been valuable and salutary. It remains for them both, or D'Arcy alone, or Arden alone, to produce a truly convincing play. Arden's point of view is set out clearly in his book of essays, *To Present the Evidence* (1978). As technicians these two writers have been well ahead of their time, and their innovations have been used by others far less talented.

Few approach the level of seriousness sought for here, although there are many skilful dramatists who can put together effective theatre pieces. **Harold Pinter** (1930), originally a Jewish actor from the East End, wrote several original plays before losing his gifts in the tedious labyrinth of theatrical politics. Pinter is an ironic super-realist whose first three plays hold up a mirror to nature – to life as she is really lived – with a quite remarkably artful artlessness. When asked what his work was about he replied: 'The weasel under the cocktail cabinet': in 'real life' there are weasels under cocktail cabinets; but not in fiction. ... Again, the oddness of Pinter's dialogue is simply that it reproduces everyday speech – which, in dramatic contexts, seems very odd indeed. The 'Kafkaesque' (q.v.) elements in Pinter's plays, the hired killers, the strange instructions given down the shaft of a dumb-waiter, the menacing atmosphere (of the first three plays: *The Room, The Birthday Party, The Dumb Waiter*) – all these are super-realistic: the author merely withholds the 'explanation': why is Stanley to be killed in *The Birthday Party*? Who gives the instructions in *The Dumb Waiter*? You only need to be supplied with a limited number of answers, and you have solved the riddle. Pinter, then, is a very different kind of 'absurdist'. There are elements of caricature (of reality), and an atmosphere of horror as well as comedy – but the dramatist's position is still basically realist. There is no 'great mind' working here, as some have imagined: the plays are simply *tranches de vie* with ellipses and some variety – music-hall-derived material thrown in. These plays were published in 1960 under the title of *The Birthday Party*.

The Caretaker (1960) is even more overtly realist. Although the play is strange in atmosphere, and one of the characters is (medically) depressed, there is a perfectly acceptable 'explanation': Mick wants to get rid of an old tramp his depressed brother has picked up – but without offending the latter. *Tea Party*, written like a number of Pinter's other plays, for television, is a study of a man descending into catatonic schizophrenia – it ends with his complete paralysis. Again, this is absolutely realist once we have the explanation (which in this case we do have). *The Homecoming* (1965), written for the stage, is also realist; it moves yet nearer to the conventional realist formula. The notion that Teddy – who comes home, having achieved success in America, to confront his awful family – is a liar has no more evidence to support it than any other unverifiable statement by anyone else. ... That is one of Pinter's points. And in the case of this play we can even begin to discuss it in 'Bradleyan' terms: in terms of the characters' psychological motivations. With Arden (q.v.), Pinter stood head and shoulders above his contemporaries in the theatre. But since *The Homecoming* he has had nothing to add, and new plays are self-parodic. He has written a number of screenplays for pretentious novels, and is eminently professional. He also works in the theatre, and is now a predictably 'establishment figure'. He has just announced that he is now 'politically committed'.

The third substantial post-war English dramatist, **John Whiting** (1915–63), died prematurely. He did not, in fact, fulfil his potential – nor did he ever have a real commercial success. *Saint's Day* (*Three Plays*, 1957), winner of the Festival of Britain Play Competition, anticipated a good many future techniques: 'absurdity', deliberate lopsidedness of structure, abandonment of realist intentions. *Marching Song* (*Three Plays*, 1957) is one of the few really outstanding post-war plays: so much so that John Russell Taylor calls it 'formidably intelligent' but 'a little cold and lifeless': it 'could never take an unprepared audience by storm' (for Taylor, this would be an enormously 'exciting' event, the desideratum – but he is a critic of the theatre, not a playwright). For *The Devils* (1961), commissioned by the Royal Shakespeare Company, Whiting drew on Aldous Huxley's (q.v.) study of mass hysteria, *The Devils of Loudun*, but treated the material in the light of his own unusual preoccupation with man's tendency to undermine his material position – in which process Whiting discovers much poetry. *The Devils* should not be judged by realist standards: it needs (like Shakespeare's histories) to be judged in its own, not in historical, terms. Probably Whiting was the most gifted of all the playwrights of his generation – but he lacked sufficient spirit of compromise.

Arnold Wesker (1932) is less gifted, but his *Wesker Trilogy* (1960) – *Chicken Soup with Barley* (1958), *Roots* (1959), *I'm Talking about Jerusalem* (1960) – deserves to survive. The first of these is set in Wesker's native East End, the last two in Norfolk. These are sprawling, muddled – but passionately alive. They do not succeed in portraying the post-war working-classes, but they do present some convincing characters – notably Beatie in *Roots*. However, the plays, for all their vitality, do not stand up well to close examination: the Norfolk speech is badly done, there are some pointless faults of construction and inconsistencies, and at times Wesker's simplistic idealism is revealed in all its stupidity – not as innocently lovely or Blakean, but as something a little awkward. ... *Chips with Everything* (1962), a portrait of life in the RAF, has its moments – but in general Wesker's attitudes (which are not the result of processes one would normally describe as intellectual) are obtrusive. During the Sixties Wesker worked hard on his impossible and noble Centre 42 project, and his plays of that period (*The Four Seasons*, 1966; *Their Very Own and Golden City*, 1966) have increasingly reflected his over-optimistic view of society – a view that unfortunately has less and less, of a lyrical nature, to sustain it. None the less, he is the warmest and most likeable of the playwrights of his time.

John Spurling (1936) combines hard neutrality of outlook with interest in Latin-American possibilities, and is already technically adept. *MacRune's Guevara* (1969) is a relentless and comic examination of a legendary character. Spurling is an excellent arranger, with a good sense of theatrical technique. Yet he has not yet had a major theatrical production: a West End 'run'. It is possible that if he had this encouragement, which he surely deserves, he would go on to something rather more substantial than he has so far achieved. All (or nearly all) his plays are based on unoriginal material, and some are simply exercises (e.g. *Romance*, produced 1971). Certain of them are foolishly ambitious, like *The British Empire, Part One* (1981), in which he starts to examine the nature of the foundation of the British Empire – but without, apparently, any feelings of his own about it at all. One would like to say that he is admirably 'uncommitted'; but one does not say so because it is hard to find out, in the absence of anything about love or art or its function, just what he does believe, feel or think. He is committed to the necessity of creating an effect, but so far he has been unable to move his audience – you cannot move any audience in the theatre to a coldly sceptical point of view, and this is what Spurling seems to possess. That is excellent – but does his coldly sceptical eye ever need to subdue unruly passions? Unruly passions are a part of the history of the world, and, even in his best plays, such as *MacRune's Guevara* and *While Rome Burns* (produced 1976), he seems unable to depict them. Yet he is a superb technician, and one feels that his point of view – only apparently icy – could in some way be presented effectively. One therefore judges his work from the highest standards, and hopes that he will find more commercial success in the theatre than he has so far done – he is possibly too intelligent to mix well into theatrical theatres. *On a Clear Day You Can See Marlowe*, produced in London in 1974, a joke about the various views of Marlowe now prevalent (including the absurd ones, such as that he 'wrote' Shakespeare), is far above the heads of an average London audience. Yet it would be tragic if Spurling were to be forced to become a closet dramatist: he is head and shoulders above his rivals.

Tom Stoppard (born Tom Straussler in Czechoslovakia, 1938) has attracted perhaps more spurious and empty-headed adulation than any other writer of his time. He offers us the quintessence of boulevard culture (q.v.). Granted his skill as a theatrical craftsman – and this is considerable – he offered the thoughtful reader or playgoer nothing but illusion, most especially that of 'deep cultural experience'. When he made his name with *Rosencrantz and Guildenstern Are Dead* (1967) the shallow-minded columnist Harold Hobson, for too long the irascible, ingratiating and egregious *éminence sans couleur* to the boulevard audience, stated that this was 'the most important event in the British professional theatre for nine years' (what had happened in the amateur theatre is a mystery – but Hobson, a reactionary conformist who has consistently played at being a non-conformist, clearly meant that the last 'important event' had been *Look Back in Anger*, q.v.). In fact this play (it was Stoppard's seventh, and he had also published a bad novel) was based on a brilliant stage idea; but it said no more than Beckett had said, with much greater vigour and linguistic power, in *Waiting for Godot* (qq.v.), on which it was too clearly a clever and ambitious variant. After this followed a series of clever plays which capitalized upon, and trivialized, current issues: the difficulty of defining what is real, problems of identity, and 'absurdity' (q.v.) served up in a manner that would please West End audiences and could be explicated by criticasters – such as the tortoise in *Jumpers* (1972) called Pat because Hamlet says 'Now might I do it, Pat' – this sort of humour hugely pleases and flatters boulevard audiences and those who feel obliged to follow them. *Travesties* (1975), which provided a not wholly unenjoyable means of passing a few hours, exposes his limitations: this farce suddenly collapses when it has to deal with the personality of Lenin – Stoppard cannot deal with such people, for all his other characters are simply non-people, in the fashionably Pirandellian (q.v.) sense (though few trouble to remember Pirandello). One of Stoppard's critics has suggested that he is 'questioning the nature of reality'. Certainly he knows how to quote from philosophers. But he as certainly lacks the equipment even to begin to question the nature of reality, something which has stood up remarkably well throughout the centuries. This is therefore a vacuous statement – and a disingenuous one when it is remembered that Pirandello does raise such issues, though with characters he can convince us are 'real'. The *farceur* with the minuscule imagination cannot deal with real people (some people being more real than others, so it seems, and that is partly what the drama is about): as a flashy entertainer Stoppard is excellent for those who are satisfied by feeble wit and shallow ingenuity – but to the thoughtful he has nothing to offer.

David Mercer (1928–80) was more serious than Stoppard, but not at all as skilful. His plays, of which *A Suitable Case for Treatment* (1966; in *Collected TV Plays*, 1981) is the best known, were too early marred by his attachment to the ideas of R.D. Laing (q.v.), which are not consistent, and which present a view of madness more dangerous than humane. Mercer unwisely allowed himself to be analysed (a dubious procedure), and came to the Laingian conclusion that 'madness' is a 'psychological revolution'. This led him into the confusion which I have outlined in further detail in my introduction. In his last play, *Cousin Vladimir* (1978), he seems to have been breaking out of this stranglehold, and might easily have become the most interesting 'political playwright' of his time, for he was also developing new techniques.

Edward Bond (1934) is sincere but not, as not a few critics have described him, 'great' – that is a heavy word, if it means anything at all, and presents problems as to what we should call Shakespeare or O'Neill (q.v.) or a few other playwrights. Many of his plays are based on histories and biographies, and their relationship to facts is highly tenuous. However, this may not much matter. His land-enclosing Shakespeare, in *Bingo* (1974), may easily be viewed as Bond's idea of a man of genius who will not practise social justice. Any notion that this Shakespeare, or the poet Clare in *The Fool* (1976), resemble their real-life counterparts is preposterous, and one hopes that the author realizes this. Bond lacks the equipment to throw any light on characters or on history, of which his ideas are crude; but he does have a passion for social justice that is deeply felt, and which sometimes comes across in his angry plays. His devotion to what he calls the Rational Theatre need not be discussed. In general his polemic (and one does not have to dislike this to state the fact) vitiates his plays: the notorious sensationalism of the baby stoned to death in *Saved* (1966) or the somewhat immature high jinks of *Early Morning* (rev. *Plays* I, 1977 – *Plays I* and *2*, 1977–8 collect *Saved, Early Morning, The Pope's Wedding, Lear, The Sea, Narrow Road to the Deep North, Black Mass, Passion*) don't come off except to audiences much too easily prone to 'shock'. But Bond's chief failure is his language, which is dead. It has been called 'lapidary', but one must wonder if the critic who thus described it knows the meaning of the word, which in any case hardly suggests energy. Yet, for all the irritation which Bond arouses in educated people, he does provide a genuine drama of protest, unsophisticated in a worthy way – and, above all, he has never sold himself to the commercial theatre. He is a more forceful playwright than the amiable **Alan Ayckbourn** (1939), who has written a large number of effective but superficial drawing-room comedies: he is essentially a wholly inoffensive and skilful entertainer.

IV

D.H. Lawrence (1885–1930), despite his international reputation, was one of the most English of all English writers. He wrote novels, stories, drama (at the end of the Sixties this was revived, in London, with some deserved success), travel books, criticism and poetry. Much of his best poetry (the fullest edition is *Complete Poems*, 1964) is about birds, beasts or flowers; but in this form he tends to be over-diffuse: very few of his poems are wholly successful. They aim at truth to feeling, but too often language fails. However, judicious selections from his poetry show clearly that it cannot be lightly dismissed: apart from any other consideration, it contains invaluable indications of his attitudes. His criticism (conveniently assembled in Anthony Beal's *Selected Literary Criticism*, 1955) is frequently whining, self-indulgent and unfair; it is, quite as frequently, piercingly brilliant in its insights.

Whether one ultimately likes Lawrence or not, he is undoubtedly a writer of immense importance, indisputable genius, and power. He lived and died poor; although a sick man – he suffered from tuberculosis for much of his life, and it killed him – the concept of compromise with commerce was totally unknown to him. He was the most honest of all writers. Moreover, there are some things he could do perfectly (like the sketch 'Adolf', about his father; and some of the short stories): things that no one else has done. 'There was', his friend Richard Aldington (q.v.) said, 'no taming him'. And so even if he could be vicious (as in his letter to Kathleen Mansfield, q.v., as she was dying), unkind, prejudiced, a would-be sex-mage whose practical grasp of his subject was notably imperfect – still, this century has needed and still needs more like him: untameable, dedicated to their project, undeflectable from it by any pieties – political, academic, polite or dogmatic. ... The price of all this is likely to be a personality difficult to deal with; but it is a price worth paying – even if one is sometimes led to doubt this.

Lawrence's father was a Nottingham miner married to a woman who was – and felt herself to be – a little above him socially and intellectually. For the whole of his life Lawrence sought (unsuccessfully) to resolve his fierce Oedipal feelings, which were complicated by his extreme (and equally unresolved) difficulties in relating to women. The fact that he probably 'mercy killed' his mother when she was in intolerable pain could not have made things easier for him. Almost always a petulant, small-minded egoism undermined his marvellous tenderness. He refused to recognize his limitations – which in terms of technique (as his poetry demonstrates) were considerable – and too frequently tried (angrily and aggressively) to express his attitude in its entirety in single works. His marriage to Frieda Lawrence, originally the German wife of an etymologist at Nottingham University, was probably about as stable as any marriage he might have made; but neither Frieda, nor any other woman, could have supplied his demands, which were unquestionably neurotic. In so far as Lawrence is a creative writer, he is liberating; but in so far as Lawrence was a sexual prophet, he was a dangerous man, insensitive to the effects of the tyranny of himself and others. His philosophy, that what is right is what feels right – in the 'solar-plexus', the 'blood' – is certainly much more dangerous and ambiguous than Nietzsche's (q.v.) philosophy, which was the result of intellectual processes far more complex, and of a much deeper self-insight. Lawrence acted on his instincts and intuitions, but, at some relatively early stage, his sexual self-exploration became arrested: he became identified with the position in which he found himself. He furiously and truculently generalized from this position, refusing to try to create better balanced books. Even though he preached instinctive life, his own instinctive life was evidently more crippled than that of many men; the power of his message surely derives from the fierceness of his compensation for this – in the Adlerian sense. He seems to have suffered from some kind of impotence (his friend John Middleton Murray, the critic, Utopian and 'professional sufferer', stated that he did), and the descriptions of love-making in his novels are embarrassing and unconvincing, decked out with vulgar and pretentious language. However, his descriptions of male contacts are often authoritative (the wrestling in *Women in Love*, the massage in *Aaron's Rod*): there was a quality in women that sent him into a retreat whose ignominy, like his concomitant homosexual inclinations, he entirely refused to face. Thus, in the middle of *The Rainbow* (1915), in which the characters have been allowed a life of their own, Lawrence hysterically intrudes with something entirely personal to himself. ... 'What is the meaning', asks David Daiches, 'of the incident' in which 'Ursula and Skebrensky have some sort of tremendous crisis ... symbolized by Ursula's compulsive desire to lie on her back ... and by the particular way she accepts Skebrensky's love-making?' The meaning is that Lawrence is substituting himself for his imagination at the point where this fails. ... He was, in fact, sexually ignorant: his defensive sexual dogmatism destroyed his sexual freedom. It is strange that so few critics have thought it worth while to examine this discrepancy. But it is interesting, in this connection, that Lawrence's wholehearted admirers are seldom only critics, but also themselves committed to sexual or moral prophecy. Since it is Lawrence whom Dr. F.R. Leavis (1895–1978) set above all other writers of this century it is appropriate at this point briefly to discuss this influential and gifted critic – whose own excellence is so similarly flawed. Leavis was a self-assertive moralist, and he chose to select what he liked from Lawrence's work, and then to erect this as a kind of monument of twentieth-century genius – while 'wilfully' (Daiches) ignoring Lawrence's limitations. Now Lawrence's faults, which are bad ones, go along with great virtues – the chief of them is the intuitive capacity to present hidden truths about human beings and their relationships in terms of their apprehensions of nature – but the faults need to be mentioned.

Leavis as a critic suffered from similar limitations: he was a critic of great gifts, insight and integrity; but those who were not entirely for him he felt to be wholly against him; he sought not pupils but 'disciples'; those disciples he attracted who did not break away have been, like the master, rancid and fanatic in manner: the chip on the shoulder of every 'Leavisite' (as his followers are called) is a splinter of the cross upon which the master himself was crucified by society's less than absolute acceptance of his creed.

It is no wonder that Lawrence has been raised up, in this atmosphere, as a God. And it is a pity: while Leavis in his book on Lawrence's novels, *D.H. Lawrence: Novelist* (1955), gave a valuable account, he was also responsible for an uncritical acceptance of Lawrence's dangerous, because so confusingly presented, ideology: that life is a mystery, not to be solved by dogmas, and only to be known by itself: by acceptance of itself, by vitality. It is not often seen that the Lawrentian vitalism is in fact itself dogmatic. ...

There are of course inspired passages in every one of Lawrence's twelve novels; but each one is flawed in the same way as Daiches points out that *The Rainbow* is flawed: by a sudden, raw, personal, ideological intrusion into the imaginative texture. The best of the novels are *Sons and Lovers* (1913), for which he drew on the experiences of his childhood – and in which he managed to be fair to his father (who appears as Morel); *The Rainbow*; and *Women in Love* (1920) in part – but this is ruined by his attempt to judge Gerald Crich instead of explaining him, and by the untruthful presentation of Birkin (himself) as a sexually self-fulfilled man.

But Lawrence's supreme achievement is in the best of his short stories, which were collected in three volumes in 1955 (the short novels appeared in two volumes in 1957). Here, in this relatively short compass, he did not always feel impelled to intrude, and his sense of humour (in Lawrence's writing this seldom manifests itself more specifically than as a sense of general relaxation) emerges. In 'The Prussian Officer', one of his greatest stories, he is able to draw upon his homosexual proclivities without strain: writing it, he did not have time to become upset and confused about this problem. It is in the stories that Lawrence reached perfection uninterrupted by the sort of neurotic turbulence that led him, in his final novels, to authoritarianism and (in *Lady Chatterley's Lover*, un-expurgated version 1961) hysterical manipulation of a female character – the noble lady in the arms of the gamekeeper, a wishful portrait of Lawrence – under the disguise of writing a hymn to the life of the instincts. It has been said that although we must condemn 'the murk and unassimilated excitement' when 'it comes into the novels', we nevertheless pay the price 'for the Lawrentian genius ... gladly'. We do pay it; but not 'gladly': we are 'glad' only when we discover the genius unpoisoned, as in the best stories.

Virginia Woolf (1882–1941) was a very different sort of writer. The daughter of the Victorian man of letters Leslie Stephen, and the wife of Leonard Woolf – a liberal and humane journalist, publisher and (latterly) autobiographer – she suffered for most of her life from a type of manic-depression. Eventually she drowned herself. That Virginia Woolf was a genuinely innovatory novelist, critically aware of the changes in sensibility that were taking place around her, goes without question. The extent of her actual achievement, however, has been challenged. Just how much more conventional was she than she thought? Are her innovations chiefly technical?

Her theories will sound familiar to anyone who knows something of modernism. The novel was not to be a photograph, not even a critical photograph, of life: it was to be a recreation of experience. 'Clock'-time was to cease to dominate it. But Virginia Woolf's work frequently suffers from her own lack of experience. She understood that trivialities were only apparent, but – herself always rich and protected – she tended to underrate the obviously non-trivial: 'it's not catastrophes, murders, deaths, diseases, that age and kill us; it's the way people look and laugh, and run up the steps of omnibuses'. One knows what, in reaction to the realism practised by Bennett and Wells (qq.v.) and by a host of poorer novelists, she meant; but these things do age and kill (too) – and all the more amongst the poor, about whom Virginia Woolf failed to be as sensitive as she would (to her credit) have desired. She would have done better if she had worried less. One might say, without being wholly unfair, that her awareness of the inadequacy of conventional realism was an advantage to Virginia Woolf: she employed it as a strategy to avoid the 'cruder' aspects of life (murder, death, diseases – poverty) with which she guiltily could not deal. (The issue might not come up if her criticism did not so frequently show her guilt on this score.) She remains, despite her immense potentialities, very 'literary'; she could not quite escape from that into literature, as other greater modernists (Joyce, Céline, qq.v.) have done. Joyce chose the stuff of 'normal' life (to reveal that it was there, rather than anywhere else, that abnormalities were to be found). Virginia Woolf was less at ease about her subject matter. In her two most important novels (*Mrs. Dalloway*, 1925; *To the Lighthouse*, 1927) her technique suggests new and rich possibilities; but clearly the imaginative stuff on which she is concentrating, even in these books, is somewhat lacking in substance: her imagination cannot quite visualize a world, a society: her characters swim in water that has been sterilized and distilled – its salt, its fish, its teeming life destroyed – by purely literary considerations. Thus, those significant moments that it was her so intelligent intention to capture are not always particularly revelatory; her world seems impoverished because it is composed of people like herself. The ghost of her father's Victorian rationalism is nearly always lurking in the shadows: as a 'philosophy' to console us for our loss of belief; thus the imagination's freedom is curtailed: the scepticism of the imagination is terrifying because belief is as powerful in it as is nihilism – the lurid force of the clash is absent in Woolf, perhaps because she needed to dampen her manic terrors. But *Mrs. Dalloway* succeeds at least in its vivid, impressionistic evocation of London and in its consciously Proustian (q.v.) revelation of life-as-flux. Her finest novel, *To the Lighthouse*, is much influenced by Romains' *Death of a Nobody* (q.v.), which her friend Desmond MacCarthy had co-translated: although it is in no sense a product of 'unanimistic' thinking, its theme is the influence of a person after death, and its concept of time is the Bergsonian (q.v.) one of Romains. And although it is limited by Virginia Woolf's usual lack of substance, by an emphasis on sensibility that is made at the expense of robustness, it is none the less a beautiful book. *The Waves* (1931), which consists of a series of interior monologues keyed in with the progress of the sun over the sea, has its admirers; but it is too self-conscious, the life-substance ebbs away like the waves. Virginia Woolf was not a poet, and when she tried to be she tended to be embarrassing. Throughout the Thirties, except for occasional flares, the flame of Virginia Woolf's genius guttered; her last novel, *Between the Acts* (1941), shows all the old intelligence, but lacks power and conviction (although it is worth noting that Walter Allen, q.v., seldom a critic to dismiss lightly when he has had time to consider, regards it as her best novel).

Less need be said of **Dorothy M. Richardson** (1872–1957) – for a time one of H.G. Wells' (q.v.) many mistresses – whose sequence of twelve novels *Pilgrimage* (1915–38) is rather lucky to have attracted the amount of attention that it has. She was certainly a pioneer of the stream-of-consciousness (q.v.) method; but in an ultra-realist rather than a phenomenological direction. Dorothy Richardson's protagonist Miriam is not an interesting woman, and the progress of her life is (alas) made more dull and more monotonous by the author's dogged and humourless refusal to leave much of it out. The method is of course interesting; but it is not as interesting as some have made it out to be. After all, it cuts out the physical; it ignores (as Walter Allen has pointed out) the entire implications of what Freud and others of his generation brought out into the open. Dorothy Richardson held feminist views; but her feminism is impoverished by her refusal to acknowledge woman's sexuality (she herself was not short of sexual experience: she was married, and in any case H.G. Wells would have educated her in any shortcomings – if that term may be used advisedly and without offence: Wells was after all in a certain sense a feminist *par excellence*).

The most important of experimental writers of his generation in English literature is **James Joyce** (1882–1941), a Dubliner who lived in exile from 1904 until the end of his life – in Zurich, whither he had fled from France after an operation. Joyce has often been attacked for his insensitivity to contemporary history, but in his case this is hardly just: his subject-matter was not the life of literary people (far from it), but of 'ordinary' people (he wanted above all – he, too, saw the awful, tragic irony of it – to reconcile the function of good-bourgeois-husband-and-father with that of writer): he saw that he could not do this in a priest- and politician-ridden Ireland, and he left it. *Ulysses* (1922) is a celebration of, a monument to, the life of ordinary, 'vulgar' people; had Joyce directed his energies to polemical indignation over Irish – and, later, European – politics he could not have created this monument, which in itself is an antidote to the dehumanized and dehumanizing efforts of politicians, who are now rapidly attaining the status of demons. (Joyce's admirer Eliot, q.v., cannot be acquitted of the same charge: in his work there is no pity.)

Joyce received a good although painful education in Jesuit schools. He soon rejected the ideals of the Irish literary revival as being too nationalistic; he even went to Paris with the intention of studying medicine. The poems of *Chamber Music* (1907) – the pun is, of course, intentional – which went unnoticed, reveal the lyrical springs of his genius. He had already written the stories in *Dubliners* (1914), but could not find a publisher for them. These describe the Ireland from which he had deliberately chosen to exile himself, from which he had painfully torn up his roots. They render it with perfection: the prose loves compassionately the dreary awfulness, even while it comments ironically upon it. Joyce had already taken the guts and bone out of Catholicism: he left behind only the bloated skin of its tired dogmatic insistencies. He had learned from Ibsen (q.v.) to be realistic; his awareness that life consisted of moments of continuous 'sin' (the official and life-murdering Roman Catholic word for a constellation of emotions including guilt, shame, anxiety, lovelessness) redeemed by equally continuous moments of joy and blessedness was his own. Until after *Ulysses* he was an optimistic writer.

The protagonist of *A Portrait of the Artist as a Young Man* (1916) is Stephen Dedalus, who reappears in *Ulysses*, which, in tracing the progress of an artist to maturity, represents him as necessarily uncommitted and free – and lonely.

In *Ulysses*, a masterful combination of realism (of an undeniably naturalist, q.v., flavour) and symbolism, we find Stephen confronted with Leopold Bloom, an 'ordinary' man. Gradually, throughout the twenty-four hours of time covered by the novel, these two come together. Bloom is the father whom Stephen seeks; but he must finally refuse his offer of hospitality (a bed for the night). Significantly it is Bloom, Ulysses, the 'ordinary', 'dirty', 'little' man, whose experiences are the richest: the artist is represented as the calculating son of the universal, decent, threatened man. This is Joyce's resolution of the universal problem of what I have called *Künstlerschuld* (q.v.). Even Joyce, one of the most dedicated writers of the century, once thought of being a physician. ... *Ulysses* is a colossal celebration of life – including its miseries – biologically (in Marion Bloom's final thoughts as she goes off to sleep), emotionally (in Bloom's mind) and intellectually (in Stephen's mind). To describe his technique as an exploitation of 'stream-of-consciousness' (q.v.) is inadequate; his own theory of 'epiphanies' is more revealing. In scriptural terms an epiphany is a 'showing-forth'; for Joyce it was 'a sudden spiritual manifestation, whether in the vulgarity of speech or of gesture or in a memorable phase of the mind itself'. *Ulysses* is a subtle and rich book, but it is not a difficult one. It is, at once, a despairing, amoral, drunken Irish joke, a retelling of an ancient myth in symbolic terms, an immense, rueful parody of Catholic 'order', a quasi-naturalist tragi-comedy. ... Yet the question of whether it wears as well as what went before it – is it too long? – puzzlingly persists.

Joyce's wife (they lived together from 1904, but did not get legally married until 1931), Nora Barnacle, was a non-literary woman ('Why don't you write sensible books that people can understand?') – as 'ordinary' (but how extraordinary she was!) as one would expect from the author of *Ulysses*. She bore him two children, a son and a daughter. The latter, Lucia, became schizophrenic, and eventually had to be permanently hospitalized. This broke Joyce: it touched off his enormous guilt. The guilt was not connected with his leaving the Roman Catholic Church, but with the price (paid by others) for his devoting himself to creative writing. Like most of the great writers of this century, he blamed himself for being creative. In *Ulysses*, as I have suggested above, he had been able to some extent to resolve this problem. The progressive dissociation of Lucia's personality, which he early registered, revived his guilt. *Finnegans Wake* (1939) is his anguished response to his daughter's gradual retreat from reality. He took her to Jung, who told Joyce that she had schizophrenic tendencies. Desperately he objected: why were her verbal games not just like his own? 'You are both going to the bottom of the river', Jung replied, 'but she is falling and you are diving'. Joyce had his own troubles, too: fame had by no means made him rich; he was almost blind; *Ulysses* ran into censorship trouble in almost every country in which it appeared. He may well have felt that he was being driven deeply into himself. *Finnegans Wake* is the dream of H.C. Earwicker (*Here Comes Everybody*) and of Joyce himself, written in multiple puns. Although it has become a book to which a number of scholars have written 'keys', it is an inaccessible or almost inaccessible failure, the work of a man whose masterpieces had already been written. It is fascinating, comic, ingenious; but as a whole it fails. Joyce's associative technique becomes a desperate parody of Lucia's disastrous compulsion: the guilty father searches the bottom of the river for the daughter he feels he has abandoned, and allowed to drown in a meaningless unreality. Joyce seeks with huge vigour to perform the impossible: to give meaning to a fragmented personality. *Finnegans Wake* is wonderful food; but we cannot really eat it. 'I could not', he wrote of this book, which was seventeen years in the making (scrawled out painfully, between eye operations), 'I felt I could not, use the words in their ordinary connections. ... When morning comes of course everything will be clear again. ... I'll give them back their English language. ...' But morning (Lucia's miraculous recovery; his own clear sight) never did come. The project of *Finnegans Wake* arose as an intuitive response to the oddness apparent in the fifteen-year-old Lucia: to the effect that Joyce saw himself having, as a dedicated writer, upon his family's life. But the answer to his doggedly private and bitter attempt to turn words into nothing but counters is to be found in the humanity of *Ulysses*. Joyce's letters have been collected (1957), and his *Critical Writings* (1959). Richard Ellmann's excellent biography appeared in 1959. *Giacomo Joyce*, a short but interesting story from about 1914, was published in 1969.

As important (and exciting) a writer as Joyce, though few have recognized it, was **Percy Wyndham Lewis** (1882–1956). Although Joyce learned much from Lewis, no two writers could be more different. Lewis was a painter of genius, as well as a writer; he, too – although much later in life – went blind. Wyndham Lewis (who is not to be confused with an often witty humorist, Catholic apologist and biographer called D.B. Wyndham-Lewis, also blind in his old age and now also dead) was literary critic, art critic, polemicist, satirical poet – and, above all, novelist. In general Wyndham Lewis has been, and is, ignored; when granted a place in surveys of literature it is usually as a right-wing obscurantist. But discerning critics (T.S. Eliot was one of them; Pound, Grigson, Walter Allen, C.H. Sisson, qq.v., are others) have recognized his strange genius.

Lewis embarrassed everyone, including – in the end – himself. His faults are soon dealt with – sooner, indeed, than some virtues, because of the lack of attention he has suffered. But these must be enumerated.

He frequently tried to do too much at the same time: some of his polemical writing is inexcusably slapdash and inaccurate – as well as being irrelevant to his real concerns. He became too involved in his function as polemicist, and neglected to develop his imaginative and intuitive gifts – until it was almost too late. For much of his life (until he found himself exiled in Canada, during the Second World War) he used the intellectual side of himself as a protective shield against compulsions that can only be described as romantic. These he nervously rationalized as 'privacy': it is as well to remind his detractors that, while he wilfully over-indulged his paranoid tendencies, he also enjoyed a tenderly happy marriage, though it was by no means a conventional one, or one unmarred by infidelities. But in his capacity as the hard-headed, self-styled 'Enemy', this (personally) timid, kind and gentle man wilfully refused (1931) to see Hitler as anything but a comic 'gutbag', and even appeared to praise him. This was a worse case, as Lewis finally saw, than merely doing it to annoy because he knew it teased the left. He failed to discern the humanity and sense of alarm that were genuine elements in the liberal protest against Hitler. He cannot be defended on the grounds that he baited the sillinesses of the left. *The Hitler Cult* (1939) was his official apology; but he later examined, imaginatively, the causes of this failure (and what it implied) in one of the most self-castigating novels of the century: *Self-Condemned* (1954), published only three years before he died. He lived to suffer for his excesses, and to expose his failures to himself – and in the process to write a work, *The Human Age* (1955–6), that, although it is unfinished, will in due time be seen to be a classic (as T.S. Eliot said, alluding to the treatment of people as puppets – 'hallucinated automata': here 'the puppets begin to get the better of the puppet-master'). So Lewis' grave faults did not destroy him as a creative writer. He is ultimately a giant of letters not in spite of them but – like all such giants – because of them. Most of Lewis' novels are in print, and there are two selections from his work: E.W.F. Tomlin's *Wyndham Lewis: An Anthology of his Prose* (1969) and Raymond Rosenthal's paperback *A Soldier of Humour and other Writings* (1966), which contains much otherwise inaccessible early work.

What Lewis the critic, satirist and sociologist was interested in was what he called, in *The Art of Being Ruled* (1926), 'the life of the intelligence'; the pride of 'its servants', he wrote, 'if they have it, is because of something inside themselves which has been won at no one else's expense, and that no one can give them or remove from them'. Lewis the satirist was, at his best, an apostle of the life of the intelligence unique in his time. Savagely humorous (usually over the heads of his targets), he used thought where most literati slackly used fashion or facile emotion. He cast himself into isolation partly by exercising his human right to objectivity, and so descending into the iciness of a hysterical indulgence of his eccentricities and paranoid tendencies (these were not psychotic – though he sometimes made them appear such by over-indulgence of them). His thinking about time, flux, and the role of the intellect may most conveniently be found in *Time and Western Man* (1927), a book which anticipates and transcends many of the more important ideas of the five decades that followed its publication; here he is at his least rigid in his application. The basis of his notions about art arose from his practice as a painter: '... I am for the Great Without', he wrote, 'for the method of *external* approach'. And he tended to describe his people in wholly external terms. So far as satire was concerned, this was effective: in the massive *The Apes of God* (1930), a fearful account of the silliness of literati, the dehumanizing process is justified. But that was Lewis functioning as the Enemy – and in him there lurked an enemy of the Enemy. ... Even in his most ferocious satire, Lewis was always straining after something else, something imaginative and creative; but this was not really compatible with his dehumanizing descriptive technique. His satire became phantasmagoric horror: the romantic element cannot express itself, but is held rigidly down by the cold technique (in such paintings as 'The Surrender of Barcelona' the romantic richness is more apparent, because Lewis was able to use actual colour). Lewis' powerful imaginative yearnings hid beneath the cool or comic surface, a metaphor for the graphic, a result of the ruthless and behaviouristic exploitation of the 'eye' – like red-hot lava waiting to erupt. It has been asked why the strangely original early writings – 'Bestre', 'The Cornac and his Wife' – 'had no later fulfilment'. But they did: partially in *Self-Condemned*, fully and linguistically in the last great unfinished tetralogy. Lewis was in 1914 a pioneer of the short-lived vorticist movement: in other words an English cubist. Vorticism (of which Pound, q.v., was the chief champion) in painting and literature was essentially an anti-mimetic movement (it did not last long): the artist was urged to invent in his own right (cf. cubism, q.v.). As Walter Allen has remarked, 'Lewis's prose at its best is as exciting as any written in English this century'. And in Lewis' earlier prose we may see the germs of an astonishing experimentalism. Consider the beginning of 'Cantleman's Spring Mate' (1917):

> Cantleman walked in the strenuous fields, steam
> rising from them as though from an exertion,
> dissecting the daisies speckling the small wood,
> the primroses on the banks, the marshy lakes,
> and all God's creatures. The heat of a heavy
> premature Summer was cooking the little narrow
> belt of earth-air, causing everything innocently
> to burst its skin, bask abjectly and profoundly. ...

Or this from the 'advertisement' to 'The Enemy of the Stars' [it is not possible here to reproduce the startling typography]:

> DRESS. ENORMOUS YOUNGSTERS, BURSTING
> EVERYWHERE THROUGH HEAVY TIGHT
> CLOTHES, LABOURED BY DULL
> EXPLOSIVE MUSCLES, full of
> fiery dust and sinewy energetic
> air, not sap. BLACK CLOTH
> CUT SOMEWHERE, NOWADAYS, ON
> THE UPPER BALTIC.
>
> VERY WELL ACTED BY YOU AND ME.

Lewis tinkered with this amazingly original style, in which disparate elements seem to clash, diverge and come together, until *The Childermass* (1928), in which he tried to discover where it might lead in a full-scale work. Then, in illness and possibly in despair, he abandoned it and fought his battles in a different way. (This negative phase of his creative life is perhaps best described as one of collapse into a much less energetic behaviourism.) But towards the end of his life he resumed the task, with renewed lucidity and courage: *Monstre Gai* and *Malign Fiesta*, which, with the revised *Childermass*, form *The*

Human Age, explore the meaning of existence. The mass of humanity, in a limbo outside heaven, awaits examination by the Bailiff. This visionary work, 'magnificent and dreadful' (Walter Allen), which will undoubtedly be seen as one of the major achievements of the present century, was written by Lewis when he had become (by a savage stroke of irony) blind (the pressure of an inoperable tumour on his optic nerve) and was dying.

Other notable works by Lewis, one of the major art critics of his time, include *The Demon of Progress in the Arts* (1954) and the novels *Tarr* (1918) and *The Revenge for Love* (1937). He has not yet had his critical due, nor has his astonishing personality – a compound of the demonic and the visionary – been adequately explored.

L.H. Myers (1881–1944), like T.F. Powys (q.v.), has long been championed by F.R. Leavis and his school (q.v.); without the critical attention thus accorded to him he would perhaps have been forgotten – which would certainly be critically unjust. Myers, especially in the trilogy *The Root and the Flower* (1927–35) – *The Pool of Vishnu* (1940), a sequel, is not on the same level – is a distinguished philosophical novelist; in fact, he is so distinguished that he clearly shows the limitations of this genre. Myers, son of F.W.H. Myers the psychical researcher, was rich, fastidious and mystical. As a young man he had a mystical experience: a sense of the goodness of man as seen from the eye of God. This – together with his guilty hatred of his own class – remained his guiding light until his suicide. He began as a verse dramatist, and did not publish his first novel, *The Orisers* (1922), until he was forty-one. Myers failed to resolve the problem of his sense of alienation from his environment until he set his fiction in the past (in an Elizabethan India). Even here he does not entirely succeed in a creative capacity, for, subtle and intelligent as he is, his real purpose is didactic: briefly, it is to demonstrate that personality, and all that man does to form it and exercise it, is an obstacle to his self-realization. In *The Root and the Flower* a young prince, Jali, is shown as being presented with various temptations, the main one being that of becoming a 'personality' instead of a fulfilled person. Myers' thinking is interesting and important – but it precedes his invention and conception of character. Finally, assailed by black depressions, he rejected art and fiction altogether, became a somewhat desperate communist, and tried to pinpoint the evils of society in an autobiographical study; he destroyed this before destroying himself, thus incidentally answering the question that had plagued him for the whole of his life: why do men choose to live? Like Martin Buber, the author of *I and Thou*, to whom he owes much, Myers fiercely resisted the tendency of the modern, commercial world to treat people as objects – and, as G.H. Bantock has remarked, 'he has ... a sense of evil'. Judged by the highest standards, he failed; but no novelist of greater imaginative power has yet tackled this (essentially Hindu) subject-matter in our literature. He is a major neglected figure.

A. E. Coppard (1878–1957), a short-story writer who never wrote a novel, is nowadays almost as neglected as Myers (q.v.). His *Collected Tales* appeared in 1948; it was followed by *Lucy in her Pink Jacket* (1954). Coppard came up the hard way: apprentice to an East End tailor, office boy, professional athlete, clerk. He was well over thirty before he began writing poetry and stories seriously. His poetry is not successful; but his best short stories are among the most poetic of his time. Although self-educated, he was an exceedingly cunning and studied writer, who worked very hard (sometimes too hard) to gain his apparently spontaneous effects. A grand anarchy lay at the heart of his work; his most deeply felt stories (such as 'Dusky Ruth') involve characters whose real concerns are entirely anti- or non-social. The solitary protagonists of a few stories are Edward-Thomas(q.v.)-like figures. Coppard, who came from Kent, is one of the most English of writers; failure to keep to his roots is his only serious lack.

Caradoc Evans (1879–1945), although one of the most ferocious satirists of Wales (he was a Welsh-speaking Welshman writing in English), was as Welsh as Coppard (q.v.) was English. His first collection of short stories, *My People* (1915), was remarkably original, even though the author went back to the style of the Bible for his sharp, gleefully realistic and honest accounts of the dark idiosyncrasies of his people. After two more volumes of stories he brought out a satirical play, *Taffy* (1924), which caused a stir when it was produced in London: a critic said it 'hit, hurt and heartened'. His first novel, *Nothing to Pay* (1930), embodied an even more deliberate and angry caricature of the Welsh than he had yet attempted – and it did not increase his popularity in his own country. Evans was above all the denouncer – often in its own brand of powerful rhetoric – of the Welsh nonconformist institution known as Chapel. It is in Evans' novels and collections of stories that we may find a more morally engaged, less self-indulgent, less derivative version of the more popular *Under Milk Wood* (q.v.). He wrote four other good novels: *Wasps* (1933), *This Way to Heaven* (1934), *Morgan Bible* (1943) and *Earth Gives and Takes All* (1947). His final collection of stories is *Pilgrims in a Foreign Land* (1942). He deserves to be read and assimilated.

Ronald Firbank (1886–1926), a cultivated taste if ever there was one, presents a complete contrast. He was a pathetic and yet genuinely agonized trivialist, a chic fugitive from life who hid, in aestheticism, what his giggling response to terror could not neutralize; his substanceless fiction attracts fellow-homosexuals – and writers whose roots are in, or half in, the Nineties. His technique and mood have influenced writers as diverse as Osbert Sitwell, Anthony Powell, Carl Van Vechten, Aldous Huxley, William Gerhardie, Evelyn Waugh, Ivy Compton-Burnett (qq.v.). He wrote twelve novels and a play; the best known novels are *Valmouth* (1919) and *Concerning the Eccentricities of Cardinal Pirelli* (1926); *The Works* appeared in 1928, later to be supplemented by *Santal* (1931), stories, and *The Artificial Princess* (1934). Firbank cannot be called serious, and he was also silly – but it must be conceded, even by those who are repelled by the pointlessness of his concinnity, that, in Evelyn Waugh's words, he 'negligently stumbled' upon 'technical discoveries': the efficacy of dialogue, conversational nuance, the withdrawal of the kind of cause and effect associated with conventional mimesis. ... *Sorrow in Sunlight* (1924), called *Prancing Nigger* in America, played an important part in the cult of things negro which swept France in the Twenties – and which indirectly influenced the progress of negritude (q.v.). Firbank's work, always valetudinarian, hovers between the ingenuous and the cunning; its tittering nihility has no more than a touching, childish quality – but in Waugh it becomes a blackness, in Powell an observational position, in Van Vechten a self-caressing pussiness, in the early Huxley a cleverness. ... Firbank belonged inexorably to the Nineties, but he managed to anticipate – largely by influencing – that twentieth-century vein which exploited, more or less successfully, the subtle survival of decadence.

Another source for these writers, as for Firbank himself, was Frederick Rolfe (1860–1913), self-styled baronet and priest, who was both more comic and more poisonous than Firbank. He was a confidence-man, pauper, tutor, blackmailer, paedophile, translator – and author of seven novels and a number of short stories. Rolfe was a trickster whose failed life stank to himself as to the few friends whom he had and betrayed. But he was a fascinating figure: a bore, but also a pseudo-Borgian freak whose vindictiveness and paranoia have deservedly become legendary – largely through A. J. A. Symons' famous and unsurpassable biography, *The Quest for Corvo* (1930). Rolfe's one decent novel, *Hadrian the Seventh* (1904; 1950), is by no means the 'masterpiece' Symons called it; but it is a psychopathological *tour de force*, an autobiographical fantasy about a man who, rejected as a priest (as Rolfe was), is elected Pope and proceeds to revenge himself upon – or to reform? – the Church. ... Even this novel, told in an over-mannered and hysterical prose, depends upon our knowledge of Rolfe himself to gain its full effect: it is the self-recorded case-history of a remarkable patient. A number of Rolfe's other works are now again available, and there is a cult of him amongst male paedophiles, who find him an admirable hero, which he was not.

Ivy Compton-Burnett (1892–1969), whose novels are constructed entirely out of dialogue, is a unique phenomenon in English fiction: a very respectable and aristocratic lady (one thinks of Marianne Moore, q.v.) whose one 'moral failing' (in purely Victorian terms), her lesbianism, gave her uncannily sharp intelligence a window onto the world of real human evil: this bitter and severe intelligence, in the privacy of the author's consciousness, made its ironic decision some time between the publication of a first, wholly conventional tale, *Dolores* (1911), and that of *Pastors and Masters* (1924), the first genuinely 'Compton-Burnett' novel. Ivy Compton-Burnett was an artful prestidigitator: her bland procedure – the recording of dialogue – conceals: the very highly melodramatic nature of her plots; her lack of interest in realism – all her 'characters', after all, share in their creator's delight in style and epigram; her limitations (the late Victorian upper middle-class world), which are as severe – she recognized it – as her opinion of existence; her lack of psychological expertise – of knowledge of actual mental process; the strong, uncreative, mushy elements of sentimentality in her. ... Here is a case of the triumph of a self-prescribed, drastic therapy. Greek tragedy is an obvious influence, although she was not interested in this within its own context. Her theme, most broadly defined, is exploitation: she sees her specimens as exploiters or exploited – but the former may prove to be the latter in disguise, or the position may become transformed. One can be sure of only one thing: that the surface of the story will remain conversational, an imperturbable parody of the ravaged and ravaging minds of the protagonists. Her plots almost invariably involve such vicious, violent or sensational crimes as incest, murder, forgery and so on. Ultimately these are not, perhaps, novels at all – but marvellously entertaining Indic fantasies, in which nothing really happens except in peoples' minds. As she has said, with a characteristically misleading, sardonic directness: 'real life' is 'of no help at all'. This hardly matters, though: ultimately the quality we gain from these observations is as tragic as their classically educated progenitor intended. There are more than twenty novels, from which one might select *Brothers and Sisters* (1929), *Parents and Children* (1941), *Manservant and Maidservant* (1947), called *Bullivant and the Lambs* in America, and *A Heritage and its History* (1959) as being particularly excellent.

Aldous Huxley (1894–1963) was more versatile and, during his lifetime, very much more widely read than Ivy Compton-Burnett (q.v.). In the years following his death his reputation has slumped drastically, doubtless because he had throughout his career – right from clever young man through fashionable mystic to psychedelic vulgarian – a journalistic flair. This may seem odd in so esoteric and highly educated a man; but Huxley bristled with contradictions – his failure to resolve them prevented him from progressing from brilliance to the seriousness of a major writer. He is certainly not as accomplished or as rewarding as Compton-Burnett. The adroit, studiedly cruel young imitator of Firbank (q.v.) jostled in Huxley with the aesthete of guiltily ascetic tendencies; the theoretical hedonist with the deficient monk. Because Huxley began as an entertainer and ended as a mystic it is often supposed that he changed drastically; such is not the case. As D. S. Savage, one of the most astute of modern critics, has pointed out, both the early attitude of 'Pyrrhonic hedonism' and the later mystical one – essentially this amounts to a rejection of the ego and its works, including 'time', for the sake of 'union with the absolute' – 'originate in a common dislocation of being'. The early Huxley of those bright comedies of manners, *Crome Yellow* (1921), *Antic Hay* (1923) and *Those Barren Leaves* (1925), felt himself to be as detached from the crude, raw stuff of life as did the later mystic. The early writer has no mercy on his characters; he caricatures the disgustingness of human physicality in them; the later writer has dropped caricature and learned compassion (although he was never able, in his fiction, to achieve warmth) – but he still rejects physicality.

The three early novels are coruscating, farcical, worthy successors to the Ben Jonson of the 'humour' plays. *Those Barren Leaves*, more serious, is more questionable because its characters, which ought to be endowed with their own vitality, are rather too obviously vehicles for Huxley's own reflections on futility. *Point Counter Point* (1928), a *roman à clef* that owed a good deal to Gide's *The Coiners* (q.v.), is Huxley's best, most felt, novel – although it is significant that even here the most moving episode revolves around a Beethoven quartet. Huxley lacked warmth as a novelist; but he had decency and gentleness, and *Point Counter Point* does succeed to a limited degree in exhibiting sympathy towards that humanity which does not aspire but simply suffers and lives. Huxley examines himself in the person of the novelist Philip Quarles and finds himself wanting: 'All his life he had walked in ... a private void, into which nobody ... had even been permitted to enter'. He throws himself (humbly) up against the vitalistic Mark Rampion (D. H. Lawrence, q.v., a friend of Huxley's), and in the book gives Rampion the edge. 'The intellect', Quarles ends by believing, 'ought to humble itself ... and admit the claims of the heart, aye and the bowels, the loins. ...'. But that was to falsify the true state of affairs. Savage calls the novel an inept failure, shoddily written, 'puerile in conception and presentation'. ... There is something to this judgement, and even to the charge that here, more than anywhere, Huxley betrays 'the fatal juvenility which ... vitiates his understanding of life'. But it is none the less too severe. Huxley is juvenile as a novelist only when compared to, say, Lawrence at his very best; at times *Point Counter Point* is far from inept; the sincerity and, perhaps more to the point, the seriousness of Huxley's project is evident on every page, and Rampion is realized with power and some understanding. After this, however, Huxley's powers as a novelist collapsed: *Eyeless in Gaza* (1936), *After Many a Summer* (1939) and all its successors are intelligent; but they are thesis-fiction, written in an entire absence of imaginative pressure. *Brave New World* (1932) is a clever but somewhat cold dystopia and it owed more than a little to Zamyatin's superior *We* (qq.v.), which for some reason Huxley pretended not to have read. Of Huxley's retreat into mysticism the less said, perhaps, the better: it never seems, even to a reader of good faith who is interested in mysticism, and not prejudiced against it, to be more than journalistic; one assumes, or at least hopes, that his personal experience was of a more substantial calibre. His two best later books are historical studies: *Grey Eminence* (1941) and *The Devils of Loudun* (1952). *Texts and Pretexts* (1932) is one of the most lively and provocative anthologies – linked by commentary – of its time. His *Letters* (1971) are interesting and reveal much.

William Gerhardie (1895–1980) – the final 'e' was his own recent reversion to an older family spelling – was a better novelist, who never had his due; even a uniform edition initiated in the late Sixties has not really established him. He did in truth 'go off' (like the ladies in Mrs. Oliphant's Victorian novel *Miss Marjoribanks*) very badly during the Thirties, and his latter-day manner (in letters to the press and so on) was irritating and off-putting; but this is not an excuse for the neglect of his accomplished and unusual early novels. The 'masterpiece' upon which he was supposed to be working in his last years, *God's Fifth Column* (1982), turned out to be rubbish. But it is to the early Gerhardie that attention is due. His originality owed much, no doubt, to the fact that Gerhardie – an Englishman – was brought up in Petrograd: he looked at things from a very unusual point of view. That is his strength. *Futility* (1922) and *The Polyglots* (1925) are both true English-Chekhov – and both deal with Englishmen abroad. Here Gerhardie is both sad and comic, with a certain modest deftness of touch that he later mistakenly sacrificed in the interests of a wider scope. *Resurrection* (1934), about a young man who has the mystical experience of becoming divorced from his body, is his attempt at a major novel, and it almost comes off. But Gerhardie is too ambitious and self-consciously experimental, as if he wishes to produce a rival to *Ulysses* or *Point Counter Point*; and it is here, too, that a self-defeating tone of superiority begins to creep in (just the same kind of preening but mistaken self-delight that wrecks Nabokov's *Ada*, q.v.). *Of Mortal Love* (1936), a sentimental love story of the Twenties, shows his talent stretched to its utmost – and fragmenting under the strain. The remainder of his life was, in creative terms, a waste.

Evelyn Waugh (1903–66), another admirer of Firbank (q.v.), has the same horror of life as Huxley (q.v.); he has more energy, Dickensian inventiveness, but is sicker – he early (1930) rationalized his guilty inability to respond to people into an all-embracing orthodoxy: Roman Catholicism. Essentially, however, his world is the nihilistic one of Firbank; but it was enriched by the manure of an intelligent and religious gloom. It is obvious enough that Waugh dwelled darkly and at length upon the mysteries of Christ; but it is equally obvious that, whatever he achieved in his own life, self-centredness deflects his work from the true seriousness it continually promised. Religion in his work seldom functions as more than something to console his sense of hatred (not dislike or distaste) for the world – and everyone in it. His aggressive Catholicism has assured him of many more readers than Huxley – but he is not really a very much better novelist, even if he looks like one (and it must be conceded that he usually does – and that he had by far the richer imagination): his religion is seen, by his readers at least, as his excuse for condemning not merely the modern world, but also the people in it. Waugh's early novels differ from Huxley's in that they are fantasies where Huxley's are farces; they are less brilliant, but more crazy. In *Decline and Fall* (1928) and *Vile Bodies* (1930) there is a sense of autonomous life missing in even the earliest Huxley; the atmosphere is entirely antinomian. Only the kind of seriousness that expresses itself in the form of solidity is absent – present, instead, is an indifference of which the author is obviously unaware. It might have been youth; later books showed that it was not. *A Handful of Dust* (1937), the story of a man's falling apart under the strain of his broken marriage, has been admired as Waugh's best novel, and a masterpiece; but it is neither. It is rather a piece of elaborate and skilful fakery: Waugh uses his famous detached manner – much vaunted as 'objectivity' – to cover up his own incapacity for that psychological understanding which amounts to compassion. Whereas in the comic novels (*Scoop*, 1938, and *Put Out More Flags*, 1942, are to be included in this category) Waugh could to some extent rationalize his terror into shuddering, quick laughter, here he inhibits himself by attempting to deal with ostensibly realist material. All Waugh's later fiction – with the exception of the scarifying satire, *The Loved One*, 1948, on the Hollywood cult of death – is spoiled in this way. The trilogy formed by *Men at Arms* (1952), *Officers and Gentlemen* (1954) and *Unconditional Surrender* (1961) is an imitation of Ford's *Parade's End* (q.v.), and collapses by the side of it: Guy Crouchback is a wistful technicoloured photograph of Waugh, whereas Tietjens has an existence independent of Ford. It is true that in this trilogy, especially in the concluding book, Waugh tried to assert interest in humanity; but it came too late to make any difference to his achievement: the relevant passages read like sermons preached by worthy but linguistically ungifted parsons. The best of the later novels is *The Ordeal of Gilbert Pinfold* (1957), a treatment of his own experience of a series of hallucinations induced by the paraldehyde he took in order to alleviate his manic-depressive illness. A gifted writer – but either neutral or nasty in just the places where niceness counts. However, there is no chance that he will ever be unread: he has too much sheer energy. Only the last works, intended to be more substantial, are likely to be forgotten.

*

Joyce Cary (1888–1957) did not publish his first novel, *Aissa Saved*, until 1932, when he was forty-four years old – so that as a writer he belongs to a generation later than his own. He is an exuberant novelist, whose poor sense of form is sometimes more than counter-balanced by his remarkable gift for identifying with his characters. What matters to Cary is vitality and integrity: these are more important than morality – and in the life of an individual they are more important qualities than success. Cary's earliest novels, written out of his experiences in the Nigerian Political Service, are as good as anything he ever did. *Aissa Saved* is an objective account of the effect of missionaries upon those they convert, *Mister Johnson* the memorable story of an African who tries, with first pathetic and then tragic results, to live like an Englishman. The sequence *Herself Surprised* (1941), *To Be a Pilgrim* (1942) and *The Horse's Mouth* (1944) is a study in different sorts of innocence and integrity; the novels are narrated, respectively, by Sara Monday, Mr. Wilcher and Gulley Jimson. The first and the last of these are criminal; Wilcher is a senile exhibitionist. But all three represent life to Cary, and whether they irritate the reader or not, there is no mistaking the gusto and the energy which have gone into their making. *A House of Children* (1941) recreates an Irish childhood with great charm and verve. It is true that the actual world of Cary's novels is unvaried and limited, and even that he is unimaginative ('there is ... much less ... than meets the eye' in his writing, wrote Anthony West); but he is inventive, and he does convey the sense of life in which he so desperately believed. Cary is a representative of the same religious tradition as Bunyan, but in his hands it becomes secularized into a kind of humanism, a combination of pragmatism and ecstasy that for many readers is unsatisfactory – but is nevertheless a fact of British life, and is not artificial. He was not at all a profound writer, but he was an energetic one. His books seem much less good when re-read after a period of years.

Rose Macaulay (1889–1958) was a humane, shrewd and witty novelist whose best work will assuredly survive. Her best novels are *Potterism* (1920), an excellent, rather Forsterian (q.v.) satire on the society of its time, and her last, *The Towers of Trebizond* (1956), the self-told story of a woman who goes to Turkey to escape from an adulterous love-affair – an unusual and sad comedy.

Stella Benson (1892–1933), who died young of tuberculosis, should not be forgotten. Probably her diary, which is now allowed to be published, is her most important work; but *The Poor Man* (1922) and *Tobit Transplanted* (1931) are both original, painfully self-probing, witty novels; the latter tells the story of Tobias and the Angel in a modern Manchurian setting.

Rebecca West (ps. C. I. Fairfield, 1892–1983) was very much a novelist of her period: intelligent, solid, sensibly feminine, determinedly enlightened. She was a brilliant journalist – though in this field her work, of which *The Meaning of Treason* (1949) is the most notable, remains journalism. She tended to be self-righteous and to lack charity in her judgements of traitors – indeed, her work in this field remains journalism precisely because she never properly examines the psychology of treachery, but rather discon-certingly takes it for granted as completely evil, which it is not. Her second novel, *The Judge* (1922), was hailed as the 'best psychoanalytical novel'; and so it was then, but now it reads just a little too pat. In fact Rebecca West's best novel is the comparatively late *The Fountain Overflows* (1956), which is the first of a sequence which remained unfinished. This is a retrospective account of an Edwardian family broken up by the defection of the brilliant but self-destructive father. *Letters to a Grandfather* (1933) is an unusual work about the religious impulse, in which God appears as a tired Negro in faded scarlet evening dress. *The Birds Fall Down* (1966) was a comparative failure: she seems here to have lost energy. She was a brilliant conversationalist, shrewd, witty and malicious; but while she possessed shrewdness and wit in abundance, it is arguable that she lacked real depth. For some years she lived with Wells (q.v.), by whom she had one son, **Anthony West** (1914), who has, in *Heritage* (1955; 1984), written in 1949, given one version of the relationship – he believes his mother to have been a monstrous and treacherous woman.

More gifted as a novelist than any of these, and now unduly neglected (not a single book of hers is in print), is Rebecca West's (q.v.) older contemporary **May Sinclair** (1865– 1946). Like Rebecca West, she is very much of the Edwardian period (she was a suffragette, or at least took part in some marches), but her grasp of character is greater; clever, again like Rebecca West, in her best fiction she transcends this. *Mary Olivier: A Life* (1919) and *The Life and Death of Harriett Frean* (1922), both acute psychological studies of women, are probably her finest novels; but *A Cure of Souls* (1924), the portrait of a sybaritic vicar, runs these very close. May Sinclair was also a very good writer of short stories; one of these, 'Where their Fire is not Quenched', is a small masterpiece of the supernatural. Other novels include *The Flaw in the Crystal* (1911) and *Arnold Waterlow* (1924). The supernatural tales, which ought to be collected, are in *Uncanny Stories* (1923), and in other volumes (she wrote thirty-six books).

Elizabeth Bowen (1899–1973), as obviously a minor disciple of Henry James as L. P. Hartley (qq.v.), wrote about a dozen worthy novels, full of delicate and sensitive descriptions of moods and places, but has never equalled *The Death of the Heart* (1938), the story of the destruction of a young girl's sensibility and capacity to love by a group of cold-hearted, affected people. In her other novels, one of the best of which is *The Little Girls* (1964), Elizabeth Bowen is better, so to speak, at description than psychology. And she made her incapacity to deal with any but a specific type of upper-class person into a more severe limitation than it needed to be by trying, from time to time, to overcome it.

David Garnett (1892–1981), after starting with a potboiler called *Dope-Darling* (1919) by 'Leda Burke', wrote some unusual novels of fantasy. *Aspects of Love* (1955) was successful at the time but has not lasted. He wrote no fiction between 1935 and 1955; when he began again he had lost his touch: his achievement had been to express his genuine habit of seeing people as animals – that was his own way of seeing, and was truly extraordinary. His volumes of memoirs are highly informative, and very readable, but – naturally enough – omit a great deal. He knew almost all of his contemporaries, and a good biography of him is needed. Probably his best novel is *Pocahontas* (1933), a very individual treatment of a historical figure which is often reprinted.

J. B. Priestley (1894–1984) has been a best-selling novelist since the panoramic *The Good Companions* (1929); he has also had successes as a playwright – sometimes an interestingly experimental one. It has long been fashionable to dismiss him from serious consideration – but this is not absolutely fair. Priestley does have certain middlebrow vices: long-windedness, over-heartiness – an insecure, bluff, Yorkshire manner – sentimentality; and he is in the realm of fiction an entirely conventional realist. But he has virtues: and he is a better novelist than his master and close friend Hugh Walpole (q.v.), with whom he collaborated in a letter-novel. Even *The Good Companions*, the tale of a concert party, has virtues: strong characterization, a good sense of place, a sense of the comic. But he has written better than this: good, intelligent thrillers (*Black-Out in Gretley*, 1942, is the best) and *Lost Empires* (1965), a knowledgeable and quite moving story of the old-time music-hall. His plays are well made, and the 'time' plays – *Time and the Conways* (1937) and *I Have Been Here Before* (1937) – and *Dangerous Corner* (1932) are as good as anything seen in the commercial theatre in their decade.

L. P. Hartley (1895–1972) was an uneven writer – some of his tales of the supernatural are really shoddy – but at his best he just earned the comparison with Henry James (q.v.) that is often made. *Simonetta Perkins* (1925) is as much an exercise in the manner of James as Lubbock's *The Region Cloud*. Hartley's strength lies, rather surprisingly, in his stern morality. His attitudes are what would be called 'old-fashioned', and one assumes that he would reject such things as psychoanalysis as tending to 'excuse' 'evil' conduct. And yet his own work is very 'Freudian': it gains its power from the fact that the evil in it is never really defined: like James, he was homosexual, and, again like James, he did not at all like being so. *The Go-Between* (1950) is a Jamesean tale of the adult world interpreted by a boy. The *Eustace and Hilda* trilogy – *The Shrimp and the Anemone* (1944), *The Sixth Heaven* (1946), *Eustace and Hilda* (1947) – is the subtle and beautifully told account of a brother and sister doomed, by their characters, to destroy each other; terror and comedy are perfectly blended here. Although Hartley is himself a moralist (his feeble, badly argued non-fiction work leaves this in no doubt) he is not in fact a moralist as a writer, but rather what Paul Bloomfield has described as 'the transmitter of a civilized ethos'. He has not only an awareness of evil but also an awareness of inevitability; moreover, he makes no judgements in his novels.

L. A. G. Strong (1896–1958) never fulfilled his early promise. A prolific and successful writer of competent and intelligent novels, the really substantial novel just eluded him. He was highly professional – perhaps too much so – but could only create types, rather than developing characters. His best work is to be found in the early novels *Dewar Rides* (1929), *The Garden* (1931) and *Sea Wall* (1933), and in his short stories of Irish rural life. He was a graceful minor poet: *The Body's Imperfection* (1957) collects his poems.

Charles Morgan (1896–1958), once regarded by the French as a leading British novelist, has gained the unenviable reputation of the middlebrow novelist *par excellence*: he is pretentious, 'deep' without depth, politely mystical – and pompous (one of his favourite phrases was 'the eternal verities'). 'X marks the spot where I read *Sparkenbroke*' (1936) V. S. Pritchett (q.v.) said of his most pretentious book. But Morgan did write one terse, decent novel: his first, *The Gunroom* (1919), based on his naval experiences. This was relatively simple, and came out of real suffering. Within six years, with *My Name is Legion*, Morgan had learned how to get himself compared with Dostoevski in *The London Mercury*. His elaborate prose style is as bad as his 'philosophy': he became a Golf-Club novelist, and almost deserved his bad reputation. But he was not a bad man, wrote some perceptive theatre criticism, and was no worse in his pretentiousness than Fowles (q.v.) or Le Carre (*q.ne v.*) are in our own time.

The Irish writer **Liam O'Flaherty** (1896–1984) wrote some excellent short stories and several novels, of which *The Informer* (1925) is the best known, but dried up in mid-career. The stories in *Spring Sowing* (1924) were lyrical, elemental, highly readable without, however, making any concessions to popularity. They marked him out as one of the leading writers in this form of his generation; but the two collections since *The Short Stories* (1937; 1948) have not been on the early level. There has been a strong revival of interest in his work, much of which has been reprinted. His best novel, a scarifying one, which will certainly survive, is *Famine* (1937). This is much less self-indulgent than his other work in the novel. *The Wilderness* (1978) is a more recent novel, which adds little to his achievement.

Another writer who lost his fine early form, perhaps because he decided to tackle novels – for which he had a commercial but not really an artistic capacity – is **H. E. Bates** (1905–74). Bates' early stories, in such volumes as *Day's End* (1928), *The Woman who had Imagination* (1934) and *The Beauty of the Dead* (1940), are almost unsurpassed in English in their time. 'The Kimono' for example, a magnificent story, could have been written by no one else. But after Bates' service in the RAF during the Second World War his work coarsened considerably, although it remained highly professional. The earlier Bates is a

sensuous, powerful writer, expert in portraying women and their moods and the atmosphere of the countryside or the small country town. Latterly he became mannered, and
sometimes declined into self-parody.

V. S. Pritchett (1900) was never, perhaps, as good as Bates (q.v.) at his best. But he is
more versatile, and his work has not fallen off. His stories – *Collected Stories* (1982),
followed up by *More Collected Stories* (1984) – are often about eccentric characters or
absurd situations. His novels, which contain passages of exquisite comedy, are studies of
tormented puritans: *Nothing Like Leather* (1935), *Dead Man Leading* (1937) and *Mr. Beluncle*
(1951), the best, a sympathetic and penetrating study of an enthusiast for odd and out-of-
the-way nonconformist religions. Pritchett is one of the very few good contemporary
literary journalists, and has written memorable volumes of autobiography.

Sean O'Faolain (originally **John Whelan**, 1900) is an Irish writer who is overall
(though he has written nothing of the power of *Famine*) superior to and more consistent
than O'Flaherty (q.v.). He has written four novels and eleven books of stories (one of
these a *Selected Stories* of 1978); his *Collected Stories I* (1980) will be continued. It is in the
story that he excels; the best of the novels are the first, *A Nest of Simple Folk* (1933), and the
most recent, *And Again?* (1979), a lighthearted (and good-hearted and intelligent)
treatment of his impressions of old age, or, to be more accurate, treatment of human
nature written from the vantage of old age. Although he served with the IRA in the early
Twenties, O'Faolain has always been at odds with society, as he showed through his
editorship of the influential Irish journal *The Bell*, which he founded in 1940; it ran until
1954. O'Faolain edited it from its inception until 1946, and would accept only what he
felt to be good as literature (rather than propaganda). He is unusual among Irish story
writers in that he concentrates less on narrative than on essential detail: he is above all
economical, and his master is certainly Chekhov (q.v.), about whom he has written
illuminatingly. He has been said to lack warmth, but this is an unfair charge: he writes in
a markedly non-moralistic manner, and with great although detached sympathy. He
likes psychological situations and relationships to emerge of themselves, and prefers not
to add much comment of his own. His criticism looked much to the past, and lamented
the loss of the hero in modern writing (*The Vanishing Hero*, 1957); but he has published
and encouraged many writers more modernistic in outlook than himself. The bitterness
of his early stories gave way to an earned mellowness about human frailty. The tales
almost tell themselves, and their modesty of tone and economy should not mislead their
readers into thinking that he is not a master of technique. He has written many valuable
biographies, and an autobiography, *Vive Moi!* (1964).

*

We now come to the two novelists, born in the first decade of the century, who are
generally regarded as the most important of their generation: Graham Greene and
Anthony Powell.

Graham Greene (1904) is, like Waugh (q.v.), with whom he is sometimes bracketed
because of it (he admires him greatly), a convert to Roman Catholicism. But he is a very
different sort of Catholic. For one thing, while Waugh was obviously of a Tory mentality,
Greene is aggressively left-wing; again, where Waugh revered orthodoxy and decorum,
Greene is openly against the conservative elements in his Church – and in his obsessive
concern with seediness and evil he has even appeared to many of his fellow Roman

Catholics to be heretical. However, Greene's Catholicism is an even more essential element in his fiction than Waugh's. Essentially Greene is concerned with what, in Catholic terms, is the idea of the mercy of God; but we do not need to be Catholics ourselves to respond to his work – for this idea functions in it as human compassion. Thus, in *Brighton Rock* (1938), the first major novel, the young gangster and murderer Pinkie is presented as in some sense 'holy': he is at least dedicated to evil, whereas his pursuers are merely decent – they lack Pinkie's faith in God, which continues to exist in spite of his desperate project to deny it. This is not in fact a realist novel (how would a semi-literate young gangster remark 'Credo in unum Satanum'?), although the seedy realist background is superbly filled in. Greene has never seriously sought to imitate life (as, say, Snow, q.v., did so industriously). *Brighton Rock* is a thriller-as-metaphor (Paul West calls it a 'structural oxymoron'!), a superb novel that misses real distinction only because of a certain patness on the part of the author, a professionalism which, most unfortunately, functions as an over-simplifying, even a coarsening, agent. This criticism applies in more or less degree to all Greene's novels, and is perhaps the reason why they do not wear as well as one expects them to. And yet I think it is truer to put it in this way than in the way the Leavis-inspired (q.v.) F. N. Lees (1952) put it. He spoke of 'popular fiction ... crude analysis, the obtrusive and deformed emotionalism ... defective presentational technique. ...' That is to say, I believe Greene's view of life has more power and creative validity than this approach allows: one does see it as modified by sensationalism, but at least its power is always there. His view of life, repellent to so many people, is not really 'popular' (i.e. middlebrow): it involves no manipulations of reality, and it cannot be called sentimentality.

His first novel, *The Man Within* (1929), was influenced by both Robert Louis Stevenson and – thematically – Conrad (q.v.), a novelist whom he closely resembles. Even here Greene's hero is educated by guilt into grace. And for those who are not Catholics, and doubtless for some of those who are, grace in Greene often means simply being human rather than being moral-before-the-event: defensively rigid, reaching forward aggressively into the texture of life to make judgements (an element in middle-browism, though seldom overt). Greene's whisky-priest in *The Power and the Glory* (1940) is a coward, dirty, the father of a bastard – but he is none the less a priest. He represents man, doomed to sin (always depicted in Greene as various kinds of squalor or shabbiness), redeemed by grace. He is the only priest in a Mexico that has prohibited both Catholicism and alcohol, and his enemy is a policeman who is as dedicated as himself. Before the priest is shot the two come together, in a passage whose irony is sometimes missed, to recognize each other's type of goodness. (In fact the situation in Mexico was at least by implication over-simplified by Greene, although he never actually specifies the country.)

Greene has tended to parody himself in some of his later novels, in particular in *The Heart of the Matter* (1948), which is technically one of his finest achievements. This dramatization of theological abstractions (how can a sinner in the eyes of God's Church be a saint in the eyes of God?) is almost convincing; but Orwell (q.v.) was right to charge that it led to 'psychological absurdities'. However, although the context into which Greene has put his hero, Scobie, is unsatisfactory, the man himself is nevertheless invested with a kind of life. The best of the later novels are *The Quiet American* (1955), which contains a masterful portrait of a hysterically bad man, and *The Comedians* (1966), about Haiti under the malevolent regime of the late Duvalier, 'Papa Doc'. Novels after this have been lively but lightweight. *The Human Factor* (1978) is almost as poor as the appalling, Stoppard-scripted movie made from it.

Anthony Powell (1905) provides a complete contrast. He wrote five novels before the

Second World War, of which the last, *What's Become of Waring?* (1939), is perhaps the best. They established him as the best comic novelist of his generation; but recognition of this fact has been slow to come, despite the fame of his twelve-novel sequence *A Dance to the Music of Time*, begun in 1951 with *A Question of Upbringing* and finished with *Hearing Secret Harmonies* (1976). Powell's method in the early novels is decidedly aristocratic and omniscient; but he knows not to try to do more than expose the follies and stupidity of his characters. There is more than a touch of Wyndham Lewis (q.v.), although the tone is softer, and the laughter elicited considerably less strident.

A Dance to the Music of Time continues the comic work with confidence, brilliance and an admirable coolness; it is also a technical *tour de force*. Certainly, for all that certain insensitive critics have tried to dismiss it as snobbish, it is one of the greatest *roman fleuves* of the century in any language, and as certainly, Powell should have had the Nobel Prize – were that consistently awarded for literary merit, which it is not. Powell is one of those novelists who make a virtue of their limitations. While it is true that his attitude is un-mistakably upper-class (though it is incorrect to assert that he cannot deal with lower- or middle-class people, as the movingly related suicide of Biggs in *The Soldier's Art*, 1966, clearly demonstrates), it is to his credit that he has not tried to change this: *A Dance to the Music of Time* never purports to be narrated by other than an aristocrat, and Powell is an aristocrat. But viewed as a whole, the sequence is clearly more than the bird's-eye view of an aristocrat. Powell is a Tory, but his masterwork has no political bias. He has succeeded in giving us a view of the whole of English life – though at one stage it looked as though he would not be able to achieve this.

Powell's narrator, Nicholas Jenkins, is evocatively unobtrusive, a worried ironist whose own personality is for most of the time in the background. His narrative consists of carefully selected recollections; objectivity is attained by a balletic scheme in which 'human beings, facing outwards like the Seasons, move hand in hand in intricate measure'. The spell of the storyteller is always present. Powell's type of comedy has been compared to Evelyn Waugh's (q.v.); but the hypomanic and cruel element in Waugh is absent; where he is frenetically gleeful, shrieking the truth of (his own) religion, Powell is thoughtful, as if in his attitude he were trying to define of what social sanity might consist. And in this effort he transcends the political.

The sequence opens with *A Question of Upbringing* (1951). After a Proustian (q.v.) introductory paragraph, Nicholas Jenkins is back at school, at Eton. Its successors are: *A Buyer's Market* (1952), *The Acceptance World* (1955), *At Lady Molly's* (1957), *Casanova's Chinese Restaurant* (1960), *The Kindly Ones* (1962), *The Valley of Bones* (1964), *The Soldier's Art* (1966), *The Military Philosophers* (1968), *Books Do Furnish a Room* (1971), *Temporary Kings* (1973) and *Hearing Secret Harmonies* (1976).

Few fictional techniques employed in the English language today convey as well as Powell's the sense of life as it actually passes before us: hence the apparent plotlessness, the wild improbabilities and coincidences, the flatness of narrative manner. This is in fact reality. The passing of time is for once seen – without metaphysics or passion – as it is: without even such feelings about it as Powell himself possesses. But this does not create a sense of boredom. Widmerpool, one of the true monsters of modern fiction, is anything but a bore. There is residual wisdom enough in the sequence for us to want to know what life (not Powell) will do with the characters. Widmerpool is a major comic-evil creation, and the account of his death one of the finest tragi-comic passages in English fiction. Behind Powell's comedy and irony, and perhaps behind the Proustian ambitions, lies a serious concern with what human obligations are, or might become. The American critic Charles Shapiro's judgement, 'England's best comic writer since Charles Dickens', is probably right, but it does not go far enough. Powell is one of the most serious and technically adroit novelists since Dickens. His procedures are in fact unobtrusively modernistic, but are in the interests of an essentially conservative (with a small c) morality: a morality based not on puritanism but on freedom and on the exceedingly complex notion of, to put it necessarily crudely, decency. Jenkins is sceptical, but – despite his coolness – obsessed, in his apparently casual way, with decency. He is almost paralysed by decency, as Powell shows us. Widmerpool is the foil to him: the ambitious go-getter, amoral, wanting to have his cake and eat it. Each book betters its predecessor, but only because of its predecessor. ... At the end we recognize that the old charges against Powell – he could not deal with the lower classes, he was a snob, he was limited, and so on – have all been dealt with by him: they are no longer valid. Like Dickens, although in a different way (Dickens published in periodicals), Powell has very intelligently employed reader-reaction as feedback, and has succeeded in accomplishing almost all of the things he was supposed not to be able to do. This fundamental modesty has helped him to achieve one of the masterworks of his time, and he has not received even half the credit for it that he deserves. *A Dance to the Music of Time* is humane, poetic, and moving: not a comic work, as is so often supposed, but a tragi-comic one of enormous sensibility, subtlety and compassion.

It used to be necessary to put **C. P. Snow** (1905–80) in his place: his work was grotesquely over-valued and was even set for examinations. At one time he was a (Labour) minister, and was eventually created Baron. In this capacity he was a failure. His heart was in the right place, but he was not a very intelligent man, even though he had a good deal of information at his fingertips. He ended by getting far too angry about the so-called 'permissive society', and whatever creativity he possessed (it was not much) he squandered in the interests of good-hearted but pointless crusading. He was a consistently atrocious critic, valuing such writers as Daphne du Maurier (*q. non v.*) and Cozzens (q.v.) above others far superior, of whom he had often not heard. His best book was a modest one: his first, a detective story called *Death Under Sail* (1932). Had he stuck to this genre he might have been as good in it as, say, Freeman Wills Crofts. Instead, in 1940, after writing two other novels, he began the eleven-sequence autobiographical work known as *Strangers and Brothers*: *Strangers and Brothers* (1940), *The Conscience of the Rich* (1958), *Time of Hope* (1949), *The Light and the Dark* (1947), *The Masters* (1951), *Homecoming* (1956), *The New Men* (1954), *The Affair* (1960), *Corridors of Power* (1964), *The Sleep of Reason* (1968) and *Last Things* (1970). This is the correct reading order. The material upon which this sequence draws is of the greatest interest: Snow's own experience (in the sequence he is Lewis Eliot, a flattering portrait of himself, though with the best of intentions towards himself) as scientist, civil servant and government minister – a man from the provinces who reaches the top. Unfortunately the treatment is poor: the prose is bad, the psychology is unsubtle, the assumption behind it is evil – that everything would really be all right if only people could enjoy committees, and stop criticizing public men. Snow showed no signs of having read or understood Durkheim or Romains (qq.v.), and he unwittingly, and rather sadly, gives us a self-portrait as a drab, humourless, desiccated and severely limited man. Snow tried to be humane, and had humane aspirations – and he ended (but not in the *roman fleuve*) as a convinced pessimist, but not for good reasons. He received high praise from critics who should have known better; it was simply not due to him, for he was an unimaginative writer with little flair. He had no notion of the function of the poetic or the religious side of man, and he appears to have had the haziest ideas about anthropology – yet that would have been essential to the successful author of so monumental a project as he planned. His one apparently saving grace was that he could retain some readers' interest by telling a story. But the story soon becomes tedious. And the readers needed to feel that they were being told how the country was run –

which they were not. If his work survives at all – and it ought not to – then it will be for the information it purports to give about public life. Or for its almost spectacular drabness. One should probably grant that Walter Allen's comment to the effect that Snow was 'massively fair' is just. Unfortunately this cannot apply to his imaginatively impoverished work; perhaps, as well as being pompous, he was too massively fair. . . . (God, it should be remembered, is frequently regarded as massively unfair – and the novelist is a kind of God.)

Richard Hughes (1900–76), a pioneer of radio drama as well as a novelist, wrote so little that he probably did not obtain full due, even though he was invariably treated with respect. Each of his novels is excellent and highly original. The first, *A High Wind in Jamaica* (1929), is the story of some children in the Sixties of the last century; on their way home from a Jamaican plantation they are captured by pirates; eventually they are rescued, and learn to accept an adult version of their experience. But the subject of the novel is the truer nature of this experience: its nature as seen from the viewpoint of a child. This lucid tale of children, brutal and yet strangely gentle, is poetic in the best sense. Hughes' now unjustly forgotten poems (they are collected in *Confessio Juvenis*, 1926) were successful – they are influenced by Skelton and by Hughes' friend Robert Graves (q.v.), yet are original and eloquent, though lightweight. *In Hazard* (1938), equally unusual and beautifully accomplished, is about a steamer caught in an unexpected hurricane. The narration seems to be artless, but is in fact highly sophisticated and carefully planned – one presumes that Hughes wrote so little because he revised at length. The revelation of the true characters of some of the ship's officers and crew is done with consummate skill and subtlety; the descriptive writing is masterly. Hughes' third novel, *The Fox in the Attic* (1962), the beginning of a planned four-volume work with the rather unhappy title of *The Human Predicament*, is 'a historical novel of my own times'. A young Welshman, just too young to have fought in the First World War, comes down from Oxford and goes to the Germany of the Weimar Republic. Here we meet Hitler, Goering, Röhm and other historical personages; the hero, a curiously innocent and bewildered creature, understands little of what is going on around him. *The Wooden Shepherdess* (1973), all that Hughes had time to complete of his trilogy, shows signs of strain, although the account of the Night of the Long Knives is brilliantly vivid and deservedly famous. *Collected Children's Stories* (1977).

Edward Upward (1903) was a close friend at Cambridge of Isherwood (q.v.), with whom he devised the private, satirical world of 'Mortmere' – as Isherwood recounts in his autobiography *Lions and Shadows* (1938), in which Upward appears as Allen Chambers. Upward was the only British writer of fiction – as Gascoyne (q.v.) was of poetry – successfully to absorb both Kafka and surrealism (qq.v.). This was in the novel *Journey to the Border* (1938), and in a few short stories (now collected, together with the novel, in *The Railway Accident*, 1969). This early work is brilliant and exciting, but it has been a little overrated; the stories are better than the novel because the latter peters out into crude communist propaganda. Communist dogma is what frustrates Upward's very different novels *In the Thirties* (1962), *The Rotten Elements* (1969), and *No Home But the Struggle* (1977) – a trilogy published complete as *The Spiral Ascent* (1977). They trace the progress of Alan Sebrill, who, like Upward himself, joins the communists in the Thirties but leaves them in the Forties because he believes that, under Soviet influence, they have deviated from Marxist-Leninism. Finally Sebrill and his wife commit themselves to the CND. Sebrill is an unsympathetic character: a humourless puritan, rigidly devoted to his creed. The writing is deliberately muted: it is as if Upward had determined to sacrifice all his imaginative gifts. However, the account of Sebrill's dedication to communism is of historical interest. In effect Upward recounts the process of a man's destruction by his lack of humour and flexibility; but he does it unwittingly, since the story is almost certainly his own. The trilogy as a whole lacks art or grace, and parts of it are, though not deliberately, hilariously funny. But it demonstrates a certain courage and determination, as well as sincerity, and it may yet be read for its sociological and historical values.

Upward's early prose was more effective than that of **Rex Warner** (1905). Warner is a gifted stylist and a classical scholar of distinction, but in his fiction he has consistently failed to find a satisfactory objective correlative (q.v.). It is obvious that he has feelings and ideals, but his fiction is spoiled by coldness and over-intellectuality. In the earlier, Marxist books – *The Wild Goose Chase* (1937) and *The Professor* (1938) – Warner created, with undoubted skill although little conviction, a Kafkaesque (q.v.) atmosphere; but this tended, in fact, to obscure his intentions – which were simply allegorical, whereas Kafka was no allegorist. In *The Aerodrome* (1941), his least unsuccessful novel, the allegory becomes more explicit, although an over-complicated plot interferes with its impact. Since the end of the war Warner has written efficient, readable but less ambitious historical novels demonstrating his conversion to Christianity.

Arthur Koestler (1905–83) has treated the problems of fascism and communism with more success. He was a Hungarian whose better fiction was written in Hungarian and German rather than English. Before becoming an Englishman and settling in England Koestler spent some time in gaols in Spain (under sentence of death) and France; he wrote books about this. After temporarily giving up fiction Koestler wrote a series of useful, influential books on sociological and religious subjects. His first two and best novels were written in Hungarian and German respectively: *The Gladiators* (tr. 1939) and *Darkness at Noon* (tr. 1940). The first is an intelligent and moving account of the slaves' revolt of Spartacus in ancient Rome; that it examines it in twentieth-century terms does not subtract from its power and force of characterization. *Darkness at Noon* is Koestler's finest novel: it is the story of an old-guard communist who falls victim to Stalin's purges. He is a 'just' victim to the extent that in his heart he regards Stalin as a betrayer of communism. This was one of the earliest really lucid revelations – in the West – of the true nature of Stalin's rule. But its political implications are incidental – they gain their strength from Koestler's very matter-of-factness. Rubashov, the protagonist, is presented not only as a victim of a tyrannical system and a mad logic: we see him attaining an ultimate freedom as he contemplates his destruction. That the book is so psychologically convincing is a strong argument against those who hold that it is not really a novel at all. Koestler's later novels are in English. None is dull, and all are acutely intelligent; but they lack the power of the two already discussed. *Thieves in the Night* (1946) is an impassioned but propagandist tale of the struggle of the Zionists in the Palestine of 1937–9; *Arrival and Departure* (1943) tries to demonstrate that ethical imperatives transcend neurosis – a secret agent is shown by psychoanalysis that his motivations are private, but he continues the fight. Here the bones of the argument show through the thin psychological skin and flesh much too obtrusively. Later in life Koestler became an eminent essayist, and showed intelligent interest in the paranormal. Some of his work on the latter subject tends to be scrappy and journalistic, but he has undoubtedly been a useful influence in the battle against barren scientism. It has been a serious and wilfully unjust error to ignore this aspect of his writings even if one does not agree with him: a refusal to take serious arguments seriously. He took his own life when threatened by a constellation of painful diseases – this decision, too, has had and will have much influence.

George Orwell (1903–50), who died young, of tuberculosis, has been much discussed since he published *Animal Farm* (1945), his satire on the Soviet Union; but his fiction apart from this has been consistently underrated. He has been called many things: leftist, conservative, sick satirist and now, very oddly, 'sexist'. ... His last great novel, *Nineteen*

Eighty-Four (1949), has been systematically denigrated, despite its great power: it is too near the truth. David Daiches predictably calls it 'masochistic' and tiptoes backwards into the safety of the drawing-room (home of 'serious political reflections') as he gasps, 'as a criticism of English socialism it is fantastically irrelevant and even as a picture of the ultimate evil of the totalitarian state it is too obsessed and self-lacerating to arouse serious political reflection'. *Nineteen Eighty-Four* is not a criticism of English socialism, but a warning of the consequences of contemporary 'politics' in general. What Daiches, an intelligent but polite critic, failed to realize is that it is possible that Orwell's warning has actually postponed or even prevented some at least of the horrors that he foretold. This novel represents an entirely valid resolution of Orwell's conflicts. Big Brother and the rest are convincing: the critics have shrunk back in horror. Irving Howe is right when he observes that the book 'trembles with an eschatological fury that is certain to create ... the most powerful kinds of resistance'. Once that fury is recognized, the timid little Aristotelian and other objections of the awed critics can be seen for what they are – and ignored. For, as Howe points out, of course we shall all 'feel more comfortable if the book could be cast out'. It is certainly, to employ C. P. Snow's (q.v.) unforgettable term for satire, 'cheek'; but it will take more than Snow or even Daiches to transform the nature of twentieth-century affairs into something genteel and acceptable at office- or cosy seminar-level. *Nineteen Eighty-Four* is a vision of Swiftian proportions which belongs, horribly, to our time.

Orwell was a fine (if often confused) journalist; most of his occasional writing is in *The Collected Essays, Journalism and Letters of George Orwell* (1968). He can be obtuse (what columnist is not from time to time?) but he makes up for this with his many unique insights. He is, in fact, for decency and readability and intelligence combined, the best journalist of the century – and it is by studying his journalism all together that we can best see that his potentialities, in the realm of psychological fiction, were enormous. But his best work is in *Down and Out in Paris and London* (1933) and in his novels (a fact not sufficiently recognized), chiefly of course in *Animal Farm* (a classic), and the final book. It has been said that Orwell was not interested in character; but to condemn him as a novelist because of this is to misunderstand both his purposes and the type of fiction he wrote – as well as to ignore his actual achievement. After all, *Animal Farm* is an animal fable. And a characterization of Winston Smith, the protagonist of *Nineteen Eighty-Four*, would be wholly out of place: the man is fighting for the right to have a personality. Thus he makes effective his ultimate verdict on those who are not interested in character. His autobiographical sketch of pre-school life, *Such, Such Were the Joys* (it is in the *Collected Essays*), shows considerable aptitude for presenting character, and suggests that, had he lived, he could have carried out his intention of breaking away entirely from polemics to write about 'human relationships' – this is what he told his wife in the last days of his life. But his earlier novels are better than is often admitted: *Burmese Days* (1934), *A Clergyman's Daughter* (1935), *Keep the Aspidistra Flying* (1936), *Coming up for Air* (1939): all these have lasted for over a quarter of a century or more – and they will survive as invaluable and sensitive portraits of the Thirties where more ambitious books will fall into oblivion. They are the nearest we have in fiction to the novels of Gissing (q.v.): they evince a similar kind of disgust at all the manifestations of modern life, and a similarly obstinate belief in integrity. But I cannot agree with Walter Allen that Orwell resembles Gissing in deficiency of 'human sympathy'. True, some (not all) of Gissing's novels are thus deficient; but I do not think one feels this in Orwell. He is not concerned with the compassionate portrayal of character; but he is concerned with the portrayal of the conditions that cause men to lack compassion. Did Swift lack compassion? Allen admires *Burmese Days*, but feels that an impression of misanthropy 'finally chills'. But how was the young

Orwell, fresh from Eton and service with the police in Burma, to deal with such conditions? Was there anything at all likeable about the British administration there? I think that what Allen calls misanthropy is in fact despair of Swiftian proportions: compassionate concern. Orwell achieved more in his fiction than almost any critic has so far been prepared to allow.

Christopher Isherwood (1904 – 86), once a great hope of English fiction, petered out into a skilful and intelligent entertainer – a novelist of high quality, but not of the first or perhaps even the second rank. His genius all but vanished, possibly under the pressure of personal problems, in a cloud of mysticism: like Huxley (q.v.), he took up the study of Eastern religion – which he at first combined with writing film scripts in Hollywood. Isherwood, as all his novels and his autobiography (*Lions and Shadows*, 1938) show, writes very well indeed – too well, perhaps, for his own good, since he is able to make trivialities pass for more substantial stuff. Between 1928 and the outbreak of war (and his departure to America, where he has eventually settled – as an American citizen) Isherwood wrote four good minor novels. He was as gifted in prose as his friend Auden (q.v.) was in verse. But, again like Auden – many of whose characteristics he shares – he has never really grown up. Hence his retreat into an unconvincing mysticism. The early novels were comic and brilliant, but depthlessly so: the later ones well describe the miserable lives of immature men, but fail to explain the misery or the immaturity. For all the recommended mysticism (or Quaker austerity), one's strongest impression is of a clever, seedy, hopped-up kid. ... The first two novels, *All the Conspirators* (1928) and *The Memorial* (1932), are clever and well observed Audenesque indictments of the bourgeois for their sickness of mind and acceptance of falsity; they do not go deep psychologically, but are technically adept. *Goodbye to Berlin* (1939) is Isherwood's best novel (the third, *Mr. Norris Changes Trains*, 1933, is an amusing, in-joke novel partly based on the exploits of a real-life homosexual): a series of sketches that superbly evoke the atmosphere of pre-Hitler Berlin; Isherwood is the neutral observer – and is at his best in this relaxed and undemanding position. *Prater Violet* (1945) was a disastrous attempt at a Hollywood novel; its successors are more readable and amusing, but entirely fail to account for their protagonists' inability to come to terms with themselves or the world.

A less clever, stylistically inferior, vastly more substantial (and, alas, more neglected) novelist is **James Hanley** (1901–85). Hanley is an irritating writer: he has obstinately refused to learn much about technique through over forty years of writing; he is diffuse and humourless; but he has a power and intensity of vision that all but a very few of his contemporaries lack. In certain respects he may be compared with Thomas Wolfe (q.v.); but he does not run to length, and is generous and outward-looking where Wolfe was egocentric – however, he has the same kind of crude energy, and is moved by the spectacle of life in somewhat the same way. *Boy* (1931), the stark tale of the ordeal and death of a twelve-year-old boy on a sea voyage, was foolishly banned, which discouraged the sensitive Hanley – who, however, continued with the first of his *Furys* tetralogy, about a Liverpool-Irish family (Hanley was born in Dublin): *The Furys* (1934), *The Secret Journey* (1936), *Our Time is Gone* (1940) and *Winter Song* (1950). This suffers from Hanley's usual faults of diffuseness and clumsiness – but it does have the inestimable advantage of reading like an account of a 'real' family. His most sombre work, however, is *Say Nothing* (1962), which deals with the despairing inhabitants of a boarding-house; this has a truly Dostoevskian power. Hanley's adaptation of this novel provided British television's finest play of the Sixties. Hanley's technique has not advanced, but he has developed into one of the subtlest exponents of inarticulate emotion; it is time that he gained the recognition that he deserves. Henry Green (q.v.) thought him, on the strength of such sea novels as *Hollow Sea* (1938), the best sea novelist since Conrad (q.v.); Faulkner (q.v.) admired *Boy*;

Forster, Read (qq.v.) and many others have given him intelligent praise. His *Collected Stories* appeared in 1953, and was followed by *The Darkness* (1973). His failure to find readers, despite his clumsiness, is inexplicable. The best of his later novels is *Levine* (1956), but *The Kingdom* (1978) shows no flagging of energy.

*

Cyril Connolly (1903–74) was not primarily a novelist; but *The Unquiet Grave* (1945), the book for which he will be remembered, is certainly an imaginative work. For many years Connolly – editor of the widely read magazine *Horizon* (1940–9) – was, with Pritchett and Grigson (qq.v.), one of the few literary journalists whose critical opinions were worth noting. His best criticism is collected in *Enemies of Promise* (1938 rev. 1949), *The Condemned Playground* (1945), *Ideas and Places* (1953) and *Previous Convictions* (1964). He is often provocative, and is unreliable on poetry – but always civilized (in the best sense) and worth reading. Like Jocelyn Brooke, Isherwood, and Rayner Heppenstall (qq.v.) he writes with a rare lucidity. He is an ironic pessimist of the civilized Irish variety ('It is closing time in the gardens of the West' ...), puckish, an expert parodist, an authoritative historian of the educated sensibility of his age. Most of what may be said against him has been said by him in *The Unquiet Grave*, which he published under the pseudonym of 'Palinurus'. Since for his last few years Connolly (no longer much stimulated by what he read) was the chief literary columnist of the London *Sunday Times*, this book is in danger of being forgotten – or at any rate of being ignored by a generation too young to remember it. It is a work of courageous self-revelation, whose chief achievement is to cut self-love out of the self-portrait it renders. It is said that many intellectuals of Connolly's generation immediately recognized themselves in *The Unquiet Grave*; what is more surprising is that almost any cultivated person born not later than 1932 (or thereabouts) can still recognize something of himself in this wry, rueful and self-mockingly sensitive account of an intellectual's attempt to lead a tolerable existence. Connolly found it hard to be at his best – the novel *The Rock Pool* (1935), about a young man's disintegration when he falls into the hands of an arty group in France, is amusing but resolutely minor – but *The Unquiet Grave* is a classic, and it has not dated. *The Missing Diplomats* (1953), on Burgess and MacLean, both of whom he knew well, is a superb piece of journalism. Connolly, who produced little because he did not want to produce mediocre work, was almost the last of a dying breed: the genuine man of letters.

    Flann O'Brien (ps. **Brian O'Nolan**, 1911–66), a civil servant, journalist and Gaelic scholar, who was born and lived all his life in Dublin, is a very different kind of Irishman, but is similarly unclassifiable in the context of the conventional novel. O'Brien's prose combines Joyce (q.v.), who praised his first book, with the great nonsense writers – Lear, Carroll and Morgenstern (q.v.); only his tendency to whimsicality prevents his being a major comic writer. His lightness of touch, however, does not detract from his achievement: it is, indeed, a relief to have one of the most familiar of modern themes (a novel about a man writing a novel about men writing a novel, which is the subject of O'Brien's best book, *At Swim Two Birds*, 1939) treated lightly rather than heavily. *At Swim Two Birds* is funny in a unique manner. It is the quintessence of Irish responsibility, which means that it lacks serious emotional substance, but not wisdom. A characteristic notion introduced by O'Brien is that the water we drink is too strong. ... Other novels, *The Hard Life* (1961), *The Dalkey Archive* (1964), *The Third Policeman* (1967), are excellent comic tales on a smaller scale. There are a number of selections from his shorter pieces.

*

Henry Green (ps. Henry Yorke, 1905–73), a Midlands industrialist, is a major novelist
who pursued the trivial, of which he had an exquisite sense, to the point where his
subject-matter disappeared and he stopped writing. But his achievement is a major one.
Living (1929) is about life in a Midlands foundry such as Green worked in after he came
down from Oxford; it is a joyfully optimistic novel, simply celebrating the fact of life
against a background of drabness, personal disappointment and hard work. Although it
was for years taken as a proletarian novel, *Living* is concerned essentially with what Green
considers the proper subject of modern fiction: 'the everyday mishaps of ordinary life'.
Green is often called a symbolist; but the fog (*Party Going*, 1939) and birds (*Living, Party
Going, Loving*, 1945) and other entities that haunt his novels are both more and less than
symbols: they 'stand for' qualities just as such entities do so – if they do so – in 'real life'.
Green, for all his carefully selective technique and lyricism, is a realist more than a
symbolist. In *Party Going* a group of idle parasites are waiting to set off for France, but are
delayed by fog in a hotel that becomes surrounded by workers waiting to go home. The
scales are not weighted: this is a realist treatment. The metaphor for the 1939 situation is
all the more effective for not being contrived – as in the novels of Rex Warner (q.v.) or
some of the poetry of Auden (q.v.). *Caught* (1943) is about life in the London fire-service
just before the German Blitz began in earnest; this is boring because it gets bogged down
in detail. *Loving*, set in an Irish country house in the early years of the Second World
War, is Green's most beautiful and subtle novel. It is the love story of the English butler,
Raunce, and the housemaid Edith. Raunce is one of the most complex and solid portraits
in modern British fiction. Raunce emerges so clearly because morality (judgement) never
intervenes: the result is a product of pure imagination, a character as rich in contradictions as a real man. Green was not able to maintain this standard; in *Loving*, one of the
most original novels of its time, he exactly caught the elusive poetry of 'everyday life'; his
work was done. Its successors – *Back* (1946), *Concluding* (1948), *Nothing* (1950), *Doting*
(1952) – concentrate, Pinter-like (q.v.), on capturing exact nuances of speech, and
become slighter and slighter.

Jocelyn Brooke (1908–66), another writer of unusually lucid prose, never achieved
anything near the recognition he deserved, although his highly original autobiographical
works – *The Goose Cathedral* (1950) and *The Dog at Clambercrown* (1955) are the best –
received good notices. His finest book is *Private View: Four Portraits* (1954), four beautifully
delineated, shrewd portraits of people whom he had known well. Brooke was at his best
in this shadowy area between fiction and reminiscence, but one of his straight novels
comes nearer to creating a genuinely Kafkaesque (q.v.) atmosphere than anything except
Edward Upward's (q.v.) fiction of the Thirties: this is *The Image of a Drawn Sword* (1950), a
beautifully written account of a nightmare that begins when the protagonist is awakened
in the middle of the night and drafted into an unknown, mysterious army. ... This at
least of his fiction should survive; and his autobiography will be remembered. At the end
of his life he became ill and his work went off – another volume of autobiography and a
book on Proust were never published.

Rosamund Lehmann (1901) derives, like Elizabeth Bowen (q.v.), from Henry James
(q.v.) as much as she derives from anyone. She is a sensitive writer, gifted with compassion and psychological understanding; but it sometimes seems that she seeks, vainly,
to escape from her own intensity. She has never found a suitable style, and her
main subject – the sufferings of women in love – often becomes cloying and over-
obtrusive. The faults in her style – mushiness, lack of precision, reliance on cliché –

point up her failure to write a wholly successful novel. She has maintained a high standard, but probably has never done better than her first novel, *Dusty Answer* (1927), and *The Weather in the Streets* (1936). Both of these are excellent period pieces. In the much later *The Echoing Grove* (1953) her real intentions (to dissect and perhaps destroy, or reveal in its full unworthiness, the male object of female suffering) seem to be at odds with the story she tells, in which her gentleness and reconciliatory nature operate against her impulses. Her brother **John Lehmann** (1907) has written fiction, autobiography, criticism and graceful minor poetry; but he is most famous for his discriminatory help to young writers through his magazines (*Penguin New Writing*, *The London Magazine*) and his publishing firm, which issued the works of many important writers, including Pavese (q.v.).

William Cooper (ps. **Harry S. Hoff**, 1910) is a disciple of C. P. Snow (q.v.), but a more gifted novelist. The Joe Lunn of his *Scenes from Provincial Life* (1950) is the first of the unlikeable nonconformist heroes of whom Kingsley Amis' (q.v.) Jim Dixon is the most famous. Before this he had written four less interesting novels under his own name. In *Scenes from Married Life* (1961) Joe has settled down into a useful member of the community as a civil servant (he is also, of course, a well known writer) and accepted that what he once disliked and rebelled against is really the best of all possible worlds. ... In this and his other novels Cooper is only as funny as an establishmentarian can be. In a 1983 novel he took Joe Lunn into his old age – but his attitudes had hardened and the book lacked energy. There is, however, one exception: *Disquiet and Peace* (1956), a most perceptive and moving study of a woman afflicted with depression, set in Edwardian times. This is a distinguished and delicate novel, and stands in strange contrast to the mixture of crude, cocky brashness and conformity (Cooper's views resemble those of his erstwhile friend Snow, although he possesses more humour) that characterize the other, markedly inferior, books. It is perhaps significant that he stated that anyone who did not find one of his novels 'simple, lucid, attractive and funny' should ask himself 'Should I be trying to read books at all?' (1972). There is a distinctly repulsive flavour to this immodest statement: writers do best to leave praise of their work to others.

Patrick Hamilton (1904–62), famous as the author of the excellent stage thriller *Rope* (1929), and of a really remarkable and under-estimated play – it was far too good to succeed on the London stage – called *The Duke in Darkness* (1943), was a novelist who never received the critical attention he deserved. He was an expert (and envenomed) castigator of the speech habits and stupidity of the pseudo-gentry – the sort that congregate in the saloon-bars of large pubs (exactly the kind of people who refer to the lower classes as 'the great unwashed'). This infinitely foolish and pathetic section of society is triumphantly well represented in *Mr. Stimpson and Mr. Gorse* (1953), but too facetiously in the trilogy *Twenty Thousand Streets under the Sky* (1935), the important parts of which, however, are entirely successful – and compassionate. Hamilton realized the poetic side of his genius most fully in *The Duke in Darkness*, and in the novel *Hangover Square* (1941). The latter is psychiatrically 'wrong' in the sense that it confuses the rare – and hysterical – phenomenon of dual personality with schizophrenia (basing itself on the *Black's Medical Dictionary* 'definition', still disgracefully perpetuated in the latest edition). But the hero, or anti-hero, an alcoholic psychopath and hysteric, is nonetheless convincingly presented. Hamilton was himself an alcoholic – and a communist – and in this powerful novel he predicts his own tragic decline with great subtlety. He is a writer who needs to be looked at again very carefully, for *The Duke in Darkness* is really one of the most important plays of its time; and his prose is brilliantly revealing of middle-class public-house habits – no one did it so well. *Gaslight* (1939) deserves its fame as a thriller, and *The Slaves of Solitude* (1947) is another excellent novel about loneliness.

Storm Jameson (1891) has never been accorded the praise she deserves, although she is at her best superior to Lehmann, Bowen and even West (qq.v.), all of whom were discussed by reviewers in far more serious terms. She has written too much (some forty-seven novels), but certain books stand out. She knows this, and is characteristically forth-right about it. She also feels, perhaps correctly, that her autobiography *Journey from the North* (1969–70), about her Yorkshire nonconformist roots and her interests in European literature and her notion of the novel, is her best book: it is certainly required reading for anyone who wants to know about women and literature in this century, and is worth more than a thousand pseudo-feminist tracts written by facile self-advertisers trying to become men (Jameson remains resolutely what she is, a woman, and was a true feminist long before the modern movements were thought of). Another important book is *Parthian Words* (1970), a declaration of her faith in writing. Her best novel, and a very good one, is *Cousin Honoré* (1940). Honoré is a Frenchman, a selfish and sensual man, but energetic and cunning in a not altogether unattractive way. Jameson brings out his character with great skill. This novel gives portraits-in-depth of several other French people – never, in this case, types, but always individuals. It is rare for an English novelist to write so well and so revealingly about other nations, and Jameson is perhaps better at it than any of her contemporaries. The novel is set between wars, and is incidentally a subtle study of the French mentality in the face of the Nazi threat. All Jameson's novels are readable (she deprecates them a little too much), but ones especially worth looking at include *The White Crow* (1968) and *The Early Life of Stephen Hind* (1966). Much of her non-fiction is valuable, especially *The Decline of Merry England* (1930). She is a very distinguished woman of letters, and deserves far more honour than she has received. That Drabble (q.v.) should receive the CBE and Jameson be ignored provides a gloomily accurate index of just how worthless such decorations are, as of our declining standards. But you get what you work for, and Jameson, among other things, has made a virtue of modesty and decently accurate self-appraisal: if some have their decorations from the Palace, others have what Graves (q.v.), in another context, called the 'obscure proud merit' of the admiration and deserved affection of a discerning minority.

A. L. Barker (1918), much admired by Rebecca West (q.v.), is another very fine writer whose later, and always developing work, has lacked the attention given to her first story collection, *Innocents* (1947). She is quite unclassifiable, although wrong-headed attempts have been made to link her work to that of Angus Wilson (q.v.). She has been taken as a caricaturist, but in fact she explores, with a compassionate and yet detached sensitivity, the phenomenological worlds of odd or eccentric people. The compassion exists in the loving and exactly observed detail. She takes a stance, as writer, of disliking no one. There are no nice or nasty people for her, while she is writing – though afterwards she (and the reader) may well make the inevitable judgements. She deals with the naïve, the ego-centric, the lonely, the sick – and with their perceptions of reality, which she captures as no other contemporary writer can capture. Bainbridge (q.v.) tries to do something like this, but lacks the intelligence and the insight. The idiocies of Barker's characters are by no means her own, and she employs a subtle self-control in the place of an unprofessional self-indulgence. Barker's novels include *John Brown's Body* (1969); and there are several volumes of stories, including *Lost Among the Roundabouts* (1964), but as yet no complete edition. Her world, odd but sharply real, is not describable except in her own terms – one might pay her the tribute of saying that only her characters could recognize it. Her style is impeccable, her aims more modest than they need to be. It has been said, fairly enough, that hers is a talent to be treasured; but genius is the more accurate word. Poets who con-centrate, however honourably, on the 'everyday', become tedious (Creeley, q.v., is an example); but prose writers such as Barker demonstrate that there is energy everywhere:

polemic is alien to them, because their eye is always on the real. Thus they give us a true reality to argue from. Feminists of 'radical' disposition would do well to read this author, who portrays women as they are, and never as they allegedly ought to be, or as they cannot be. Her men are often monsters, as men indeed often or even usually are; but she never strains to gain this effect, and one feels that she is as detached about them as any woman of insight can be expected to be.

*

Malcolm Lowry (1909–57), born in England and educated at Cambridge – but resident abroad (America, Mexico, Canada) for most of his life, although it was at the little village of Ripe in Sussex that he finally put an end to his life – was a heroic alcoholic who succeeded, more than any other who resembled him, in resolving his terrible problems in creative form. His *Selected Poems* (1962) show him to have been a gifted poet; his posthumous fiction – which includes *Hear Us O Lord from Heaven Thy Dwelling Place* (1961) and *Lunar Caustic* (French tr. 1956; 1968) – reveals massive gifts; his early hallucinated sea-story *Ultramarine* (1933), which was influenced by and written with the help of Conrad Aiken (q.v.), is full of promise. But his masterpiece, one of the most powerful novels of its time, is *Under the Volcano* (1947). Lowry dedicated himself to work on this as desperately as he dedicated himself to self-exploration and self-destruction through drinking. Its setting is Mexico – a Mexico that symbolizes Hell – on the Day of the Dead, and its hero is an alcoholic, Geoffrey Firmin, the last day of whose life this is. Firmin is dedicated to his own death, and *Under the Volcano* is the terrific vision that his voluntary sacrifice of his life vouchsafes him. Finally he is murdered and thrown into a ravine; but it is of course drink, or rather what drink stands for, that kills him. Lowry knew his subject well, and only ten years after finishing this novel he killed himself. Firmin, British Consul in a Mexican town between two volcanoes, represents Lowry himself – and, on the level that matters to the reader, the artist. If Vallejo (q.v.) and some other writers have given us a positive answer to the problem of what I have called *Künstlerschuld* (q.v.), then Lowry certainly gives us a terribly negative one. Perhaps it is a limitation. And yet Firmin – himself in deliberate flight, to hell, from all those who love him and seek his salvation (his ex-wife, his anti-fascist brother) – knows of heaven as well as hell. His self-destructive drinking (a Faust figure, he has taken drink to gain the power of insight – and now he must pay) enables him to see heaven – as well as to anaesthetize him from a rotten world that (1939) is destroying itself just as he is. *Under the Volcano* operates successfully on both the realist and the symbolic planes; Firmin is a true modern Faust, a tragic figure of our times. Lowry, after all, endured the agonies of alcoholism (some details appear in Aiken's *Ushant*, where he figures as Hambo) to some purpose: perhaps in his own terror-haunted mind Lowry did equate the Faustian drunk Firmin with an ineluctably guilty artist; but in relentlessly recording his anguish he showed a courage and sense of compassion (this, of course, is apparent in the characters of those who desire to save Firmin) that merit our gratitude.

A writer who has something of Lowry's power, and who is regarded by some as Britain's leading living novelist, is **William Golding** (1911). He received the 1983 Nobel Prize. Although he had published a volume of poetry as early as 1934, Golding did not attract attention until he was forty-three, with *Lord of the Flies* (1954), still his most famous novel. This is a savage gloss on the Victorian writer R.M. Ballantyne's *Coral Island*, in which some British boys are wrecked on a desert island, and create a decent Christian society. Golding's boys create as memorably horrible a dystopia as anyone has thought up since Wells' Rampole Island (q.v.). There is something modish about Golding's vision of these prep-school boys' vileness, and I am not even sure that all 'the disagreeables', in Keats' famous phrase, fully 'evaporate'; but there is no denying his conviction and force. He is, however, a writer who requires to be separated rather firmly from the many fashionable critics that his work has attracted. These critics have represented him as every kind of writer: allegorist, fabulist, realist, mythographer, Christian – and so on. This is, as Walter Allen has pointed out, 'a considerable confidence trick'. Here there really is a negative vision – and one in which, when we think about it, Golding has cheated somewhat: this is fantasy. Yet, because of the modishness I have mentioned, because of a certain element of pretentiousness, *Lord of the Flies* escapes the censure that *Nineteen Eighty-Four* (q.v.) attracted. ... It is at least interesting that *Lord of the Flies* is anthropologically 'wrong' – as was actually demonstrated when some boys were wrecked on an island and did not behave as the boys do in the novel. ... Of Golding's later novels *The Inheritors* (1955), *The Spire* (1964) and *The Pyramid* (1967) seem to me to be the best. *The Inheritors*, about Neanderthal man, is flawed by the same wilfully negative attitude (I mean that the negativity seems to be contrived, to deliberately omit something from the author's response, in the interests of fashion or rhetoric), but it is a *tour de force* by virtue of its brilliant presentation of his Neanderthal people – the Neanderthal people were nothing like that. Golding gives no reason why *Homo Sapiens* (supplanter of his Neanderthal Man) should be vile, murderous and predatory; but his picture of his 'predecessor' does have a kind of gentleness. *Pincher Martin* (1956) and *Free Fall* (1959) fail to cohere, although they contain superb passages; *The Spire*, a medieval novel about the erection of a phallic spire, without proper foundations, to the glory of God, is another study of the evil grounds upon which the apparently good establishes itself. It is his most powerful and original novel, and perhaps the finest visionary work to have been written since the war. In *The Pyramid*, Golding appears to take up a realist approach; but closer examination reveals that it is as symbolic, if less obtrusively so, as its predecessors. However, the treatment of the background, a provincial town (Stillbourne) in 1930, and its Operatic Society's production of *The King of Hearts*, is well done in a realist mode. Golding has sometimes been overrated; his symbolism is strained; but he remains one of the most interesting of contemporary novelists. His later novels show an extreme falling off. *Darkness Visible* (1979) is wilfully negative; *Rites of Passage* (1980), though well written, is actually perverse in its angry and ill-based nihilism. Golding has said that his greatest regret is that he cannot write poetry, and in *Poems* (1934) the key to his failure is to be found. However, *The Spire* is a triumphant exception – for all that Golding's protestations, in his criticism, that he believes in God sound hollow and self-justificatory. Few would dispute his right to the Nobel Prize amongst writers in English – but Powell, Hanley or Narayan (qq.v.) would have been more appropriate.

Golding's contemporary **Rayner Heppenstall** (1911–81) is yet another neglected British novelist. Heppenstall, like Connolly and Jocelyn Brooke (qq.v.), is an excellently lucid writer; but he has always been uneven – and latterly he became off-puttingly eccentric in views, putting forward such opinions as that the pornographer Ian Fleming (perpetrator of James Bond) is the finest stylist of our time and that Hardy (q.v.) was no good because he was untranslatable in French. ... This must be ignored, for Heppenstall is almost the only English novelist to have properly absorbed the influence of the modern French novel. He has written well on Léon Bloy and Raymond Roussel (qq.v.). Heppenstall's best novel is *The Connecting Door* (1962), which renders the surface of things with great acuteness and feeling. *The Lesser Infortune* (1953) and *The Greater Infortune* (1960) are also interesting novels. *The Fourfold Tradition* (1961) is one of the most illuminating books on the differences between French and English fiction – and on the French 'new novel' (q.v.). His best novel, however, may well have been his last: *Two Moons* (1977). This is a technical triumph which went totally unrecognized. It was based on the notion of the real moon and what in astrology is called the 'progressed moon'. Once this basic idea is explained – and it is not difficult – the book becomes easier to read. It is not necessary to 'believe in' or even to have an open mind about astrology to appreciate it, as it is not about astrology. Heppenstall had become somewhat tiresomely obsessed with the increase of crime and violence in the modern world (tiresomely because political crimes and wars did not worry him) – but here he found an objective correlative (q.v.), and his imagination took over. It is a remarkable and powerful work.

Walter Allen (1911), author of deservedly standard books on the novel in English, is in danger of being ignored as a good novelist in his own right. This would be unjust, for he is a master of colloquial understatement and an unusually careful observer of society. His modest, almost casual manner is deceptive. His first mature novel was *Rogue Elephant* (1946), a comic and ironic study of an ugly and unpleasant writer. *Dead Man Over All* (1950), which gained scant appreciation, is one of the best of modern novels about technocracy. Allen does not have Snow's (q.v.) reverence for the public, official, over the private, individual, life, and he traces the real lives of his characters with a compassionate psychological adeptness. But his best novel is *All in a Lifetime* (1959), which traces, through a bedridden narrator, the changes in British working-class life since the latter years of the reign of Queen Victoria. This is a subtle sociological study, in which Allen's knowledge of fictional techniques has stood him in good stead. It is moving, as well as shrewd and skilful: the most successful working-class novel since Green's *Living* (q.v.). It is something of a loss that Allen has not written any new fiction for the past twenty-five years; but he has written a number of indispensable studies of fiction. He is one of the few critics to have properly appreciated Wyndham Lewis (q.v.), about whom he was once going to write a book – unfortunately this never appeared.

Lawrence Durrell (1912) was for many years best known as a poet and youthful friend of Henry Miller (q.v.). His *Collected Poems* (1960; rev. 1968) contains, in fact, his least unenduring work. An Irishman born in India, and for much of his life a British government official in the Middle East, Durrell's most consistent characteristic is his anti-puritanism, and his best poetry presents an Anglicized, thoroughly heterosexualized, wafer-thin but genuine slice of Cavafy (q.v.): it is an achievement. What brought Durrell real fame, however, was the tetralogy known as the Alexandria quartet: *Justine* (1957), *Balthazar* (1958), *Mountolive* (1958) and *Clea* (1960). This has been an enormous popular success, hailed by modish critics; it amounts, however, to little more than what Leslie Fiedler has called 'warmed-through Proust'. The French see the same kind of profundities in it as they once saw in Charles Morgan (q.v.). The clue to its lack of real quality is contained in Durrell's pretentious prefatory note to the second novel in the series: 'Three sides of space and one of time constitute the soup-mix recipe of a continuum. ...' The vulgarity of 'soup-mix' is characteristic. How could the coffee-table public fail to fall for something that was not only as 'deep' as this pompous statement implies, but also sexy and overwritten ('beautiful' or 'poetic' writing)? Durrell based the series on a vulgarization of the relativity principle. As Pursewarden, one of the characters, pronounces: 'We live our lives based on selected fictions. Our view of reality is conditioned by our position in time and space – not by our personalities, as we like to think. ... Two paces west and the whole picture is changed'. The quartet is full of such gobbets of 'wisdom'. The four books deal with the same material – a series of (mostly sexual) incidents in Alexandria – from different viewpoints. The whole is supposed to be an investigation of modern love (of physical sex as the true reality), or perhaps a representation of life as significant only when it becomes art. He was much influenced by Groddeck, and is a sort of Reichian *sans* Reich (q.v.). The quartet is muddled, and the self-consciously lush writing is an indication of its essential meretriciousness. The characters have no solidity; the entire conception is robbed of whatever atmospheric power it might have had by its author's ambitious, polymathic vulgarity: his adolescent obsession with decadence, his preoccupation with occultism, his fatal penchant for potted wisdom. This is the kind of thing that naturists read aloud to one another after sunset and before exchanging sensual essences (or whatever). If Colin Wilson – who perpetrates a rather similar though vastly less well educated mixture of Nietzsche-and-water, sexiness, personal immortality, 'superman crime' and the occult – is the mage of the lounge, then Durrell is the savant of the drawing-room. By 2000 his quartet will be as dead as *Sparkenbroke* is today – and orgasms will still be non-philosophical. The successors to this work, all as modish, are not worth serious discussion – and have not attracted it.

Angus Wilson (1913) is an altogether more serious and substantial writer. He has been much misunderstood ('scrupulously prolongs the tradition running from Trollope to Hugh Walpole') for two reasons: he can write in a genuinely realist manner, and he has made attempts to revive the solid, Victorian novel. He has not been taken seriously enough, perhaps, by critics. In fact he is not a traditionalist – and even if his attempts to create a twentieth-century equivalent of the nineteenth-century novel are over-ambitious failures, they are nevertheless experimental failures, for Wilson is a sophisticated critic, well aware of the difficulties confronting him in his project. Wilson is a very gifted novelist and one eminently justified in harbouring major ambitions: he is a deadly satirist of the stupid and the pretentious, he has the sort of compassion that goes with a capacity for self-criticism (this is all too clearly what the latter-day Durrell, q.v., has lost), he can construct his big novels properly. ... But his very ambitiousness is (or at least was) in a sense his worst enemy: it led him to attempt the impossible, the construction of massive realist novels, when his real gift is for the fantastic, the grotesque – the richly imaginative. His best novel, *The Old Men at the Zoo* (1961), is in fact satirical fantasy: set in (what was then) the future, 1970. We see England invaded by Europe and the Zoo taken over so that the new rulers can throw their opponents to the beasts. All this is presented as if it were 'ordinary' subject-matter; but the result is merely an increase of ironic tension. It is a work of considerable feeling and compassion. Wilson's first novel, *Hemlock and After* (1952), is his most successful purely realist work (outside the short story); it suffers from its failure to build up a complete enough portrait of the hero, Bernard Sands, a novelist who falls victim, in middle life, to the homosexual impulses that he has so far successfully repressed. Wilson has a Dickensian gift for caricature, and this has never been seen to better advantage than in his devastating picture of London's homosexual underworld. This is hardly, alas, an advertisement for 'Gay Liberation' – it portrays a society which is the enemy of the decent, unobtrusive, oppressed homosexual such as Sands; it reminds us that the mindless taking-over of the euphemism 'gay' has provided shallow exhibitionists with an excuse to indulge themselves at the expense of real homosexuals. *Anglo-Saxon Attitudes* (1956), full of excellent things, and an acute character study, is nevertheless too long; it tries to achieve what is today a sociologically inappropriate kind of solidity. *The Middle Age of Mrs. Eliot* (1958) is, as has often been pointed out, too near to clinical case-history. *Late Call* (1964) is less novel than satire – on the deadness of modern life as lived (or not lived) in a British New Town. *No Laughing Matter* (1967) is long, like *Anglo-Saxon Attitudes*, but more successful in its language and in conveying the vitality of the crowded canvas the author loves. It is also more genuinely experimental than the earlier works. This vein is continued in *As if by Magic* (1973) and *Setting the World on Fire* (1980). He has written well on Zola, Dickens and Kipling (qq.v.). As a short-story writer Wilson is formidable: *Death Dance* (1969) contains twenty-five of his best, but is at present available only in America. His work has not had the examination it deserves.

P.H. Newby (1918) is an excellent minor comic novelist, but when he has tried to be more ambitious he has not succeeded in writing more than a few superb but isolated scenes. The context is always highly intelligent, but it is not really imagined; one feels that Newby has taken too much thought, that he lacks a single vision of his own because of his awareness of others'. And yet the potentiality is there to such an extent that one wishes that Newby would abandon his nervous, play-safe pastiche of other writers' life-views (Conrad's, Lawrence's, qq.v., in particular), and abandon himself to himself. As it is, a certain meanness of spirit (a deliberate avoidance of robustness), an over-prudence, seems to vitiate what could clearly be – and in part is – a major achievement. If only, one feels, Newby could sustain the power and sensitivity of *A Step to Silence* (1952), the first of two books about Oliver Knight (the sequel is *The Retreat*, 1953): the descriptions of Midland landscape, of the teachers' training college which Oliver attends before joining up, of (in particular) Oliver's older friend Hesketh's model geography lesson, given to satisfy the examiners of his efficiency as a teacher. But even this novel fails to hold together: Newby is too reticent with Knight; and he is too eager in the sequel to turn him into a freak, to disown him as a character and transform him into a stock symbol of alienated man. What has happened is that Newby's empathy has failed: he is too nervous to attempt further self-portrayal. In later novels the intentions are excellent, and there are always well rendered scenes; but there is a lack of psychological conviction. In *The Picnic at Sakkara* (1955) Newby has set his sights lower: the result is superbly executed light comedy. Later work is mostly obstinately over-ambitious: rather obviously the novels of a bitterly disappointed man. The diluted Christianity of the more serious novels is unconvincing and clearly factitious – as in *A Season in England* (1951) and *One of the Founders* (1965). *Revolution and Roses* (1957) is a return to farce, but is not as funny as *The Picnic at Sakkara*, though it has its moments. *A Lot to Ask* (1973) is an even feebler assertion of religious faith. Newby seems to have lost his way – yet when he started he had real promise. But he has forgotten the difficult things he had to say, and relapsed into a dull competence. He had a long and successful career at the BBC, ending as Managing Director of Radio – a position requiring a very high degree of compromise.

Denton Welch (1917–48) died at thirty-one as a result of a road accident sustained when he was a boy; he lived in extreme discomfort and, in the last stages of his illness, acute pain. His books, *Maiden Voyage* (1943), *In Youth is Pleasure* (1944) and *A Voice Through a Cloud* (1950) – there was also a volume of stories and sketches, *Brave and Cruel* (1948) – are candid, subjective explorations of his self-pity and homosexuality. His was only a minor talent, but a sufficiently exquisite one to have kept his work alive for a quarter of a century. Like Jocelyn Brooke, who edited some of his literary remains, Welch wrote autobiography in the form of fiction; his unbaring of his personality is quite remarkable – even unnerving. His technique consists of a series of extremely detailed impressions; there is no generalization. Welch's narcissism and hypersensitivity sometimes obtrude into his work (especially in *In Youth is Pleasure*), but when these are under control his writing provides a unique insight into the homosexual mentality.

Anthony Burgess (1917) is the most naturally gifted English novelist of his generation; but he has not yet produced the major novel of which he is so clearly capable. He is a talented musician, learned in linguistics, and a genuine polymath. He is also an active journalist and critic. No writer of our time is more obviously highly intelligent – and aware of the essentially subversive function of the writer. No contemporary novelist more clearly displays genius. And yet no single book has yet contained all this genius and sensibility. This is partly because he is too clever, too aware, too self-conscious, too versatile: swarms of objective correlatives present themselves to him, and become too articulate too soon; he can't help knowing too well what he is doing. But in too many cases this extremely sentimentive (q.v.) type of writer has allowed himself to be inhibited into complete silence; we were for a time grateful for Burgess' prodigious output, for the fecundity for which he has unfairly been blamed. Notable among his novels is the *Malayan Trilogy* (1956-9), which is essentially a tragedy on the subject of Britain's withdrawal (of interest as well as power) from its empire. Burgess is a Tory (in the old, Johnsonian, sense) unable to recover from the shock of realizing that Toryism died with Ford's (q.v.) Tietjens (a statement with which he would certainly agree). This horror has led him into over-frenzied journalistic activity, into a no-nonsense, professional approach to his craft that tends to obscure his seriousness, dedication and stature – and into excursions into the area where horror merges with comedy. *Nothing Like the Sun* (1964) is a *tour de force* on Shakespeare's life – the only tolerable novel on the subject – which seems to be based on Fripp's rather than Chambers' better known biography. Perhaps his most powerful novel, in which we see more of the author himself than elsewhere, is the devastating *Honey for the Bears* (1963).

Burgess did finally attempt his mammoth novel, with *Earthly Powers* (1980). This met with a chorus of extravagant and uncritical praise from reviewers – but what was said could hardly have pleased an author of Burgess' intelligence, since it consisted of superlatives, and did not at all even describe the book he had written. It is in fact a ragbag, containing some passages of brilliance but others of tedious muddle. His more recent novels preceding this had exploited his cleverness and his ingenuity rather than his narrative powers: one had the sense of a man constructing breathtaking crossword puzzles, drawing knowledgeably on every new set of ideas (in particular, structuralism, q.v.), and yet forfeiting the very traditionalism in which he felt rooted, and with which he felt he must compromise rather than destroy. He had the heart and the skill to write something of the calibre of Ford's *The Good Soldier* (q.v.), though set in these even more dishonourable times. But *Earthly Powers*, despite its fascinating theological and genuinely comic passages, and its pyrotechnics, does not cohere. It seems uneasy on the problem of homosexuality, which it does not resolve. Furthermore, much of the language is dead. From so imaginatively gifted a writer, *Earthly Powers* is curiously synthetic, and a disappointment. When the adulation of the reviewers has faded – and it always does – it is likely to be seen as more lightweight than it should have been, than, indeed, its undoubtedly serious material itself suggests. It seems to have been written too quickly and carelessly. It is in part an admirable book; but to write admirable books is not enough. Burgess' intelligence and energy seem for the moment to be too widely dispersed: were he to gather his powers together, and concentrate them into one novel, he might still achieve a masterpiece. Of course, as he knows, there is a price to pay for writing the script of the soap opera *Jesus of Nazareth*.

James Stern (1904), born in Ireland and educated at Eton, is known only to a few connoisseurs of the short story; yet his *Stories of James Stern* (1969) – he had published three previous collections, in 1932, 1938 and 1951 – contains nothing so esoteric that it would not appeal to a wider readership. He has led a varied life: farmer in Rhodesia in the Twenties, bank clerk, editor, journalist in Europe, sixteen years' residence in the USA: few men's experience could have been wider. He has translated many books, and written an autobiography called *The Hidden Damage* (1947), which never appeared in England. There are some dozen uncollected stories: enough for a new volume. He has always resisted offers from publishers to write a novel, since he feels that, as he puts it, he wants his fiction to be '*short*'. Already in his first volume he was writing prophetically and humanely, though not polemically, about the racial situation in South Africa: he had the sensibility to see what was to come. Many of his other stories deal with boyhood, and may be autobiographical. He is a terse writer, modest, highly intelligent, able to give a sense of the time, the place and the feelings of the characters he is describing. One uncollected story, set in Africa, from a magazine of 1933, 'Strangers Defeated', about a horse and its owner and the feelings of the natives about them, has the power and vigour of Quiroga (q.v.) at his best. It is odd that he has not easily taken his place as a leading, and highly effective, practitioner in this difficult and little appreciated form.

Fred Urquhart (1912) is another excellent writer of stories, although he has written novels as well. His *Collected Stories* were published in two volumes (1967–8), and have been followed by two more collections. His chief strength lies in his ear for Scots dialogue in all its various forms: as Naomi Mitchison has said, 'he is a wonderful listener'. He has a touch of Caradoc Evans (q.v.), though is never so bitter: he tells his fellow Scots what they do not much like to hear. He is very good at portraying women; and most of the characters he treats are in some way humiliated or eccentric. Like almost all good story writers, what he has to tell us comes through speech or thought – there is little description. His novels are really stories that grew to a length: *Jezebel's Dust* (1951) is the best of them. He is the sole surviving member – except for Pritchett (q.v.) – of that group of story-writers of the Thirties which comprises the golden age, in this century, of the short story in England. Many who must go unmentioned in this book were then turning out better stories than we have seen since. His first book did not appear until 1938 – the novel *Time Will Knit* – but he was well known in Scotland for years before that, and it was then that he really began. He has known most of the writers of his time, and his autobiography would make a fascinating book – but perhaps it would be impossible for him to write it as he would wish, since he would be saying too much about too many still living people. He is therefore the kind of writer whom it is necessary to know.

*

It is the habit of literary journalists to compare all women novelists with Jane Austen – which is both an injudicious and a foolish procedure. Three writers who have had too much pseudo-critical attention paid to them are Muriel Spark, Iris Murdoch, and Margaret Drabble (qq.v.).

Muriel Spark (1918) is clever and sometimes amusing (her jokes go less far than her admirers claim, however), but her Roman Catholicism seems to function as something more distinctly personal than universally divine (if one may so put it). She writes well and concisely, and this has tended to obscure the psychological superficiality and sheer petty malice of her content. Like Evelyn Waugh (q.v.) she indulges herself in callousness; but she doesn't have Waugh's intelligence or weight. Her stature is exactly summed up (if unwittingly) by a phrase once thrown off by the ladies' columnist Katherine Whitehorn: 'top-notch Spark'. This mock-critical ejaculation exactly echoes her real voice – even if it filters out the uncanny and incongruous literary adroitness. *Memento Mori* (1959) is the most successful of her novels. She lacks wisdom, emotional substance and all compassion, but the surface of her novels was until quite recently attractive. Her limitations were not fully revealed until she attempted a large-scale novel, *The Mandelbaum Gate* (1964), in which most of the writing is simply dull. *The Hothouse by the East River* (1973) showed up her limitations even more severely: a portentous allegory with an attempt at theological seriousness. With *Loitering With Intent* (1981), a feeble attempt at a comic novel, she seemed to fade out of even the public reckoning. She wanted to be like Evelyn Waugh, but she had no unhappy depths to her malice.

Although considerably less adroit, **Iris Murdoch** (1919) is more serious. She (unlike Muriel Spark, q.v.) has the potentialities of a novelist; but she has in effect refused to write a novel, and has instead resorted to desperate tricks: pretentious symbolism and crass sentimentality. At times both her characterization and her dialogue are at a woman's magazine level (as in *The Nice and the Good*, 1968); she leaves us with the impression that she dares not contemplate her true attitude towards life, but instead must hurry on to the next novel. She was a teacher of philosophy by profession, and her own philosophy (it is outlined in the astonishingly entitled pamphlet *The Sovereignty of Good Over Other Concepts*, 1967) gives a useful indication of her fictional intentions. These are not (apparently they dare not be) imaginative – but philosophical. Alas, philosophy has never been a satisfactory *raison d'être* for the creative writer. And Iris Murdoch's philosophy is not distinguished: a pallid and sentimental Kantian substitute for Christianity. In the later novels some of the characters search for Murdochian virtue; the results are as mediocre as the philosophy, and they are not improved by the author's insertion of clothes- and pet-notes of interest only to an audience for whom the public library is now a (doubtless unsavoury) substitute for the defunct circulating library. The earlier novels are superior – the least organized, *Under the Net* (1954), is in some ways the best of all because it has no pretentious control superimposed on it, and the hero is simply allowed to wander. For in Iris Murdoch control is nearly always pretentious in terms of the creativity – the ability to create autonomous character and situation – that has been revealed. She can descend to such depths as this piece of dialogue, supposed to be exchanged between a very young man and woman after their first sexual encounter:

'Was that really it?'
'Yes.'
'Are you sure you did it right?'
'My God, I'm sure!'
'Well, I don't like it.'
'Girls never do the first time.'
'Perhaps I'm a Lesbian.'...
'Oh Barb, you were so wonderful, I worship you.'

The single novel that demonstrates that Iris Murdoch is above the kind of thing she has been content to perpetrate is *The Bell* (1958), which most critics have agreed is her best. Here the action, which concerns a homosexual founder of a religious community, is convincing in itself – with the result that the author's symbolic intentions do not seem to be contrived. This is by no means a good novel – it is too muddled – but it is Murdoch's least unserious novel. Otherwise, despite excellent passages, the 'mysteriousness' of Iris Murdoch's fiction, even if it is regarded as 'deep' in some quarters, is no more than meretricious trickery. What has happened to this talented writer by now is that she cannot see her people as people, and so in her despair she has become increasingly reckless, using every modish cliché – spying, sex, incest, mythological allusion, the Gothic, whips – to distort her and her reader's attention from her inability to imagine situation. Nothing she has written in the Seventies or Eighties really adds anything.

Margaret Drabble (1939) has been consistently overrated, to the detriment of her development as a journalist. But there is a group of women readers – quite a substantial one – who intensely dislike her work. She is intelligent and quite fluent, but essentially her novels are romances dressed up in realistic clothes, trying to do for the self-styled liberated woman what the straightforward pulp romance does for the woman who is to all intents and purposes unaware of even the existence of any kind of feminism. Drabble is pure middlebrow (q.v.) because her characters are manipulated to appeal to a certain kind of market: imagination has no play whatever in her work, and her style is drab and without energy (though competent enough). What she is saying is what certain sorts of women want to hear – and what certain men would like to hear about women. But it does not look like that at first sight, and it has been quite an artful performance. She took George Eliot as a model, and tried to construct sound, traditional novels dealing with contemporary life. But she lacks George Eliot's moral seriousness – and, indeed, that kind of moral seriousness no longer works in novels about contemporary life. She has no sense of humour, and little wit. Yet she says that she writes about 'privilege, justice and salvation'. Were she truly gifted (she is certainly talented), she might have been highly interesting as a woman writer who, by her imagination, was striking deep blows at the heart of, not feminism, but of polemical feminism of the sort that wants woman to become a kind of man. However, her position remains undefined, and, while we ought not to expect fiction to become polemic, we can expect to infer something from it. This we cannot do.

Drabble has tried to write about intelligent women such as herself, and has made it her speciality to describe the conflicts between their aspirations and their motherhood. *The Millstone* (1965) is about a scholarly woman who has an affair not important to her, becomes pregnant, and then discovers that she has maternal feelings – which, to her surprise (as she has been only a scholar), she finds she shares with 'ordinary' people. But scholarly people are not really always cut off from the real world, and Drabble's Rosamund Stacey (a suspiciously George-Eliotian name) is not a very convincing figure: she is, rather, a manufactured one. Some feel that while the two successors to *The Millstone* – *Jerusalem the Golden* (1967) and *The Waterfall* (1969) – are close to 'woman's magazine fiction', Drabble in that novel, and in *The Needle's Eye* (1972), does transcend this genre. But close examination reveals that even in those books she is engaged in writing thesis romances. They are books describing how women would like to picture themselves as feeling, but they never penetrate to the depths of how they actually feel. They are clever, sometimes well observed, but essentially shallow. Drabble is writing not from herself, but wholly with an audience in mind. *The Middle Ground* (1980) was, more simply, tedious. It is a pity that in an age when good journalists are almost non-existent, this clever author should have chosen fiction. It is a greater pity that she should have been taken so seriously.

Her elder sister, **A.S. Byatt** (1936), has tried to do exactly the same thing with the novel: write about contemporary life in a traditional manner. She has not succeeded, but her books are more serious, her sense of character deeper – and she has much less of the journalist about her. With her third novel (the first two were competent and readable, and far outstripped her sister's in achievement), *The Virgin in the Garden* (1978), she began a planned series. It owes much to Powell (q.v.), and is not altogether comfortable in that sense: it is clearly very ambitious, and it brings in a great deal too much modernistic-looking allusion of a fashionably mythological and literary sort. It covers the period 1952–3, and there are some quite good passages evoking the atmosphere of the year of the coronation (1952). But it smells of the lamp, and one does not feel very confident about what is to follow. It seems as though this is to be a work that will attract praise from academic critics for academic virtues; great labour has gone into its construction, but of vitality there is little.

More gifted and more eccentric is **Angela Carter** (1940), who, although it has frequently been diverted into what seem to many to be foolish or trivial channels, possesses genuine energy. Her book about pornography, *The Sadeian Woman: An Exercise in Cultural History* (1979), is interesting, but no more so than any not unintelligent woman's writing on this subject might be. It does not define cultural history very clearly, and is sometimes wilful. Her fiction relies very heavily on the puerile or even the infantile: rape, murder, castration, and the rest of the stuff to be found in Sade's interminable accounts of tortures (the least interesting aspect of him). But she is relevant to a certain degree, because her preoccupation with woman-as-masochist-trying-to-be-sadist often leads her into imaginative paths, although these always have dead ends. So far she has remained far too reliant on the world of pulp horror fantasy. People read this mainly because of their need to pretend that real horrors and sado-masochistic impulses do not exist: that is to say, they can play at being horrified, but then 'dispose of' the books. The process seems to be cathartic but is not cathartic enough: true dread keeps on returning — and truly horrifying books are not wanted, because these set up genuinely disturbing resonances. But it has to be admitted that her writing is far superior to that of the run-of-the-mill (and disgusting) perpetrator of pulp horror fantasy, and that she is making an attempt to dispose of a problem that cuts deeply into woman's conception of herself. The better novels are *Shadow Dance* (1966), *The Magic Toyshop* (1967) and *Love* (1971). There are a few interesting stories in *The Bloody Chamber* (1979). *The Passion of New Eve* (1977), a novel, is peculiarly silly inasmuch as it gets itself lost in polemic: the Amazons who turn the protagonist into a woman in order to demonstrate to him the results of his exploitations of women are wholly unconvincing, both anthropologically and imaginatively, since they don't want to be exploited, even if some women do. Are they manipulations made by the author in order to avoid the consequences of her own erotic make-up? Angela Carter would like to try to tell us, imaginatively, why so many women are affected by the bleak and uncompromising *Story of O* (q.v.); but she comes nowhere near to solving this problem. On the other hand, she should receive many more marks than, say, Drabble (q.v.), both for having energy and for making a serious attempt. She is exploring very dangerous territory, and she deserves congratulations for doing this. It is at least understandable that she feels herself forced to draw on the debased and debasing material of talentless writers who are content to purvey evil for money (the pulp horror writers, who are moral criminals), and who have no understanding of what they are doing, and no writing skills – such as would actually undermine their commercial intent – whatsoever. Curiously, most of these hacks are paedophiles, misogynists, or both.

Beryl Bainbridge (1934) is less talented and less interesting. Much of the criticism of her has depended upon the male critics injecting such qualities into her work as they feel desirable in women novelists: for example, she is not really a 'black comedian', and she does not possess 'increasing mastery of style'. As she has written: 'I am not very good at fiction ... it is always me and the experiences I have had'. There is nothing wrong with such a confession. But it might suggest a deficiency of the imagination. Graves (q.v.) often said that he did not possess the right kind of inventiveness to be a novelist of the conventional type – and that was true enough, with the exception of one novel, *Seven Days in New Crete*. But this did not disqualify him from being a novelist at all: as he implied, he preferred to draw upon, and then embellish, history. The question of deficiency of imagination did not come up here, of course: Graves wrote poetry. In addition, there is always the fact that all fiction, if only in the manner in which an author has selected and presented his or her material, is in a sense autobiographical. It bears its author's signature. If it tries not to bear his signature, or even if it actually does not bear it (if that were possible), then that, of course, is in itself a signature. Proust (q.v.) deals with this problem, mentioning Hardy (q.v.), in the course of *Remembrance of Things Past* (q.v.). But in the particular case of Bainbridge there certainly is a lack of imagination – there is also a lack of any kind of controlling intelligence. One feels that she has had a very sympathetic editor, one who greatly helped her to put her books into shape. That might be the case. Assessment of this editor's role in Bainbridge's novels could present a problem to anyone wishing to spend time in investigating her *oeuvre*.

I am not, of course, suggesting that Bainbridge cannot read, or is an idiot – though I find certain passages in her slackly written novels idiotic, as if the author were following the most wilfully foolish line that she could. Her first five novels were modish, exploiting the ill-defined vein called 'black humour' – an excuse for a good deal of writing neither amusing in any way, nor horrifying, but rather exposing its perpetrator's lack of humour, taste and originality. (The same could never be said of Evelyn Waugh, q.v., however one might judge him.) Bainbridge relates 'shocking' incidents in a flat manner, as though they were 'ordinary'. *Harriet Said* (1972), which was her first novel, but the third to appear, is characteristic: there is an accidental killing by a girl of thirteen. But this is about all there is to it. The author appears to be amused by it, and yet to hint that somewhere or other there is something 'evil'. But the reader, while he or she may be amused by this amoral, rambling, silly story, is given no sense that Bainbridge herself has any true awareness of such a concept: it is as if someone has told her that fiction often deals with moral issues and that she ought to consider that. Bainbridge's weakness, a lack of control and a lack of any imaginative insight into evil, is also (if in a very limited way) her one strength. Here is a writer narrating series of events without any notion of what they are about. And this, of course, is just how some people seem to be in their behaviour, and how some people register experience. But the idiot's eye view of the world has been given to us most memorably by Faulkner in *The Sound and the Fury* (qq.v.), and of any such notion as that idiots are 'hallucinated automata', in Wyndham Lewis' (q.v.) memorable phrase, there is no trace. Nor is there a trace of any other attitude. Bainbridge's 'firm belief' that anyone can write (and it doubtless is easy for her) is very revealing. She has adopted the mask of the aliterary, self-indulgent 'scribbler'. And this, after one has looked through a few of her novels, is exactly what she is. The whole enterprise becomes intolerable. She does make some readers laugh, although it is hard to accept that she makes anyone think. One does not blame Bainbridge for the attention she obtains; but one wonders how critics fail to be accurate in their accounts of what she is doing. To call her 'tragically oriented' leaves us in some difficulty when we come to describe (say) Faulkner. *The Bottle Factory Outing* (1974) is a tolerably amusing tale of a group of people (she usually deals with groups). *Young Adolf* (1978), which has been supposed to make a 'comment on history', is a total failure, and very dull to read. Bainbridge's voice is that of the slapdash child; but her candid autobiography, unedited, might make a fascinating spectacle. Here she could fulfil her own programme: 'Once the grammar has been learnt it is simply talking on paper and in time learning what not to say'. Where ignorance is bliss 'tis folly to be wise, as Bainbridge might learn not to say.

Brigid Brophy (1929) is older and more gifted, although she may not yet have written her best novel. So far her best book is *Prancing Novelist* (1973), a brilliant study of Firbank (q.v.) with which one does not have to agree to appreciate: it is really more about its author than about Firbank. Brophy is a follower of Shaw and Freud (qq.v.), although she has modified the ideas of both: she is a vitalist. I do not believe that her 'philosophy', which is essentially non-sceptical – it amounts to a rationalist certainty – is what has given Brophy her distinction. I believe that she has done well what she has done well in spite of her beliefs. But this is true of so many novelists and writers in general that it cannot, and is not meant to, be taken as an insult. Brophy's criticism is sharp and useful, her stand on 'animals' rights' admirable; but neither of these is dependent on the holding of a rationalist position. Where she is rationalist or highly polemical she can be very silly indeed (as in her part of the absurd *Fifty Books of English and American Literature We Could Do Without*, 1967, a damp squib if ever there was one: it sets out to destroy such writers as Spenser and Jonson, but gives no cogent reasons for its depreciations – I doubt if she would want it reprinted now), but also very effective, as in *The Longford Threat to Freedom* (1972). But there is in Brophy a powerfully irrational – imaginative – streak; when this gets the better of her she writes quite beyond herself. She has written eight novels, but the best is *Palace Without Chairs* (1978). This puzzled the regular critics: they regarded it as a political allegory, and could not make sense of it. Brophy had already suggested, in *The Adventures of God in His Search for the Black Girl* (1973), that those who received imaginative information were not likely to understand it. ... In fact *Palace Without Chairs* transcends the merely political, and is an ironic comedy in which a royal child survives as an enigmatic symbol of hope because of her 'vitality': she is a pachydermous lesbian whose parents, King and Queen of an imaginary country, have, along with their other four children, either committed suicide or vanished, giving way to a military dictatorship. *In Transit* (1969) is an experimental novel with some interesting passages; *The Snow Ball* (1964) is her fictional tribute to Firbank (q.v.), but is of less universal interest, although it is very clever and knowing part-pastiche. The didactic in Brophy is strong, but separate from her creative achievement – hence her commitment to Freud as well as to Shaw: the two men do not sit happily together. She has written a fascinating and unusual book about Mozart. *Don't Never Forget* (1966) collects reviews and essays, some of them invaluable guides to their subjects.

Maureen Duffy (1933) has written many novels about the sad, the outcast, the subversive, of which the best is *Londoners* (1983). She finds it hard to escape from the drabness of her settings, but she knows them well. She has written some rather elegant lesbian love poetry – *The Venus Touch* (1971) – which rivals Bishop's (q.v.), and is less self-conscious and arch.

Anita Mason (1942) has so far written two unusually promising novels. The first, *Bethany* (1981), deals with a strained relationship and the destructive effects of those who make Utopian claims. The result is uncanny, disturbing and psychologically interesting. The second, *The Illusionist* (1983), although awkwardly written in parts, boldly takes on a theme that no one else has directly attempted: gnosticism (q.v.). It is about Simon Magus, the heretical magician who figures in the Apocryphal New Testament. With considerable courage, and a great deal of research, she resolved to set Simon in his own times. The result is not a complete success – it fights shy of the gnostic issues and plumps for a rationalistic attack on religious 'magic' – *The Illusionist* is a unique book by an author with a highly original mind, one who does not move in 'literary circles', and who follows her own nose in a most refreshing manner. She has come much nearer to the spirit, though by no means the manner, of Kafka (q.v.) than any of his so called explicators, let alone his imitators. Her next task is the very difficult one of exploring the nature of her own religious convictions which she distrusts to the extent of denying them. It could be a major novel.

Philip Toynbee (1916–81) was, like Heppenstall, Connolly and Jocelyn Brook (qq.v.), an exquisitely clear stylist, as he demonstrated in *Friends Apart* (1955), reminiscences of his early years. He was one of the most interesting of modern English novelists, but never realized himself. He was for the whole of his life a dedicated alcoholic, which caused him much misery. However, he did experiment intelligently (*Tea with Mrs. Goodman*, 1947; *The Garden to the Sea*, 1953), and is thus more deserving of attention than most of his contemporaries. The latter is marred by an obtrusive Jungian (q.v.) symbolism, which Toynbee seemed to be exploiting rather than convinced by; but it is nonetheless an arresting novel. His series of novels with the overall title of *Pantaloon* (1961–) in free verse, which he left unfinished, is a failure – partly, but not wholly, because he could not handle free verse. This was, in essence, an autobiographical project, and Toynbee admitted that in it he was trying to combine Proust (q.v.), Cervantes, Wordsworth, Goethe (and possibly Marlowe, too). ... This was far too ambitious. The work is diluted and feeble, and seems to have been written without energy. At the end Toynbee was moving towards a sort of Weil(q.v.)-like Christianity; but unhappily, sincere though he undoubtedly was, this looks much more like the last gesture of a desperate man than a serious or robust experiment. Toynbee may well have been a major novelist lost to us by alcohol. It is impossible to say. But his prose was at its best lucid, an excellent example to others.

Stanley Middleton (1919), who was born in Nottingham and has lived there all his life, has written a score or so of novels, but not one has been published in America. This is extraordinary, since he has often been compared to D.H. Lawrence (q.v.), and is in any case occasionally discussed in America as an important English regional novelist. He has been turning out well-crafted, intelligent, readable novels since 1958, and has never written a bad one. He is much subtler as a writer than he has been taken to be, and has received scant recognition.

His novels are usually set in the Midlands, and deal with crises in people's lives from which they learn but do not profit, or from which they fail to learn at all. His narrative is not stodgy or dull, but is unsensational. His thoughtful shifts of viewpoint are unobtrusive: he is a quiet novelist. He is exceedingly scrupulous in the way he deals with his characters, having to make them, as he has admitted, 'act out of character' in just the way people do – but at the same time to show that they 'live out what they are said to be'. Few novelists would even recognize the paradox. ... His characters are not extraordinary people; but this is one of this neglected novelist's strengths. He aims, not to report, but to illuminate the lives of 'ordinary' people. His imagination does not show itself in his language; but he has more imaginative powers than he is credited with, and his novels are more complex than they are normally taken to be. He is also important in that he has successfully carried on writing in a solidly realistic tradition. One can think of very few novelists in Britain or in America who have so consistently and successfully written in this quite straightforwardly realistic mode without their work's suffering for it.

Middleton does not write about nice people at all – there are hardly any of these in his books. Rather, they are inglorious and even second-rate; at best they are humdrum. There is an almost naturalist (q.v.) streak in him, in his determination to show that 'most people', and these are the people he writes about, are unamiable muddlers (c.f. e.e. cummings', q.v., 'mostpeople'); but he is not didactic enough to be a real neo-naturalist, and one cannot insult him by suggesting that he ever writes to a programme: he writes truthfully to his view of life, which is a pessimistic one. His people are the ones (unlike him, certainly – and this is part of his achievement) who do not obtain consolation from or even respond much to literature. And anyone to whom novels really mean something and who has been a teacher (Middleton's own job for the whole of his life), or an actor, or a business man, or a professional man – these are typical 'Middleton people' – will know very well that such people are commoner than those who do. They are a dreary lot. Yet Middleton humanizes them, gives them all the human status they possess. He is perhaps the only novelist who could write a fair-minded novel about a VAT man – and this is a great tribute to him, and means that he can depict, quite sympathetically, rigid characters who lack warmth, humour or humanity, people who would be as happy in Berlin in 1942 as they are in Great Britain in 1984. There is a sense in which he, and he alone, is writing interestingly about the drab world 'outside' what we call literature. Thus I should claim a higher status for him than he has. One of his most successful novels is *Terms of Reference* (1966), in which two differing types of family dither fascinatingly over the failed marriage of their respective children, neither of whom they can see as themselves. They are too preoccupied with their own position in society, and nothing really happens; but they act out 'interest in the situation' like robots. It is a dispiriting book, and yet in its quiet way a very powerful one. And, as always in Middleton, it demonstrates how courageous even weak or wretched people can be. Other excellent novels are *Harris's Requiem* (1960), *Apple of the Eye* (1970), *A Man Made of Smoke* (1973) and *The Other Side* (1980).

Kingsley Amis (1922) caught a universal post-war mood in his very funny novel *Lucky Jim* (1954). In this book the Pooterish Jim Dixon represents honesty; a university lecturer, he rejects culture not so much because of what it is as because of its snobbish and hypocritical associations. He is not likeable: he is not only exasperated, anti-phoney and furious, but also a sly and ambitious go-getter. He resembles Denry of Arnold Bennett's (q.v.) *The Card*, but lacks his mobility and warmth: there is something feral about his snarl – this is a deprived young man who is going to be revenged. The high comedy does not obscure the inner determination. But Jim Dixon is real, and his preoccupations are powerfully conveyed. Nor are we entitled to assume that the author has put Dixon forward simply as a hero: on the contrary, I doubt if Amis minds in the least if we object to his boorishness, and pity his accident-proneness. We laugh at him as much as we laugh with him. This was an unusual novel, a necessary variation on the theme initiated in *The Card*. It is all the more unfortunate, then, that Amis' fiction has, over the past thirty years, tended to deteriorate. This seems to be because Amis has identified with the simplistic, materialist side of himself – at the expense of the sensitive side, as is sometimes presented in his earlier poetry. In a word, he is coarse; rather than be driven by his comic imagination and his dislike of sham, he has allowed himself to be taken over by the aggressive, conservative *bon viveur* which is his public persona. But he is more than just a popular novelist who turns his private conflicts to good commercial account. One might claim that Amis was not intellectually capable of developing the *Lucky Jim* theme any further than he did; that the succeeding novels simply exploit various kinds of smartness and cynicism until the author became tired and settled into a straight novel-a-year man. ... The key to Amis, though, is his sentimentality, which he has had some success in resisting. There are good poems in *Collected Poems 1944–1979* (1979), and one would expect this: sentimentality usually has, as one of its components, true feeling. But Amis in fiction has tried both to eliminate this altogether, confusing it with 'soppiness', and also to accommodate it. *Jake's Thing* (1978) is a good satire on currently fashionable 'sex therapy'. *The Alteration* (1976) may, however, have owed too much to someone else's earlier novel to be as successful as it ought to have been. On the whole Amis' espionage and speculative fiction has not been very good, though fans of James Bond liked his post-Fleming Bond story *Colonel Sun* (1968), which he wrote as 'Robert Markham'. *The Green Man* (1969), a ghost story, has more to it than meets the eye. He writes well, and few of his novels are less than interesting – but they are not as interesting as they should be. He is certainly an effectively observant comic novelist (*Ending Up*, 1974); but he has sacrificed true seriousness to gain his comic and satirical effects: he seems to be afraid of serious-ness, confusing it with the earnestness he satirized in his first novel. Yet there is still a very good, and not merely comic, novel in him. He is now perhaps more to be classified as a semi-popular rather than a serious writer – except that he remains a poet, which is what matters.

John Wain (1925) is less accomplished but more straightforward. *Hurry on Down* (1953) was – as Anthony Burgess (q.v.) seems to have been the only critic to note – an inept performance, ill-written and badly constructed; but its subject matter, the rejection of bourgeois values by an educated anti-hero, was fashionable; and, as far as it went, it was well-meant. The successors of *Hurry on Down* have been, if anything, less distinguish-ed; and his poetry has degenerated through want of direction; but in his short stories Wain exhibits some of the control he so badly lacks in his other work. He seems in this form to be able to master his excitement about himself, and his sensitivity and feeling are given fuller expression.

Thomas Hinde (ps. **Thomas Chitty**, 1926), who has been somewhat neglected by the critics, is a master-delineator of the British at their nastiest and most small-minded, and is one of the best realist novelists of his generation. *Mr. Nicholas* (1952), his first novel, is also his best – and one of the best to appear in England since the Second World War. He set himself a very high standard with it. It is about the tyranny of nastiness, age and insanity – a memorable and deeply-felt portrait of an impossible-to-love, and yet pathetic human being, together with an account of how the young struggle in the cruel nets laid by their elders and betters. Hinde conveys the sense of decency (this is not, alas, definable in public-school, Christian, or any other moralistic terms), the decent man's helplessness in the face of bourgeois malice or ill-will, better than any novelist of his time. He shows this in many of his later novels, including *Happy as Larry* (1957), *For the Good of the Company* (1961) and the African novel *The Cage* (1962). It is possibly a matter of regret that he has latterly turned to a self-conscious symbolism, for his social observation is so acute that one misses it – and the symbols do not arise from the action, but are arbitrary. But clearly he still has potential, more probably as a satirist, however, than a Jungian symbolist.

The novels of **Alan Sillitoe** (1928) are all more or less wrecked by their author's extreme simplicity of mind. Few writers who have managed to acquire his reputation can have been so much at the mercy of crude emotion. The nature of his difficulties is probably best illustrated by an equation made in one of his crass verses – between 'cancer' and 'racism'. His first novel, *Saturday Night and Sunday Morning* (1958), is as atrociously written as Wain's (q.v.) *Hurry on Down*, and is not particularly psychologically plausible, but has the power and freshness of youth. *Key to the Door* (1961) is distorted by wishful thinking and poor construction; the succeeding novels consist mostly of puerile anti-authoritarian fantasy, although there are flashes of good description. More recently he has taken to writing sentimental romances of no literary interest. Sillitoe is better in his short stories, and has never been more powerful than in *The Loneliness of the Long Distance Runner* (1959): in this narrative of a Borstal boy Sillitoe's hatred of injustice, hypocrisy and exploitation found an effective objective correlative (q.v.). He has written other simple, precise and moving stories; one of the best is *The Ragman's Daughter* (1963), also the title of a collection. But he now seems, to all intents and purposes, to be written out. His imagination has failed him, and he has none of the sort of intelligence that can sustain a writer.

John Fowles (1926) is an intelligent man who has become a paradigmatic hero of boulevard culture (q.v.), though like all such heroes his time is passing. It even got to the point when the 'profundities' of his 1969 novel *The French Lieutenant's Woman* could be savoured to the full only after the Pinter (q.v.)-scripted film version had been issued some years later. Many spoke of the book in terms of the film and of its stars. Fowles is by no means without talent, but this has become increasingly misdirected in the interests of that pseudo-'depth' which is a requirement of the middlebrow reader, until with *Mantissa* (1982) he has almost vanished into himself, victim of his own too high self-assessment. He is a minor novelist who has wrecked his novels by trying to be a Dostoevsky or a Hesse (qq.v.) – or whatever other heavyweight comes to the boulevard mind. And once a writer tries to be 'profound', or takes himself too seriously too early, he is doomed: his work declines into arch-pretentiousness.

Fowles became, after his first relatively straightforward novel *The Collector* (1963), the middlebrow's recherché 'questioner of the nature of fiction'. He well understood the fiction of such as Gass (q.v.) and other Americans, and he also picked up the mood that characterized the *nouveau roman* (q.v.). He made shrewd use of the 'enigmatic female' theme. He followed his first novel with *The Magus* (1965), of which he made a solemn revision (1977), thus treating himself as a top heavyweight engaged in, so to say, Prousting-off his earlier meta-Alain Fournier (qq.v.). This book is the tale of a young Englishman who gets himself embroiled in mystery and magic on a Greek island; he undergoes various experiences and is then given a mock trial at the end, and thinks he is getting what he deserved because all his life he had been holding reality at bay by making everything into fiction. This is easy enough to explicate in fashionable critical terms. But in the novel itself it means nothing, and it does not say anything about the nature of fiction. This is not really a subject that Fowles wants to be interested in (even if he is interested in it privately): what he wants is to create the illusion that he is discussing 'highbrow' topics in order to allow readers to feel that they have had deep philosophical experiences, and are 'in' on the latest 'thinking'. *The French Lieutenant's Woman* is a clever and more accomplished piece of work, although it means nothing and is not at all memorable. Fowles lets his readers know (as though they did not know it already – and perhaps they did not) that novelists intervene into the stories they tell, that they play God, that they arrange things. All this is an exercise in mock modernism. The style is largely pastiche of Thackeray, though there are many quotations and reports slipped in – just to demonstrate once more that novelists do arrange their material, and that this does not just come into being. Naturally, the novel has three endings, supposed to illustrate that Fowles' characters might have themselves 'arranged' things in those three different ways. Unfortunately, Fowles has little real sense of character, and is not interested in it. His interest lies in using his novels to illustrate current preoccupations about the nature of fiction (but these are as old, and even older, than Cervantes) in a palatable manner. As a popularizer of such preoccupations he is partially successful. But since everything is to that end, the astute reader discovers that, when he has understood what Fowles is really doing, there is no actual novel left. Everything is to a pseudo fictional purpose: this is popular criticism (with its inevitable over-simplifications) disguised as fiction. In *Daniel Martin* (1977) this process becomes tedious and wholly pretentious.

The other lucubrated line Fowles pushes is that men don't understand women ('What does a woman want?' asked Freud a long time before Fowles was born). But then feminism is in the air in all sorts of forms. If he could add any cogent comment, Fowles would be welcome; but he seems only to be exploiting an at present much ventilated puzzlement. This is a pity, because Fowles is inventive, might have imagination if he chose to exercise it (*The Collector* suggests this), and is clearly capable of writing at above the level he has chosen. Of course he is superior to Stoppard (q.v.): a novelist cannot get away with what a playwright can get away with – the latter has the abilities of actors, more rhetoric and showmanship to play with. But Fowles could be better than he is – and one day he might become so. No serious critic has written on Fowles (there are a few obscure books about him), though Bradbury (q.v.) has; and it is instructive to discover that what discussion of him there is, by criticasters, consists of elementary discussion about the status of fiction, either directly, or in the terms of Fowles' 'characters'. Curiously, he does not escape being criticized for pretentiousness, but this is so far only in whispers: it was the film version of *The French Lieutenant's Woman* that gave him his prominent place in the boulevard hierarchy. But such positions are always temporary, and the more people read *Daniel Martin* the less likely they will be to want to persevere with him. One therefore hopes that he might become serious, and write for himself. But with *Mantissa* (1982), a monotonous display of gobbets of undigested 'erudition', even reviewers began to be exasperated with him.

Malcolm Bradbury (1932), a university teacher (and still engaged in this pursuit for part of his time), is another novelist who owes much of his reputation (less heavy than that of Fowles, q.v.) to a dramatization of one of his novels, although *The History Man* (1975) was a television serial, not a film, when it started to be talked about. The book had been well received, but became really widely discussed (i.e. 'Bradbury', if without an initial capital, became accepted currency on the cultural market) only when it was adapted for television some half-decade after its initial publication. One cannot fairly characterize Bradbury as a product or a perpetrator of either gutter or boulevard culture (qq.v.), although he exploits both – the former in radio plays about football. Rather, with his professed 'anti-historicism', his appreciative explications of such as Fowles – one of whose stories he adapted for television, as homage to the master – and his depthless distrust of the left (distrust of it is another matter), he is the Social Democratic Party's cultural hero. Bradbury, one might say, is a luckier William Rodgers *de la littérature*; but he has no more staying power. His book of parodies, *Who Do You Think You Are?* (1976), treats its 'victims', predictably enough *bon ton* writers such as Murdoch, Snow (at that time), Amis, Durrell (qq.v.), with the utmost respect: the element of real parody, such as Beerbohm (q.v.) used to such deadly effect, is absent.

Bradbury is a predictable critic, though his scholarship is nothing out of the ordinary. He has been quite informative about Forster, Twain (qq.v.) and others, but provides no real insights; his book (edited in collaboration) dealing with *Modernism 1890–1930* (1976) is feeble in most of its parts, and cannot be described as ever truly illuminating. He does not appear, here, to have been really engaged with his task. His first two novels were, likewise, sound and dull; his style lacks vitality, and his language lacks poetic vitality and does not really pretend to it – his published verse, *Two Poets* (with Allen Rodway, 1966) makes this evident, though he makes a decent enough attempt to be coherent. *Eating People is Wrong* (1959) and *Stepping Westward* (1965) were campus novels, trying to combine a rather fuzzy, post-Forsterian 'liberal sense of decency' (this did not come across as strongly as it does in even the 'weak' Forster novels), with social comedy. Both novels owed too much to Amis (q.v.), and abounded in set comic pieces (such as academic parties); but they lacked Amis' bite, and are not satirical or sharp or funny enough: they are, rather, what those people who are satirized in them would most like to read. True satire needs venom; but venom does not pay, and is doubtless bad for the liberal mind.

Bradbury's *The History Man*, about a go-getter called Howard Kirk, a sociologist, went less heeded until the actor playing him in the television version gave him an apparently flesh-and-blood existence. He does not really possess this in the novel. This sly caricature, unkindly believed by a few of Bradbury's colleagues to be a partial self-portrait, is developed by Bradbury from a character in *Stepping Westward* called James Walker: in that novel we had a liberal who refused to sign an American loyalty oath when he found himself as 'writer-in-residence' at an American university. He was seen sympathetically, although Bradbury could not manage to endow him with a convincing moral strength of his own – again, he was trying to follow Forster, and was more confused than Forster. Bradbury would never say that if he were forced to betray his country or his friend he would wish to have the guts to betray his country; it was muddled of Forster to say it, but courageous in its provocativeness – Bradbury would never like to be provocative in this way, and clearly does not like the idea of being lonely, which is one key to his lack of creativity. He swims with any strong enough current, and will continue to do so, however it may change direction.

Kirk, then, is frankly set up as the 'historicist enemy'. However he is not a character, but rather a stereotypical 'rat': we must infer that 'historicists' always act like rats: lie, cheat, betray, and manipulate. But the manner in which Kirk does these things creaks, is not psychologically real. The technique is really smear by association: give a man a certain constellation of views (by no means coherently stated), and then simply deny him humanity. Kirk has become the paradigmatic new-university-sociologist monster; but Kirk does not exist. The awful earnest sociologists with their abbreviated names (Stan, Jackie, Ron, and so forth) are both more comic and more touching than Kirk. Bradbury must be given credit for anticipating the actual collapse of the radical left in the late Seventies. He tries to make all socialists, Marxists and 'progressives' seem like Kirk, and thus helps to create an intellectual atmosphere suitable for the formation of the senti-mental, milk-and-water Social Democratic Party.

The point I am making, in devoting such space to so meagre a novelist, is not a political one, but a moral one. Bradbury is sometimes discussed (invariably at a low critical level) as a writer concerned above all with 'moral values': just like the SDP, which has never achieved any coherent statement, but collects votes from those whose con-sciences won't allow them to support the hard, non-Tory right, and who are afraid of Marxism. Bradbury has no moral centre in a creative sense; he rather pretends to have one. Boring academic go-getting didacts might or might not be menacing figures; but since Kirk is a caricature disguised as a character we cannot know anything about this one. It would be a novelist's job to show us what made this one tick. *The History Man*, purporting to demonstrate to us how a man who believes that the social sciences can predict long-term political trends (the Popperian, q.v., view of historicism, which Popper invented), actually seems to show us that such a man does not really believe in this doctrine at all, that he is an odious opportunist, and so forth. It fails to acknowledge that there are sincere and humane historicists. In other words, it does not demonstrate (as Bradbury actually stated in 1972 that he wished to do) that 'true' historicists – if there be such creatures – are by definition swinish opportunists, that historicism is really only a mask for human nastiness: Kirk simply is not one at all. This is wholly modish: not a genuine symptom of the anxieties engendered by the splitting of the left into doctrinaire militant, Marxian socialists of various sorts, and wandering centrist liberals, but rather an opportunist gesture towards a soft centre which has all the vices of politics as we now increasingly horribly know them, and not a single one of its consolations. It is thus, in truth, a contribution to the new situation, in which what Orwell (q.v.) called 'accomplices of fascists' (the terminology is not quite right, since no fascist-style constitution is pro-posed; but it will do here) rule in the name of Toryism, defying every precept ever set forth by that real Tory Dr Johnson – and are opposed, not by robust defenders of the humane values, but by authoritarians hoodwinking a gang of bewildered liberals. The heartless lack of centre, the fundamental unfunniness, of *The History Man* is exactly the literature suitable to this fake opposition, and doubtless it is written by one of its dupes, for its tens of thousands of other less astute dupes.

Rates of Exchange (1983) confirms the preceding judgement, and one reviewer even went so far as to suggest that each of Bradbury's preceding novels, published in the

Fifties, Sixties and Seventies, were 'decade novels' – a polite way of saying 'modish'. In this new novel a university linguist goes to 'Slaka', which might as well be Russia as anywhere – it is an imaginary place 'liberated' by the Soviets in 1944 – to lecture for two weeks.There are the usual bad jokes about East European critical pretensions: one thesis is on 'anarchistic nihilism of the proletarian novel of A. Sillitoe' (a nice tribute to Sillitoe, q.v., for his own shift to the empty centre); are such jokes really funny enough, or original enough? I doubt it. One needs a writer who can throw some actual sad light on the icy earnestness of 'Marxist-Leninist correctitude'. Predictably, Bradbury draws heavily on another hero of the social-democratic nullibiety: Le Carré. Bradbury has said of the novel that it is 'anti-Thatcherite, anti-Keynesian', an attack on money: this is perplexing, for it is nothing of the sort. It is vague, full of jokes about the alleged ridiculosities of linguistics – jokes made by someone who is no master of linguistics, but who is rather making poor fun out of the fact that few linguisticians can write English. Bradbury is popular because he lacks a first-rate mind, which is bound to please an audience which is made to feel inferior by so complex a subject as linguistics in any case: *Rates of Exchange* is again empty, malleable (later it could be claimed to be anti-whatever was required at the time for middlebrow consumption), without characters, full of lucubrated weak comedy about the awfulness of 'conducted tours' of any part of the Soviet Empire: old stuff. Of course Bradbury the novelist is not worth a quarter of the space I have assigned him. But the nature of his mediocrity and its proportion to his popularity amongst supposedly serious readers are important if bleak issues. The very apotheosis of middlebrowism, it turns out, is an academic. Now academicism has its regular vices – though there is a remarkably high proportion of exceptions – but it seldom has that vice. (Erich Segal of *Love Story* was a mutation without significance: it may even have been the parodic aberration of a tasteful man.) The author who was supposed, in *The History Man*, to be attacking the 'new university' (he denied this; but the point was that his book was crying out to be so defined) turns out himself to be a sort of 'new academic'. Howard Kirk hardly exists as a character, but whatever he is supposed to stand for (and it was the comparative energy with which he was presented, though more by an actor than by his inventor, which led people into the illusion that anyone, even Bradbury himself, could be like him) is certainly preferable to the infinitely flexible, flaccid works of Malcolm Bradbury. Not one of these could ever be any kind of fragment to shore up against our ruin.

Francis King (1923) is uneven as a novelist, but the best story-writer of his generation. His best novels are *The Custom House* (1961) and the still too neglected *A Domestic Animal* (1970). He spent time in Japan, and is the English writer who most resembles – and thus has most profitably learned from – Japanese novelists such as Soseki and Toson (qq.v.). His stories, lucid, beautifully shaped, tender and exact, simply require to be read. The best volumes are *So Hurt and Humiliated* (1959), *The Brighton Belle* (1968) and *Indirect Method* (1980). A collection of them is overdue.

V.S. Naipaul (1932), a Trinidadian of Hindu parents who settled in England, has written about the Caribbean; but he writes in the tradition of the English and not the West Indian novel, and is therefore to be considered as an English writer.

Naipaul began by finding Trinidad impossible and cynical: when very young he 'set' (for himself) the works of Wells (q.v.), Austen and other English writers 'in Trinidad'. Disgusted, he set off for England, where he read English at Oxford and experienced further disillusionment ('the course had little to do with literature', he said). His first three books of fiction were *The Mystic Masseur* (1957), *The Suffrage of Elvira* (1958) and *Miguel Street* (1959), sketches about Trinidadian life which he had in fact written before the first two published books. *The Mystic Masseur* was the most mature of the three books: it is a comic satire on a man who rises, through use of popular superstition, from failed masseur in Trinidad to an English-named and decorated mystic and politician. It consists partly of the subject's own autobiography, which he has suppressed in the interests of his false position, and of the author's own narrative. All these books were attacked by West Indian writers, particularly Lamming and Hearne (qq.v.): they felt that Naipaul was ashamed of his heritage, and had betrayed it by taking up a 'castrated' satirical position. But they missed the point. There is an element of self-criticism (and anguish) in *The Mystic Masseur*, and Naipaul sees his roots simply as he really sees them – he is no more 'appreciative' of English or any other society. The attack on him was ill-founded. True, he does not celebrate the vitality of Caribbean life in the way that some native writers can; but his range is wider – and he was in any case the child of Hindu parents, so that there is a sense in which he owed no more allegiance to Caribbean life than to the Indian mysticism which he so bitterly attacks (less for what it is – this has proved his Waterloo – than for the way in which it is exploited by everyone everywhere). *A House for Mr Biswas* (1961) established him as a truly major novelist. This is set in Trinidad, over three generations, but it is no more, in essence, a satire on the life there than it is on life anywhere, though it is true in its particulars. And it is in any case more than satire. Biswas, who has an extra finger (a peculiarly potent symbol), is an imaginative man who can find no outlet for his imagination. He exists both as a convincing – and very unfortunate – character in himself, and as a symbol for not merely the 'artist' (as is usually stated), but for all those whose creativity (the expression of this does not in fact require the composition of novels, poems, pictures, music, or anything else, but rather the realization of individuality in harmony with whatever it is 'society' ought to be and is not – and Naipaul is a writer with the rare modesty to understand this) is trapped, buried, frustrated, obscured, defeated. It has thus been correctly described as being of 'epic proportions', and it remains and will remain as good a book as Naipaul has ever written. *Mr Stone and the Knights Companion* (1963) is an English comedy about a retiring librarian who aims to form a club for all the veterans of his firm; in reality he is trying to come to terms with his old age and approaching death. It is touching, but slighter than *The Mystic Masseur*. *The Mimic Men* (1967) combines English and Caribbean themes, and is rich in implication; but it cannot quite come to terms with the problems it sets up: Naipaul finds himself caught between nihilism and true holiness in the Hindu sense, and does not resolve the two – it would have been a major achievement if he had; but he lacks quite that degree of genius. *A Bend in the River* (1979) is masterfully written, but depends rather too much on Conrad (q.v.), in both its African setting, some of its details, and its nihilism: Conrad was not really, at bottom, a nihilist, and it seems that Naipaul is, or, rather, that he has not found a voice of affirmation. So that this novel is a trifle factitious – but only by the highest standards, which he has himself set. Naipaul's fiction should be read in conjunction with his non-fiction, which is quite as important: *India: A Wounded Civilisation* (1977) is perhaps the most revealing book on this difficult subject written in the past twenty-five years. The essay on Eva Perón, *The Return of Eva Perón* (1980), with other essays, is also excellent. Naipaul is a rewarding writer, who has hardly ever written a bad sentence: a serious man (and therefore humorous as well) who has been a rich Caribbean gift to English letters.

Paul Bailey (1937) wrote one outstanding novel, his first, *At the Jerusalem* (1967), but has failed to equal it. It was an unpretentious, imaginative, impeccably written study of old age, written with great but unobtrusive compassion, and was rightly praised. Its successors are nowhere near it in quality, although one would like to be able to say that at least one approached it. In fact they are highly competent, factitious exercises, which have attracted the sort of convoluted criticism which they simply don't deserve, although Bailey is himself highly sophisticated. 'Bailey is almost as sparing of words as Webern was of musical notes.' The truth is that, in *A Distant Likeness* (1973), he tried this technique, and intelligently; but it was not effective, for the book was not compelled. There is no reason why he should not write again as he did in his first book, and he probably will; he has after all paid the price of a truly spectacular debut. Latterly he has taken to journalism and useful radio criticism, particularly on Italian authors such as Bassani (q.v.). There is still no potentially better novelist of his age in Great Britain.

Robert Nye (1939) is a gifted novelist – but he is probably more gifted as a poet – whose best novels are his least well known. *Falstaff* (1976) was a popular success, and is very bold – but the reasons for which copies of it were burned in the Shakespeare Department of one prominent university are not wholly obscure. Nye, a successful pasticheur, is original in spite of himself. His best novels are *Doubtfire* (1966) and *The Voyage of the Destiny* (1982), the latter about Sir Walter Raleigh. A few of his poems are very moving. He is much better than his frantically over-enthusiastic but attractively written book reviews suggest.

Martin Amis (1949) is a novelist who observes well, and has an eye for what can justly be satirized; but so far one cannot infer from his novels any imaginative position. It is as though he were a journalist – a good one – constructing more or less elaborate moral fictions. Sometimes he lapses into over-sick comedy, as in *Dead Babies* (1975), which is clever but distinctly unpleasant and directionless. It is hard to see where he will go. So far he has used his intelligent awareness of various literary modes to put fictions together; but there has been too little of himself at the centre. He is therefore not 'compelling', as he has been called; but he is interesting, and would be more so if he found a voice of his own. He is rather more like his father Kingsley Amis (q.v.) than probably either would really like.

V

The Thirties in Britain were dominated by the four poets whom Roy Campbell (q.v.), in an otherwise weak and clumsy satire, conflated as 'MacSpaunday'. Actually Cecil Day Lewis, Louis MacNeice, W.H. Auden and Stephen Spender (qq.v.) were never all together in one room until after the Second World War, and the notion of them as a genuine foursome is wrong. But all four, like many intellectuals in the Thirties, were Marxist (or at least left-wing), and all four were associated in the public mind. What they had in common was age, an admiration for Hopkins and Eliot's *The Waste Land* (qq.v.), and a feeling that revolutionary changes were needed. They were, however, very different. The Irishman **Cecil Day Lewis** (1904–72), despite his gestures towards modernism, was not a modern poet at all, and was never able to deal with modern issues. He was a sincere but unsophisticated left-winger, and felt embarrassed by it when patriotism and World War Two drew him enthusiastically into the Home Guard. Presumably his odd penchant for writing bad but competently executed verses on public occasions got him the laureateship. Day Lewis had energy and strong feeling, and was a brilliant pasticheur (Hardy, q.v., Emily Bronte and others); but diligent search through his *Collected Poems* (1954) and its successors yield all too little poetry in Day Lewis' own voice. His best poetry appears in the wartime collection *Word Over All* (1943) and in his translations – from Valéry (q.v.) and Virgil. As early as 1939 Philip Henderson noted that Lewis is 'only a poet ... when he forgets the Marxist mountain ... and allows his natural, and after all quite Georgian, lyrical talent free play'. Day Lewis is the sort of poet one would like to praise more than one is able to; even in his modest neo-Georgian vein he is too frequently tepid or over-parodic, his rhythms metrical rather than personal (they have even been called slick). But as a popular poet he was not bad, and in *Word Over All* he actually looked good – it was only in retrospect that one saw it was all out of other people, and a little specious.

Louis MacNeice (1907–63), also an Irishman, was the most extroverted of the poets of the Thirties: as well as being a student of the classics, he was a keen player of games and (like Norman Cameron, q.v.) a popular boon-companion. He was a minor poet who never really took poetry quite seriously enough; when, at the end of his life, he wanted to do so, he was out of the habit. A good deal of his output, particularly *Autumn Journal* (1939) and *Autumn Sequel* (1954), consists of prosy pseudo-philosophical rambling. But he was intelligent and honest: if his poetry gives most pleasure to members of the middle classes who feel doomed, bewildered and sorry, but still continue as they are, he cannot fairly be called a middlebrow – in the sense that Day Lewis (q.v.) is middlebrow, a suitably 'serious' substitute for 'difficult' poets: poetry was for MacNeice a limited instrument, and he was never pretentious, although he was frequently vulgar. But his poetry does little more than reflect the fears, hopes and anxieties of his class; it describes much, sometimes felicitously, but illuminates nothing. His work abounds in the tired, sophisticated clichés of the audience at which it is aimed; whenever he becomes serious the atmosphere becomes highbrow-taproom. His best poetry is satirical-funny, as in the famous 'Bagpipe Music' – he exploited the same vein very successfully in one or two of his radio plays. It is often said that in his last poems, most of them published in *The Burning Perch* (1963), he reached a new intensity; and certainly he succeeded here, at last, in purging his language of its unfortunate Chelsea-like glibness ('May come up with a bouncing cheque,/An acid-drop and a bandage') and professionally blasé tone. These poems do, too, expertly describe what it is like to be middle-aged, in love, intelligent, tired, possessed by forebodings of death, and suffering from advanced alcholism; but the slick, journalistic manner had been with MacNeice too long: none is more than neat and appealing, although there is a desperate yearning for a depth he knew he could not achieve. The elements of surprise, a truly individual voice and technique, the capacity to express the intensity of feeling that was, I think, potentially there, are missing. MacNeice, whose *Collected Poems* appeared in 1967, could entertain poetically, and he could touch the heart; he could be appealing; but his poetry is not really durable.

The early *Poems* (1930) of **W.H. Auden** (1907–73) was the most energetic and promising collection of its time (there had been a privately printed volume issued by Spender, q.v., before this); its excitement still casts a spell – and there are many of Auden's own generation who have never escaped from this spell, and who consequently have never been able to judge his achievement dispassionately. The poems in his first collection are frequently incoherent, and their author is clearly hopelessly confused between a Kiplingesque (q.v.) imperialism and a Marxist–Freudian revolutionary attitude; there are echoes of, and even lines lifted from, other poets – Blunden, De la Mare, Graves, Laura Riding (qq.v.), and so on. But excitement and feeling are also present: this is a poet of technical brilliance who has a genuine lyrical gift. *The Orators* (1932), which again mixed Freud, Groddeck and Kipling, was just as confused – the peculiar charade 'Paid on Both Sides', frequently childish, contains some of his most genuinely promising work; but in *Look Stranger* (1936) Auden had reached his lyrical apogee, and had purged himself of some of his more irritating public-school mannerisms. However, he was careless with his technical gifts, and never finished a poem off properly; he has nothing personal he dares to say, and a real voice is uncannily absent.

His subsequent poetic career is a story of steady decline and disappointment: like his friend Isherwood (q.v.), he never grew up. One is presented with the extraordinary spectacle of a man of very great facility, with fine intuitions about poetry (Auden is one of the best anthologists of our time), who has nothing of intellectual and little of emotional substance to say. For all his energy and versatility and intellectual curiosity, Auden has no more to offer than the following messages: that poetry changes nothing (he agreed, in fact, with Laura Riding, q.v.); that poetry should be entertaining above all else (this is consistent: entertainment is all it is good for); and that life should be led as graciously as possible. Thus, Auden's 'philosophical' poems, the poems in which he tries to make 'major' statements – *New Year Letter* (1941), 'The Sea and the Mirror' (1945: included in *For the Time Being*, 1945), *The Age of Anxiety* (1948) – are essentially superficial. *New Year Letter* contains Auden's ideas (of that time) about all subjects; it is rather like a glossy 'dictionary of thoughts', and when it surprises it does so because Auden is so adept at the expression of truisms. *The Age of Anxiety* is just what it seems: the prelude to a conversion to Christianity that can make sense only to Auden himself. But not many critics claim that the later Auden, the Auden of the Fifties and Sixties, carries real weight. It has been said that he taught the twentieth century that poetry can be philosophical; but this is not demonstrable in any way – neither is any notion that he is 'great', which he is too often and too carelessly called. If he is really the major poet he has for so long been supposed to be then this is for the poetry collected in the earlier *Collected Shorter Poems* (1950) and perhaps for the poems in *The Shield of Achilles* (1955). Now if vigour and the ability to move the reader without the reader ever knowing why (Auden lost both these qualities during the Fifties) were enough to make a major poet then Auden would be major. But they are not. Again, if what Alfred Alvarez has called 'catching the tone of the age' ('catching the tone' is just right: it does not imply explaining, exploring or illuminating) were the attribute of a major poet, then certainly Auden would be one. But it is not; and he is not. He is an important phenomenon; he had excellent qualities; but he failed to develop – and became the greatest disappointment of his age. Even in the most celebrated of his poems – the elegies on Yeats (q.v.) and Freud, 'Musee des Beaux Arts' – there is a spurious quality. In the best poems the superbly memorable phrases are isolated, have no context: they are the notes and impressions of a clever and sensitive adolescent, not of a mature man. The immaturity of which the clowning was a symptom in the earlier poetry has persisted: this poet has failed to examine his personal situation, and his casual stance towards poetry may be more the result of this than of conviction. And yet until about the mid-Fifties – when his poems began to deteriorate into facetious trivia – Auden concealed his emotional rawness and intellectual superficiality with remarkable skill. Sometimes he did this by apeing another poet – he is a superb mimic. A good example of this is 'Their Lonely Betters' (1951), which is, as one would say, 'pure Graves' (q.v.) – but without being pastiche-homage in the really more candid and honest manner of Day Lewis (q.v.), since Auden injects his own casual manner. He has real feeling for the poets whose procedures he appropriates. Indeed, those of his best poems that are not imitative owe what viability they have to their quality of sincerity. *Spain* (1937; rev. 1940), on the Spanish Civil War, remains moving in spite of its rhetoric; 'In Praise of Limestone' (1951), when one looks carefully at it, has little meaning – but does embody a fascination with England. A great deal of the responsible admiration that Auden attracts is actually admiration of his performance rather than of his achievement; future critics who cannot be dazzled by his performance will assuredly wonder why we saw so much in him. But, as his friend Richard Crossman said, the trouble was that Auden was ashamed of his homosexuality. In other words, though he played the furtive buffoon about it, he never even began to face the issue – and a poet of the range Auden tried for cannot fail to confront the issue of his own sexuality and succeed as a poet. For a man without a first-class mind putting himself across as a man with one – in truth he was flash – he made himself look very impressive. But he was, ultimately, meretricious.

Humphrey Carpenter has written an excellent biography of Auden.

Stephen Spender (1909) had markedly fewer technical resources than Day Lewis, MacNeice or Auden (qq.v.); his ear is considerably less sure, but his poetic impulses were deeper and more serious – and have survived longer. He has written much lush, tentative, over-sensuous poetry, but his best has qualities more enduring than those of most of his contemporaries. In recent years he has been able to integrate his sense of humour – often in evidence in his criticism – into his poetry. Spender has written a truly outstanding and now neglected novel about life in an unpleasant preparatory school, *The Backward Son* (1940), and a book of stories, *The Burning Cactus* (1936); two later stories, published under the title *Engaged in Writing* (1958), are less successful. He is also an uneven but always stimulating critic.

The poems in Spender's first collection, *Poems* (1933; there were two earlier, privately printed pamphlets), were altogether more emotionally *réussis* than the earlier poems of Auden, MacNeice or Day Lewis. There are obvious faults – lack of humour, obscurity resorted to in order to avoid sentimentality, confusion – but one is drawn into the unmistakable presence of a poet. And although Spender has remained a poet (in a way that Auden and Day Lewis quite certainly did not) – has not become corrupt or tired or mechanical, has retained his sensibility, has learned to do certain things better – I doubt if he has ever written a more exciting and appealing book. There is a sweetness and a breathlessness about Spender's early poetry that he has never quite been able to recapture. He is the one twentieth-century poet of whom one can genuinely say that he was 'Shelleyan'. It is not altogether an easy thing to be without actually being Shelley (who found it difficult enough); but he survived it with some dignity, and without drowning. This quality is seen at its most vulnerable but nevertheless most potent in the very early 'Epilogue':

> Time is a thing
> That does not pass through boredom and the wishing,
> But must be fought with, rushed at, over-awed,
> And threatened with a sword:
>
> For that prodigious voyager, the Mind,
> Another self doth find
> At each hour's stage, and riven, hewn and wrought
> Cannot foretell its port.
>
> Let heart be done, shut close the whining eyes,
> And work, or drink, or sleep, till life defies
> Minute, month, hour and day
> Which are harrowed, and beaten, and scared away.

Spender charmingly foresaw the weaknesses of his later poetry: he 'expected always', in a manner genuinely Shelleyan, 'Some brightness to hold in trust,/Some final innocence/ To save from dust'. But this was not always apparent: Spender's lyricism and sensitivity were not usually strong enough to shore him up against the shocks of war and of the kind of personal sexual difficulties common to all. He lacks the less often acknowledged, sceptical, scientific, toughly intellectual side of Shelley. But he also lacks Shelley's fatal hysteria. *The Still Centre* (1939) and *Ruins and Visions* (1942) showed a falling off after *Poems*, and there was not quite enough in *Collected Poems* (1955) to state positively that

Spender had either fulfilled his promise or developed satisfactorily. But adjudgement of his performance now means less to him, and in more recent poems, now collected in *The Generous Days* (1971), he has notably succeeded in integrating his subtle sensibility and his intellectual intricacy, although everything has been transposed into a minor key. Whereas Spender had previously always been open to the charges of clumsiness, emotional over-indulgence and unnecessary ambiguity, the author of these less grandiose poems is firmly in control. Is this new modesty a gain? One can only repeat what George Barker said of the *Collected Poems* ('... if you come across a cripple walking you can be ... sure that he wants to get somewhere') 'the true presence itself ... moves and operates'. With Spender this has always been the case, and one has learned to be grateful for it. He has been a generous if sometimes irritable man, has been much hated by people whom most of us would be proud to be hated by (he was once attacked for being photographed 'in a cricket shirt', though it was not a cricket shirt) and more younger writers have reason to be grateful to him than is generally known.

However, just as the homogeneity of 'MacSpaunday' was false, so was the concept of their dominance of the Thirties. There were poets as good – or better. Prominent among these was **Norman Cameron** (1905–53), whose genius is only just now in the process of being recognized – though he has had imitators since the Fifties. Cameron, a Scot with a Calvinistic conscience and a penchant for occasional reckless behaviour, wrote a witty and metaphysical poetry – frequently laced with deep feeling – that foreshadowed the style of the so-called Movement (q.v.) of the Fifties. He resembled Graves and was a close friend of his and of Laura Riding's (qq.v.) – but he was not substantially influenced by either; this can be demonstrated but is seldom believed. He formed his style while still at Oxford, as the sequence of poems included by Auden (q.v.) in *Oxford Poetry 1927* shows. Perhaps nothing illustrates the general insensitivity to real quality in poetry of official, academic or fashionable critics, anthologists and literary historians so much as their neglect of Cameron, whose excellence and originality are evident to anyone who truly cares for poetry. Cameron made the best English translations from Villon and Rimbaud; his *Collected Poems*, a slim volume, appeared posthumously in 1957. He did not really develop (he was doubtful and suspicious about the importance of poetry) – in this respect he resembles his compatriot Andrew Young – but his sardonic, tender sensibility was always capable of dealing with problems as they arose. Cameron's was the perfect twentieth-century traditional manner: he had no innovatory ambitions and was (over-) modest about his achievement – but cliché and poeticism are so entirely absent from his poetry as to render it exemplary in style alone. Its emotionally dense texture is the result of stubborn honesty and of intellectual and emotional self-appraisal. Cameron's is a poetry that will appear increasingly strong and original as work more ambitious in scope, but ephemeral, falls away.

When one compares the achievement of **Ronald Bottrall** (1906) (*Collected Poems*, 1961; *Poems*, 1975; *Against a Setting Sun*, 1984) to, say, that of MacNeice (q.v.), one is again struck by the obtuseness of the regular critics. For Bottrall far exceeds MacNeice both in dedication and performance. Possibly his reputation was harmed when both F.R. Leavis and Edith Sitwell (qq.v.) – a notoriously hysterical and unreliable critic – praised him. At his best he has real style and feeling; above all, he truly feels the pressure of the modern world (Auden, q.v., tended to enjoy his own success in it, however he may have protested), and it evokes a complex and lively response from him. Moreover, he has an original lyric gift, as he shows in 'Four Orders':

> I am a trembling leaf
> I am a withered arm

I am a sunken reef
I am a trampled worm.

Leaf, be the caterpillar's joy
Arm, enfold the new-born boy
Reef, flower into a coral isle
Worm, fertilize the soil.

A serious critical exploration of Bottrall's poetry would reveal a versatile and immensely well-informed mind, a linguistic turbulence frequently controlled, and an exquisite humour. He is a versatile technician, and the author of one of the most successful long poems in our time, the autobiographical 'Talking to the Ceiling' (in *Poems*, 1975). Some of his later poems have the enigmatic quality of Vallejo (q.v.). He is very uneven, and does not often produce memorable single lines – but the impact of his work as a whole is that of a shrewd friendly man of great sensibility. The chief influence on him has been Cavafy (q.v.), but he never tries to imitate him.

John Betjeman (1906–84) could have been a poet but, in Spender's (q.v.) words, he was never able to escape being 'the schoolboy who pretends that he is only pretending to be a poet'. Betjeman is bound to irritate serious readers of poetry for this reason: so much wilful silliness, thumping metre, and deliberate pastiche of earlier and now inadequate modes from a writer so clearly capable of sensitivity and rhythmical tact. By silliness one means the sort of impulse that led him to say – on one of his too frequent appearances on television – that he preferred 'Tom Moore' to Donne. ... This refusal to be serious haunts and ultimately vitiates his verse, which is enjoyable but none the less coffee-table. One has to be crass to be a best-selling poet in these days, and Betjeman was crass; but he had qualities that other best-selling poets have not usually possessed. He was capable of real feeling; his nostalgia has style. One is not inclined to praise him for this, however: he squandered his gift – and, even worse, used it slyly to persuade those who buy his books that they are reading serious poetry. Most reprehensible is the cunning manner in which he indulges his own sentimentality: some of his lines move his non-literary readers, while his sophisticated audience may take them as satire. The most complete edition of his *Collected Poems* appeared in 1970. He was Poet Laureate, although the 'official' verses he produced were laughably banal. There is, however, a case to be made out for his earlier poems (not the autobiographical *Summoned by Bells*), and anyone who reads poetry should read Betjeman, to make up his own mind.

Geoffrey Grigson (1905–85) published his first *Collected Poems* in 1963; most unusually, he has written nearly all his best poetry since then. Grigson, a tough, scholarly and always provocative critic, is another of that dying breed, the genuine man of letters. Grigson edited the influential poetry magazine *New Verse*, which he had founded, throughout the Thirties. Since then he has supported himself by a series of critical and other works of a high standard; outstanding among these is the autobiographical *The Crest on the Silver*. His early poems were impressionistic, even imagist (q.v.) – and correspondingly slight. During the Sixties he broadened his scope without sacrificing the precision and luminosity that, at his best, he had always had. *Collected Poems* (1983).

It is through Grigson that the memory of Clere Parsons (1908–31) has been kept alive. Parsons did not have time to fulfil his promise, but what he did accomplish shows that he was potentially a major poet. He was mainly influenced by his contemporaries at Oxford (Auden, Spender, qq.v.) and by Laura Riding (q.v.).

Curiously, since he was famed for his cerebral qualities, the keynote of the poetry of William Empson (1906–84) is repressed passion. His output was small. He published two collections; his *Collected Poems* appeared in 1961. He was best known as a critic – for *Seven Types of Ambiguity* (1930; rev. 1953), *Some Versions of Pastoral* (1935) and *The Structure of Complex Words* (1951). And he was, too, one of the most suggestive and subtle, although recondite, critics of his time. But he was also a good poet, and one who was consistently misunderstood. The reason for his extreme intellectuality was his extreme intensity and depth of feeling, both political and personal; this feeling is apparent, but has not been searched for diligently enough by his critics and even his disciples. Thus, Alfred Alvarez, who began as a disciple of Empson and then swung (predictably enough) to D.H. Lawrence (q.v.) – and then to confessionalism and suicido-confessionalism – called his subjects 'impersonal'. Now it is true that from time to time Empson indulged in 'crossword puzzle' poetry – his enthusiasm for this, as a critic, sometimes led him into an indiscriminating attitude – as in such poems as 'Rolling the Lawn' ('You can't beat English lawns. Our final hope/Is flat despair. Each morning therefore ere/I greet the office, through the weekday air,/Holding the Holy Roller at the slope. ....'). But the essential Empson was 'learned', as the last line of 'This Last Pain' announces, 'a style from a despair'. This is not, however, as Alvarez insists, a limited achievement. Empson was concealing deep feelings – but not a rich lyrical gift. The achievement has been important because it kept 'wit' alive over a period when it counted for little in poetry: Empson's best lines – 'Not to have fire is to be a skin that shrills'; 'Twixt devil and deep sea man hacks his caves' – have an Augustan toughness as well as a metaphysical concentration of feeling. Empson had his reasons for turning poetry into a minor project – it is one of the features of his minor poetry – and it was not his fault that the poets of the Fifties imitated his manner and produced no more than a series of drab anti-romantic statements. He himself disliked his influence, and pleaded, by implication, for 'honey' and for 'a singing line'; but how 'Re-edify me, moon, give me again/My undetailed order' sings!

W.R. Rodgers (1909–69), an Ulsterman who had been a Protestant priest and who wrote highly praised radio features, was at one time held up as a possible rival to Dylan Thomas and George Barker (qq.v.); but his poetry has now, it seems, been almost forgotten. (The drunken Thomas, in BBC pubs, would point out Rodgers and say in a hushed, awed voice: 'That's the man to watch!'). In his first poems, collected in *Awake* (1941), he was over-intoxicated by words and too heavily influenced by Hopkins ('Now all our hurries that hung up on hooks'); verbal pyrotechnics, assonance and dissonance and rhetoric too often obscured the fact that he had something to say. He was always plainer than Thomas and Barker, though: a strong-thewed Augustanism lay behind even the comparative exuberance of the earlier poems. The American poet and critic Kenneth Rexroth compared him to Marvell; this is not too far-fetched, as the poems in *Europa and the Bull* (1952) demonstrate. But Rodgers failed to develop: his poetry was too uneven, too unexcitingly 'physical' (it remained difficult to justify most of his verbal effects), too little worked out. The strength and unfashionable openness were there; but so was an unaccountable carelessness. His best poetry is simple, like his description of the airman who must be pitied because 'he'll/Halt, hang hump-backed, and look into his crater'.

Bernard Spencer (1909–63) was associated with Lawrence Durrell (q.v.) in Cairo during the Second World War; a few of his poems had appeared in such magazines as Grigson's *New Verse* (q.v.) in the Thirties, but he did not publish a book – *Aegean Islands* – until 1946. He seems to have killed himself – or not to have cared whether he lived or died: he disappeared from a hospital and was found on a railway track with a fractured skull. He had been feverish and may well have suffered from some now undiagnosable neurological damage. His *Collected Poems* appeared in 1981. His poems resemble him: well-bred, restrained, fastidious, acutely sensitive (to the point of breakdown) behind a tight-lipped reserve. Unfortunately, this reserve characterizes even the last and most powerful poems, robbing them of immediacy. His early poetry is elegant, unpretentious, over-civilized, passive; but a note of menace begins to creep in about 1950 (he ends a poem of that year by asking 'what towns born on what darker coast of sleep,/how many histories deep?'). It is a profounder note; but Spencer never gave it a quite full expression. But he did find single images into which he concentrated his feelings of sexual guilt and shame, and his premonitions of death: for example, in 'By a Breakwater' he sees what he takes to be lovers – but the man, 'middle-aged', is emptying a syringe into the woman's arm. ... Spencer's work was never trite, and it deepened in intensity as he grew older, although by then he lacked the will to pull it all together into a piece. He is most likely to be remembered for his later poems; but *Collected Poems* is a distinguished volume, a testament to integrity and seriousness and purpose.

Kathleen Raine (1908), who published her *Collected Poems* in 1956 – *The Hollow Hill* followed in 1965 – has since the Forties been an uncompromising Platonist and symbolist. Her poetry is limpid, musical, deeply serious; frequently it is so removed from life that it hardly touches the ground (after all, even the Platonist is rooted in life); but when Kathleen Raine writes of the real mystery she helps to restore meaning to it:

> We look up and the sky is empty as always; only
> Assembling the scattered for-ever broadcast light
> Here, or there, in his creatures, is seen that Face.

Poetry written since *The Hollow Hill* is really too ethereal to add much to her achievement: immateriality has become an obsession to her.

James Reeves (1909–78) is widely read but has not had the attention of critics. For long it was commonplace to hear him referred to as of the 'school of Graves' (q.v.), on the strength of his friendship with the older poet and because Laura Riding (q.v.) prefaced his first collection, *The Natural Need* (1936). In fact the early poems included in this owe at least as much to Eliot, Pound, Richard Aldington and the imagists (qq.v.) as they do to Graves or Laura Riding. On the other hand, Reeves' later poems owe more to Edmund Blunden, Andrew Young and John Crowe Ransom (qq.v.) than to Graves – whose consistency of energy and 'attack' his poetry has never pretended to have.

Reeves, perhaps the only genuinely crepuscular (q.v.) poet in the English language – yet he had never heard of the *crepuscolari* – writes in three distinct manners; but, as Edwin Muir (q.v.) wrote in reviewing one of his volumes, 'Perfection does not call attention to itself': the surface of the poems is not striking. Most approachable of Reeves' manners is his quiet pastoralism, which in its way is as authentic as Blunden's, although it is less observant of natural detail, and frequently takes a wryly satiric look at human obtrusions. In 'Ghosts and Persons' he writes of 'slow heads drowsing over sums' and the 'mower's distant sound' whining through high windows, but also of 'The forward smile and stupid eyes/Of a youthful village charmer'. Human 'progress' in its urbanizing forms amuses Reeves, but finally, especially in pastoral settings, arouses his resentment.

Reeves' angry, Kafkaesque (q.v.) manner, as beautifully exemplified in 'Greenhallows' – ostensibly an account of a journey to an interview for an important position – is less familiar, more original and harder to interpret. In this vein, Reeves appears violently to reject his normally calm acceptance of – even refuge in – his bourgeois backgrounds and to express attitudes quite alien to his usual self as expressed in poetry. The same kind of uncharacteristic energy is to be found in the sequence 'Letter Before a Journey' and in some of the satirical poems included in *The Questioning Tiger* (1964).

Finally, Reeves is the author of a handful of deeply felt, and powerfully expressive lyrics, such as the guiltily homosexual love poem 'All Days But One', which begins:

> All days but one shall see us wake to make
> Our last confession:
> Bird notes at dawn revive the night's obsession. ·

Guilt, regret, anger, desire for stability – these are among the staple elements in Reeves' best poetry. Few have more memorably portrayed the pains, pleasures and sinister or unhappy nature of the conventional life than Reeves; few are more startling beneath a tranquil surface. *Subsong* appeared in 1969, *Poems and Paraphrases* in 1972; *Collected Poems* in 1974. Reeves chose to be or to seem conventional; but beneath this mask he was furtive, unhappy and sexually very disturbed – however, much of his best poetry expresses this furtiveness and Schubertian fright, and in selection it will survive.

*

'MacSpaunday' and those whom they influenced (Kathleen Raine, who had not discovered her true manner, and Bernard Spencer, qq.v., were among them) were sometimes in the early days called the 'New Country' school: this was the name of an anthology, edited by **Michael Roberts** (1902–49), a distinguished intellectual – he wrote a good book on T.E. Hulme (1938) – and a minor poet of some distinction (*Collected Poems*, 1959). Roberts went on to produce what is arguably the most influential anthology of this century, the original (the revised versions of it are worthless) *Faber Book of Modern Verse* (1935). Roberts included in this excellent collection three poets whose work was recognized at the time as reacting away from the socio-political concerns of the so-called 'New Country' poets. It was not that George Barker, Dylan Thomas and David Gascoyne (qq.v.) were anti-left-wing – all three were sympathetic, for example, to the elected government of Spain – but that their main concerns in poetry were non-political.

Of the three, **George Barker** (1913) is at once the most uneven and the most gifted. It is unfortunate that he has had to write under the shadow of his more immediately striking but also more meretricious contemporary Dylan Thomas (q.v.). The general verdict is that Thomas is the better poet; but this is not the case. Barker is a prolific, hit-or-miss poet who can write quite indescribably badly – and with great power and authority. Barker was not much influenced by surrealism; his confusions came naturally to him, and harked back to Smart and the Blake of the prophetic books rather than to France. His early poetry was tragic and guilt-laden, consisting of great clusters of words that are flung at the reader with a deliberate lack of tact. In many ways Barker anticipated Berryman (q.v.), who looks somewhat less original when put by his side. Barker distrusts neatness and can inflict hideous cacophonies upon his readers – 'Satan is on your tongue, sweet singer, with/Your eye on the income and the encomium' – he has not really developed his procedures since his early days, but he scores a rather higher proportion of successes. However, it is perhaps fair to say, as David Daiches does, that he has never integrated 'his talents into a wholly satisfying poetic complexity'. But he is not that kind of poet: we have to look for his best and most integrated work in single poems. Barker, a most original poet (he is in fact more original than Thomas), is in love with the oxymoron – sometimes too facilely, but at others with surprising authority. Not afraid to be absurd, he can be more successfully elemental than almost any of his contemporaries:

> Step, Primavera, from your bed,
> Dazzling with existence;

> Put the Sun and the Moon and the Systems right;
> Hang heaven on circumstance:
> Lean from all windows like waterfalls,
> Look, love, on us below:–
> And so from their somnolence in sense
> All things shall rise to you.

Barker needs rigorous selection (his *Collected Poems* appeared in 1957). There is no doubt that he is one of the most rewarding and interesting of contemporary poets – and one who deserves a great deal more critical attention than he has had. Although the generally accepted notion of Barker as an uneven poet is correct as far as it goes, there is more to him than this: he has plenty of wit and skill, and quite often his failures are considerably less disastrous than they appear. But it must be said that Barker's professed feelings towards others, and his sometimes hysterical elegies for dead friends, are thoroughly specious. However, he has done things in English that only Bottrall (q.v.) has even dared to try. Incomparably his best poem is *The True Confessions of George Barker* (1950; rev. and complete version, 1965), in which he for once subjects himself to an analysis less than self-indulgent.

Dylan Thomas (1914–53) has been overrated and overpraised, largely, no doubt, because of his somewhat spectacular life and death. He was a simpler and less prudent man than Barker (q.v.); despite the many books – particularly in America – that have been written about his poetry, this is usually not well accomplished, and leans heavily on violent rhetoric. Thomas' early inspiration came from James Joyce (q.v.), translations of Rimbaud (perhaps – although in typescript versions – by Norman Cameron, q.v., who became his close and unwilling friend – he wrote a poem about him in which he said that when Thomas sat on a sofa he left a stain) and the Bible: the wild and whirling, irrational manner of his early volumes (*Eighteen Poems*, 1934; *Twenty-five Poems*, 1936) was certainly highly original. But, as his leading critics themselves admit, he is never lucid (Barker very often is). If, then, he is the major poet that we are so often invited to celebrate, we should need to discern a method in this lack of lucidity. But there is none. When we have conceded the powerful effect of the rhetoric and the unfamiliarity of his surrealist-like verbal juxtapositions (but he is always closer to a Welsh revivalist spell-binder than to a genuine surrealist), we have to admit that Thomas is frequently irresponsible in his use of words. There is a strong though inchoate emotional pressure behind his poetry, and a feeling for the sound of the words (though his ear was faulty, as in 'There is a saviour/ Rarer than radium. ...'); but Thomas suffered from an insensitivity to the meanings of words, a result of his inability to come to terms with reality. Like many alcoholics, he was at bottom an appealing man; but he never grew up, or even tried to. He was no Baudelaire or Rimbaud; his counterparts are to be sought in the nineteenth century, among similarly immature men: Swinburne, Dowson, Francis Thompson. Where Thomas is comparatively lucid, as in the elegy for Ann Jones, he is usually weakly adjectival: strip the poem of its not, on second inspection, so striking adjectives – and nothing is left. Thomas is in some respects a dirty little boy, and the imagery of the earlier poems (many of them about masturbation) is simply 'dirty'. The much vaunted complexities and profundities of his work invariably prove to be the projections of critics.

But Thomas does have vitality – and, where he is not too ambitious, some small successes, such as 'The Hand That Signed the Paper'. But it is a pity that this vitality, and his sensuousness, have led sensible critics to over-praise him, and to regard him as a profound thinker. Accounts of his 'thought', in fact – invariably by people who never met him – unwittingly reduce it to the series of commonplaces that it is. Thomas' later poems

– 'Over Sir John's Hill', 'In Country Sleep' – do attain a greater simplicity than his earlier in that they are less clotted and wilfully sexual in their imagery; but the kind of simplicity they seek is rhetorical, and their individuality is restricted to tone. The most complete edition of Thomas' *Collected Poems* appeared in 1971. He wrote some exquisitely funny prose, printed in *Quite Early One Morning* (1954) and *Adventures in the Skin Trade* (1955); but the success of the radio drama *Under Milk Wood*, skilfully done though it is, is not artistically deserved: Joyce is plundered, T.F. Powys (q.v.) is imitated – the script is ingenious rather than felt, and a lack of real clarity is everywhere apparent.

   David Gascoyne (1916) was more directly influenced by surrealism than either Barker or Thomas (qq.v.) – or, indeed, any other English poet. Gascoyne's first book of poetry, *Roman Balcony*, appeared when he was sixteen; his novel *Opening Day* followed in 1933, when he was seventeen; *A Short Survey of Surrealism* (1936) was published when he was twenty. When he published *Poems 1937–42* (1943) he had reached his maturity, although he was not yet thirty. Influenced by Jouve (q.v.) and by the early manifestations of the philosophy of existentialism (q.v.), Gascoyne is a most unusual phenomenon in English poetry; yet his 'Europeanness' does not give his poetry an un-English flavour. On the contrary, he remains the most English of poets, a genuine visionary writing in the tradition of Blake and Dante Gabriel Rossetti's 'The Woodspurge'. His early surrealism, where successful, achieves innocence. Unfortunately, however, the latter stage in Gascoyne's development is wanting: his later poetry has the strength of sincerity, but is grey, defeated and lachrymose:

> Not from a monstrance silver-wrought
> But from the tree of human pain
> Redeem our sterile misery,
> Christ of Revolution and of Poetry,
> That man's long journey through the night
> May not have been in vain.

This is too deeply felt and dignified to be platitudinous; but it is disappointing in the light of the earliest poetry, and lacks real energy. Gascoyne's *Collected Poems* appeared in 1965. He has written little in the past thirty years, but has published interesting personal diaries – and is still much read.

   Vernon Watkins (1907–69) was considerably older than Thomas and Barker (qq.v.), but did not become known until the Forties. His first book, *The Ballad of the Marie Lwyd*, appeared in 1941. Watkins was the best of the British poets to be associated with the so-called romanticism of the Forties, and until the end of his life he continued to write in his own unfashionably lyrical or Platonic styles. He began as a self-consciously Celtic imitator of Yeats (q.v.); but at his best his manner is seventeenth- rather than nineteenth- or twentieth-century. He is humourless and often takes himself too bardically seriously; much of his poetry is monotonous and dull; but every so often he is pellucid, illuminating and original. It is ironic that so heavyweight an effort as Watkins' should in the end produce only a few lyrics; but it is also an object-lesson. A *Selected Poems* appeared in 1967; another selection is *I Was Born in Wales* (1976).

   Henry Reed (1914) has published only one collection of poems, *A Map of Verona* (1947), but this is widely read – it remained in print for a quarter of a century. There are a few good uncollected poems. He has earned his living as a translator and writer of radio scripts – including the famous 'Hilda Tablet' series. Reed has written several distinctly different kinds of poem: the metaphysical, influenced above all by Marvell; a narrative, contemplative poetry influenced by Eliot (q.v.); parody – as in 'Chard Whitlow', which was Eliot's own favourite parody of himself; a narrative poem influenced not by Eliot but by Hardy (q.v.) – such as 'The Auction Sale'. Reed's justly famous 'Lessons of the War' sequence is in his metaphysical vein, exploiting *double entendre* to its limit, varying the tone from the wistful to the broadly comic (as in the third poem of the sequence). The less well known 'The Auction Sale' handles narrative as well as it can be handled in this age. Reed is a poet of greater range than is usually recognized; only his Eliotian contemplative poetry really fails to come off, and even this is eloquent and rhythmically interesting.

*

Two Irish successors of Yeats (q.v.) are outstanding: **Patrick Kavanagh** (1905–69) and **Austin Clarke** (1896–1974). Yeats had preferred **F.R. Higgins** (1896–1941), but Higgins never really progressed beyond a pleasantly expressive occasional poetry. Kavanagh (*Collected Poems*, 1964) wrote a narrative poem about the poverty of the land and the people in his home county, Monaghan: 'The Great Hunger'. He also wrote a good autobiographical novel, *Tarry Flynn* (1949); he was for some years a newspaper columnist. His best poetry is subtler than his ostensibly careless, conventionally romantic attitude ('... this soul needs to be honoured with a new dress woven/From green and blue things and arguments that cannot be proven'), combining self-satire with lyricism in an unusual and moving way. Clarke (*Later Collected Poems*, 1961) was a fastidious minor poet who over the years performed a number of technical experiments, within the tradition, of interest and importance. He was above all a classical poet, and is an honourable example of one; but although his integrity is beyond question, the usual fault of his work is that there seldom seems to be sufficient emotional impulse to draw it together. However, Ireland has not yet produced – leaving aside the more robust Kavanagh – a worthier successor to Yeats.

The recent troubles in Ireland have produced a large crop of poets: violence usually does. But only one is of serious account: **Seamus Heaney** (1939). In *Death of a Naturalist* (1966), his first collection (there had been a pamphlet, *Eleven Poems*, in the previous year), he wrote some sensitive, original rural poems in traditional verse. Some of these were moving and striking; clearly the work of a poet whose metaphors (often yoking writing with farm or manual work) were unforced and natural to him. He tells in the poems of this volume of how the world of nature menaced him as a child, and of how hard he found writing poetry to be. But it was an un-self-conscious book, whose complexities were not imposed from outside, or from reading, or from critical ideas. It looked as if Heaney was going to be a true poet: true, that is, to his own voice, and to his own sense of the rightness of his words in describing his experience. There were many good poems, too, in *Door into the Dark* (1969). But the successive volumes, *Wintering Out* (1972), *North* (1975) and *Field Work* (1979), showed him departing from his old principles, and becoming 'literary' in the wrong sense. The real moral of this – the important one – is that poets have to learn to remain silent when a poem does not demand to be written: poetry is initially a compelled thing, even though the work on what has been compelled may take much longer than what was first 'given'. If nothing is given, there is usually no poem. In his first book Heaney could write (it is the first stanza of 'Poem'):

> Love, I shall perfect for you the child
> Who diligently potters in my brain

> Digging with heavy spade till sods were picked
> Or puddling through muck in a deep drain.

This was felt and genuine – and the rest of the poem is as good. By the time of *North* he
can, too, still write a very good poem – for example, 'A Constable Calls', a memory of a
policeman calling on his father to check that his farming was 'correct'; it ends:

> A shadow bobbed in the window.
> He was snapping the carrier spring
> Over the ledger. His boot pushed off
> And the bicycle ticked, ticked, ticked.

But there is a disturbing new note, here, too, as in 'Exposure':

> How did I end up like this?
> I often think of my friends'
> Beautiful prismatic counselling
> And the anvil brains of some who hate me
>
> As I sit weighing and weighing
> My responsible *tristia.*
> For what? For the people?
> For what is said behind-backs?

The poem ends with a peculiarly pretentious line, 'The comet's pulsing rose' – and,
although a poetic impulse was there, peters out into something that a likely critic might
describe as 'deepening into a new complexity'. Heaney himself does not feel in the way
he pretends here: with his own voice he would never say 'My responsible *tristia*'. And this
'continental manner' (q.v.), which Heaney increasingly adopted, causes a naturally
concrete poet to become abstract and meaningless. Behind his newer poems there is
seldom an occasion – other than the desire (not need) to write a poem, an aspiration
shared by too many people. Very few poets indeed continue to write at their best for a
period of ten years, and very many do fill up the gaps by manufacturing pseudo-poetry
(translation is a much more sensible activity, and keeps the hand in). That is all that
Heaney has done – and even amongst his more recent verse there are a few poetic
successes. But he is perhaps good enough to learn true tact: to keep his manufactured
poetry to himself. It is evident that he knows the true from the false, although whether he
would acknowledge this is another matter altogether. *Selected Poems* (1975).

During the Second World War itself, it was the loss of **Sidney Keyes** (1922–43) that
attracted the most attention. Keyes (*Collected Poems*, 1946) was certainly promising, but it
is hardly possible to prophesy what he might have done: his poetry is (understandably) a
hotch-potch of influences (Rilke, Yeats, Eliot, qq.v., and others), and there are hardly as
yet the glimmerings of an original manner. Two other poets, lucky enough to have a little
more time to develop than Keyes was allowed, were more important: the Welshman

Alun Lewis (1915–44), whose *Collected Poems* (but this is really a selection) finally appeared in 1966, and **Keith Douglas** (1900–44): *Collected Poems* (1951 rev. 1966).

Alun Lewis, who died while serving in Burma – the 'accident' in which he shot himself seems to have been deliberate and was possibly the result of persecution by another officer – had time to develop, to purge his poetry of triteness and over-romantic diction (often apparent in his first collection, *Raider's Dawn*, 1941). His greatest difficulty lay, it seems, in knowing when to stop. But he was a poet of great power, who described the loneliness of military life in the early Forties with unique eloquence and accuracy; he wrote, too, exciting and original love poetry. He has yet to obtain his due as a love poet; but he will ultimately be seen as one of this century's best. He has not been an important influence; but his intrinsic importance is greater than that of any other English poet killed in the Second World War.

Douglas did not achieve nearly as much (he had less time), but his extrinsic importance would probably have been greater. In him we see romanticism not rejected, but tempered by intellectuality – and a poetic intelligence not equalled by any poet since. His poems often lack finish, but this does not obscure his tough fusion of feeling and 'wit', his generous awareness of the world around him.

Roy Fuller (1912) also made his reputation during the war, in which he served but which he fortunately survived – he had in fact been publishing poetry, criticism and fiction since the mid-Thirties. His *Collected Poems*, which appeared in 1962, established him as a major poet among the younger generation: it was generally felt that here was the best living poet of his generation, one just a few years younger than that of MacSpaunday (qq.v.). But his poetry does not make as clear an impression as it should, and is certainly in no way major. He is intelligent and sensitive, but lacks power and drive. His early poetry is too evidently influenced by Auden (q.v.), his later by Yeats (q.v.); this is particularly important, because here he apes a manner that rather clearly does not suit him. He began well, but chose a disappointing direction in which to develop. For all his later poetry's interesting and intelligent unravelling of small Freudian knots, its chief function seems to be to keep any real kind of poetic vision at bay. Thus Fuller – in his weakest type of poem – mourns his political impotence and bourgeoisdom (he is a Marxist), but does absolutely nothing about it. His parodies of Yeatsian richness do not complement this apathy, because they entirely fail to convince. And yet there is enough that is good in Fuller to compel us to judge him from high standards: he has always tried to deal honestly with his experience, and even his latter-day posturing is rhetorical in intention, rather than self-deceit. He has written enough to make us regret that his ultimate stance should be to defend so limited a position.

It is difficult to understand why Fuller's near contemporary, **C.H. Sisson** (1914), who did not become known until the publication of his first collection of poems, *The London Zoo*, in 1961, is not better appreciated. The author of an extraordinary novel, *Christopher Homm* (1965), Sisson's voice is unquestionably contemporary. His diction is chaste, sometimes almost puritanical in its clarity and savage directness; but beneath this temperamental severity fires burn – fires which throw up passionate and memorable lines, such as 'If we have reasons, they lie deep'. The 'if' here is characteristic: Sisson appears to be an extreme pessimist – intelligence and gloom have never, of course, been fashionable attributes – part of whose theme is corruption, or, in theological terms, original sin. But the careful reader of his poems (*Numbers*, 1965; *Metamorphoses*, 1968; *In the Trojan Ditch*, 1974 – a retrospective collection; *Anchises*, 1976) will discover that they are coloured by an extreme, though subtly ironic, good humour. For another part of his theme is grace: both the grace inherent in the human creature to endure its terrible corruption, and the grace that is therefore inherent in the situation itself. The 'if' in the line quoted above is characteristic, then, because Sisson refuses, with unobtrusive courage and a poetic sharpness of intelligence, to exploit his own certainties, to step beyond the known grounds. Sisson's poetry displays a tough, curious, informed mind under continuous pressure from experience; it ranges from exuberant and deliberately villainous scatology ('The Theology of Fitness' is the prime example of this) to sustained passion. He has made many translations (Catullus, Horace, the whole of *The Divine Comedy*), and is an essayist of wit and keen perception: *The Avoidance of Literature* (1978) collects the best of these. He has been fascinated by the manifestations of the right, but is a Johnsonian Tory who has no time for modern politics. *Anglican Essays* (1983) explain his disenchantment with the Church of which he is now hardly a member. He is an important poet and an important thinker.

*

Scotland has not yet produced another poet of the calibre of MacDiarmid (q.v.); but at least three poets writing in Lallans, and four in English, are worthy of note. **Robert Garioch** (ps. **R.G. Sutherland**, 1909–82) was a witty, acerb poet in Scots; many of his best poems are satires. He is well represented in *Selected Poems* (1967). He uses Lallans as though it were his own language, not a literary device, and expresses comic and outrageous emotions in it that could not possibly be expressed in any other language. **Sydney Goodsir Smith** (1915–74), who also wrote in Scots, was more ambitious and more uneven. Many regard him as the natural successor to MacDiarmid; but MacDiarmid's own lyrical successes very often show up his lyrics as forced and artificial. Nor does his Rabelaisian, comic verse always succeed. But when it does it is revelatory; 'Sydney Slugabed Godless Smith', whom 'Auld Oblomov has nocht on', can be genuinely exhilarating. What one finally misses in his work, however, is the ability to modify his romanticism (in which he over-indulges himself under the disguise of linguistic gusto) or his sense of fun, which spills over into facetiousness. **Tom Scott** (1917) is altogether more austere; but his use of Lallans, while not as exuberant as Goodsir Smith's, is ultimately more responsible. He began by writing in English, but in 1953 produced his remarkable *Seeven Poems o Master Francis Villon made owre into Scots*.

W.S. Graham (1917–85) had verbal energy, best displayed in *The Nightfishing* (1955), an obscure but exciting sequence; *Malcolm Mooney's Land* (1970), in which he indulges his intellectual confusions rather than purges them, shows that he has failed to develop. **G.S. Fraser** (1915–80) wrote, in *Home Town Elegy* (1944) and *The Traveller Has Regrets* (1947), some of the most honest and carefully wrought poetry of the Forties; readers will turn back to it when the time comes to reappraise the period. At his best, when he is not susceptible to the influence of Yeats (q.v.), he is a gritty, subdued poet – certainly one of the best of his generation, as his posthumous *Collected Poems* (1981) makes clear. He was writing well until his premature death. **Ian Crichton Smith** (1928) is an uneven poet; but no one writes more densely or compassionately than he does at his best. His main collections are: *The Law and the Grace* (1965), *In Bourgeois Land* (1970), *Selected Poems* (1971) and *The Notebooks of Robinson Crusoe* (1975). He combines a subtle humanitarianism with a brooding, self-deprecatory Calvinism that gives his poetry great strength and originality.

*

The Fifties saw a reaction to the romanticism of the Forties, although the name of the 'Movement' given by a journalist to such poets as Davie, Gunn, Larkin and Amis (qq.v.) was unhelpful. The Sixties and early Seventies saw a great proliferation of versifiers of all kinds (mostly bad because lazy, careless, ignorant or derivative). It remains here to pick out the more outstanding. **Elizabeth Jennings** (1926) has been cruelly used by fashion. Her first collection, *Poems* (1953), was rightly praised for its modest and sober strength, and its unusual way of looking at landscape and experience. The chief influence on these early poems was Edwin Muir (q.v.), whom Elizabeth Jennings also resembled in lacking a personal, 'attacking' rhythm. Throughout many volumes (*Collected Poems*, 1967), she has sustained her sobriety and honesty of tone – but has run out of experience. It is as if she gave up all to be a poet, and now has nothing to write about except her approach to the writing of poetry and her acute disappointment at not remaining in the public eye. But to be written out – as she now certainly is – is not dishonourable, and a certain plodding courage characterizes her more recent unenergetic volumes.

Donald Davie (1922), once one of the most intelligent and aware critics of his generation, has never been able to escape from his didactic inclinations. His poetry is sometimes clever, but nearly all of it is factitious – verse not as poetry (which is produced under the kind of pressure that cannot be faked) but as various kinds of didactic criticism. He has wit, ingenuity and technique – but his work is controlled by what he prescribes as necessary ('for poetry') at the time of its composition: everything is for 'the good of poetry'. The best poetry does not come into being in this way: experience is primary in it, and its author is first a poet – and then (if he likes) a critic. Davie is first a critic. But there is a wry and bitter feeling which takes over in some earlier poems; and no critic illustrates his prescriptions more cleverly or more interestingly. His wit and the remarkable movement of his intellect are his own; it is a pity that the emotion in his poetry should so often be non-existent or aped. Much of his best work was in *New and Selected Poems* (1962), *Events and Wisdoms* (1964). *Essex Poems* (1969) was less good.

In the Seventies his work took a disastrous nosedive. After *Collected Poems* (1972) he has published embarrassingly bad neo-Georgian verse, or, worse, craven pastiche of Pound (q.v.). And he has issued remarkably obtuse books trying to explain his shift to Anglicanism and support for such figures as Mrs. Whitehouse. It is as though unhappiness at his failure to be regarded as a major poet had driven him into nervous collapse. He is no longer to be taken seriously.

Davie's exact contemporary **Philip Larkin** (1922–85) aptly reveals his severe limitations (it is a matter of the difference between actually being moved, and simply being in a state of admiration or intellectual fascination); it is ironic that he, in his turn, should exhibit severe critical limitations, the chief of which is his refusal to consider European poetry as being of interest. But the student of true poetry becomes used to such ironies. Larkin's first collection, *The North Ship* (1945), is not more than promising (it was Charles Madge, q.v., alone who prophesied his future from this volume); *The Less Deceived* (1955) and *The Whitsun Weddings* (1964) contain his important poetry; it has traces of Hardy and Graves (qq.v.), but there is no doubt of its originality. *High Windows* (1974) was less good. That this is apodictically as good as it is demonstrates the sceptical quality of the imagination. Larkin faces what seems to be a merely squalid predicament ('truth', for him, is a 'trite truss advertisement'), and yet he moves us. His best poems remain on the right side of sentimentality. One may sympathize with Charles Tomlinson (q.v.) when he complains that 'a movement in which he is the star performer can scarcely be thought of as having the energy to affect the ultimate destinies of English poetry'. But it may well not be for poets themselves to worry about any 'ultimate destinies'. But Tomlinson, like Davie (q.v.), is a critic-poet and not a poet-critic: the 'ultimate destinies' of any poetry exist only retrospectively; meanwhile, poets do what they can. As Tomlinson points out, Larkin's subject is 'largely his own inadequacy' (true: but why not? The test of a poet is not what he is but how truthful he can be about himself – Tomlinson will not acknowledge his own inadequacies and is not nearly as moving as Larkin can be); he goes on to deplore 'Larkin's refusal to note what had been done by the French before 1890 in the ironic self-deprecating mode'. But if Larkin could 'note' Laforgue and Corbière's poetry then he would certainly not be capable of the fine, ironic, self-deprecating poetry he wrote in English in the Fifties and Sixties. ... So much for criticism.

A poet quite as good as Larkin, and perhaps better because he has had more experience of life, is not yet at all well known, although he will be: this is **Cliff Ashby** (1919), an aggressively anti-literary Yorkshireman who possesses an uncanny ability to write directly and movingly. His poems are in *In the Vulgar Tongue* (1967), *The Dogs of Dewsbury* (1976) and *Lies and Dreams* (1980). Ashby, who has also written two laconic, sour novels, is probably the most powerful, spare poet of his generation; recognition of his genius cannot be much longer delayed.

Charles Tomlinson (ps. **Alfred Tomlinson**, 1927) is, like Davie (q.v.), an excellent and sensitive critic. He has a fine sense of landscape, a fascination with decay (which he seems not to acknowledge), and he is a good craftsman. An American admirer of his perception and his intelligence, however, has characterized him as 'no poet'. One sees what he means. Tomlinson has all the equipment of a poet except the capacity to deal with emotion. This has led him to try to realize himself in other men's styles: he has thus imported the procedures of Williams, Vallejo (qq.v.) and other poets into English poetry – but he has not absorbed them, and he has been unable to compensate for his own deficiencies. He is a frustrated painter, and his best effects have been gained from poem-pictures, where landscape acts as a metaphor for mood; but self-satisfaction or complacency (reflected in the prissy and exasperated tone of his criticism) seem to preclude the self-criticism, the self-exploration, the irony and the humour to which he would need to subject himself if he were to succeed in recording more than a series of moods. This is a loss to poetry. But as it is his poetry is far too cool and delighted with itself; one can hear the taps of the ferule as he sets about instructing his calm little world in how to organize itself – all ignorant of another, rougher world outside. His books include *The Necklace* (1955), *Seeing is Believing* (1958), *A Peopled Landscape* (1963), *The Way of a World* (1969), *Selected Poems* (1978).

Brian Higgins (1930–65), by contrast, was a hit-or-miss poet (somewhat in the manner of his friend George Barker, q.v.), who had too little time to exercise control over his considerable intelligence. His poems were published in *The Only Need* (1960), *Notes While Travelling* (1964) and *The Northern Fiddler* (1966). There are many good poems which remain unpublished, as yet, in book form. His best poems were full of urgency (an urgency that now seems poignant), primitive energy and directness of purpose. They combine passion, humour and subtlety. 'Genesis' demonstrates something of his quality:

> Language is the first perversion of the senses.
> The alphabet was written on the gates of Eden.
> Reason is an angel in mathematics, a castration
>   in literature, and a devil in life.
> The first and last speech was a curse.
> When the moon was numbered the stars grew pale.
> It was God who conspired with Satan in that garden
> When, lowering the snake, he sent words to prove
>   the Fall.

The two poets of Higgins' generation most discussed have been Ted Hughes and Thóm Gunn, although the latter, partly through having settled in America and partly through a failure of powers (he has become simply tedious), is not now mentioned so frequently.

Ted Hughes (1930) is a Yorkshireman whose first inchoate poems, in *The Hawk and the Rain* (1957) , showed signs that he might develop some sort of power, though of what sort was quite uncertain. From the beginning, he displayed a lack of ear and a remarkable lack of the ability to think in a coherent manner. Thus, if he were to develop as a poet at all – at this point his source was all too obviously D.H. Lawrence (q.v.) – it would have to be as a naïve poet; in this age that would not have been easy, although a few, by keeping away from over-literary influences, have done it. In fact he decided to become a heavy-weight 'primeval' poet, one who could elicit from his admirers such remarks as 'I love Ted Hughes, he is so evil' – this is a quotation. Although apparently incapable of writing even a series of rhyming couplets, and thus unequipped by any technique, or even a sense of rhythm, he extended his sources, none of which he has ever displayed the least indication of understanding. They include highly coloured (translated) foreign poetry, gnostic texts, the *I Ching*, various kinds of occult lore (both mush and otherwise), and the same puerile world of the pulp horror writer which I have described in discussing Carter (q.v.). His earlier poems offered a certain sort of whimsical sense, if you liked 'the magic of animals'. But they meant nothing. Nor did the pseudo-pantheistic 'philosophy' he was self-consciously developing. Eventually his poems came to mean nothing at all, so that *Crow* (1971; rev. 1972), a series of poems about a vaguely mythological figure, offered critics (some of whom fell for it, while others did not) the chance to make whatever comments they liked. The ideas behind the sequence were suitably vague: a misunder-standing of the notion of the 'survival of the fittest' (the fittest are not in fact the most violent and rapacious: not even in conventional Darwinism), a reliance on the incorrect facts that 'nature' is all violence, lust, cruelty, atrocity, and a mushy and muddled set of paradoxical precepts drawn from all kinds of theological, anthropological and other material. Hughes needs above all to demonstrate that his insistence on the 'necessity of the diabolic' is something he really feels, suffers and has somehow worked out. Yet what one gets from his verse is a sense of mindless self-destruction, a snarlingly opportunistic parody of despair, a woefully stupid failure of an imagination to proceed further than a lucubrated dwelling, without consideration or humanity, upon the merely bestial and evil. There is no vision here, only the parody of a vision. In *Gaudete* (1977), a long poem (it was an attempt at a film scenario) whose 'story' is almost comically dependent on T.F. Powys (q.v.), Hughes reached his nadir. The prosy verse lurches here and there, and depends for its effects on heavily over-used images of blood and violence. It all comes down to, it seems:

Horrible world

Where I let in –
As if for the first time –
The untouched joy.

The successors to *Gaudete*, and there are too many (Hughes is losing his nerve), try to restore a balance: after horror there can be a return to 'the arcadian dream', as a 'critic' put it. Hughes' reputation has been so inflated – and that is not altogether his fault – and his work so little subjected to hard criticism, that to read it with a severely critical eye would seem to be asking people to do something atrociously unfamiliar, such as spitting on an altar. Yet when it is thus read, it collapses into a factitious heap of semi-surreal notes, careless jottings about the writer's inner experience of animals – all presented in the most shoddy manner. What is dismaying is that so self-indulgently negative, unconvincing, intellectually tawdry, derivative and synthetic a 'vision' should ever have been taken seriously at all. A heavy pall hangs over Hughes' pseudo-gnomic utterances: clearly he has never thought about the material he rifles with such unheroic abandon. A faith that there is a meaning to Hughes' verse is what has kept his reputation alive so far. But when this is properly questioned, and when the sheer stupidity and unpleasantness of what for him and a few critics passes for thought has been exposed for what it is, a huge balloon will collapse with a whimper.

Thom Gunn (1929) wrote some promising undergraduate poems in *Fighting Terms* (1954; rev. 1958; 1962); but his progress from British conventional poet to frankly American homosexual poet has not been convincing or even very interesting. He has tried to be honest, and has much better technical equipment than Hughes (q.v.): he deserves to be called a poetaster (q.v.), which means that he is all right but not good enough. ... His homosexual poetry, and his self-conscious evocation of the American worlds of Beat (q.v.), leather jackets and pop, are uneasy – and he has sacrificed a great deal of his energy by writing in loose forms which, while they resemble those of Frank O'Hara (q.v.) and many others, do not suit him. There is much, too, in the later work that is both sentimental and 'downright silly', as one critic has pointed out. *Selected Poems* (1979) contains some of the better poems from his early phase. But there can be no doubt that he has slumped from being quite a bright English poetaster to the ghost of a boring and out-of-date American beatnik; yet if he could write of whatever it was that pulled him into this dead world, and in the forms he was wont to use, he could still produce a startling poetry. But the decision he has made has robbed him of the need to think, or to consider the possible benefits of taste. And this world of his, even in America, died, to all intents and purposes, some years back.

Geoffrey Hill (1932) is a superior poet, but one who has vitiated his gifts by over-restraint and too heavy reliance on books. He uses literary deceits to undermine his passionate disturbances. Yet he avoids rhetoric, and seems simply to acknowledge his limitations. The results are still worth while – and he is one of the best poets now writing, though he denies us the less indirect utterance he gives us reason to believe we should value. Those who read him with respect, as I do, are none the less infuriated by his wilful hermeticism and his implied admission that he wants to express feeling directly but cannot do so. If he were simply an oblique (q.v.) poet, then this would hardly arise; but it is all too evident that he is an oblique poet who wants to be a direct one. In his poetry feeling, a moral concern for others, a sense of the dramatic, a refusal to conform to conventional thinking: all these are also evident. When he is not too literary (and at times he has been too derivative; readers of Barker's *True Confessions*, q.v., just the kind of poem Hill would like to write and cannot, will note uncomfortably close echoes), he can be stately, dignified and moving. His invention of a poet, Arrarruz, from whom he makes translations ('The Songbook of Sebastian Arrarruz'), learned mainly from Pessoa (q.v.) rather than from Pound or Tate (qq.v., as has been suggested), is too convolute to quite come off: Arrarruz remains, after all, too reticent 'himself'. So that it is in his 'public' poems that Hill succeeds best, since he cannot write personal poems in the way he desires: *Mercian Hymns* (1971) is his most impressive collection, with its mournful but accurate attempts to rediscover the sense of the religious in English history. To an extent, this volume does collect what little remains of our real heritage. It is thus very distinguished in a true sense. *Somewhere is Such a Kingdom* (1975), which has appeared only in America, collects the poems to 1971.

The problem confronting **P.J. Kavanagh** (1931) is that of placing suffering, which he understands, into his poetry. He has sometimes been prepared to be banal or senti-mental: not to evade suffering, but to expel it because it seems indecent to his impeccably religious heart, which is an impressively kind one. One is sympathetic to this, especially in an age when disgust is relished for its own sake (Kavanagh has written a superb satire on a tourist coachload of people going to watch the pseudo-guru Hughes being publicly disgusting under the guise of 'truth-seeking') and very often his poetry is sinisterly precise and disturbing. He has deepened and developed – emotionally rather than intellectually – and ought to mean something to every sensitive reader. *Selected Poems* (1982).

Only one poet remains who has been consistently interesting – others have briefly promised, but collapsed – and this is **Tony Harrison** (1937). Harrison is well known for his versions of Aeschylus for the National Theatre, and for other adaptations and trans-lations. But his chief work remains in his own poetry, collected in *The Loiners* (1970) and *The School of Eloquence* (1978). Harrison knows that poetry is difficult, and is determined not to write (or at least not to publish) his bad poetry. He is a most accomplished tech-nician. It is true that he does not yet work from what is 'given': rather, he seems to clothe an idea. But he is exceptional because verbal excitement is created in him by the sorts of ideas he has – and he is cautious about making a fool of himself, an admirable trait in the days of Hughes (q.v.). He has poetic integrity. His poems work by 'wit' in the Empsonian (q.v.) sense; they are elegant and delicately angled. Many recent ones have been obses-sively, but not over-obsessively, concerned with his father. At his best, as in 'On Not Being Milton', he is compressed, moving, brilliantly intelligent and sardonic. David Wright (q.v.) was justified in once describing him as a 'white hope of English poetry'.

Sean Haldane (1943), the Anglo-Irish poet who has written a book about Trumbull Stickney (q.v.), *The Fright of Time* (1970), collected his early poems in *Skindiving* (1972), which he published in Canada. These are imaginative and always intelligent, but at times over-lyrical: occasionally they even spill over into sentimentality, because this poet is searching for valid means of overcoming negative feelings. In later poems, soon due to be published, he has stumbled upon his own voice: he has at last allowed himself to be overtly satirical (something he had previously forbidden), and to express his sense of evil. But he has sacrificed none of his lyricism. The recent poems, more dramatic than the earlier ones, are often impressive and moving.

Bulgarian Literature

The Bulgarian language is South Slavic, quite close to Russian, from which it borrowed extensively in the nineteenth century. The modern state of Bulgaria came into being in 1878, as a Turkish principality which was in effect autonomous. It became an independent kingdom in 1908. Before this the literary activity, in a culturally backward country, directed towards national liberation and the foundation of a literary language, was mainly in the hands of the patriotic but also, at bottom, nihilistic poet Hristo Botev (1848–76), the poet and educationist Petko Slaveykov (1827–95) and the story-writer and populist Lyuben Karavelov (1835–79). Of these men only Karavelov showed much concern for art and psychological truth; Botev, understandably overrated in his country's literature, was killed after the 1876 uprising. **Ivan Vazov** (1850–1922), who was a minister of education for a short while in the closing years of the nineteenth century, became the leader of the traditionalist and nationalist group which dominated Bulgarian literature until the end of the Second World War. Vazov, a just and never narrow-minded critic, believed literature should be devoted to the interests of the whole people. His novel *Under the Yoke* (1889–90; tr. 1893; 1955), written in exile, deals with the savagely crushed April Rising of 1876 which led to the war of liberation from the Turks. It made the world suddenly aware of Bulgaria and, to a lesser extent, of Bulgarian literature. Although (with the exception of his epic novel) his work now inevitably seems dated, he remains the dominant figure in modern Bulgarian literature. (MBL)

Konstantin Velichkov (1855–1907), who was minister of education before Vazov (q.v.), was the most notable poet in the traditionalist group. His chief contribution to Bulgarian poetry was his expansion of its techniques – for example, he wrote the first good sonnets in the language. This facility he gained from his French education. His best work, however, is in his travel books.

Stoyan Mihaylovski (1856–1927), also educated in France, was the satirist of the Vazov circle. He was by turns Christian believer and decadent nihilist. He appointed himself the Bierce (q.v.)-like castigator of all the evils of the new Bulgaria. He was in fact a savage pessimist, with a fine technique and a vituperative style. His chief work, *Book of the Bulgarian People* (1897), is totally despairing: there is no compromise possible between anarchy and enslavement. He was thus a prophetic writer.

Venelin (ps. **Todor Vlaykov**, 1865–1943), although also a follower of Vazov (q.v.), was caught for the whole of his long life between his social and his individual aspirations. He wrote some of the first realistic stories of Bulgarian village people, using colloquial language and dialect. He was dedicated to the interests of the peasants all his life, and was a member of the radical peasants' party which took power in 1919, but was overthrown by a right-wing military coup in 1923. This government, which was headed by Alexander Stamboliisky (murdered in the coup), has been neglected by historians. It was the only peasant dictatorship that has ever existed. It was hostile to the left, and to liberalism. The right overthrew it because it was trying, in collaboration with Yugoslavia, to suppress the powerful Macedonian terrorist organization called IMRO. From 1923 Bulgaria became a dictatorship under the nominees of King Boris, a shrewd and devious man, who defied Hitler and may have been killed at his orders (1943). The monarchy was abolished in 1946. Dimitrov (Georgi Dimitrov, Bulgaria's first post-war communist premier) put through the Stalinization of Bulgaria with ruthless zeal, slaughtering agrarian and social democratic members of what is still called the Fatherland Front after show 'trials'. Then he seemed to want to emulate Tito, and 'died' in hospital in Moscow in 1949. The rulers of Bulgaria since have been Chervenkov – and then Zhivkov, an able psychopath.

Anton Strashimirov (1872–1937) wrote stories of peasant life, though in a less colloquial language, and with sometimes more conventionally literary 'colour' and plot. He was more prolific than Vlaykov (q.v.); many of his novels and plays (the outstanding one is *The Vampire*, 1902) are vivid evocations of the history of Bulgaria at the end of the nineteenth century. (MBL)

Naturally, there arose a school of writers who were sharply opposed to Vazov's nationalist conception of the function of literature – not that Vazov did not have his own doubts. Its leader was the poet **Pencho Slaveykov** (1866–1912), the son of Petko Slaveykov; its organ of expression was the magazine *Thought*. His aim, he said, was to 'extricate the man from the Bulgarian'. He travelled abroad, mainly in Germany, and imported into the literature of his country ideas from German idealism, English romanticism and Russian humanism. Naturalism (q.v.) he rejected altogether. Slaveykov was crippled from youth, and tended to see his country's predicament as his own. The myth of Prometheus is central in his work. From Nietzsche (q.v.) he extrapolated the notion of 'exalted personality', which he equated with 'aesthetic man'; he saw Bulgarian destiny as involving a transcendence of national dogma. His best work by far is an anthology, *The Isle of the Blessed* (1910), of works by fictional poets to whom he gave full fictional biographies.

One of the most gifted poets associated with this group was **Peyo Yavorov** (ps. P. Kracholov, 1878–1914). Yavorov was the first truly tormented soul of Bulgarian literature. He became disillusioned with populism and socialism in 1903, after having fought (though not a Macedonian) on behalf of Macedonia, withdrew more and more into himself, and finally committed suicide (after one unsuccessful attempt). The poetry of the years 1904–11, which was written much under the influence of Russian and then French symbolism (qq.v.), is his best. The characteristic title of his 1907 collection is *Insomnia and Intuitions*. In order (it is said) to please his wife he turned to poetic drama, and wrote *At the Foot of Mount Vitosha* (1911), *When the Thunder Rolls* (1912) and *As the Echo Replies* (1912), misty Chekhovian (q.v.) plays with an undertone of menace and despair.

The works of **Petko Todorov** (1879–1916) consist of 'idylls' (a form he took from Schlaf, q.v.) and plays. The idylls are symbolist (q.v.) recreations of ancient folk tales in which heroes tragically fail to achieve reconciliation of their own aspirations with the needs of society. His plays combine Ibsen's (q.v.) techniques with folk themes. But *The First* (1912) is more straightforward, about the wealthy Bulgarians who collaborated with the Turks.

The poet **Kiril Hristov** (1875–1944) was certainly of an individualistic persuasion, although in fact he took Vazov's (q.v.) side in the controversy between him and Slaveykov (q.v.), who was his friend. He spent most of his life in exile – the lot of many Bulgarians. Hristov was the first uninhibited poet of Bulgaria: personal, fresh, erotically descriptive, he shocked the readers of the Nineties. The poems are now dated; but they served their purpose. He also wrote plays and novels.

Elin Pelin (ps. D. Ivanov, 1877–1949), one of Bulgaria's greatest writers of short stories, became the best known Bulgarian writer after Vazov's (q.v.) death. He wrote little after 1923. In his writings he conducted a love-hate relationship with the Bulgarian peasants of the countryside around Sofia; but, although he travelled and lived abroad in

France and Russia, he could never come to terms with urban life. Whereas Todorov and Vlaykov (qq.v.) had in their different ways portrayed the peasantry as they had always been, Pelin portrayed them under the impact of modern life: he saw them under the threat of change. He understood them better than Todorov and Vlaykov, and portrayed them not in any romantic spirit but in that of psychological realism (q.v.). He is Bulgaria's first realist – and a good one. He never attached himself to a political group, but accepted the communist take-over. He remained in favour with the exceedingly repressive Bulgarian communist party. (MBL)

Yordan Yovkov (1880–1937) is another writer still in communist favour. His subject is usually the same as Pelin's (q.v.), but his approach – while never urbanly slanted – is more cosmopolitan. He wrote a fine satirical comedy about the greed and nastiness of provincials which would have been quite beyond Pelin's range: *The Millionaire* (1930). He wrote many stories and story-cycles (which amount to novels) about Bulgarian peasants and the impact upon them of war and other circumstances outside their control. Pelin analyses the effects of change; Yovkov does the same, but his range is wider. His style is still held up as a model. (MBL)

Dimcho Debelyanov (1887–1916), who was killed in Greece during the First World War – into which Bulgaria's rulers had led it on the side of Germany – was the leading symbolist (q.v.) poet. He saw French symbolist doctrine as a key to the mysteries of Bulgarian history. He left just a handful of rhythmically haunting poems, in some of which he has premonitions of his early death; he has been highly influential because of their quality, their evocation of the Bulgarian past, and their peculiarly Bulgarian unhappiness – that wholly justified sense of having been cheated by history of the primitive right to one's own roots. This unhappiness was to emerge as a cynical-seeming bitterness in the prose of Stamatov (q.v.).

Nicolay Liliev (ps. N. Mihaylov, 1885–1960) was Debelyanov's (q.v.) friend and fellow symbolist (q.v.). He had a powerful influence in post-war Bulgaria; in 1934 he became the director of the National Theatre in Sofia. His knowledge of foreign literatures, particularly English and French, was unsurpassed. He wrote comparatively few poems; most of them are collected in *Poems* of 1932. A sad man, hating the modern world and loving only the memory of his childhood, his search for an inner world manifested itself mainly in his emphasis upon form, melody and delicate elegance of utterance.

Hristo Jasenov (ps. X. Tudžarov, 1889–1925), murdered by police for his leftist sympathies, was another symbolist (q.v.) with considerable mastery of style. Also murdered in this repressive year was **George Milev** (1895–1925). He began as a symbolist and decadent (qq.v.), but then embraced communism and wrote *September* (1924; tr. 1961) in Mayakovsky's (q.v.) style. Had the rightists not seized power in 1923 he would probably not have turned to communism.

Elisaveta Bagryana (ps. E. Belcheva, 1893) is Bulgaria's leading woman poet. She travelled much abroad, saying that she 'had a husband in every country', and generally titillated the Bulgarian bourgeoisie between the wars by enjoying many love affairs and writing about them with candour. One of her best cycles of love-poems is about Britain, where she had what pseudo-tolerant polite critics once used to call 'a passionate liaison'. She has written beautifully of the Bulgarian landscape, and against modern technology and the insensitivity of the men who implement its inhuman and menacing programmes. She is a prolific poet, sometimes too content to express conventionally romantic sentiments; but at her best she is vital and impressive. She is a direct, and anti-symbolist poet. Her books include *The Eternal and the Saint* (1927), *The Sailor's Star* (1932), *Five Stars* (1953) and *From One Bank to the Other* (1963). The two latter volumes contain a good deal of 'socialist' poetry, in which genre Elisaveta Bagryana is clearly uneasy. Many of her first poems appeared in the magazine *Golden Horn* (*Zlatorog*, 1922–44), which was, in general, devoted to perfection of form and simplicity of expression. This offered a haven to those writers who did not want to be murdered or called 'communist' for being critical of the repressive government, which ripened the country for communism. *Golden Horn* was an eclectic and anti-dogmatic magazine, intelligently edited by the critic Vladimir Vasilev, and was the most important in Bulgaria in its time.

The leading novelist of this period, and after the First World War, was the Macedonian **Dimitur Talev** (1898–1966). His main works are *The Years of Proof* (1928–30), the trilogy *The Iron Candlesticks* (1952) and *The Bells of Prespa* (1954). These are historical works, tracing the difficult and exciting history of the Macedonian peoples. Talev has narrative power and what has been called an 'epic serenity'; his style, already formed, was not much affected by the advent of socialist realism. The historical novel is of course an excellent defence against socialist realism (q.v.), though it always has to contend with ignorant pseudo-Marxist 'historiographers' – corrupt bullies who enjoy keeping their superiors 'in order'.

Bulgaria's most successful writers of urban fiction are the misunderstood **Georgi Stamatov** (1869–1942), **Georgi Raychev** (1882–1948), whose psychological novel *Sin* (1923), which had the merits of sexual candour, was much praised, and **Dimitar Shishmanov** (1889–1945), whose *Shadows on the Acropolis* (1938), on the relations between the ancient and the modern, reached a new level of sophistication. All these writers have been described as 'sterile' or 'cynical', but only by polite critics whose optimism about human nature is (alas) unjustified. Stamatov introduced psychological analysis into Bulgarian fiction. His tales of city life are pitiless, revealing the corruption of officials and the misery of the poor. First an army officer and then a judge, Stamatov was one of the most sharply gloomy of all Bulgarian writers; but his sense of psychology is acute, and his bitterness justified. He is probably the best Bulgarian writer of fiction of this century. As a judge Stamatov opposed capital punishment – his fiction is as 'cynical', at bottom, as that. Raychev carried on in the same tradition. Shishmanov, liquidated by the communists for his 'conservatism' at the end of the Second World War, treated eccentrics in a markedly unconservative manner.

Nikolai Vaptsarov (1909–42), murdered, by firing-squad, by the opposite party as a resister of fascism, has aptly been called 'Bulgaria's Mayakovsky' (q.v.). He was indisputably the most gifted poet of his generation, and would no doubt have been shot by the communists if the Germans had not done it for them. He was no more subject to slogans or clichés than was Mayakovsky at his best. And, again like Mayakovsky, his feeling for everything modern and mechanical is suffused with genuine optimism and energy. In the hours before his death he wrote some remarkably moving poems to his wife. His only collection was *Motor Songs* (1940); but his *Collected Works* appeared in 1959.

After 1944, when the communists dominated government (they had liquidated all opposition by July 1948), the freedom of the Bulgarian writer was effectively curtailed: Bulgaria is so near to Russia that dissension need not be tolerated, and so remains underground. The exiled minor writer **Georgi Markov** (1929–78) was murdered in London: the Bulgarians who run this part of the Soviet Empire are the most savagely zealous of all puppets. Yet no major Bulgarian writer has gone into exile. There was a tiny relaxation in 1956, though it made little difference. In that year writers looked to the poet **Atanas Dalchev** (1904), who had resisted Stalinism and survived, as their leader and exemplar. Dalchev had been publishing since the Twenties, and although he is not a very gifted poet his courage has proved historically important, and might become more so. The short-story writer **Nikolay Khaytov** (1919) has been able to criticize communist bureaucracy without mercy, and yet be accepted as a 'communist critic' of local communist shortcomings, but he is a minor writer. A good deal has been done, however, in the historical novel. **Anton Donchev** (1930), perhaps following the example of Talev (q.v.), wrote an outstanding allegory in *Time of Parting* (1964; tr. 1968): the subject is ostensibly the forcible conversion of Bulgaria to Islam by the Turks. **Dimitur Dimov** (1909–66) wrote *Tobacco* in 1951, was forced to amend it, and was then allowed to re-issue the original. But it is not possible to write a truthful novel about contemporary Bulgaria, and the work of party hacks is intolerably comic: they lack the occasional technical proficiency of their Soviet counterparts. **Emilian Stanev** (1907) wrote a fine and sensitive story, *The Peach Thief* (1948; tr. with other Bulgarian stories, 1968), about the conditions in Bulgaria in 1919. But he was soon forced into such historical novels as *Antichrist* (1970). No substantial poet has emerged.

*

The theatre has flourished in Bulgaria since the communists took over. Playwrights have not. Before this the one competent playwright was Yovkov (q.v.), whose *Albena* (1929) was a worthy domestic drama. Almost the only play criticizing the Sovietized system appeared in the very brief Bulgarian Thaw (1956): *Fear* (1956), by **T. Genov.** This showed an opportunist climbing through the ranks of the communist party. In 1957 controls were brutally applied again. **Kamen Zidarov** (1902) wrote some sharp and dramatic historical plays such as *Ivan Shishman* (1959 rev. 1963), in verse. *The Public Prosecutor* (1964) by **Georgi Dzhagarov** (1925) is an anti-Stalinist trial-drama which was allowed through by the censor.

Bulgarian writers have been as repressed as any in the world. Socialist realism (q.v.) is absolute dogma, and literature is directed by a set of semi-literate culture clerks. There are innumerable and interminable pseudo-polemic discussions, conducted at a low cultural level. Approved writing is monotonous, repetitive, lacking in psychological depth: the writer's situation is an abject one. Bulgaria's literature in exile is, unfortunately, an undistinguished one: 'hampered', says an exile, 'by its old-fashioned ideas and polemics – continually turning back to the past instead of looking towards the future'. Yet there is probably a major writer somewhere in that country. The only one with claims to this status is Donchev (q.v.), but he is effectually gagged. Stamatov's (q.v.) black vision has come true.

Canadian Literature

The pressures on Canadian writers have been more diverse than in some of the other ex-colonies: there have been two 'home cultures', French and British – as well as the presence of the strongly-developing American culture to the immediate south. The fact that the French and the British (one should perhaps say English and Scottish) cultures exist side by side raises the question of whether there is, even now, such a thing as a single, indigenous Canadian culture. Certainly it is only very recently that young Canadian writers have felt anything like confidence that there is – and this is largely owing to the emergence of an international feeling (among young people) that racial and political differences belong to an older generation. ... And yet from this supposedly 'boring', archaic and 'square' society emerged the first 'unsquare', new-style prime minister in the history of the modern world: Pierre Elliott Trudeau (Olof Palme of Sweden was the next). It is true that when a Canadian politician was kidnapped and subsequently killed by Canadian separatists Trudeau in mid-crisis looked (and spoke and acted), suddenly, much like any other conventional politician – but although now tired and bowing out, he was once different.

There is not much in the poetry and fiction of the nineteenth-century Canada that can be offered as interesting except in a historical or local sense. The one exception, Isabella Valancy Crawford, whose poetry contains some magnificent lines and passages, died in 1887, aged thirty-seven. It was not until during and after the war that a Canadian literature began to develop. It is true that **Stephen Leacock** (1869–1944) began writing his humorous sketches in 1910 (he also wrote serious works on politics), but he was seldom more than an Englishman commenting on Canadian life. The exception is *Sunshine Sketches of a Little Town* (1912), in which the narrator's ambiguity of attitude betrays the stirrings of a truly Canadian consciousness.

As is usual in colonial literatures, it was the poets who first made themselves heard – in the Twenties. But two early French-Canadian poets should be mentioned. The invalid **Albert Lozeau** (1878–1924) was not a modernist, but his short lyrics – written from his bed – were, when not sentimental, elegant and moving records of a life necessarily devoted to reverie. The precocious **Émile Nelligan** (1879–1941), born in Montreal, had an Irish father and a French-Canadian mother; before he was twenty he had become hopelessly insane, and spent his last forty years in an asylum. He can justifiably be thought of as Canada's Rimbaud or Campana (q.v.). He is really a part of the French rather than the French-Canadian tradition, but q this makes him all the more important: he introduced symbolism to Canada, whose English poets, however, then made nothing of it. He read his poems aloud, but they were not published until 1903; the *Complete Poems (Poésies complètes)* appeared in 1952. The chief influences on his work were Rimbaud and Verlaine, and the theme of his lush but suggestive poetry, which is astonishingly precocious in accomplishment, is the inaccessibility of beauty in the ordinary world. (OBCV)

The English-Canadian poets became active in the mid-Twenties, but their group anthology, *New Provinces*, did not appear until 1936. Canadian publishers were not much interested in issuing poetry until the years of the Second World War. The father-figure of modern Canadian poetry is **E.J. Pratt** (1883–1964), born in Newfoundland. Pratt, who began as a Methodist priest, is a good, forceful narrative poet who has affinities with Masefield and Roy Campbell (qq.v.). He had little lyrical gift, but his language is admirably lucid and his versification masterly within its severe limitations. He broke with the old, mechanically picturesque procedures to form a poetry that actually observed both natural and urban processes. He is a truly dynamic poet, who will introduce any kind of relevant scientific information into his work. In this (alone) he resembles MacDiarmid (q.v.); but he is never prosy. He takes public themes (*Towards the Last Spike*, 1952, is on the building of the Canadian Pacific Railway) but spices them with irony. Pratt never found a language of resolution, and therefore lacks that ultimate wisdom which characterizes the work of a major poet. He came nearest to it in *Brébeuf and His Brethren* (1940), the narrative of a Jesuit priest who is martyred by Indians. The fullest retrospective edition of his work was published in Canada in 1944: *Collected Poems.*

The poets of the so-called 'Montreal School' (or 'Maple Leaf School') of the Twenties learned from Pratt to widen their scope to include all aspects of life; but they employed shorter forms. **A.J.M. Smith** (1902–80) was important as an influence and anthologist as well as a poet. He was essentially a cautious modernist, and his work remains more or less in the formal tradition, often reminding one of the Sitwells (qq.v.), and drawing on the English metaphysical tradition. His deliberate pastiche of such poets as Yeats (q.v.) and Vaughan is educated and displays sensitivity and skill; but since his best efforts are in this kind of poetry one wonders if his function is not predominantly critical. He had an admirably hard style in his 'own' poems, but too often lapsed into rhythmical obviousness and a tone slightly false to his own educated sophistication. **F.R. Scott** (1899) is a satirist, a love poet and a nature poet – in that order. But his chief function has been as a critic. As a young man at McGill University he played a large part in making his contemporaries aware of Pound and Eliot (qq.v.). He has led a public life, as Professor of Law at McGill and as an active socialist (he was chairman of the CCF, the Canadian socialist party, 1942–50), and has been a lively figure. (OBVC)

By far the most interesting and gifted of this Montreal group was the Jewish poet **A.M. Klein** (1909–72), who remained poetically silent after 1948, when he published *The Rocking Chair*, his fourth collection. Probably he is the most important Anglophone Canadian writer of this century. His first volume was called *Hath Not a Jew . . .* (1940). This was followed by the *Hitleriad* (1944) and *Poems* (1944). *The Second Scroll*, an experimental novel, appeared in 1951. Klein, 'a Jewish poet in the sense that Claudel [q.v.] was a Catholic poet' (A.J.M. Smith), is the poet of Quebec, whose French-Canadian conservatism he views from his own Hebraically conservative position. He is very much an odd man out, although his work is held in high regard. He wrote from the point of view of a sophisticated but committed Jew: even when dealing with such themes as an Indian Reservation he considered them – if only obliquely – in the terms of an alienated, tortured Jew who yearns for Jerusalem. But he is unique because of his involuntary (and still very Jewish) irony, and his remarkable use of language. One feels that he did not go to secular Israel (he worked in public relations in Montreal) because, under such circumstances, he preferred to work in a less frustratedly secular Canada. Nevertheless, he was zealously concerned with the establishment of Israel as well as with protest against the Nazi atrocities. His latest poetry achieved an idiosyncrasy of diction which was necessary for the complex feelings it expressed. Was Klein an influence on John Berryman (q.v.)? He ends his poem 'Montreal', in *The Rocking Horse*:

> City, O city, you are vision'd as
> A parchemin roll of saecular exploit

> Inked with the script of eterne souvenir!
> You are in sound, chanson and instrument!
> Mental, you rest forever edified
> With tower and dome; and in these beating valves,
> Here in these beating valves, you will
> For all my mortal time reside!

Here is the same kind of mixture of heroic poetry, old high manner, archaism and quaintness that characterizes much of Berryman's later work. Certainly Berryman's own manner differs from Klein's; but this approach, among others, could well have provided him with the confidence to go forward. Despite his long silence – his mental health gave way in the Fifties, and he became a recluse – Klein was Canada's most original English-language poet, and perhaps the only one of his generation who, although so rooted in the past of his race, was entirely unsatisfied with the poetic procedures of the nineteenth century. His work stands squarely behind names now better known than his, and in time it will be studied in depth. (OBCV) *Collected Poems* (1974).

The younger poets whose work began to appear in the Forties had less creative confidence than Klein, and consequently a more eclectic and 'international' approach. They were galvanized into activity by an energetic Englishman, **Patrick Anderson** (1915), who became a Canadian citizen, but eventually returned to Great Britain. He was in Canada only for ten years. What Anderson really did was to export to Canada the styles and pre-occupations of the English poets of the late Thirties; his own poetry was a sensitive instrument for the recording of these (particularly of Auden, MacNeice, Barker, Gascoyne, qq.v.) rather than an *oeuvre* in its own right. But his application of this Thirties-style sensibility was intelligent and fluent, and his presence in Canada beneficial. His best published work is contained in autobiographies (*Snake Wine*, 1955) and travel books. Although called, with justice, 'a kind of tea-drinking Dylan Thomas', on account of some of his over-fluent Canadian poems, Anderson is an exceptionally intelligent man who has an engaging line in criticism of his earlier selves. (OBCV) Anderson, who while in Canada joined forces with Scott (q.v.), established the magazine *Preview*, and it was there that the work of **P.K. Page** (1917) first appeared. P.K. Page was born in Swanage, Dorset, England, but was educated and grew up in Canada. A characteristically rigorous selection of her best work, with new poems, was included in *Cry Ararat!* (1967), which was followed by *Poems, Selected and New* (1974). Her start as a poet of social protest under the influence of Scott and Anderson (qq.v.) was in fact a false one; her real concerns emerged in the poems of *The Metal and the Flower* (1954): satire of lonely bourgeois personalities merges into psychological and biographical concern. These were perhaps her most successful poems: her more recent work, for all its purity of line, is not entirely convincing. Such thoughts as 'A single leaf can block a mountainside;/All Ararat be conjured in a leaf' are better left where they belong: with William Blake. (OBCV)

Earle Birney (1904), a noted scholar and critic, born in Alberta, was in his early years a farm labourer, logger, bank clerk and sailor; later he became an academic, though no conventional one. He has been one of the most independent of Canadian writers, and is now a universally respected veteran. But it is his geniality rather than his poetry which appeals: the latter is too open to too many influences, and is sprawling and ungainly. He has written two novels: the picaresque *Turvey* (1949) and *Down the Long Table* (1955), on the depression years. (OBCV)

Another Canadian original is **Irving Layton** (1912), who was born in Rumania. His parents emigrated to Canada when he was only one year old. Layton is a gifted poet, a 'natural', who seems compelled to mix his sillinesses and rushes of blood to the head with

his more straightforward lyrical poems. He can seldom express himself without a childish
rage or petulance; his wisdom is deliberately withdrawn. But when he writes of that
experience which ought to temper his opinions he is a bright minor poet, and almost
justifies the comparisons – often made – between himself and Blake and Whitman. He
has been overrated (he is nowhere near so accomplished a poet as Klein, q.v., even
though he has been referred to as 'great') because his immense energy tends to obscure
his incapacity, even at his best, to organize his emotions. The concluding stanza of 'The
Birth of Tragedy' gives a good sense of his achievements and his limitations:

> A quiet madman, never far from tears,
>   I lie like a slain thing
>   under the green air the trees
> inhabit, or rest upon a chair
>   towards which the inflammable air
> tumbles on many robins' wings;
>   noting how seasonably
>   leaf and blossom uncurl
> and living things arrange their death,
> while someone from afar off
> blows birthday candles for the world.

There is more cliché here than the sincere vitality of the surface suggests there might be,
and there are confusions; the last two lines insufferably indulge a penchant for whimsy;
but the emotion which the poet is not altogether successfully trying to capture is pure,
and the line 'and living things arrange their death' has been its reward. The most
complete collection of his work, of which there is far too much, is *The Poems* (1977).
(OBCV; CWT)

The Montreal poet **Louis Dudek** (1918) has been a helpful influence on Canadian
poetry without contributing to its permanent qualities. He originally appeared in the
Preview anthology, *Unit of Five* (1944), which introduced P.K. Page (q.v.). Dudek's friend
Raymond Souster (1921) is another useful, generous and lively influence; his verse is
direct, pleasant and prosy. For many years he was also at the centre of Montreal literary
activity. A *Selected Poems* appeared in 1956, and he has published many other collections.

Later English-Canadian poets have divided themselves into academic and USA
schools. **Jay Macpherson** (1931), a university teacher who stated that she stopped being a
poet in 1957, but then published two more volumes, makes poetry out of previous
poetries, of which she has extensive knowledge. She was first taken up by Robert Graves
(q.v.), who printed her *Nineteen Poems* (1952) on his long-defunct Seizin Press; but her
best-known, and much acclaimed, book is *The Boatman* (1957). These poems represented
one of the cleverest and most attractive literary retreats from sexuality of their decade.
Reluctantly influenced by Graves' pagan beastliness (as one might, from the general tone
of the poems, put it), they combined elements of fable and learned Biblical reference with
great skill and charm. The subtly organized scholastic surface does not conceal a wistfulness for robust experience, a wistfulness which again emerges in *Welcoming Disaster*
(1974). (OBCV) **James Reaney** (1926) founded, and edited, a magazine called *Alphabet*
(1960–71), which followed the theories of the important Canadian critic **Northrop Frye**
(1912), a minister of the United Church of Canada and university teacher who has been
described by Mordecai Richler (q.v.) as 'our keeper of true standards'. Frye's most
ambitious and influential book is *Anatomy of Criticism* (1957), in which he contentiously
attacks value judgements and makes a prophetic bid to reduce literature to its socio-

anthropological and mythopoeic components. His project has interesting, though tenuous, affinities with the programme of the Russian Formalists (q.v.). Frye is an intelligent critic; but his manic reductionism is a reaction to his own creative failure, and readers should be wary of accepting his theories – his comments on actual works, though, are frequently valuable. Reaney's poetry seeks to order his experience into recognizably Fryean categories, and to subsume them under a general and very unconvincing Christianity. The most interesting and original of his books are *Twelve Letters to a Small Town* (1962), written in a mock-infantile style, and *A Suit of Nettles* (1958), satirical mock allegory. Despite some surrealism, Reaney has yet to burst out of his over-scholastic theorizings and to face himself in his poetry; but it already displays the lineaments of experience. He is very active as a writer of verse plays, but all of these read poorly. (OBCV; CWT)

Bertram Warr (1917–43), killed in the Second World War, should also be mentioned. He did not have time to realize his gifts, but the poems in *Yet a Little Onwards* (1941) display remarkable sophistication and potential – as the final lines of 'The Deviator' illustrate:

> And as I sat here this morning, thinking my thoughts amid the sounds,
> Suddenly, all these, the definables, began telling their meanings to me,
> Saying there is no aloneness, there can be no dark cocoon,
> With room for one, and an empty place, if love should come.
>
> (OBCV)

Little need be said of **Leonard Cohen** (1934), who long ago smothered his small talents in whimsical, sickly lushness. (OBVC; CWT) Some used to point to **Alfred Purdy** (1918) as one of the first of the younger Canadian poets to find an expression for 'the emergence of a new nation', but this seems over-confident: his sprawling verse entirely lacks a rhythmical coherence, and suggests that his natural form is autobiographical prose. (CWT)

Nothing interesting has happened in Anglophone Canadian poetry since Klein (q.v.). The ascendancy of **Margaret Atwood** (1939), described irreverently as the current 'queen bee of Canadian literature', has been a depressing phenomenon, and will remind readers with perspective of Mary Gilmore (q.v.), who became a Dame and 'cannily sucked homage from the environment'. John Metcalf said of Atwood's *Survival: A Thematic Guide to Canadian Literature* (1972) that it 'set back literary appreciation by a decade'. Curiously enough, for so avowedly modernist a writer, this is an old-fashioned book: nationalist and feminist – but in the old-style, outdated manner of, say (once again), Dame Mary Gilmore. With her novel *Surfacing* (1972), and with the strident *Survival,* Atwood began to establish a high reputation as a novelist – and this tended to eclipse the one she already had as a prizewinner for her verse. Here she is giving her version of the dialogue between the French and the English Canadas:

> Your language hangs around your neck,
> a noose, a heavy necklace:
> each word is empire,
> each word is vampire and mother.
>
> As for the sun, there are as many
> suns as there are words for sun:
>
> true or false?

To this arhythmical, pretentious and insipid magma of cut-price linguistics, anthropology and philosophy, one is tempted to add 'And what does it matter?'. If a critic can call this 'intense' and go unchallenged, then clearly 'literary appreciation' is away and somewhere else. But there is nothing better in Canadian poetry today, unless it be the thin skill of Jay Macpherson (q.v.).

Canadian novels in English in this century have been poor, and Atwood's novels and stories certainly do not improve on those of MacLennan or Wilson (qq.v.) – by the side of the great Morley Callaghan (q.v.), which they now outsell, they are pale indeed. But they are better than her verse. *The Edible Woman* (1969) was a negligible exercise in comic Gothic which entirely failed to come off; this was before Atwood attained her considerable professional skills. *Surfacing* (1972), which became a cult novel, is a clever, self-consciously experimental account of an 'I' woman who is supposed to regain her being. The 'surfacing' of the title, fashionably involving Indian paintings and the corpse of her father (*mais naturellement*), and owing not a little to Jung (q.v.), is unconvincing. But the emotional deadness of the protagonist, ostensibly transformed – in fact only transformed in a manner suitable to prescriptive critics – is rather horribly convincing, and the element of self-mockery is wholly genuine. *Lady Oracle* (1977) is good light entertainment and Atwood's best because least pretentious novel: this time the Gothic is exploited to comic effect. *Life Before Man* (1980) is strangely repellent and reads as though it had been written by the untransformed 'I' of *Surfacing*. It is a mixture of fake nihilism and, as a critic has said, a negation of the 'presupposition on which the novel has traditionally been based, that the lives of men and women ... have a value ...' There are novels which validly challenge that proposition, but their authors have imaginations richer than Atwood's. *Bodily Harm* (1981) is the synthetic novel of a self-satisfied writer, and has neither feeling nor style. *Dancing Girls* (1977) collects glib but admirably professional stories.

*

In French-Canadian poetry the first really important poet after Nelligan (q.v.) was **Hector de Saint-Denys-Garneau** (1912–43), whose volume *Gazes and Games in Space* (*Regards et jeux dans l'espace*, 1937) initiated the modern movement in Canadian poetry. Saint-Denys-Garneau did almost all his poetic work between 1934 and 1937 – he suffered from a heart condition – and, like Nelligan, was more a part of the French than the French-Canadian tradition. He was aware of Rilke (q.v.), and his poetry is more individual and more pioneering in its use of free verse than any of his Canadian-English counterparts. His *Journal* (1954; tr. 1962), which explores both his own spiritual unease and Canadian problems, is one of the great modern examples of the genre.

Saint-Denys-Garneau's cousin **Anne Hébert** (1916) has written with similar purity and insight, although she succeeded in transcending her invalidism where Saint-Denys-Garneau ultimately failed. She is highly regarded; and now publishes mainly in France. 'Manor Life', in F.R. Scott's (q.v.) version, is one of her most characteristically sombre, austere and exact poems. It concludes:

> See, these mirrors are deep
> Like cupboards
> There is always someone dead behind the quicksilver

Who soon covers your reflection
And clings to you like seaweed

Shapes himself to you, naked and thin,
And imitates love in a long bitter shiver.

(CWT)

Anne Hébert has also written two delicately evocative novels, *The Wooden Rooms* (*Les Chambres de bois*, 1958; tr. *The Silent Rooms*, 1974) and *Kamouraska* (1970; tr. 1973). A third novel was rightly rejected as over-sensational: the influence of Julian Green (q.v.) had been taken too far. (OBCV; CWT)

The best known French-Canadian poet of the younger generation is **Jean-Guy Pilon** (1930), whose poetry is, however, more deliberately cosmopolitan than personal. (OBCV; CWT)

*

Fiction that is not merely provincial has been even slower to establish itself than poetry in Canada. The chief places of honour must go, in English to **Morley Callaghan** (1903), and in French to Gabrielle Roy (q.v.). Callaghan, a Canadian newspaperman, was first encouraged to write fiction by Hemingway (q.v.), who later introduced him to the American expatriates in Paris, about whom he has written understandingly in *That Summer in Paris* (1963). Callaghan is a realist novelist of very high quality, whose achievement has not been fully recognized except in his native Canada, and then belatedly. His harshness is somewhat modified by his devout Catholicism, but this is never polemically to the fore (unless compassion be a solely Christian quality). *Strange Fugitive* (1928), his first novel, was about a bootlegger. Much better was *It's Never Over* (1930), a haunting account of the sufferings of the friends and family of a man hanged for murdering a policeman. His first major work is *Such is My Beloved* (1934), dealing with a Roman Catholic priest's attempt, which leads to his destruction, to redeem two prostitutes. Here Callaghan dwells upon the dangerous resemblances between Christian love and opportunistic lust. His attitude towards his prostitutes is, especially for the Thirties, refreshingly unsentimental and unhysterical. *The Loved and the Lost* (1951) examines, with the same poignancy, Negro-white relations in Montreal; this shocked Callaghan's fellow Catholics. *A Passion in Rome* (1961) is a story of a love affair between two Canadians living in Rome, and raises the same issue as the earlier work: to what extent is love sexual opportunism? The magnificent short stories are collected in *Stories* (1959). Callaghan's earlier novels, and the two longer ones of 1951 and 1961 which I have mentioned, have been called 'gauche, tentative and implausible' by George Woodcock, a critic of whom it is always worth taking note. Woodcock's thesis is that Callaghan began his significant work with *Such is My Beloved*, continued it with the two superb novels *They Shall Inherit the Earth* (1935) and *More Joy in Heaven* (1937), and then faltered and tried unsuccessfully to become 'a novelist in the full-figured nineteenth-century manner' – and recaptured his earlier form only with *Close to the Sun Again* (1977). In essence Woodcock is right; but I believe that he underrates the longer novels – though most would agree that *A Fine and Private Place* (1975), about a neglected novelist, was a lapse. However, there is no doubt that it is in the *récit* (q.v.) and short story that Callaghan is at his greatest. *They Shall Inherit the Earth* is about a son who ruins his father by allowing a false charge to go unchallenged, and is a study in sin every bit as compelling as anything in Green, Greene, Bernanos or Mauriac (qq.v.). *More Joy in Heaven*, more American than Canadian, is quite simply one of the best crime stories ever written – although it is on the lucubrated theme of a criminal who is unable to reform because of his associations. *Close to the Sun Again* is as powerful as – and probably more laconic than – anything he has written: about an old tycoon who comes alive as death and lack of memory claw at him. Of his thirteen novels, just four have appeared in Great Britain. Yet he is one of the most versatile, moving, dense and poetic of any contemporary novelist in any language. There is plenty of room for disagreement about what is his best work, and critics do disagree – as they should about so great a writer. Those who have yet to know his books have a rich and rewarding experience before them. Callaghan, an immensely superior writer to the overrated Hemingway (q.v.), grasped early the lessons of naturalism (q.v.), Christian humanism of the most straightforward sort, and, above all, truth to inner and outer life. Even the first books are badly flawed only by the high standards he later set himself. The publication of his works in a uniform edition, and full critical attention, are now some thirty years overdue.

Gabrielle Roy (1907–83) was born in Manitoba; she was a teacher and an actress before becoming a writer. Her first novel, *The Tin Flute* (*Bonheur d'occasion*, 1945; tr. 1947), is a humourless but moving study of slum life in Montreal, with a bitter undertone of social accusation. *The Cashier* (*Alexandre Chenevert, caissier*, 1954; tr. 1955), her subtlest book, presents a bank-clerk, a character reminiscent of Duhamel's Salavin (q.v.). The well-written *Street of Riches* (*Rue Deschambault*, 1955; tr. 1957) consists of autobiographical sketches. *The Hidden Mountain* (*La Montagne secrète*, 1961; tr. 1962) tries to trace the mainsprings of artistic inspiration through the career of a painter who seeks beauty in Canada and then in Paris; this excursion into symbolism is unconvincing. *The Road Past Altamonte* (*La Route d'Altamonte*, 1966; tr. 1967), short stories many of which have their source in childhood experience, shows a return to form. Gabrielle Roy's strength as a novelist lay in her uncluttered view of ordinary lives, and her refusal to regard commercial 'progress' as a true human benefit.

Hugh MacLennan (1907–80), born in Nova Scotia, was another writer who from the beginning showed an awareness of the real problems facing Canadians; he continually urged his countrymen to abandon their collective inferiority complex and to face their problem of a divided culture with realism and maturity. After Princeton MacLennan went on to Oxford as a Rhodes Scholar, and while there travelled widely in Europe. He wrote, but did not publish, two novels in the early Thirties, while teaching in Canada; but then became aware that there was 'no known contemporary fiction being written in Canada' (either he had not read, or had misunderstood, Callaghan, q.v.), and so set himself the task of rectifying the omission. The result was *Barometer Rising* (1941), about the great munitions ship explosion in Halifax Harbour in 1917 (which he witnessed). *Two Solitudes* (1945) was the first Canadian novel to explore in depth and with real understanding the conflict between the descendants of the British and the French. *The Watch that Ends the Night* (1959) is a rather over-solemn novel about communism and Canadian intellectuals; but it is intelligent and humane. Like Gabrielle Roy (q.v.), MacLennan had little humour; in this respect both writers are overshadowed by the more cosmopolitan Callaghan. *Each Man's Son* (1951), however, is a major novel, in which compassion and insight fully compensate for the author's lack of a comic sense. This is one of the outstanding English-language studies of a too enclosed community. The portrait of the gentle smashed-up boxer Archie MacNeil is unforgettable and gives the lie to the charge that MacLennan is too trapped in his classical background and his university training to give a true account of 'ordinary' life. He followed this novel with *Return of the Sphinx*

(1967), and *Voices of Time* (1981), both worthy but less imaginative than his earlier books. He wrote with great sincerity on an old-fashioned 'grand scale'; it did not quite succeed, but he provided a service to Canadian literature which no one else did – and in *Each Man's Son* wrote a book which everyone ought to read.

Although of an older generation, **Ethel Wilson** (1890) did not publish her first novel, *Hetty Dorval* (1947), until she had reached almost sixty. The wife of a Vancouver doctor, Ethel Wilson is justly honoured by the younger generation as a shrewd, ironic and intelligent novelist. *Hetty Dorval* is a subtle study in promiscuity. All its successors are about love or emotions and attitudes that pose as love. *Equations of Love* (1952) describes a love affair through the eyes of a number of people, and then examines it in terms of the person who experienced it. *Love and Salt Water* (1956) is more overtly satirical. Ethel Wilson shares at least an acerbity of mind with Ivy Compton-Burnett (q.v.). Her stories, collected in *Mrs Golightly* (1961), are full of acute insight, but are disconcertingly glib in style.

The French-Canadian novelist, **Roger Lemelin** (1919), once 'the bad boy of present-day Canadian literature', began brilliantly with two realistic novels about the Lower Town of Quebec, where he had worked. Like Gabrielle Roy (q.v.) Lemelin compels attention by his refusal to settle for a complacent view of French-Canadian society. *The Town Below* (*Au Pied de la pente douce*, 1944; tr. 1948), a disrespectful and satirical tale, won a prize in France. *The Plouffe Family* (*Les Plouffe*, 1948; tr. 1950) – taken up as a weekly serial on television – is about an opera-singer who becomes a monk but then leaves his monastery to fight Nazism.

Two minor novelists, exact contemporaries, who share a concern with the Canadian creative predicament, are **Ernest Buckler** (1908) and **Sinclair Ross** (1908). Buckler's most outstanding novel is his study of a mute artist in *The Mountain and the Valley* (1952). Ross is less pessimistic; *As for Me and My House* (1941) is about a clergyman's and his wife's struggle to exist physically and spiritually in a prairie town. More interesting and vivid is the analytical *The Well* (1958), which deals shrewdly and sympathetically with a young man of criminal mentality. His two later novels are of less account.

Younger prose writers include Mordecai Richler, who long made his home in London but is now back in Canada; Brian Moore, who lives in America; Jack Ludwig, who works as a university teacher in the state of New York; and Margaret Laurence (qq.v.), who lived in Africa before settling in England. The fact that these and other highly self-consciously Canadian writers live abroad must mean something; it is probably, however, an indictment of the social rather than the strictly cultural environment. The French-Canadians tend to stay at home, although most of them publish in France – a few, such as Anne Hébert (q.v.), in France only.

Mordecai Richler (1931), a lively and intelligent writer much concerned with Jewish problems, has not yet – despite massive and somewhat irrelevant publicity campaigns – written the novel of which he is capable. His novels deal with the same kind of material as the poems of Klein (q.v.): he was brought up in a Jewish family in Montreal. He has not bettered his second novel, *Son of a Smaller Hero* (1955), about Jewish life in Montreal. *The Apprenticeship of Duddy Kravitz* (1959) is less sure in touch, but is written with verve and humour. The satirical *The Incomparable Atuk* (1963), about an Eskimo writer's success with Toronto intellectuals, is slighter but extremely funny. *Cocksure* (1968) is more ambitious and less effective; and the novels which followed it have not equalled *Son of a Smaller Hero*.

Brian Moore (1921) is a Belfast Irishman who emigrated to Canada after the Second World War. *The Lonely Passion of Judith Hearne* (1955) is a tender-tough study of an alcoholic spinster. His best known book, *The Luck of Ginger Coffey* (1960), is also his most specifically Canadian. Ginger Coffey is a middle-aged Irish immigrant in Canada: he finds himself bereft of wife, job and a sense of virility, and he can only respond by fantasizing and self-deceit. The processes through which he discovers the truth about himself and his situation are described with acute psychological penetration and feeling, although not without sentimentality. He has not yet bettered this novel; but its successors, which include *The Emperor of Ice-Cream* (1965) and *The Mangan Inheritance* (1979), have been of a high standard. (CWT)

Jack Ludwig (1922) is more experimental, and has learnt from Saul Bellow (q.v.), with whom he has collaborated on a periodical. Of his novels, the earliest, *Confusions* (1963), is by far the best. Especially notable in this study of an American Jew who goes to teach in California is Ludwig's grasp of the speech-habits of North American Jews (one of Bellow's special provinces). (CWT)

Margaret Laurence (1926) sets the best of her five novels, *Jest of God* (1966), in a small Canadian prairie town, Manawaka. The story of an unhappy and unfulfilled teacher's abortive love affair is told by herself with dignity and insight. The relationship between erotic and religious disturbance is delicately explored, and, as in all Margaret Laurence's fiction, small-town pressures on decency are rendered with fearful exactitude. She has written three books of short stories. (CWT)

*

A good deal of theatrical activity goes on in Canada, but there have so far been few really successful dramatists worthy of consideration. The French branch has had more vitality than the English. The dominant theatrical personality in Canada for the past thirty years has been the versatile actor, producer and playwright **Gratien Gélinas** (1909), known as **Fridolin** because of the series of revue sketches he wrote and played in between 1938 and 1946: these featured himself as the Chaplinesque Fridolin. *Lil' Rooster* (*Tit-Coq*, 1948; tr. 1950), a shrewd comedy about French-Canadians in the overseas Canadian armies during the Second World War, was more substantial, and enjoyed an immense and widespread success (except in New York). *Bousille and the Righteous* (*Bousille et les justes*, 1959) was another success in both English and French. Other French-Canadian playwrights include **Guy Dufresne**, **Félix Leclerc** (1914) – both authors of fairly successful plays – and the more serious **Paul Toupin**, whose *Brutus* and *The Lie* are interesting, but have not attracted the public. However, **Jacques Languirand**, a close disciple of Beckett and Ionesco (qq.v.), has aroused some interest. The leading playwright of the younger generation is the prolific **Marcel Dubé** (1930) whose *Zone* (1955) and *Florence* (1950) are black farces of some originality.

English-Canadian drama is sparse on the ground, although there are numerous performances in many cities. Canada's most distinguished English-language playwright is **Robertson Davies** (1913), also a novelist (whose work has been overpraised by Bellow, q.v.). Davies, an ex-actor who became an academic, gained success with the one-act *Eros at Breakfast* (1948), which he followed with the full-length *Fortune My Foe* (1949). His novels portray small-town Canadian life satirically but lovingly. He adapted *Leaven of Malice* (1954), a satire on intellectuals, for the stage in 1960. He is an intelligent writer whose work is unfortunately not free from a sentimentality and a heavy mock-profundity that too often masquerades as wisdom. He was an amusing light satirical novelist who lost his touch when he tried to become serious.

Chinese Literature

Modern Chinese literature begins late: in 1919, with the movement called the Literary Revolution. This was a logical development from the political revolution of 1911, which, although not really successful (Sun Yat-sen was unable to establish his authority over the whole of China), created a climate of change. Of all the literary languages of the world not yet supplanted by the colloquial, the Chinese was probably the most hopelessly out of touch with the actual life of the first two decades of this century. It was a language foreign to the common people. It is thus waste of time to discuss writers of this century whose works are in classical Chinese: they are accessible to no-one – and the serious efforts are not in effect superior to the titillating semi-pornographic 'Mandarin Duck and Butterfly' fiction – stuff about prostitutes – which flourished in the first decade of the century. All that can be said is that the fiction of the period 1900–17 paved the way for later, more serious work in the vernacular. A heap of novels satirical of the maladministered Chinese society of the time helped make the linguistic breakthrough inevitable. Only the crude theatre, performed by students, of the Spring Willow Society (1907), was in the vernacular. It cannot be said that since 1919 Chinese literature, whose past poetry, at least, is one of the glories of the world, has attained much distinction (except in one case, Wen-i-to, q.v.). Between then and 1937 China was torn apart by civil war and then by the war with Japan (1937–45); there followed four more years of civil war. In 1949 the communists came to power. Little is known in the West, and less understood, about their impact upon Chinese society. But literature has, for the time being, been a casualty, if we are to rely on the translated material that is sent out of Pekin, which consists of abject socialist realist (q.v.) fiction that is quite certainly more simple-minded than was the government of Mao Tse-tung, himself once a very minor poet, and until recently advertised in his own country as a major one.

It is necessary, before discussing the very few Chinese twentieth-century writers of any distinction, to make some remarks on the political background. Too frequently it is assumed that the peasants – still the vast majority of the huge population of China – have been plunged, by communism, into a hell that contrasts with an idyllic past. Whatever one may feel or think about communism, this is not so. When Sun Yat-sen died in 1925 he was trying to accommodate the communists into his Kuomintang party, whose 'three principles' were already 'nationalism, democracy, socialism'. Chiang Kai-shek seized the leadership and proceeded to violate these principles. Until 1937, when it became necessary for the Chinese to unite against the common enemy, the country was alive with war: not only the civil war, but also feudal wars between warlords – for power and plunder.

On 4 May 1919 Chinese students, supported by intellectuals, rose in violent protest against the Versailles Treaty decision to cede former German territory in Shantung to the Japanese. Intellectuals were putting forward their claims to judge and to control foreign policy. Magazines in the colloquial began to appear. The young suddenly felt emancipated. Their spirit was Chinese – this is often misunderstood – but the ideas came from the West. Eventually this led to confusion: the Chinese civilization is not Western, and the greatness of its literature is based in Chinese and not Western concepts. This, perhaps, underlies some of the difficulties experienced by the Chinese in adapting themselves to the complex and self-contradictory theories of a complex and self-contradictory nineteenth-century German Jew; it also explains the complex nature of Chinese political attitudes towards the West, which are not simply 'Marxist', and are certainly not as simply hostile and aggressive as many of us may be led to believe. One of the problems is translation. Mao went against Marxist theory in carrying through a peasant, not a proletarian, revolution.

The leading spirit in the literary revolution was the critic, versifier and scholar **Hu Shih** (ps. **Hu Hung-hsing**, 1891–1962), who studied at Cornell University in the USA, and then at Columbia. Hu studied under Dewey (q.v.), and was much influenced by T.H. Huxley. He was Chinese ambassador to the USA 1938–42, and ended his life in Taiwan. Hu Shih pronounced the literary language (*wen-yen*) to have been dead for two thousand years, and proposed to substitute for it a form of the vernacular (*pai-hua*) that had been employed in the popular literature, which was regarded as vulgar by the classical writers. He was a professor at Pekin University from 1917 until 1926, and was thus in a position to get his ideas put into practice. But he was not revolutionary by temperament, and was glad to leave the polemics to his friend and supporter, the essayist Ch'en Tu-hsui (1879–1942), a founder of the Chinese Communist Party, who wrote (1917): 'Down with ornate toadying aristocratic literature to build a simple and lyrical literature ... a fresh and sincere realistic literature ... a clear, popular social literature'. New translations into the vernacular of important European writers, including Ibsen, Chekhov and Strindberg (qq.v.), followed. All this was part of the great process, begun under the impact of the West, of the breaking down of the supremacy of the intellectual élite: both Confucianism and the old examination system had gone; now young Chinese, as young Japanese almost fifty years before them, were anxious to acquire knowledge of foreign languages and Western technology.

By the beginning of the Twenties the language battle had been won, and the vernacular (now renamed *kuo yu*, or national language) was established. There was a spate of social realism in the drama and in fiction (nearly always in the form of the short story). Poetry did not fare so well, as Hu Shih's *Experimental Verse* (1916) had already made clear. In this less than thirty years of freedom (until 1949, when socialist realism was imposed) modern Chinese literature did not have time to develop. The literature of its classical period had lasted for nearly three millennia; it is not yet time to judge that of its modern period.

The political background in those thirty years was not conducive to the growth of a new literature. Civil war existed between Chiang Kai-shek's ruling Kuomintang, the warlords and the Chinese Communist Party (formed 1921). Chiang made a deal with the warlords and turned on the communists in 1927. By then writers had become disillusioned. In 1922 the Creation Society had been formed, chiefly inspired by the poet and critic Kuo Mo-Jo (q.v.). The writers of this group were influenced by European romanticism and, like their earlier Japanese counterparts, by *fin de siècle* decadence (qq.v.); but all were social revolutionaries, if of varying hues. The group was proscribed in 1929 by Chiang Kai-shek, who thus dealt a blow to the development of his country's literature – just as his autocratic rule disguised, for the benefit of gullible Americans, as democracy prepared the way for the communism which he (at all times) maintained would ruin China. His rule from the beginning was corrupt and based on corruption. A number of the Creation writers and critics returned to Japan (until 1937), the country where they had originally learned about Western literature.

The outstanding figure in modern Chinese literature, and the fullest artist so far to manifest himself outside poetry, is **Lu Hsin** (ps. **Chou Shu-Jen**, 1881–1936). (His name is variously written, as Chinese is variously transliterated; he often appears as Lu Xun.) Lu Hsin was dissatisfied with Chinese society from his earliest student days, and he set out to be a writer in order to provide a cure. Until his disillusioned last days, when he cooperated with the communists, he was remarkably consistent in his objectives. As a young man he studied medicine in Japan, taught at various universities, and translated some Russian stories. He wrote his first short story, 'Diary of a Madman', in 1918, especially for the inaugurators of the literary revolution; twenty-five more followed. Besides this first one, 'The True Story of Ah Q' (tr. 1926; 1956) is his most famous. He was an important critic, whose *Brief History of Chinese Fiction* remains the best Chinese criticism of this century. Three of his stories are translated in *Modern Chinese Stories* (1970), from which useful publication, containing many stories by younger writers, the reader may judge the quality of modern Chinese fiction.

Lu Hsin spent his last years issuing polemics from Shanghai, under various pseudonyms, against the nationalist government. He was continually in danger of assassination by Chiang Kai-shek's hired killers. But he never joined the communist party – although he is still revered by it – and a year before he died of tuberculosis he wrote: 'Once a person gets inside the Party he will be bogged down in meaningless complications and quarrels. ...' Lu Hsin was an individualist, whose social indignation was essentially nondogmatic. No writer of modern Chinese prose can match either his economy or the degree of human feeling that he gets into stories. Such a writer would now be stifled, which suggests that one of the many faults of the Chinese communists is that they have not yet learned to cope with imaginative literature.

Mao Tun (ps. **Shen Yen-Ping**, 1896), in favour until the Sixties – and Minister of Culture 1949–64 – wrote some competent realistic novels in the Thirties, including *Midnight* (1933; tr. 1957). He was severely censured for allegedly supporting the ownership of private property in *The Lin Family Shop* (written before the revolution but translated in Pekin in 1957).

Ting Ling (ps. **Chiang Ping-Chih,** 1907–85), who vanished from the literary scene in 1957 when she was accused of rightist tendencies (this was not long after she had unsuccessfully denounced her ex-husband **Shen Ts'ung-Wen**, 1903, a popular storyteller, as 'bourgeois'), wrote some of the best Chinese fiction in the period before the Japanese invasion of 1937. It is sensationalist by Western standards; but the subject-matter of *Water* (1933)–group-life–and of certain short stories–sexual incompatibility between communists and non-communists–represented a sincere attempt to deal realistically with the personal problems of people living in politically disturbed times. *The Sun Shines over the Sangkan River* (1948; tr. 1954), which got a Stalin Prize, is about land reform. She has recently been declared rehabilitated, somewhat like the last Manchu Emperor, who after 're-education' lived as a private citizen in Peking–he had been puppet-Emperor of Manchuria, 'Manchukuo' (1932), for the Japanese, and imprisoned in Siberia 1945–50, which demonstrated the value the Chinese put on rehabilitation. But whereas ex-Emperor Henry Pu-yi (died 1967) was occasionally invited to receptions for foreigners, Ting Ling lived quietly.

Pa Chin (ps. **Li Fei-Kan**, 1904), at one time an anarchist (PA ━ BAkunin, CHIN ━ KropotKIN), is best known for his trilogy *Torrent* (1933–40), of which the first volume, *Family* (1933), was translated in 1958. This effectively describes his own struggles against, and escape from, his traditional upbringing in a wealthy family; but it is excessively sentimental. Since 1949 he has written little fiction.

Of this group of novelists the best known in the West was **Lao She** (ps. **Shu Ching-Chun**, 1899–1966), because he made contacts when he was living in London 1926–37.

His use of Pekin dialect was much admired. He also wrote plays. Some of his novels are *City of Cats* (1933; tr. 1964), *The Quest for Love of Lao Lee* (1933; tr. 1948), *Rickshaw Boy* (1937; tr. 1945) – his best known and most successful book – and *The Yellow Storm* (1946–50; tr. 1951). Lao She was slight, professional, a slick portrayer of character, and pleasantly humorous.

No major novel has been written in China since the Revolution. The Cultural Revolution (a brutal movement, 1965–8, to assert Maoism against 'revisionism' – it proved a mistake, both economically and intellectually) silenced many writers. Some of these reappeared, but it has made no difference. If writers can write only about specific subjects, literature is temporarily dead. Mao's 'Hundred Flowers' policy of 1957 ('let the parties contend') was far too short-lived to achieve results.

*

At first the new poetry seemed crude. One of the earliest poets was a politically very flexible one, although he was less insincere than excitable. At the same time, **Kuo Mo-Jo** (1892–1978) was talented and knowledgeable, and far superior to the man who ran literature, Chou Yang – a trivial writer. He was never a really interesting poet – he could be described as a Chinese Lundqvist (q.v.). First he co-founded the Creation Society (1921), which advocated art for art's sake in a fairly simplistic fashion. Then he fled to Japan when the purge of communists began, at the time of the nationalist-communist split in 1927. In 1937 he came back to China: at this time the warring factions formally joined together to resist the Japanese attack. After the communist victory in 1949 he became an important cultural figure; but he was a genuine scholar of ancient Chinese social customs. Somehow he survived – being, so to say, genuinely sympathetic towards each new development in Chinese government. At heart he was an excited and enthusiastic romantic, good at the art of verse craftsmanship – and not at all the villainous opportunist he could be made out to be. Part of his early and zestful reformist volume, firing out Utopian dreams like bullets from a machine gun, was translated as *Selected Poems from the Goddesses* (1958). It is not a bad social verse, influenced by Tagore as well as Whitman (qq.v.). Later he became a sort of Becher (q.v.). His poems of old age were in a sober and classical mode; his vitality had gone.

Ai Ching (ps. **Chiang Hai-Cheng**, 1910) is more interesting as a poet. His best poems come from the period 1935–41: these are propagandist, but manage to say better things than 'The glorious future awaits!', a slogan which is scattered, in various forms, throughout Chinese poetry of these and the post-revolutionary years. One feels that Ai Ching wanted to say more than this – and his anxieties are often apparent in the language of his poetry. Ai Ching had been steeped in the poetry of Rimbaud and the French symbolists (q.v.), and this influence never left him. 'The dried pond is like the blind eye of our earth' is not at all typical of propagandist poetry – and Ai Ching's is full of such images: nervous, tending to describe the suffering incurred by revolutionaries, instead of the benefits of revolution. Of villagers: 'Their eyes are dulled and blank with endless disappointments and sorrows'. He concentrated on the negative side of life – because that was his nature – but was not able to find his own way through to any sort of substantial affirmation. Instead he had to 'confess his faults', and try to write a dreary verse which he did not believe in. He was purged in 1957, and unheard of until 1977, when he was 'rehabilitated' after the fall of the 'gang of four'. He was even allowed to go to America.

Hsu Chih-Mo (1895–1931) and **Wen I-to** (1899–1946), founders of the 'Crescent School', which wanted to combine traditional influences with romantic foreign ones, were the two most gifted poets of the century; but the latter was very much more so than the former, 'the Chinese Shelley'. Hsu was killed in an air crash. He had been a friend of H.G. Wells, Katherine Mansfield (qq.v.) and a pupil of Harold Laski. He studied at Cambridge, and acted as Tagore's (q.v.) interpreter when he toured China (1924). Outside China he is better known than Wen, which is a pity, since his gift lay in technique rather than in poetry itself – whereas Wen has the broodingly acrid integrity of a Hagiwara (q.v.). The gifted Hsu himself spoke of the 'meticulously executed works of I-to' and of his own comparative lack of self-control. He was attracted by the English limerick form, and would experiment in this to write perfervidly sentimental love lyrics (his love life was 'scandalous'). Even at his best he could write of 'melting' into a woman's breasts in a general atmosphere of lotuses and floating snowflakes. Yet technically what he did is very interesting. Like Wen, he knew that the Chinese poetry of the time was exhausted, and he wanted to reinvigorate it. But his poetry is not as quintessentially Chinese in spirit as Wen's. People were impressed by his Chinese enthusiasm for English romantic poetry, and by his fervent nature – and so tended to overrate his well wrought but over-romantic poetry. His best work is to be found in the posthumous volume *Wandering in the Clouds* (1932). In the famous poem 'Love's Inspiration' he seemed to be getting nearer to originality and to his own voice – and he was only thirty-five:

> It isn't important: you just sit down first,
> The instant's not right – I think it's
> Already finished, already totally
> Vanished, from this world. Floating, without care,
> I don't know where I am. As if there's
> A cloud like a lotus, gripping me
> (On her face is a smile like a lotus)
> Imprisoning me in the remotest land ...

The trouble is that the original is marred by inversion and other bad habits Hsu picked up from his devotion to nineteenth-century English poetry. Both he and Wen had seen how fatal an influence Whitman (q.v.) could be – but in his case he could have profited from following Whitman at least in using words in their natural, and not in a 'poetical', order.

Wen-I-to was a quite different case. From the start he saw that some kind of form was inevitable in poetry: 'no poem can be written without form', just as 'no game can be played without rules'. Wen's Western model was Keats; but he had a Chinese model, too, very firmly in his mind – the ninth-century poet Li Shang-yin. His superiority over all other Chinese poets of his time is immediately apparent, even in early poems:

> Angular from the green arch are some hard thin
> Elm boughs which have not yet quite caught up with spring.
> They are printed on the fish-scale sky,
> Light-blue, clouded writing-paper
> On which the monk Huai-ssu has inscribed
> His aduncous script of iron and silver sweeps.

But his greatest poem gave the title to his second and last book of poems: *Dead Water* (1928) bears an uncanny resemblance to Quasimodo's poem (q.v.) of the same title – though it is conceivable that the Italian could then have known of Wen's poem, it is unlikely:

This is a ditch of hopelessly dead water.
No fresh breeze can disturb its surface.
Why not throw in some bits of rusty metal
Or even some of your surplus food and soup?

Perhaps the copper will transform the green into jade,
Perhaps the rust on the can will bloom like peach –
So let the grease reticulate a silken braid,
And bacteria spew out clouds of colour.

Let this dead water ferment, into a ditch of green wine
Crammed with floating foam like white pearls,
The blatter of tiny pearls transmuting to huge pearls
Though they'll be pricked when gnats alight to taste the wine.

So a ditch of hopelessly dead water
May still arrogate an iota of glory.
And if the frogs cannot endure the solitude
Let them burst into songs of praise.

This is a ditch of hopelessly dead water,
A place where beauty could never live.
May as well let evil have its way here:
Examine what sort of world it can make.

The ditch was, of course, China – but it may as well have been the world. Frightened of his own pessimism, Wen more or less abandoned poetry to preach a cautious and not altogether convincing theory of literary 'commitment'. He became increasingly critical of Chiang-Kai-shek's handling of the corrupt government, and was mentioned as a possible prime minister who could unite the country. But that was too correct a judgement: in 1946 he was riddled with bullets at the orders of the Kuomintang leader, who thus put himself into the position of the assassins of Lorca (q.v.): the inflated war-lord put the seal of dishonour on his name for ever.

The most successful aspect of the Chinese theatre since 1949 has been the lavish and of course re-vamped Peking Opera, which had been dominant since the early nineteenth century; but these socialist realist (q.v.) vehicles, while very highly effective, have no literary merit. After 1919 sometimes grotesque versions of plays by Ibsen, Shaw and even Galsworthy (qq.v.) provided social protest drama. In the Thirties there were many more or less spontaneous street plays; the communists also encouraged agitprop 'living newspaper drama', which flourished in other countries. These manifestations have not continued since 1949, as their very spontaneity might produce criticism of a wrong-headed nature. **Tien Han** (1898–1968), another founding member of the Creation Society (q.v.), who was savagely attacked during the cultural revolution (q.v.), was the leading communist dramatist. He wrote the words of the communist national anthem. He worked for the Opera, but also produced many plays and films – including a twenty-act didactic tragedy with performers, slides, and film clips. He began to get into trouble with

Hsieh Yao-Huan (1961) – the Tang protagonist is executed after asking the Empress for political reforms. The play which really established the vernacular drama, though, was written by **Tsao Yu** (ps. **Wan Chia-Pao**, 1910) in 1934: *Thunder and Rain* (tr. 1936), which he followed with two more plays to make up a trilogy. The whole trilogy has now been better translated – *Thunderstorm* (tr. 1958), *Sunrise* (tr. 1960), *The Wilderness* (tr. 1979). These plays are the first and almost the last to adapt Western methods successfully to the Chinese stage, and, although highly ideological, they would still play well anywhere. They created a great stir in China; it has been rightly said that they still haunt the mind with 'emotional conflict'. **Hung Shen** (1894–1955), one of Baker's (q.v.) students, did a great deal for the Chinese theatre and film, and wrote several credible plays on rural themes. In later times the plays of **Ho Ching-Chi** (1924) have been popular, especially *The White-Haired Girl* (1945; tr. 1953), which he wrote in collaboration with another less well-known dramatist. Tsao Yu's plays of the Fifties were not as good as his earlier trilogy, but *Bright Skies* (1956) and *Gall and Sword* (1962) contained original elements. Lao She's (q.v.) plays of the same period were both popular and effective. With the advent of the cultural revolution the traditional Peking Opera was abolished completely. There was even a crackdown on all drama – but it is now being revived and there are some signs of greater freedom. The Red Guard episode was in part unleashed by a play written by **Wu Han** (1909), a deputy-mayor of Peking. In *The Dismissal of Hai Jui* (1961) he implied that the past is instructive: this was dangerously revisionist. *1500 Modern Chinese Novels and Plays* (1948) contains a great deal (perhaps too much) information up to its date of publication; it emanated from the Peking Catholic University Press, so that it has its point of view. *Modern Drama from Communist China* (1970) is informative. But, as with fiction, this is a theatre which is more interesting from the sociological and historical viewpoint than from the literary.

The Chinese literature of exile, or from Taiwan (formerly Formosa), has not produced much. The first wave of 'literature' from Taiwan matched that of the mainland in tendentiousness. **Eileen Chang** (orig. **Chang Ai Ling**, 1920) has provoked controversy. Her father was a member of a family once prominent in the service of the Manchu dynasty, her mother a cosmopolitan. How accurate she has been about her father's ill treatment of her is open to question, since she was clearly over-devoted to her mother. She has been called the greatest Chinese writer of the century, but by unthoughtful anti-communists – she is certainly not 'great' at all. She left China for Hong Kong in 1952, and after that went to America, where she has taught in several universities. She at first made her living by romances published in popular magazines; these are worthless, and even their chief admirer has referred to their 'intimate boudoir realism'. They were collected in 1944 (*Romances*). In Hong Kong she wrote *The Rice Sprout Song* (1954; tr. 1955), which she translated herself. This is a story of peasants being asked for more than they can afford to pay towards the Korean war effort. It is more dissident than literary, though what it depicts probably happened – but the story is not well told, the author being more indignant than imaginative. *The Naked Earth* (1954; tr. 1956) is more sophisticated, but is, again, more in the nature of polemic than literature. Chang's creative achievement – such as it is – hardly lies within the scope of this book: it is rooted in the romances she wrote as a young woman. She uses unpleasantness to revenge herself for being Chinese at all, as *The Rouge of the North* (1967), based on an early short story about pre-revolutionary China, demonstrates. She has shown no real concern for China in her disguised polemic; but it is hard to justify the remark that in her romances her use of imagery is 'compelling and subtle'. Essentially she has tried to make use of the traditional literature, and has misunderstood it (perhaps as her Westernized mother did) and failed.

In another category **Chen Jo-Hsi** (1938), who lived in the republic for many years, has written a serious and thoughtful account of the cultural revolution in *The Execution of Mayor Yin* (1976; tr. 1978): anyone who wants to understand the impact of this episode should read this book. She has written the best novel of dissent – whether the reader agrees with her position or not – so far; and it stands up as a book in strictly literary terms.

Czechoslovakian Literature

I

The modern Republic of Czechoslovakia came into being in autumn 1918. However, a vigorous literature was already extant in Czech and, to a lesser extent, in Slovak. Literary Czech was fully developed in 1348, when Prague University was founded; the nineteenth-century patriots had the rich tradition of the earliest great Slavonic literature to draw upon. Czech and Slovak are similar (the Czecho-Moravian dialect is actually a transition between the two languages, with a largely similar vocabulary). The Czechs have dominated the modern period (with the exception of the immediate post-1945 period), but there have been a few important Slovak writers. The only two writers to have achieved a truly international reputation are Hašek and Čapek (qq.v.).

Czechoslovakian literary development parallels that of Europe: liberalism and nationalism were followed in the Nineties by scepticism (the future first President of the Czechoslovak Republic, **T.G. Masaryk**, 1850–1937, then Professor of Philosophy at Prague University, was the leading anti-romantic), which existed side by side with the decadent *fin-de-siècle* mood common to every country. Jaroslav Vrchlický (ps. **Emil Frida**, 1853–1912), often contrasted with Čech (q.v.) – because where the latter represented 'nationalism' he represented 'cosmopolitanism' – was receptive to all these phases, and then to symbolism (q.v.). His epic poetry is marked by skill and superb craftsmanship, but is bogged down in solemnity. However, his technical influence, and the example he set of going to French and English rather than to German literature, have been of importance in the development of Czech poetry. Undoubtedly his influence is more important than his work. For the last four years of his life he was mad.

The beginning of Czech poetry is always dated from Karel Hynek Mácha's (1810–36) epic poem *May* (1836; tr. 1949): this not only embodies the romantic revolt of the individual against society, but also foreshadows the Nietzschean revolt against God – and even the universe itself. This attitude conflicted with the upsurge of Czech nationalism that followed Mácha's death; but it is always as well to remember that this (philosophically) thoroughgoingly negative epic lies at the back of all the Czech poetry that followed it. This applies in approaching the work of **Otokar Březina** (ps. **Václav Ignác Jebavý**, 1868–1929), the first major Czech poet after Mácha. Březina, born in southern Bohemia, became a schoolmaster. In him we see the impact of Schopenhauer and Nietzsche (q.v.), and then of French symbolist procedures (q.v.) on a mind wholly Czech. It was Březina who imported symbolism into Czech poetry. The usual account of him claims that he convincingly transformed his bleak pessimism into an optimistic vitalism; this is somewhat misleading. His first book of poetry, *Mysterious Distances* (1895), is immature in content – decadent, Nietzschean, sorrowful – but assured in style. By the time of *Polar Winds* (1897), his third book, he had found his own voice: in a highly disciplined free verse, which has had a great influence, he expressed a Spinozan acceptance of all things, including evil and suffering, as part of an incomprehensible pattern. *Builders of the Temple* (1899; tr. 1920) concentrates, however, on the suffering rather than the pattern – and is his best book. *Hands* (1901), his last collection of verse, has possibly been misunderstood; it is not his best work, as it is too intellectualized, and he withdrew into a disgruntled twenty-eight-year silence after it. It returns to the earlier mood of Spinozan acceptance, but its return to more traditional forms and hymning of life are not altogether convincing. The essays in *The Music of the Springs* (1903) are much more so, and their subtlety has hardly been noticed. Březina was a true symbolist in that he preferred his inner world to the outer one: his real message is not more optimistic than Mácha's – but ultimately he felt obliged to mute it in the interests of a specious mysticism.

The opposite tendency is to be found in **Karel Toman** (ps. **Antonín Bernášek**, 1877–1946) and **Viktor Dyk** (1877–1931). Both began as ironic decadents, but then turned into nationalist poets – melodious but superficial. The latter became a politician and conservative polemicist during the last decade of his life. Toman lived to see himself, in the last year of his life, promulgated as 'national poet'.

More frequently read now than either of these are the unashamedly decadent poet **Jiří Karásek ze Lvovic** (1871–1951) and, more important, **Petr Bezruč** (ps. **Vladimír Vašek**, 1867–1958), who continually revised his one book *Silesian Songs* (1903 rev. 1909; rev. 1937; tr. 1966). He was a spokesman for the Silesians, but his poetry is not really political – rather it is simply regional. His pseudonym (not the only one he used) means 'Peter without Hands' and, although a shy man, it was as local bard that he began and ended. His poetry is as effective as the poetry of protest can be, and is superior to that of his friend **Josef Machar** (1864–1942), who influenced him. Machar's 'minor' poems are now seen to be his best – together with his verse novel *Magdalena* (1894; tr. 1916), about a prostitute who fails to make a marriage because of small-town gossip and hypocrisy.

The Czech version of expressionism (q.v.), the most important phase of which was 'poetism' (q.v.), at first took the form of an earthy naturalism, the chief exponent of which was the communist **Stanislav Kostka Neumann** (1875–1947), who wrote novels and influential criticism as well as poetry. His best poems – personal and relaxed – are contained in *Love* (1933); his most influential book, however, was *New Songs* (1918). He had begun as a crude vitalist, then developed, under pressure of war, into a poet of everyday things: *Love* represents his early sexual vitalism modified by experience. He was essentially shallow; but was for long a very popular and admired poet. **Josef Hora** (1891–1945) was a more interesting and complicated poet. His expressionism at first took a political form – his first volumes reveal him to be a proletarian and even unanimistic (q.v.) poet. *A Tree in Blossom* (1920) and *Working Day* (1920) are devoted to wartime Prague: its collective will to freedom and independence during the First World War, and its individual workers. Hora became a communist, but both the ruthless programme of the party and the pull of his native countryside induced him to leave it in 1929. He had also been reading Bergson and James (qq.v.), who appealed to his essentially metaphysical sensibility. Then, consciously following the romantic pessimism of Mácha, he wrote his most convincing poems, especially those in *Variations on Mácha* (1936), one of the most overwhelmingly Czech of all modern collections, in which nineteenth-century Gothic (tombs, witch-lovers, death) is subjected to a thoroughly modernistic sensibility. Eventually, under the pressure of the betrayal of Czechoslovakia and the pending Nazi occupation, Hora tried to regain some of his faith in life. *Jan the Fiddler* (1939) subsumes under its story of a musician who leaves his homeland for many years of exile, only finally to return, Hora's own development. He meets the lover he parted with years before, long married, as a stranger:

> A black piano. Katie dressed in black,
> black hair above her forehead braided high.

So was it that she met her friend come back
after some twenty years had passed them by.
His lamp-lit room seemed darkened to her eye.
'Autumn? Let us not think of that tonight.'

(PP)

But in truth this is a gloomy poem, concealing profound despair. Hora was never shallow like Neumann (q.v.); but ideas vitiated most of his poetry, which is only occasionally entirely his own. He exercised a strong influence after his death.

Jiří Wolker (1900–24), who died of tuberculosis, was eventually a more thorough-goingly proletarian poet. Convinced that he was of English descent (from a family named Walker), he was a typically expressionist figure, and reminds one slightly of Georg Heym (q.v.), in that he was a keen open-air type and loathed, or said he loathed, all forms of bohemianism. And, just as Heym kept a skull on his desk, so he read and studied Oscar Wilde (q.v.). He came to Prague to study law, but the misery of the working classes, contrasted with the ancient magnificence of the city, called forth from him the extra-ordinary poetry of *The Guest in the House* (1921), which is not only unanimist (q.v.) and Tolstoian in its call for universal love and brotherhood but also shot through and through with Czech country lore and magic. One is reminded of Esenin (q.v.) in his optimistic phase, and of Else Lasker-Schüler (q.v.). But the main inspiration is Wolker's own. Čapek's (q.v.) important anthology of French poetry in translation (1920) also played a decisive part in Wolker's development – as it did in that of many other Czech poets. Then Wolker came under the influence of Hora's *Working Day* (q.v.), and produced the classic collection of the proletarian movement: *The Difficult Hour* (1922). The viewpoint behind this combines a Dostoevski- or Bloy-like (q.v.) reverence for the poor – God's chosen ones – with a new radicalism, religious in its fervour. Wolker was intensely naïve, but this does not spoil his poetry. For the poems are beautiful in their intensity and their radicalism resembles Soviet poetry in its great early phase – not in its 'socialist realist' phase. Wolker was not an innovator in matters of form; but, more important, he created his own poetics. He was attacked, even by his friends, for his ideological views – and not wrongly – but in the best of his own poetry he entirely transcends these. The notion of human brother-hood transcends any possible notion of 'politics' even as practised by the relatively humane Masaryk (q.v.); and even if Wolker embraced these as an entity on the literary scene, his poems go beyond them.

Czech 'poetism', *poetismus*, whose chief spokesman was the critic and art-critic Karel Teige (1900–51), arose out of two previous rival groups: the *Devětsil* ('Colt's Foot'; 'Nine Powers') group – dedicated to revolution in all spheres of life – and a more conservative one, which produced the magazine *Host* (*The Guest*) and of which Wolker was the leading spirit. Teige had been the leading theoretician of the proletarian *Devětsil* group; but in 1924, following the poetic example of his friend Vítězslav Nezval (1900–58), he returned to the anti-dogmatic, non-political attitude from which he (rightly) deduced that the best of Czech poetry had emerged. Teige felt that he could not advocate pessimism, and so he defined 'poetism' as 'airy and playful, full of fantasy, unfettered and unheroic, with a bias towards love'. This provided the right kind of basis – a better one than social or socialist realism (q.v.) could have offered – upon which individual poets could build: nearly all the important Czech poets of the Twenties were associated with poetism, which later (1928) transformed itself into surrealism (q.v.) – a surrealism which had only tenuous links with Breton's (q.v.) movement, since the Czechs had their own rich past of love-horror, miracles and magic to draw upon. Prague itself in the period immediately before the break-up of the Austro-Hungarian Empire was to a certain extent 'surreal':

beauty, the past, the present, absurdity, and terror all co-existed uneasily in the great old city, as Hašek and Kafka (qq.v.) both show in their different ways. It is important to realize that the Czech modernist poets of the period between the wars did not personally reject political socialism and communism, even if they reserved the right to go their own way poetically. This can be seen most clearly in the work of Nezval: its contradictions are instructive.

Nezval, whom some still believe to be the most important Czech poet of the century, began with *The Bridge* (1922), a collection reflecting 'proletarian' intentions but shot through with the poet's own Czech vision, and much influenced by his reading of decadent poetry. The effect is already proto-surrealistic. His justification for making and living in his own world came from his conviction – crystallized when he heard **Jaroslav Seifert** (1901–85), a minor poet (and man of courage who raised his voice against the limitations of Stalinism) whose style has intelligently changed with the times, read a paper in 1922 – that truly revolutionary poets could reach the uneducated common man only through 'lowbrow' art: what was wanted was not Marx, incomprehensible to the worker in his bourgeois environment, but fantasy – fantasy that he would take as entertainment but which was really training him for the socialist millennium. In other words, Nezval, like Seifert, was one of those who anticipated pop-art. (Pop-art has now become a commercial parasite on true folk art, as Nezval would have seen.) But in fact Nezval, a truly gifted poet, was suffering from an acute case of *Künstlerschuld* (q.v.) – a disease which also troubled his fellow-Czechs Rilke and Kafka (qq.v.). The silent cinema, the Czech folk-heritage of fantasy and fairytale: all this had not yet been devitalized by commerce; besides, it offered him the excuse he needed to create his own world. His massive output between this time and 1938, when he broke with surrealism, is characterized by a violent and guilty confusion between two moods: an individualism undoubtedly felt as morbid (death, night, horror), and a lyrical affirmation of the brotherhood of man. In these ten years of frenzied activity Nezval reflected one of the confusions that haunt the heart of modern man. Thus his ideal poet of the remarkable epic *The Amazing Magician* (1922) is conceived in optimism; but he is really a tortured figure, who gains his power at the expense of his reason. Eventually the strain of fulfilling this role proved too much for Nezval, and he turned to communism and to the writing of patriotic poems. During the immediate post-war years he wrote routine hymns to Stalin and 'peace' (*Song of Peace*, 1950; tr. 1951), which display verbal dexterity but no poetic conviction. But he quickly became disillusioned (the suicide of his fellow-poet and close friend Konstantin Biebl in 1951 deeply disturbed him), was associated with elements hostile to socialist realism, and tried to intervene in cases of writers imprisoned under the Stalinist regime. His situation was not an easy one. His *Collected Works* appeared in twenty-four volumes (1950ff.). (TMCP)

František Halas (1901–49), the greatest modern Czech poet, also began in the proletarian movement and passed through a poetist phase; but he abandoned himself more fully than any other poet of his generation to what, in so highly political a context, must be known as 'subjectivism'. That 'subjectivism' in poetry is not necessarily equivalent to indifference to events is suggested by his eloquent collections *Wide Open* (1936) and *Torso of Hope* (1938). His collections between *Sepia* (1927), his first, and these had indeed been 'morbid' (one of the official Stalinist adjectives to be applied to his work after his death, when 'Halasism' became a word of opprobrium among the mediocre lackeys in charge of 'culture'), most particularly *The Cock Scares off Death* (1930), in which he wrote:

The world grown so familiar
lies on your dream
The grub within the rose.

(PP)

But in *Wide Open* (1936) he had so withdrawn from the external world as to picture himself being borne away, helplessly, by his dream. So that his return to a care for his country in *Torso of Hope* is not unconvincing: the only alternative would have been silence, and silence (as the poems indicate) was not his response to the disaster that threatened Czechoslovakia and the world. His war-time and post-war poetry certainly reflects a deepening pessimism, but it is never irresponsible or stupidly nihilistic. Probably his most characteristic volume of poetry is *Old Women* (1935; tr. 1947), where he mixes brutality with charm to illustrate the meaningless tragedy of ageing. He worked to help bring about the communist takeover. His death in 1949 may be taken, in George Theiner's words, as a 'symbolic event': his kind of poetry could not exist under Stalinism. He spoke of being 'whored up' after the communist takeover, which destroyed his illusions immediately. He died in great bitterness.

The tradition of Catholic mysticism, strong in Czechoslovakia, was represented by the Moravian **Jakub Deml** (1878–1961), a renegade priest who spent much of his time 'feuding', in Alfred French's words, 'with its living officers'. Deml reminds one in certain respects of Bloy (q.v.) whose work he knew well: his onslaughts on his enemies (including at one time or another everybody) were characterized by a similar convoluted bitterness, if not scatology. Like Bloy, Bernanos and Jouhandeau (qq.v.), Deml sees life on earth as a conflict between God and Satan; but his vision is of course Czech. His poetry recreates the world of the nineteenth-century romantics and of Březina (q.v.) in his own peculiar but none the less modern setting. One is often led to feel that his Catholicism was only another name for the inner world which he regarded as paramount. However, his work would be impossible to understand without the idea of a single God at its centre: a God who beckons him into this inner world. Deml, who translated Rilke (q.v.) into Czech, was regarded by Nezval (q.v.) as his master. The neglect into which he has fallen is due not only to his own scorn for readers and critics but also to the fact that he refused, after 1948, to have anything to do with the communists, and published no more in the remaining years of his life.

The main argument amongst the modernist Czech poets between the wars revolved around the question of social commitment; Catholicism was frequently seen as politically reactionary and conducive to artistic self-withdrawal or 'ivory-towerism'. The polemics were as transitory as most such polemics are; and the advent of socialist realism (q.v.) put paid to them for more than a decade. The more seriously a poet was identified with a position the less serious his work: the best poets were, like Nezval or Halas (qq.v.), confused and inconsistent in their attitudes – for it is in poetry, not polemical prose, that poets resolve their confusions.

Vladimír Holan (1905–80), whose first book appeared in 1926, emerged in the Thirties as a representative of 'pure poetry'; he styled himself a 'sombre poet, an apocalyptic poet'. It was not until the brief Thaw in Czechoslovakia that his poetry could be collected and appraised. He is now a dominant figure in Czech literature. He owes more than any other contemporary Czech poet to Valéry (q.v.), though the main influence in his work is Rilke (q.v.), whose grand 'flow' he could emulate. His earlier poetry was more abstract and intellectual than anyone else's of the time, and this cut him off from potential readers. But he developed into a much more accessible poet in his later years.

His most impressive and dense poem is *A Night with Hamlet*, which he wrote in 1949 and then revised continually until he was able to publish it in 1964. It is translated in *Selected Poems* (tr. 1971). Unusually, Holan's work has gained in authority as he has got older; but he is not a major poet as Halas (q.v.) obviously was. (NWC)

Several new poets emerged in the Sixties – it would have been impossible for them to do so before. The position for the Czech writer now, since the 1968 Russian invasion and the establishment of a government subservient to Moscow, is again depressing. The leading poet of the younger generation is (or was) **Miroslav Holub** (1923), who is as distinguished a scientist (he is an immunologist) as he is a poet. He has been translated into English extensively (*Selected Poems*, tr. 1967; *Although*, tr. 1971; NWC), which might give the impression that he is a more important poet than, say, Halas (q.v.) – who has not. This is not the case. He is not important at all. Like Seifert and Nezval (qq.v.) long before him, he wants to create a poetry that 'ordinary people' can read 'as naturally as they read the papers, or go to a football game'. But, unlike Seifert or Nezval, Holub is not a poet. He is against the lyrical-romantic Czech tradition, and uses a stark free verse. A. Alvarez (q.v.) has put him forward as a matter-of-fact poet of the electronic and industrial present, refusing to commit himself but rather accepting reality as it is. Be this as it may, his tedious, feeble verse has been enormously overrated outside Czechoslovakia – possibly because of Alvarez' over-enthusiasm. Clearly a man of intelligence and sophistication, Holub's poetry lacks robustness and linguistic excitement. It is as over-cerebral, in its way, as Holan's (q.v.) earlier work. He made (1973) a long and sickening 'recantation' of his support for the 1968 government, which may have been his response to some threat – but may not.

A much less frivolous poet than the tiresome Holub is **Ivan Diviš** (1924), whose language has energy, and who is perhaps the only poet in Czechoslovakia of this generation who is really interesting. (NWC) The initiative has otherwise passed to prose writers, though claims have been made – at a rather low level – for several young writers of a verse that is well meaning, readable, but simply uninspired.

*

In this century the Czechs have until recently probably achieved more in poetry than in fiction, with the exception of Hašek and Čapek (q.v.). **Jaroslav Hašek** (1883–1923), joker, anarchist and great novelist, was in himself a paradigm of the subversive artist. No wonder Brecht (q.v.) loved him. He would not have been happy for long under any authority. Hašek drank a good deal and frequently engaged the attention of policemen, whom he regarded with disfavour; he edited a fortnightly magazine called *The Animal World* in which he would from time to time invent animals or to which he would contribute articles with such titles as 'The Rational Breeding of Werewolves'; he twice seems to have falsely notified the authorities of his death, and to have composed an obituary of himself headed 'A Traitor'; he ran a dog-stealing business, forged pedigrees for mongrel dogs for which he would invent exotic names, and even wrote a guide on how to steal dogs; he stood as parliamentary candidate for his own Party of Moderate Progress Within the Limits of the Law (voters were promised a pocket aquarium); worst of all, his most famous book had to be banned to the armies of three countries (Czechoslovakia, Poland, Hungary) as 'detrimental to discipline'. ... Hašek's famous demotic masterpiece *The Good Soldier Švejk* (1920–23; tr. 1974) was left unfinished; the conclusion by Karel Vaněk is trivial.

Hašek wrote a great deal other than *Švejk*, of which only *The Tourist Guide* (tr. 1962) and the selection *The Red Commissar* (tr. 1981) are available in English translation; his other work – short stories, sketches, humorous and subversive essays – has been hidden for years, but is slowly becoming available and will presumably be translated in due course.

Švejk, for which Hašek wrote three sketches as early as 1908, is based on Hašek's experiences in the Austro-Czech army in 1915, before he deserted to the free Czech armies in Russia, where for two years he was an efficient commissar. The correct interpretation of the hero is undoubtedly that he is an anarchistic, anti-social figure and that he is not stupid (Hašek himself said that those who thought he was stupid were mistaken). He is also, of course, a Czech making fun of his Austrian masters. But this fat dog-fancier who entered the hearts of the people long before he entered the minds of the critics (the Masaryk regime, rather pompous, could not really take such irreverence) is essentially a man who despises authority and who knows how to get round it. Hašek and all his works certainly should be banned from any respectable society. For years *Švejk* could be written off as irresponsible fun; events have caused it to be revealed for what it is: a comic exhortation to individuals to defy the tyranny of officials and oppressors. It is magnificently there – as are the multiplying officials: a bible for the decent. But it is not a simple work. It reflects the absurd collage of its society in its structure, a collage of quotations, tall stories, flat narrative, dialogue; but Švejk is avenging, lonely, callous – and homeless. Although very funny, it is at heart a bleak book, which gives one pause to reflect on the despair which lies behind anarchy.

Karel Čapek-Chod (ps. **K. Čapek**, 1860–1927) lacked Hašek's comic genius, but shared, though from a socially more viable stance, his point of view. Čapek-Chod was a naturalist (q.v.), but only because he enjoyed demonstrating man's pointless struggles. The happy chronicler of the decay of the Prague bourgeoisie, he is Hardyesque (q.v.) in that he projects his own nihilism into Fate, making it into a teaser. But this is because he has aspirations to challenge his sense of absurdity; eventually he stopped short, merely telling bizarre tales of trapped men. Sometimes called 'the Zola of Prague', his gusto in describing decline is far greater than Zola's (q.v.), and he incorporates into it much Czech grotesquerie – although, as I have pointed out, the Czech situation under the Austro-Hungarian Empire was in itself grotesque – Slovakia, being simply a part of Hungary, escaped this, though it lost its identity as a price. *Antonín Vondrejc* (1917–18) is a satirical portrait of Prague intellectuals and bohemians; his best novel, *The Turbine* (1916), which was translated into French in the year of its publication (*La Turbine*), is a prophetic account of the impact of technology, with comic pictures of the kind of men who believe in it. *The Jindras* (1921) is a less satirical novel about a father-son relationship. Čapek-Chod published many excellent collections of novellas and short stories, such as *Five Novels* (1904) and *Four Audacious Stories* (1926). He was a tough, mocking and excellent writer who awaits an English translator.

Ivan Olbracht (ps. **Kamil Zeman**, 1882–1952), originally a lawyer, and a lifelong communist, became a fairly important politician after 1945. His father was a minor realist novelist. Although politics tempted him from his literary function, he was once regarded by many critics as Czechoslovakia's leading novelist. *Of Evil Solitary Men* (1913) consists of sketches about tramps and circus people, and rather uneasily combines the attitude of the early Gorki (q.v.) with an almost kitsch romanticism. It was his novel *The Strange Friendship of the Actor Jesenius* (1919) that established him. This is the story of a comedian, Jesenius, and his double, the actor Veselý; it is divided between the battlefront and the world of the Prague theatre. *Anne the Proletarian* (1928), simple-minded propaganda, is a tendentious failure. His best novel is *Nikola Šuhaj – Bandit* (1933; tr. 1954): here Olbracht projected his less respectable and more anarchistic feelings into the hero, a bandit of sub-

Carpathian Ruthenia who lived by his own laws, but who was a popular hero among the poor people of the area because he divided much of his booty among them. This has an epic sweep, and incorporates much Czech and Jewish lore. The stories of *The Bitter and the Sweet* (1937; tr. 1967) are set in the same region; some of them recall Babel (q.v.). He also wrote *The Darkest Prison* (1916), a powerful psychological novel of a blind man's jealousy, *Valley of Exile* (1937; tr. 1965), again set in Ruthenia, and *The Conquerors* (1947), ostensibly about the conquest of Mexico but really about the Nazis. During the occupation he wrote children's books, until arrested and imprisoned by the Nazis, in 1942.

Karel Čapek (1890–1938), who died, it was said, of a heart pierced by Chamberlain's umbrella, was one of the most intelligent of Czechoslovakian writers. The creative life of Čapek, who was novelist, playwright, essayist and journalist, exactly paralleled the life of Masaryk's Czech republic, which was also killed by 'Chamberlain's umbrella'. Čapek was the chief dramatist of the republic, but his novels are superior to his plays. He was Masaryk's close friend. Čapek at first studied science, and his early novels owe much to H.G. Wells (q.v.). His important and influential volume of translations from French poets has already been mentioned; in spite of this, he chiefly turned to English and American literature. He threw himself heart and soul into the affairs of his country, but his real attitude to life is expressed in his dictum that 'A short life is better for mankind, for a long life would deprive man of his optimism'. His brother Josef Čapek, primarily a cubist and primitivist painter but the co-author of some of the earlier works, perished in Belsen.

Čapek's plays include *R.U.R.* (1920; tr. 1923), *The Macropoulos Secret* (1922; tr. 1925) – made into an opera by Janáček – and, with his brother, *The Insect Play* (1921; tr. 1923). *R.U.R.*, written in the spirit of, and anticipating, Huxley's *Brave New World* (q.v.), gave the name 'robot' (*robotit*: to drudge) to the world. The robots revolt against their masters.

Čapek's novels, written in a clear language, try to educate his countrymen into democracy and vigilance against fascist aggression by means of Wellsean fantasy; but they involuntarily express a profound pessimism. *The Absolute at Large* (1922; tr. 1944) tries to deny the absolute – which is released among mankind as a gas. *Krakatit* (1924; tr. 1925) prophesies the atomic bomb. But Čapek's finest novel is *War with the Newts* (1936; tr. 1937), in which he satirizes and foresees both the coming Nazi holocaust and post-war European capitulation to commerce. A Czech sailor discovers some newts which resemble human beings; humanity exploits them; they revolt (led by a mad corporal) and triumph.

Čapek cannot be called a great writer. His work lacks real substance and vision. But he was a good man. Banned by Nazis and Czech Stalinists alike, he was 'rehabilitated' in Czechoslovakia only in the late Fifties, when his work had been made available in Moscow.

Jaroslav Durych (1886–1962), a doctor, was a neo-Thomic Catholic historical novelist whose sympathies with the working classes never wavered. He was an excellent critic, and was in fact a greatly superior writer to Čapek (q.v.). This led him into inconsistencies – his enthusiasm for the Counter-Reformation, for example, is hard to reconcile with his hatred of oppression – but his most outstanding work, the fantastic and expressionistic *The Descent of the Idol* (1929; tr. 1935), is strengthened by the tensions thus generated. This is set in the Thirty Years' War, and is the best of the many novels (and biographies) that have been written about Wallenstein, with whose career it deals. Durych's poems and dramas were unsuccessful, but in his best novel he succeeded in creating the kind of symbolist art advocated by his master Březina (q.v.). Durych was silenced by the government of 1945, and banned by the communists (except 1956–70); but Czechs still read him. He was aggressively Catholic and aggressively right-wing, but one of the most important of neo-Baroque writers.

Vladislav Vančura (1891–1942), also originally a doctor, was a steadfast communist throughout the Twenties and Thirties; he was shot by the Nazis as one of the reprisals for Heydrich, who had been killed by Czech patriots. Although his last novel, *The Family Horvat* (1938), shows some signs of the crudities which often characterize the socialist realist (q.v.) approach, Vančura was in fact a highly experimental writer, who introduced both colloquial and archaic words into the literary language. His books differ markedly from one another except in the densely baroque nature of their style. Though on the left, he is not as far from Durych (q.v.) as one might expect: both are expressionists, both struggle against intellectual ideologies. The best of his many novels are *The Baker Jan Marhoul* (1924), which although not always convincing in its portrayal of a man dedicated to communism is none the less powerful, *Markéta Lazarová* (1931), an adventure story set in medieval days, *The End of Old Times* (1934; tr. 1965), another adventure story – this time more satirical and with debts to the eighteenth-century French novel – and *Three Rivers* (1936), an analysis of a Czech intellectual's response to communism during and after the First World War. Vančura was proscribed by the Stalinists, but his works have had a strong influence on such writers as Kundera (q.v.).

The most readable socialist realist (q.v.) was **Marie Majerová** (ps. **Marie Bartošová**, 1882–1967), who although crude and sentimental was talented, a fine story-teller, and sincere. *Ballad of a Miner* (1938; tr. 1960) has genuine pathos because it was voluntary socialist realism – after the takeover she failed to perform to the Stalinists' satisfaction.

Milan Kundera (1929), born in Brno, was the first of the younger Czech novelists to react sharply against the dreary socialist realism of the Stalinist years. His chief novel is *The Joke* (1967), a proper English translation of which – replacing an inaccurate one – appeared in 1974; this is at once a satire on the fake communism of the Stalinists, on the opportunists who thrived under it, and on the Czech character itself. *Life is Elsewhere* (1979; tr. 1974) was published by Škvorecký on his émigré press – it first appeared in a French version in 1973 – long after Kundera had left Czechoslovakia (1975), since he was not allowed to publish there. *The Farewell Party* (tr. 1976) seems frivolous by the side of this study of a poet who sells out to Stalinism; but *The Joke* remains Kundera's best novel. (NCW) **Josef Škvorecký** (1924), now in Canada, wrote the first novel to look dispassionately at the Red Army's 'liberation' of Czechoslovakia in 1945: *The Cowards* (1958; tr. 1970). This differed considerably from the official version of these events, and was soon banned. One of the chief official objections was that the liberating army were described by Škvorecký as 'Mongolians'; from Canada he has retorted that he sees no objection to this, since he is not a racist. He has written a number of other books, including *Reflections of a Detective Story Reader* (1965) and *The Lion Cub* (1969). (NCW)

Bohumil Hrabal (1914), now one of Czechoslovakia's most distinguished writers, did not begin to publish until he was well over forty. He studied law, but the Nazi occupation made practice an impossibility. He was obliged to take a variety of manual jobs. But in 1962 he decided to devote himself to literature. *A Pearl in the Depths* appeared in 1963. His best-known work is *A Close Watch on the Trains* (1965; tr. 1968), which became famous as a movie under the title *Closely Observed Trains*. This is narrated by its anti-hero, Miloš Hrma, who works on the railways (on which Hrabal worked) as the Nazis are rushing troops through Czechoslovakia to their collapsing eastern front. It is hilarious, moving and heroic by turns, and leaves the reader in no uncertainty as to why its author shot suddenly to fame. He writes in a colloquial, apparently uncontrolled language which is highly effective for his debunking purposes. He is the Czech writer who has made most effective use of Hašek (q.v.). He supported Husák publicly, as Hašek would have done, but has unpublishable material circulating. The authorities allow him to publish conventional material. *The Death of Mr. Baltisberger* (tr. 1975).

The most distinguished Czech writer in exile was **Egon Hostovský** (1908–73), who resigned from the diplomatic service in 1948 after the communist coup, and went to the USA. He was also in exile during the Second World War. His exciting novels, whose plots are sometimes as melodramatic as those of thrillers, deal with the experiences of alienated and displaced personalities, and with the problems of Jewish assimilation. His earlier fiction – *The Closed Door* (1926), *The Case of Professor Körner* (1937) – dealt with the plight of alienated Czech Jews. His finest work – *Missing* (tr. 1952), *The Charity Ball* (tr. 1957), *Three Nights* (1964), *The Plot* (1964; tr. 1961) – probes the inner world of refugees from tyranny with intensity and understanding but without self-pity. He is one of the few contemporary novelists who have learned from Dostoevski without parodying him; but the chief influence on him has been Greene (q.v.), as he admitted. He is underrated, though quite widely read.

II

The Slovaks had been separated from the Czechs since 906; the creation of Czechoslovakia in 1918 was a bringing together of two natural cultural partners; but while the Czechs had had their own state under Austria, the Slovaks had been part of Hungary. Until the middle of the eighteenth century the Slovaks used Latin, Hungarian or Czech to write their literature; a standard Slovak was devised in the mid-nineteenth century. Slovak literature is less confident than Czech because the people allowed themselves to be 'Magyanized' relatively willingly – though of course there were exceptions.

The father of Slovak realism, the prolific novelist **Martin Kujučín** (ps. **Matej Bencúr**, 1860–1928), a doctor, spent most of his life abroad: in Dalmatia, then in Chile, and finally back in Yugoslavia. He was in Czechoslovakia for a few years after 1918. He had a confident style and his fiction is solid, well observed and humorous. His early work deals with Czech life, but his best novels – *The House on the Slope* (1903–4) and the five-volume *Mother Calls* (1926–7) – deal with Dalmatia and the lives of Croatian emigrants in South America.

Janko Jesensky (1874–1945), like Hašek (q.v.) and other future Czechs loyal to their aspirations, deserted from the Austro-Hungarian army during the First World War and joined the free Czech army in Russia. A lawyer, he held a political post in the republic; during the Nazi occupation he circulated anti-fascist verses, collected in *Against the Night* (1945). Though Jesensky thought of himself primarily as a poet, and had been associated with Krasko (q.v.) as one of the leading poets of the pre-1914 Slovak 'modern' school, his chief work is the novel *Democrats* (1934–7; tr. 1961), a scathing satire on upperclass Slovak life under the republic. Like Čapek (q.v.), Jesensky was dedicated to the republic without much hope of its survival. Always an enemy of Slovak separatism, he made cruel fun of the Nazi puppet-state, the 'independent' Slovak Republic of 1939–45.

Peter Jilemnický (1901–49), a Czech by birth, began to write in Slovak when he went to Slovakia as a schoolmaster in 1922. Jilemnický was a good socialist realist (voluntary) who wrote well of the Slovak peasantry in *The Step that Rings* (1930), *The Fallow Field* (1932) – his best novel – and *Our Compass* (1937). He was taken by the Gestapo in the Second World War and spent three years in concentration camps. He spent the rest of his life – shortened by his sufferings – as Czechoslovakia's cultural attaché in Moscow, and as a model for younger writers to emulate.

Milo Urban (1904) was originally a brilliantly realistic observer of the process of transition from Hungarian to Czechoslovak rule. He has never bettered *The Living Scourge*

(1927), a novel about Slovak peasants during the First World War. A Slovak separatist, he collaborated with the Nazis as a journalist during the Second World War, and was imprisoned at the liberation; but by 1958 he was allowed to publish a (poor) socialist realist view of the Chamberlain-Hitler dismemberment of Czechoslovakia: *The Extinguished Lights* (1958). His later work is inferior. Two other Catholic writers remained faithful to separatism and now live in America: Andrej Žarnov (ps. F. Šubík, 1903) and the priest Rudolf Dilong (1905). Their work is pious and sickly, unlike that of the early Urban.

A long novel by **František Hečko** (1905–60), written before he became hamstrung by socialist realism (q.v.), is even more successful in the same genre as *The Living Scourge*, though it deals with a later period: *Red Wine* (1948).

Ladislav Mňačko (1919), who visited Israel in 1963, supported the Stalinist line in the early years of communism, but later (1964) publicly recanted, confessing his own guilt. *Death is Called Engelchen* (1959; tr. 1961) is about the resistance to Nazism; *The Taste of Power* (1968; tr. 1967) describes the life of a top communist with understanding – it is a depressing book. Mňačko now lives in Austria, and publishes in German. He is probably a more interesting writer than Kundera (q.v.), but is not half as well known.

*

Svetozár Hurban Vajanský (ps. **Svetozár Hurban**, 1847–1916) was equally important as poet and novelist, but it is probably his poetry that will survive the longer. He was an ardent and mystic Slavophile who believed that the West was morally corrupt; he was nevertheless influenced, especially in his poetry, by German models. His lyrics introduced a new lucidity into Slovak poetry. Although he was himself a staunch fighter for Slovak liberty, several times imprisoned by the Magyars, his novels are remarkably objective in their account of the difficulties of wealthy Slovaks, torn between a convenient loyalty to the authorities and loyalty to their own people.

The reputation of **Hviezdoslav** (ps. **Pavel Országh**, 1849–1921) has perceptibly declined; but during and for a quarter of a century after his lifetime he was regarded as the doyen of Slovak poets. As a precocious boy poet he was a Hungarian patriot, but from his nineteenth year all he wrote was in Slovak. He was a lawyer, but gave up the profession early in order to devote himself to literature. He undoubtedly enriched the language and range of Slovak poetry, and he broadened his themes; but his work has dated. His best poetry is probably contained in the *Bloody Sonnets* of 1917 (tr. 1950), a protest against all war and the First World War in particular. He was influenced by Vrchlický (q.v.), and did perhaps more than any other Slovak writer to internationalize his literature. He translated *Hamlet* and many other classics.

Ivan Krasko (ps. **Ján Botto**, 1876–1958), although all his work is contained in two volumes – *Nox et Solitudo* (1909) and *Poems* (1912) – was a superior poet. He was an important political functionary in the Masaryk republic. But his poetry, usually described as 'decadent', is in fact based on a recognizable system of symbols; he can certainly be called a symbolist (q.v.). The influence of his pessimism has been as great as that of Hviezdoslav (q.v.), but more subterranean. Where Hviezdoslav extended Slavonic poetry, Krasko broke more decisively with its traditional forms, substituting for them ones taken over from French and Italian poetry.

Emil Lukáč (1900–79) and **Ján Smrek** (ps. **Ján Čietek**, 1899) were the two leading poets of the Twenties and Thirties. Lukáč was widely influenced: by Hviezdoslav, French symbolism, Valéry, Jammes (qq.v.) – he spent two years at the Sorbonne – Rilke and

Ady (qq.v.). His translations from French poetry – *Trophies* (1933) – were influential. Lukáč, a religious but profoundly pessimistic man, condemned as a 'cosmopolitan decadent' in 1948, remains an 'old-fashioned' symbolist. Smrek underwent the same kind of influences, but was more responsive to the wave of surrealism which manifested itself in both Czech and Slovak literature between the wars – and which was also to be condemned in 1948. Where Lukáč – like Urban (q.v.) – supported the short-lived 'independent' German-protected Slovak state of the priest-traitor Josef Tiso, Smrek opposed it.

Laco Novomeský (1904), born in Budapest, took an active part in the great Slovak uprising against the Nazis in 1944; he is now considered to be the chief older poet. Like most of the better poets of the between-wars period, Novomeský was strongly influenced by the Czech proletarian and poetist (qq.v.) phases; he was a leading light in the communist and avant garde Masses (*Dav*) Group, whose magazine of that name ran from 1924 until 1926. Novomeský came to reject 'committed' in favour of 'pure' poetry, but his work of the period reflects confusions and tensions similar to that of Nezval's (q.v.). His books include *Sunday* (1927), *Rhomboid* (1932) and *Open Windows* (1935). At the liberation he gained high office in the Ministry of Slovak Education, but was one of the victims of the Stalinist purges of the early Fifties: his offence was 'bourgeois nationalist deviationism'. He was released and 'rehabilitated' in 1963: the state went so far as to promulgate him (1964) a 'national artist', a high Czech honour accorded posthumously to the murdered Vančura (q.v.) and others. He has since written informatively on the Slovak avant garde between the wars.

Since the early Sixties the Czech and Slovak cultures have tended to move nearer together; the number of translations to and from the two languages has increased. At present, however, the rulers of Czechoslovakia can get little change from their writers. 'Offer them more money', advised Moscow some years ago. 'But we do', a harassed culture-lackey is reported to have answered: 'We offer them Hollywood salaries, but they just won't write'. ...

The situation is still hopeless in 1983, although Husak is now tired and fading. Writers either use a samizdat means of communication, or pretend (e.g. Hrabal) to accept the rule, or they are in prison.... Those such as Holub who are favoured were for the most part trivial in any case.

III

Čapek (q.v.) is undoubtedly the best known Czechoslovak playwright of this century; whether he is an important one is another matter. His plays are ingenious and enjoyable, but his fiction is of considerably more interest – and the plays add nothing to theatrical development. The Czechs are enthusiastic theatregoers; but much intelligent and imaginative theatrical activity has failed to produce a dramatist of major stature. The best theatre of the Masaryk republic was probably the 'Unfettered' Theatre of the two actors and playwrights **Jiří Voskovec** (ps. **Jiří Wachsmann**; 1905) and **Jan Werich** (1905), and the experimental theatre of E.F. Burian (1904–59). On the advent of communism, Voskovec chose exile, and became an American character actor, but Werich and Burian remained. Both played some part in the theatrical revival after Stalin's death. There was also a short-lived 'Dada Theatre' in the Twenties. The only tolerable socialist realist (q.v.) in the Stalinist period was the lively **Jan Drda** (1915), who skilfully used the folk-tale tradition to gild the bitter pill. The most promising avant garde dramatist **Jiří Frejka** (1904–52) killed himself.

In the Sixties a new avant garde theatre grew up. The best known young playwright is **Václav Havel** (1936), who has worked in the theatre for most of his life, and was until 1966 literary manager of the important Balustrade Theatre in Prague. *The Garden Party* (1963; tr. 1969), his first play, was an international success. *The Memorandum* (1966; tr. 1967) is a memorable satire on bureaucracy, in which a deputy outwits his boss by introducing into the business a synthetic language, Ptydepe, which revolutionizes communication. This is one of the funniest, most penetrating and disturbing satires to come out of the communist world since the war. Since then he has written many plays, all offensive to the Soviets, who, through their servants, have imprisoned him. He has at present just been released (March 1983) – a blow to the tiring Husák, who wanted to keep him in gaol. Havel's plays transcend the Theatre of the Absurd (q.v.), though they were influenced by it. Some of the later plays, not published in Czechoslovakia, are more or less realistic – and very moving and powerful.

Ivan Stodola (1888–1977) was the dominant figure in the Slovak theatre in the between-wars period, with such plays as *The Shepherd's Wife* (1928), a tragedy, the historical *King Svatopluk*, on the Slovak anti-Hungarian uprising of 1848–9, and *Tea with His Excellency the Senator* (1929), social satire. The leading post-war playwright is **Peter Karvaš** (1920), who has applied himself as intelligently as the times have allowed to the individual psychological problems of 'socialist man'. *The People of Our Street* (1951) and *The Scar* (1963) are among his plays.

Dutch Literature

I

The literature of the Netherlands differs from that of the Flemish Belgians, which is treated in a separate section – though under the general heading of 'Dutch', for the two languages are very similar. Flemish was a Frankish dialect which after the sixteenth century fell into disuse and was revived by Belgian writers in the nineteenth century; these drew, however, on literary Dutch as well. The spelling of Flemish is more archaic than that of Dutch. Dutch is gaining ground amongst Flemish speakers, but the University of Ghent continues to be a centre of Flemish learning and literature. The two literatures are gradually coalescing; but important differences are still manifest.

In the Netherlands many people speak English, German and French; the Dutchman's literary education is considerably higher than that of his British counterpart. But he tends to have a somewhat low regard for his own literature. This may account for Dutch literature's relative lack of self-confidence. The feeling is unjustified: the Netherlands in this century have produced two, perhaps even four, major novelists, and two major poets; and a host of important minor talents.

II

The Dutch literary revival of 1880, in the hands of the Eightiers (*Tachtigers*) as they called themselves, paralleled similar movements in other European countries; but it was – and had to be – more drastic. The way had been prepared by the classic novelist Multatuli (the pseudonym, meaning 'I have suffered much', of Eduard Douwes Dekker, 1820–87). The Eightiers, whose magazine, founded in 1885, was called *The New Guide* (to distinguish it sharply from the well established *The Guide*), attacked the effete romanticism, then too solidly established, for its sentimentality, conventional religiosity and unctuousness. They changed the Dutch literary language by their insistence upon precision and eschewal of cliché. The Flemish priest, poet and polemicist Guido Gezelle (q.v.), who had looked to Keats and Shelley in the Sixties, anticipated the so-called Eightiers, but whereas he was Christian and moralistic they were aesthetes.

The chief poet of this group was **Willem Kloos** (1859–1938), whose cult of beauty and art for art's sake now seems dated, but whose influence on Dutch poetry was great because of his originality of diction, his evocative rhythms, and the consistency of his critical thinking, which is basically Shelleyan. For him the function of art is the creation of beauty, and his position in Dutch poetry may fairly be described as similar to Shelley's in England, but it must be remembered that he was consciously following in Shelley's footsteps. (The Keats of the Netherlands is certainly Jacques Perk, Kloos' close friend, who died in 1881 at the age of twenty-two. Perk was a better poet than Kloos: his sonnet-sequence to a Belgian girl he met briefly is one of the best things in the Dutch literature of the nineteenth century, and is far less lucubrated than anything by Kloos. Nonetheless, the latter rewrote many of the sonnets before he printed them in 1882 – *The Guide* had refused them.) Kloos' first book, *Poems* (1894), is famous for its sonnets, which are, in their over-literary way, extremely beautiful. Kloos declined into an emotionally lifeless perpetrator of turgid philosophical verse; but his cult of worship of the elevated self was a necessary reaction to the complacency that had characterized Dutch literature before the Eighties. He is a vital figure in Dutch literature, though not a truly important poet.

Albert Verwey (1865–1937), like Kloos, was one of the early editors of *The New Guide*, but he severed his connection with Kloos in 1889, becoming critical of his worship of the irrational and his views about the non-political nature of literature. He was a friend (not a disciple) of George's (q.v.), and his manner is often reminiscent of the German poet's. He ended by seeing the function of poetry as a social binding of all peoples and times. Verwey was a skilful but largely artificial poet, at his best when he felt that his 'eternal self' was 'doomed to solitude' – a view against which he later reacted. Verwey underwent many changes in mind, and gives the impression of continually forming groups only to break away from them. But his progress was intelligent, and he, too, was an essential figure.

Dutch late nineteenth-century prose was directly influenced by Zola's naturalism (q.v.); but it also drew upon its own great pictorial tradition. There was a tendency to try to turn writing into a kind of painting, in which everything was to be described with minute photographic accuracy. One is inevitably reminded of Holz (q.v.) and his search for an art that would exactly reproduce life. This is realism at its utmost limits; it sometimes even appears modernist because its syntax is stripped down until it resembles a diagram. **Lodewijk van Deyssel** (ps. **K.J.L.A. Thijm**, 1864–1952), Kloos' (q.v.) friend and a fellow 'Eightier', began with an admiration of Zola (q.v.), although his aestheticism led him to condemn Zola's moralism. His two early novels, *The Little Republic* (1889) and *A Love Story* (1887), are not really so much naturalist as defiantly realistic; they included some descriptions of sexual scenes which caused a twitter then, but which nowadays seem innocuous. He broke with Zola in 1891, and turned to reproducing the 'sensation' which arose from proper 'observation'. His impressionistic prose poetry, attempts at making pictures with words (they are collected in *Apocalypse*, 1893), are failures. Until about this date he could profitably be compared to Holz (q.v.) in his tendencies; but soon afterwards he drifted into a whimsical mysticism on the pattern of Maeterlinck (q.v.). He was influential in Dutch literature, but left no really successful book except for his biographies, one of which (1891) is of Multatuli (q.v.). But his best book is his *Memoirs* (1924). There is a book on him by H.G.M. Prick.

The Dutch novel of this period seldom transcends national boundaries: the photographic accuracy of its portrayal of bourgeois society lacks psychological penetration, and the prose is clumsy. These novels are to literature precisely what sober, competent and unexperimental photography is to painting. 'Naturalist' should really be used of this kind of fiction only in its (in literature) misleading sense of 'like nature'.

There are exceptions amongst this generation of realists: the main one, **Louis**

Couperus (1863–1923), is the only Dutch writer of this century to achieve a truly inter-national reputation. He was a cosmopolitan character, of Javanese blood, who lived in Italy until the beginning of the First World War; he said of himself that although he loved the Netherlands he felt more Italian than Dutch. He began as a realist-naturalist under the influence of Flaubert, Zola and, to some extent, Tolstoi (qq.v.); but Zola did little more than provide him with a method. In *Footsteps of Fate* (1890; tr. 1891) the characters are the victims of inexorable fate in a manner typical of naturalism, but even here there is a hint that character is not destiny. For Couperus had an oriental bent in his make-up that led him to view man as unnecessarily concerned with his fate: he who resigns himself may find peace. Couperus was a dandy who would have liked to have been a transvestite (perhaps he was); he was also a homosexual, and in *Footsteps of Fate* and *Ecstasy* (1892; tr. 1892) he tried to explore this theme. It is complained that in the latter the portrayal of the two main characters' feelings towards each other is 'inadequate', and that the relationship is 'hysterically platonic'. This is true, and the novel is not one of his best – not as good as *Eline Vere* (1889; tr. 1892), a social novel about the collapse of a woman (really Couperus himself) through lassitude – it has to be remembered that he could not be open. But it is true that his greatest weakness is his tendency to powder and manicure his novels as he did his body. Throughout his life his quest was for heterosexual love – but he could not find it. *The Hidden Force* (1900; tr. 1922), set in Indonesia where Couperus went to live for a year, shows him at the top of his powers. An administrator is destroyed by a magical force which the natives understand but which he refuses to accept. The tetralogy *Small Souls* (1901–4; tr. 1914–18) gives a picture of Dutch family life on the scale of Galsworthy's *Forsyte Saga* (q.v.), but is infinitely more subtle and sensitive than that overrated work. Here Couperus compassionately traces the progress of a mentality from pettiness to desire, through suffering, for wisdom – and incidentally gives an incomparable picture of Dutch middle-class life. *The Mountain of Light* (1905–6), a study of Heliogabalus the Androgyne, could have been a masterpiece, but Couperus could not face up to its impli-cations, and it disintegrates. *Old People and the Things that Pass* (1908; tr. 1918; 1963), the story of the effect on three very old people of a murder committed sixty years back, in the colonies, shows him at his best. Although its impressionistic prose is sometimes unneces-sarily hard to read because of its over-manneredness, it is masterly in its presentation of a present haunted by memories of the past. Couperus is a fascinating writer who needs only comprehensive republication in the English-speaking world – in better translations than are available – to draw attention to his genius.

Another exception to the general mediocrity of the Dutch novel at this period was the more thoroughgoingly naturalist **Marcellus Emants** (1848–1923), who was of an older generation than Couperus (q.v.), but had started as a poet and dramatist. His fiction, however – the first appeared in 1878 – is his best work. He was a naturalist of Zola's (q.v.) sort; and he put great emphasis on hereditary factors, but carried the relish in squalor much further. His 'philosophy' is not very interesting: it is simply that life is meaningless. But his masterpiece, *A Posthumous Confession* (1894; tr. 1975), quite transcends his programme (if life is meaningless, of course, then why write about it? – doing so can only confer meaning upon it, unless one assumes that what one has written is also meaning-less). It is a vivid, superbly written account of one Willem Termeer, who has killed his wife. His motives and feelings are analysed with uncanny skill and power; and *A Pos-thumous Confession* is certainly a pioneer psychological novel. Frederik van Eeden (q.v.) was to be influenced by it. The terse and concise quality of this book stands in contrast to some of Emants' other work: grandiose dramatic epics, sensationalist novels, historical works. But he did find his own voice later: first in *Miss Lina* (1888), then in his finest novel, and then in *Initiation* (1901) and *Love Life* (1916).

J. van Oudshoorn (ps. J.K. Felybrief, 1876–1951) was neglected in his lifetime. He is a mysterious, rewarding writer, whose *Alienation* (1914; tr. 1965) – its Dutch title is *Mirror of Willem Merten's Life* – about a man who feels himself to have been ruined through masturbation, is a pioneer masterpiece. After the Second World War his work was taken up by a new generation; but he had exercised an influence already, especially on Bordewijk (q.v.). Other important books by Oudshoorn include *Purifications* (1916) and *Tobias and Death* (1925).

Another (long-lived) member of this generation whose work was not to make an impact until later was Nescio (ps. J.F.H. Grönloh, 1882–1961). His volume of novellas, *Little Poet, The Sponger, Little Titans*, was re-published in 1933 (the middle title had appeared in 1918), and the *Forum* group took it up rather as the percipient Du Perron (q.v.) took up the contemporary Slauerhoff (q.v.). Grönloh's work is, as the critic R.P. Meijer has rightly said, the 'greatest small *oeuvre* in Dutch literature'. He followed up his first novellas with *Mene Tekel* (1946) and *Above the Valley* (1961). 'Life has taught me hardly anything, thank God,' he wrote. His short fictions tell of men whose aspirations come to nothing, who are defeated, and they do so in a delicate, unobtrusively throwaway, colloquial style which steers an exquisite course between the pompous and the absurd. Only Elsschot (q.v.) equals him in his wise irreverence; but he must have influenced all the best of his successors.

The poet, dramatist and novelist Frederik van Eeden (1860–1932), a psychiatrist who had medical qualifications – he set up a psychotherapy unit in Amsterdam – was a co-founder of *The New Guide*, but soon reacted to Kloos' (q.v.) dedication to art for its own sake. More interestingly than Kloos, he oscillated between social conscience and individual realization, discovering – in so doing – a language of his own. But this tension between opposites, evident in his novel *The Deeps of Deliverance* (1900; tr. 1902; 1974) did not last. To combat the anti-social villain in him, which produced his best work, he founded a semi-communist community, which (because of his admiration for Thoreau) he called Walden; this collapsed, as all such communities do, and eventually (1922) he fell into Roman Catholicism. He came to see himself as a second Jesus (*Called or Chosen?* is the title of a 1924 novel); but, surprisingly, he could relax out of this unfortunate vision. He had become popular in the late Eighties with *Little Johannes* (1887; tr. *The Quest*, 1907), a woolly *symboliste* novel which has now dated. But *The Deeps of Deliverance*, a study of a young girl's development, is in bourgeois terms 'morbid', although it struggles out of such morasses into a false pleasantness before it finishes. Its best passages emphasize the difficulties of reconciling female sexuality with a male world, and are full of the kinds of insight one might expect from a psychiatrist; when it rationalizes these into 'joy' it becomes programmatic and is as unconvincing as it is dated and boring. He wrote with humour and understanding of the failure of his Tolstoian (q.v.) community in *The Promised Land* (1909). He was an interestingly confused man; Erich Fromm contributed to a study of him.

The most important playwright of this generation – indeed, he has not been equalled, let alone surpassed – was Herman Heijermans (1864–1924). Influenced in his technique mainly by Ibsen (q.v.), he was a socialist who depicted, in a naturalist manner, the miseries of the poor. His most famous play, about oppressed North Sea fishermen, was *The Good Hope* (1901; tr. 1928), which was played all over the world. At the very end of his life he wrote a poignant novel, *The Little Dream King* (1924), about a boy's growing up in a slum. He was a Jew, and his comic sketches about (mostly) Jewish life in Dutch cities, published under the name of Samuel Falkland, are unique in the language for their raciness and insight. His play *The Way Out* (1909–11), in which the action arises from the thoughts of a dying child, showed that – like Ibsen – he could be as poetic as he could be realistic. *Links* (1904–5; tr. 1927), about the greed and insensitivity of a business man, influenced Hauptmann (q.v.).

The writer who eventually most decisively broke with photographic realism was **Arthur van Schendel** (1874–1946), who was born in Java. Van Schendel wrote of events in the external world, but described them through the eyes of a dreamer. He spent some years teaching in England and then in Holland before devoting himself entirely to writing. Curiously enough, although he was the first major novelist to break completely with the naturalist manner, one of the chief themes of all his fiction is man's impotence against his destiny. His first stories and novels, set in medieval times, were Pre-Raphaelite in mood. And yet the germ of his future work is contained in his first story, *Drogon* (1896): a dreamy, eccentric young man is 'fated' to seduce his brother's wife. *A Wanderer in Love* (1904) and *A Wanderer Lost* (1907) tell of a monk and his struggles against sexual desire. These have an irresistibly lush quality, somewhat reminiscent of Rossetti; but they are self-indulgent, and the pseudo-medieval background palls. Van Schendel continued in this vein, more or less unprofitably, until 1921, when he went to live in Italy. His Italian stories show signs of change. The period of his maturity begins in 1930, with *The 'Johanna Maria'* (tr. 1935), the biography (set in the nineteenth century) of a sailing vessel. This is written in the impassive style for which Van Schendel became famous: there is no dialogue, and the events described have an oneiric quality. There followed more novels of high quality, in which Van Schendel more seriously explores his fatalistic theme: *The Waterman* (1933; tr. 1963), *The House in Haarlem* (1936; tr. 1940), *Grey Birds* (1937; tr. 1939). *Oberon and Madame* (1940) and other books of this period are actually gay in their romanticism. The posthumous *The Old House* (1946) is perhaps Van Schendel's finest work of all. Van Schendel was at his best when imposing a fierce restraint on his innate romanticism: when, as in *The Waterman*, he is showing how destiny – in the form of unobtrusive but stifling social pressure – overrides such romanticism. It was in *The Old House* that he brought this to near perfection. He is a difficult writer – as difficult to come to terms with as such Japanese as Toson and Soseki (qq.v.) – but an original and compelling one.

Poetry immediately before the First World War was represented mainly by Gorter, Holst and Verwey (qq.v.), though there were other poets whose work has now dated. **Herman Gorter** (1864–1927) was a member of the Eighties movement, and up until *The School of Poetry* (1897) he indulged himself in an entirely subjective verse. This accorded with Kloos' (q.v.) prescription, but Gorter was in earnest in a way that Kloos could never have known: he flung himself into his own feelings and conducted an exploration of them so frenzied that he nearly lost his reason. The resultant poems were in freer verse than anything the Netherlands had seen. At this point Gorter, by far the most gifted of the poets of his group, really left the best of himself behind. After a study of philosophy he became a Marxist – but a curiously rigid one. His epic *Pan* (1916) is a grandiose work, highly doctrinaire – and hopelessly remote from ordinary experience, let alone that of the proletariat. But ultimately Gorter became a proto-'Eurocommunist': he broke with Lenin, whom he knew, and resigned from the Party in 1921. His best poetry is in the long *May* (1889), and in *Verses* (1890). This was innovative, and some of it still excites the mind.

The early work of **Henriette Roland Holst** (1869–1952) appeared in *The New Guide* (q.v.), but, in company with Gorter (q.v., of whom she wrote a biography, 1933), she became an adherent of William Morris socialism and then of communism. In the mid-Twenties she turned to a religious socialism. Her poetry suffers from lack of control, but its irregular forms and burning sincerity had a deserved effect on Dutch poetry.

The symbolist poetry of **Jan Hendrik Leopold** (1865–1925), whose output was small, resembles an island half-enveloped in haze: nothing is quite in focus or quite discernible.

No doubt this remoteness (not at all like that of Gorter's, q.v., epic) arose largely from the deafness from which he suffered. Like that of another deaf poet, David Wright (q.v.), his poetry has a sensuous musical quality. He was deeply influenced by the philosophy of his countryman, Spinoza, as well as by ancient Sufic poetry. During most of his lifetime he was not well known; now there is a revival of interest in his poetry. Verwey (q.v.) described his lyrics as 'like the swelling and fading of a wave that never breaks'. His world, particularly as expressed in the long poem *Cheops* (1915), is eminently worthy of investigation: he is not a successful poet, but he is a deeply interesting one.

A. Roland Holst (1888–1976), one of the most lively literary members of the underground war against the occupying Nazis in the Second World War, is another important symbolist, who combines the Celtic esotericism of Yeats (q.v.) with the kind of pre-temporal paradises of which we catch so many glimpses in the French poetry of the first thirty or forty years of this century. Writing from the viewpoint of innocence (though not assuming it) he either celebrates the eternal lost world or, with perhaps more effect – and in a more hallucinated poetry – records visions of himself in the corrupted temporal world. His imagery is elemental, and in this and in his paganism he is reminiscent of Saint-John Perse (q.v.). Some earlier collections are *The Confessions of Silence* (1913), *Beyond the Distances* (1920), *A Winter By the Sea* (1937); more recent is *In Danger* (1958). Dutch literature needs only to be better known for Roland Holst to have an international reputation. His language, like that of Saint-John Perse, matches his grand theme, though whether he is a major poet is open to doubt: poetic energy is too diffused throughout his work, which is, ultimately, less moving than impressive.

Dutch expressionism was imported from Germany and re-named 'vitalism' by its leader **Hendrik Marsman** (1899–1940), who was supported by the humanist critic Dirk Coster (1887–1956). Marsman's vitalism differed very little from the second phase of German expressionism, which he had imbibed while in Germany as a young man; but he was one of the first outside Germany to perceive the genius of Trakl (q.v.). He also helped translate some of Nietzsche (q.v.) into Dutch. His *Poems* (1923) and *Paradise Regained* (1927) contain explosive and implosive poetry, too experimental and program-matic to be effective, but suffused with undoubted energy. In 1930 he began to revise his ideas; the resultant collection of essays, *The Death of Vitalism* (1933), marks the beginning of his maturity. When the young Germans who had influenced Marsman in 1921 became Nazis, he looked into himself, rejecting the nihilistic and violent side of expressionism. His consistent self-consciousness saved him from his grandiose tendencies, but robbed most of his later poetry of spontaneity. In the Thirties he led a wandering life, searching for but not really finding a faith; always pursuing his idea of 'Gothic ardour'. His last poem, *Temple and Cross* (1939), on the theme of the conflict between Christ and Dionysus, comes down in favour of the pagan God. Perhaps the best of all his creative works is his novel *The Death of Angèle Degroux* (1933), the strange tale of a love affair between two 'superior' beings. The boat in which Marsman was escaping to England from France in 1940 was torpedoed, and all but his wife and one other passenger were lost. He has been said by Seymour F. Flaxman to have had a 'very high-handed tone' as a critic; but his tone is not in fact as high-handed as Flaxman's, and he is always interesting.

Eddy du Perron (ps. **Charles Edgar du Perron**, 1899–1940), Marsman's (q.v.) exact contemporary, was one of the liveliest and most valuable members of this generation. The son of rich parents, he came to Paris to work as a journalist when they lost their money. Malraux dedicated *The Human Condition* (qq.v.) to him. He had an especial admiration for Stendhal, whom he physically resembled, for Multatuli (q.v.), whose work he helped to popularize, for Larbaud and for Simenon (qq.v.). Of the very best type of tough, intelligent, individualist left-wing intellectual, Du Perron exercised a strong influence on the generation that came after him; his death from heart disease at only forty-one was a tragedy. His poems are amusing, deliberately lightweight and in the intentionally matter-of-fact, colloquial '*parlando*' style that he and his *Forum* (q.v.) associates cultivated. But Du Perron wrote one classic, a book that demands to be better known outside Holland: *The Country of Origin* (1935). This autobiographical novel consists of descriptions of his life in Paris alternated with extraordinarily vivid memories of his Javanese childhood. There are few books as good on the East Indies; and few books recapture the mind of a child so exactly. It is partly modelled on Multatuli, of whom Du Perron wrote an excellent biography, and it remains one of the best modern novels in Dutch. Du Perron also wrote two other novels, some short stories, and much interesting informal critical prose.

Du Perron was the co-founder, with **Menno Ter Braak** (1902–40) and the Flemish Roelants (q.v.), of the *Forum* group, which was originally formed as a counter to Marsman's (q.v.) 'vitalism'. This group, which advocated lucidity, objectivity and quietude in place of expressionist rhetoric and noise, almost exactly parallels the German 'new objectivity' (q.v.), although it manifested itself rather later: it was in fact a modified expressionism, but wanted to shed the frenetic aspects while retaining the ground that had been won. Ter Braak killed himself when the Nazis invaded the Netherlands. The leading figure of the group was **Simon Vestdijk** (1898–1971), who became the Netherlands' most important writer after the death of Van Schendel (q.v.)

Vestdijk studied medicine (in which he qualified), psychology and philosophy before he became a writer. He was among the most prolific: translator of Emily Dickinson, R.L. Stevenson and others, he found time to write thirty-eight novels, ten collections of short stories and twenty-two books of poetry – as well as twenty-eight non-fiction books. He wrote, it was said, 'faster than God can read'. He combines in his novels (his best work) a lust for life with a psychiatrist's objectivity. After the Second World War he was put forward as an exemplary writer by the Dutch existentialists (q.v.), whose leader was the poet and critic **Paul Rodenko** (1920), a left-wing polemicist (who compiled the standard anthology of the work produced by the 'experimental' poets of the Fifties, q.v.). Vestdijk's outstanding work is the eight-novel autobiographical sequence *Anton Wachter* (1934–50). This is generally characterized by Vestdijk's special, and at first off-putting, combination of vitalism and cerebral analysis. He has been unlucky in his translations: the only good novel of his that has appeared in English is *The Garden Where the Brass Band Played* (1950; tr. 1965). This is an account of how beauty and trust are destroyed in a small Dutch town at the beginning of the century. Nol, a judge's son, loves his piano-teacher's daughter, Trix; but trivial prejudices triumph. Vestdijk is more consistent in the shorter forms, however, when his ideas are most subordinated to his imagination, which gets free range. At one time put forward as the Netherlands' candidate for the Nobel Prize, Vestdijk undoubtedly diffused his gift by too great a prolificity; but his best fiction will survive. He is an important essayist, and a man who had a truly open mind – he wrote on all the subjects that interested him, from Freudianism through astrology and music to his fellow writers.

Ferdinand Bordewijk (1884–1965), a genial joker who took in earnest critics more than once, was an independent writer who successfully developed certain aspects of nineteenth-century Gothic. His *Fantastic Tales* (1919–24) combined the elements of Poe and the modern detective story. After this, becoming aware of surrealism, he turned to a more fantastic manner. *Groaning Beasts* (1928) is about a motor-race. *Bint* (1934) exposes the fascism latent in vitalism, and was itself accused of fascism: it is the study of a terrorizing teacher, and is in no way 'fascist'. His finest novel, *Character* (1938; tr. 1966), is written in a more conventional style. Grandly evocative of Rotterdam, the port of its setting, it tells of a father whose method of bringing up his (illegitimate) son is to oppose his every whim. Bordewijk was a versatile and eccentric writer, the main function of whose work is to reveal the inadequacy of social structure and morality to human needs. He is notable as a recreator of the atmosphere of old places.

The figure of **Martinus Nijhoff** (1894–1953) stands behind much of the Dutch poetry written since 1945, even though Achterberg and Slauerhoff (qq.v.) are more important. Nijhoff passed through a semi-expressionist phase, but by 1924, with *Forms*, had discovered the resigned and melancholy manner natural to him. He is a religious poet, searching for a means of redemption from adult corruption, which he sees in sexual terms: he postulates a Christ who is the equivalent of the child-in-the-man, through whom the man may gain salvation. Wise innocence may illuminate the adult's mundane and degenerate life. His language is deliberately sober and non-poetical. It is his awareness of the existence of an inner world rather than any specific poetic procedure that has made him important to the poets of a later generation.

Jan Slauerhoff (1898–1936) was the most independent and gifted member of the *Forum* group, though he was never active in literary debates. He trained as a doctor and became a ship's surgeon. Slauerhoff was an anti-social outcast, a wanderer who could accept nothing that life seemed to impose upon him; he was also, although extremely uneven, one of the most gifted Dutch poets and novelists of this century. One critic spoke of the 'hoarse, shy' tone with which all he wrote is imbued. He was a master of poetic technique, and therefore irritated some by his frequent carelessness. His most enduring works, apart from his wild poems – the work of a *poète maudit* thirty years out of his time, and aware of it – are the strange novel *The Forbidden Empire* (1932), in which the life of the Portuguese epic poet Camoëns is counterpointed with that of a ship's radio operator (Slauerhoff himself), and *Life on Earth* (1934), about a man who loses himself in opium dreams. Slauerhoff was one of the most original writers of his time in any language.

Gerrit Achterberg (1905–62) was the most gifted of the Dutch modernist poets. Words for him are in themselves magical, and his poetry is to be approached firstly for its necromantic qualities. He suffered from incapacitating mental illness, and wrote his poetry for therapeutic reasons; but he regarded it as therapeutic only because he thought of it as spiritually efficacious. He believed in the transmuting power of poetry, which he regarded as prayer. This belief gives his work a surrealist (q.v.) air. He eschews the ordinary materialistic meanings of words and tries to return to their true, primitive meanings – which centuries of corrupt usage have obscured and distorted. His central theme, expressed in various ways, is a version of the Orpheus myth: Orpheus does not want to bring Eurydice back to life, but to join her in death. This is Achterberg's response to the actual loss of his beloved. Inasmuch as a poet 'is what he prefers', Achterberg is a poet of earth. He wryly contrasts the trivial nature of 'ordinary' life, with its little projects, with the depth of being itself. His verse became increasingly traditional in its forms. At his most eloquent he is a poet of purity and magic; but some of his work is spoiled by an eccentricity – arising from mental instability – that is irrelevant to his central vision.

On 15 December 1937, after he had published two volumes of poetry, Achterberg killed his landlady and wounded her sixteen-year-old daughter (with whom he was having an affair) with a revolver. He was sentenced to spend time in a psychiatric hospital, and was released in 1943. He thereafter married. Since pre-1937 poems deal with the theme of union with the beloved in death, one can only assume that Achterberg reached a state in which he felt he must test out his theories; but his wife survived. In one of his most important poems, *The Ballad of the Gasfitter* (1953; tr. 1972), Achterberg sees himself as a compulsive closer of holes (a *dichter*, which also means 'poet' in Dutch as in

German; and it implies 'closer to'). This is one of the most eccentric and powerful of all contemporary poems: densely metaphysical and yet down-to-earth, satirical and ironic. His poems were collected in 1963, and about a tenth of them constitute a body of work unique in our time. *A Tourist Does Golgotha* (tr. 1972).

Lucebert (ps. **L.J. Swaanswijk**, 1924) tries, like Achterberg (q.v.), to create an objective reality of language; but the process is less natural to him, the pressure to write less intense. He is an abstract painter and photographer as well as a poet, and since the Fifties has turned to drawing in preference to writing. He was then the most important representative of the 'experimental' school of poetry, with *The Triangle in the Jungle* (1951) and *Of the Abyss and Aerial Man* (1953). He is a cheerful rebel against all kinds of conformity, who writes a lightweight, playful neo-surrealist verse that mixes humour in equal proportion with social indignation. 'Atonal' (the author's term), it is full of neologisms, nonsense-propositions and startling juxtapositions – sometimes clothed in parodically solemn, hymn-like forms.

Willem Frederik Hermans (1921) was for a time looked upon as the leading contemporary Dutch writer of experimental fiction. His initially sceptical approach may be compared to that of Robbe-Grillet (q.v.), from whom, however, he differs in other respects. However, like Robbe-Grillet, he was trained as a scientist: a physical geographer. Hermans began as a poet, but changed to fiction in 1949 with *The Tears of the Acacias*, a savagely cynical, scatological story set in occupied Amsterdam and in Brussels at the time of the liberation. Hermans, whose exasperated tone – in fiction and polemics – often recalls that of Céline (q.v.), has written in various experimental forms, but his main theme is the unavoidability of human chaos and individual anomie. With *The Dark Room of Damocles* (1958; tr. 1962) Hermans begins a new and less desperate approach: man's situation is the same, but the existence of values is obliquely conceded. *Memoirs of a Guardian Angel* (1971) reflects the same concerns. Later work more trivially reflects the earlier nihilism, and has been disappointing.

After the war the individualist tradition of Du Perron (q.v.) was continued in the magazine *Libertinage*, edited by the poet **H.A. Gomperts** (1915). This has steered a middle course between the socialism of *Podium* and the aesthetic *The Word.* The chief 'experimentalist' was Lucebert (q.v.); the most interesting poet of a more traditional bent is **A. Marja** (ps. **A.T. Mouji**, 1917), a 'committed' writer who calls his poetry 'anecdotic'.

Jan Hendrik Wolkers (1925), who is also well known as a sculptor, is a best-selling author – and was a serious one. There is an element of sick meretriciousness in his work; but this is no more than incidental and irritating. He has a sense of wry and ironic humour that is genuine – and more understandable than his fiction as a whole, which is perhaps the reason for his wide appeal. Wolkers' novels that have been translated into English are characteristic work. *A Rose of Flesh* (1963; tr. 1967) is a study of a self-pitying, guilty man whose daughter has died in a scalding accident by his neglect (and that of his wife). He continually re-enacts this trauma, his own spirit scalded. *The Horrible Tango* (1964; tr. 1970) is also about a sick man. Wolkers is one of the most gifted of his generation; as yet he has not wholly realized it. *Turkish Delight* (1969; tr. 1974) is inferior, as are *The Dodo* (1974) and *The Kiss* (1976).

Gerard Kornelis van het Reve (1923), a gifted homosexual exhibitionist who dissolved his gift into buffoonery, wrote *Evenings* (1947), a description of a week in the life of an adolescent 'drop-out'. This plotless narrative compassionately traces the anguish that lies at the heart of his unease, and is one of the best studies of the younger generation written in the post-1945 period. Van het Reve then published an autobiographical novella *Werther Nieland* (1949), his best work. He wrote a book of trivial stories in English, *The Acrobat* (1956), and his writing became merely entertaining. However, *The Language of*

Love (1972), a non-fiction book containing a novel, is extremely interesting about voyeuristic homosexuality, which the author now calls 'Revism'. He is now known simply as Gerard Reve, but has only repeated himself in recent work.

Harry Mulisch (1927) is self-consciously European. *The Stone Bridal Bed* (1959; tr. 1962) is a semi-surrealistic study, of sometimes horrifying power, of the post-war mentality. His fictionalized account of the life of Wilhelm Reich (q.v.), *The Sexual Bulwark* (1973), is interesting, as are a few of his plays – but he has lost the power of *The Stone Bridal Bed.*

III

The magazine *From Now On* was the vehicle for the Flemish revival, which closely paralleled those of the French-speaking Belgians and the Netherlands. The Flemish literature being insecure, the magazine was all the more fiercely assertive of its uniqueness. The father-figure for all Flemish writers at this time was the poet-priest Guido Gezelle (1830–99), who had, almost alone, re-created Flemish as a literary language. The poetry of Gezelle, a lovable man, persecuted for his love of Flemish by government and Church alike, is unlikely to survive except as a demonstration of linguistic skill and virtuosity. But as a whole it breathes warmth and simple faith in nature.

Gezelle had a tragic life, full of reactive depressions and disappointments; the spirit of his work was transmitted in a more dynamic form by **Pol de Mont** (1857–1931), who discovered and paganized Gezelle's work, and caught his countrymen's imagination with his facile but sincere and musical lyrics.

Cyriel Buysse (1859–1932), Maeterlinck's (q.v.) close friend, was equally French in outlook. But unlike his associate he decided to write in Flemish in order to enrich and invigorate a literature he felt had become impoverished. He was a prolific author of short stories, travel books and essays; but did his best work in fiction and the drama. He published his first novel in the Dutch *New Guide* (q.v.) in 1890. Resembling Maupassant in lucidity, but influenced by Zola (qq.v.) as a kindred spirit, he depicted farming and middle-class life without sentimentality. His most famous novel is the early *The Right of the Strongest* (1893), a portrait of a coarse farmer who gets his way with his girl and everyone else; this is naturalist, but with the emphasis on the 'Darwinian' doctrine of the survival of the fittest. A later and better novel, into which Buysse injected more of the romanticism natural to him, was *The Life of Rosy van Dalen* (1906). As a dramatist Buysse, who was made a baron in the last year of his life, was influenced by Hauptmann and, closer to home, the Dutch Heijermans (qq.v.). He wrote neat comedies and, most notably, *The Paemel Family* (1903), about a farmer exploited by landowners and his struggle against them. He had much contact with Dutch writers, including Louis Couperus (q.v.). Buysse, Streuvels, Teirlinck and Van de Woestijne (qq.v.) were the main forces behind the establishment of modern Flemish literature, which they advocated in the magazine *Today and Tomorrow* (*Van Nu en Straks*).

Gezelle's (q.v.) nephew **Stijn Streuvels** (ps. **Frank Lateur**, 1871–1969), who rivalled Chiesa (q.v.) in longevity, was for fifteen years a village baker. He read widely, and his natural countryman's fatalism was reinforced by Dostoevski, Hamsun, Zola, Hardy (qq.v.) and the other novelists he devoured. Ultimately, however, he eschewed literary influence and found that he could most effectively record the life he saw around him in

Western Flanders. His early book of stories described life in the depressed flax-growing areas: *The Path of Life* (1899; tr. 1915). All the ingredients of his later work are apparent: fatalism, delicacy of observation of human aspirations, a poetic sense of inexorable, beautiful, cruel nature. He has in his succeeding fiction – short stories and short novels – no lesson to teach, only a fact to demonstrate. Like Hardy, whom he somewhat resembles – though he lacked Hardy's poetic vision – he sees man as at the mercy of blind destiny, in this case the natural cycle of the seasons. Those who rebel suffer; it is better to be like Jan Vandeveughel in *Old Jan* (1902; tr. 1936), and endure. Although he does not have Hardy's massive sense of tragedy, and often takes refuge in an assumption that God's in his heaven and all's right with the world (in which his shocked imagination does not believe), Streuvels deserves to be better known and more widely translated. There is an element of Flemish mysticism or fatalism running through his work that raises it above regionalism. *The Flax Field* (1907), for example, a drama of the conflict between father and son, is so intense and psychologically accurate that it transcends mere regionalism. Fortunately some of Streuvels' earlier work is available in a French collection, *August* (*L'Août*, 1928), and there are other translations into French (e.g. *Poucette*, 1934) and German (e.g. *Des Lebens Blütezeit*, 1947).

Herman Teirlinck (1879–1967), son of **Isidoor Teirlinck** (1851–1934) – who with **Raimond Stijns** (1850–1904) wrote *Poor Flanders*, a truthful picture of poverty and social injustice – expanded the horizons of the Flemish novel. He was first led to experimentalism by his failure to write with real effect about the peasants, whom he approached with urban preconceptions (he was born in Brussels). He became famous for *Mijnheer J.B. Serjanszoon* (1908), an over-mannered tale of an eighteenth-century hedonist; this is witty and amusing but is now as hopelessly dated as most of Anatole France's (q.v.) books. It is certainly not his best work, though too often claimed to be. In 1915 he and Van de Woestijne (q.v.) began to write an epistolary novel, *Towers of Clay*, part of which was published in a magazine; unfortunately it was never finished.

As a dramatist – he was an outstanding one by European standards – Teirlinck set himself the task of revitalizing, on broadly expressionistic lines, the Flemish theatre. His *Slow Motion Picture* (1922) is one of the most successful of all the later expressionist plays. Two lovers jump into a canal. As they drown they re-live their experiences together, including the birth of their child; when the police rescue them they part as strangers – cured of love. This was one of the earliest plays to make effective use of cinema techniques, and Salacrou (q.v.) was clearly influenced by it in his *The Unknown Woman of Arras* (q.v.). *The Bodiless Man* (1925) employs the familiar expressionist technique of splitting one man into his component parts. Influenced by Pirandello (q.v) as well as by expressionist drama, this play has a Flemish element which is all Teirlinck's own. *The Magpie on the Gallows* (1937), perhaps Teirlinck's most powerful play, demonstrates both the evils of puritanism and the discomforts of old age (a theme he would take up again when he was old).

The novel *Maria Speermalie* (1940) gives the history of a passionate and polyandrous woman who rises to the aristocracy. *The Man in the Mirror* (1955; tr. 1961), which addresses its old banker hero in the second person throughout, is a tragi-comic masterpiece. The protagonist sees his past self, with its transgressions of bourgeois values, as someone else (an irony often missed); he does not change from his false and hypocritical ways. Essentially this is an account of the writer-as-confidence-man, an analysis of *Künstlerschuld* (q.v.); but the portrait is not of the author. *The Struggle with the Angel* (1952), which ranges over six centuries, is less successful as a whole. Teirlinck remained active until the end of his life, and was even cultural advisor to the King on Flemish language problems. He lacks Streuvels' (q.v.) robustness, and is probably too intellectual, as a novelist, for most tastes: a writer's writer, perhaps, but certainly an intelligent, imaginative and rewarding one.

The leading Flemish poet, and the only other major twentieth-century poet in Dutch besides Achterberg (q.v.), was **Karel van de Woestijne** (1878–1929). Van de Woestijne was initially influenced by the narcissistic decadence of Kloos, by George and Rilke (qq.v.), and, above all, by the ideas of Baudelaire. He was also a follower of Moréas (q.v.), and approved of his post-symbolist (q.v.) call for a return to a new classicism. But Van de Woestijne's critical ideas played little part in his actual achievement, which, while clearly within a decadent (q.v.) ambit, is markedly original. In his best poetry he achieves a manner entirely his own, compounded of nostalgia for childhood, sexual guilt and un-relieved bitterness. He died of tuberculosis. A robust, not to say lush, sensuality is challenged and penetrated by a cruel and almost metaphysical shrewdness. He was very much of his age, a typical tormented soul of the first quarter of the century. He is particularly interesting because he felt his symbolist procedures, at which he grasped like a drowning man, to be continually threatened by his lack of faith in the Platonic assumptions underlying them. This explains much of the intensity of his bitterness and his supposed obscurity. He saw his own lust as a luxurious and hellish dissolver of the beauties of nature. He saw himself as a hazel-nut and, simultaneously, as the greedy worm within it; as it devours his robust centre he becomes 'an emptiness that does not speak or heed'; but, touched by a child's hand, he sings. His epic, systematizing poems of the Twenties, for all their interesting baroque monumentalism, are less successful than the early ones, but contain many fine passages. He truly hated himself, and was at his best when he was completely honest about it; when he was sorry for himself he wrote badly. He wrote several volumes of literary criticism and prose, all of which are suffused with his own unhappy and melodious style. His most significant story is 'The Dying Peasant' (1918), in which he reaches a genuine affirmation of life. Some idea of his poetic genius may be gained from *Poèmes choisis* (tr. 1964).

No later Flemish poet of Van de Woestijne's stature has emerged. Elsschot (q.v.) wrote some good poems, but was primarily a novelist. **Paul van Ostaijen** (1896–1928) was an expressionist and experimentalist who did not live long enough entirely to fulfil his gift. *Music Hall* (1916), however, was a really remarkable and original first collection of poems from a man of only twenty. The chief influence was the unanimism (q.v.) of Romains and the *Abbaye* group (qq.v.); but the poems in it, all evoking a great city, incorporate (and frequently anticipate) elements of the grotesque; Van Ostaijen is never starry eyed – as were some of the *Abbaye* group – on the contrary, he is deeply and naturally cynical in an extremely modern, 'light', specifically urban manner. After the surrealism of *The Signal* (1918) and *The Occupied City* (1921), Van Ostaijen did in fact reach a more sombre and idealistic mood in *The First Book of Schmol* (1928), in which he essays a self-styled poetry of 'organic expressionism', which amounts to an attempt to combine words irrationally, in order to attain new meanings. He wrote a number of Kafkaesque (q.v.) prose works, such as *The Brothel of Ika Loch* (1925). Van Ostaijen exercised a strong influence on the post-1945 Flemish poets. His verse is extrinsically important because he was the first thoroughgoingly modernist poet in Dutch; but it has little real substance. Tubercular, he raced through too many moods and styles of thought. But his prose (e.g. *Outlawed*, 1927; *Self-Defence*, 1933) is more suggestive.

The more traditional Flemish poets since the Thirties have not written very well, but the post-war modernists who looked to Van Ostaijen are as superficial as he was, without being as lively. An exception may be **Paul Snoek** (ps. **Edmond Schietakat**, 1933), who is also a painter; but his poetry is distinguished only by isolated lines of some beauty and by a diffuse charm. A critic wrote that his 'verses ... carry an occasional proverbi:

Greene (q.v.), specifically about the problems raised by Catholic rigour.

Maurice Roelants (1895–1966) was a novelist and critic who tried to take Flemish letters in the direction of Dutch internationalism: away from provincialism and local elements. He wrote psychological novels in the French classical tradition: there are few characters, and nothing much happens except in their minds. The short story collection *The Jazz Player* (1928) contains his best work; but his few tense, intelligent novels are excellent studies of middle class *angst*. They include *Come and Go* (1927), *Life as We Dreamed It* (1931) and *Prayer for a Good End* (1944). The poems he wrote at the beginning and end of his life are not only revealing but well accomplished.

Louis-Paul Boon (1912–79) began as a vitalistic follower of Walschap (q.v.), and has remained a severe critic of society. But he is more modernistic in method, and his long novels are more reminiscent of Céline's (q.v.) than of Walschap's. He is concerned, without in the least disguising his own angry and exasperated feelings, to reveal the moral and physical corruption that underlies modern life. His novels are peopled with scores of characters, and in this at least seem to have been influenced by Dos Passos (q.v.); although his technique is modernistic, there is more than a trace of the old, pessimistic naturalist about him. His people are not usually intelligent or nice – and they are, of course, his choice. His finest books are the ironically entitled *My Little War* (1946), the vast *Chapel Road* (1953; tr. 1972) and *Summer in Ter-Muren* (1956), the moving story of a little working-class girl. Boon introduces himself into his own novels as a participant in the action and by holding conversations with his characters. Prolific and bursting with energy, Boon, the worthiest of all Céline's successors, was Belgium's most gifted Flemish novelist of his generation, and he contributed greatly to the renewal of the novel after the Second World War. *Brothers in Arms* (1955) tells the story of Reynard the Fox, but leaves the boundary between man and animal poignantly open. Later novels and 'non-fiction novels', telling of the history of socialism in Belgium in various ways, are less imaginatively coherent – but all Boon wrote was lucid and moving.

Boon's contemporary **Johan Daisne** (ps. **Herman Thiery**, 1912) is a more cerebral writer. He describes himself as a 'magic realist' (q.v.), and the label is useful inasmuch as he has the power to compel belief in his fantastic narrations. *The Stairway of Stone and Clouds* (1942) rather too sentimentally relates aspirations to reality: but the cinematic *The Man Who Had His Hair Cut Short* (1947; tr. 1965), narrated by a man on the verge of madness, is more convincing. The long Joycean narration describes, at one point, the postmortem of a girl whose body is rapidly rotting. It is all very well for a critic to say that this is an 'excellent example of Daisne's "magic realism" … through which he penetrates beyond the ideal and the illusory in order to reach the ultimate reality of life'; but this begs a few questions. Does he reach it? Of course not (but the critic evades this). The book is just one more example, better than most, of a wild monologue: better than most because it possesses certain persuasive powers.

Marnix Gijsen (ps. **Jan-Albert Goris**, 1899), a diplomat, has written a remarkable modern reinterpretation of the Susanna and the Elders story, *The Book of Joachim of Babylon* (1946; tr. 1951); like his near-contemporary Vestdijk (q.v.) Gijsen is Freudian in his approach and uses much autobiographical material. He is also bitterly anti-clerical, intellectual, sceptical and anti-nationalist. *Telemachus in the Village* (1948) is a vivid, shrewd, sad picture of life in a Belgian provincial town; *Lament for Agnes* (1951; tr. 1975) is a nostalgic story about an unhappy love-affair. His many later novels showed no signs of declining powers.

*

Teirlinck's contribution to the Flemish theatre has already been discussed; the leading figure of the younger generation of Flemish writers is the versatile poet, novelist, film-maker and dramatist **Hugo Claus** (1929). A poet highly experimental and modern in style, he seeks to reinstate man in a context of pre-'civilized' innocence. His theatre is powerful and highly coloured: in particular *The Dawn Fiancée* (1955), which enjoyed success' in a French version, is a robust treatment of a brother-sister incest theme; society's attitude to incest, rather than incest itself, is regarded as corrupt. His novel *Dog-Days* (1952) resolutely describes a young man's doomed quest for existential purity. *Shame* (1972) cleverly explores the emptiness of a Belgian TV team who are filming a Passion play on a Pacific island. *Astonishment* (1962) is a novel which contains passages of real power, transcending the rather feeble and fashionably 'mythological' structure.

Eastern Minor Literatures

Colonization by various European countries – the Netherlands, Great Britain and France among them – has meant that most Eastern countries have produced little more than embryos of indigenous literatures. The native languages themselves – let alone their scripts – have had little opportunity to develop. Those that have been insubstantially productive (e.g. Buryat literature), and have shown no true development, have only been briefly discussed, although (as in the case of Malta) sometimes individual writers have been mentioned. (Eastern literatures of countries within the USSR have been assigned to Western Minor Literatures.)

Burmese modern literature – written in the now official language of the Union of Burma, Burmese – has not been particularly substantial, nor has any writer of real stature arisen. Its development, however, started relatively early: with the introduction of printing, which began about 1870, and the fall of the monarchy in 1886. British rule provided fewer impediments than are usual to the development of a popular colonial literature. From 1875 onwards popular works began to appear, particularly the dramatic form known as the *pya-zat* – a kind of musical play – and sentimental romances.

The traditional Burmese drama has had a long and distinguished history; but by the beginning of this century it had entirely vanished. The modern novel in Burma begins in 1904 with a very free adaptation of an episode in *The Count of Monte Cristo* by **James Hla Gyaw** (1886–1920). Only two or three other novels appeared, however, in the first two decades of the century: **U Kyi**'s *The Rosette Seller* (1904) and *The Ruler of the Golden Land* (1914), about young Burmese who rejected traditional values only to be disillusioned by visits to the West, by **U Lat** (1866–1921).

By 1920 literature was fast deteriorating; the foundation of the University of Rangoon in that year partially halted the process. Between then and the Japanese invasion (1942) there arose a new generation of writers, who began to write in a Burmese not too far removed from the colloquial. A number of adequate translations from European literatures were made; prose fiction was developed; poems that were at least serious in intention were written. The major influence in these years was the Experiment for a New Age (*Khit-san*) movement. This, based on Rangoon University, attempted to hold the balance between Western and Burmese. The most substantial literary achievements were the novel *The Modern Monk* (1936) by **Thein Pe**, and the fiction of Burma's first woman writer, **Dagon Hkin Hkin Lei** (1904), which included a quite realistic portrait of the peasantry called *A Woman's Life* (1931).

Since 1948, with the creation of the republic and the replacement of English by Burmese as the official language, interest in the national literature has increased. **U Nu** (1907), one-time prime minister, then political prisoner (now released), is one of modern Burma's better known writers. Apart from political essays and translations of Western novels, he has published a memoir, *Five Years in Burma* (1945), and a Western-style play, *The Victorious Voice of the People* (1953; tr. 1953). Two leading novelists have been **Min Aung**, who wrote *The Earth under the Sky* (1948), and the woman novelist **Ja-Ne-Gyaw Ma**

Ma Lay (1917), author of *Not that I Hate* (1955). But censorship is now very tight, and the members of the Press Scrutiny Committee continue to stifle writers, of whom they are rightly afraid.

*

The modern literatures of Cambodia, Laos and Viet Nam (both South and North) are in general exceedingly impoverished, although there is no lack of trash in the form of detective stories, romances and semi-pornography (usually cast in a highly moral framework). In certain of these countries the ancient literatures are being made available once again; this is probably the most significant aspect of their literary activity. This is certainly the case in Bali (now, however, increasingly under the influence of the Indonesians), in Cambodia, and in that part of Lower Burma inhabited by the Buddhist Mons (where worship of the ancient literature actually inhibits the creation of a new). In the earlier modern period many paraphrases of Western – mostly French – realistic novels were published; these have no independent literary merit.

*

It is owing to Truong Vinh Ky, known as Petrus Ky (1837–98), that nearly all Vietnamese literature today is written in Quoc Ngu, a romanized script. In this century most of the better writing emanated from the literary group calling itself Tu-Luc Van-Doan. This group, influenced by French realism, flourished in the Thirties. No outstanding single work was produced, but the whole direction of Vietnamese fiction was changed, and a new kind of novel could emerge were it not for socialist realist (q.v.) demands.

*

The main exceptions to the general picture of Oriental literary impoverishment (the oriental Russian states being dealt with in the Western section) are Indonesia, Persia and the Philippines; but Thailand (formerly Siam) has a fairly flourishing literature. The main influence has been Buddhist; but the Hindu influence has not been negligible. It was the circle of the King of Siam, Rama VI, **Vajiravudh** (1881–1925) and of the Prince **Bidyalankarana** (1876–1945) which first introduced modernism into Thai literature. Vajiravudh translated from the French and the English (he went to Oxford), wrote stylish short comedies that were original at least in Thai literature, and an intelligent epistolary novel called *The Heart of a Young Man*. Bidyalankarana was more creatively gifted: his short stories – clever and humane – count among the best of Thai prose.

One of the most gifted of modern Thai novelists has been **Si Burapha** (ps. **Kulap Saipradit**, 1904). Si Burapha, influenced by Marxist theory though not a thoroughgoing Marxist, has persistently opposed the tendencies to sentimentality that disfigure most of Thai fiction – even that by relatively talented writers. *A Man Indeed* (1928), a bitter story of a man's struggle to overcome his inferior social position, introduced a new note of realism into Thai literature. *Behind the Picture* (1938) and *The Struggle of Life* (1944) treat of sexual themes with great restraint and subtle psychological understanding. His later work was not of a similarly high quality; he devoted himself to attacks on the way literature was going in Thailand.

Dok Mai Sot (ps. **Mom Luang Bubpa Sukich Nimmanheminda**, 1906–63) was the leading woman novelist. Her theme – the social and other harms resulting from crude and mechanical Westernization – is best illustrated in *Thus the World Is* (1935); she wrote nine other novels, all of them containing intelligent and often amusing writing.

The versatile **Mom Ratchawong Khu'krit Pramoj** (1912), a leading liberal journalist and satirist, is still the most lively figure in contemporary Thai literature. He is a critic, short-story writer and playwright as well as a novelist. *Four Reigns* (1953), a long saga, intelligently reconciles the past with the future, the ancient and oriental with the new and Western. *Many Lives* (1955) shows acute awareness of social differences in modern Thailand.

*

Maltese is a language with affinities with Tunisian Arabic, ancient Phoenician and Sicilian. It replaced Italian as Malta's official language in 1934. So far only one man has written in it with distinction: this is **Dun Karm** (ps. **Carmelo Psaila**, 1871–1961), a Roman Catholic priest. In Psaila's poetry, which can be read in the original by fewer than half a million people, many of the unique characteristics of the Maltese literature of the past are preserved: among these are conciseness, dignity and lack of sentimentality. Psaila turned from Italian to Maltese poetry in 1912. His predecessor **G. Muscat Azzopardi** (1853–1927) was less gifted, but deserves mention as a pioneer and as Psaila's teacher – and the one who persuaded him to write in Maltese. Others who contributed to the development of Maltese poetry are **A. Cuschieri** (1873–1962) and **Ninu Cremona** (1880–1972), who was, however, best known as a playwright. But Psaila, or Dun Karm as he is usually called, is the outstanding Maltese poet. He is not a great author, but his poetry is original and interesting. Fortunately, a selection of it has been translated by A.J. Arberry in *Dun Karm: Poet of Malta* (1961).

G. Aquilina (1911), although not as gifted as Psaila (q.v.), has done more than any other towards the development of Maltese prose, particularly in his historical novel *Under Three Regimes*, and in his plays.

*

The literature of modern Korea has been serious as well as energetic in its aspirations; but few writers of originality have emerged. The so-called Era of Enlightenment, involving imitations of European and American realism, began in 1876, when Korea began to make contact with other countries. It represents a clean break with the literature of the past, which had stretched back over two thousand years. Until 1910 Korean literature was dominated by the 'New Novel', which, while crude, melodramatic and nationalistic, did introduce the use of the colloquial. The most notable examples are novels by **Yi In-Jik** (1862–1916) – *Tears of Blood* (1906), *The Voice of the Devil* (1908) – who inaugurated this type of fiction.

In 1910 Korea was forced to accept the 'annexation' to Japan; from this time dates the second modernist phase known (for reasons obvious enough) as the Independence era. **Yi-Kwang-Su** (1892–?), whose fiction has still not been surpassed in this century, became active at this time. (The date of his death, or even whether he is dead – although presumably he is by now – is not known: he was captured by the communists during the Korean War and taken off to North Korea.) *The Heartless* (1917) is the first truly modern Korean novel: apart from attacking the Japanese annexation, it attacks the injustices inherent in Korean society itself, and yet maintains a high standard of psychological accuracy. *Love* (1936) is even more outstanding. Yet Yi-Kwang-Su, for all his personal success in restoring a partially non-propagandist role to fiction, none the less believed in the dogmatic, nationalistic function of literature.

After the Japanese suppression of the Korean revolt of 1919 a group of writers arose who felt that literature, by working for independence, was betraying its true purpose. The members of this 'Creation Circle' (called thus after their magazine, *Creation*) admired the achievement of Yi-Kwang-Su, but opposed themselves to his theory of literature's social function. These writers, on the whole pessimistic and anti-political in mood, fell under the influence of Zola (q.v.) and other late nineteenth-century naturalists.

At roughly the same time as the Creation Circle was formed, however, a proletarian group arose; this became stronger within a few years, and by 1923 there was an active New Trend group, practising social realism. Less good writing came from this than from the Creation Circle; in any case the whole left-wing of Korean literature was rigidly repressed, by the Japanese, by 1935. After the Second World War and, again, after the Korean War in South Korea (the writers of North Korea practise a crude form of socialist realism, q.v., or nothing; there is no discussion), the debate between those who believe in literature as a social and political instrument and those who believe in it as a means of revealing truth has continued. South Korea is an unhappy country, ruled by virtual dictators; there are indications that a novel and a drama heavily influenced by European radical modernism will emerge; but as yet there is no substantial writer.

Modern Korean poetry has been superior in quality. Ko Won has compiled and translated an excellent selection from it in *Contemporary Korean Poetry* (1970). Modern poetry begins with **Ch'oe Namson's** (1890–1957) free verse poem 'From the Sea to Children', a vernacular poem that seemed – with its ironic levity of tone and its idiomatic language – as modern to Koreans as 'Prufrock' (q.v.) did to Americans and Englishmen. As a poem it is not more intrinsically important than, say, Jakob Van Hoddis' 'World's End' (q.v.); but it happened to inaugurate a new poetry and a new poetics. Later, after 1919, symbolism (q.v.) began to play its role. **Kongch'o** (ps. O Sang-Sun, 1894–1963), a 'nihilistic wanderer, never married', educated in Japan, introduced a resigned, Buddhistic note in his free verse poetry. **Yi Chang-Hui** (1902–28), who killed himself, was Korea's leading symbolist and hermetic poet of the early period; he wrote poems of elegant despair and solipsist ecstasy. **Chong Chi-Yong** (1903–*c*1951), probably killed in the Korean war, cultivated a similar note, and is influential today. The best of the younger poets is **Kim Ch'Un-Su** (1922), who combines Japanese with Western influences in a poetry that evokes the modern sensibility with sensitivity and feeling.

*

Modern Persian literature has for the most part reflected the political situation. This has not yet been resolved, since the regime now in power is still reactionary: there is no freedom of speech or opinion. The literature of the early period (1905–21) is one of liberal revolt against tyranny and religious obscurantism. There seemed to be some hope for a liberal constitution until the coup d'état of 1921, when the reign of Riza Shah was inaugurated. The dominating figure of this period is the poet **Malik Al-Shu'ara** (ps. **Muhammad Taqi Bahar**, 1886–1951), who was forced (some less cautious contemporary poets were murdered) to take refuge in scholarly activities. He had been a leading member of the liberal revolution (1905–12), and was an MP. Always a classicist, he was nevertheless a tireless experimenter within the limits of the traditional forms, and he believed in both free discussion and the abolition of privilege. In retrospect his character and the example he set are more intrinsically important than his own poetry, skilful and often eloquent though this is.

Contemporary Persian poetry resembles Turkish, but there are fewer and less gifted practitioners; and the situation for writers is worse. Most of the poetry written under the late Shah was trite or unintelligible – in imitation of pretentious Western models.

The two most important prose writers have been **Muhammad Hijazi** (1899) and **Sadiq Hidayat** (1902–51), Persia's most important modern novelist, and a major figure by international standards. Hijazi managed to attain, and to retain, popularity during the reign of Riza Shah; his subject was the nature and the lot of Persian women. His first mature novel, and the one that brought him fame, was *Ziba* (1931). This, the most penetrating and detailed portrait of twentieth-century Persian life yet to appear, deals with Ziba, a charming *femme fatale*, and a young theological student who is driven to delinquency by his involvement with her. *Ziba* is a devastatingly ironic exposure of Persian bureaucracy. Unfortunately Hijazi himself became increasingly involved with the world he depicted in this early novel; nothing he has written since – skilled and clever though it is – comes near to equalling it.

Sadiq Hidayat, originally a student of dentistry, visited France and absorbed much of its culture. The chief influence on the younger generation of Persian writers, he was profoundly aware of the Persian past (he was learned in its folklore) and yet as receptive to Western influences. At bottom a nihilist, thrown into despair by the fierce obscurantism still (twenty-five years after his death) the dominant factor in Persian life, he gassed himself in a Paris apartment in 1951. He is a fascinating writer, who combines in his fiction (one novel and several collections of short stories) brutal naturalism (q.v.) with the magical and fantastic elements of Persian folklore. He also wrote plays. One of his earliest books had a theme unusual, even unique, in modern Oriental fiction: *Man and Animal* (1924) deals with mankind's cruelty to animals. His best stories were written between 1930 and 1937. His short novel *Haji Aqa* (1945) is a study of a charlatan. Hidayat's masterpiece, however, is *The Blind Owl* (1936; tr. 1957; 1974 – the new version is much better). This is an extraordinary mixture of poetry and naturalism: the unenlightened owl, endowed with human wisdom, becomes sick as it recognizes silence. This strange and unique book was first circulated in India in a duplicated form – a copy must be worth a fortune. It is an indescribable work, of great power: compulsive reading.

One of his most distinguished successors is **Ali-Muhammad Afghani** (1925), about whom little is known save that he was an army officer and that he spent much of the Fifties in prison because of his interest in freedom ('leftist tendencies'). Afghani has written (it is said in prison) the enormous novel *Mrs Ahu's Husband* (1961). This may well be the masterpiece that some Persians (but not the conservative majority) claim it to be. It describes the decay of the last thoroughgoingly reactionary generation (born around the turn of the century) of Iranians. It deals unerringly and movingly with the position of Persian women. The main plot concerns the eventually successful efforts of a woman to win her husband, a worthy baker, from the clutches of an adventuress. The book is over-long, but it represents the best in Persian literature since the death of Hidayat. It was followed by another novel in 1966.

Sadegh Chubak (1916), who began publishing in the Thirties, combines decadent influences from the Nineties with an ill-absorbed modernism, although he can achieve power in isolated passages. *The Patient Stone* (1966) is characteristic: as a novel it does not hold together; and each element is nihilistic or decadent: a corpse eaten by worms; an impotent junkie; brutal murder; sexual orgies. The younger **Esmail Fasih** shows more promise, and his first novel, *Sharab-e Kham* (1969), although uneven, is more psychologically convincing. **Ferydoun Hoveyda** writes in French. His best novel is *The Quarantines* (*Les quarantaines*, 1967). A notable work by a Persian written in English is **F.M. Esfandiary's** *Identity Card* (1966), which gives perhaps the grimmest picture of the Shah's Persia yet available; the book had to be smuggled to America. What is now happening in literature cannot be seen for the dust of the strange revolution and deposition of the Shah; it cannot be good yet.

*

The literature of modern Indonesia is a comparatively flourishing one; among the literatures dealt with in this section only that of the Philippines can rival it. A few natives of the modern Indonesia write in Balinese (q.v.), Javanese and Malay; but the vast majority write in the modernized form of Malay now described as Indonesian. One of the more talented of the earlier pioneers, the first modern poet in Indonesian, was **Muhammad Yamin** (1903–62), a Sumatran who played some part in the creation of modern Indonesia. His first collection of poetry, *Fatherland*, appeared in 1922. But Yamin is in no way modern in his use of language, and his forms are traditional and conservative; his poetry was new only because of its nationalistic content. **Roestam Effendi** (1903) is more versatile and sophisticated; as a communist MP between the two World Wars he spent much time in the Netherlands. His poetry draws much on European models, but is none the less rooted in his experience of his native West Sumatra.

Even more influential, however, were the brothers **Sanusi Pané** (1905) and **Armijn Pané** (1908), and **Sutan Takdir Alisjahbana** (1908). Sanusi Pané wrote some attractive lyrical verse as a young man, then turned to drama and finally to literary journalism. His brother, whose language assimilates European constructions to Malay in a remarkable manner, is a gifted novelist: *Shackles* (1940) is the first true psychological novel in Indonesian. Takdir Alisjahbana is a more polemical writer: he has always fervently believed in the assimilation of Western techniques as the chief means of raising Indonesia to her rightful position in the world, and his advocacy of an Indonesian culture based on European rather than Hindu concepts has given rise to much controversy. His own creative work (poetry, fiction) is less important than his influence as a critic and essayist (he posits a version of social realism, as well as nationalism, against the artistic self-sufficiency of a writer such as Sanusi Pané); he has held high cultural posts since independence. He, Armijn Pané and the poet **Amir Hamzah** (1911–46) – killed in pre-independence fighting – founded a magazine in 1933 that was to prove the rallying-point of Indonesian literature over the next nine years: *New Man of Letters*.

The 'Generation of 1945', upon whom Du Perron (q.v., born in Indonesia) was an important influence, has so far produced a handful of outstanding writers. The poet **Chairil Anwar** (1922–49) – who died of a combination of syphilis, alcoholism, typhus and tuberculosis – was undoubtedly the most gifted writer Indonesia has yet produced.

Anwar, another 'nihilistic wanderer', and 'agony writer', was a natural expressionist who used Rimbaud and the Dutch Marsman (q.v.) as his models. His poetry, disturbed, vital and powerful – it has something in it of the haunted quality of Campana's (q.v.) – was published in collected form after his death. *The Complete Poetry and Prose of Chairil Anwar* appeared in 1970, but these translations were sharply criticized by scholars. Although haunted by despair and restlessness, Anwar found some hope in the aspirations of his people, in whose destiny he was able (at times) to believe, since he could project into it his own dynamic, if chaotic, spirit. Anwar was able to create an Indonesia in which he projected the entire gamut of his confusions – and his insight. He has been overpraised; but no other Indonesian writer has possessed his energy.

Three outstanding contemporary Indonesian poets are **W.S. Rendra** (1935), **Sitor Situmorang** (1924) and **Ajip Rossidhy** (1938).

Pramoedya Ananta Toer (1925) is the leading contemporary novelist. He is an objective realist who deals – in such novels as *A Guerilla Family* (1950) and *It's Not an All Night Fair* (1951; tr. 1973) – with the themes of the Japanese occupation and the post-war struggle against the Netherlands. As Toer became more communist, his fiction coarsened. After 1965, when right-wing forces took over the country, Toer was imprisoned, not to be released until 1979. He wrote the massive *Man's Earth* (1980), an important story of Indonesia in the earlier years of this century. It was so popular that in May 1981 the government banned it. **Mochtar Lubis** (1922) has written, in his loosely constructed, episodic *Twilight in Djakarta* (1963), the most savage indictment of Indonesian life under the now deceased Sukarno.

*

Literature in Malay has received some stimulus from that of Indonesia; but rather more of intrinsic value has been produced in the non-Malay literatures of Malaya and Singapore: those written in English, Chinese and Tamil. **Wong Phui Nam** (1935) is the leading poet in English – and he is a talented and aware one, if somewhat given to facile imitation of fashionable European and American models. Some of his poetry may be found in *Bunga Emas: an Anthology of Contemporary Malaysian Literature* (1964). Good short stories have been written, notably by **Lee Kok Liang** (1927), who received his university education in Australia and has been influenced both by Australian realists such as Leonard Mann (q.v.) and by Faulkner (q.v.). Nonetheless, the background of his stories is strictly regional. Chinese prose writing in Malaya is represented by **Wei Yun**, originally from China, and **Miao Hsiu**, who writes mainly of the period of Japanese occupation. The best poet writing in Chinese is **Tu Hung** (ps. **Tay Ah Poon**, 1936). All the Tamil writing consists of short stories, radio plays and poetry. The most gifted of these writers in the Indian language is **B. Subba Narayanan** (1929), who came to Malaya from India in 1940. He is chiefly a playwright, but has also written short stories and poems.

*

The modern literature of the Philippines, the third largest English-speaking country in the world, has been and continues to be flourishing and individual, although many younger writers find it hard to establish themselves. Doubtless this vitality has much to do with the American occupation, which followed that of the Spanish and was benign and encouraging to the development of the native culture ('Filipinization'). Although the literature of the latter half of the nineteenth century was in Spanish – even the important novels of the nationalist José Rizal (1861–96), who was murdered by the Spaniards – the Spaniards' influence ceased abruptly, as soon as they were driven out by the Spanish-American war (1898). The nationalist phase had produced a flowering of native talent (in Spanish); and there were, of course, works in Spanish published in the first twenty-five years, and later, of American rule. But most of the important Filipino writing has been in English. However, there are two writers in Filipino, the national language derived from Tagalog (the language of Manila and its environs) and nine other regional vernaculars. These are **A.G. Abadilla** and the social realist **Amado V. Hernandez**. Abadilla is a novelist; Hernandez a playwright and poet as well as the author of one novel. These are the only writers so far to have given life to a language that is still under attack for its artificiality.

Modern Filipino literature of the earlier phase, beginning in the late Twenties and maturing in the mid-Thirties with the granting of commonwealth status (1936), was best represented in the short story. Contemporary Filipino literature is mainly distinguished by its interesting and original poetry. Good novels remain an exception. One of the first and most gifted of the writers of short stories was **Manuel Arguilla** (1911–44), executed by the Japanese when they discovered he was working against them. Most of his best stories are collected in *How My Brother Leon Brought Home a Wife* (1940). Influenced – but not to his detriment – by Hemingway (q.v.), Arguilla was at his best in telling stories through the eyes of a child. At the same time as he was active José Garcia Villa (q.v.) was also writing short stories; but Villa is primarily a poet, and is something of an odd man out. His stories were published in America, but not in his own country. Other important pioneers in fiction include **N.V.M. Gonzalez** (1915), author of some of the best Filipino novels, including *The Bamboo Dancers* (1959); the physician **Arturo B. Rotor** (1907), who writes vivid stories based on his own experiences in his first and best collection, *The Wound and the Scar* (1937); and **Kerima Polotan**, whose *The Hound of the Enemy* (1962) is one of the best novels to appear since 1945.

Nick Joaquín (1917) is a subtle, if stylistically lush, writer of fiction and drama that mostly searches for the Filipino essence in the Americanized present. He was once going to be a priest, and he has been concerned all his writing life to reconcile the pagan past of his country with the spirit, not of any modern Church, but of the Gospels. Filipino drama has been slow to develop; Joaquín's *Portrait of the Artist as Filipino* (1953) is the best of the plays so far written. He has written one novel: *The Woman who had Two Navels* (1961). This was developed from a novella Joaquín completed shortly after the end of the Second World War, and published in *Prose and Poems* (1952). It juxtaposes two stories, one set in the Spanish past and one in the present, in a skilful and meaningful manner. There is a *Selected Stories* (1962). If we leave Villa aside, Joaquín is undoubtedly the leading Filipino writer of the century.

José Garcia Villa (1914) is the first Philippine writer since Rizal to gain a truly international reputation. His early and promising short stories, mostly about his boyhood and strict upbringing, were collected in *Footnote to Youth* (1933) and published in New York. Villa had enrolled at the University of New Mexico at the age of sixteen. He has made his home in America since this time, although he has held teaching posts (including one at the University of Quezon, which had expelled him at the age of fifteen for publishing a poem it considered obscene) in the Philippines. Not many Filipino critics rate him highly: they accuse him of solipsism and prophesy that the novelty of his poetry will quickly wear off. Yet Marianne Moore (q.v.), among others less distinguished, has given serious critical attention to his poetry, which is unquestionably serious. His famous 'comma poems', in which the words are separated from one another by commas, are by no means ineffective or merely 'novel'. (An experiment that came after the 'comma poems' is 'reversed consonance': Villa claims that, for example, the word 'sings' 'mirrors' the word 'begins'.) What at first may look a specious rhetoric in his best poetry (the most substantial selection is in *Poems 55*, 1962) is in fact the product of an original and often astute mind. At the back of much of the poetry is his early rejection of his wealthy father and all he stood for (Villa rejects, not the Philippines, but his family). He is a genuine eccentric, a poet of interest and some fascination; he may not possess major status, and he may have disfigured some of his poetry by over-ingenious tricks; but his integrity has never really been in doubt. He truly prefers public madness. The genuine puzzle his work offers is well exemplified in 'Inviting a Tiger for a Weekend':

> Inviting a tiger for a weekend.
> The gesture is not heroics but discipline.
> The memoirs will be splendid.
>
> Proceed to dazzlement, Augustine.
> Banish little birds, graduate to tiger.
> Proceed to dazzlement, Augustine.
>
> Any tiger of whatever colour
> The same as jewels any stone
> Flames always essential morn.
>
> The guest is luminous, peer of Blake.
> The host is gallant, eye of Death.
> If you do this you will break
>
> The little religions for my sake.
> Invite a tiger for a weekend,
> Proceed to dazzlement, Augustine.

There is an *Essential Villa* (1965), a *Portable Villa* (1962), and a *Selected Stories* (1962).

The outstanding poet of the younger generation – and he deserves a higher reputation than he has so far gained outside his own country – is **Alejandrino G. Hufana** (1926). Hufana studied in America, and has assimilated all that he needs from twentieth-century American poetry (for example, the epigrammatic gravity of Masters, q.v., the narrative mastery of Robinson, q.v.). His best theme, like that of Joaquín (q.v.), is the quest for whatever is authentic in the Filipino past. He writes (in a clean verse that most would-be narrative poets contemporary with him should envy) of both the past and the present of 'primitive' peoples. There is a touch of Villa (q.v.) in him, so that we should not be as sure, perhaps, as most Filipinos are that Villa is to be written off as unrepresentative.

Federico Lilsi Espino Jr. is the leading writer in Tagalog; he also writes in English. So far his work, collected in *Pasternak's Balalaika* (1967) and *A Rapture of Distress* (1968), and other small volumes, is self-consciously experimental: cosmopolitan influences have not yet been fully absorbed. But Espino clearly has something to give to Filipino literature. His best work so far has been in English prose, in the tense and well-written tales of *The Country of Sleep* (1969). **Edelberto K. Tiempo**, who writes in English, shows a similar promise in the stories in *A Stream at Dalton Pass* (1970). The outstanding writer in Spanish is the woman poet **Adelina Gurrea**, whose most substantial collection is *Other Paths* (1967).

Finnish Literature

Finnish, a Uralian language with nothing in common with Swedish – Estonian (q.v.) is its closest relation – is now the vernacular of nine-tenths of the population of Finland. Modern Finnish literature proper dates from 1880: the Young Finland ('Nuori Suomi') movement.

Finland was united with Sweden from the twelfth century until 1809, when it was made into a Grand Duchy of the Russian Empire. Until 1899, when there was sudden Slavophile pressure exerted from Russia ('russification'), and when existing arrangements were rudely violated, Finland had enjoyed relative autonomy, and there had been no opposition to the development of Finnish nationalism. This was a romantic movement centred on the Finnish language and its folklore (the epic *Kalevala* was reconstructed by Lönnrot in 1849), the richest elements of which were discovered in Russian Karelia (the Karelian element became exaggerated later), a fact which was to have consequences. The movement was heavily oriented towards German idealist philosophy, and was anti-Swedish because the ruling classes of the eighteenth century were mainly Finland Swedes, who spoke Swedish (the Swedo-Finnish minority literature is dealt with under the Scandinavian heading, because this book is classified by language). The new native literature was at first realistic but in a romantic manner. It was influenced by both Swedish and Russian literatures, but looked elsewhere in Europe. Its main aim, however, was to create a genuinely Finnish literature. Yet there was an important writer, much too early to be a member of Young Finland, who in many ways foreshadowed all the developments in Finnish literature until at least the middle of this century, and, essentially, later. The sources of many 'new' styles and attitudes may be traced back to his enormously varied work: the swing to realism in reaction to romanticism and decadence, the comic novel dealing in confusions and confabulations, the pervasive influence of the *Kalevala* – and both the heroizing of the 'primitive', 'noble', pagan Finn, and the reaction to that. ... He was Alexis Kivi (ps. A. Stenvall, 1834–72), novelist and story-writer (chiefly), playwright and poet. Kivi wrote in Swedish as well as Finnish, but his epic work *Seven Brothers* (1870; tr. 1929) is in Finnish. In this story of seven brutal and violent northern Finnish brothers, which is interspersed with folklore elements, and is written with a majestic sweep, all the contradictory features mentioned are present. There is humour (a characteristic of almost all Finnish writing), lyricism, romanticism, harsh realism, and a resolution of confusions. *Seven Brothers* is a European masterpiece which should be back in print in the English language (Matson's version only needs editing). The ghost of Kivi is behind most of Finnish literature, and Finland has not yet produced a greater writer.

The leading writers of the Young Finland movement were Minna Canth (ps. W. Johnsson, 1844–97), story-writer and playwright, still recognized for her ear for authentic dialogue, **Juhani Aho** (ps. **Juhani Brofeldt**, 1861–1921) and Arvid Järnefelt (q.v.).

Aho, a parson's son, got to know Daudet, Maupassant and Zola (q.v.) in Paris in 1889. He began as a romantic realist; but his discovery of sterner French realistic (q.v.) procedures did him nothing but good. Prior to going to Paris he had written *When Father Brought Home the Lamp* (1883; tr. 1884), *The Railway* (1884) and *The Parson's Daughter*

(1885). The last of these deals sensibly with provincial middle-class life, and touches on the emancipation of women – a theme as common in Finnish as in Swedish literature, in which there are more women writers than elsewhere. But his first mature work was started in Paris: the sketches he called *Shavings* (1891–1921; Fr. sel. tr., *Copeaux*, 1927). Realism here is still tinged with romanticism, or vice versa; stylistically these sketches influenced later writers, and they are still attractive and readable. Clearly Aho had read Turgenev. With the novel *Panu* (1897; tr. 1899) Aho reached his Finnish-nationalist, romantic peak: this is a tale of Christianity's conquest of paganism, and is his not very impressive tribute to the Finnish heathen past. He found his head again to an extent in the backwoods love story *Juha* (1911), which is still over-romantic, but far more psychological. In his last phase he was influenced by Selma Lagerlöf (q.v.). *Squire Hellman* (tr. 1893) is a collection of stories.

Arvid Järnefelt (1861–1932), a lawyer who early came under the influence of Tolstoi (q.v.), is less interesting, though in his time he was taken with great seriousness. He described his Tolstoian change of heart in *My Conversion* (1894). For thirty years he was regarded as an eccentric Utopian recluse, even though some of his concerns were Finnish (feminism, sexuality, the future of the peasantry). Then, in 1925, he had a best-seller with the religious novel *Greeta and his Lord*, which he followed up with the three-part *Novel of my Parents* (1928–30). He has dated badly and is not much read today: he reacted intelligently against the worst excesses of the 'noble pagan Finn' legend, but was too determined to edify his readers.

The leading lyrical poet of this generation was the neo-romantic **Eino Leino** (ps. **Armas Eino Leopold Lönnbohm**, 1878–1926), who became involved in the Young Finland movement while at university in the mid-Nineties. He was the first poet of real skill and flair since Runeberg, 'Finland's national poet' who died in 1877. But Runeberg wrote in Swedish, as did Leino's truly important Swedo-Finnish near-contemporary Edith Södergran (q.v.). Leino did not clearly understand what could be done with the Finnish language in poetry, but his instinct told him that a change had to be made from a prosody ingeniously but unhappily based on German models, though he was greatly influenced by Heine. Leino began as a brilliant journalist and youthful national romantic; but his personal life became clouded when his first marriage broke up towards the end of the first decade of the century (he made two more), and he moved from a nationalist to a confused and unproductive Nietzschean (q.v.) position. The brilliant lyrics of the young Leino, collected in *Songs of Man* (1896), represent the spearhead of the neo-romantic reaction to the naturalism already evident in the work of Aho (q.v.) and others. His chief work, *Holy Songs* (1903–16), contains elements from folklore – particularly from the *Kalevala* – and combines patriotism with menacing, decadent undertones of a personal nature; here, drawing on the old oral tradition, he came near to creating truly Finnish rhythms. He wrote some twenty verse plays, fiction and criticism.

Maria Jotuni (1880–1943) was important both as a novelist and as a playwright, though she received less attention than was her due in her lifetime, and was rediscovered and republished by modern Finnish critics. Her earliest short stories, influenced by Aho (q.v.), dealt with simple people, and were written in a clipped, laconic style which combines humour, an acute feminine psychological insight and a sense of tragic destiny. She later turned from naturalism (q.v.), but never lost her underlying sense of the tragic. Eventually she refined her techniques to a distinctly modernistic degree of concentratedness. Her use of dialogue is celebrated for its skill. Perhaps the finest of her work is to be found in *The Young Girl in the Rose Garden* (1927), a collection of short stories. She has been accused of 'cynical eroticism' – but by a male critic. Actually she looks at men with rightly disenchanted eyes.

Maiju Lassila (ps. Algoth Untola, 1868–1918), the leading leftist polemicist during the savage civil war of 1918, wrote one novel (out of many) which was popular precisely because it was unedifying: the richly comic *Borrowing Matches* (1910). This has recently and deservedly been revived, as prophetic of the kind of humour and craziness that Finland was then without (few Finnish writers have lacked humour altogether, but it was frequently of a heavy sort). This book is in some ways in the Hašek (q.v.) class, and should certainly be translated. Lassila led a mysterious life; he made a fortune as a businessman after 1900, then had a hand in an assassination in St. Petersburg, and vanished for a time. He warned of reprisals after the Civil War, and was himself to be executed in a special ceremony to please exultant Germans. But on the way he got himself shot. ... He is now a cult figure, and the subject of an inaccurate but effective film.

Volter Kilpi (ps. Volter Ericsson, 1874–1939), the Finno-Swedish son of a ship's captain, who chose to write in Finnish, began as a decadent aesthete, but developed from this manner in a way uncannily reminiscent of the Dutch novelist Arthur van Schendel (q.v.), who was his exact contemporary, and whose work he could hardly have known (though he was a librarian, at Turku). Kilpi is a very difficult author, whose work has never been really popular, and who has possibly been neglected because of his political position during and after the civil war, when he was a monarchist, and then a right-wing pamphleteer. His progressive deafness from an early age is one of the keys to his frequently fantastic and at times totally hermetic style. His most substantial work, set in southwestern Finland, is the trilogy *In Alastalo's Hall* (1933), *Humbler Folk of the Parish* (1934) and *On the Way to Church* (1937). This has been compared to Joyce and Proust (qq.v.), but then so have too many other works. However, it is an exercise in memory, and he did indulge himself in neologisms and fantastic coinings. More to the point, it anticipates, as has been pointed out, the 'tropisms' of Sarraute (q.v.). It is about a patri- archal community just after the middle of the nineteenth century, and is remarkable in that it is full of silences and rages which are most effectively conveyed. Neologisms and strange constructions are mixed in with (mostly) interior monologue (q.v.) to tell this strange story of a whole community; the last novel dwells on a group of islanders as they go to church on a midsummer Sunday morning. In this book Kilpi is a modernist entirely unrecognized outside his own country. He sweeps his own memory along the swiftly changing, plotless story-line: it is as though he absorbs all his recollections like a sponge, leaving at the end only a death-haunted present – a church, and the graveyard with which the whole work begins. *At Closed Gates* (1938) is a series of inexplicable and impenetrable meditations which yet have an eerie, sullen power. The unfinished *Gulliver's Journey to Fantomimia* (1944) is a failure: a poor attempt, made too late, to find a popular audience by combining social criticism with science-fiction adventure. Kilpi was exceedingly learned, and is a fascinating writer – he recalls Henry Williamson in his reactionary fury, but he produced fiction much more interesting, impersonal and lasting. About the trilogy there is something strangely hushed, resentful – but moving, and in a way towering. It is a grave error to be influenced against Kilpi's work by his politics – he did not understand the dangers of extremism (and nor did the communists).

The political struggle in which Finland became enmeshed at the end of the First World War, and its history between wars, was not calculated to bring the best out of people; and yet out of some, somehow, it did – even, ultimately, out of Mannerheim. The 'russification' programme begun in 1899 of course aroused Finns to an anti-Russian hatred which (understandably) soon gathered unpleasantly racist overtones. But there had been industrialization in the nineteenth century – very rapid after 1870 – and this had led to socialism. Since there was a ready-made opposition to the Tsar present in

Russia, many Finns turned to it zealously. There was a degree of co-operation between the mainly German-oriented nationalists and the socialists in the first decade of the century, when for a short while (for a year or two after the 1905 Revolution in Russia) liberal concessions were wrung from the Tsar. But the two factions hated each other as much as they hated the Tsar (who re-started russification in 1907). When the 1914 war came the Finns enjoyed a burst of economic prosperity – and hopes of an end to Russian domination. But in 1917 tensions built up: many of the Marxist socialists decided to defy the electorate, who had just voted in bourgeois parties and taken away their majority in parliament. But they were split, and the new government declared an independent Finnish republic on 6 December 1917. Just under two months later the extreme left tried to take power in an armed coup, and thus precipitated the civil war, which lasted until May. The left were supported by Russia, the right by Germany: it was a battle between Reds and Whites (led by such military heroes as Mannerheim and Walden), and it has of course never been forgotten. When the Whites won, they embarked on a savage repression – causing many to fly to Russia. This bloodbath was as unwise and ill-advised as the attempted insurrection of the Marxists and their sympathizers had been. It created martyrs such as Untola (q.v.). The Whites were unable to hold on to power, owing to Allied opposition, and it was a democratic government which signed the Treaty of Tartu with Soviet Russia: they did not get Karelia back, but they did get a promise that it was to be granted autonomy. In fact it was used by communist Finns, backed by Russians, as a base of operations against democratic Finland, which the Soviets wanted (and still want) as a part of their empire. The extreme right in Finland would not accept this treaty, and formed themselves into various power groups; the so-called coalition party *Kokoomus* (which means coalition) was their political front. But *Kokoomus* held only a handful of seats in parliament; the Communists made the anti-democratic faction up to about fifty. The rest of the 200 seats were held by parties of the centre and by the social democrats. A few seats were held by the Swedish minority, the Agrarians and the most intellectual of the parties, the Progressive. Left and right worked against the government, an uneasy coalition which kept changing (between 1919 and 1966 Finland had had sixty governments). The left had their base in Soviet Karelia – and control of the unions. The right had a partially government-funded private army, the Defence Corps (SK), and a kind of masonic 'non-political' association called the Academic Karelia Society (AKS), which enlisted almost all the students at the universities and exercised enormous power throughout the country – since almost all Finns of the ruling classes were (and are) university-trained. The AKS was a model fascist organization – but it came into being before fascism. It was nationalist, authoritarian, held communism out as the proverbial bogey in an impracticable manner, racist, and regarded all democracies as weak forms of government. There was also 'Industrial Peace', a big business organization with a corps of strike-breakers ready to go anywhere.

So the situation was ripe for a fascist-style coup. But it never quite happened. This is one of the most remarkable political facts of the century, particularly as the SK could not be disbanded, and as AKS had successfully created the perfect ideological background. Worst of all, the communists were in most ways a mirror-image of their opponents; the threat of Soviet occupancy was not an idle one.

Obviously this is relevant to literature: the sort of literature that got written, the sort of criticism that was – and is – made of it. Very few people could take no side at all: the always cowardly position of being 'resolutely non-political' was impossible. No one could be but confused as to where his or her interest truly lay. A.F. Upton comments: 'Isolated by geography and language, given to introspective brooding on their own problems [one thinks of Kilpi, even if he was or thought he was a 'White'], the Finns have tended to be scornful of patent solutions for their difficulties imported ready-made from abroad. They do not accept that anyone from outside could teach them much about what directly concerns themselves.'

There is a legend in some quarters that all these developments, especially the civil war, were taboo in Finnish literature between the wars; but this is not the case. The Finno-Swedish literature, by a minority who were by now feeling oppressed, was the most explicit and the most objective; but there were other writers who held a more or less neutral position, and who tried to see the causes and the consequences of the war. **Ilmari Kianto** (1874–1970) wrote *Joseph of Ryysyranta* (1924), about the poverty of the peasants. Kianto, **Frans Eemil Sillanpää** (1888–1964) and Joel Lehtonen (q.v.) took the White side in the war, and were anti-socialist; they have therefore often been called 'fascist' propagandists. But, while their fiction entirely ignores urban workers, they were not as partisan as they have been made out to be. It is true that Sillanpää would not have received the Nobel Prize in 1939 had Russia not attacked Finland; but because he never tried to come to terms with industrialization, and cannot be called a social novelist, does not mean that he was a 'fascist'. A friend of Aho (q.v.) and of the composer Sibelius, he was (like the latter) almost as famous for his capacity for alcohol as he was for his books. But he was an overrated writer, and his work fell off after 1930, when it became increasingly escapist. He studied biology (although he took no degree), and became a vitalist after the manner of that time: for him, the universe was one single living entity, and it expresses itself most fruitfully through the lives of humble people. *Life and the Sun* (1916), influenced by Hamsun (q.v.) – but it quite lacks the sly brilliance of the earliest and best Hamsun – is a love story in which two urban lovers merge together according to the dictates of nature. Far superior is *Meek Heritage* (1919; tr. 1938), the best constructed of all Sillanpää's works; this deals with the events of the Finnish civil war. The central figure is a tenant-farmer, a character who is resigned to his fate. Sillanpää's treatment is not profound; but it is humane. After this Sillanpää came under the influence of Maeterlinck (q.v.), and entered a more mystical period. He became famous with *Maid Silja or Fallen Asleep While Young* (1931; tr. 1933), his least satisfactory book. Sillanpää's short stories are possibly superior to his novels: better constructed and with a deeper psychological penetration. Here Sillanpää displays his genius for noting tiny inner movements of the mind and heart, and for suggesting unconscious motivation. Sillanpää's minor gift is usually expressed in massive forms, which makes him a disconcerting writer.

Joel Lehtonen (1881–1934) began as a typical romantic nationalist, but became more realistic as events in Finland impinged on him. *Putkinotko* (1919–20; Fr. tr. *La combe aux mauvaises herbes*, 1962), the name of an estate, studies a single day in the life of a poor sharecropper. This is less ponderous and more humorous than *Meek Heritage* (q.v.): a sharper book, but hardly an adequate analysis of the causes of the civil war, since it treats urban people as superficial, and almost robs them of their humanity. But people without roots are not in fact less 'deep' than peasants; they are simply more 'neurasthenic' – nor is socialism necessarily a taint. Still, Lehtonen was aware of his insufficiencies, and there is much implied criticism in *Putkinotko*. His last book, *The Battle of the Spirits* (1933), is more critical of chauvinism than anything by Sillanpää (q.v.).

Toivo Pekkanen (1902–57) is in some ways a more interesting and enigmatic writer. He was Finland's first major 'proletarian' writer, though his work has been subjected to various interpretations. Is he a naturalist, a realist or a symbolist? The answer is that he has been all three. *My Childhood* (1953; tr. 1966) is a starkly objective account of the struggle of a working-class family. Pekkanen would not attach himself to any political faction, though this may have been owing to circumspection. *My Childhood* came late in Pekkanen's surprisingly versatile writing career. Earlier had come the undoubtedly naturalistic *On the Shores of my Finland* (1937), describing a strike, and *Black Ecstasy* (1939), a psychological novel about love between peasants. His novel-cycle about his native port of Kotka (1957–8) employs the techniques of Dos Passos (q.v.), presenting its inhabitants in the dreary world in which they live, but also showing them in moments of true humanity, when their resignation changes to desire for a better life.

Pentti Haanpää (1905–55) paid for his accurate savaging of the life of Finnish conscripts in the short-story collection *Field and Barracks* (1928) by being ostracized as red, godless and an enemy of security. Influenced by English literature (particularly by Lawrence, q.v.), he was not a proletariat writer: his theme was the dehumanizing effects of industrialism. He could not find a publisher after *Field and Barracks* for seven years. Haanpää's work later became accepted; but he compromised only to the (reasonable) extent of supporting his country against the Russians when they treacherously attacked it. *War in the White Desert* (1940) is the most vivid of all descriptions of the Russo-Finnish 'winter' war over whose fierce fifteen weeks the Red Army was humiliated – before using sheer extra might to force Finland to cede nearly 16,000 square miles of land. *War in the White Desert* was translated into French (*Guerre dans la désert blanc*, 1942). Thereafter Haanpää became a brutally powerful and ironic writer, uncompromising in his pessimistic view of life. After his death by drowning (presumed to be suicide) there appeared *Magic Circle* (1957), perhaps his greatest achievement. When the protagonist vanishes into the Soviet Union at the end some critics seized on this as significant: actually Haanpää, always a peasant writer at heart, meant it as a gesture of despair – but he chose water rather than the Soviet Union. Haanpää's view of life resembles that of Camus (q.v.); but he is not interested in solutions or protests. He relishes the comedy of human aspirations, played out against the wholly indifferent, and yet mockingly beautiful, background of nature. In this he recalls Bunin (q.v.). He again is a more interesting writer than Sillanpää. He was not a communist, and is called one only by reactionary critics who objected to his telling the truth about the army.

Although not as gifted a writer, the escapist **Mika Waltari** (1908–79) has attracted much more attention outside Finland with his skilful, well-written, intelligent but kitsch historical novels, most of which have been translated (*Sinuhe the Egyptian*, 1945, tr. and abridged 1949; *The Secret of the Kingdom*, 1959, tr. 1960; etc., etc.). Waltari, like Pekkanen and Haanpää (qq.v.), was associated with the *Tulenkantajat* (Torchbearer) group when a very young man. The Torchbearers, 1924–9, were a left-wing, outwards-looking group; their motto was 'The largest windows open onto Europe'. This group contained most of the Finnish writers influenced by expressionism (q.v.) but it also belatedly incorporated some elements of futurism (q.v.). It quickly dissolved, although an influential left-wing magazine bearing the same name continued until 1939. Finnish publishers were either run by or in fear of the fascist AKS until 1936.

Though Waltari caused something of a stir with his precocious first book, *The Great Illusion* (1928), about rebellious youth, he soon calmed down. His most interesting work is to be found in *Moonscape* (1953; tr. 1954), short stories. Here the cinemascope effect and relentlessly mindless piling up of historical detail are lacking, and there is some understanding of psychology. But essentially Waltari remains a good-natured purveyor of middlebrow fodder; his seriousness is continually swallowed by his reprehensible desire to fill the lounges of the West with pseudo-mystical consolation.

Aino Kallas (1878–1956), who married an Estonian and who lived in London from 1922 until 1934, was a better historical novelist, though she chose to write about Estonia. Her work has aptly been described as 'ballad-like'. The best books are *Barbara von Tisenhuson* (1923; tr. 1927) and *The Rector of Reigi* (1926; tr. 1927): here she discovered an authentic language, based on old Estonian, in which to describe the past. These books are a little shrill in their mystical praise of love – which comes over as something of a generalization – but succeed in anatomizing the paradoxes of the past. They are hardly for the squeamish. Stories are collected in *The White Ship: Estonian Tales* (tr. 1924). She wrote *Diaries* covering the period 1897–1956 (1952–6) and these are of indispensable value even if not 'artistically meritorious', as a polite critic has called them.

Väinö Linna (1920), originally a farm labourer, caused one of the biggest post-war sensations in Finnish letters with the publication of *The Unknown Soldier* (1954; tr. 1957), the story of a grousing soldier in the winter war. This sold half a million copies, which was unprecedented in a country of under five million. It is a vivid and vigorous book, making brilliant use of dialogue; polite society was shattered by its candour, but also fascinated. The trilogy *Under the Polar Star* (1959–62; Fr. tr. of I and II, *Ici, sous l'étoile polaire*, 1962–3) deals with the war of 1918, and again provoked controversy. Linna's views of the extremely complex issues behind the war are controversial, but they are undoubtedly more penetrating than those of the historians. He has been particularly anxious to dispel what he believes is the myth of a disinterested White army.

Veijo Meri (1928) shares the post-war generation's disillusionment with war and bourgeois war-values (such as 'heroism', which he considers a mythical quality). He is more modernist than Linna (q.v.). *The Isolated* (1959) and *Events of 1918* (1960) – on the Civil War – portray individuals lost and isolated in the hell of war. *The Manila Rope* (1957; tr. 1967) is set in the First World War. Meri has also written about modern Helsinki. His novels represent a move away from realism to political disenchantment and neo-expressionism: written in a deadpan style, they describe bizarre events – the effect is less objective than cynical and blackly humorous. **Antti Hyry** (1931) is an experimentalist, who cultivates a similarly naïvely objective style that is interesting, but apt to become monotonous. His best novel is *The Edge of the World* (1967).

Such writers, as well as **Paavo Rintala** (1930), have aroused the wrath of right-wing critics – including some outside Finland – who feel that they are not aware of the 'Russian menace'; but this is a mistaken attitude. Rintala's relentless de-mythologizing of the Mannerheim cult and other relics of pre-war Finland – they were, naturally, perpetuated by the 'Continuation War' of 1941–4, when the country fought alongside the Nazis – is a necessary critical step. *The Long Distance Patrol* (1963; tr. 1967) is an excellent example of his harsh style. His point that much that was unpleasant in the Finnish character was involved in the Continuation War is not really destroyed because it may have been inevitable, though he is a critic of the concept of 'inevitability', a rationalization made by many right-wingers ashamed of their encouragement of fascism.

*

Despite the genius of Leino, Finnish poetry has adapted slowly to this century. What the Finnish poet **Anselm Hollo** (1934) – he now writes in English and lives in America – has called 'Finnitude' grew up, and 'was liable to bog poetry down in either of two kinds of neo-romanticism: the "cosmic" . . . or the folk-loristic. . . .' This was understandable in a new nation. But almost all poets until the Fifties tried to write Finnish poetry in predominantly German forms; since, as Hollo points out, Finnish is a Uralian and not an Indo-European tongue, the results were often 'somewhat repulsive'. The modernist poets of the Fifties therefore had less use for the Torchbearers (q.v.) as pioneers than they otherwise might. One cannot say that any of the Twenties poets discussed below really understood their reading of Nietzsche and French poetry. Like Ady (q.v.) in Hungary, they brought back something; but Finnish soil was less fertile than Hungarian.

Most of Finland's leading poets of the between-wars period were associated with the Torchbearers group. **Uuno Kailas** (ps. **Frans Uuno Salonen**, 1901–33), who died – like so many of his countrymen – from tuberculosis, was its leading spirit: he introduced the German expressionist poets into Finland in a volume of translations published in 1924. For a whole year (1928–9) he was mad. He prophesied his early death with phthisic ecstasy. His earlier poetry is violent and tormented in a typically expressionist style; after his illness he reacted against this, to produce a more controlled – although not less disturbed – poetry. His first mature collection was *Sleep and Death* (1931); here for the first time his turbulent guilts, anguished self-scrutiny and hallucinations are subsumed under an iron discipline – representative, of course, of Kailas' need for restraint and fear of mental collapse. His thinking about poetry was influenced by that of **Juhani Siljo** (1888–1918), who was killed in the civil war on the White side. Siljo believed unconvincingly in poetry as a means of self-revelation and of achieving a perfect life; Kailas clung to this without believing in it. (TCSP) **P. Mustapää** (ps. **M. Haavio**, 1899–1973), a distinguished scholar, drew on Finland's early literature. The surface of his poetry is deliberately light and easy; but this conceals a clever adaptation of early manners to modern needs, and a playful humour, the chief future of his insubstantial but readable poetry. (TCSP)

Lauri Viljanen (1900), another leading light in the Torchbearers (q.v.) group, is more important as an influence than as a poet. He is an intelligent conservative humanist, sometimes intolerant in his more recent criticism. He has kept Finns in touch with European developments for nearly fifty years. His poetry is well-made but conventionally humanistic in content.

The leading woman poet of the Torchbearers (q.v.) was **Katri Vala** (ps. **Alice Wadenström**, 1901–44), who is often compared, for her intensity, to Edith Södergran (q.v.). Like the latter, Katri Vala died of tuberculosis. She introduced free verse to Finland. Her poetry of the late Twenties is her best – 'I cycle my hunger's orbit/Bare and dreary as a prison yard./My senses and thoughts are rough from work' – because of its freshness, spontaneity and firmness of line. The later, more politically radical poetry is less important. Katri Vala died in Sweden; her *Collected Poems* appeared in 1945.

Aala Tynni (1913), Mustapää's (q.v.) wife, is an interesting poet, who has assembled an anthology of European poetry – translated by herself – from A.D. 1000 to the present: *A Millennium of Song* (1957). **Lauri Viita** (1916–65), who died prematurely in a car crash, was a predominantly urban poet (his first collection was called *Concreter*, 1947) who alternated between a grandiose 'cosmic' poetry – ineffective – and a simple, ballad-like style of great charm. He graduated into an impressive novelist; *Moraine* (1950), set in the Civil War, a study of urban life, is successful on sociological and psychological levels. **Helvi Juvonen** (1919–59) was influenced by Emily Dickinson and, above all, Marianne Moore (q.v.): she projects herself into various animals in the same way, although her manner is considerably more personal. With Haavikko (q.v.) she was the leading Finnish modernist of the Fifties.

The most gifted Finnish post-war modernist is the publisher **Paavo Haavikko** (1931). With *Ways to Faraway* (1951) he may fairly be said to have 'brought Finnish poetry up to date'. A selection of his poems has been translated into English: *Selected Poems* (1968; 1974). Haavikko is an extreme modernist: his poetry combines hermeticism with a strong sense of, as he puts it rather pretentiously (in the form of a question), 'How can we endure without falling silent when poems are shown to mean nothing?' He has indignantly repudiated the reactionary 'Finnitude' of his elders, and he shares his contemporary Meri's (q.v.) view of war. His poetry rejects any kind of easy way out, any neatness, and consequently often runs the risk of being found impenetrable. His poem-sequence 'The Winter Palace' is his most impressive work, and has attracted praise from

Enzensberger (q.v.) and other poets. His absurdist play *The Superintendent* (1968) was translated in 1978. He is a cold poet – his *nouveau roman* (q.v.) style novels reflect this coldness – who is given to making trite generalizations ('The whole world is history') but he is very inventive, technically adept, and often funny. He has put forward the intelligent view that the Finns survive their 'in betweenness' by their pragmatism.

Juha Mannerkorpi (1915), who was born in Ohio, is a more run-of-the-mill modernist, whose poetry, drama and short stories seldom transcend their influences (mainly Beckett, q.v.); but he has made translations from Beckett and other French writers into Finnish. Tuomas Anhava (1927), a more original poet, has absorbed the influence of classical Chinese and Japanese poetry, which he has translated. A substantial retrospective selection appeared in 1967. There is a translation of some of his poems into English: *In the Dark, Move Slowly* (1969). Marja-Liisa Vartio (1924–66), first wife of Haavikko (q.v.), began as a poet but then went on to write a series of highly poetic novels: essentially she was a poet. Her early death was a serious loss to Finnish letters. The posthumous *The Birds were Hers* (1967) is her finest novel, and one of the best to come out of post-war Finland, the subtle and original story of a widow who, obsessed with birds, can relate to others only through her maid. With Haavikko (q.v.) at the forefront of the modernist movement is Eeva-Liisa Manner (1921), who has graduated from the traditional to surrealist free verse; she has written fiction and drama.

*

Most Finnish writers have tried their hand at drama, but this has nonetheless been fairly described as of 'negligible international significance'. The best plays have come from Finno-Swedes (q.v.).

Maria Jotuni (q.v.) was as distinguished in the theatre as in fiction. She began as an Ibsenian (q.v.) but soon branched out into comedy – her forte – with such plays as *Man's Rib* (1914). Her most powerful tragedy is her drama dealing with Saul, *I am to Blame* (1929). Lauri Haarla (1890–1944) wrote a number of successful dramas (and novels) on medieval subjects. Haarla was influenced by German expressionism (q.v.) in these plays; *The Two-Edged Sword* (1932), an attempt to depict the civil war, was a failure. A number of Finnish writers best known for their work in other fields – Waltari and Haavikko (qq.v.) among them – have written plays, but no major dramatist has emerged. However, *The Lappo Opera* (1967) by Arvo Salo (1932), with music by Chydenius, was an enormously successful send-up of the fascist *Lapua* movement of the Thirties, and would play well in any country where fascist-style thinking is in the air and is resented.